ERIC ALTERMAN

# WE ARE NOT ONE

## A HISTORY OF AMERICA'S FIGHT OVER ISRAEL

BASIC BOOKS

New York

Basic Books
Hachette Book Group
1290 Avenue of the Americas, New York, NY 10104
www.basicbooks.com

Printed in the United States of America

First Edition: November 2022

Published by Basic Books, an imprint of Perseus Books, LLC, a subsidiary of Hachette Book Group, Inc. The Basic Books name and logo is a trademark of the Hachette Book Group.

The Hachette Speakers Bureau provides a wide range of authors for speaking events. To find out more, go to www.hachettespeakersbureau.com or call (866) 376-6591.

The publisher is not responsible for websites (or their content) that are not owned by the publisher.

Print book interior design by Amy Quinn.

Library of Congress Control Number: 2022940791

ISBNs: 9780465096312 (hardcover), 9780465096329 (ebook)

LSC-C

Printing 1, 2022

*To my brave, strong daughter, Eve Rose Alterman, who
taught her old man more in one year about grace and courage
than he managed to learn in the previous sixty-one.*

*"In a world so hard and dirty
So fouled and confused
Searching for a little bit of God's mercy
I found living proof."*

—*Bruce Springsteen, "Living Proof," 1992*

Levin had often noticed in arguments between the most intelligent people that after enormous efforts, an enormous number of logical subtleties and words, the arguers would finally come to the awareness that what they had spent so long struggling to prove to each other had been known to them long, long before, from the beginning of the argument, but that they had loved different things, and therefore did not want to name what they loved, so as not to be challenged.

—Leo Tolstoy, *Anna Karenina*, Book
IV, chapter XIII, 1877


A man hears what he wants to hear and disregards the rest.

—Paul Simon, "The Boxer," 1970

# CONTENTS

INTRODUCTION

# WORKING ON A DREAM

The space that Israel occupies in US political debates is, by any measure, extraordinary. In land area, the Jewish state ranks 149th in a list of 195 independent nations—it is smaller than Belize and El Salvador and only slightly larger than Slovenia. And yet, despite its size, and despite its distance from the United States, Israel, and particularly its conflicts with the Palestinians and surrounding nations, remains one of the most intensely debated topics in all of American politics. The participants in these debates often treat competing arguments not as matters of policy, but as challenges to their personal identities. This tendency has long been evident among American Jews, but in recent decades it has also become true of millions of conservative Christians. More and more, it is evident in Israel's opponents as well. This identity-infused inflexibility is one of many causes of the debate's intensity and one reason why arguments so often veer away from any recognizable reality experienced by the people who actually live there.

Just as extraordinary as the degree of attention paid to Israel in the United States is the level of support it receives. This support takes countless forms. Most obviously, it can be seen in opinion polls, in which Americans demonstrate significantly more sympathy for Israel, as opposed to the Palestinians, than do citizens of any other nation on earth. This is true for liberals, conservatives, and moderates alike. And it is true not only for Jews, but also for Protestants and for Catholics. It is true— or at least it has been, until recently—for almost everyone, with just a few significant exceptions.[1]

Israel's popularity with US citizens, however, does not begin to explain the degree of indulgence it receives from the US government. After all, gun control, strict environmental regulation, and higher taxes on the super-wealthy also poll extremely well with the public but are not at all reflected in congressional legislation. In addition, "foreign aid" is just about the most unpopular cause, at least in the abstract, that any pollster can identify. And yet America's generosity to Israel is literally unparalleled, not only in US history, but in the history of any nation. Since its founding in 1948, Israel has been by far the largest US foreign aid recipient, despite the fact that it has grown to be among the world's dozen wealthiest nations (as measured by per capita gross domestic product). What's more, Israel receives this aid, as policy scholars Amnon Cavari and Elan Nyer have put it, "earlier than other countries, with fewer limitations on how to use the funds and minimal bureaucratic oversight (essentially unaudited allocation) and is one of the very few countries that benefit from laws permitting tax deductions for contributions to foreign charities." Since 1997, the United States has had a law that demands that it vet the human rights records of all military units in any nation that enjoys US aid. Alas, according to a 2021 study published by the Carnegie Endowment for International Peace, Israel is "the only country in the world for which the United States does not have tracking mechanisms to determine which weapons go to which military unit," and hence is free to ignore this requirement.

US law ensures that Israel receives sufficient military support to maintain a "qualitative military edge" over any and all combinations of its potential adversaries. Israel is invited by law to receive preferential treatment as a bidder on US defense contracts, and it is often given surplus US equipment at minimal (if any) cost. Under President Barack Obama, the United States signed a Memorandum of Understanding (MOU) in which it committed itself to providing Israel with $38 billion in military aid over a period of nine years. This pledge is unlike any other US foreign commitment. Diplomatically, the US government has often treated Israeli priorities as indistinguishable from its own. Between 1946 and 2012, for instance, fully more than half of the vetoes the United States employed in the United Nations Security Council were devoted to the defense of Israel.

This book is a history of the debate over Israel in the United States: about its founding, its character, its conflicts—both internal and external, especially as they relate to the Palestinians—and many other issues. It pays particular attention to the actions and concerns of American Jews, as historically they have stood at the center of the debate, oftentimes defining its terms and policing its borders. It is not a book about Israel itself, US diplomacy in the Middle East, or the fate of the Palestinian people inside or outside Israel's borders (however one might define these). My shelves are already groaning from books on those topics, and, as I hope to make clear in the coming pages, actual events in and around Israel and the arguments that Americans have about them are birds of decidedly different feathers. While Middle Eastern realities undoubtedly do play a role in determining the contours of the US debate, they do so in unpredictable, often irrational ways. Over time, the American debate over Israel ultimately turns on its own axis, with a center located not in Jerusalem or Tel Aviv, but in midtown Manhattan and Washington, DC. It is in this "public sphere," as defined in 1962 by the German philosopher Jurgen Habermas, where I find my focus.

Even to use the singular form for the word "debate" with regard to Israel, the Arab nations, and the Palestinians can be misleading. Over time, countless debates have arisen, and these have spilled into one another in complicated ways, psychologically no less than politically, to the point where it becomes virtually impossible to make sense of any of them without taking at least some account of all of them. And as an Israeli policy analyst, Calev Ben-Dor, observed in 2021, "All essays, books and documentaries about the Israeli-Palestinian conflict or peace process will inevitably be criticised for perceived bias. Do they give too much or too little attention to any number of factors…?" "Objectivity" and "comprehensiveness" are words that have no meaning in a conflict such as this one, where views are held intensely, and where they frequently seem impervious to contradictory evidence. I don't doubt that this work will invite considerable criticism by those who see their own side treated in a manner they consider to be unsympathetic or lacking in the crucial fact or insight that would, in their eyes, undermine my entire analysis. It is my profound hope, however, that we—reader and author—will be able to transcend these moments and ultimately come to see this work, to borrow a frequently misused phrase, to be both "fair and balanced" in its treatment of the topics I seek to address.[2]

The wildly disproportionate amount of attention Israel receives in American political discourse today is not exactly a historical anomaly. Even before the state was born, its future first president, Chaim Weizmann, wrote to President Harry S. Truman that "Palestine, for its size, is probably the most investigated country in the world." And that has been true across approximately two thousand years of human history. As the historian David Nirenberg reminded us, the ancient Egyptians, the early Christians, the first followers of the Prophet Muhammad, and medieval Europeans all "invoked Jews to explain topics as diverse as famine, plague, and the tax policies of their princes." In their writings, the words *Jew, Hebrew, Semite, Israelite*, and *Israel* appear with a frequency stunningly disproportionate to any populations of living Jews in those societies."[3]

People all over the world have marveled for millennia at the imagined mystical power of the Jews over the societies in which they have found themselves following expulsions from their previous homes. Dedicated to scholarship and spiritual salvation, Jews judged their condition to be one of endless episodes of political impotence and vulnerability. They viewed themselves as an "ever-dying people," in the words of the mid-twentieth-century Polish-born American Jewish philosopher Simon Rawidowicz. Indeed, it was hardly unusual for the members of a diaspora community in any time or place—even before the Holocaust—to see themselves as "the final link in Israel's chain." Aside from the lucky few who relocated from Germany to the United States in the early to mid-nineteenth century, they consistently adopted what the Columbia University Jewish historian Salo Baron termed a "lachrymose" interpretation of their own history. Although Baron had in mind the nineteenth-century Polish Jewish historian Heinrich Graetz, the view he was criticizing was perhaps enunciated most cogently by a historian who also happened to be the father of Israel's longest-serving prime minister. Speaking to *The New Yorker*'s David Remnick in 1998, Benzion Netanyahu explained that "Jewish history is in large measure a history of holocausts."[4]

The creation of a Jewish state was a dream few ever dared to seriously propose before the founder of modern Zionism, Theodor Herzl, came along, at the end of the nineteenth century. Or, if they did, the task of its realization was understood to be the business of the Almighty rather than mere mortals. Even when, in the aftermath of the Shoah, the dream miraculously came true, it nevertheless continued to function as a dream. Ironically, this process mirrored a deeply rooted Jewish tradition. The Talmud draws a distinction between "the Jerusalem of above" and "the Jerusalem of below"—between the Heavenly Jerusalem, the one of hopes and dreams, and the Earthly Jerusalem, the one of walls and stones.

Addressing this phenomenon, the secular Israeli novelist Amos Oz advised that the "only way to keep a dream rosy and intact is to never live it out." Would Israel be "a moral light unto the nations," or a "nonstop macho show"? Or, better yet, "an incarnation of the Jewish shtetl from Eastern Europe"? As Oz so wisely observed, for Jews, at least, Israel is "a conglomeration of dreams, fantasies, blueprints and master plans." Rather than attempting to unpack, and therefore understand, this extremely complex society and the problems it faced, American Jews imagined an Israel that bore only a passing resemblance to the actual country under construction. When the dream has appeared to conflict with a far messier reality, it has almost always been the dream that carried the day.[5]

The question of how well Israel has managed to live up to the myths created for it—leaving aside the fact that no nation possibly could have done so—is one that most members of the American Jewish community have long sought to avoid. The political scientist Leon Hadar tells a story that nicely illustrates this dynamic: In the late 1980s, an American Jewish women's organization sponsored a screening in New York of a young woman's critical documentary, at least in part financed by the Israeli government, about how the Israeli military treated its female soldiers. Even though the film was shown to what one would have expected to be a sympathetic audience, made up of young, well-educated, and presumably feminist-oriented Jewish women, the reaction, when the filmmaker was introduced following the screening, was polite applause followed by deafening silence. Eventually, a woman stood up and said something along the following lines: "Look, you are obviously a very talented producer and I am sure that you presented an accurate picture. But you have to understand that for us Israel is a fantasy, and we would like to keep it that way. So please don't come here and try to destroy this fantasy for us!"[6]

Before Herzl published his landmark 1896 pamphlet *Der Judenstaat* (*The State of the Jews*, usually mistranslated as *The Jewish State*), support in the United States for the notion of Jewish sovereignty in the Holy Land came almost exclusively from Christians. America's Jews at the time constituted a largely assimilated, well-to-do community of mostly German origins whose members feared that any sympathy for the cause of a separate nation for Jews could easily lead their Christian neighbors to question their patriotism. Beginning in the early 1900s, however, this stance softened considerably, and in the mid-1940s it changed entirely as the horrific consequences of Nazi atrocities came to light. News of the Shoah provided a kind of last straw for Jews who had hoped they might someday be welcomed to live in relative safety and security anywhere outside the United States (which, in 1924, had also closed its doors to virtually all immigrants). If Jews were to survive in the future, they would need their own homeland.

Once this "miracle" came to pass with Israel's founding in 1948, for many American Jews, that was that. They contributed funds to help settle new immigrants, plant forests, and build schools, but they did not much visit, and they certainly did not "make aliyah"—that is, move to

Israel—in significant numbers. Nor did they encourage their children to do so. Nor did they feel a need to involve themselves in Israel's political or diplomatic disputes. As Jewish Americans, their concerns were with America. In one of the great ironies of perhaps all human history, "after 2000 years of exile and persecution, the Jews had become a success story," wrote the Israeli journalist Anshel Pfeffer. In reality, it was not just one success story, but two simultaneous stories, and each contradicted the other. "American Jews were finally proving that, in the land of the free, there was no need for a Jewish homeland and Israeli Jews were proving that only in their homeland could Jews be truly free." For American Jews, as Philip Roth put it, "Zion was the United States."[7]

But even without Israel looming nearly as large as it later would in the minds of most American Jews, discussions in Congress and the media and in most communities in the United States in the decades following May 1948 were still largely "pro-Israel" arguments. This was due in part to the political savvy of American Jewish organizations; in part to a durable, if muted, loyalty among the Jewish population at large; and in part, and most significantly, to the cultural and (especially) financial power exercised on behalf of Israel's cause.

A fundamental change in American Jewish attitudes took place in the immediate aftermath of the 1967 Six-Day War as fears of a "second Holocaust" gave way to an emotional embrace of Israel that shocked even those who experienced it. Before 1967, save for the years immediately surrounding the founding of the state in 1948, the agendas of America's major Jewish organizations were shaped by the traditional concerns of American liberalism, with a focus on social services together with issues related to racial discrimination and the legal separation of church and state. By choosing liberal causes that were "good for the Jews," but not only for the Jews, they managed to elude the traditional divide between Jewish "particularism" (that is, concern only for fellow Jews) and "universalism" (the desire to "repair the world," or *tikkun olam*, in Hebrew), embracing both simultaneously.

But the polite, law-abiding version of liberalism to which American Jews had attached themselves following the New Deal began to come under siege from both left and right in the period leading up to the

1967 war. Jews often felt themselves caught in the crossfire. On one side were calls for "Black Power" and growing identification with an Israel-skeptical third world among their erstwhile allies in the civil rights movement, along with New Left condemnations of "Amerikkka" from some of their own children, a reference to the Ku Klux Klan and racism in America. On the other were seductive declarations of an aggressive America faithfully standing by her allies emanating from an increasingly influential American right wing, a group that American Jews had hitherto been uncomfortable with politically, culturally, and religiously. Following the shock of Israel's smashing six-day victory, however, literally everything—race relations, social justice, social services, Jewish education, and anything else you can think of—immediately took a distant back seat in Jewish communal life to support for Israel. The attachment to Israel became what Rabbi Alexander Schindler, a widely respected twentieth-century leader of Reform Judaism, American Jewry's most popular denomination, compared to "a kind of kidney machine, without which [American Jews] cannot live."[8]

The other cause that appeared to excite funders and Jewish leaders inspired by the Six-Day War was Holocaust remembrance. This, too, however, can be understood as an aspect of the community's arsenal of arguments for Israel. The horrific history of the Shoah became inextricably intertwined with arguments in defense of Israel's increasingly harsh treatment of Palestinians and its apparently endless occupation of the West Bank. Jews did not forfeit their liberal beliefs, but most were willing to lay them aside whenever they were understood to come in conflict with support for Israel. This transformation reshaped the meaning of secular American Jews' cultural and religious identities, as these became synonymous with an enthusiastic embrace of Zionism together with angry efforts to excommunicate anyone who dared dissent from this consensus. As the Jewish scholar and rabbi Shaul Magid has written, "The Jewish discourse about Zionism [became] Jewish identity itself." Zionism now defined Jewish legitimacy. It was "no longer part of a larger conversation. It define[d] the conversation."[9]

As just one example of how powerfully this phenomenon manifested itself in the world of professional Jewish organizations, take Kenneth

Stern, scholar of antisemitism, who joined the (formerly non-Zionist) American Jewish Committee in 1989 and spent the next twenty-five years laboring in its vineyards. He later recalled that "no one felt less a part of the AJC family because of how, or if, they observed the Jewish religion." Staff members were never asked whether they planned to attend High Holiday services. But he and his colleagues (including those who were not Jewish) felt "tremendous pressure" to attend New York's annual "Salute to Israel" parade. "There were multiple memos, the tone and content of which suggested it would hurt one's career not to show up, even though the parade was on Sunday, a day off," he wrote. At the same time, Stern saw his organization "sacrifice an instinct for serious thought, discussion and self-reflection in favor of ardent pro-Israel advocacy." The need to appear "'strong' in defense of the Jewish people, as both a political end and a fundraising necessity, trumped nuance," and "even private, internal questioning of the wisdom of public positions on Israel became more difficult."[10]

Prior to 1967, Israel enjoyed broad support in the United States, especially among liberals and leftists. It was perceived to be a Spartan, socialist, anti-imperialist nation and very much an underdog in its constant battle with the surrounding Arab nations that sought its destruction. The image of an Israeli David fighting off the Arab Goliath—memorialized in the enormously popular 1958 book and 1960 movie *Exodus*—was more misleading than illuminating, but it lived on as a tool for Israel's supporters in the debates they faced. Once the world separated itself into competing camps during the Cold War—almost simultaneously with Israel's creation—Israel's leaders took advantage of multiple opportunities to prove their new nation's usefulness to the United States in its Manichean struggle with the USSR. Israel's ability to call itself "the only democracy in the Middle East" earned it considerable credit with the non-Jewish American public, which, in any case, was decidedly not, under almost any circumstances, predisposed to identify with darker-skinned Muslim nations.

The debate about Israel's character began to shift in the 1980s. Tens of millions of evangelical Christians, newly empowered in US politics by

Ronald Reagan's 1980 election victory, took up Israel's cause. In doing so, they joined the mostly secular, mostly Jewish neoconservative pundits and politicos who had seized on an all-but-unquestioning defense of Israel as a fundamental ideological precept. (Israel's 1977 election of the conservative Likud Party, led by Menachem Begin, to replace the socialist-oriented Labor Party served to smooth the path of both parties into this political space.) The evangelical/neocon alliance was knit together in part by the Israeli government and in part by the growing power of what has come to be called the "Israel lobby." This alliance was accompanied, however, by a gradual sense of distance and disillusionment on the part of many American Jews, especially younger ones, who became increasingly alienated by the rightward direction of Israel's politics and its harsh treatment of the Palestinian populations under its (apparently permanent) authority.

In the 1940s, the Zionist leader Rabbi Abraham "Abba" Hillel Silver had defined Reform Judaism as inhabiting "the common ground between Zionism and liberalism, Judaism and America." But as Israel came to be perceived as more and more a conservative cause, liberals and leftists evinced growing sympathy for the plight of the displaced Palestinians, who, now stateless and oppressed, had come to occupy the underdog role that history had previously assigned to the Jews. Among intellectuals and inside America's universities, their cause was often likened to the cause of Black South Africans against their country's apartheid system. Secular American Jews remained stubbornly liberal compared to almost all other ethnic and religious groups. Indeed, sociologists Charles S. Liebman and Steven M. Cohen have found that for these American Jews, "liberalism is not merely a characteristic but clearly a major component of their understanding of what it means to be a Jew."* But the contradiction between

---

* I should note here that Steven M. Cohen, whose sociological studies of American Jewry are referenced here and elsewhere in the book, was named in 2018 as a serial sexual harasser by multiple women. He was also accused of using his position as the most influential researcher of American Jewry, as well as his professorship at Hebrew Union College, to do so. Cohen admitted to these charges and lost his position at the college, and he has since been generally (though not completely) spurned in the Jewish scholarly community. He is not, however, the only person quoted in this book about whom such allegations have been made. Similar charges were leveled against former *New Republic* literary editor Leon Wieseltier (in 2017), as well as against Michael Steinhardt, the billionaire

support for an increasingly illiberal Israel and for liberal struggles at home, especially in the age of Trump, presaged yet another potential transformation.[11]

If the Israelis had chosen a motto for their country, they could have done worse than to use a statement that the nation's first prime minister, David Ben-Gurion, repeated often: "It matters not what the Goyim say, but what the Jews do." To an awe-inspiring degree, Israel, a tiny, initially quite poor, beleaguered nation, consistently chose its own path regardless of the obstacles that lay before it. From the moment of Israel's victory in its war of independence—what the Palestinians call the "Nakba," or "catastrophe"—its leaders have rarely proved willing even to entertain the demands of the Palestinians, the Arab world, or the majority of the members of the United Nations. In resisting these demands, it has always been able to count on the unswerving support of the US government.[12]

Aluf Benn, editor-in-chief of Israel's *Haaretz* newspaper, summed up the history of this relationship in 2021, writing, "From the day [Israel] was granted independence, and even before that, relations with the Palestinians have been the central topic on the agenda of the Zionist movement and the State of Israel. And since 1948, every American president and administration has acted in accordance with Israel's stance without exception." This was true "even as [the presidents] grumbled about the

---

Jewish funder of various schools, scholarships, and Jewish programs (in 2019 and earlier). In addition, Steinhardt has admitted to purchasing millions of dollars' worth of stolen ancient artifacts. Wieseltier and Steinhardt have admitted to certain allegations made against them while insisting on questioning the circumstances and interpretations of others. A number of scholars whose work and arguments I respect have drawn connections between the despicable actions of these men and the agendas each one pursued regarding the debate over Judaism and Israel. And while I agree that in many cases these connections may very well matter, I have chosen not to pursue this line of argument when referring to them or to their work in this book, in each case for the sake of the continuity of my more central argument. But I wish to make it crystal clear that I made this choice because I remain uncertain about how their behavior might be relevant to their arguments, not because I question the women who have come forward to tell their stories. I do not, and I remain grateful for their bravery in having done so. On the larger issue, see Lila Corwin Berman, Kate Rosenblatt, and Ronit Y. Stahl, "Continuity Crisis: The History and Sexual Politics of an American Jewish Communal Project," *American Jewish History* 104, nos. 2/3 (April/July 2020): 167–194.

settlements or sought to restrain the Israeli army in Lebanon or Gaza or mediated the peace process." Never, Benn continued, has any US administration asked Israel "to dismantle the settlements or grant the Palestinian refugees from 1948 the 'right of return'—issues which are the foundation of the Arab stance on the conflict." Moreover, "despite the wide-ranging support of the international community to end the occupation and establish a Palestinian state, the American veto in the UN Security Council has impeded any plan for international pressure or sanctions against Israel aimed at changing Israeli policy."[13]

Much of Israel's success in securing the support of so many US administrations has been due to the efforts of American Jews and their practice of what the Cornell University political scientist Benedict Anderson called "long-distance nationalism." Anderson coined the term to define the relationship between exiles, immigrants, and the offspring of any individual home nation. The relationship between the American Jewish community and Israel represents a unique political achievement, but what is most extraordinary about it is that this nationalistic commitment is dedicated to a country where few American Jews have ever lived, where a language is spoken in which precious few are fluent, and that many have not even visited.[14]

Israel's sixth president, Chaim Herzog, paid tribute to the remarkable accomplishment of American Jews in 1985 when he observed, "Never have Diaspora Jews been so politically powerful since Joseph sat next to Pharaoh's throne." Though they barely constitute 2 percent of the US population, American Jews—or at least their self-appointed leaders and spokesmen—have fervently supported Israel in politics as well as in the media and in their home communities, and they have met with remarkable success. Once conservative Christians joined them in the 1980s, the two communities, while sharing little else politically and almost nothing at all culturally, created one of the most powerful political forces in all of American politics—one that politicians resisted at the risk of their careers. In December 2018, Democratic House Speaker Nancy Pelosi proudly proclaimed to a Jewish audience that if the US Capitol ever "crumbled to the ground, the last thing that would remain is our support for Israel."[15]

Another advantage Israelis enjoy in the context of American politics is patience. Whatever unhappy noises a US official might feel compelled to make about any Israeli government action—whether building new settlements or bombing an Arab neighbor's nuclear reactor—Americans will eventually give in, or, more likely, lose interest. In a secretly recorded 2001 discussion with West Bank settlers, Israel's Benjamin Netanyahu explained this commonly held view. "I know what America is," he told them. "America is a thing that can be easily moved, moved in the right direction.... They will not bother us." At the same time that Israelis have depended on American Jews to ensure the political and financial support they needed to carry out their aims, they have tended to view these same Jews with only barely disguised contempt. This is a view consistent with Zionist ideology, which sought to rebel against what its writers and thinkers held to be the shameful history of Jewish diasporic living. The early twentieth-century Zionist poet and author Joseph Chaim Brenner, for example, called diaspora Jews "Gypsies and filthy dogs." The view spanned the Zionist ideological spectrum, with thinker A. D. Gordon, considered one of Labor Zionism's most influential early writers and thinkers, describing diaspora Jewish life as the "parasitism of a fundamentally useless people"; Vladimir Ze'ev Jabotinsky, the founder of Revisionist Zionism, calling them "ugly, sickly Yids," and insisting that Zionists must "eliminate the Diaspora or the Diaspora will eliminate you"; and the great liberal novelist A. B. Yehoshua mocking American Jews for only "playing with Jewishness" while Israelis lived it every day.[16]

In 2014, Rabbi David Ellenson, president of Hebrew Union College, which trains American Reform rabbis, called for a Zionism "built upon the dialectical foundations of universalism and particularism," in which both were accorded "religious legitimacy." But this was the last thing Israelis had in mind. As the ultra-religious grew ever more influential in Israel, the society created there further distanced the two sets of Jews with a turn toward ever more restrictive religiously based laws and culture. American rabbis saw their marriages and conversions unrecognized in Israel, and their religious authority mocked not only in synagogue, but also in that nation's laws. In 2017, Shlomo Amar, Israel's former Sephardic Chief Rabbi, called Reform Jews—by far the largest religious denomination for American Jews—"worse than Holocaust deniers." This followed on the 2016 comment by Israel's deputy minister of education, Meir Porush, that "Reform Jews should be sent to the dogs."[17]

American Jews have sometimes challenged the Israelis on these matters, but their protests have rarely produced results. Despite pride in their heritage, American Jews have often, though sometimes secretly to themselves, shared the Israeli view of their second-class status. The famed American Jewish literary critic Alfred Kazin wrote in his 1978 memoir, *New York Jew*, of growing weary over what he deemed to be "Zionist contempt for Jewish life elsewhere in the world." And yet Kazin, the author of a foundational text of American literary criticism—one that holds a special place in the history of Jewish cultural assimilation into the mainstream of American intellectual life—had admitted, in an entry in his journal five years earlier, that "the State of Israel reminds me of myself," and "myself reminds me of the State of Israel." Saul Bellow, the Nobel laureate American Jewish author, added a measure of militant pride to this common but often inchoate sense of psychological connection felt by so many American Jews of his generation when he observed, in a 1988 lecture, that "the founders of Israel restored the lost respect of the Jews by their manliness. They removed the curse of the Holocaust, of the abasement of victimization from them, and for this the Jews of the Diaspora were grateful and repaid Israel with their loyal support."[18]

As Bellow implied, Israel's military prowess is often employed as an expression of Jewish power in American Jewish life and Jewish literature. One can see the role it plays as a kind of psychological antidote for the humiliations of Jewish history, as well as for the personal feelings of inadequate masculinity that many American Jewish men have experienced growing up in a culture that did not value their commitment to scholarship over physical prowess. In an infamous 1963 essay, "My Negro Problem—and Ours," *Commentary* editor Norman Podhoretz spoke of being "repeatedly beaten up, robbed, and in general hated, terrorized, and humiliated" by Blacks as an adolescent. Podhoretz, having been faced with "Negroes" who were "tougher than we were, more ruthless," and who "on the whole...were better athletes," and forced, in lieu of fighting back, to "retreat, half whimpering" in a "nauseating experience of cowardice," later reveled in Israel's military victories over its darker-skinned Arab adversaries. He would celebrate, for instance, what he termed "the most brilliant institution of a reestablished Jewish sovereignty in the Land of Israel" to be the fact that the Israelis had overcome "the pacific habits...of the past two thousand years" of Jewish history. The same tendency can be seen reaching an almost comical apotheosis in the macho rhetoric of the likes of longtime *New Republic* owner Martin Peretz, who, following one of Israel's occasional military incursions into Gaza—this one in 2008—warned, apparently in all seriousness, "For centuries, Jewish blood was cheap. The message is: don't fuck with Israel."[19]

During a 2012 interview on NBC's *Meet the Press*, host David Gregory addressed Israeli prime minister Netanyahu as "the leader of the Jewish people." Gregory, who is Jewish, later clarified his remarks on Twitter, explaining that it would have been "better to say he's leader of jewish state," but in voicing the unstated assumptions of most American Jews and many of his colleagues in the mainstream media, he was right the first time. Certainly, Israelis have received little or no pushback from American Jewish leaders on this point. Instead, prominent American Jews have tended to take their orders from the Israelis and run with them. In 2021, for instance, the liberal ice-cream impresarios Ben Cohen and Jerry Greenfield announced that they would no longer allow their ice cream to be sold in the occupied territories, though it remained widely available across Israel itself. In doing so, they spoke in the traditional terms of American liberal Zionists. Describing themselves as "proud Jews" and "supporters of the State of Israel," they said they simply wished to voice their opposition both to the "Boycott, Sanction and Divest" movement, which targets all of Israel, and to an Israeli policy that "perpetuates an illegal occupation that is a barrier to peace and violates the basic human rights of the Palestinian people who live under the occupation." Israel's foreign ministry, however, immediately sent out instructions to mainstream American Jewish organizations demanding a mobilization against the ice-cream businessmen, and these groups fell into line, denouncing them as "ugly," "shameful," "bigoted," "antisemitic," and "dangerous," among other epithets.[20]

In his 2022 book *It Could Happen Here*, Anti-Defamation League CEO Jonathan Greenblatt called Cohen and Greenfield's decision "an insidious effort to delegitimize the Jewish state." Pro-Israel lobbyists demanded—and won—divestment from whatever investments their pension funds held in the ice-cream company's parent company, Unilever. These and other punitive actions were taken because the two men took a position that Israel and the occupied territories should be treated as separate entities—that the West Bank was not "Israel," and vice versa, even though they did so at a time when most Americans, including 58 percent of American Jews, wanted the United States to restrict its aid to Israel to prevent it from being spent on settlements. The purpose of the response, as William Daroff, CEO of the fifty-three-member Conference of Presidents of Major American Jewish Organizations, the umbrella group for mainstream Jewish leaders, explained, was intimidation. "With Ben & Jerry's, it's not just about Unilever," he explained in a February 2022 interview. "It's about every other multinational company that may come under pressure from fringe elements. And we want them to see the *tsuris* (Yiddish for suffering)—that's the technical term—that has been caused for Unilever in state capitals, where 33 states have effected some sort of action to push back against boycott, divestment and sanctions." (Their tactics succeeded when Unilever, over the objections of both Ben and Jerry, who sued their parent company to express their objections, agreed in June 2022 to sell its Israeli operations to a local corporation that planned to service settlements in the occupied territories.)[21]

The Jewish journalist J. J. Goldberg noted in 1996 that American Jewish leaders were becoming "ever more incomprehensible to the majority of their fellow [American] Jews." Today this is truer than ever. While the leaders of American Jewish organizations are constantly on planes traveling to meet with their counterparts in Israel, fewer than half of all American Jews have ever visited the country, to say nothing of the tiny percentage who could communicate in Hebrew if they had to. And yet, despite their names, groups such as the American Israel Public Affairs Committee (AIPAC), the American Jewish Committee (AJC), and the United Jewish Appeal (UJA) are not in any democratic sense accountable to the community for whom they claim to speak. They are answerable only to the wealthy donors who control their boards of directors. According to a 2018 study conducted by conservative financier Sanford

Bernstein's Avi Chai Foundation, just a "small pool of deep-pocketed donors" accounts for between 80 and 90 percent of all Jewish institutional funding. As a result, "the Jewish community is becoming even less of a representative democracy than it ever was," said Jack Wertheimer, a politically conservative American Jewish history professor at the Jewish Theological Seminary, who wrote a lengthy essay accompanying the study. Wertheimer argued that this development has undermined the "consensus-driven approach to Jewish communal life... because these larger donors want what they want."[22]

None of this should have surprised anyone who was paying attention. During the Trump presidency, according to the Pew Research Center, 92 percent of Israeli Jews considered themselves political centrists or on the right, while 78 percent of American Jews identified with the center or the political left. The 2020 presidential election found more than three-quarters of American Jews preferring Joe Biden over Donald Trump, but among Israel's Jews, these views were almost perfectly reversed, with 70 percent favoring Trump (a view that was shared by the roughly 10 percent of American Jews who count themselves as "Orthodox"). According to a 2022 survey, Israel was literally the only major Western nation in the world to hold that preference. And yet on Israel-related matters, the political priorities of the best-funded and most politically influential American Jewish organizations often reflect the views of Israeli Jews, together with the tiny minority of conservative and ultra-religious American Jews who share those right-wing, hawkish ideas, rather than those of the dovish majority for whom they ever more anachronistically claim to speak.[23]

Thanks to a few extremely wealthy Jewish funders and the commitment of millions of Christian conservatives, Republicans remain firmly in the hardline, pro-Israel camp. Democrats, however, are moving away from lockstep fealty to Israel on all matters, and even electing the occasional openly pro-Palestinian candidate. On campus, the movement to boycott Israel—sometimes led, and often supported, by Jewish students—continues to grow, causing parents and grandparents to panic and raising questions about the future of both American Jewry and US foreign policy. For the moment, despite having experienced a shaky period during the short Israel/Hamas war of May 2021, the pro-Israel consensus among US political elites remains intact, especially when judged by the support Israel continues to enjoy in Congress and elsewhere in the US government.

Meanwhile, the Israeli/Palestinian conflict remains a wound that continues to fester. Hopes for peace among American Jews and others may rise and fall with events, but the willingness, by either side in the region, to commit to the compromises necessary to create a genuinely stable peace has never come remotely close enough to reality to be tested. As longtime US negotiator Aaron David Miller admitted, "The politically inconvenient truth is that the three factors necessary to have any chance of ending the Israeli-Palestinian conflict—strong leaders who are eager to get things done fast, a workable deal, and effective U.S. mediation—have never been present." What is left in the wake of the constant failure to find a peaceful solution to the conflict, therefore, is a fight about how to best distribute the blame. And while other issues of Middle Eastern politics come and go, the fierceness of this particular fight has never subsided.[24]

What follows is a combination of exploration and analysis of America's apparently endless series of arguments about Israel, together with an interrogation of their implications for the future of the United States, its Jews, the state of the world, and many aspects of global politics and culture that the debates have influenced since they first entered our political life and culture well more than a century ago.

# CHAPTER 1

# ZIONISM FOR THEE, BUT NOT FOR ME

At midnight on May 14, 1948, in Tel Aviv, the Jewish Agency chairman, David Ben-Gurion, proclaimed the founding of the first Jewish nation-state in nearly two thousand years. Barely ten minutes later, at 6:11 p.m. Eastern Standard Time in Washington, DC, the White House issued a statement recognizing "the provisional government as the de facto authority of the State of Israel." The proclamation followed on President Truman's decision the previous November to instruct the US delegation to the United Nations to vote in favor of the partition of the British protectorate of Palestine into separate, independent Jewish and Arab states, joining in the 33–13 majority. Ten nations abstained, and six Arab nations walked out, refusing to take part in the vote.

The following day's *Washington Post* carried the headline "Recognition of Israel Stuns U.N. Delegates" on its front page, but it shouldn't have stunned anyone. Recognition was a long time coming. And however painfully arrived at, it was a decision that left Truman prouder than just about any other he had made as president. Truman took it seriously, if not literally, when Hebrew University president Eliahu Elath promised that his name would be "inscribed 'in golden letters in the four thousand years' history' of the Jewish people." "I am Cyrus, I am Cyrus," the president proudly proclaimed, comparing himself to the Persian king who had liberated the Israelites from Babylonian exile, inviting them to return to Israel in the sixth century BCE. Truman claimed to have read the Bible cover to cover three times by the time he turned 14.[1]

Reality has a way of ruining a fantastic storyline. The return of the Jewish people to Palestine, the revival of the Hebrew language, and the creation of the modern economic and military powerhouse that is Israel is a story so unlikely that for over a thousand years—short of prayer for Divine intervention—nobody much even entertained the belief that anything like it might ever be possible. Palestine had been inhabited by Jews since the fall of the Persian king Cyrus the Great in 539 BCE, when the period of the Babylonian exile ended and the restrictions on a Jewish presence in the land then called "Judah" were lifted. Sovereignty over the land remained in flux under various rulers. The Roman general Pompey the Great conquered Jerusalem in 63 BCE; the Romans ruled Palestine until 66 CE, when the Jews rebelled. Rome had reconquered the land by 70 CE, destroying the city's Second Temple. The temple's protective Western Wall, now the holiest site in the Jewish religion, was the only thing left standing. Many Jews fled, but many were also captured and enslaved or perished in the siege preceding the Roman victory. The Jews who remained, limited by their circumstances, left the question of state sovereignty to others. Most simply wanted to ensure a Jewish presence in their homeland, should the Messiah decide that it was time to make an appearance.

Different Jewish sects had wildly differing views on the question of whether humans had (or should have) any role to play in the timing of God's decision about the Messiah's appearance, especially given the prevailing theological belief that the Israelites had been exiled for their sins. Almost all the rabbis endorsed the view that "if the Jewish people repent they are redeemed, and if not they are not redeemed," as stated in the Talmud, the multivolume text of rabbinical interpretation on how to live Jewish life. But just what this meant in terms of actual behavior remained in dispute, subject, as always, to the unfathomable intentions of God. Jews may have chanted "Next year in Jerusalem" each year at the close of their Passover seders. But it was not until the end of the nineteenth century that almost any Jew anywhere dared utter these words with the intention of bringing about a collective, purposeful objective for the Jewish people in their ancient city.[2]

The modern-day Zionist political movement began in Basel, Switzerland, in August 1897, when Theodor Herzl (born Benjamin Ze'ev Herzl in Budapest), then thirty-seven years old, managed to assemble a group of like-minded Jews at the First Zionist Congress. In the 1880s, the Jewish population of Palestine, then under the gradually crumbling rule of the Ottoman Empire, had already begun to swell with emigration from the Russian "Pale of Settlement"—an area with strict borders subject to rules about where Jews were and were not allowed to live. During the "First Aliya"—from 1882 to 1903—the Jewish population of Palestine roughly doubled, rising from 25,000 to some 50,000. Those who arrived had many different backgrounds and motivations, however. Some were Marxists, anarchists, or other types of radicals; others were religious Jews; and quite a few embraced capitalism, purchasing land and hiring local Arab labor. Almost all were escaping a Russia in which pogroms, together with Jewish expulsions, sometimes of entire villages, had become an almost regular feature of daily life. As these attacks intensified, a "Second Aliya" would later bring another 35,000 to 40,000 Jews from the Pale in the years before the beginning of World War I. By 1914, their numbers had reached about 85,000 out of a total Palestinian population of roughly 700,000. At the time of the First Congress, Jews in Palestine were still considered to be an anomaly. Of the roughly 2,367,000 Jews who eventually left Europe during the late nineteenth and early twentieth centuries, an estimated 2,022,000 chose America as their destination.[3]

Herzl himself was a nearly perfectly assimilated Jew. While he had been confirmed on his thirteenth birthday, he had never been Bar Mitzvahed, and once he said he wanted nothing so much as to have been born into the Prussian nobility. (Herzl's own son converted to Christianity.) A prominent, well-traveled, and culturally sophisticated editor and former correspondent for *Neue Freie Presse* (New Free Press), a leading European newspaper, he was deeply affected by the spectacle of what would become

France's Dreyfus affair, which began in 1894 and was not resolved until 1906. In this incident, a French Jewish military officer had been repeatedly tried for allegedly betraying the nation to its enemies. The antisemitic fury unleashed at the innocent Captain Dreyfus disabused Herzl (and many Jews with him) of the belief that the 1791 political emancipation of France's Jews would end their persecution.

Herzl published his now famous pamphlet calling for the creation of a modern Jewish homeland, with the subtitle *Versuch einer modernen Lösung der Judenfrage* (*Proposal of a Modern Solution for the Jewish Question*), in February 1896, just fourteen months after Dreyfus's first trial and (later overturned) conviction. The first English translation appeared in May of the same year. His was not the first call for Jews to begin establishing a homeland, and Herzl was agnostic about its location. Sometimes he entertained the idea of Argentina, at other times what is now Kenya. But when it became clear that support could only be built for the Jews' biblical homeland, he settled on Palestine. It is no exaggeration to say that Herzl saw himself as a modern-day Moses. "I shall do something for the Jews, but not with them," he told the philanthropist Baron Maurice de Hirsch. With tireless dedication and a history-changing combination of chutzpah and charisma, he somehow succeeded in not only forging an extremely unlikely movement across multiple borders, but also earning the support of an impressive array of world leaders and influential thinkers and funders.[4]

Herzl's success was, initially, almost entirely confined to Europe. In the United States, Jews were enjoying a historically unrivaled sense of physical security, legal protection, and future promise. The earliest American champions of Jewish resettlement in Palestine were almost all Christians, who believed it would hasten Christ's return. William Eugene Blackstone, a real estate entrepreneur and best-selling author of religious texts, who adhered to the doctrine of "premillennial dispensationalism," the idea that Christ will reign for a thousand years on the earth following his Second Coming, dedicated much of his life to promoting the notion that the US government should "restore [the Jews] to the land of which they were so cruelly despoiled by our Roman ancestors." He managed to garner over four hundred signatures of prominent Americans, including those of Joseph Medill, publisher of the *Chicago Tribune*, and Melville W. Fuller, chief justice of the US Supreme Court, to an 1891 petition supporting the return of Jewish sovereignty over the Holy Land. Nothing came of it, however, and Blackstone would spend the rest of his life agitating, ineffectively, for the cause. He died in 1935, thirteen years before his dream came to fruition and about half a century before his views became a passionate enthusiasm for millions of American evangelical Christians.[5]

Zionism was a popular, if far-fetched and largely rhetorical, cause among American politicians in the interwar years. Among American Jews, however, it inspired little more than denunciation and denial. Until the early 1880s, most American Jews were either German immigrants, who had begun arriving in the 1830s, or their children. Their leaders were almost exclusively well-to-do members of Reform congregations, a liberalizing religious movement that had begun in Germany and reflected the ideals of the Enlightenment applied to traditional Jewish texts and teachings. The basic tenets of Reform Judaism could hardly have conflicted more sharply with those of Zionism had the latter been invented specifically for this purpose. Reform Judaism rejected any hint of Jewish nationalism or peoplehood. The first Reform temple in the United States, founded in Charleston, South Carolina, was dedicated in 1841 with the words, "This country is our Palestine. This city our Jerusalem."[6]

To the Reform rabbis and lay leaders, the religion shared by Jews consisted exclusively of a set of theological beliefs and extremely lightly worn religious practices. Jews could be Jews anywhere and everywhere, without concerns about where their loyalties lay so long as they dedicated themselves to spreading the ideals of social justice and universal cooperation among all peoples. Their all but unchallenged religious leader in mid-nineteenth-century America was Rabbi Isaac Mayer Wise, the founder of a series of cornerstone Reform institutions, including the Union of American Hebrew Congregations (later the Union for Reform Judaism), Hebrew Union College, and the Central Conference of American Rabbis (of which he became president). In 1897, the same year Herzl and company met in Basel, Wise addressed a different conference. His message could hardly have been clearer: "We are perfectly satisfied with our political and social position.... We want freedom, equality, justice, and equity to reign and govern the community in which we live. This we possess in such fullness, that no State whatever could improve on it. That new Messianic movement over the ocean does not concern us at all."[7]

The composition of American Jewry changed radically, however, in the final years of the nineteenth and the first years of the twentieth centuries. Thanks to war, revolution, and increasingly violent persecution, community life in the Pale of Settlement was becoming increasingly untenable for Jews, with persecution spreading to a geographical area that today would encompass Poland, Russia, Ukraine, Latvia, Lithuania, Belarus, and Moldova. The mass emigration that followed led to a dramatic increase from these nations in the number of Jews in the United States, from roughly 250,000 in 1880 to approximately 3.5 million in 1920. The population density on the largely Jewish Lower East Side of Manhattan reached historic proportions, and many of these new immigrants were attached to radical ideologies such as socialism, communism, and anarchism that promised to deliver the Jews from their unhappy historical predicament. Many also remained faithful to their traditional Orthodox religious precepts. A significant number merely hoped to succeed economically and provide a better life for their children, without concern for politics. "Zionism" therefore became many zionisms, comprising myriad disparate groups with often conflicting ideologies.

The Orthodox Mizrachi Zionist Organization, for instance, sought to found a Jewish state with a legal system based on rabbinical interpretations of the Torah—the first five books of the Hebrew Bible—and the Talmud. Still others shared the goal of Ahad Ha'am (born Asher Zvi Hirsch Ginsberg in 1856), a Russian Jewish scholar who first envisioned what we now term "cultural Zionism," a movement that focused not on statehood or political power per se, but on Palestine as the home of a Jewish spiritual and cultural rejuvenation. The Poale Zion workers movement, in contrast, sought to meld socialism with support for Zionism. But most of the new immigrants were understandably more intent on going about their own daily lives, struggling for food, shelter, and their own futures, rather than concerning themselves with events in distant Palestine.[8]

Enter Louis Dembitz Brandeis. Born in Louisville, Kentucky, and educated at Harvard Law School, Brandeis rose through the legal and political worlds faster and higher than any American Jew before him. In 1916, he became the first Jew to be appointed to the US Supreme Court. Ironically, Brandeis was not religious even by the lax standards of his fellow German Jews—he ignored almost all the traditional religious rituals, belonged to no temples, participated in no Jewish community activities, and celebrated Christmas at home. Speaking to the Century Club in New York in 1905, shortly before he turned forty, the man liberals called "the People's Lawyer" declared, "There is no place for what President [Theodore] Roosevelt has called hyphenated Americans.... Habits of living or of thought which tend to keep alive difference of origin or to classify men according to their religious beliefs are inconsistent with the American ideal of brotherhood, and are disloyal."[9]

The reasons for Brandeis's conversion to Zionism are much contested among historians. The upshot is that he came to believe that Zionism—which he interpreted to mean support for Jews who, unlike American Jews, required a refuge from the political persecution so common elsewhere in the world—was consistent with both his philosophical beliefs and his commitment to fighting for the underdog (he had been a leading lawyer for Russian Jewish workers). Brandeis would explain that "the Zionist meanings came to me rather in terms of the American Idea than in terms of what I had learned of *Torah* at home or in *cheder*."[10]

Brandeis agreed in 1912 to join America's still tiny Federation of American Zionists (later renamed the Zionist Organization of America). Soon afterward, he agreed to chair the organization. Given the respect he had earned in progressive legal circles as well as his distance from the traditional model of Zionist agitator, the movement could not have created a more compelling champion if it had set out to do so under laboratory conditions. In a 1915 speech titled "The Jewish Problem: How to

Solve It," delivered before the Conference of the Eastern Council of Reform Rabbis, Brandeis reversed the arguments that Isaac Mayer Wise had made seventeen years earlier by fusing his version of Zionism with American patriotism. Just as a man could be "a better citizen of the United States for being also a loyal citizen of his state, and of his city; for being loyal to his family, and to his profession or trade; for being loyal to his college or his lodge," so, too, "every American Jew who aids in advancing the Jewish settlement in Palestine, though he feels that neither he nor his descendants will ever live there, will likewise be a better man and a better American for doing so." Indeed, he continued, "loyalty to America demands...that each American Jew become a Zionist. For only through the ennobling effect of its strivings can we develop the best that is in us and give to this country the full benefit of our great inheritance."[11]

Brandeis risked much here. When Woodrow Wilson announced his appointment to the Supreme Court in 1916, the president's predecessor, William Howard Taft, complained to a friend that Brandeis had "adopted Zionism, favors the new Jerusalem, and has metaphorically been re-circumcised," and speculated as to whether "he would have grown a beard to convince those bearded Rabbis...that he was a Jew of Jews." Such musings among many were no doubt what kept Brandeis's confirmation vote relatively close, given the standards of the time, at 47–42 in favor.[12]

Brandeis's leadership changed the face of American Zionism in the eyes of both Jews and gentiles. He rejected the idea of encouraging American Jews to make aliyah in favor of advocacy for helping persecuted Jews around the world to do so. This shift in focus helped to defang the arguments of those who might otherwise question the commitment of Jews in America to their own nation. If Zionism was understood, as originally intended, to inspire an "ingathering of exiles" to the land of the Bible, then its support in the United States became (and would remain) a matter of "Zionism for thee, but not for me." Moreover, Brandeis had frequently represented Russian Jewish immigrants in their legal struggles as laborers to earn decent working conditions and other legal protections, thus gaining the respect of a broad swath of Jewish Americans. He seemed to be just the right man to elevate the Zionists' status. He helped the movement to form a bridge between the German and Russian Jewish cultures that would fuse them together in decades to come. By 1919, the dues-paying membership of the Zionist Organization of America had increased to 176,000 from a mere 12,000 five years earlier.[13]

According to popular, though likely apocryphal, lore, after the 1897 First Zionist Congress, two Viennese rabbis sent two scouts on a fact-finding mission to Ottoman-ruled Palestine. Reporting back on its suitability as a future Jewish homeland, they wrote, "The bride is beautiful, but she is married to another man." If true, the report dissuaded almost no one. The British Jewish author Israel Zangwill visited Palestine a year later and wrote that "Palestine has but a small population of Arabs and fellahin and wandering, lawless, blackmailing Bedouin tribes." He proposed that the world should "restore the country without a people to the people without a country." Zionists almost always demonstrated remarkable confidence that they would eventually outnumber the Arabs there. But following a half century of immigration, coupled with a frantic effort "to conquer the country, covertly, bit by bit," via a strategy of "buy, buy, buy" (in the words of Eliezer Ben-Yehuda, now known as the father of modern Hebrew), Jews still made up no more than about a third of Palestine's population at the moment of Israel's 1948 creation.[14]

One of the most important leaders of that community was the scholar and rabbi Judah Leon Magnes who had been leader of two of New York's most prestigious Reform temples before emigrating to Palestine. A Zionist, a pacifist, an eminent scholar of Judaism, a champion of the Jewish working class, and son-in-law to the famed American constitutional scholar and German Jewish leader Louis Marshall, Magnes became the first chancellor of Jerusalem's Hebrew University in 1925. Ten years later, he became its president. He joined with the philosopher Martin Buber, the historian Gershom Scholem, and Henrietta Szold, the health-care pioneer and founder of the Jewish women's organization Hadassah, to establish the Ihud (Unity) movement in August 1943. Its members insisted that a Jewish homeland worthy of the name could only be successfully achieved with the peaceable cooperation of the local Arab population, expressed in a binational rather than a specifically Jewish state. "The Jews have more than a claim upon the world for justice," Magnes explained. "But...I am not ready to try to achieve justice to the Jew through injustice to the Arab."[15]

Ihud inspired political support immediately among German Jews in the United States following its founding. The Sulzberger family proved so enthusiastic about it that the newspaper they owned—the *New York Times*—hired an Ihud staff member to be its Jerusalem correspondent. The US State Department was similarly supportive. Its officials would frequently consult with Magnes on possible ways to head off the Zionist plans for statehood. What always eluded Ihud, however, was any hint of reciprocity among Arabs anywhere, much less those in Palestine. There was simply none to be found.

Zionists experienced a moment of elation when, as they were still fighting the Germans in November 1917, the British government issued its "Balfour Declaration" endorsing the establishment of a "national home for the Jewish people" in Palestine. The British then accepted responsibility for Palestine governance under a League of Nations "mandate" amid the collapse of the Ottoman Empire, first in July 1920, following the Allied San Remo conference, and more formally in August 1922, following the signature of the Treaty of Lausanne. The Balfour Declaration became the official policy of the United Kingdom, and not long afterward, Brandeis succeeded in helping to convince President Wilson to endorse it as well. The president even predicted, albeit mistakenly, that "the Jewish Homeland was one of the two primary achievements that would come out of the war."[16]

But in their euphoria, the Zionists ignored the declaration's caveat that in the event of the creation of any such homeland, "the civil and religious rights of existing non-Jewish communities in Palestine" had to be respected. This condition has remained impossible to achieve to this day. The inability of both Arabs and Jews to share Palestine became increasingly evident during the period of heavy, though legally restricted, Jewish immigration. Arab riots broke out in 1920 and 1929 and again in 1936, when an Arab general strike degenerated into an explosion of violence that resulted in the deaths of more than three hundred Jews, Arabs, and

British soldiers. The scope of the violence gave lie to the oft-proclaimed Zionist contention, going back to Herzl, that peaceful Zionist colonization of Palestine was possible. Even those leaders who had still believed it now had to face reality.

In the wake of its legal mandate, the British came up with a number of plans for Palestine, none of which ever came to fruition. Led, or perhaps pressured, by Jerusalem's grand mufti, Mohammed Amin al-Husseini, Arab leaders rarely, if ever, would agree to engage with any of Britain's proposals, regardless of how favorable to the Arab side they might have been. Their first refusal came with British High Commissioner Herbert Samuel's 1921 proposal for what he termed "a legislative council in which Arabs would constitute ten of twenty-three positions, with Jews occupying three positions and the British the remainder." Next, in June 1922, Winston Churchill, then British secretary for the colonies, issued a white paper restricting Jewish immigration and legal land purchases in Palestine. Though it did not withdraw British support for the eventual creation of a Jewish homeland, the Churchill White Paper insisted that it only be done with the cooperation of its Arab inhabitants.[17]

In 1937, the British issued the Peel Commission Report, which admitted for the first time that their mandate had become unworkable, and so, too, had the idea of a unified Palestine shared by Arabs and Jews. According to its authors, "the continued impact of a highly intelligent and enterprising race, backed by large financial resources, on a comparatively poor indigenous community, on a different cultural level," was no formula for peaceful coexistence. The result was "an irrepressible conflict." In hopes of avoiding this, the commission therefore recommended a partition of Palestine into Arab and Jewish enclaves. This first proposal of what would become known as the "two-state solution" rested yet again on the impossible dream of Arab agreement, however. It happened again when Prime Minister Neville Chamberlain's government issued a white paper in May 1939. The Chamberlain White Paper, which suggested sharply limiting Jewish immigration to Palestine as well as Jewish land purchases, became the basis for British policy—tragically, as it happened, given the horrific fate awaiting Europe's Jews at the time. Even these immigration quotas, however, were never fulfilled. The white paper also called for a transition to majority, and therefore Arab, rule. But just as they would continue to do in the near future and to this day, as the historian John Judis has observed, "the Arabs turned down a plan that under the circumstances was very favorable to them." Then as now, "the Palestinian Arabs suffered from a profound lack of national leadership."[18]

## CHAPTER 2

# THE HORROR

HITLER'S RISE CONFRONTED ZIONISTS WITH WHAT FELT LIKE AN ENDLESS series of wrenching decisions. The Jewish people were facing a catastrophe that dwarfed all those that had come before it. At the same time, the opportunity to create the first Jewish sovereign state since biblical times—one that built on the revival of the Hebrew language and an unprecedented commitment to the defense and uplift of the Jews—now felt achingly close to fruition. The problem was how to pursue that goal while at the same time doing whatever was possible to save their brethren in Europe. This meant undermining Great Britain in one arena and supporting it in another. The question divided Jews as few have before or since, but it ended with a near consensus: that while saving Jews from Hitler was likely impossible, the creation of a Jewish state in Palestine was attainable—and it would be the only way to defend Jews from future Hitlers, whatever form they might take. Zionist activist Nahum Goldmann expressed this near consensus with admirable economy: "Hitler has proved a Jewish homeland is necessary and the Jews in Palestine have proved that it is possible."[1]

The old joke "Ask two Jews, get three opinions" spoke a truth that manifested itself on a nearly hourly basis among the ever-expanding list of ideological schisms that arose among the various groups within the Zionist movement of the early 1940s. Hadassah, the women's Zionist organization that Henrietta Szold had founded in 1912, had grown into a fund-raising and organizational juggernaut, in part because it avoided politics and focused exclusively on service to the needy. Szold, still its leader, was dedicated to peaceful coexistence between Arabs and Jews and eager to find whatever kind of accommodation might be possible before even considering the possibility of statehood. She was also among the founders of Ihud, which was dedicated to this same vision. The Zionist Organization of America (ZOA) disagreed, arguing instead for the conquest of as much territory as possible and evincing almost no concern about whatever consequences this position might hold for the Arabs already living there. The Orthodox Religious Zionists of America (also known as Mizrachi), meanwhile, found themselves forced to deal with the socialists of Poale Zion of America (and vice versa), and both had to find a way to work with the socialist-Orthodox-Zionist Poale Mizrachi, which enjoyed support from both Orthodox garment workers in New York and religious kibbutzim in Palestine. That so many groups with competing agendas were able to reach agreement on anything at all and go on to assemble what may be the most impressive lobbying effort in the history of democratic politics would be impressive enough. But it would also turn out to be among the most significant contributions to the realization of what had, for millennia, appeared to be a fantastic, barely even imaginable goal: the creation of the first sovereign Jewish state in two millennia.

Rabbi Stephen Wise, formerly a trusted lieutenant to Louis Brandeis at the Zionist Organization of America, was an unabashed champion of the belief that social justice lay at the heart of American Jewish identity. Born in Budapest, he came to New York as a child and received a PhD from Columbia University before becoming a rabbi. A rare Zionist within the Reform rabbinate, Wise helped to found the American Jewish Congress in 1918 as an alternative to the elitist, non-Zionist orientation of the German Jews who led the American Jewish Committee, which had been founded in 1906. Among the first to organize marches, mass rallies, and boycotts against Hitler, beginning in 1933, Wise was also a founder, in 1936, of the World Jewish Congress, which sought to unite Jewish communal organizations worldwide in opposition to the Nazis. He was a consistent confidant of US officials as he desperately sought to inspire action to save Europe's Jews. Both passionate about the Zionist cause and committed to Jewish unity, Wise frequently found himself juggling the demands of competing groups and ideologies. Moreover, as a friend and devotee of President Franklin Roosevelt, he was unwilling to distance himself too much from his president. His de facto position on almost everything therefore was compromise. On the Palestinian side, he allied himself with the storied British chemist and Zionist moderate Chaim Weizmann, whose devotion to the British ruling class mirrored Wise's commitment to FDR and the Democrats.

Wise's nemesis in the movement was Rabbi Abba Hillel Silver. Born in what was then Poland (now Lithuania), Silver grew up on New York's Lower East Side and began agitating for the Zionist cause in 1907 at the age of fourteen. Although he remained a congregational Reform rabbi, "Jewish statehood and Hebrew culture," in the words of one biographer, "were the highest values of his career." Senior rabbi for forty-six years at Temple-Tifereth Israel in Cleveland, he was a spellbinding speaker. Like Wise, he was an early champion of labor rights, workers' compensation, and civil liberties. Otherwise, he was Wise's opposite. Silver was a lifelong Republican. He often exhibited a harsh demeanor, and he had a famously quick temper. And his views were maximalist in every respect: he allied with the militant David Ben-Gurion on matters concerning Palestine, in opposition to the moderate Weizmann/Wise wing of the Zionist movement. Silver promised at a 1935 ZOA convention to build an Israel that reached "beyond the Jordan, stretching north and stretching out on the shores of the Mediterranean."[2]

Schisms formed within schisms among Zionists as the horrific news from Europe began to trickle into the United States in early 1942. The Reform movement was well into the process of jettisoning its commitment to Judaism as exclusively a religion, like Christianity, in favor of a new view of Jews as a religious community, like Irish or Italian Catholics.

Such distinctions came to appear tragically irrelevant given Adolf Hitler's strong feelings on the subject. Despite disagreements over the details, however, the imminent danger to Europe's Jews, coupled with the refusal of any Western democracy to accept significant numbers of Jewish refugees—the United States had closed its doors to almost all immigration in 1924—led to a communal near consensus that mass emigration to Palestine was the Jews' only hope.

Following on scattered stories in the Yiddish press, the first well-publicized (albeit unconfirmed) English-language report of the mass murder of Jews underway in Europe came from the exiled German novelist Thomas Mann. Mann relayed this news on BBC radio, with one of his reports being as early as November 1941, before Japan attacked Pearl Harbor and Germany declared war on the United States. "The news sounds incredible, but my source is good," he said in January 1942. "Four hundred young Dutch Jews have been brought to Germany to serve as objects for experimentation with poison gas.... They are dead; they have died for the New Order and the martial ingeniousness of the master race." Mann's report was largely ignored, though the *New York Times* printed a story titled "Extinction Feared by Jews of Poland" four months later, buried on page 28.[3]

The process of "knowing" and "doing" worked its way slowly through Jewish organizations and then through official US agencies, never with sufficient swiftness to save those living in the shadow of mass death. The amazing audacity of the Nazi killing machine exercised a near-hypnotic effect on virtually everyone who heard the news for the first time. Felix Frankfurter, Brandeis's protégé (and successor on the Supreme Court), spoke for many American Jews and some gentiles when, upon hearing one such report from an escaped eyewitness, he lamented, "I did not say that he is lying. I said that I don't believe him. There is a difference. My mind, my heart, they are made in such a way that I cannot conceive it. No, no, I do not have the strength to believe it."[4]

As Hitler's minions were murdering tens of thousands of Jews every day across Nazi-occupied or -controlled Europe, US officials refused to address the crisis. The State Department's Division of European Affairs continued to suppress the news, owing to what it termed the "fantastic nature of the allegations." Finally, on November 24, 1942, Undersecretary of State Sumner Welles summoned Wise to Washington in order to authorize him to release the horrific news of the ongoing murder of millions of European Jews. The confirmed number was already over two million. Even this information barely made a ripple in the US press. As late as December 1944, a majority of Americans, according to a Roper poll, still did not believe that the mass murder of European Jews was taking place.[5]

President Roosevelt, so beloved by American Jews, displayed little interest in saving those being slaughtered in Europe. He spoke with Jewish leaders about the topic just once, in a December 1942 meeting that lasted twenty-nine minutes. The president offered sympathetic words but promised no concrete action. And he took none, not even to ensure that the State Department met its minuscule quota for refugee admission. Officials in both the War and State Departments were almost unanimously opposed to anything that smacked of giving the Jews special treatment—whether in Europe, in Palestine, or before American refugee boards—irrespective of the special threats they faced. Roosevelt's closest advisers, including the Jewish ones, thought it best to play down the significance of the Holocaust as well as the potential of a Jewish state as a cure for the age-old Jewish Question in Europe. All wished to avoid inspiring antisemites to condemn the war effort as being fought for "the Jews."[6]

The ease with which American Jewish organizations came to embrace the Zionist cause in this crucial moment has since given rise to enormous controversy among historians over whether the intense focus on Palestine came at the expense of rescuing Jews from the Nazis. The reasons for the change in focus within American Jewry are easily understood if sometimes difficult to forgive. American Jews saw refugees as victims, a source of Jewish shame and a symbol of Jewish impotence. The Zionists, in contrast, made American Jewish breasts swell with pride. As the Hollywood screenwriter Ben Hecht explained in 1942, the Palestinian Jew had become a "champion... bringing a healthy and glamorous sound to that world-battered word 'Jew.'"[7]

Among American Jews, the desperately difficult cause of "rescue" could not compete with the thrilling potential of the first Jewish state in nearly two millennia. The "rescue" issue did not even make the original agenda of the American Jewish Conference of 1943, and when it was belatedly added, it received little attention. Abba Hillel Silver cautioned his colleagues at the American Zionist Emergency Council, in May 1944, not to "overemphasize" the plight of the refugees, lest doing so enable opponents to say, "If it is rescue you are concerned about, why don't you concentrate on that and put politics aside?" He worried it was "possible for the Diaspora to undermine the Jewish state."[8]

The historian Aaron Berman has argued that the Zionists' decision to give first priority to efforts in Palestine weakened the ability of American Jewish organizations to focus on the crisis in Europe: "Concentration on the statehood issue meant that few resources were left for the rescue campaign." This may be true, but any other approach was unlikely in any case. Not only did few people know of the extent of the genocide underway, but it was (and remains) difficult to imagine how American Jews might have prevented or mitigated it. A public campaign in the United States was not going to sway Hitler and his allies, and the United States could hardly demand that other nations take in refugees while refusing to do so itself. Roosevelt and many Jewish leaders remained nervous about the potential for an explosion of antisemitism that might threaten both support for the war and the Jews themselves. No major Jewish organization proved willing to demand that more Jewish refugees be allowed into the United States, at least in a public campaign. With few exceptions, Jewish leaders were unwilling to challenge the president's clearly delineated solution of saving Jews by simply winning the war. Nahum Goldmann again put a painful reality—as it was then understood—into succinct terms: "One half of the generation is being slaughtered before our eyes, and the other half has to sit down and cannot prevent this catastrophe.... Nothing can be done to check them; we can only work for victory."[9]

Might it have been possible to save significantly larger numbers of Jews if that had been the sole focus of American Jewry's efforts? A group calling itself the Emergency Committee to Save the Jewish People of Europe certainly thought so. Led by "Peter Bergson"—the pseudonym adopted by Hillel Kook, a hardline acolyte of the Revisionist Zionist thinker Ze'ev Jabotinsky, and energetically aided by Ben Hecht, this group sought to ignite a campaign that would simply save Jews, without reference to the future of Palestine. It succeeded in pulling off star-studded galas in 1943 in six cities. With the motto "We Will Never Die," they featured several Hollywood stars, including Marlon Brando, Paul Muni, and Edward G. Robinson, with original music composed by Kurt Weill. The Bergson group proposed to create emergency refugee shelters in Palestine for Jews who managed to escape from the periphery of Hitler's rule, such as from Hungary, Romania, or Bulgaria.

Mainstream Zionist organizations did everything in their power to discredit these efforts and the people behind them. Rabbi Silver insisted that "Zionism is not a refugee movement." Stephen Wise testified before Congress that the Bergson group was not a responsible part of the American Jewish community. During the height of the Holocaust, the American Zionist Emergency Committee, the movement's main political arm, went so far as to make plans to oppose a congressional resolution calling on Britain to ease restrictions on Jewish entry into Palestine, because it did not include a commitment to Jewish sovereignty. To explain these remarkable maneuvers, historian Michael N. Barnett lays responsibility on the various interlocking, albeit unspoken, forms of guilt torturing American Jews as they learned the facts of the Shoah. They suffered "survivor's guilt" together with "guilt that they had never fully grasped what was happening in Europe until it was too late." Add to this the guilt that they "had never found the right words, or tried harder, to convince their relatives to flee while it was still possible," and "were still not doing enough for the survivors." And finally, "there was guilt that, once again, they were living comfortable lives in America while Jews were fighting and dying an ocean away." Compared to the images of "emaciated bodies being bulldozed into nameless pits," the Zionists' counter-image of brave men and women fighting for "Jewish independence," Barnett noted, "became a moment of expiation and redemption." And so the wholehearted embrace of Zionism became, for most American Jews, the only option they could imagine.[10]

*     *     *

As tensions increased in Palestine, the specter of the Shoah had another, less frequently discussed effect on Zionist debates in the United States: it inspired a remarkably indulgent attitude toward Jewish terrorists. This was rarely acknowledged in public. Ben Hecht was now acting as de facto press secretary for the Irgun Tvai Leumi (National Military Organization, more commonly known as the Irgun), which was led by future Israeli prime minister Menachem Begin. Its more radical offshoot, Lohamei Herut Yisrael (Fighters for the Freedom of Israel, more commonly known as Lehi, or the Stern Gang), was led by another future prime minister, Yitzhak Shamir. Hecht placed a series of newspaper advertisements in May 1947 celebrating the Irgun's murder of British officials and soldiers in Palestine, declaring, "Every time you blow up a British arsenal, or wreck a British jail or send a British railroad train sky high or rob a British bank... the Jews of America make a little holiday in their hearts." He called the turn toward terrorism "the sanest and healthiest thing that has happened to the battered Hebrew cause in 1500 years."[11]

Mainstream Zionist organizations issued statements of stern disapproval. The primary complaint, however, was that the expression of pro-terrorist sentiments "confused the public," as Nahum Goldmann put it, as spokesman for the Jewish Agency. Worried that news of these terrorist attacks would turn the US public and Congress against the Zionists, the American Jewish Committee softened its position opposing Jewish statehood. In a confidential staff memo, AJC staff researcher Milton Himmelfarb expressed the hope that "after the state was created, the daily papers in New York at least would no longer carry headlines screaming of King David Hotel explosions and hangings of British sergeants; in short, 'better an evil end than an endless evil.'"[12]

The question of the morality of the Jewish terrorists and their willingness to murder civilians in order to intimidate their adversaries, both British and Arab, rarely arose in American Zionist circles. The implication—sometimes voiced, sometimes implicit—was that after the horrors inflicted on the Jews by the Nazis, and the refusal of the rest of the world to take much notice, such scruples were a luxury Jews could no longer afford. What's more, it seemed to work. Bruce Hoffmann, author of a comprehensive history of the topic, described the Jewish terrorist campaign as "the first post–World War II 'war of national liberation'" and credited its success with hastening the British government's ultimate decision to end its mandate and withdraw its troops, thereby paving the way for the Zionist victory.[13]

Not all American Jews were eager to hop aboard the Zionist express. The most vociferous voice of the movement's Jewish opponents undoubtedly belonged to Elmer Berger, a prominent Reform rabbi in Flint, Michigan. Funded by some of the great fortunes of American Jewry, including Lessing Rosenwald, son of Sears, Roebuck magnate and philanthropist Julius Rosenwald, Berger organized anti-Zionist Jews into the American Council for Judaism (ACJ) in 1942. ACJ literature deplored "the racist theories and nationalist philosophies that have become prevalent in recent years," by which Berger meant not only fascism, but also Zionism. The literature attacked what it called the "Hitlerian concept of a Jewish state." The ACJ's members "look[ed] forward to the ultimate establishment of a democratic, autonomous government in Palestine," with Jews, Muslims, and Christians "enjoying equal rights and sharing equal responsibilities": "Our fellow Jews shall be free Palestinians whose religion is Judaism, even as we are Americans whose religion is Judaism." While the group's membership was small and geographically concentrated, and even in those places remained a minority, it continually punched well above its weight politically. In part this was due to the fact that its views were very much appreciated within the US national security establishment, and especially the State Department. Only slightly less significantly, the ACJ also enjoyed the enthusiastic support of the Sulzberger family's newspaper, the *New York Times*.[14]

Although *Times* publisher Arthur Hays Sulzberger never formally joined Berger's organization, his newspaper continued to treat the group as a serious political and ideological force long after this might have been journalistically defensible. He forbade use of the phrase "the Jewish people" in the paper, preferring unwieldy substitutes such as "people of the Jewish faith"; later he vetoed all use of the term "the Jewish state." Following in the footsteps of Adolph Ochs, his father-in-law and predecessor in the publisher's chair, who, perhaps ironically, was married to the daughter of the famed Reform rabbi Isaac Meyer Wise, Sulzberger consistently resisted putting Jews in "showcase" editorial positions at the *Times* regardless of their qualifications. He urged his fellow prominent German Jews to follow a similar practice in the businesses they oversaw. In 1938, he tried to convince Franklin Roosevelt not to nominate Felix Frankfurter to succeed Benjamin Cardozo on the US Supreme Court, lest the appearance of a "Jewish seat" on the court provoke an antisemitic backlash. Sulzberger's anti-Zionism became so extreme that he complained in a 1946 speech that "thousands dead might now be alive" had the Zionists put "less emphasis on statehood." This concern for the fate of Jewish victims of Nazism, however, is invisible in the *Times'* coverage of the issue, which consistently downplayed the danger to Europe's Jews, buried stories about the Shoah, and, in short, ensured that America's "paper of record" made no attempt whatsoever to do justice to the historic crimes then underway.[15]

A more significant obstacle to the Zionist conquest of mainstream American Jewish institutions than the uncompromising anti-Zionism of the ACJ were the more measured concerns expressed by the non-Zionists who led the American Jewish Committee (AJC). These were some of the wealthiest and most admired Jews in America. The AJC operated as a self-appointed executive committee for (mostly) German American Jewry, protecting both its interests and its image as it committed itself to the kinds of good works that its members understood to serve both goals simultaneously. Initially spearheaded by the lawyer Louis Marshall (Judah Magnes's father-in-law), together with the banker Jacob Schiff and the scholar Cyrus Adler, it was formed in 1906 at least in part to address the crises faced by Russian Jews (both those seeking to emigrate to the United States and those who had already arrived). The help, while crucial to the remarkable success of the immigrants in rising through American society, came with a mixture of ambivalence and condescension. The German Jews' fear was that these unclean, unkempt masses would discredit all Jews in the eyes of Protestant America. The sheer numbers of the Russians—an immigrant wave that would eventually reach more than two million before it was shut down by Congress's restrictive Immigration Act of 1924—meant, moreover, that they would soon overwhelm the comfortable, authoritative position of the 250,000 or so German Jews who had previously defined the community. With the countless philanthropic institutions they formed, the Germans sowed the seeds of their eventual displacement by the very people they believed themselves to be rescuing.

Constantly worried about the possibility of an explosion of antisemitism, AJC members remained wary of Zionism and its implications for Jewish peoplehood as well as its potential for dividing Jewish loyalties. And while AJC's position was simpatico with that of President Roosevelt and the US State Department, it was not one shared by most East European Jews. The latter were growing increasingly dedicated to Zionism as news of the horrors of the Holocaust traveled through family and village networks. No doubt concerned about the increasing political distance between his organization's orientation and that of the Jewish masses in whose name it purported to speak, Joseph M. Proskauer, a lawyer and former New York Supreme Court judge, who became head of the AJC in 1943, scrambled to try to bridge the gap. He had a partner in the Zionist stalwart Stephen Wise, who shared his commitment to both FDR and at least a pretense of Jewish unity. While insisting "on principle" to be "unalterably opposed to any plan that would seem to set up the Jews as a separate political enclave," Proskauer proposed a "conference" of Jewish groups in the hopes of moderating Zionist demands and retaining the AJC's position as first among equals in Jewish organizations.[16]

A previous meeting, held at New York's Biltmore Hotel in May 1942, with 600 delegates and Zionist leaders from 18 countries attending, had demonstrated the dominance of one view in particular. Those demanding the creation of a Jewish "commonwealth" among Zionist leaders, together with a shift of its political focus from the United Kingdom to the United States, had prevailed. Now, on August 29, 1943, 504 representatives of 65 national Jewish organizations and institutions, claiming to represent fully 1.5 million American Jews, gathered at the Waldorf-Astoria in Manhattan. Because of its deliberately limited membership, the AJC was granted only three delegates. The Zionists, meanwhile, had secured the votes of over 80 percent of the delegates in advance.

As the proceedings began, moderate Zionist leaders, led by Wise, sought to work out a compromise with Proskauer in the hopes of preserving Jewish unity. When the AJC leader agreed to drop his organization's blanket condemnation of the idea of a Jewish state, merely terming its proposed creation "untimely," Wise was willing to make a deal. Abba Hillel Silver, however, was not. Grabbing the podium via a complicated parliamentary maneuver, he denounced the compromise even before Wise had finished proposing it. Rising to spellbinding oratorical heights, Silver thrilled his audience by asking, "How long is this crucifixion of Israel to last?" "From the infected typhus-ridden ghetto of Warsaw, from the death block of Nazi-occupied lands where myriads of our people are awaiting execution," he thundered, "from a hundred concentration camps which befoul the map of Europe, from the pitiful bands of our wandering ghosts over the entire face of the earth comes the cry: Enough!" When he concluded that "there is but one solution for national homelessness. That is a national home!" the room burst into a spontaneous rendition of "Hatikvah," the Zionist national anthem. All serious talk of compromise ended then and there. Among organizations represented at the conference, only the AJC voted against the creation of a Jewish commonwealth (before its delegates walked out). Silver had effectively elbowed the aging Wise from his position as the de facto leader of the American Zionist movement, and his program soon became the all-but-unchallenged program of mainstream American Jewish organizations and the millions of Jews they could fairly be said to represent.[17]

Its embrace of Zionism transformed the American Jewish community, providing both a common cause and sense of purpose. It served simultaneously to unite and democratize the community. It blunted the oversized influence of Jewish wealth and power as previously exercised by the AJC and uplifted the East Europeans to equal and ultimately dominant status. Simultaneously, it united Conservative, Orthodox, and Reform Jews as never before. In doing so, moreover, it helped to bring back into the fold many "who otherwise would have been lost to Judaism," as the seminal theologian of Conservative Judaism, Solomon Schechter, had predicted it would back in 1906. For a growing number of Jews, the tenets and rules of the religion itself were losing their appeal, but commitment to the cause of what became known in the wake of the Holocaust as Jewish "peoplehood"—essentially ethnic solidarity—rose accordingly.[18]

Almost irrespective of whatever religious or theological beliefs they held, this sense of community revived a feeling of pride among American Jews and affirmed their commitment to Jewish identity. At one meeting of the Jewish National Fund, an organization founded in 1903 to purchase land in Palestine in order to settle Jews there—a young rabbi asserted, without challenge or protest, "I was born in Palestine; the Jews of Palestine have status and dignity; the Jews of the Galut [exile] have no status and no dignity." Such sentiments were common among American Jews as they learned of the tragedy in Europe. They experienced a profound sense of helplessness in its wake, which helped to fuel the Zionists' success within the community. But winning over American Jews was one battle; convincing the US government to support the Zionist agenda in the face of powerful opponents inside and outside the country was a task of an entirely different order.[19]

# CHAPTER 3

# IN THE ARENA

HARRY TRUMAN'S DECISION TO RECOGNIZE THE STATE OF ISRAEL JUST minutes after David Ben-Gurion's midnight announcement on May 14, 1948, was the culmination of one of the most ambitious and successful lobbying campaigns in political history. It pitted the mostly Jewish member organizations and individuals of the Zionist movement against virtually the entire burgeoning US foreign policy and military establishment. Although Truman had initially been reluctant to support the idea of a Jewish state, once he had decided to do so he saw himself as choosing not only the most politically expedient option, but also the one that might just add his name to a story begun thousands of years earlier in the Bible.

The question of Palestine had not loomed large in the minds of American leaders during World War II. When it did arise, President Roosevelt had genially juggled competing interests with sympathetic-sounding promises without committing himself to them. On February 18, 1945, as Allied troops were closing in on Berlin, FDR met with the Saudi king, Ibn Saud, aboard a US navy cruiser in the Suez Canal. For Roosevelt, it was a pit stop on his way home from Yalta, the Crimean port city where he, Winston Churchill, and Joseph Stalin sought to shape the postwar world. Roosevelt told an aide that he planned to "point out to Ibn Saud what an infinitesimal part of the whole area was occupied by Palestine and that he could not see why a portion of Palestine could not be given to the Jews without harming in any way the interests of the Arabs." Alas, Ibn Saud informed the president that the Arabs would die "rather than yield their land to the Jews." He suggested instead that the Germans should pay for what they had done by giving the Jews part of their own country. Roosevelt promised to include both Jews and Arabs in any policy the United States eventually endorsed. In the few weeks before his death on April 12, Roosevelt occupied himself with other matters. But he still found time to send mixed messages, both confirming his support for the Zionists and reassuring the non-Zionist leaders of the American Jewish Committee that he shared their discomfort with the notion of a Jewish state in Palestine.[1]

Harry Truman did not much concern himself with Palestine before becoming president. He had been a county judge in Jackson County, Missouri, and had owned a haberdashery—which had failed, leaving him with debts—before becoming a US senator. He owed his political career to the father of an army buddy, who happened to be the boss of a Missouri political machine. A popular senator and loyal Democrat, Truman became Roosevelt's 1944 running mate as an unlikely compromise candidate after the Roosevelt team decided to dump FDR's increasingly proSoviet former vice president Henry Wallace. During the eleven weeks of his vice presidency, Truman met with FDR only twice and never alone. Palestine, as far as we know, never came up in their discussions.

As president, Truman appeared at sea when faced with the need to deal with complex, competing priorities. Unlike Roosevelt, he had no gift for hiding his plans and potential machinations until the proper moment arrived to spring them. Often appearing to change his mind on key questions depending on who happened to be the last person to brief him, Truman gave his inherited team of long-serving Roosevelt aides the impression that he could be cajoled into doing whatever they thought best, however much he might complain along the way. This inspired a constant tug-of-war between his advisers until decisions became impossible to reverse. The buck may have stopped with Truman, as the plaque on his desk said, but it bounced around quite a bit before finally settling down in one place.

Truman also brought his small-town prejudices from Independence, Missouri, to the White House. Writing in his diary, he would call New York City "kike town" and complained about Jews being "very selfish" and always "demanding special treatment" without concern for other victimized groups. He even compared them to Hitler and Stalin "when they get power, physical, financial or political." Despite his preconceptions, however, Truman formed deep relationships, both personal and professional, with individual Jews. The most famous of these was with Eddie Jacobson, his army buddy and former business partner, and the Zionists would constantly call upon Jacobson to try to convince the president to see things their way. That they ultimately succeeded is a major reason why there is a country called "Israel" today.[2]

The first postwar attempt to solve the matter of the future of Palestine came in January 1946 with the appointment of an eleven-member joint British-US committee meeting in Washington, DC, the Anglo-American Committee of Inquiry Regarding the Problems of European Jewry and Palestine. These "problems"—that is, the future of Palestine, given that it was becoming increasingly clear to most observers that Arabs and Jews were not going to be able to share the country peaceably—were considerably exacerbated by the still uncertain fate of an estimated 220,000 Jewish refugees who had survived the Holocaust, and who were now living in miserable conditions in Allied-overseen refugee camps across Europe. The committee recommended allowing 100,000 Jews to immigrate to Palestine immediately. Committee members hoped for the eventual creation of a single binational state. It would be "neither a Jewish state nor an Arab state," and it would "fully protect and preserve the interests in the Holy Land of Christendom and of the Moslem and Jewish faiths." In the meantime, however, the country would continue to be governed by the British. The committee deputized a two-man team, a British parliamentarian and a US diplomat, to draft an implementation plan, which became the "Morrison-Grady Plan," named after its authors,

British deputy prime minister Herbert Morrison and US diplomat Henry Grady, and was issued that July.[3]

Zionists did not much like the Morrison-Grady Plan, but rather than refuse to engage at all, they began a massive lobbying campaign for terms that would lead to the creation of a Jewish state. At one cabinet meeting, Truman showed the assembled a sheaf of telegrams "four inches thick." Every single one was opposed to the implementation of the report's recommendations. "Jesus Christ couldn't please them when he was here on earth, so how could anyone expect that I would have any luck?" Truman was heard to complain. But it wasn't just angry telegram writers that Truman was worrying about. It was Jewish voters located in Democratic urban strongholds across the Northeast and Midwest, as well as Jewish financial contributors on both coasts. Truman would never stop telling people that he thought this had been the best plan for the region, and he was heard to blame "British bullheadedness and the fanaticism of our New York Jews" for undermining it.[4]

Truman felt that unless the United States and Britain could secure agreement between the Jews and Arabs, "the situation [would be] insoluble," and the result could be a catastrophic war. His concerns were not unwarranted: even future Israeli prime minister David Ben-Gurion, who since 1935 had chaired the Jewish Agency, the Zionist's proto-governmental organization in Palestine, appeared to share them. Working under the cover of deepest secrecy, he was willing to delay the realization of the cause to which he had devoted his entire adult life, fearing that although the Jews now made up slightly more than a third of Palestine's population, they were not yet strong enough to win a war against their potential enemies. Those enemies were not just the Arab inhabitants of Palestine itself but also the five neighboring Arab nations, which had already promised to invade in the event of a declaration of statehood.

Ben-Gurion tried to convince British prime minister Clement Attlee's lord chancellor, Sir William Jowitt, to retain British troops in Palestine for another five to ten years, and thereby give the Jewish community a chance to strengthen itself before the ultimate battle. But Britain no longer had any interest in remaining in Palestine to enforce such a deal, even in the extremely unlikely case that one could be reached. It had emerged from World War II in dire financial straits and was in the process of drawing down its global obligations, not deepening them. Not only was policing Palestine financially costly, but British soldiers there were under increasingly effective siege from Jewish terrorist militias. In the winter of 1947, Britain announced its planned withdrawal and dumped the problem in the lap of the fledgling United Nations.[5]

The various institutions of the nascent, usually fractious US national security establishment demonstrated a rare unanimity and consistency when it came to Zionism: they were opposed. As early as 1942, Allen Dulles, who was running the Office of Near Eastern and African Affairs at the State Department at the time (and would later become director of the Central Intelligence Agency), had voiced his objections to a merely rhetorical pro-Zionist resolution in Congress. He backed down only after it was clarified that the resolution would commit the United States "to no foreign obligation or entanglement." Reasons for this opposition shifted with the times. In October 1945, Loy Henderson, in Dulles's seat as chief of the Bureau of Near Eastern and African Affairs, insisted that US support for Jewish emigration to Palestine "on humanitarian or other grounds" would undermine US interests in the region. He believed it would inevitably cause "resentment...towards the United States" in the Middle East. In articulating his position, he said, "There are four hundred thousand Jews and forty million Arabs. Forty million Arabs are going to push four hundred thousand Jews into the sea. And that's all there is to it. Oil—that is the side we ought to be on." Assistant (and future) secretary of state Dean Acheson concurred, telling President Truman that a Zionist victory would "imperil...all Western interests in the Near East."[6]

The newly formed CIA powerfully reinforced these views with a report on the likely Arab reaction to US support for the Zionists. With rare and impressive prescience, its authors predicted, among other results of a potential US pro-Zionist policy, that Arab leaders would fear Jewish expansion—that, from the Arab perspective, the Jews would probably seek to "consolidate their position through unlimited immigration" and then "attempt to expand until they become a threat to the newly won independence of each of the other Arab countries." Operating from these assumptions, those countries could declare war on the new Jewish state and attack Jews living in the Arab nations themselves. A pro-Zionist tilt, furthermore, risked the loss of US oil concessions in those Arab nations; Islamic religious authorities might even issue a call to jihad, urging all Muslims "to fight the invader, regardless of country of origin." Finally, and perhaps most important to the authors of the CIA's response, was the fear of "a Soviet attempt to exploit all of the above."[7]

In their struggle to build support in the United States, Zionists naturally looked to the folks who were already invested in the cause for a helping hand, especially those American Christians who, thanks to their reading of the Bible, had already bought into the Zionist cause. But instead of the merely rhetorical support they had received from Christians in the past, Jews now began asking for specific commitments on the basis of the idea of restitution. The Holocaust had been perpetrated in an ostensibly Christian nation—with some forty million Protestants and twenty million Catholics, among other Christian denominations, in a 1933 population of about seventy million—and there had not been much protest from either its religious leaders or the Vatican. Zionists therefore argued that Christendom owed the Jews their own country in reparation. As the Zionist firebrand Rabbi Abba Hillel Silver put it, "Our six million dead are a tragic commentary on the state of Christian morality and the responsiveness of Christian conscience." On this point, if not many others, the more moderate Zionist leader Rabbi Stephen Wise concurred: "My people deserve reparation from a Christian world if there be a Christian world."[8]

Prewar Zionist Christian organizations had been mostly front groups boasting illustrious signatures but little genuine substance. Emanuel Neumann, who had worked under Justice Brandeis at the Zionist Organization of America but later became Silver's top lieutenant, had put together the so-called American Palestine Committee, an organization that was chartered in 1932 but existed largely on letterhead. Ten years later, however, he created the Christian Council on Palestine, which boasted two of America's leading theologians, Paul Tillich and Reinhold

Niebuhr, on its executive committee. Niebuhr, in particular, would prove to be a remarkably dedicated foot-soldier for the cause in multiple arenas simultaneously. As early as May 1933, he was already publishing articles with titles such as "Germany Must Be Told!," and proposing Palestine as a potential solution to Germany's Jewish problem. He would continue to speak and write on the topic over the ensuing years. In 1941, now comfortably ensconced at New York's Union Theological Seminary, and a dedicated Roosevelt-supporting Democrat, Niebuhr founded the magazine *Christianity and Crisis*. He then used it to advocate for the Zionist cause over the objection of the magazine's editorial board. Toward the end of World War II, after joining with other prominent Christian leaders to found the American Christian Palestine Committee, he traveled the country lecturing on its behalf.[9]

Niebuhr's passion for the Zionist cause inspired him to wait for hours outside the 1946 meeting of the Anglo-American Committee of Inquiry in the hopes of being invited inside. Just before the committee called it a day, they did invite him in, and he was asked to speak in place of his own boss from the Union Theological Seminary, the intensely anti-Zionist Reverend Henry Sloane Coffin, who was mysteriously absent. Niebuhr used the occasion to argue for a position so extreme that barely any Zionists had dared to voice it. About the efficacy of a binational Jewish-Arab commonwealth, Niebuhr called it a likely formula for war and instead suggested, "Perhaps ex-President Hoover's idea that there should be a large scheme of resettlement in Iraq for the Arabs might be a way out." Asked if this implied the forcible removal of the Arabs from Palestine, Niebuhr said yes, before adding, with almost comical understatement, "It may not appeal to the Arabs as being immediately just."[10]

By raising the possibility of what we now call "transfer," Niebuhr contradicted the official Zionist position. Ben-Gurion had told the committee, "There will not only be peace between us and Arabs, there will be an alliance between us and Arabs, there will be friendship." But Ben-Gurion himself knew this to be nonsense. Although Ben-Gurion may once have hoped for a peaceful solution to the problem of a shared Palestine, by the time of these hearings, it was clear from the violent riots of 1920, 1921, 1929, and 1936 that the Arab inhabitants would reject such an alliance or possibility of friendship. In those incidents, the Arabs had protested both the British presence and the likelihood of further Jewish immigration. In a 1937 letter to his son, Ben-Gurion had written, "A partial Jewish state is not the end, but only the beginning.... We must expel Arabs and take their places, if necessary...with the force at our disposal." Although he would often speak sympathetically of the hardships Zionism inflicted on the Palestinians, his position on strengthening and expanding the Jewish community in Palestine never wavered. Back in Washington, Stephen Wise, a movement moderate, privately wrote Niebuhr to thank him for going "beyond where we dared to go, though not beyond where we wished to go."[11]

In addition to the position he occupied among Christian clergy, Niebuhr claimed a uniquely influential voice within America's liberal intelligentsia. *The Nation* magazine was ground zero for the debate over who were the imperialists and who the anti-imperialists in Palestine. Were the Zionists the good guys as they fought to eject the British, while coincidentally, and regretfully, displacing the local Arab population? Or was it the Arabs themselves, who sought to defend their homes and way of life against the technologically superior, Western-supported colonialists, who were the good guys? Writing at length in the magazine in early 1942, when the full truth of the Final Solution had not yet reached American shores, Niebuhr insisted that because Jews were "the chief victims of Nazi fury," they needed a "'homeland' in which they will not be simply tolerated but which they will possess." Niebuhr admitted that Zionist leaders were "unrealistic" in pretending that their demands would entail no "injustice" to the Arab population, but he also did not much seem to care. Zionist organizations distributed Niebuhr's essays far and wide.[12]

At the dawn of the debate over Jewish statehood, liberals made their choice, and they chose the Zionists. *The Nation*'s editor-in-chief, Freda Kirchwey, discovered what she called "the miracle of Jewish Palestine"— the Jewish men and women who had emigrated to Palestine to help shape the future of the Zionist state, she said, were "'free' in the full moral meaning of the word." They had resisted imperialist interests driven by "oil and the expectation of war; oil and the fear of Russia; oil and the shortage in America; oil and profits." Lillie Shultz, director of Nation Associates, a nonprofit organization created to accept tax-deductible donations on behalf of *The Nation*, accused Ernest Bevin, Britain's secretary of state for foreign affairs, of enjoying "a little bloodletting—particularly of Jewish blood," as his nation sought to protect its "oil empire and... to advance the plans of the Anglo-America alliance for containing the Soviet Union." Kirchwey accused the grand mufti of Jerusalem, Mohammed Amin al-Husseini, who had spent much of World War II in Berlin, of being "responsible in large part for the Nazi program of extermination of the Jews." There is no reason to doubt the sincerity of *The Nation*'s editorial support for the Zionists. Yet these beliefs were not the only motivations for its frequent forays into battle on behalf of the cause. Shultz secured secret payments from the Jewish Agency to Nation Associates, made in the names of individuals so as to hide their origin. She would continue to facilitate this sub-rosa financial support after the state's founding by helping the Israelis to secretly fund and arrange visits of Christian luminaries who were likely to report back favorably on issues of concern, such as Israel's hardline diplomatic stance vis-à-vis the return of Arab war refugees to what had been their homes in Israel.[13]

America's other leading liberal publication, *The New Republic*, covered Palestine much as *The Nation* did, though with less intensity. Its early coverage was heavily critical of the British. In December 1946, former vice president Henry Wallace took over as the magazine's editor before quitting, in July 1948, to run for president as far-left challenger to Truman. While at *TNR*, he took a tour of Palestine in the winter of 1946–1947 and returned home to announce that "Jewish pioneers" in Palestine were "building a new society" there. Wallace found the Zionists in Palestine ready to teach "new lessons and prov[e] new truths for the benefit of all mankind." They sought to do this, moreover, not from a "somber spirit of sacrifice," but with "a spirit of joy, springing from their realization that they are rebuilding their ancient nation."[14]

Also reporting from Palestine for *The New Republic* was the legendary leftist journalist (and former Washington correspondent for *The Nation*) I. F. Stone. Working for an ever-changing series of left-wing publications, depending on who would pay for him and his travels, as well as whose political lines he crossed one too many times, Stone sought to combine the human drama he was witnessing with his Marxist-infused interpretation of world history. He published a series of moving newspaper columns later collected in the now classic work *Underground to Palestine*, and later a celebratory book with the photographer Robert Capa titled *This Is Israel*. Stone traveled on the crowded, barely seaworthy vessels secured by the Zionists to smuggle refugees from Europe to Palestine, eluding British warships on the way. He sought "to provide a picture of their trials and their aspirations in the hope that good people, Jewish and non-Jewish, might be moved to help them." More than any other contemporary journalist, he succeeded in capturing the desperation of Zionist pioneers as well as their passionate optimism. Stone became enraptured by the "tremendous vitality" of those who just months earlier had been "ragged and homeless" survivors of Nazism, and who were now building Jewish Palestine. "In the desert, on the barren mountains," and in "once malarial marshes," he wrote, "the Jews have done and are doing what seemed to reasonable men the impossible. Nowhere in the world have human beings surpassed what the Jewish colonists have accomplished in Palestine, and the consciousness of achievement, the sense of things growing, the exhilarating atmosphere of a great common effort infuses [their daily lives]."[15]

Stone's reporting created a sensation. He single-handedly lifted the circulation of the intensely pro-Zionist, left-wing daily newspaper *P.M.*, where he filed a number of these reports, to a brief period of profitability. He cared desperately about the fate of the refugees and thrilled to the fact that as they had been "kicked around as Jews...now they want to live as Jews, to hold their heads up as Jews." He was proud to call them his "kinsmen" and "brothers," and said they were an inspiration to "all who prize human courage, devotion, and idealism." And yet Stone did not ignore the fate of the Palestinian Arabs who had been displaced. He scored the Jews for failing to devote "one-tenth" of the attention to Arab relations that they had to building up the land. He refused an enormous offer of publicity funds for *Underground to Palestine* because it was conditioned on his willingness to remove the endorsement the book carried of

Israeli-Palestinian binationalism. He would spend the next half-century of his career searching in vain for a just solution.[16]

One of the most intriguing publications to be found anywhere when it came to Palestine (and much else) was *Commentary*, the extremely ambitious intellectual magazine founded and funded by the American Jewish Committee in 1945. The magazine served multiple purposes. It helped to domesticate and assimilate the socialist sons and daughters of the Lower East Side into the liberal mainstream of American Jewish life, for example, but it simultaneously showcased the brilliance and originality of this first-born generation of American Jewish intellectuals before that same mainstream. This was during a period when established American institutions of higher learning and young Jewish intellectuals approached each other with mutual feelings of mistrust. By providing a prestigious forum for the young Jewish writers and aspiring intellectuals to display their talents, the AJC offered a way for each side to traverse at least some of the distance necessary to bridge this gap. It also helped to create a more inclusive intellectual culture for Jew and gentile alike. For *Commentary*, the question of Palestine was intimately tied up with the self-identity of American Jews and the image of Jews and Judaism that the Zionists were likely to create in the eyes of American gentiles. As its founding editor and guiding spirit, Elliot E. Cohen, explained in *Commentary*'s first issue, with millions of the Jews of Europe murdered—"Not killed in battle, not massacred in hot blood, but slaughtered like cattle, subjected to every physical indignity—*processed*"—it had fallen to American Jews to embrace "a far greater share of the responsibility for carrying forward, in a creative way," their "common Jewish cultural and spiritual heritage."[17]

The young Jewish intellectuals in the magazine's orbit did not much share in the enthusiasm for the Zionist project, save for a rather distant and casual admiration for Zionist essayist Ahad Ha'am's notion of Israel as a cultural center for Jews worldwide. The young intellectuals' distaste for Zionism was not, however, simply a matter of the age-old conflict between Jewish particularism and universalism. It was, at bottom, visceral, as if Zionism represented one more skin of the old world to be shed in the new. "The idea of a Jewish state was abhorrent," recalled Alfred Kazin decades later. "The world of Jews was what we were trying to escape." It was surely no coincidence that the young, and then still radical, Norman Podhoretz first came to the attention of *Commentary*'s editors when, in 1951, he penned a condescendingly hostile letter about the Israelis to his mentor, Lionel Trilling. Following a six-week visit there, he called Israeli Jews "a very unattractive people," finding them to be "gratuitously surly and boorish" as well as "arrogant" and "anxious, and therefore had little hope "to become a real honest-to-goodness New York of the East," as if this had been—or ought to be—the Zionist ideal. Trilling passed the letter on to then-editor Elliot Cohen, and Podhoretz was invited into the magazine's inner circle.[18]

*Commentary*'s earliest coverage of the conflict tended toward the views expressed by the far-left Zionist fringe Ihud group, where Judah Magnes, Martin Buber, and Gershom Scholem, among others, could be found. Cohen considered Zionism to be a distraction from his mission of shaping young Jewish minds to simultaneously serve the cause of American Jewry and the cause of American culture itself by proving themselves to be the equals of any of America's leading intellectual lights. His primary correspondent in Palestine was the Prague-born Robert Weltsch, former editor of the distinguished *Jüdische Rundshau* (Jewish Review), the best-read Jewish publication in Germany until it was forced to shut down in 1938. A close friend and ally of Chaim Weizmann, he cast an extremely critical eye on the Zionist militants preparing for war and statehood. In New York, the democratic-socialist-minded journalist Sidney Hertzberg—father of Hendrik Hertzberg, the famed liberal editor of both *The New Republic* and *The New Yorker*—covered the machinations of Zionist politics with a similarly skeptical eye.

By far the most pessimistic reading of the Zionist future to appear in *Commentary*, however, was Hannah Arendt's 1946 essay on the occasion of the fiftieth anniversary of the publication of Herzl's *State of the Jews*, the pamphlet that had launched the modern Zionist movement in 1896. Arendt, a brilliant German refugee and passionate binationalist, who, after escaping the Holocaust in Germany, had worked for a Zionist organization in Paris before being forced to leave there before the Germans arrived, now compared the Jewish infatuation with Zionism to that of a medieval Jewish community's disastrous embrace of the false messiah

Sabbatai Zevi. Paying precious little heed to what was actually taking place between the already-warring Jews and Arabs two years later in May 1948, Arendt's tone reached a fevered pitch. Just as Ben-Gurion was announcing the creation of the state, she declared the mood of the Yishuv (the Jewish community in Palestine) to be one in which "terrorism and the growth of totalitarian methods are silently tolerated and secretly applauded." The likely result would be that "the unique achievements of Zionism in Palestine"—by which she meant collective agricultural farms and other manifestations of its socialist spirit—would be "destroyed." The new state, Arendt predicted, would be "surrounded by an entirely hostile Arab population, secluded inside ever-threatened borders, absorbed with physical self-defense to a degree that would submerge all other interests and activities." It would therefore "degenerate into one of those small warrior tribes about whose possibilities and importance history has amply informed us since the days of Sparta." The net result would be that "Palestinian Jewry would eventually separate itself from the larger body of world Jewry and in its isolation develop into an entirely new people." She called on the United Nations to impose a solution on the two warring sides—a solution, as she proposed it, that would feature "mixed Jewish-Arab municipal and rural councils."[19]

More than seventy years after it was written, Arendt's missive seems sadly divorced from reality. As the scholar Susie Linfield noted in her 2019 study *The Lions' Den: Zionism and the Left from Hannah Arendt to Noam Chomsky*, from the moment it was published, none of her demands seemed remotely practical. There were no Arab counterparts to the Jewish binationalists in Magnes's Ihud group, and there was no interest in the United States or Britain in imposing peace in Palestine by military force. She also failed to address the fundamental problem that made statehood necessary: the need to find a home for the nearly quarter of a million post-Holocaust Jewish refugees who remained stranded in displaced persons (DP) camps in Europe. And yet despite all these flaws, her predictive powers appear no less remarkable: the historical development of the Jewish state, and with it the Zionist project, has proceeded very much along the lines she predicted. Arendt had her flaws, no doubt, as a political pundit, but at the same time, she demonstrated a tragically impressive gift for political prophecy.

Within the more conservative establishment media in Washington, debate over Palestine tended to reflect the prejudices of the national security bureaucracy. Insider columnists Joseph Alsop and Stewart Alsop, who were brothers, warned their readers in February 1948 that Palestine would face a "catastrophe" after the scheduled British departure in May. US officials had two "unthinkable alternatives." The first was to do nothing. In that event, "at best, the experts anticipate that most of the great economic progress achieved by the Zionists will be destroyed; that the Jews will be driven from eastern Galilee and the Negeb [sic] strip around Tel Aviv." But the second alternative was no picnic either. It involved sending US troops into Palestine, for "if the blood bath begins, no force will enter Palestine without American (or Russian) troops at its head." Yet this could not be done, the Alsops claimed, as it would "inflame the entire Arab and Moslem world."[20]

The *New York Times*' most influential voice on foreign policy matters, reporter and columnist James "Scotty" Reston, argued in favor of what he termed "a non-partisan approach," which he unfortunately declined to define. Reston did, however, give voice to State Department–style fears that the new Jewish state would be "likely to seek the support of this country for many of its external policies and constantly may attempt to enlist the political support of pro-Zionist organizations here to gain that assistance." Other groups, such as "pro-British, Italian and Polish organizations," he said, had made similar efforts. But according to "officials," Reston wrote, the Zionists were "better organized, financed and located than the others, and must be neutralized by a Democratic-Republican decision to treat Palestine...on a nonpartisan basis."[21]

Reston had a point, if not a solution. The League of Arab States, now called the "Arab League," formed a lobbying group to pursue Arab interests in 1945, but it remained underfunded, understaffed, and overmatched by the Zionists in every way. It was also wracked by infighting both among the leaders of the Arab nations and between those nations and the largely disorganized and politically leaderless Palestinian population at the time. As a result, the most influential anti-Zionist voices outside the US government likely belonged to former US government officials working with—and often funded by—the oil industry. Ex–US intelligence official Kermit Roosevelt—a grandson of President Theodore Roosevelt and a future CIA officer, who would go on to mastermind a 1953 coup against the democratically elected government of Iran—joined with fellow former spies, State Department officials, and oil business executives to launch the Committee for Justice and Peace in the Holy Land in 1948. Writing in the scholarly *Middle East Journal*, Roosevelt complained that while virtually every American he knew with any diplomatic, educational, missionary, or business experience in the Middle East opposed the Zionists, President Truman was setting the country on a course that was clearly antithetical to its national interests. Why? Zionist pressure had been "exerted systematically and on a large scale." This was bad news for Jews, Roosevelt warned. There was a "gap between Zionist Jews and those considerable numbers of American Jews who fervently oppose setting their race apart as a national group." The Zionists risked making Americans "increasingly conscious of the presence of Jews" in their midst and thereby raising "the specter of increased anti-Semitism."[22]

American Jews, however, now appeared ready to shed this concern in favor of the chance to make the Zionist dream a reality. According to a November 1945 Roper poll, over 80 percent of American Jews agreed that "a Jewish state in Palestine is a good thing for the Jews and every possible effort should be made to establish Palestine as a Jewish state or commonwealth for those who want to settle there." Nearly half a million American Jews were now dues-paying members of at least one Zionist organization, and many more contributed funds and passionately shared their views. What was now called the American Zionist Emergency Council—the political arm of the Zionist groups working together to support Israel in the United States, originally created in 1939, but now vastly energized and expanded—was given the means to conduct a lobbying campaign. The size and scope of the organization had no parallel in the history of democratic politics. Despite constant infighting inside the council between supporters of Rabbi Silver and Rabbi Wise—who traded its chairmanship depending on who was up and who was down— its success outpaced not only that of its opponents, but quite possibly of every lobbying organization either before or since.

In 1941, Ben-Gurion had said, "We must storm the American people, the press, the congress—senate and house of representatives, the
churches, the union leaders, the intellectuals—and when these will be
with us, the government will be with us." By the end of 1945, forty-one
governors and state legislatures had signed letters calling on Truman "to
open the doors of Palestine." Fully twenty-seven speeches on Palestine
were heard in the Senate in just one forty-eight-hour period in February 1947, with another thirty-four senators adding statements of support
to the Congressional Record. Mailings ran into the many millions: one
Connecticut town boasting just 1,500 Jews managed to send 12,000 pre-
printed pro-Zionist postcards to US officials. That same year, there were
mass demonstrations in thirty cities in a single month. Together with
the countless other municipalities that sent the same message, these pro-
Zionist politicians and voices could be calculated to represent 90 percent
of the US population at the time.[23]

Jews in Palestine were also making their case with great effectiveness. When
the British announced that they were definitely ending their mandate and
withdrawing their troops, the question of Palestine's future was left to the
UN Special Committee on Palestine (UNSCOP). When the eleven members of the committee visited Palestine, "crowds of Jews turned out to greet
them" everywhere they went, according to an internal American Jewish
Committee report. Arab leaders, on orders from the grand mufti, refused
even to acknowledge the visits. After two weeks of this treatment, the committee gave up all attempts at communication with Palestinian Arabs, and
its report reflected this.[24]

The final plan for the proposed partition of Palestine was drafted by
Paul Mohn, Sweden's deputy representative for UNSCOP. Mohn was
the son of a philosemitic Swedish Protestant minister who had taught his
son about the trials and tribulations of Jewish history. Mohn loved "the
Holy Land" and admired the "Jewish intellect." He was deeply moved
by a visit to the DP camps in Europe and sympathized with the desire of
the people he met there to build a Jewish homeland. Mohn had hoped
to "enable the Jews and the Arabs to live side by side both as friends in

peaceful times and as enemies in times of tension." As it became obvious that this goal was impossible, however, he found he had no trouble deciding which side to favor.[25]

Mohn's partition plan favored the Jewish population in every respect. In 1947, at the time he was drafting the UNSCOP plan, the United Nations calculated the Jewish population of Palestine to be about 608,000, or slightly less than a third of its inhabitants. Under the UN's plan, however, the Jews were to be accorded 55 percent of the land, including the crucial seaport of Jaffa, with its Arab population of 70,000 as against just 10,000 Jews. Forty percent of Palestine was given to its Arabs, with the remaining 5 percent, which included Jerusalem and parts of the Negev desert, to remain under UN sovereignty until such time as everyone could agree on how it might be divided. What had been Palestine was to be split into seven separate zones—divided between Jews, Arabs, and UN control—with a proposed economic union uniting them. But given its complex structure, together with its dependence on mutual goodwill and a spirit of compromise among the two warring sides, the plan might just as well have depended on a herd of unicorns. A vote in the General Assembly was planned for November 29, 1947, the day the British mandate was to be terminated.[26]

As both Jews and Arabs in Palestine prepared for war, US national security officials refused to give up on their delusional hope for some sort of agreement that might prevent the Zionists from declaring a Jewish state. Even less sensibly, they continued to look for guidance to those Jewish elements who, sharing this hope, had forfeited all influence within the movement. Foremost among these was Judah Magnes. The rabbi, who was still chancellor of Hebrew University, spoke freely, condemning the Zionist "totalitarianism" that sought to unite the Jewish people "by force and violence." As late as April 1948, he would travel from Jerusalem to the United States on a State Department–sponsored trip to try to dissuade President Truman and Secretary of State George Marshall from recognizing the Jewish state once it was declared. Magnes went so far as to argue for the implementation of sanctions against the Palestinian Jews in the hopes of somehow avoiding war. Nothing, however, could have been less likely. Not only was the rest of the Yishuv already preparing for the coming Arab invasion, but the British were refusing even to consider extending their mandate—they "cannot," as the US consul general in Jerusalem telegraphed home, "get out of Palestine too soon."[27]

Harry Truman was no Zionist. He thought that nations based on religion and/or ethnic exclusivity belonged to the past. But more than anything he wanted to avoid a war that would either end in the slaughter of more Jews or require the commitment of US troops on the ground in Palestine. Even the most optimistic scenario, the successful creation of a Jewish state in Palestine, was undesirable, because it would forever be a thorn in the side of the United States with regard to its relations with the Arab world. Yet Truman was also deeply moved by the increasingly desperate plight of the hundreds of thousands of stateless Jewish refugees— survivors of Nazi death factories, or those who had emerged from hiding places in attics and the like—who had now been shunted off to squalid, unsanitary DP camps. Truman's "basic approach," as he described it in his memoir, "was that the long-range fate of Palestine was the kind of problem we had the U.N. for. For the immediate future, however, some aid was needed for the Jews in Europe to find a place to live in decency." He hoped to provide such aid, however, without simultaneously granting the Zionist demand for Jewish sovereignty.[28]

In June 1945, barely sixty days into his presidency, Truman sent Earl Harrison, the former commissioner of immigration and naturalization and then dean of the University of Pennsylvania, to Europe to report on the state of the Jewish refugees there. Harrison found that the Jewish DPs were still living "under guard behind barbed-wire fences...amidst crowded, frequently unsanitary and generally grim conditions, in complete idleness." He wrote Truman, "As matters now stand we appear to be treating the Jews as the Nazis treated them except that we do not exterminate them." His recommendation was a "quick evacuation of all the non-repatriatable Jews in Germany and Austria, who wish it, to Palestine."[29]

Truman agreed and forwarded the report, together with his own endorsement, both to the US supreme commander of the allied forces,

General Dwight D. Eisenhower, and to British prime minister Clement Attlee (whose Labour Party had just defeated Churchill's Conservatives in a landslide). He asked that immediate measures be taken to
allow 100,000 Jews to immigrate to Palestine. "No other single matter
is so important for those who have known the horrors of concentration
camps for over a decade as is the future of immigration possibilities into
Palestine," the president said. Ernest Bevin, the British foreign secretary,
was heard to complain that Truman apparently "did not want too many
Jews in New York."[30]

The conflict between the president's head and heart would be a consistent theme of his management of the problem of Palestine. Truman's
heartfelt sympathy for the refugees' plight, together with his admiration
for the people of the Old Testament, constantly tugged at his conscience.
His political instincts, along with those of his political advisers, also
pulled in the direction of the Zionists. His national security team felt
otherwise, though, concerned that the conflicts that could arise in a Jewish state would mean problems for the United States in the region in the
future, and logically, Truman knew this to be true.

The electoral concerns were real. New York City, where half of America's Jews already lived, was understood to be crucial to Truman's hopes
for both retaining a Democratic Congress in 1946 and winning the presidential election two years later. Rabbi Silver, a rock-ribbed Republican,
was always looming as a potential opposition organizer should Jews grow
dissatisfied with Truman's response to the problem. This concern was
exacerbated by the fact that New York's popular governor, Thomas E.
Dewey, looked to be his most likely Republican opponent in the presidential election.

A pattern established itself relatively quickly. When the president
found himself with a choice between acceding to the Zionists' demands
or siding with his own national security bureaucracy, he would let loose
with a fusillade of complaints about how infuriating the former were being before he ended up siding with them. Bevin recalled Truman saying,
just before the 1946 election: "They [the Jews] somehow expect me to
fulfill all the prophecies of the prophets. I tell them sometimes that I can
no more fulfill all the prophecies of Ezekiel than I can of that other great

Jew, Karl Marx." On, October 4, 1946, as the Jewish holy day of Yom Kippur was about to begin, and with the US midterm elections coming up in November (and just after Dewey had demanded that "hundreds of thousands" of Jews be allowed into Palestine), Truman announced US support for the Jewish Agency's proposal for "a viable Jewish state in control of its own immigration and economic policies in an adequate area of Palestine." Confusing as it may have been, this process would repeat itself many times over in the lead-up to 1948, the year both of Israel's founding and of Truman's first election contest as the Democratic candidate for president.[31]

Truman's closest friends and confidants worked hardly less relentlessly on behalf of the Zionists than the Zionists themselves. The president was heard musing, not long before the 1948 election, "I am in a tough spot. The Jews are bringing all kinds of pressure on me to support the partition of Palestine and the establishment of a Jewish state. On the other hand, the State Department is adamantly opposed to this. I have two Jewish assistants on my staff, David Niles and Max Lowenthal. Whenever I try to talk to them about Palestine, they soon burst into tears." But these two were hardly the only members of his staff fighting internally for the Zionists. Samuel Rosenman had been a close adviser to FDR and his favorite speechwriter, and Truman viewed him as a valuable voice of reason and experience. Rosenman, who was the first aide to earn the title of "White House counsel," frequently consulted with Rabbis Wise and Silver. But when Rosenman returned to private practice in February 1946, his replacement, the savvy young gentile attorney Clark Clifford, would turn out to be the key player in the president's decision-making. Clifford, as it happens, was not particularly interested in Zionism, but he was very much interested in winning elections.[32]

Clifford's calculations convinced him that it would be impossible for Democrats to retain the White House without a sweep of the heavily Jewish cities in the Northeast and Midwest. He received a steady stream of memos from Eliahu Epstein (who later Hebraicized his name to the aforementioned "Eliahu Elath"), the influential Washington representative of the Jewish Agency, and turned these over to Max Lowenthal in order to provide more arguments for the president. Lowenthal, born "Mordechai" to Orthodox Jewish immigrants from Lithuania, had made his way to Harvard Law School and befriended future Supreme Court justice Felix Frankfurter there. That acquaintance had led to an invitation to become a member of the rarefied circle of Justice Brandeis's political protégés. Lowenthal had advised Truman in the Senate and after Truman became president during the final stages of the war. He now preferred to stay in the shadows and worked out of the comfortable confines of Washington, DC's, tony Cosmos Club.

Clifford explained in a private memo to the president, on November 19, 1947, as UNSCOP debated the partition, that "today the Jewish bloc is interested primarily in Palestine and somewhat critical of the Truman Administration on the ground. . . . Unless the Palestine matter is boldly and favorably handled there is bound to be some defection on their part to the alert Dewey." Truman and Clifford had good reason to be concerned. Not only had Dewey been the state's governor, but New York City looked to be fertile ground for Henry Wallace, who was challenging Truman from the left on the 1948 Progressive Party ticket. Whenever the administration appeared to deviate from Truman's stated pro-Zionist position, Wallace would speak of the "gift of a million votes" from their Progressive ranks. Truman needed little convincing on this point. As early as 1945, he explained to four US ambassadors to Arab countries that whatever their objections to a pro-Zionist policy, he had "to answer to hundreds of thousands who are anxious for the success of Zionism": "I do not have hundreds of thousands of Arabs among my constituents," he told them.[33]

Clifford's goal was to nail down the support of America's Jews for Truman's 1948 election by steering the machinery of US foreign policy toward the swift recognition of the creation of Israel as soon as it was announced. But his task was made significantly more complicated by the fact that Truman had appointed George Marshall as secretary of state in January 1947. With the single exception of General Eisenhower, Marshall—a former US Army chief of staff; US envoy to China in 1945–1947, in charge of negotiations between China and Chiang Kai-shek's

Nationalist forces; and a future US secretary of defense—had no rivals in stature or public influence. Having appointed him to head up the State Department, Truman had no choice but to defer to him on most foreign policy questions. In September 1947, Marshall instructed the US delegation at the United Nations to do whatever was necessary to prevent the adoption of the UN partition plan, which he feared "would mean very violent Arab reaction" and "precipitate their rapprochement with the Soviet Union." Stoking the president's worst fears, he advised Truman that partition would likely force the United States to "put troops into Palestine" in order to avoid an Arab massacre of the Jews. But Marshall's greatest concern was the possible expansion of Soviet influence in the region. The departure of British troops, combined with the socialist orientation of Israel's leaders, he thought, might open the door to this scenario.[34]

The arguments continued to rage in public. Henry Morgenthau Jr., Franklin Roosevelt's longtime treasury secretary and now head of the United Jewish Appeal, authored a series of articles attacking the State Department for having "suppressed vital information" that might have led to "the liberation of the Jews kept in Hitler's death camps." That line of reasoning not only appealed to Truman's still strong feelings about the plight of the DPs, but also enjoyed the advantage of being true. New York governor Herbert Lehman, Dewey's successor, who was both a Democrat and a Jew, made the same charge in the *New York Times*, demanding that the United States at least begin the process of repaying its debt to the Jews victimized by "persecution and hatred and bestiality," and adding that it could do so by arranging for the immediate immigration of 150,000 refugees to Palestine. The State Department retaliated by leaking its alleged evidence, supplied by the British, that the Yishuv was being run by "handpicked Communists or fellow travelers" eager to do Moscow's bidding in the Middle East. This, too, was reported in the *New York Times*, which had previously warned, in a January 1, 1948, story, that a "Red 'Fifth Column' for Palestine [was] Feared" by US and British officials as ships carrying Jewish refugees arrived on its shores. Fortunately for the Zionists, however, this particular concern failed to gain traction with Truman.[35]

Internally, Clifford relied on Lowenthal and Epstein to draft responses to the apparently never-ending barrage of State Department objections to the UN partition plan; he would then put his own gloss on them and pass them on to Truman. In this manner, he met Marshall's arguments on their own terms while leaving unspoken the assumption that the outcome of the 1948 election might depend on the president's decision. He did this by cleverly insisting that he would never even think of ever raising the topic: "One's judgment in advising as to what is best for America must in no sense be influenced by the election this fall," he wrote. Partition, he argued, was "the only hope of avoiding military conflict for the United States in the Middle East," and "the only course of action with respect to Palestine that will strengthen our position vis-à-vis Russia." His point was that a trusteeship requiring US troops would only serve to alienate both sides and play into Soviet hands. (Silver had more than once intimated that, if necessary, Zionists would fight US troops just as they had fought the British.)[36]

Borrowing an argument initially made by Hubert Humphrey, who was then the mayor of Minneapolis, with his senatorial career and term as vice president under Lyndon Johnson still in the future, Clifford also insisted that to oppose the UN partition plan would undermine the world body at a time when it desperately needed a show of support. The United Nations, he explained, was "a God-given vehicle through which the United States can build up a community of powers in Western Europe and elsewhere to resist Soviet aggression." Meanwhile, the president should feel free to ignore threats of an oil embargo, because "the Arab states have no customer for their oil supplies other than the United States." Perhaps the British might have to worry about offending Muslims, because of their colonial interests, but the United States had no such obligation. Rather, the opposite was true. Why, he asked, wouldn't the "ridiculous" sight of the United States "trembling before the threats of a few nomadic desert tribes" lead Russia or Yugoslavia to "treat us with anything but contempt in light of our shillyshallying appeasement of the Arabs?"[37]

Despite these careful calculations, the pull toward partition for Truman was at least as much emotional as it was political. He had received a letter from his old friend Eddie Jacobson, who had first met the future president when he served under Captain Truman during World War I. In his memoirs, Truman would call Jacobson "as fine a man as ever walked." The experience led to the two men becoming partners in the haberdashery business after the war. Dean Acheson would later observe that what would eventually become Truman's "deep convictions" regarding the fate of the Jews in Palestine were "in large part implanted by his close friend and former partner" Jacobson, whom a frustrated Acheson described, with considerable exaggeration, as "a passionate Zionist." Jacobson had, in truth, been uninvolved and largely uninterested in the cause until the Zionists recruited him—but he did prove more than happy to help. He was especially useful to another key member of Clifford's team, the pro-Zionist FDR holdover David Niles, in reaching the president when Truman felt he could not stand to hear another word on the topic.

The planned November 29, 1947, UN vote on UN General Assembly Resolution 181 approving the partition plan required two-thirds of the member states to pass. On November 25, by the Zionists' own count, they were one vote short. Arabs and Jews employed every means of pressure at their disposal. Future secretary of state Dean Rusk, who was then in charge of the department's UN desk, would later call the "pressure and arm-twisting applied by American and Jewish representatives" in various national capitals on behalf of the resolution "hard to describe." So, too, was the level of world attention: the *New York Times* ran eighteen stories on the partition the day after the vote, and fully 360 stories in the following seven weeks, averaging roughly seven stories every day. But the vote on November 29 hardly settled matters. Indeed, it hardly settled anything at all. The final tally was 33 in favor, 13 opposed, and 10 abstentions. Both the Arab nations and the State Department continued to try to find ways to undo what had just been done. The Zionists accepted it, though at the same time they were planning to seize whatever opportunity arose to improve the already extremely generous terms accorded them.[38]

US national security officials detested the UN partition plan and were furious over the results of the vote, to say nothing of their orders from the president to support it. Robert McClintock, director of the State Department's Office of UN Affairs, privately predicted that if the partition were actually allowed to proceed, "the Jews will come running to the [UN]

Security Council with the claim that their state is the object of armed aggression and will use every means to obscure the fact that it is their own armed aggression against the Arabs inside Palestine which is the cause of Arab counter-attack." The US officials consistently sought to undermine the proposal or alter it in favor of the Arab position. Secretary of State Marshall looked forward to one day seeing the construction of a transnational oil pipeline from the Persian Gulf states to the Mediterranean seaport of Jaffa. He urged Truman to ensure that Jaffa and Safed, two strategic Arab-dominated cities that would have provided a direct line to the sea, remained under Arab control. Zionists strenuously resisted this idea, and their constant pressure had the effect of further infuriating the president, who wanted nothing more than to be done with the issue. Truman particularly detested Rabbi Silver, and not without reason. At a meeting Truman held with Zionist leaders in January 1948, Silver literally banged on the president's desk. A furious Truman ended the discussion and confided to his diary, "No one, but no one, comes into the office of the President of the United States and shouts at him, or pounds on his desk. If anyone is going to do any shouting or pounding in here, it will be me." He then issued instructions that he had "had it with those hotheads." "Don't ever admit them again," he told staff, "and what's more, I also never want to hear the word Palestine mentioned again."[39]

The Zionist camp could have saved itself a great deal of effort and infighting if it had understood that Truman wanted to deal with the aging former president of the World Zionist Organization, Chaim Weizmann, and only Chaim Weizmann, on the issue. The aged, aristocratic British chemist shared the president's hatred for Silver, whom he often compared to Hitler; to Truman's ears, his voice was honey compared to the bombastic Republican rabbi's vinegar. When Weizmann finally got in to see Truman on March 18, 1948, entering through a side door so as not to be seen by the White House press corps, he excited the president with visions of Truman's heroic role in history. According to the recollection of Truman's daughter Bess, Weizmann's "vivid description of the Jews' [agricultural achievements in Palestine] ignited the enthusiasm of the ex-senator who had toiled for years to create regional development and flood controls in the Missouri Valley." Truman then gave the man he so admired his most solemn promise: "You can bank on us." That same day, the president ordered the State Department to cease its efforts to improve the Arabs' position in the planned partition.[40]

Truman may have made up his mind, but his foreign policy team refused to concede this. Advised by the anti-Zionist State Department director of policy planning, George F. Kennan—later credited with authoring the US Cold War strategy of "containment"—together with a battery of Arabist ambassadors and foreign service officers, Secretary Marshall and Undersecretary of State Robert Lovett instructed US ambassador to the United Nations Warren Austin to offer the General Assembly a proposal that would suspend the partition plan and replace it with yet another temporary trusteeship. Although Austin's February 24, 1948, speech was short on specifics, it was clear that the department intended the British to oversee the trusteeship, ignoring the fact that Britain had no interest whatever in returning to this thankless task.[41]

What is perhaps most remarkable about the position of the entire US security establishment is the degree to which it was completely out of touch with the reality not only on the ground in Palestine, but also in London and even on Pennsylvania Avenue. Lovett and the State Department's Loy Henderson from the Bureau of Near Eastern and African Affairs discussed ways to bring "moderate and temperate" individuals to Washington to "break the president's logjam." This would have included, for example, the Ihud stalwart Rabbi Judah Magnes from Jerusalem. But it was yet another indication of how distant the State Department's plans for Palestine were from both Truman's political calculations and the increasingly chaotic situation in Palestine itself. Magnes had long ago forfeited whatever influence he had among Zionists. Britain was adamant about leaving, and Truman would not even consider replacing its troops with Americans (who, in any case, were unavailable in sufficient numbers, thanks to the nation's rapid postwar demilitarization).[42]

Austin's speech, meanwhile, caused chaos within the UN delegation. Eleanor Roosevelt, the passionately pro-Zionist former First Lady and perhaps the most prominent voice of the Democrats' still-strong idealistic liberal internationalist wing, threatened to resign her post as the first chair of the UN Commission on Human Rights if the policy he announced was not reversed. Truman could not immediately reverse the State Department's own reversal, however, without creating the impression of an administration whose foreign policy was out of the president's control, though here he failed as well. A *New York Times* editorial noted that the speech came "as a climax to a series of moves which has seldom been matched for ineptness in the handling of any international issues by an American administration."[43]

Truman grew predictably furious when he finally came to pay attention to the speech he had, in fact, approved in advance without apparently understanding it. (He would later claim, as he often did in such situations, that he had been blindsided.) In his diary, he blamed the State Department for "pull[ing] the rug [out]" from under him, reversing his stated policy, and making him out to be "a liar and a double-crosser," and he vowed privately to get even with those "striped-pants conspirators." Truman did agree to an off-the-record meeting with Magnes at Marshall's request. But the president was far more concerned that Chaim Weizmann would now likely think him a "shitass." Truman told Clifford to fix it. Clifford knew better than to contradict the president's contention that he had been given no advance knowledge of the speech. What mattered now was Truman's belief that he had been double-crossed and his desire for revenge.[44]

With the partition plan now dead in the water, Truman's day of decision came on May 12, 1948, when he met with Marshall, Lovett, and Clifford to decide whether to recognize the new state of "Israel" when the time came two days later, when David Ben-Gurion was to declare the state into existence. Lovett and Marshall argued against recognition, citing three essential points: it was questionable under international law whether they could offer recognition when there was no actual state to recognize; the president could damage his reputation by making what might appear to be a transparent attempt to win the Jewish vote; and, given US intelligence reports about Soviet infiltration of Jewish communists into Palestine once the British departed, he had to deal with the fear that recognition might enhance Soviet interests in the region.

Clifford responded with a series of arguments designed both to counter these claims and anticipate additional ones. His 1991 memoir notes that as he spoke, General Marshall displayed signs of increasing

anger and discomfort, and finally exploded. "Mr. President," he demanded, "I thought this meeting was called to consider an important
and complicated problem in foreign policy. I don't even know why Clifford is here. He is a domestic adviser, and this is a foreign policy matter."
He accused the young aide of "pressing a political consideration with
regard to this issue," saying, "I don't think politics should play any part
in this." Truman defended his decision to invite his political adviser, and
Clifford continued with his multipronged attack on the national security
establishment's anti-Zionist consensus.[45]

Clifford noted how impractical its plans for trusteeship had become,
given the fact that the Jews and Arabs were already fighting as the mandate drew to a close and the British were already on their way out the
door. Regarding the Soviets, the United States had lost an opportunity
by allowing them—through their allies, the Czechs—to be the lone
weapons supplier to the Zionists, and thereby to confer de facto, if not
de jure, recognition to the state. Clifford also played to the president's
sympathies regarding the awful experience of the Jews in recent times, as
well as the West's failure to fulfill Britain's 1917 Balfour Declaration in
support of the creation of a Jewish state there—one that subsequent US
presidents had endorsed. He went on to argue that early recognition was
consistent with the president's policy from the outset, that a Jewish state
already existed for all practical purposes, and that a trusteeship—even
if one were possible—would postpone the promise of actual statehood
indefinitely, letting down and discriminating against the Jews, and encouraging the "Arabs to enlarge the scale of violence."[46]

Clifford also tied his argument to the need to support both democracy
and the new United Nations. "Where there is not now and never has
been any tradition of democratic government" in the Middle East, he
explained, "it is important for the long-range security of our country, and
indeed the world, that a nation committed to the democratic system be
established there, one on which we can rely. The new Jewish state can be
such a place. We should strengthen it in its infancy by prompt recognition." For his pièce de résistance, Clifford appealed to Truman's love of
the Israelites of the Old Testament, rather than the ones who were presently making his life miserable. Quoting Deuteronomy 1:8, he recited,

"Behold, I have set the land before you: go in and possess the land which the Lord swore unto your fathers, Abraham, Isaac, and Jacob, to give unto them and to their seed after them."[47]

Sensing that Truman had been mightily impressed by Clifford's arguments, and unaware of the president's promise to Weizmann, Marshall grew ever angrier. He announced that "if the President were to follow Mr. Clifford's advice, and if in the elections I were to vote, I would vote against the President." This retort understandably angered Truman, but it also boxed him in. He could not order Marshall around the way he routinely did everyone else who worked for him. So, he caved. "I understand your position, General, and I'm inclined to side with you in this matter."[48]

But Marshall had said he would vote against Truman; he had not said he would resign or even criticize the president in public. And when Truman finally reversed himself yet again and defied his advice, Marshall's resistance simply evaporated. On May 14, Clifford and Lovett labored for a deal on behalf of their respective bosses in time to respond when Ben-Gurion made his announcement declaring the creation of the state of Israel. Zionists had argued at the United Nations that the Jewish Agency, headed by Ben-Gurion, was about to become the only operational governmental authority once the British departed. Clifford used this fact to argue that US "recognition" of the state of Israel was merely the "recognition" of reality. What's more, given Britain's departure, the state of Israel would become the only legally constituted body in Palestine able to secure order. By the end of the day, Clifford had received Lovett's word that the secretary would not publicly speak out against Truman's decision. He was, after all, the president, General Marshall likely reasoned, and had a right not only to choose his own policies but also to expect the loyalty of those below him once he had done so.[49]

Truman signed the letter of recognition shortly after 6:00 p.m. Eastern Standard Time, giving de facto recognition to the new state and its government. In his prepared statement, which had been written even before the name of the state was announced, he crossed out the words "the Jewish State" and wrote "Israel." He inserted the word "provisional" before the word "government." After Rusk notified Warren Austen, who was still heading the American team at the United Nations, the defeated diplomat got into his limo and left the premises without even bothering to inform his delegation of the president's decision. They heard about it with the rest of the world, on the radio.

What ultimately determined Truman's decision? He was obviously worried about its political implications, which, thanks to the Zionist lobbying and propaganda campaigns, pointed in a single direction. He also cared deeply about the feelings and opinions of his old friend Eddie Jacobson, as well as Chaim Weizmann and his present and former aides David Niles, Max Lowenthal, and Sam Rosenman. He admired George Marshall, Dean Acheson, and others, too, but for them, the emotional pull was lacking. Truman was not immune to the flattery of the Zionist leaders, and he may have believed he was playing a role in a new chapter extending biblical history, a history he took seriously.

Finally, if Truman had one consistent concern as he ricocheted between the competing sides in this debate, it was for the fate of the hundreds of thousands of Jews who were sitting in DP camps, desperate to go either to America or to Palestine. America was out of the question. And to Truman, so was letting them rot in the camps while Britain, the Arab nations, and the US State and Defense Departments tried to ignore their plight. He was deeply moved by their desperate situation and remained consistent in believing they should be allowed to emigrate to Palestine. Had Britain or the Arab nations allowed their entry into Palestine, they might eventually have lost control of the country to the Jews, but there would have been no need to declare a state, and no need to fight a war over it. And yes, predictions of a possible massacre could not be ruled out. But if Ben-Gurion and the Jews were willing to risk it, then so, dammit, was Harry S. Truman.

# CHAPTER 4

# JEW VS. JEW

Israel never did develop into the "normal" country so many of its supporters hoped and prayed it might. But during its infancy, it was hardly the cultural, political, religious, and ideological battleground it would eventually become. Within the United States, the young nation enjoyed press coverage that was generous to the point of purposeful propaganda. A 1949 article in *The New Republic* found Israelis to be "like Americans... aggressive, competent and impatient to get things done." Three years later, *The New Yorker*'s John Hersey described Israeli children as "regular Californians—sturdy, open-faced, sun-coppered," and "potentially bigger, it seems, than their parents, and perhaps bolder too." The rosy view of the young country was decidedly bipartisan. The historian Bat-Ami Zucker noted that the Congressional Record of the 1960s is replete with comments from senators and congressmen from both parties saluting Israel as a "democratic oasis in a desert of dictators" and "a solid bastion of freedom and democracy against the forces of aggression and totalitarianism."[1]

Israel's intellectual achievements and democratic character were often pitted against what was implied to be the backward and barbaric

character of the Arab nations surrounding it. Eleanor Roosevelt visited
Israel in 1952 and found it to be "like a breath of fresh air after the Arab
countries." And on Israel's tenth birthday, in 1958, speaking at a rally in
New York, the liberal historian Henry Steele Commager described it as
"devoted to peace," while surrounded by peoples ruled by "chauvinism,
militarism, and territorial and cultural imperialism."[2]

As no diaspora community had ever had to deal with a sovereign Jewish nation in two millennia, the nature of the relationship between the
American Jewish community and the Israeli government required definition. It should have come as no shock that despite the best of intentions,
an entirely new set of challenges arose—ones for which few, if any, historical precedents, much less roadmaps, could be found.

To Israel's first prime minister, David Ben-Gurion, the biblically based
call for the ingathering of exiles in the nation's Declaration of the Establishment of the State of Israel (aka Declaration of Independence) was not
merely rhetorical. Ben-Gurion was not remotely religious, but he believed
that God had given the land of Israel to the Jewish people, and that only
by living there and working the land could the Jewish people redeem
themselves from the shameful combination of timidity and powerless-
ness that had led inexorably to the tragedy of the Shoah. To this end, he
would sprinkle his arguments with Talmudic quotes, such as the famous
admonition from Ketubot 110b: "He who dwells outside of the land of
Israel is like one who has no God."[3]

But precious few American Jews chose to take up the call. American
Jews' embrace of Zionism had been predicated on the formula enunciated by Justice Louis Brandeis in the 1920s. It focused exclusively on the
dire need to find a home for Jewish refugees. American Jews liked America just fine. Not much more than 1 percent—six thousand of roughly
five million American Jews—had chosen to emigrate to Israel after its
founding. One Israeli reporter at a World Zionist Congress meeting described raising the topic of "aliyah" in the United States as inappropriate
"in polite company"—like speaking of "sex in Victorian England." Pollsters were reporting a significant diminution of American antisemitism
in the wake of the discovery of the Shoah, and the doors opening to Jews
for the first time in American society made the postwar future appear

brighter than ever. The Jewish sociologist Theodore Sasson would later characterize the relationship between American Jews and Israel in this period as "attending Israel day festivals and parades, dancing the hora, and decorating their homes with Israel-related art and artifacts," along with the occasional "tightly scheduled synagogue mission or denominationally sponsored youth tour." This distance, added his Brandeis University colleague, the historian Jonathan Sarna, allowed American Jews to imagine Israel as an "idealized dream world."[4]

The crisis was over, and the hard work of nation-building was underway, but the problems Israel now faced, understandably, were not foremost in the minds of American Jews or high on the list of priorities for American Jewish organizations. While the latter did raise funds and awareness about Israel, they were primarily concerned with problems closer to home. Israel usually appeared near the end of the American Jewish Committee's annual reports, under the heading "Overseas Concerns." In his popular study of American Judaism, originally published in 1957, the sociologist and former *Commentary* editor Nathan Glazer could not but be mystified by his own observation that "the two greatest events in modern Jewish history, the murder of six million Jews by Hitler and the creation of the Jewish state in Palestine, have had remarkably slight effects on the inner life of American Jewry."[5]

Anti-Zionism receded considerably among American Jews. Nonetheless, thanks to the strong support of the Sulzberger family, the intensely anti-Zionist American Council for Judaism continued to enjoy coverage in the *New York Times* that could only be explained by the owner's own obsessions. The constant complaint of the ACJ's executive director, Rabbi Elmer Berger, regarding the alleged Zionist plan "to retain a medieval control over a so-called 'world-wide Jewish people'" also won the council favor in the US State Department. Its officers employed ACJ press releases to pretend that such beliefs enjoyed significant support among American Jews. But the primary purpose of the council seemed to be to heighten the blood pressure of the leaders of more mainstream Jewish organizations. Among these was the non-Zionist American Jewish

Committee, whose grandees slowly made peace with the notion of Jewish "peoplehood." But its members still struggled to find their footing when dealing with the reality of an actual Jewish state. Their politics notwithstanding, their hearts were stirred by what they saw in Palestine. As AJC officer Milton Himmelfarb wrote in a confidential memo to his board of directors, "Those of our contemporaries who fear Jewish nationalism cannot avoid being stirred by the establishment of a Third Commonwealth two thousand years after the destruction of the Second and three thousand years after the founding of the First."[6]

Mordecai Kaplan, perhaps American Jewry's most influential theologian of the twentieth century and a self-described Zionist, thought that Jews in the diaspora would "likely...act as a brake on the chauvinistic tendencies that the Israeli struggle for survival is only too apt to arouse in the Jews of Israel." AJC members concurred and began to lobby the Israeli government to accord its Arab population more rights and greater respect. They even took an interest in monitoring the harsh treatment meted out to both Arab refugees and those Arabs who remained inside Israel, for a brief period paying staff to document it. But they found they had little leverage with the Israelis on such matters and eventually decided to keep their concerns to themselves.[7]

Despite having been out of step with the Zionist sympathies of most American Jews at the time of Israel's founding, the AJC managed to maintain its central role in Jewish politics. Israel could not hope to survive, much less thrive, without significant financial support from America's Jews, together with low-cost US government loans. Ideology aside, these contributions were understood by both sides to come from a place not only of generosity but also of guilt. American Jews had not done nearly enough to try to save the Jews of Europe and were terrified of making the same mistake twice. In the aftermath of the worst catastrophe ever suffered by the Jewish people, Israelis were embarked on what appeared to be an unprecedented and heroic experiment in the reinvention of an ancient, battered people. They were birthing a new, egalitarian society under constant threat of destruction, with the benefit of few of the sorts of luxuries American Jews took for granted. The least American Jews could do was to help pay for it. Beyond writing checks, however, Israelis expected American Jews to shut up and salute.

After all, if they wanted a voice inside Israel's political debate, Ben-Gurion and company were always more than happy to remind them, they were welcome as immigrants. Israeli leaders, journalists, intellectuals, and especially poets did not hesitate to term American Jews to be living in the latest iteration of traditional *Galut* (exile) and mock their concern with acceptance by their gentile neighbors. The conflict between the "New Jews" of Palestine and all others was a fundamental precept of Labor Zionism, the founding ideology of Israel's ruling party for the first thirty years of its existence. A. D. Gordon, one of the movement's ideological forefathers, had written, as early as 1911, "Every one of us is required to refashion himself so that the Galut Jew within him becomes a truly emancipated Jew; so that the unnatural, defective, splintered person within him may be changed into a natural wholesome human being who is true to himself."[8]

American Jewish leaders squirmed over Israeli statements that consistently likened them to quislings frightened before their Christian overlords. The Anti-Defamation League of B'nai B'rith (ADL)—which had been founded the wake of the 1913 "Leo Frank Affair," in which Frank, a Jew, was arrested and falsely convicted of a rape and murder in Atlanta, and then lynched by a local mob—had undertaken the mission of fighting all discrimination. But its particular focus was antisemitism. Its national chairman, Meier Steinbrink, complained to the Israelis of the "danger implicit in" such pronouncements, as they could "only form the basis of the continued charge made against us by our enemies that we of American birth and American citizenship are guilty of dual loyalty." The AJC's president, Jacob Blaustein, warned the Israelis that the "misunderstandings" such talk caused could only result in "headaches." It would have an "adverse effect on obtaining maximum cooperation (funds and otherwise) for Israel from American Jews," he said, and strengthen the mutually detested American Council for Judaism.[9]

Internal AJC documents evince considerable concern about "the allegation of conflicting loyalties" returning to haunt American Jews, should

Israeli leaders continue to speak as if they owed their primary allegiance not to their home country, the United States, but to the Jewish state. This concern was naturally heightened by the fact of the socialist orientation of Israel's ruling political party. The increasingly paranoid political atmosphere in Cold War America, especially given the anti-Communist right's obsession with the activities of Jewish radicals in New York, Hollywood, and elsewhere, also played a role. AJC representatives consistently advised Ben-Gurion to identify with US Cold War aims lest resentment "be vented on American Jews who would be charged with Communist sympathies." Thus began the decades-long public relations campaign by American Jews on behalf of "the only democracy in the Middle East." But the Israelis didn't care. Over and over, they would repeat some version of their contemptuous demand that American Jews cease their whining and "come home." "Our next task," Ben-Gurion announced just before Labor Day, 1949, "consists of bringing all Jews to Israel.... We appeal chiefly to the Jews of the United States."[10]

Following painstaking negotiations of the kind associated with postwar treaties between formerly warring nations, in August 1950 Blaustein managed to secure significant, albeit entirely rhetorical, concessions from Ben-Gurion. The Israeli prime minister declared, "The Jews of the United States, as a community and as individuals, have only one political attachment and that is to the United States of America. They owe no political allegiance to Israel." To further clarify the point, Blaustein felt compelled to add in a response that he "would be less than frank" if he did not say "that American Jews vigorously repudiate any suggestion or implication that they are in exile." Here Ben-Gurion refused to agree. Even so, he was consistently pilloried inside Israel for the concessions he did make, especially when he agreed to reaffirm the remarks eleven years later.[11]

Establishing a tradition to which future Israeli prime ministers would studiously adhere, Ben-Gurion proceeded to ignore whatever the Americans believed they had been promised. For instance, in December 1960 he declared that the "Judaism of the Jews of the United States and similar countries is losing all meaning," before adding that "every religious Jew has daily violated precepts of Judaism and the Torah by remaining in the Diaspora." He kept this up for decades, calling Zionist support groups outside of Israel "wandering Jews." Such statements would provoke outrage among American Jewish leaders, and then the process would repeat itself. The Americans would complain that the Israelis were giving aid and comfort to American antisemites, but the Israelis did not care. As far as they were concerned, American Jews' fear of antisemitism was just one more reason why they should stop their whining and make aliyah. Israelis shared a deeply—one might say religiously—held belief in the moral decadence and likely disappearance of the diaspora, via some vaguely defined combination of assimilation, prejudice, persecution, and personal self-indulgence that was somehow inherent in the conditions of Galut. This attitude proved especially painful for those American Jews who were paying attention—admittedly a small number—because the Israeli attitude was inextricably linked to the widely held Israeli belief that diaspora Jews shared some responsibility for their own passivity in the face of the Nazis. As the great Israeli historian Zeev Sternhell once observed, Zionist ideology, with its doctrine of *shlilat ha'golah*—the negation of the diaspora—"at times resembled [that] of the most rabid anti-Semites."[12]

The Blaustein exchange with Ben-Gurion remains in many respects a puzzling document. The AJC leader, historian Jack Wertheimer would write in an AJC-sponsored history of the organization, "was trying to work out an understanding between the Israeli government, on the one hand, and a population with no political or legal connection to the Jewish state, on the other." He might have added that Blaustein had no specific authority over that population, and, as a non-Zionist, did not even share its most fundamental beliefs. What's more, by choosing the AJC as his interlocutor with American Jews, Ben-Gurion was snubbing those organizations that had stood with the Zionists during the struggle for statehood. But money talked then, as it undoubtedly does in the moment you are reading this. As the owner of American Trading and Production Corporation, then America's fourteenth-largest company, Blaustein was possibly the wealthiest Jew in America. His fellow grandees were also no slouches in the fund-raising department.[13]

The Israelis agreed to Blaustein's language, according to an AJC publication, in the hope that it would "yield certain economic results." The AJC, with Ben-Gurion's public promise in its pocket, could rest easy that anyone who questioned the loyalties of America's Jews got their answer, even if they lacked the ability to enforce its contents. Meanwhile, dedicated American Zionists had little to bring to the table save their desire to stick their noses into how the Israelis governed themselves—something for which Ben-Gurion had no patience. Publicly scorned by Ben-Gurion for their failure to put their feet where their hearts were said to be and move to Israel, those who pledged their loyalty to the ideology of Zionism but did not participate in its realization as citizens of the Jewish state were viewed by Israelis as impotent hypocrites. The then twenty-seven-year-old rabbi Arthur Hertzberg framed the dilemma in a 1949 issue of *Commentary*: "What shall I do with my Zionism?" he asked in an article titled "A Movement in Search of a Program." To this question, he had no answer, and the Israelis had no interest.[14]

The frustration of American Zionists grew significantly as Blaustein successfully inserted himself as the go-between for the Israelis and American Jews. President Truman confided to the AJC leader in early 1949 that he had become "thoroughly disgusted with some of the high-pressure groups" acting on behalf of Israel, adding that it was "in spite of the obstructive efforts of some of them" that he had had chosen to support the Zionists in the end. The president also no doubt appreciated the fact that Blaustein managed to keep the contents, and even the fact, of his presidential conversations to himself. That was a decidedly rare quality in a Jewish American leader, then as now, but one that would soon be especially prized by US presidents as conflicts erupted between Israel and the United States in increasingly greater quantity and intensity.[15]

# CHAPTER 5

# STANDING UP AND STANDING DOWN

ONCE ISRAEL WAS FIRMLY ESTABLISHED, HAVING WON ITS WAR FOR INDE-pendence and signed four armistice agreements with its Arab adversaries in July 1949, the new state's relationship with the United States settled into a pattern of continual repetition. US diplomats would ask Israel to compromise on something, often having to do with the repatriation of the Arab refugees who were expelled or had fled during the war. The Israelis would listen patiently and then proceed to do whatever they had intended in the first place. The secretary of state would complain to the president, and there the matter would end.

Inside the Truman White House, according to the US diplomat Richard Ford, writing in 1951, one found "an informality not normally associated with the high-level ties found between two sovereign states." This casualness was the product of the long-standing relationships between Zionist leaders, Truman's advisers, the leaders of both US political parties, and countless members of Congress. And these connections, combined with the political and financial support of American Jews, left the Israelis free to pursue whatever goals they felt appropriate without concern for too much pushback. Assorted Jewish leaders, and often the president's close friends and political advisers as well, countered every State Department complaint. Inevitably, President Truman would decide he did not need another domestic headache and leave the Israelis to do whatever they likely would have done anyway.[1]

Israel's refusal even to entertain the notion of the return of any significant number of the roughly 750,000 Arab refugees created by the war proved a massive thorn in the young nation's side. In the US national security establishment, Israel was viewed as an inconvenient complication for US relations with the Arab world. Inside the State Department, the refugees' plight was understood to be problematic less for humanitarian reasons than for the fact that Arab leaders felt the need to make a show of caring about them. Whatever motives were at work, the Palestinians never—and still have never—lost their longing to return to their homes, villages, lemon groves, etc. The sight of them forced to live in horrifically unsanitary conditions in refugee camps spread across Jordan, Lebanon, Syria, and the Egyptian-held Gaza remained a permanent wound in much of the Arab world. This was in addition to the fact that Israel proved a perfect focus of anger for what became known as the Arab "street," and therefore an extremely convenient way to divert whatever political energies that might otherwise have been channeled into resistance to these regimes' repressive rule. "From the time of Israel's birth as a state, talking about Israel has been, in part, a way that Arabs talk about their own world," the late Arab historian Fouad Ajami wrote, but it has also been a way of avoiding that discussion.[2]

US-Israeli disputes arose even before the war's end. A March 1949 State Department analysis had advised Secretary of State George Marshall that the failure to "liquidate or materially reduce the magnitude of the Arab refugee problem" would increase regional instability and possibly invite the Soviets in to take advantage of the instability. But Chaim Weizmann, Israel's first president, acknowledged to James McDonald, America's first ambassador to Israel, that the Arab exodus had created "a miraculous simplification of our tasks." When McDonald passed this comment along to Marshall, the secretary replied, "The leaders of Israel would make a grave miscalculation if they thought callous treatment of this intractable issue could pass unnoticed by world opinion." He added that "hatred of Arabs for Israel engendered by [the] refugee problem would be a great obstacle" to any hopes the Jewish state had for peace with its neighbors.[3]

But the Israelis believed themselves entitled to what foreign minister (later prime minister) Moshe Sharett described as "spoils of war," as compensation for the conflict they insisted they had tried to avoid. And these included "the lands and the houses" given up by Palestinian Arabs, regardless of whether they had left voluntarily or been expelled. Indeed, within Ben-Gurion's cabinet, discussion focused on methods of inspiring more such departures, both in order to make room for the Jewish immigration necessary to ensure the survival of the state and to significantly reduce the threat of a potential fifth column inside the country.[4]

The 150,000 or so Arabs who remained in Israel after the war lived under martial law and needed travel permits—often denied—to move from one village to another. Their towns and villages were placed under permanent curfew, and large regions of the country where they had lived before 1948 were now closed off to them. Ben-Gurion was heard to worry aloud that if they were permitted to move more freely around the country, "those 600,000 or more refugees living on our borders will cross the border and enter the villages that have emptied." When speaking publicly, he slyly argued that it was all being done for the Palestinians' own good, "just like the first reservations" the United States had set up for Native Americans. In 1950, Israel enacted the Absentee Property Law, which transferred ownership, without compensation, to the state of any property previously belonging to "anyone who spent any time in an enemy country or 'in any part of the Land of Israel that is outside of the area of Israel.'" Records show that most of the property of 372 separate Arab villages was expropriated and turned over to the Jewish National Fund, which defines itself as a "trustee on behalf of the Jewish People." In its place, 116 parks were established. The Israel Land Authority was thus accorded 93 percent of the land inside Israel's pre-1967 borders. Virtually all of it was distributed to Jews.[5]

As would become the norm for virtually all matters relating to the Jewish state, the actual situation in Israel and on its borders bore precious little resemblance to the Israel imagined in US debate and discussion. Writing in 1995, the "post-Zionist" Israeli historian Avi Shlaim described what he termed the "conventional account" of the war and its aftermath:

> With the expiry of the Mandate and the proclamation of the State of Israel, seven Arab states sent their armies into Palestine with the firm intention of strangling the Jewish state at birth. The subsequent struggle was an unequal one between a Jewish David and an Arab Goliath. The infant Jewish state fought a desperate, heroic, and ultimately successful battle for survival against overwhelming odds. During the war, hundreds of thousands of Palestinians fled to the neighboring Arab states, mainly in response to orders from their leaders and despite Jewish pleas to stay and demonstrate that peaceful coexistence was possible. After the war, the story continues, Israeli leaders sought peace with all their heart and all their might but there was no one to talk to on the other side. Arab intransigence was alone responsible for the political deadlock.[6]

This narrative has little in common with the complex reality of events that led to what Palestinians and their supporters now call the "Nakba," or "catastrophe," of 1948. The roughly 750,000 Arabs who fled did so for many different reasons, but orders from other local and foreign leaders were hardly their primary inspiration. In a 1948 study undertaken by the Israel Defense Forces (IDF), Israel's unified military service, the IDF itself took credit for forcing out 70 percent of the Arabs who left. David Ben-Gurion would later be so haunted by these expulsions that, as prime minister, he would speak to their imaginary presences, à la Macbeth. Jewish pleas for Arabs to remain were few and far between, and decidedly overwhelmed by numerous threats, expulsions, and acts of deliberate terrorism, including rape and mass murder. (Jews, it needs to be mentioned, were also the victims of Arab attacks and massacres during the war, both inside Palestine and in the bordering Arab nations, where they, too, had lived for centuries.)[7]

Eager to minimize the Arab presence inside their nation and quickly arrange for the immigration of the vulnerable Jews stuck in now hostile Arab nations, Israelis evinced zero interest in proposals that demanded a return of Arab refugees to Israel or the return of lands conquered by Israel in the 1948 war. Israel did make an offer to Egypt at the 1949 UN Conciliation Commission on Palestine meeting to accept Gazan refugees as Israeli citizens. The catch was that Israel insisted as well on annexing Gaza, in addition to all the territory it had captured in the war, beyond that included in the partition agreement. This was hardly to be taken seriously, as no Arab leader could possibly justify turning over additional lands to Israel if he wanted to remain breathing, much less leading. (Jordan's King Abdullah, who in 1948 had come to "a tacit understanding" with the Jewish Agency "to divide up Palestine between themselves at the expense of the Palestinians," as Shlaim put it, was assassinated in 1951 for just this reason.) And the offer's lack of seriousness was consistent with a fundamental aspect of Israeli policy that has remained unchanged from the moment of the war's end to the present day: Arab refugees would not be returning to their former homes; their resettlement was an Arab, not Israeli, responsibility. As for conquered lands, as Ben-Gurion made clear in December 1955 in instructions to Foreign Minister Sharett, "Israel will not consider a peace offer involving any territorial concession whatever. The neighboring countries have no right to one inch of Israel's land."[8]

US State Department officials never tired of attempting to convince the Israelis to soften their stance. When Marshall retired as secretary of state in January 1949, he was replaced by Dean Acheson, who shared his predecessor's impatience with what both men perceived to be Israeli intransigence. Acheson was an unusually influential secretary of state, and the issues upon which Truman refused his counsel were few and far between. But when it came to Israel, the president rejected his secretary's advice with unusual forcefulness. Acheson advised Truman that the refugees "constitute[d] a serious political problem" and consistently urged that "a considerable number be repatriated." He made the case on "moral" grounds, no doubt because the president liked to think of himself as making decisions on that basis, but US influence in the Arab world, together with potential Soviet inroads that might result, was obviously Acheson's primary concern. The State Department repeatedly advised the president to condition US aid on Israel taking back Arab refugees and simultaneously reducing Jewish immigration to the new state. The US ambassador to Israel, Monnett Davis, McDonald's successor in that post, urged that the president take the case to America's Jews, informing them that Israel's unwillingness to compromise on the issue was interfering with America's own objectives in the area. This, too, would become a consistent theme of the history of the Israel/Palestine debate: a secretary of state, or some other top official, would suggest to the president that he enlist American Jews to help the Israelis see the wisdom of compromise—a fool's errand every time.[9]

Israel and its US supporters fought—and won—a multipronged propaganda war both to defend its conquests and refuse the return of any refugees regardless of whatever State Department officials may have wished. To build public support, the Israelis disseminated a myth of a purely voluntary Arab exodus during the war, unabetted by forced expulsions or the threat of potential massacres such as those carried out in the villages of Deir Yassin and Lydda. (In January 2022, in the documentary *Tantura*, directed by Israeli filmmaker Alon Schwarz and premiering at the Sundance Film Festival, several Israeli combat veterans detailed their participation in another 1948 massacre, this one of an estimated two hundred to three hundred residents of the Arab village of Tantura. All reports of the event were subsequently covered up and quashed by Israeli authorities.) The Israelis also invented an imaginary series of "radio broadcasts" by influential local and regional voices allegedly instructing local Arabs to temporarily leave their homes and villages just long enough for the Arab armies to expel the Zionist invaders.[10]

The truth of what really happened never did entirely supplant the Israeli fairy tale, but much of it emerged over time. The 1979 publication of the memoir of former Israeli prime minister Yitzhak Rabin, followed up in meticulous detail by the archival research of historian Benny Morris published nine years later, would demonstrate that while the Israeli military never officially implemented its "Plan Dalet," which would have used the army to drive Arabs out of the country en masse, individual commanders were empowered to make the decision to do so on the basis of military necessity, and many did just this. For instance, in a document censored by the Israelis, but released accidentally, Ben-Gurion is quoted saying, "I am against the wholesale demolition of villages.... But there are places that constituted a great danger and constitute a great danger, and we must wipe them out. But this must be done responsibly, with consideration before the act." When the war ended in March 1949, more than three-quarters of the Arab population was gone. It is important to note that even today, documentation of these events remains woefully incomplete. The Arab nations have never opened their archives, and the Israelis have not only done so extremely selectively, but also have also started reclassifying previously released documentation.[11]

Well before any documentation was available, the insistence that the Arabs who left their homes did so without any encouragement what-soever from Israeli soldiers—indeed, against the wishes of the Israelis, who were dedicated to the dream of Arabs and Jews living alongside one another in peace and harmony—became a foundational argument for American Jews. Testifying before a congressional hearing in 1951, Isaiah L. "Si" Kenen, who headed the American Zionist Council—the first of many "Israel lobbies" to be formed in the United States—insisted on what he called "the central and incontrovertible fact... that the Arab Higher Committee stimulated, organized and directed the mass exodus." He told the congressmen present that Zionists regarded this "as a disaster," as it prevented the Israelis from demonstrating "that the Jews and Arabs could live together," a line that pro-Israel lobbyists would stick to for decades, and that many continue to repeat today.[12]

Meanwhile, just as they did during the partition debate, the Israelis sought to solve the problem of America's diplomatic discomfort with their policies and priorities by sending Chaim Weizmann to charm Truman into submission. Now occupying the largely ceremonial office of Israel's presidency, Weizmann informed Truman that the refugee problem was "not created by us," but by Arab aggression against Israel, and that it was the Arabs' problem to solve. He then informed the president who so admired him that "these people are not refugees in the sense in which the term has been sanctified by the martyrdom of millions in Europe." Truman proceeded to tell Acheson to give in to the Israelis on pretty much everything. The president came to feel so strongly about these matters that he eventually issued an edict that "no one" in the State Department "should express views of any sort outside the department [on Israel] without further direction from me."[13]

As the Cold War heated up, the Israelis discovered new arguments to support their plans. During the spring of 1950, the Knesset, Israel's parliament, was preparing to pass a "Law of Return" as part of the nation's quasi-constitutional "Basic Laws." The new law offered any Jew in the world automatic citizenship and posed Israel as a prospective place of refuge should Jews once again become a target for religious persecution, thereby binding all Jews to Israel's fate. Seeking to win new friends and influence more people, a group of high-profile American Jews, including the president's old friend Eddie Jacobson and former treasury secretary Henry Morgenthau, sent a letter to Truman that portrayed the imminent immigration of six hundred thousand Jews from Europe and the Arab Middle East to Israel as a help to the United States in its long, twilight struggle with the USSR—"a step towards consolidation of the defenses of the democratic world." Israel considerably strengthened its case as a Cold War ally when its intelligence agency was able to obtain and share the contents of Soviet premier Nikita Khrushchev's February 1956 "secret speech" denouncing Stalin and Stalinism. The theme of Israel as a Cold War asset soon became yet another staple of the arguments of Jewish American leaders.[14]

When Dwight Eisenhower won the 1952 presidential election, Israel's American supporters were understandably concerned, as barely 25 percent had pulled the Republican lever. The president once admitted that he had never even met a Jew before he turned twenty-five years old, and was surprised, after reading about them in the Bible as a child, to learn that they still existed. During the first year of his presidency, he mused, "My Jewish friends tell me that except for the Bronx and Brooklyn the great majority of the nation's Jewish population is anti-Zion," a likely indication

that the president had no Jewish "friends" at all. Though likely better informed, his secretary of state, John Foster Dulles, was perhaps even less
sympathetic. Dulles had lost a New York Senate race in 1949 to a Jewish Democrat, Herbert Lehman, and blamed Jews for his failure. Upon
meeting Ben-Gurion for the first time, Dulles thought to complain about
past "decisions [that] were often taken under pressure by the United States
Jewish groups which felt they had the right to exercise influence because
of contributions to election victory." Those days were over, he assured the
prime minister. He could hardly have been more wrong.[15]

Dulles considered "the Israel factor" to be a "millstone" around America's neck in the Arab world and judged the Jewish state's policies of
"aggressive expansion" to be a massive impediment to America's success
in the area. Henry Byroade, assistant secretary of state for Near East,
South Asian, and African affairs, told the Israelis of his having been
"beaten over the head" in Arab capitals owing to America's perceived
favoritism toward Israel. Both the president and his secretary of state
sought to implement a policy of genuine neutrality. To try to garner domestic support for this reversal, they looked to the American Council for
Judaism, as a counterpoint to more mainstream Jewish organizations.
Byroade spoke to its 1954 annual meeting, fresh off an address at the
World Affairs Council in which he importuned Israel to "drop the attitude of the conqueror and the conviction that force and a policy of retaliatory killings is the only policy that your neighbors will understand." He
added that Israel might consider "making your deeds correspond to your
frequent utterance of the desire for peace," and advised Israel to jettison
its self-image as the "headquarters" of a state offering "special rights and
obligations" to Jewish citizens the world over. While also asking Arabs
"to accept the state of Israel as an accomplished fact," Byroade further
counseled the Israelis to curb their devotion to ingathering Jews from
other nations, as this justifiably inspired "Arab fears that if the population of Israel were to expand materially through further immigration, . . .
it would be humanly impossible to maintain those people within the
confines of the present state."[16]

Byroade's speech to the ACJ had little, if any, discernible effect. For if there was one issue upon which most Jews—Zionists and

non-Zionists—could agree in the aftermath of the Holocaust, it was on the necessity of open Jewish immigration to Israel. The creation of the state of Israel had only increased the precarious position of Jews living in Arab nations in particular. And American Jews had seen—and indeed, been seared by—the consequences of persecuted Jews having nowhere to turn and no voice to plead their case. Byroade, who was named ambassador to Egypt in 1955, continued to argue within the administration for Eisenhower to deliver a presidential address designed to "break the back of Zionism as a political force."

Needless to say, there was no such speech and never would be. The soaring rhetoric in Israel's 1948 Declaration of Independence about extending "its hand to all neighboring states and their peoples in an offer of peace and good neighborliness" had been scarcely more than rhetoric. In reality, Ben-Gurion expected endless war. He explained this to the Zionist leader Nahum Goldmann in decidedly unsentimental terms not long after independence had been achieved. "Why should the Arabs make peace?" he asked. "If I was an Arab leader, I would never make terms with Israel. That is natural: We have taken their country. Sure, God promised it to us, but what does that matter to them? Our God is not theirs. We come from Israel, it's true, but two thousand years ago, and what is that to them? There has been anti-Semitism, the Nazis, Hitler, Auschwitz, but was that their fault? They only see one thing: We have come here and stolen their country. Why should they accept that?"[17]

During its first eight years, the young state's frequent military operations against its neighboring Arab nations cost the country 1,237 lives, and far more than that among their victims. Among the worst of these was a disastrous foray into the West Bank village of Qibya (then under Jordanian rule) on October 14–15, 1953, following a grenade attack that killed a Jewish mother and her two children. The Israeli response, carried out by an army commando unit led by a twenty-five-year-old major, Ariel Sharon, resulted in the death of 69 Palestinians, mostly women and children, and the destruction of 45 houses, a school, and a mosque. While most tit-for-tat attacks and retaliation occurred under the radar of the world's attention, this example of Israel's commitment to asymmetrical retaliation received almost universal condemnation in the world's media and among its diplomats.[18]

As a result of these events, when Israel conspired with Britain and France to invade Egypt's Sinai Peninsula in October 1956, it was already finding itself in far less congenial grounds in Washington than it had enjoyed under Truman and the Democrats. The attack came in response to the July 26, 1956, announcement by Egypt's president, Colonel Gamal Abdel Nasser, that he had nationalized the nearby Suez Canal and shut off Israeli shipping in the Straits of Tiran, effectively blockading Israel's southern port of Eilat and cutting off its access to the Indian Ocean. Britain and France obviously had their own reasons for wanting to seize control of this crucial shipping passage, as Nasser's nationalization of the canal could potentially threaten their trade routes and endanger their economies. It could also inspire other such moves by third world leaders were it to be allowed to succeed. The three co-conspirators kept the Americans completely in the dark, which understandably left the president furious.

This development was particularly damaging as it came at a time when President Eisenhower was preoccupied with the Soviet invasion of Hungary, which was seeking to detach itself from the Eastern bloc and praying for American intervention. Israel, France, and England had put the United States in an "acutely embarrassing position," according to the president, whose first order of business was always to ensure that "the Soviets must be prevented from seizing the mantle of world leadership." Dulles was all but apoplectic. Notwithstanding both his and the president's fondness for violent military coups in places such as Iran, Guatemala, and the Congo when engineered by the CIA, Dulles nevertheless fumed: "We do not approve of murder. We have simply got to refrain from resort to force in settling international disputes."[19]

What particularly infuriated Eisenhower and Dulles was the fact that they thought themselves to be in the process of wooing Egypt into a US-led Middle Eastern alliance to counter Soviet influence in the area. The invasion created exactly the situation the United States sought to avoid, not only offending the entire Arab world but also offering an opening to the Soviets to appear as the anti-imperialist power par excellence to the rescue. And it did so, to top it all off, at a time when the United States wanted the world's attention focused on the brutal Soviet invasion of Hungary.

To the degree that Dulles and Eisenhower felt that the invasion undermined their plans, they should have known better than to entertain them in the first place. Such a simplistic anti-Communist alliance could only have been dreamed up by someone with no understanding of or much interest in the recent rise of pan-Arab nationalism. But Dulles and Eisenhower were far from ready to admit this and blamed Israel and company for pushing Egypt and much of the Arab populace into the Soviet camp. A perceived avatar of anti-imperialism during its fight for independence, Israel was now acting as the junior partner in an old-fashioned imperial adventure. The Soviets soon took full advantage of the situation by threatening war with the Western powers and Israel in the event they refused to withdraw.

That the invasion occurred on the eve of a US presidential election only added to the president's fury. Eisenhower would confide in a special "memorandum for the record" that if Israel's leaders believed "winning a domestic election [was] as important to us as preserving the interests of the United Nations and other nations of the free world in that region," they were sadly mistaken. He instructed the State Department to "inform Israel" that the United States would proceed "as if we did not have a single Jew in America."[20]

The invasion was nothing but bad news for American Jewish leaders. The president's anger forced them to confront the dilemma they so wished to avoid: Which side were they on, Israel's or America's? American Jewish officialdom found itself pulled in multiple directions simultaneously. Speaking during a nationwide television broadcast, Zionist Organization of America president Emanuel Neumann insisted that the Israelis were simply "continuing" the same war that the Arabs had begun eight years earlier, only this time they had been forced to take on Nasser (the "Hitler of the Nile"). The group demanded nothing less than "full and forthright support for Israel's defense" from the Eisenhower administration. Another group of Jewish leaders rounded up sixty-four prominent Christian clergy and lay leaders to sign a letter decrying Nasser as "clearly imitative of the Hitler pattern, and of the present communist pattern in Hungary." Israel's ambassador to the United States, Abba Eban, huddled with the leaders of the American Jewish Committee to try to find a way to mitigate the damage. Secretly, the group asked Secretary Dulles to help facilitate direct negotiations between Egypt and Israel, so that "the status quo ante" might be restored, and the "conditions which have caused bloodshed, misery and turmoil" addressed (without naming what those conditions might have been). Behind the scenes, its members feared the public relations impact of what appeared to be Israel's "expansionist aims," while at the same time hoping to prevent the United States from supporting UN sanctions of the Israelis to ensure its withdrawal.[21]

Britain and France had no choice but to accede to Eisenhower's demands to turn around and go home, especially given the possibility of the Hungarian situation devolving into a world war. But the Israelis, per usual, stuck to their guns. They demanded access to the Suez Canal and refused to consider unilateral withdrawal without it. Once again, American Jewish organizations lined up to cause massive headaches for US diplomats. And once again, the White House was barraged with mail, with over 90 percent of it supporting Israel's position. Both Senate Majority Leader Lyndon Johnson and Senate Minority Leader William Knowland strongly supported Israel's claims as well.[22]

Like his predecessors, Dulles found Zionist pressure to be a major annoyance, which only amplified his already considerable antisemitism. He believed that the Israeli embassy was "practically dictating to the Congress through influential Jewish people in the country," and complained to colleagues that he found it "almost impossible in this country to carry out a foreign policy not approved by the Jews," particularly given what he judged to be their "terrific control" over Congress and the news media. He said he wished that, instead of circulating its "various inaccuracies and distortions" about his policies, the "Jewish fraternity" would focus its attention on "the Israeli government to try to change their policy of presenting the world with faits accomplis," and in so doing end what he defined as their policy of treating US cooperation "as a one-way street."

Almost certainly with his brother John Foster Dulles's knowledge, and possibly under his orders, Allen Dulles, who happened to be director of the CIA, even funneled secret funds to a pro-Arab interest group, the American Friends of the Middle East, made up of oilmen and former Arabist diplomats, albeit to little effect. Sherman Adams, Eisenhower's chief of staff, weighed in as well. He warned that if Israel failed to accede to US demands for withdrawal, and the United States did not sanction it at the United Nations, the president risked, in consequence, "endanger[ing] western influence by convincing Middle Easterners that U.S. policy toward the area was in the last analysis controlled by Jewish influence in the United States."[23]

The administration had initially refused to engage the Israeli demands for concessions from the Egyptians, adhering to President Eisenhower's stated principle "that a nation which attacks and occupies foreign territory in the face of U.N. disapproval could not be allowed to impose conditions on its withdrawal." In his memoir Eisenhower said he wanted to propose a UN resolution to cut off "not just governmental but private assistance to Israel" until it withdrew. Dulles was particularly interested in cutting off loans to Israel from what he considered to be "Jewish banks," a category in which he included such decidedly non-Jewish institutions as Chase Manhattan and Bank of America. He even sought to stop all transfers of funds to Israeli accounts. Undersecretary of State Herbert Hoover Jr., acting in Dulles's stead while the secretary was in the hospital for cancer treatment, suggested that perhaps Israel might be expelled from the United Nations. In his memoir, the president wrote that he even considered using US forces against Israel if its leaders did not agree to withdraw.[24]

By January 1957, however, the administration was singing a decidedly different tune. Israel's demands came to loom larger in its decision-making, and the sanctity of the administration's commitment to UN principles rather less so. Instead of a return to the status quo ante, Secretary Dulles offered Israel a guarantee of the security of the border between Israel and the Egypt-held Gaza Strip, together with a similar guarantee of safe passage for Israeli shipping in the Straits of Tiran and the Gulf of Aqaba. The United States also endorsed the Israeli position regarding "interference, by armed forces, with ships of the Israeli flag," which entitled Israel to strike Egypt again if passage through the Gulf of Aqaba and the Straits of Tiran were denied it. That was the carrot. For the stick, should Israel continue to stonewall, the president threatened to suspend all US government assistance and do away with the generous system of tax credits designed to facilitate private-sector investment in the country. He even went public with his threats, telling the country in a televised speech that "if the United Nations once admits that international disputes can be settled by using force, we will have destroyed the very foundation of the organization." These threats led, finally, to a complete Israeli withdrawal in early 1957. Moreover, the president had made his position stick both with the Israeli and the US public. A November 1956 Roper poll taken shortly after Eisenhower's landslide reelection found that fewer than 20 percent of those surveyed agreed that Israel had been "justified in sending troops to Egypt," compared to over 30 percent who felt it was not (about half of those asked had no opinion). Other polls confirmed these views, and most of the editorials on the topic published in major newspapers were largely critical of Israel.[25]


Though the Sinai debacle inspired what now stands as perhaps the strongest admonition ever given to Israel by a US president, Eisenhower and Dulles succeeded in condemning its actions without paying any discernible political price for it. Indeed, both the polls and the editorial pages supported their tough response, and Eisenhower's performance among Jews in the 1956 presidential election would constitute a high point for Republicans in this era.

American Jewish organizations had reasons to be grateful. They had helped Israel improve its position, demonstrating their worth as something more than just a money spigot. And they had done so without having their loyalty to the United States publicly called into question. In fact, the question was barely even raised in public. True, the invasion had upset America's strategy of seeking strategic partnership with the Arab world, in the hopes of preventing the Soviets from gathering up Arab allies in the oil-rich region. But this policy, too, was conducted largely outside the prying eyes of public opinion. What's more, Israel's survival was never threatened. This war really was, as the Prussian military philosopher Karl von Clausewitz had posited, the conduct of politics by other means. And in that regard, Israel achieved most of its aims at little political cost; ditto the American Jewish community. Nothing related to Israel/Palestine would ever appear so simple again.

## CHAPTER 6

# A NEW "BIBLE"

GIVEN THE POWER OF AMERICAN POPULAR CULTURE TO SHAPE PERCEP-
tions of reality, perhaps it should not be terribly surprising to discover
that one of the most important touchstones in the history of the country's
debate over Israel was a best-selling work of fiction that was later turned
into a blockbuster Hollywood film. Even so, the enduring power of
the images of the Israel/Palestinian conflict created by the author Leon
Uris for his 1958 book *Exodus*, and by director Otto Preminger for the
1960 movie version, has few parallels in the history of US foreign policy
discourse, or indeed, in the discussion of any political question. Uris's
own braggadocio—that he felt himself to be writing a Zionist sequel to
the Bible—would, rather amazingly, come pretty close to describing a
profound political truth.

It was sometime in 1955 that Uris, an ex-Marine private and moderately
successful novelist and screenwriter, decided he wanted to write a big
book about the birth of Israel. Why this became his goal remains something of a mystery. Uris thought of himself as having been "a very sad

little Jewish boy isolated in a Southern town, undersized, asthmatic." He dropped out of high school after allegedly failing English three times. He was not remotely religious. The son of communist parents, he'd had no Bar Mitzvah or Jewish education. He had married a gentile woman in a church service. Yet he had somehow grown obsessed with the fate of the Jewish state. During the 1948 war, he swore to his half-sister, "You can bet your bottom dollar if I weren't married, I'd be over there shooting Arabs!"[1]

Uris's first novel, the World War II story *Battle Cry*, published in 1953, featured a morally flawless American Jewish soldier among its rainbow cast of Marine Corps grunts and had become a best-seller. He also wrote the screenplay for the financially successful film it inspired. Uris knocked out a second novel two years later called *The Angry Hills* (1955), about Jewish soldiers fighting the Nazis in Palestine for the British army, as well as the script for *Gunfight at the O.K. Corral*, a classic 1957 western. All this presumably gave Uris the unusual idea of pursuing a film deal for his unwritten novel in order to put himself "in a position to demand more from a publisher."[2]

The idea would prove inspired, especially given the fact that Israel was hardly topic number one for American Jews at the time. What's more, while Hollywood was unarguably dominated by Jews at its highest levels, its top executives had long proven allergic to making movies with prominent Jewish characters. To a man—and they were all men—Hollywood honchos feared inspiring an antisemitic backlash or conspiracy theory should Christian America realize the truth about who was behind America's "dream factory." It was an industry, as historian Francis G. Couvares described it, "financed by Protestant bankers, operated by Jewish studio executives and policed by Catholic bureaucrats all the while claiming to represent grass-roots America." This was a moment when the US House Committee on Un-American Activities (HUAC) was headed by Congressman John Rankin, a Democrat from Mississippi, who warned of the "alien-minded communistic enemies of Christianity" who were "trying to take over the motion-picture industry." Lest anyone remain confused about who he meant, Rankin noted that the threat he identified had "hounded and persecuted our Savior during his earthly ministry, inspired his crucifixion, derided him in his dying agony, and then gambled for his garments at the foot of the cross." Now, this same group of "long-nosed reprobates" was out "to undermine and destroy America," one alien-minded movie theater at a time.[3]

Inside the studios, the fears of the Jews who really did run Hollywood but preferred that nobody take much notice of this fact came to dictate the parameters of political content in the movies made during the Red Scare. Right-wing censors were invited to scissor scripts for even a hint of pink partisanship, and anti-Communist blacklists ruled hiring at all levels. But movie moguls were willing to raise and contribute large sums to the Zionist cause; they especially enjoyed paying to smuggle arms and immigrants to Palestine as the Yishuv prepared for war. And the pervasive fear notwithstanding, Hollywood remained a place where left-wing liberalism almost always remained in ideological fashion. On the night that he recognized Israel, President Truman personally telephoned Bartley Crum, the pro-Zionist lawyer who represented the communist "Hollywood Ten" before HUAC. At a rally planned by the American Committee of Jewish Writers, Artists and Scientists, Crum joined playwright Arthur Miller and many others for a "Salute to Israel." The Black communist folk singer Paul Robeson sang two Zionist anthems— ironically, in Yiddish. But business was still business. Billy Wilder and Fred Zinnemann were both respected directors with many profitable films under their belts. Both tried to raise financing for Zionist-inspired films, and both failed.[4]

Jewish issues did briefly rise to the forefront of the moviemakers' concerns in the aftermath of the discovery of the Holocaust. The year 1947 saw the release of a film titled *My Father's House*, a tale of an eleven-year-old Polish boy's search for his lost parents in Palestine, a land portrayed as one where Jews and Arabs worked and lived together in peace and harmony. Financed by the Jewish National Fund and filmed in Palestine with amateur actors and little in the way of sophisticated equipment, the syrupy melodrama garnered few favorable reviews and did little business with moviegoers. That same year, however, boasted what would become two classic films devoted to the now red-hot topic of antisemitism. In Elia Kazan's *Gentleman's Agreement*, a gentile journalist, played by

Gregory Peck, experiences all manner of social slights and subtle forms of discrimination while impersonating a Jew for the purposes of an investigative article about antisemitism. (Ring Lardner Jr. is one of many people credited with the quip that the movie's ultimate theme was "Never be rude to a Jew because he might turn out to be a gentile.") Edward Dmytryk's *Crossfire* was the story of a deranged soldier who kills a fellow fighter in a fit of anti-Jewish hatred. Both movies were produced over the objections of professional Jewish organizations, lest they somehow stir up the feelings of Jew-hatred they were seeking to expose. The directors of both movies would eventually find themselves forced to "name names" of their alleged communist comrades to congressional committees in order to be allowed to continue to work in the field again. (Dmytryk did so after serving a jail term for initially refusing. Those actors in each film who refused to do likewise found themselves unable to find work in the industry afterward.)[5]

Six years later, Dmytryk—who had been dining with Crum on the night Ben-Gurion declared Israel into existence, May 14, 1948, teamed up with the actor Kirk Douglas, who was Jewish, to make *The Juggler*, the tale of a traumatized Jewish Holocaust refugee who attacks a policeman and escapes to Israel. There, the kindly Israeli doctor treating his psychological condition helps to cure him with the explanation, "Every person is precious to us.... That's why we have an Israel, for no other reason." This was the first—and, pre-*Exodus*, only—Hollywood film shot in the new nation of Israel. But it made little impression on either filmgoers or critics at the time. Neither did the only other film of the period dealing with Israel's creation, 1949's *Sword in the Desert*, which was filmed outside Los Angeles. In this film, directed by George Sherman and starring Dana Andrews, the British are the bad guys, and the Arabs are dirty, smelly, and without manners. Bizarrely, this terrible movie concluded with its hero being saved from capture by the sight of a star arising over Bethlehem on Christmas Eve as a chorus sings a soaring "Christ, the Lord," finale to "Oh, Come Let Us Adore Him." These two, however, turned out to be exceptions that proved a rule. It did not help a film's box-office prospects in the world's second-largest English-speaking market to cast the British as the black hats, nor to risk a boycott in the entire Arab world by portraying the Israelis as heroes. Aside from the biblical melodramas featuring the likes of Moses, King Solomon, and Samson, after these films few, if any, major motion pictures featured either an Israeli locale or a Jewish protagonist. That changed only slightly with 1958's *Marjorie Morningstar*, a tale of a young Jewish girl's romantic entanglements in which Israel figured not at all.[6]

Given these obstacles, the success of Uris's audacious plan was hardly predestined. Yet the thirty-two-year-old author made surprisingly lucrative sales, both in New York and Hollywood. MGM vice president Isadore "Dore" Schary can be considered a brave maverick in this historical moment. Like most studio executives, and most American Jews, he was a political liberal. Unlike them, he was also quite religiously observant and committed to producing "message" movies at a time when the threat of the anti-Communist blacklist had made other studios reluctant to address politics with anything but patriotic pabulum. Schary would go on to become national chairman of the Anti-Defamation League and a nearly full-time activist on behalf of Israel. His final film project was the 1975 documentary *Israel: The Right to Be*, and his final theater production was the unsuccessful 1976 Broadway play *Herzl*, which he coauthored with the Israeli writer Amos Elon. Clearly, Uris could not have found a more sympathetic sponsor. Schary promised the young author a generous advance, which Uris combined with the advance from Random House for the novel. Meanwhile, Uris arrived in Israel in time to report on the 1956 invasion of Egypt, believing, as he wrote his father, that "the good Lord sent me to Israel to write this book for my people." In this spirit, he decided to frame the story he was telling as "just another page in the story that started 4000 years ago in Genesis."[7]

These apparent delusions of grandeur would eventually turn out to be only slight exaggerations. *Exodus* would spend over a year on the *New York Times* best-seller list, including nineteen weeks at number one. Eventually, translated into fifty different languages, it would sell over twenty million copies in eighty-seven printings. The sociologist Norman Mirsky claimed that it was "virtually impossible to find a Reform Jewish home in the 1950s without a copy." Rabbi and historian Arthur Hertzberg would later write that *Exodus* had come to represent "the contemporary 'bible' of much of the American Jewish community."[8]

After being approached by Uris and then by Preminger, the Israelis treated both the novel and the film of *Exodus* as if planning a quasi-military campaign. Before the author set foot there, the Israeli consul in Los Angeles, believing that Uris intended to "cover his 'debt' to Jewry," informed the prime minister's office that the project would "work to everybody's satisfaction" so long as its author was kept in "close contact with the army" and given plenty of opportunities for "interviews with the big shots." "Operation Exodus" landed Uris a car and an official driver, along with a customs exemption for purchasing foreign foodstuff. When it came time to film the movie, the government built roads, constructed mock villages, bused in schoolchildren, provided military vehicles and soldiers dressed up in British military garb, shut down the entire port of Haifa (when necessary), and convinced forty thousand citizens to act as unpaid extras, so that the film might recreate Ben-Gurion's declaration of statehood (Preminger had requested a mere twenty thousand).[9]

And what an investment it turned out to be. When the book was published in 1958, Prime Minister Ben-Gurion admitted that Uris's work suffered from the author's "lack of talent" when judged as a work of fiction. But "as a piece of propaganda," he thought it "the greatest thing ever written about Israel." Foreign Affairs Minister Golda Meir (and Ben-Gurion's future successor) concurred. On a fund-raising trip to the United States, she found "there was no meeting where the book was not mentioned." While she admitted that the book contained "a lot of kitsch," she expected it would prove to be "of greater importance than all of the Ministers' visits and even of 60 years of Zionism, and of all the propaganda and publicity." The head of Israel's Ministry of Tourism remarked, "We could have thrown away all promotional literature we printed in the last two years and just circulated *Exodus*." The official Israeli airline, El Al, offered Americans a sixteen-day tour covering its film locations, where, according to one wag, "they swallow the novel 'Exodus' whole...and think everyone here dances the Hora constantly and goes around making courageous postures."[10]


Leon Uris would always insist that "most of the events in *Exodus* are a matter of history and public record." This is true, though not in the manner Uris intended when he said it. Yes, there had been a repurposed, dilapidated transport vessel called *Exodus 1947* filled with 4,500 DPs from a camp in the south of France that sailed to Palestine to confront British immigration restrictions. The crew was made up of mostly American Jewish veterans who had volunteered for the trip. When the British forcibly boarded the ship, they clubbed one crew member to death and shot two passengers. Then, after a brief stop in Haifa—not coincidentally, just as the UN Special Commission on Palestine, accompanied by much of the international media, was meeting in Tel Aviv—the refugees were sent not to Cyprus, per usual practice, but all the way back to France, where the passengers refused to disembark. A choir of children sang the Zionist anthem, "Hatikvah," as journalists from publications all over the world watched from the shores. The Zionist leader Rabbi Abba Hillel Silver was guilty only of minimal overstatement when he observed that the broadcast footage "filled every right-thinking man and woman everywhere with indignation and horror." The majority of passengers—women and children included—remained onboard for a month and began a hunger strike. Determined to demonstrate their toughness toward this pathetic but determined bunch, the British made the crazy—from a public relations perspective—decision to return the Jews to Germany, the site of the mass murder of their friends and families, where passengers were forced off the ship and into DP camps, resulting in 33 serious injuries and 68 arrests. It proved to be a gift from the propaganda gods for the Zionists, one they could barely have scripted if they were writing their own movie.[11]

Uris's *Exodus* hewed far closer to the experience of another ship, *La Spezia*. That voyage took place in 1946 and carried over a thousand illegal immigrants from Italy. Their hunger strike succeeded, and the British eventually allowed its passengers to disembark in Haifa and remain in Palestine. In Uris's telling, however, they became Jewish orphans traveling from Cyprus who chose to starve themselves rather than agree to orders from the British to get off the ship anywhere but Palestine. The willingness of Uris's hero, Ari Ben Canaan, to let the children starve to death is intended to demonstrate the Jews' refusal to repeat the sort of passivity they had been charged with in their response to the Holocaust (and, presumably, for the previous thousands of years of Jewish history). The faint of heart were informed that the starving orphans were "already fighters," and fortunate compared to the "six million Jews" who had "died in the gas chambers not knowing why." Uris lifted other details from the war's history but, again, twisted the facts beyond recognition.[12]

At the specific request of an Israeli Foreign Ministry official, to whom Uris turned over his manuscript for "corrections" before submitting it to his publisher, he downplayed the role of the terrorist Irgun organization and credited a prison break it arranged to its mortal enemies in the Palmach, an elite fighting force of the Jewish underground army in the pre-state years ("Palmach" is an abbreviated version of its full name in Hebrew, which translates as "strike force"). Significantly, the Uris version of the trip depicted in *Exodus* contains virtually no Americans in the crew, though, in reality, according to Ike Aronowicz, the actual captain of the *Exodus 1947*, the ship's many American Jewish volunteers were "no less determined than the people of the Palmach." But part of Uris's self-defined mission was to promote the notion of the "new Jew" under construction in Palestine (one character in the book refers to them as "a race of Jewish Tarzans"). He therefore romanticized the kibbutzniks and other pioneers at the expense of the role that postwar immigrants and European refugees played upon their arrival after the Holocaust. The latter's horrific experiences were something that both American and Israeli Jews sought to bury to the point of near silence in its aftermath, so painful and discomforting was its memory and those who represented its legacy. Aronowicz judged *Exodus* to be "neither history nor literature," and added that its character types "never existed in Israel." Uris's reply? "Captain who? . . . Just look at my sales figures."[13]

In Uris's tale, Zionism drew its moral authority from the history of Jewish persecution, justifying virtually any form of fighting back. "Nothing we do, right or wrong, can ever compare to what has been done to the Jewish people. Nothing the Maccabees do can even be considered an injustice in comparison to two thousand years of murder," explains one fighter. According to a letter the author sent his father in 1956, "Israel was won by a gun and it will be saved by a gun. If you think this spirit was gained here by old scholars, you are sadly mistaken."[14]

The book reflected these beliefs in innumerable ways, perhaps the most obvious being the author's decision to mimic Hollywood's time-honored creation of the character of the beautiful woman whose job it is to admire her man's reluctant willingness to resort to violence to protect his family and community, a trope so common in 1950s Hollywood westerns it had already become a cliché. Uris's Ari Ben Canaan, to be played in the movie by Paul Newman, "is a simple farmer, who prefers reaping and sowing to violence, but is forced to carry a gun before he can return to his farming," in the words of the Bar-Ilan University scholar Rachel Weissbrod.[15]

Seeing Ari through the eyes of the gentile American nurse Kitty Freemont, who would be played by Eva Marie Saint, readers are treated to the casually antisemitic beliefs she held upon her arrival in Israel—beliefs not uncommon in the American heartland. Kitty had "worked with enough Jewish doctors to know they are arrogant and aggressive people," she says. "They look down on us." Then she meets Ari, a Jewish *Übermensch*: a "gorgeous man" with a "hard handsome face" who Kitty says does not "act like any Jew" she has previously met. Unlike diaspora wimps of yore, Ari and his fellow freedom fighters have no compunction about defending themselves against their enemies. Attacked by a group of young Arabs, Ari whips their leader "with a lightning flick" around the neck: the lash "snapped so sharply it tore his foe's flesh apart," Uris writes. The Arabs are quieted for the rest of the story by this show of strength. The only tear Ari sheds during the entire ordeal of fighting and building a new country is when he learns that a young Jewish nurse, Karen, who survived the Holocaust, has just been murdered by Arab terrorists.

*Exodus*'s Arabs are skinny, smelly, and dishonest: "the dregs of humanity," as one character calls them. Entering one Arab village, Kitty "was not able to smell the goats but she was able to smell the women." Even their children are "pathetic" and "dirty" compared to "the robust youngsters" of a nearby Zionist settlement. The only Arabs favorably described—the ones who welcome the Jews in their midst and look forward to living alongside them in peace and harmony—usually find their lives ended painfully and prematurely by the bad Arabs, who refuse the generosity offered to them by the Jews they encounter. This saddens the Jews, but only redoubles their determination.

The book was generously received, especially given its overall trashiness—yet another indication of the well of sympathy upon which Israel could draw in the discourse of the time. In *The Nation*, novelist Dan Wakefield congratulated the "war-hardened, bestseller-proved American author" for his alleged "skillful rendering of the furiously complex history of modern Israel" in the form of fiction. Philip Roth's collection of the brilliant novella *Goodbye Columbus* and five short stories won the 1959 Daroff Award of the Jewish Book Council a year after a different group of judges gave the award to *Exodus*. But writing in *Commentary*, Saul Bellow praised Roth's literary skill and insight and contrasted it with what he described as Uris's "public relations release." Uris was inspired to complain to the press about a new "school" of Jewish authors who "spend their time damning their fathers" and "hating their mothers." He said their work "makes me sick to my stomach." He would complain in a later edition of *Exodus* about "the cliché Jewish characters who have cluttered up our American fiction—the clever businessman, the brilliant doctor, the sneaky lawyer, the sulking artist—all those good folk who spend their chapters hating themselves, the world, and all their aunts and uncles—all those steeped in self-pity—all those golden riders of the psychoanalysis couch"—that is, the far more true-to-life Jews inhabiting the lasting works of literature by Bellow and Roth—who "had no place in his work." On this limited point, he was surely correct.[16]

The movie version of *Exodus* amplified the already seismic impact of the book beyond arithmetic calculation. Uris's sponsor, Dore Schary, had by this time left MGM, and the director, Otto Preminger, had convinced the studio to sell its rights to him, arguing that an official studio release could inspire a boycott of MGM films across the Arab world. He ended up making one of the most expensive and, at 208 minutes—expansive— Hollywood movies ever filmed up to that time. (At the movie's premiere, the comedian Mort Sahl stood up late in the film and shouted, "Otto Preminger. Let my people go!"). Uris had originally been contracted to write the screenplay, but Preminger soon fired him for allegedly treating the British as "just another in a long line of Pharaohs who have been pushing [Jews] around for 2,000 years." His replacement, Dalton Trumbo, was still blacklisted at the time he got the job. But the director knew that Stanley Kubrick's *Spartacus*, a Trumbo-authored spectacle starring Kirk Douglas, was about to break the blacklist (it received an assist from President John Kennedy, who traveled across town to see the movie). This made Trumbo kosher for *Exodus* as well. Preminger, like Uris, submitted the script to Israeli officials, and, like Uris, accepted a series of "corrections," further diminishing the Irgun's role. (Its leader, future prime minister Menachem Begin, would later complain about this, both to Uris and to the movie's producers, and even undertake a nationwide US speaking tour titled "Exodus—Fiction and Reality.")[17]

The movie kept Paul Newman's beautiful, blue-eyed, blond-haired Ari Ben Canaan at the center of almost all the action. He is a warrior, a lover, a son, a brother, a protector of children, and an extremely sensitive fellow—but one who dresses as if he is still wearing the wardrobe of the uptight young lawyer he had just portrayed in *The Young Philadelphians*. Newman in fact did have a Jewish father. But the late literary scholar Amy Kaplan compared the "glistening, bare-chested" Ari, who "emerges god-like" in the film, to the "lone gunslinger" of American westerns "who protects struggling farmers from a ruthless cattle baron," often played by John Wayne or Gary Cooper. In *Exodus* the "Other" is not the Apache or Comanche, but the Arab. Along with its western tropes, the film also evoked America's struggle for independence, a common trope in Zionist propaganda before and after the state's founding. As one reviewer explained, "It's the story of our own Revolutionary War against the British, transposed to Palestine." The slogan "It's 1776 in Palestine" had been popular among Zionists in the 1940s. In the movie's trailer, Kitty, the nurse, can be heard warning Ari, "You can't fight the whole British Empire with six hundred people. It isn't possible." Her Jewish Adonis replies, "How many Minute Men did you have in Concord, the day they fired the shot heard around the world?"[18]

The film's critical reception was mixed, but its box-office business was decidedly boffo. It became the first picture ever to earn $1 million in sales before its opening, and it went on to become the third-highest-grossing film of 1960 in the United States, behind only *Spartacus* and Alfred Hitchcock's *Psycho*. It then opened across the globe, and it continued to be shown at synagogue fund raisers, Jewish community centers, summer camps, and Hebrew schools for decades to come. (The Israeli government would arrange showings all over the world throughout the rest of the decade.) Ernest Gold's shlocky theme song—lyrics including "This land is mine / God gave this land to me / This brave and ancient land to me"—was performed in the film by the evangelist heartthrob Pat Boone, and was soon rerecorded by Eddie Harris, Andy Williams, and Edith Piaf, among others. It earned the Best Soundtrack Album and Song of the Year awards at the 1961 Grammys.[19]

Writing about the film, the Israeli gadfly peacenik journalist Uri Avnery reacted to its implied politics much as Philip Roth had to the novel. He attacked what he called its "revolting kitsch" that turned Israelis into "ridiculous cowboys" manifesting "all the clichés, cheap superlatives and hyped-up descriptions parroted by tourist guides or fund raisers at Zionist *schnorer* events." He even seriously suggested that it should be banned. What most upset him, however, as it did Roth, was the manner in which both the book and the novel invited self-hatred on the part of diaspora—especially American—Jews. They incorporated, Avnery said, "all the secret longings of the conflicted *galut* Jew from the American ghetto, all the inferiority complexes of a man who deals all his life with contempt."[20]

Though Roth's and Avnery's critiques of the movie apply equally to the novel, they are particularly accurate in regard to the former. Preminger inserted a group of Nazis into the film, something even Uris, with his decidedly relaxed notions of historical accuracy, had not dared to do. In the Trumbo/Preminger telling, an Arab friend of Ari's, deemed a collaborator, is found dead with a Jewish star branded on his chest and a swastika painted on the wall. (In a ridiculous but revealing review, *Monthly Film Bulletin* credited Preminger with being "fair to all sides," as "almost the only character the script is prepared to dislike is the Nazi leader of the Arab terrorists.") The murder leads to the film's incorporation of a remarkable moment in Israel's history, one that took place while Uris was doing his research (and is included in the novel). In *Exodus*, Ari offers up a syrupy eulogy at the gravesite of the slain Arab and a young Jewish girl who are buried together in the hopes that one day their two peoples can live together in Israel in peace and harmony—if only the Arabs (and the imaginary Nazis) would allow it. Uris was no doubt inspired by a famous eulogy given in April 1956 by Moshe Dayan, then IDF chief of staff, offered in honor of Roi Rotberg, a kibbutznik killed by Palestinian infiltrators from the Gaza Strip. Yet, here again, the facts of history are perverted to suit ideological goals. The film ends, as the historian M. M. Silver noted, with the image of Karen (a Jew) and Taha (an Arab mukhtar) being buried together as Ari swears "on the bodies of these two people that the day will come when Arab and Jew will share a peaceful life, in this land they have always shared in death." Dayan's words, however, made the opposite point. "Let us not hurl blame at the murderers," he warned the assembled:

> Why should we complain of their hatred for us? Eight years have they sat in the refugee camps of Gaza, and seen, with their own eyes, how we have made a homeland of the soil and the villages where they and their forebears once dwelt. Not from the Arabs of Gaza must we demand the blood of Roi, but from ourselves. How our eyes are closed to the reality of our fate, unwilling to see the destiny of our generation in its full cruelty.... We mustn't flinch from the hatred that accompanies and fills the lives of hundreds of thousands of Arabs, who live around us and are waiting for the moment when their hands may claim our blood. We mustn't avert our eyes, lest our hands be weakened.[21]

Rotberg's murder was followed by a series of back-and-forth attacks between Palestinians and Israelis and eventually resulted in the deaths of fifty-eight Arab civilians in Gaza. But Dayan's funeral oration earned it-self iconic status in Israel, comparable to Lincoln's Gettysburg Address in the United States. With gestures toward the brutal truths of Israel's birth, it perfectly contradicted the myths embraced in the US debate that lay at the center of both Uris's and Preminger's creations.[22]

Just as millions of people around the world were viewing Israel's birth through the distorted lens provided by Uris and Preminger, Israel cap-tivated the attention of millions more via a real-life drama: the trial of Hitler's "administrator for Jewish affairs," Adolf Eichmann, for crimes against humanity. It lasted from April to August of 1961. Eichmann was sentenced to death and executed in Ramleh Prison in May 1962. Thanks to a five-part report published in *The New Yorker* by the German Jewish émigré philosopher Hannah Arendt, and later collected into her best-selling book *Eichmann in Jerusalem: A Report on the Banality of Evil*, the trial has since become a touchstone of intellectual debate on the nature of evil and the responsibility of individuals caught up in its day-to-day processes. The questions raised by the trial and by Arendt's argument belong in a different book than this one, but it is interesting to note that Ben-Gurion's stated purpose in approving the kidnapping of Eichmann in Buenos Aires, along with his trial in Jerusalem, was to teach young Israelis about the Shoah.

Setting aside the moral and philosophical issues raised by Arendt's ar-guments and the countless responses they inspired, the Eichmann trial also once again raised the issue that continued to dog Israeli-diaspora relations: To what degree did the leaders of the state of Israel represent all world Jewry? Here again, Ben-Gurion was staking his deeply con-tested claim by kidnapping Eichmann in Argentina and trying him in Israel despite the fact that whatever crimes Eichmann was guilty of had been committed in Germany. This is no doubt why the American Jewish Committee lobbied him to cancel his plans for a trial in Israel, and turn Eichmann over to Germany, or to an international tribunal. Giving voice to the view most commonly held among American intellectuals, whether Jewish or not, *Commentary* published an angry assault, by (the Jewish)

Harvard historian Oscar Handlin, on both the kidnapping and the trial. This was—again, ironically—the position of the American far right as well. No American publication objected more vociferously to Israel's trial than William F. Buckley Jr.'s *National Review*, which, in an endless series of articles, defended the Germans, especially the German Protestant church, from their association with Hitler, and insisted that only communists were likely to benefit from Israel's actions. "It is all there," its editors complained. "The bitterness, distrust, the refusal to forgive, the advancement of communist aims."[23]

These were arguments, however, for another day. During the trial, the hundreds of journalists present from publications all over the world focused their attention first on the story of the super-secret kidnapping and then on the drama of the testimony. They covered, especially, the Israeli prosecutor's attempts to get Eichmann to admit to the monstrosity of his crimes. The result, at least in the United States, could hardly have been what Ben-Gurion had in mind. A survey of daily newspaper editorials in 250 American cities showed that those condemning Israel's actions outnumbered those defending them three to one. Almost never did the authors of these pieces argue for Eichmann's innocence. But they refused to accept Israel's assertion of its right to kidnap and try him.[24]

Ironically, it was at this moment that Leon Uris thought to try to lend the Jewish state his talent for turning complex events into simplistic melodramas a second time. Having been treated to a personal audience with Ben-Gurion, and given an inscribed copy of *Exodus*, bound, Bible-style, in olive wood, Uris sought to contact the prime minister through his then chief of staff, Theodor "Teddy" Kollek (who would go on to serve as mayor of Jerusalem from 1965 to 1993, winning five consecutive elections). Uris offered to get an "exciting motion picture" made featuring Eichmann's "chase and capture." In "consideration of my past work on behalf of Israel," Uris said, he was asking the Israelis for "cleared material" from the Mossad agents who carried out the kidnapping. But the Israelis were not interested in keeping world attention focused on the kidnapping (they have kept the records secret to this day). Kollek admitted that the truth would make "a terrific adventure story and rather better than the normal gangster cops-and-robbers type," but Uris's proposal was problematic. It not only brought up the question of Israel's violation of Argentina's sovereignty again, but also detracted from the entire purpose of the operation, which was to focus the world's attention on "Nazi atrocities." These, Kollek insisted, needed to "form the major part of the *visuals* of the film." Uris came back with the reassurance that he would be "hitting hard with visual scenes of the Jewish tragedy." But ultimately he could not make good on his offer. Israel was not willing to give him the exclusive access he wanted, and anyway, nobody in Hollywood was willing to fund the film. *Exodus*, for all its commercial success, was viewed in Hollywood as a "one-off."[25]

But the influence of *Exodus* lived on with testimonial after testimonial to its power and influence over time. In 1998, the Palestinian American scholar Edward Said was heard to complain that as a novel *Exodus* remained "the main narrative model that dominate[d] American thinking" about the conflict. In the early 2000s, the World Zionist Organization maintained a website titled "The Zionist Century," which offered up a false version of the actual *Exodus 1947* voyage. It referenced the novel and the film rather than what historians know to be the truth. In early 2022, *Haaretz* reported (beneath a photograph of Paul Newman) that the Palmach Museum, which commemorates the elite fighting force, put the compass from the *Exodus 1947* on display and described it, in the words of museum director Shiri Erlich, as " 'to the best of our knowledge' the only surviving relic of the iconic ship that inspired Leon Uris' bestselling 1958 novel and Otto Preminger's epic film two years later."[26]

Rabbi Shaul Magid, a Distinguished Fellow in Jewish Studies at Dartmouth College, is one of the most cogent critics of what he terms the "Zionization of American Jewry" as "the ticket into the club of Jewish peoplehood." And yet, more than sixty years after the release of the film, he would write, "Many in my generation still well up in tears when we hear the score for Otto Preminger's *Exodus*, even those who know the film is total propaganda. We just can't help it." And in late 2021, I happened upon a discussion on a Facebook page belonging to Kenneth Bob, national president of the liberal Zionist organization Ameinu (Our People), on which he waxed nostalgic with friends about what the film had meant to them as children. One commenter said it had made him "a

Zionist at age 11." Another called it "the first film—other than The Ten Commandments," in which he "encountered the idea of the tough Jew. It was wonderfully empowering." Another such confirmation came from journalist Jeffrey Goldberg, who said he had moved to Israel to enlist in the IDF as a young man because *Exodus* set him and others "on a course for Aliyah, and it made American Jews proud of Israel's achievements."[27]

As editor-in-chief of *The Atlantic*, Goldberg would go on to become one of the two or three most influential voices in the entire US media on the issue of Israel, often helping to define the parameters of what would be considered responsible discourse. He also served, albeit informally, as the chosen interlocutor for both President Barack Obama and Prime Minister Benjamin Netanyahu when they wanted to speak to one another without speaking to one another, in the form of long, challenging interviews that inspired additional discussion all across the media. Among his sources, and those of other journalists, during Obama's second presidential term was John Kerry, Obama's second secretary of state, who headed up what remains today the last attempt to negotiate an Israeli/Palestinian peace agreement. According to what Kerry learned of Israel's founding from the movie *Exodus*, "It was the story of people fighting for a place in the world, a struggle for survival and recognition."[28]

# CHAPTER 7

# SIX DAYS THAT SHOOK THE WORLD

THE EARLY 1960S WOULD PROVE AN UNUSUALLY UNEVENTFUL PERIOD IN the history of America's debate over Israel. In retrospect, that lack of controversy during the period is surprising, especially in light of the fact that the Six-Day War that would soon erupt would fundamentally transform the debate for the next half century.

The return to a Democratic administration under President John F. Kennedy in January 1961 was a relief to most American Jews following the tense years under Eisenhower. Kennedy's opponent, Richard Nixon, had made his name as a mini Joseph McCarthy before becoming Eisenhower's vice president, and he had dutifully played the role of the administration's attack dog. Kennedy was a product of Harvard, a lover of culture who respected intellectuals and felt very comfortable around Jews. Unlike Nixon, he was not associated with any policies or priorities that would give those dedicated to Israel's welfare cause for concern.

Under Kennedy, US-Israel diplomacy resumed many of the old patterns from the Truman administration. The diplomats and professional foreign policy advisers consistently complained of Israeli intransigence, and the president listened respectfully and then ignored them. Before his first meeting with Ben-Gurion at New York's Waldorf Astoria in May 1961, one National Security staffer tried to persuade Kennedy "to talk Israel into a less belligerent attitude along its frontiers." Instead, upon meeting the Israeli prime minister, the first words out of Kennedy's mouth were reportedly, "I owe my victory to the support of the American Jews. How can I repay them?"[1]

The Palestinian refugee issue never went away, but neither did Kennedy ever take it seriously. He did not think many Palestinian Arabs really wanted to return to their homes in what was now Israel. Kennedy's top adviser for Jewish affairs, Myer "Mike" Feldman, told him that "not more than one in ten would take repatriation" if it were offered them. This made sense to Kennedy, who compared the idea of a Palestinian wanting to return to a village now in Israel to that of "a Negro wanting to go back to Mississippi." Apparently, no one close to Kennedy had any inkling of the rise of Palestinian nationalism and the refugees' yearning for return. When Assistant Secretary of State for Near Eastern Affairs Phillips Talbot offered the president suggestions for measures Israel might take to reduce area tensions and begin a path to peace, Kennedy replied, "The trouble with you, Phil, is that you never had to collect votes to get yourself elected to anything."[2]

One issue that did interest Kennedy was weapons sales. Israel wanted to be able to buy US "Hawk" surface-to-air mobile missiles, but it also wanted its own nuclear weapon, and it was secretly pursuing the latter goal with extensive help from France. It needed the United States to turn a blind eye to this, as it had no intention—and still has no intention—of admitting to this fact. Kennedy tried, and failed, to use the granting of the former in order to put a hold on the latter. The Israelis repeatedly lied to the president to cover up their nuclear program and relied on their supporters to help them get the weapons they felt they needed on both counts. As always, the relentlessness with which the pro-Israel camp pursued its goals was deeply annoying to the administration. However, it once again paid off. The State Department produced studies demonstrating that to allow Israel to purchase such sophisticated weaponry would "introduce a new, dangerous and very costly phase in an already desperate arms race." But Israel received a timely assist in the fall of 1962, when Egypt's Soviet-backed leader, General Gamal Abdel Nasser, launched an invasion of Yemen (in which his troops used illegal poison gas against their adversaries) and threatened a US ally, Saudi Arabia. During the Cuban missile crisis in October 1962, when Nasser announced his support for Fidel Castro, Kennedy lost interest in pressuring the Israelis for anything at all, and Israel got its Hawks. It is possible that, over time, he might have been less forgiving of Israel's secret nuclear bomb project and the dishonesty and dissembling that had gone into hiding it from him. But his November 1963 assassination leaves us only to speculate. Lyndon Johnson lacked Kennedy's passion for the nuclear nonproliferation issue and was even more enamored with the Israelis and their struggle. He told an Israeli diplomat, just after the assassination, "You have lost a very great friend, but you have found a better one."[3]

Late in 1966, following the death of three Israeli soldiers from Palestinian land mines placed near the border of Israel and the West Bank, the Israel Defense Forces conducted Israel's largest military action since 1956. The West Bank had remained under Jordanian control since the end of the 1948–1949 war, and the IDF operation took place in Samu and other Jordanian villages. (It is thus called the Battle of Samu.) The IDF mobilized three thousand soldiers and six hundred tanks to retaliate by attacking Palestinian guerrillas. The Israelis were unaware at the time that Jordan's King Hussein, with whom they enjoyed excellent, albeit covert, relations, had sent a condolence note to them after the soldiers' deaths. This was because the US official to whom he had given it thought it not worth bothering to forward over a weekend. Israel rained destruction on the West Bank villages, and Jordanian military forces had no choice but to try to defend against the Israeli incursion. Jordan ultimately lost sixteen soldiers, with many others seriously wounded; three civilians also died in the attack. One Israeli soldier, a commander of a paratrooper unit, died as well. Riots broke out afterward against Hussein, led by Palestinians who thought his relatively quiescent behavior toward Israel was traitorous to their cause. Israeli prime minister Levi Eshkol, who had succeeded Ben-Gurion in June 1963, understood that the operation had been an error. Jordan had been the only relatively friendly regime on Israel's borders. Privately, he averred that Israel had sought to "give the mother-in-law a pinch," but instead it "beat up the bride."[4]

Clearly, pressure for all-out war was building. On May 31, the president of Iraq, Abd al-Rahman Mohammed Aref, bragged, "Our goal is clear—we shall wipe Israel off the face of the map." The next day, a Palestinian spokesman, Ahmed al-Shukeiri, said, "We shall destroy Israel and its inhabitants and as for the survivors—if there are any—the boats are ready to deport them." An apparently apocryphal threat from Nasser that he would "drive the Jews into the sea" would haunt the discourse about Israel indefinitely into the future.[5]

Eshkol, who for weeks had resisted the increasingly insistent demands for action from his generals and ministers, now asked, "Must we allow ourselves to be worn down and killed bit by bit, if not destroyed in a future all-out war, as promised by Nasser? Must we wait for Hannah Arendt to write articles about our failure to resist?" US defense secretary Robert McNamara replied that an attack by Egypt "was not imminent," adding, "All of our intelligence people are unanimous." President Johnson told Eshkol that if Egypt did attack, "you will whip hell out of them." This time, the architect of America's disastrous war in Vietnam would be proven right.[6]

The June 1967 Six-Day War (an-Naksah, setback, to Palestinians) inspired enormous changes in almost everyone and everything it touched, beginning, naturally, with the Israelis and Palestinians. For American Jews, the transformation was only marginally less consequential for its vicariousness. The Arabs' prewar threats terrified American Jews and put them in mind, once again, of the Holocaust, with its ensuing feelings of trauma, guilt, and helplessness. While Nasser's boast has never been reliably sourced, his rhetoric offered Israelis and their supporters plenty to worry about, even though his most threatening words were frequently spoken in response to Israeli provocation. When in mid-May 1967 Israeli pilots shot down six Syrian MiG aircraft and then buzzed its capital, Damascus, Nasser, who had forged a close alliance with Syria, responded,

"We welcome the Israeli aggression. We welcome the battle we have long awaited. The threat hour has come. The battle has come in which we shall destroy Israel." That he denied the reality of the Holocaust and promoted historically discredited antisemitic conspiracy theories added further to the fears of those who held Israel in their hearts.[7]

On May 16, Egypt demanded that the UN peacekeeping force on the Sinai Peninsula and in the Gaza Strip leave the area. This international peacekeeping operation had been deployed after the 1956 invasion of the Sinai by British, French, and Israeli forces. The United Nations complied with Egypt's request, though this contravened the agreements the United States had negotiated to earn Israel's withdrawal ten years earlier. Next, Nasser closed the Straits of Tiran to Israeli shipping. The Israelis pleaded with the Johnson administration for support but received only counsel for patience, even as Jordan joined the Egyptian-Syrian military alliance. Although Johnson promised that Israel would "not be alone unless it decides to go it alone," he refrained from pledging US support in the event of an attack. Defense Secretary McNamara and Secretary of State Dean Rusk warned of what they called "Tonkin Gulfitis"—that is, allowing the United States to panic itself into a Vietnam-style war in which its fundamental interests were not threatened. What's more, General Earle Wheeler, chairman of Joint Chiefs of Staff, told the president, with remarkable prescience, that "our best estimate is that if there were a war... the Israelis would win it in five to seven days." The Israeli military shared this view, although its leaders said so only in secret. Years later, the IDF's Major General Mattityahu Peled called the threat of Israel's annihilation in 1967 "a tale which was born and elaborated only after the war." He noted that "the Egyptians concentrated 80,000 soldiers, while we mobilized against them hundreds of thousands of men." Former Israeli Air Force commander Ezer Weizman, later defense minister and after that president of Israel, would eventually explain that the belief that Israel might be destroyed in 1967 was only "endorsed by the Jewry of the Diaspora, which for its purposes wishes to see us heroes standing steadfastly with backs to the sea."[8]

Israeli intelligence reports also contradicted in real time claims that Egypt or Syria was poised to attack. As the American-born historian and future Israeli ambassador to the United States Michael Oren wrote in his history of the war, the Israelis believed at the time that Nasser "would have to be deranged" to attack. War was possible only "if Nasser felt he had complete military superiority over the IDF, if Israel were caught up in a domestic crisis, and, most crucially, was isolated internationally—a most unlikely confluence." But, given that the country was all but economically paralyzed for a full three weeks of war preparation, together with the opportunities they thought it presented, Israel's leaders decided to start the war with Egypt and Syria themselves. They secretly communicated a peace offer to Jordan's King Hussein, but the monarch intuited that his regime would not survive if he did not throw in his lot with Egypt and Syria, however ruinous the result. And ruinous it was. Both the scale and the swiftness of the destruction wrought by the IDF would shock the world.[9]

Almost overnight, the IDF killed up to fifteen thousand Egyptian soldiers and destroyed roughly 85 percent of that nation's military hardware (including its entire air force). When it was over, the area of land under Israel's control was more than four times that within its 1948 borders—to say nothing of the far smaller territory accorded it by the 1947 UN partition plan. Israel now controlled the entire West Bank of the Jordan, including East Jerusalem, taken from Jordan; what had been Syria's Golan Heights; and the Egyptian Sinai Desert. Then chief of staff Yitzhak Rabin (later Israeli ambassador to the United States, then Israeli defense minister and prime minister) bragged that the IDF could easily have conquered Cairo, Amman, and Damascus "before lunch" had the Israelis wished. The sense of swaggering self-confidence that victory brought to Israelis was astounding given the atmosphere of fear and panic that had previously gripped those not privy to Israeli military intelligence. That the apparent miracle had taken just six days—just like God's creation of the universe—inspired in many a powerful sense of Divine intervention. One Israeli newspaper reported, "The Messiah came to Jerusalem yesterday—he was tired and gray, and he rode in on a tank."[10]

The 1967 war, like virtually all wars, was filled with atrocities committed by all sides, but military censorship ensured that these remained hidden in Israel as well as in the Arab dictatorships. A book titled *The*

*Talk of Soldiers*—later published in the United States as *The Seventh Day: Soldiers Talk About the Six-Day War*—contained interviews with 140 kibbutzniks who fought in the war. They gave voice to their conflicted feelings of both national pride and moral revulsion. It was coedited by an as-yet-unknown twenty-eight-year-old writer named Amos Oz, who would go on to become one of Israel's most celebrated novelists and one of its best-known voices for the need for peace with the Palestinians. When the original transcripts were finally opened to the public nearly fifty years later, however, it became clear that they had been heavily censored to remove soldiers' references to what might be interpreted as Israeli war crimes, or comparisons of themselves to Nazis. Instead, the published versions of the interviews reaffirmed the now Exodus-imprinted Israeli image of the reluctant soldiers/scholars/farmers who held themselves to the highest possible moral standard despite the existential dangers they faced on a daily basis. And this would become the image of Israeli soldiers affixed in the minds of almost all American Jews.[11]

US media coverage of the conflict read as if it were scripted by the Israeli military itself. When the *Washington Post*'s Al Friendly was awarded the Pulitzer Prize for his reporting on the war, he sent a private note to Israel's press coordinator to say how happy he was "that the award came for stories chronicling a situation where the white hats licked the black ones, as should be the case in every proper Western." Israeli defense minister Moshe Dayan "wasn't playing dominoes" after all; "his back was to the sea," *The New Republic* reported, employing the metaphor that had so agitated American Jews before the war. "On all other sides he was eyeball to eyeball with a vicious enemy who meant to exterminate the Israeli soldiers' families, homes and country." *Life* magazine rushed out a special issue filled with photographs of ruggedly handsome Israeli soldiers—"a picture of military triumph and virile sexual appeal," in the words of literary scholar Amy Kaplan—in celebration of the fact that "tiny Israel" had triumphed "over the surrounding Arab nations that had vowed to exterminate her." Kaplan described the paradoxical way so many American Jews viewed the moment: "In Israel's swift victory over Soviet allies, Americans could vicariously experience both the dread of vulnerability and the thrill of invincibility, the irrefutable victory that was eluding them in Vietnam." As a result, "Israel came to appear both vulnerable and invincible at the same time—at risk of destruction yet militarily indomitable. Its Arab enemies were portrayed as the inverse: formidable enough to obliterate an entire nation, yet incapable of matching Israel's military forces on the battlefield."[12]

Herein lay the origins of one of many absurd aspects of American Jewish discourse on Israel. The Jewish state was now a regional superpower and would soon boast the world's fourth most powerful and possibly its second most technologically advanced army. Its military budget was greater than any four of its potential adversaries combined, to say nothing of its not-so-secret nuclear capability. And yet, because the discourse reflected emotion far more than rational calculation, the fear that these same nations would one day "drive the Jews into the sea" rarely—if ever—receded. Indeed, it remained at the foundation of almost every public pronouncement by mainstream Jewish leaders in the United States and in the literature of virtually every fund-raising pitch.

June 1967 transformed American Jews' relationship not only to Israel, but also to themselves. In a remarkably prescient *Commentary* article published just weeks after the war, Rabbi Arthur Hertzberg noted that the crisis had united American Jews "with deep Jewish commitments as they have never been united before, and it has evoked such commitments in many Jews who previously seemed untouched by them." A much-admired scholar of Jewish history as well as a congregational rabbi, Hertzberg could find "no conventional Western theological terms with which to explain this." Rather, he found that "most contemporary Jews experience these emotions without knowing how to define them," as Israel was possibly "now... acting as a very strong focus of worldwide Jewish emotional loyalty and thereby as a preservative of a sense of Jewish identity." Time would prove the accuracy of these predictions. In the immediate aftermath of the war, among American Jews, "terror and dread," said the celebrated theologian Abraham Joshua Heschel, had metamorphosed into "exultation."[13]

This transformation manifested itself in multiple ways. Few American Jews were eager to put their bodies in the line of fire, or to encourage their sons and daughters to do so. But they did donate early, often, and with great enthusiasm. The Jewish press was filled with stories of people going into debt, selling their cars, and cashing in insurance policies in order to donate the proceeds to Israel. The small Jewish congregation of Okmulgee, Oklahoma, even sold its synagogue and wired the revenues to Tel Aviv. Jewish philanthropic organizations that had formerly gone begging were now deluged with funds, with as much as a 400 percent increase above the previous year's tallies. The money came from Jews who had maintained "only the most pro forma links with Jewish religious traditions, who [knew] little or nothing of Jewish culture," the political scientist Daniel Elazar noted. These Jews wanted to "express themselves Jewishly in connection with Jewish political causes or interests." The amount of money shaken loose in Hollywood from celebrities such as Kirk Douglas, Paul Newman, Barbra Streisand, and virtually every mogul in the business appears astounding even today: $2.5 million—the equivalent in 2022 dollars of $20 million—was pledged in just one hour at a cocktail party hosted by studio executive Lew Wasserman.[14]

The war touched individual American Jews in profound and unpredictable ways. For instance, the novelist Henry Roth published the masterpiece *Call It Sleep*—a Jewish companion to James Joyce's *Portrait of the Artist as a Young Man*—in 1934 at age twenty-eight, but had put down his pen after the book was condemned by his Communist Party comrades. He had spent the next three decades as an itinerant worker, settling down to slaughter chickens for a living as a farmer in Maine. But Israel's remarkable victory reawakened his creative spark. As Roth told it at the time, he feared "the Arab states...were going to drive the Jews, the Zionist-imperialist pawns, into the sea. Jesus Christ, another holocaust of Jews!" Instead, "by skill, by daring, by valor, Israel prevailed. A miracle!...And it was Israel, a revitalized Judaism, that revitalized the writer, his partisanship, a new exploration into contemporaneity, a new summoning of the word—however inept in the service of the cause." The eventual result of Roth's revitalization was a triumphant return to writing fiction.[15]

While no doubt extreme, Roth's experience was hardly unique. Liberal intellectuals who had previously maintained an emotional distance

from both Israel and the American Jewish community were now quick
to embrace the cause. Hannah Arendt, formerly self-identified with the
Ihud's diehard binationalists who bitterly opposed Israel's founding,
joined other previously estranged Jewish writers and scholars in a prewar
plea published in the *Washington Post* that defined the crisis with what
its text termed "stark simplicity: whether to let Israel perish or to act to
ensure its survival and security, legality, morality and peace in the area."
After the war, Arendt told her friend the German/Swiss philosopher Karl
Jaspers that "Nasser should be hung instantly." On a more solemn note,
she later admitted to her friend Mary McCarthy that "any real catastrophe in Israel would affect me more deeply than almost anything else."[16]

*Commentary* flipped 180 degrees and now basked in Israel's military prowess. The sociologist Milton Himmelfarb, the American Jewish
Committee's research director, bragged that "while Jews can be pretty
good with a fountain pen and briefcase, they can also if necessary be
pretty good with a rifle or tank." Associate editor Werner Dannhauser
crowed, "Jews all over the world walk with greater pride upon the face of
the earth because of the state of Israel." In the self-consciously socialist
counterpart to *Commentary*, *Dissent*, the shock of recognition was no less
profound, however much it may have contradicted the universalist ethos
that had defined the democratic socialist publication since its founding
in 1954. Before the war, explained its guiding spirit, the literary critic
and Jewish historian Irving Howe, he had not felt much of an emotional
tie to Israel, and "no particular responsibility for its survival or renewal."
But it now thrilled him "that after centuries of helplessness Jews had defeated enemies with the weapons those enemies claimed as their own."[17]

The power of these emotions and the institutional changes they presaged would lead to a remarkably rapid remaking of American Jews'
collective identity. It had long been difficult to explain just what non-
Orthodox Jews "believed" that distinguished them from mainstream
American Protestants, save for the fact Jesus had likely been conceived
in the usual fashion. The rituals of Jewish life remained vibrant in many
families, but the theology was decidedly fuzzy. Most Jewish communal
organizations pursued agendas indistinguishable from most other liberal
organizations. Jews had their own foods, their own country clubs, law

firms, and vacation spots, but the sermons of their rabbis sounded an awful lot like a typical college commencement address. To be a secular American Jew, pre-1967, was to have faith in an America that was going to make itself better—fairer, more equal, and more peaceful—with the help of its Jews. Support for the Zionist cause had, in the past, been "one among various alternatives of Jewish identity," the Jewish scholar and rabbi Shaul Magid would write in 2019. Beginning in 1967, however, "the Jewish discourse about Zionism has become Jewish identity itself; Zionism defines Jewish legitimacy and is no longer part of a larger conversation. It defines the conversation." Rabbi Hertzberg, speaking then as president of the American Jewish Congress, confirmed this back in 1977 when he observed "the only offense for which Jews can be 'excommunicated' in the US today is not to participate in these efforts [to support Israel]. Intermarriage, ignorance of the Jewish heritage, or lack of faith do not keep anyone from leadership in the American Jewish community today. Being against Israel or apathetic in its support does." This view has only hardened over time. More than forty years later, Rabbi Sharon Kleinbaum, leader of New York City's Congregation Beit Simchat Torah, the nation's largest LGBT-oriented synagogue, spoke in almost identical terms. "A Jew today can walk into almost any non-Orthodox synagogue in America," she observed, "and profess his or her atheism or lack of Jewish practice and be embraced and accepted, but if a Jew enters that same synagogue and professes to be an anti- and even non-Zionist, he or she will likely be shown the door."[18]

This revolution made itself felt in virtually every non-Orthodox American Jewish institution. Support for Israel soon overwhelmed all other commitments, whether to social service, community solidarity, or social justice. In the everlasting battle between Jewish particularism and universalism, the former—which had been on the run among American Jews for more than century—was now threatening to wipe out the latter and do so with remarkable speed. The historian Lawrence Grossman noted that in the American Jewish Committee activities report for 1966–1967, "Israel" was buried "on page 35, yielding pride of place to 'The Spirit of Ecumenism,' executive suite discrimination, civil rights, extremism and anti-Semitism, church-state separation, Jewish identity, and reports on

Europe, the Soviet bloc, and Latin America." A year later, however, it was the lead item, "and there it remained." Within six years, Israel had blossomed into the biggest single budget item for the group, taking up nearly a third of its outgoing funds. The Anti-Defamation League of B'nai B'rith, founded as a domestic civil rights champion, now allocated nearly half of its budget to defending Israel. John Ruskay, former CEO of the United Jewish Appeal–Federation of Jewish Philanthropies of New York, described the "Israel at risk" fund-raising paradigm as having "fostered the explosive growth of the Federation system post-1967," and the numbers clearly bear him out.[19]

The Israeli triumph brought with it a new attitude for American Jews about not only themselves but also about God and Torah. Israeli leaders had long talked about their nation in the language of miracles, connecting them to the stories of the Bible as if these constituted the literal history of their nation. But following the 1967 war, the notion took on a newer, more literal meaning among both Jews and gentiles. President Johnson, like Harry Truman before him, said he saw "the hand of the Lord in the creation of Israel and... in bringing the Jews back to Israel."[20]

America's secular Jewish leaders now began to adopt the language of Divine intervention to explain the Jewish state's stunning military success, especially with regard to its conquest of East Jerusalem, where the holiest site in the Jewish religion, the Western Wall of the Second Temple that the Romans destroyed in 70 CE, still stood. At a postwar rally in Washington, DC, Morris Abram, president of the still non-Zionist American Jewish Committee, transgressed all of the rhetorical and linguistic boundaries his predecessors had so carefully observed in the past. "The people of the Book have proved the verities of the Book," he shouted to the near-delirious gathering. " 'Not by power, nor by force, but by thy spirit, sayeth the Lord.' " This theological leap would soon become fundamental to Jewish American identity. The official doctrine of Conservative Judaism would proclaim "the existence of Medinat Yisrael (the State of Israel) in Eretz Yisrael (the Land of Israel), with its capital of Jerusalem... not just in political or military terms; rather, we consider it to be a miracle, reflecting Divine Providence in human affairs." Reform Jewry would refer, no less fantastically, "to the realization of God's promise to

Abraham: 'to your offspring I assign this land.'" Each of these distinctly American Jewish religious movements soon, and increasingly, wrapped themselves in the garb of Israeli identity, with new holidays and special prayers regularly offering praise to the modern-day state. Synagogues invited an endless parade of Israeli guest speakers (often in uniform) to inform and inspire them, and many also began to sing the Israeli national anthem, "Hatikvah," in their religious services.[21]

A second, and no less important, component of the transformation of American Jewish life inspired by the war was the sudden sacralization of the Shoah. Peter Novick is among the many historians who have discerned in the reaction to the war an "immediate and most important cause of a new closeness" connecting American Jews via their "fears of a renewed Holocaust on the eve of that war." The result, after the crisis passed, was a "permanent reorientation in the agenda of organized American Jewry." A year earlier, a *Commentary* symposium titled "The State of Jewish Belief" had inspired not a single reference to either Israel or the Shoah. By a kind of unspoken but widely respected consensus, the latter had been rarely mentioned; when it was, it was only on specific occasions. Now, together with identification with Israel, recognition of the Shoah and grappling with its meaning became a pillar of what it meant to be a Jew. The theologian Marc Ellis posited the birth of "Holocaust theology" in this moment, in which a Judaism emerges that fuses its religious and cultural heritage with loyalty to the state of Israel. The perception of a second near mass death experience had a theological component. Before the 1967 war, the rabbi and philosopher Emil Fackenheim, a Holocaust refugee, famously posited a "614th mitzvah" (biblical commandment): to give Hitler no posthumous victories. In his 1982 book *To Mend a World*, he amended this precept to define the defense of Israel as the "orienting reality for all Jewish and indeed all post-Holocaust thought."[22]

Rabbi Arnold Jacob Wolf, a former assistant to Rabbi Abraham Joshua Heschel and later a friend and mentor to a young Barack Obama, would examine this dynamic in a 1979 essay, "Overemphasizing the Holocaust." In it, Wolf lamented the fact that in "Jewish school or synagogue...one does not now learn about God or the Midrash...nearly as carefully as one learns about the Holocaust." Worse, American Jewish leaders were

using "the Shoah as the model for Jewish destiny," and so "Never again"
had come to mean "Jews first—and the devil take the hindmost." Peter Novick aptly argued that "as the Middle Eastern dispute came to be
viewed within a Holocaust paradigm," it simultaneously became "endowed with all the black-and-white moral simplicity of the Holocaust"—
a framework that promoted "a belligerent stance toward any criticism of
Israel" no matter who was giving voice to it or what may have been their
inspiration.[23]

Even without the theological gloss, which, to be fair, did not interest
most Jews, the connection between the two events evinced an inescapable transformation of what it meant to be a Jew in the United States. The
constant invocation of the Holocaust's "lessons" soon became an all-but-
inescapable aspect of justifying whatever needed justification on the part
of Israel's actions, especially as the occupation of the West Bank became
increasingly and often brutally entrenched in both time and space. The
Harvard literature professor Ruth Wisse, for example, writing in *Commentary* on the twentieth anniversary of the conflict, combined Nasser's
apocryphal words with Hitler's ambitions, insisting that the former were
merely a "reformulated" version of "the Nazi theory of *Lebensraum* in
Mediterranean terms." Fortunately, she added, "what the Arabs did not
reckon on was that a people so recently pushed into ovens would not now
permit themselves to be pushed into the sea."[24]

Before 1967, many American Jews experienced the aftermath of the
Shoah "like a family secret," as one historian put it, "hovering, controlling, but barely mentioned except in code or casual reference." No
more. The war—or, more specifically, the fears that preceded it—had, in
the eloquent formulation of Elie Wiesel, turned all American Jews into
"children of the Holocaust." Not surprisingly, detailed, multivariate studies of the attitudes of Shoah survivors across the United States show that
they grew particularly attached to Israel. This powerful state, with its apparently miraculous military, became, in the words of three scholars, "the
symbol of Jewish resilience after the murder of the six million." Israel
was now perceived to be "the best means to implement the slogan 'Never
Again,' [as] the unofficial battle cry of post-Holocaust Jewry." It should
not be surprising that roughly fifty years later, when the Pew Research

Center published "Jewish Americans in 2020," it found that more Jews (76 percent) picked "remembering the Holocaust"—more than any other practice or symbol—as the "most essential" component of their Jewish identity.[25]

The Holocaust historian Lucy Dawidowicz identified a "new kind" of American Jewish pride in what she termed "the aura that radiated from General Moshe Dayan, his ruggedness, vigor, determination." She wrote that "Jews across America reveled in stories like the one about the Georgia gas station attendant who told a customer, 'I always thought Jews were "yellers" but those Jews, man they're tough.'" So, too, the gentile businessman who explained to a Jewish associate, "You Hebes really taught those guys a lesson." This "new Jew" represented a kind of corrective to the previous two thousand years of Jewish history, but most especially to the Holocaust. One Jewish woman who had been cut off completely from her religion and community told a sociologist, Marshall Sklare, "We never fought back before. We always picked up our bundles and ran. Now we can fight back." Perhaps of even greater importance for Israel's future value to US policymakers was the reaction of Harry McPherson, special assistant to President Johnson, who had replaced Mike Feldman on the "Jewish" desk. McPherson happened to be in Israel, on his way back from Vietnam, the day the 1967 war was launched. He found it "deeply moving," after "the doubts, confusions, and ambiguities of Vietnam," to witness a nation whose people's commitment to their nation's defense was "total and unquestioning." No less impressive was the way the war had "destroy[ed] the prototype of the pale, scrawny Jew." Israeli Jews were "tough, muscular, and sunburned."[26]

McPherson was a gentile, but his paean to Israel's masculine prowess mirrored how many American Jews had internalized the Israelis' oft-stated contempt for diaspora Jewish life. Israeli Jews did not commute to their law or dental offices on trains from Scarsdale; nor did they show off when it came time to pony up for the synagogue building fund. Rather, they lay aside their plowshares, and with muscular arms, tanned by hours spent "making the desert bloom" in the hot sun, mounted tank battalions and fighter jets. This was Uris's *Exodus* cast not as a movie but as real life. "American Jews said to themselves," as the journalist Thomas

Friedman put it, "'My God, look who we are! We have power! We do not fit the Shylock image, we are ace pilots; we are not the cowering timid Jews who get sand kicked in their faces, we are tank commanders.'" The American Jewish embrace of this "particular pathology," as the historian of the Holocaust Saul Friedlander diagnosed it, was a natural corollary to the triumph of Zionist ideology: "'You, the Diaspora Jews, went like sheep to slaughter; we, the proud youth of Eretz Israel, will show you what self-defense and strength mean.'" American Jews proved themselves eager to buy into this implicitly insulting bargain.[27]

Meanwhile, in the Middle East, the war had redrawn the map of Israel and offered it previously unimagined opportunities for expansion. Having conquered East Jerusalem, the Israelis immediately annexed it amid celebrations over the city's putative reunification. This move, and the subsequent attachment of all future Israeli governments to its retention, has strained and quite possibly doomed the practical possibility for a negotiated peace with the Palestinians and the larger Arab world. (As of July 2021, there were 358,800 Palestinian residents within the boundaries of the Jerusalem Municipality, constituting 38 percent of the city's population.) Even so, it was done with virtually no discussion and next to no dissent. As for the rest of its conquests, the plan was not to have a plan. Israel's 2.4 million Jews were now responsible for the governance of 1.4 million Palestinians, or roughly ten times the number that were living inside Israel proper. When Foreign Minister Golda Meir asked Prime Minister Levi Eshkol, "What are we going to do with a million Arabs?," the prime minister replied, "I get it. You want the dowry, but you don't like the bride!"[28]

Israel ended up with both. The cabinet adopted plans to do everything possible to encourage remaining Palestinians to leave voluntarily as well as to create Jewish settlements in what had been Syria's Golan Heights, Egypt's Sinai Desert, and the West Bank of the Jordan. (After initially administrating but not legally claiming the territory, so as not to appear to accept the legitimacy of the Jewish state, Jordan had annexed the West Bank in 1950, changing its earlier name, Transjordan, and had given citizenship to all the residents. The annexation was rejected internationally and recognized only by Britain and Pakistan.) Israel created its first settlement in the Golan almost immediately after the war, in July 1967, and shortly after that, established two more in the Sinai. But it was the West Bank settlements, combined with the massive military occupation necessary to sustain them, that would remake the politics of the region and redefine Israel's national identity for the coming half-century and beyond.

Owing to the ambiguous legal status of the post–1948 West Bank, the Israelis insisted that no known international law applied to its actions there, and so they began a process of land expropriation that would last, as of this writing, indefinitely. They did so, moreover, as the Palestinian American legal scholar Noura Erakat noted, "without either preserving the sovereign rights of its inhabitants or absorbing them under [Israel's] civil jurisdiction." The Israelis were well aware that they were acting on the basis of specious legal arguments (to put the matter generously). When Golda Meir became prime minister, her legal counsel informed her that, based on Article 49 of the Geneva Conventions, the erection of civilian settlements in the territories would violate international law; settlements could only be built for military purposes by "military bodies." But the fact that almost all of Israel's young people—men and women— served in its military made this distinction meaningless in practical terms, and so the Israelis sought to bend their extremely elastic interpretation of international law to suit their purposes.[29]

Israel's settler movement began as the brainchild of a small group of religious zealots who subscribed to a strand of Jewish political theology initially inspired by the first Ashkenazi chief rabbi of British Mandatory Palestine, Rav Abraham Isaac Kook, who had died in 1935 at the age of sixty-nine. Unlike almost all traditional Jews of his time and place, who had seen the Zionists not only as godless but as the blasphemous enemies of the ultimate redemption of the nation of Israel, Kook, a poet and a mystic and theologian, blessed their efforts. He understood the Zionists—however secular, and, indeed, anti-religious, their rhetoric may have been—to be God's unwitting instruments in redeeming the Land of Israel for its rightful owners, and therefore, part of his divine plan. These heretics, without understanding what they were doing, were building "the foundation upon which rests the Throne of God in this world." In Kook's theology, Zionists were crucial actors in what would become the Jews' Messianic redemption rather than the enemies of traditional Jewish practice and religion that they believed themselves to be. While Kook made his peace with the Zionists, however, he did not push them in the direction of greater militancy toward the Arabs. His teachings directed traditionalist Orthodox Jews to take an accommodationist approach to the Zionists they had previously viewed with contempt. The Zionists could hardly be defying God's will and preempting the Messiah in this interpretation, because they did not believe in God, and hence, they knew not what they said or did. Therefore, the rise of Zionism must be the echo of the Messiah's footsteps, the dawn of the Messianic era.[30]

The "miracle of 1967" touched off an explosion of religious ecstasy. Rabbi Zvi Yehuda Kook, Rav Abraham's son, taught that it was God's commandment to settle the sacred soil for the greater glory of God and Israel—and that if any West Bank territory were given away to non-Jewish sovereignty, it would preclude the return of the Messiah. Beginning not long after the Six-Day War, he led his followers to undertake the task of personally settling in all of the biblical land of Israel. They called themselves *Gush Emunim* (Bloc of the Faithful), and with their zealous commitment to the conquest of biblical Israel, they proceeded, over time, to hijack the meaning and purpose of Zionism—as they understood it—to turn it into a Messianic movement in which the state itself became sacred and the Israeli Defense Force a "holy" instrument of Jewish redemption. As Rabbi Eliyahu Avihayil, a student of Abraham Kook's, understood the moment, Israelis were now "living at the end of history," a time in which the morality of men no longer held sway. "Divine Providence no longer operates, as a rule, according to Israel's actions but according to a cosmic plan," one that was currently under way and "from which there is no backtracking."[31]

Deploying an ultimately unbeatable combination of fanaticism, psychological insight, strategic sophistication, and sheer chutzpah, the "Gush" repeatedly outlasted or undermined whatever government they faced, almost always securing official sanction and protection for their illegal land-grabs and intimidation of the local population. The group would simply seize land and buildings in West Bank areas under military occupation, claiming Divine inspiration, and leave Israel's leaders the choice: protect us and claim the land for the state of Israel, or risk our murders at the hands of the people we are displacing. With precious few exceptions, the settlers emerged victorious in this contest of wills. Successive Israeli governments almost always sent in the IDF to protect them before deciding that whatever settlement was in question happened to be necessary for "security reasons," though, in most cases, it was a matter of avoiding the accusation of having sent in soldiers of the Jewish state to evacuate Jews from what the Gush proclaimed to be "the land of Israel." In this manner, the Gush determined not only the parameters of Israel's future negotiations with its neighbors over the possibilities of peace, but also, in many respects, US policies as well. No American president has ever been willing to demand that Israel dismantle a single West Bank settlement, once established, or face meaningful consequences. Ironically, before the 1967 war, Secretary of State Dean Rusk had insisted that it was "inconceivable" that the United States "would ever support an Israeli attempt at territorial expansion." This would turn out to be one of history's worst predictions. The West Bank is, at this writing, home to nearly half a million Jews. At the same time, Israel has dispossessed Palestinian communities of more than 247,000 acres of land that were in use by them and slated for their development. In these settlements, Israelis live by their own legal system and are entitled to water allocations and other natural resources as well as archaeological sites and nature reserves.[32]

While State Department disapproval was a given, the Johnson administration had no interest in picking any fights with Israel. When it came to the issue of Palestinian refugees, the president made the same decision as his slain predecessor: forget them. Even referring to them as either "Palestinians" or "refugees" became problematic. The president relied on the same informal Jewish adviser/kibitzer that Kennedy had, Mike Feldman, who acted as a conduit to pro-Israel lobbyists and funders. In a dinner speech in honor of Israel's premier scientific research institute, named after Chaim Weizmann, he advised Johnson to speak of the "resettlement" of the "so-called refugees" and not to mention the word "Palestine," because, Feldman instructed, it "went out of existence in 1948." But to be fair to Johnson, he needed little prodding. As he put it in his memoir, "I have always had a deep feeling of sympathy for Israel and its people, gallantly building and defending a modern nation against great odds, and against the tragic background of Jewish experience."[33]

The intense new American Jewish focus on Israel naturally transformed the American political landscape. Before 1967, Israel had been understood to be a progressive cause, and the Arabs a regressive one. Israel had successfully positioned itself in the anti-imperialist camp and had enjoyed good relations with other emerging nations, especially those in Africa. The socialist orientation of its dominant party, together with the "David vs. Goliath" global image to which it had attached itself vis-à-vis the Arab world, placed it within the geography of the "good guy" camp for most liberals and leftists. That Israel had voted to seat Communist China in the United Nations, that it sided with the Soviets on some key votes, and that it opposed the apartheid regime of South Africa in almost every available instance accorded it additional capital upon which to draw in movement circles.

Conversely, before 1967, conservatives had not shown much affection for the socialist state whose leaders occasionally invoked Marxist-tinged anti-colonialist tropes about their own nation. For instance, a 1957 *National Review* editorial cautioned the Eisenhower administration about "sacrificing America's primary strategic interests to Zionist pressures at home." This pro-segregationist magazine, which termed the "white" race to be "the advanced race," nevertheless found fault with the Israelis having "the first racist state in modern history." While a few Jewish conservatives did brave the sometimes naked antisemitism that accompanied the ever-present anti-Black animosity in *National Review*, they remained largely invisible within mainstream Jewish politics. Barry Goldwater received just 10 percent of the Jewish vote in the 1964 presidential election despite having a Jewish father. Some Jews were more conservative than others, of course, but what was considered far-left liberalism in much of America was dead center among Jews.[34]

Opposition to liberalism in the Jewish community came not from the right, but from various offshoots of socialism, anarchism, and communism. Among older Jews, this was in part a vestige of the socialism-soaked Lower East Side, as well as a product of the continued prestige that Jewish labor leaders still enjoyed. But, overall, left liberalism was understood to be consistent both with the tenets of the Torah and with the marginal status Jews had occupied in virtually every society in which they had previously settled. Throughout the 1960s and 1970s, the most liberal American Jews, including, especially, Jewish intellectuals, identified with the European traditions of social democracy, while the more conservative ones saw themselves as just plain "liberal." A few important genuinely conservative thinkers did happen to also be Jews, but the most prominent among them—such as the economist Milton Friedman, the Russian-born philosopher and novelist Ayn Rand (née Alissa Rosenbaum), and *National Review* writer and editor Ralph de Toledano—did not appear to be much interested in Israel. During the 1950s, the most famous conservative Jew in America was probably the lawyer Roy Cohn, an aide to Joseph McCarthy (before becoming mentor to Donald Trump). Most Jews came to regard Cohn as a literal personification of *shande* (shame) to his people. Jewish organizations often had agendas that were largely indistinguishable from the liberal Americans for Democratic Action or the American Civil Liberties Union. Regarding Black-Jewish relations pre-1967, US civil rights leaders, including, especially, Martin Luther King Jr., were almost uniformly pro-Israel. (Incredibly, the Communist Black folksinger Paul Robeson had performed at a benefit concert for Menachem Begin's Irgun back in 1944.) This may have been partially a consequence of the fact that their movement received a significant portion of its funding from liberal American Jews, together with invaluable support from the Jewish legal community. Whatever its foundation, the alliance was real.[35]

The Six-Day War said "goodbye" to all that. The cause of the Palestinians had long been part of the Marxist-inspired "third world" international revolutionary vanguard that included North Vietnam, Cuba, Nasser's Egypt, and other nonaligned or pro-Soviet governments opposed to the Americans and their allies. These anti-colonial sentiments grew more vocal with every day that the United States continued to rain down destruction on the people of Vietnam and Cambodia. The Black-Jewish alliance had endured for more than half a century, at least since the Ku Klux Klan had begun targeting "Koons, Kikes, and Katholics." Now, the Student Nonviolent Coordinating Committee (SNCC), a New Left civil rights organization, began publishing articles reporting on what it called Israel's conquest of "Arab homes and land through terror." In one newsletter, an article noted the "fact" that "the famous European Jews, the Rothschilds, who have long controlled the wealth of many European nations, were involved in the original conspiracy...to create the 'State of Israel.'" The newsletter featured a cartoon of Moshe Dayan with dollar signs plastered to his epaulets, and another of a hand bearing a Star of David, with a dollar sign tightening a noose around the necks of Colonel Nasser and the controversial boxing champion Muhammad Ali, who had converted to Islam and supported Palestinian rights. In response to Jewish complaints, SNCC's program director, Ralph Featherstone, explained that the organization was not attacking all Jews, "only" the ones in Israel, and "those Jews in the little Jew shops in the [Negro] ghettos." Former SNCC president Stokely Carmichael's keynote speech at its 1968 convention announced that "the same Zionists that exploit the Arabs also exploit us in this country....We feel very strongly for the Commandos in Palestine....We have begun to see the evil of Zionism, and we will fight to wipe it out." These attacks left many Jews "devastated psychologically," according to Albert Vorspan, a vice president of the Union of American Hebrew Congregations. "They couldn't take the personal rejection, and they couldn't even understand, at least in theory, that even in the best organizations, blacks simply wanted to run their own show. They lost whatever ability they had had to distinguish between the shit-heads and the hotheads."[36]

A similar storm was brewing among radical New Left organizations run mostly by whites. Eric Mann, a spokesman for the Weathermen (later the Weather Underground), a violent revolutionary offshoot of Students for a Democratic Society, the mother ship of the New Left, told his comrades that "Israeli embassies, tourist offices, airlines and Zionist fund-raising and social affairs are important targets for whatever action is decided to be appropriate." Hostile assessments of what were deemed to be Israel's colonialist and imperialist intentions driven by the "mad hawks" who led it began to appear regularly in left-wing publications. George Novack, leader of the Trotskyist-affiliated Socialist Workers Party, summed up their view in this way: "The upper and middle ranges of American Jewry, comfortably ensconced in bourgeois America, some of them bankers, landlords, big and little businessmen, participate in the system of oppressing and exploiting the black masses just as the Zionists have become oppressors of the Palestinian Arabs."[37]

The views of the far left, it should be noted, were not entirely monochromatic. The primary axis of the argument rested, however, on what role Israel played in the machinations of US imperialism. In October 1967, for example, the independent and intellectually minded Marxist publication *Monthly Review* took the unusual step of publishing two editorials by its cofounders, Paul Sweezy and Leo Huberman, that took opposing views. Sweezy took the anti-Israel view dominating the New Left, while Huberman, conceding that his Jewishness no doubt influenced his position, argued that while Israel may have been "a lackey of imperialism," and given the Arab nations "just cause" to resist it, their true enemy was "not Israel, but their own feudal, reactionary, bureaucratic governments which exploit [their citizens] and Western imperialism which robs them of their wealth."[38]

One could see the full flowering of this attitude at what became an all-too-typical carnival of counterculture self-infatuation in Chicago in September 1967, called "the National Conference for New Politics." The mass meeting had been funded in significant measure by Martin Peretz's second wife, Anne Devereux (Labouisse) Farnsworth Peretz, an indirect heir to the fortune created by the Singer Sewing Machine company, whom Peretz married after divorcing his first wife—also, coincidentally, an heiress, albeit a lesser one. It ended with a speech by Martin Luther King Jr. that he could barely finish owing to constant heckling by radical critics, a walkout by the "Black Caucus," and another walkout by the "White Caucus." In a perfectly symbolic example of "Sticking it to the Man," the conference's two thousand delegates voted to support the Black Caucus's resolution calling for the condemnation of Israel's "imperialistic Zionist war," and adopted, sight unseen, all the resolutions that a Black Power conference had devised in Newark, New Jersey, months earlier—though no record of what these were ever became available.[39]

For Marty Peretz, who had long been contributing his wife's riches to various New Left causes while at the same time professing his devotion to Israel, these two warring selves demanded a winner, and that winner was Israel. He walked out, too, but purchased *The New Republic* in 1974. He then appointed himself editor-in-chief of the "flagship" publication of American liberalism. There, he was in a position to police—as well as to poison—the liberal discourse on Israel for the next forty years. Just as Norman Podhoretz would do in the American Jewish Committee–supported *Commentary*, Peretz published an endless series of personal, often abusive attacks on anyone who criticized Israel in a manner he deemed inappropriate.

In November 1967, Peretz set his sights on a then much-admired figure among New Leftists, I. F. Stone. In what had rapidly become—and today remains—the most influential intellectual publication in America, the *New York Review of Books*, Stone had written an eight-thousand-word missive that basically gave equal weight to the Arab and Jewish claims for their respective positions. But he called on the Israelis to offer concessions, because, after all, they had won virtually everything, and the Palestinian Arabs, nothing. What's more, he exploded a series of Zionist myths, most particularly the one about the "voluntary" exodus of Arabs in 1948 and the phony-baloney story of radio broadcasts demanding that the Arabs (temporarily) abandon their homes and villages so that Israel might be more conveniently defeated. In fact, he wrote, "Jewish terrorism, not only by the Irgun, in such savage massacres as Deir Yassin, but in milder form by the Haganah, itself 'encouraged' Arabs to leave areas the Jews wished to take over for strategic or demographic reasons. They tried to make as much of Israel as free of Arabs as possible."[40]

Stone's criticism stung, because he had reported so famously and sympathetically on the state's founding. His adoption of a more critical stance toward Israel was both painful and symbolic to liberal American Jews. In Peretz's estimation, as he wrote in *Commentary* at the time, "the significance for the Left of Mr. Stone's apostasy cannot be overestimated." (*Commentary*'s editors apparently agreed, as the magazine published the scholar Robert Alter's attack on the same article three months later.) Having credited Stone's coverage of Vietnam in his subscription newsletter,

*I. F. Stone's Weekly*, with having "given the peace movement much of its bearings," he was clearly concerned that Stone would be able to do the same for the Palestinians.[41]

Stone's interrogation of Israeli propaganda upset Peretz, who insisted on repeating the canard that alleged Arab "radio broadcasts" had inspired the Palestinians' 1948 exodus. But it was the larger context of sympathy for the Arab victims of Israel's victories that most piqued his ire. To Peretz, Israel was "besieged by implacable foes for two decades, hampered in its trade, and harassed by virtually continuous violence on its borders." His article sang Israel's praises: its treatment of its Arab minority as well as its "internal democracy"—which, he failed to mention, did not include these same Arabs—and proudly added that "Israel alone in the Middle East has a functioning Communist politics with representation in the Knesset—and with two Communist parties at that." The upshot? "It seems that the Left, so patient with the political grotesqueries of its favored nations, would only be satisfied with an absolutely unflawed Israel, which would mean also an Israel willing to surrender its national existence."[42]

Peretz's disappointment was understandable. Stone had famously treated the Israeli Jews as his brave brethren during the state's founding and compared them to "the men of Concord or Lexington." But his views had evolved. As Stone explained, he had devoted more space among his eight thousand words to the Arab than the Israeli side "because as a Jew, closely bound emotionally with the birth of Israel," he felt "honor bound to report the Arab side, especially since the US press is so overwhelmingly pro-Zionist. For me, the Arab-Jewish struggle is a tragedy. The essence of tragedy is a struggle of right against right." Stone had not lost his sympathy for the refugees-turned-pioneers he had so admired twenty years earlier. But Israel had betrayed his hopes by insisting, as Moshe Dayan put it, "We want a Jewish state like the French have a French state"—a quote that put Stone in mind of the expulsion of Jews from Spain in the 1400s as well as "more recent parallels." Stone also put his finger on what would become, over time, one of the fundamental contradictions of American Jewish support for Israel: "In the outside world the welfare of Jewry depends on the maintenance of secular, non-racial, pluralistic societies. In Israel, Jewry finds itself defending a society in which mixed marriages cannot be legalized, in which non-Jews have a lesser status than Jews, and in which the ideal is racial and exclusionist. Jews must fight elsewhere for their very security and existence—against principles and practices they find themselves defending in Israel." Peretz was correct to treat Stone as a weathervane. He had quoted him favorably in another article—this one aimed at New Leftists and published in the self-consciously radical *Ramparts*, titled "Israel Is Not Vietnam." That article, however, had demonstrated the graceful literary hand of his co-author, the philosopher Michael Walzer, who, over time, would emerge as perhaps the most eloquent and sophisticated defender of Israel among democratic socialists. On his own, writing in the proto-neoconservative *Commentary*, and for decades later in *The New Republic*, Peretz's disdain, mixed with faux-disillusionment with one's former allies, would almost always be the order of the day.[43]

Meanwhile, as the left was getting ready to turn on Israel just as the right was preparing to embrace it, inside mainline Christian organizations—the very ones where Reinhold Niebuhr had championed the Zionist cause so enthusiastically—Israel was becoming a villain. When Israel's survival appeared to hang in the balance before the 1967 war began, the leaders of America's Jewish organizations had looked to their allies in civil rights and antiwar marches for support in Israel's time of peril, and were met by a surprising—and depressing—silence. After the war, relations went from bad to worse. In a July 1967 letter to the *New York Times*, Henry Van Dusen, a former president of the Union Theological Seminary, wrote that objective observers must "stand aghast at Israel's onslaught, the most violent, ruthless (and successful) aggression since Hitler's blitzkrieg." He even used the word "holocaust" to describe Israel's actions. The National Council of Churches announced its opposition to what it called "Israel's unilateral annexation of Jordanian portions of Jerusalem." The editors of the *Christian Century* professed an inability to understand "the rationalistic gymnastics" necessary for those who, "having worked hard to get US military power out of Vietnam, insist that the power of the US be unleashed in the Middle East on the side of Israel." Statements like this one inspired a back and forth that led to further alienation on both sides. "Was the Christian conscience so ambivalent on the question of Jews that, once again, a pall of silence would hang over the specter of Jewish suffering, until later, condolences and breast-beating and epitaphs and the croak of guilty conscience would fill the air?" asked the Conference of Presidents of Major American Jewish Organizations.[44]

Political conservatives saw an opportunity in Israel's David-to-Goliath transformation in the public discourse. They began with the argument that if American Jews really cared about Israel's well-being, they might wish to reconsider their outspoken opposition to the exercise of US military power around the world, most particularly in Vietnam. President Johnson himself made this argument frequently even before the Six-Day War. Speaking to a gathering of Jewish war veterans in September 1966, he wondered aloud, "If you turn the other cheek in Vietnam"—an odd reference, given his audience—"what do you do when little Israel calls on you for assistance and help?" Meeting with the departing Israeli ambassador together with his replacement in February 1968, Johnson told both men "to tell their American friends at every turn that the US cannot play a responsible role in the world if they pull out on obligations like Vietnam." After all, Johnson continued, what was he to make of the "bunch of rabbis" who had come to him to instruct him "not to send a single screwdriver to Vietnam, but on the other hand, [to] push all our aircraft carriers through the Straits of Tiran to help Israel?"[45]

The philosopher Michael Wyschogrod, a member of the editorial board of *Tradition: A Journal of Orthodox Thought*, argued that the wars in Vietnam and the Middle East had more in common with those of Israel than most American Jews had hitherto been willing to admit. In addition to assorted local and historical similarities, they shared an analogous political context: "The Arab infiltrators, often of Palestinian origin, who spread death and destruction in Israeli villages, like to think of themselves as liberating their country just as the Vietcong see themselves liberating their country from the American invaders and their local supporters." And "in both cases the sympathy of the world Communist movement is on one side, while the Western world by and large supports the other." This led Wyschogrod to an argument that would soon be echoed for decades to come: that, in order for the "American commitment to the security of Israel [to] retain its credibility," the United States had to continue to maintain its war in Vietnam and its empire across the world. This was "the Jewish stake" in America's foreign wars.[46]

Though the neoconservative movement can claim many mothers and fathers, Wyschogrod's argument would join Peretz's as an essential document of its origins. One can also point to the rhetorical excesses of student protesters, violence on the part of the New Left, and increasingly open antisemitism and anti-Zionism in the Black Power movement. It is impossible to separate Jewish neoconservatism's origins from the revulsions caused by constant news reports of inner-city riots, the bombings of university research centers, the disputatious 1968 New York City teachers' strike, the chaos of that year's Democratic National Convention, the Weather Underground's "Days of Rage," and the broader societal dislocations caused by the myriad social movements of the 1960s and 1970s that these events represented. But neither can the transformation of Israel's image in the leftward precincts of American political life be dismissed.


Open criticism of Israeli actions among American Jews was decidedly rare in this period. Jews who did not face the threats that the Israeli Jews faced were instructed to keep whatever misgivings they had to themselves; their job was to write checks to pro-Israel organizations and pro-Israel letters to the editors of their local newspapers to counter any criticism that appeared. Abraham Foxman, who would go on to rule the Anti-Defamation League (ADL) as his private fiefdom for nearly thirty years, explained the diktat in simple, unambiguous terms: "Israeli democracy should decide; American Jews should support." In its 1977 annual report, the Conference of Presidents of Major American Jewish Organizations offered up a more nuanced version of the same iron law: "Dissent ought not and should not be made public because...when Jewish dissent is made public in the daily press or in the halls of government, the result is to give aid and comfort to the enemy and to weaken that Jewish unity which is essential for the security of Israel."[47]

In Israel, however, no such "not-in-front-of-the-goyim" nervousness crippled dissenters from speaking up. Among the most eloquent of these voices was that belonging to the kibbutznik and budding young novelist Amos Oz. In August 1967, he published a letter in the Israeli newspaper *Davar* pleading with his countrymen to recognize that they "were not born to be a people of masters": " 'To be a free people'—this wish must awaken an echo in our hearts so long as we have not lost our humanity." And yet Israelis were "condemned now to rule people who do not want to be ruled by us. Condemned, not merry and euphoric. The shorter the occupation lasts, the better for us, because an occupation is inevitably a corrupting occupation, and even a liberal and humane occupation is an occupation." Oz wrote of his "fears about the kind of seeds we will sow in the near future in the hearts of the occupied." And "even more," he had "fears about the seeds that will be implanted in the hearts of the oc-cupiers." Not long afterward, in the spring of 1968, the world-renowned Jewish scholar Yeshayahu Leibowitz published an essay in the newspaper *Yediot Ahronot* titled "The Territories." He prophesied that "a state rul-ing a hostile population of 1.5 to 2 million foreigners would necessarily become a secret-police state, with all that this implies for education, free speech, and democratic institutions.... The administration would have to suppress Arab insurgency on the one hand and acquire Arab Quislings on the other." He, too, begged Israelis, "out of concern for the Jewish people and its state," to "withdraw from the territories and their popula-tion of 1.5 million Arabs."[48]

But they did not listen. Or at least not enough of them did. And in the United States, meaningful debate was not even permitted among Jews of good standing in the community who wished to remain so. As the French Jewish philosopher Alain Finkielkraut has observed, "To be a hero by proxy, to ritualize the present, to need the insecurity of Israel to remain Jewish: each of these things explains why many in the Di-aspora confusedly punish themselves through an unqualified solidarity with every decision Jerusalem takes." The American Jewish embrace of their unique form of nationalism—which the scholar Benedict Anderson termed "long distance nationalism"—would only grow in the coming decades.[49]

# CHAPTER 8

# A JEW (AND AN ANTISEMITE) FOR ALL SEASONS

ANY DISCUSSION OF AMERICA'S ROLE IN THE MIDDLE EAST DURING THE Nixon presidency must begin with the complicated characters of the two individuals responsible for its conduct: Nixon, of course, and his chief foreign policy adviser, Henry Kissinger.

Richard Nixon was the kind of antisemite who hates "the Jews," but quite likes some of those he knows. Leonard Garment, the president's (Jewish) lawyer and longtime loyal friend, recalled that whenever something angered Nixon, he could be heard yelling, "God damn his Jewish soul!" Asked what kinds of people he wanted appointed to his administration during his second term, he replied, "No Jews. We are adamant when I say no Jews." Nixon bragged to the evangelist Billy Graham that Jewish leaders "don't know how I really feel about [them]." And while many Nixon defenders have excused these outbursts as the president merely blowing off steam, they are quite clearly wrong about this. For instance, one day in July 1972, Nixon was musing with his aides about the potential value of reviving the House Committee on Un-American Activities. "You know what's going to charge up an audience?" Nixon mused. "Going after all these Jews. Just find one that is a Jew, will you?"[1]

Kissinger was a Jew who found other Jews exceptionally annoying— none more so than Israelis, with whom he frequently negotiated but failed to get his way. He found them, he said at various times, "as obnoxious as the Vietnamese," "boastful," "psychopathic," "fools" and "common thugs," "a sick bunch," and "the world's worst shits." But he was not any more enamored of American Jewish leaders. Their problem was, he said, "that they seek to prove their manhood by total acquiescence in whatever Jerusalem wants."[2]

Kissinger admitted, one assumes only semi-seriously, that were it not for the accident of his birth, he would likely have been an antisemite. By way of explanation, he added, "Any people who has been persecuted for two thousand years must be doing something wrong." It is entirely possible that Kissinger did not dislike Jews any more or less than he disliked anyone else who did not defer to what he believed to be his genius; he just had to deal with them more often. We must also allow for the possibility that he spoke this way at least in part to placate his boss. Practicing what he himself called "obsequious excess," Kissinger frequently wrote notes to Nixon thanking him "for the privilege" of serving him, for "the inspiration" he experienced in observing Nixon's "fortitude in adversity and [his] willingness to walk alone." Behind Nixon's back, however, Kissinger would refer to his boss as "that madman," and "our drunken friend" with the "meatball mind."[3]

Given the fact of Kissinger's Jewishness, Nixon's feelings naturally created the potential for some sticky situations. Behind Kissinger's back, Nixon was hardly shy about his feelings. His top adviser was "Jewish, Jewish . . . Jewish as hell," and "a rag merchant" when Nixon was angry, but "my Jewboy" when the president was in a good mood. In person, Nixon enjoyed torturing Kissinger with mock-humorous references to his apparent genetic affliction. During one White House meeting following a Kissinger précis of the situation facing the United States in the Middle East, Nixon turned to the others present to ask for "an American point of view." He enjoyed complaining during meetings about "Jewish traitors" and the like before turning to Kissinger to ask, "Isn't that right, Henry? Don't you agree?"[4]

Like many German Jews of his generation, Kissinger displayed a special sensitivity to this issue. He worried that Nixon "suspected that my Jewish origin might cause me to lean too much toward Israel." When, in September 1973, Nixon appointed him to be secretary of state, Kissinger thanked him for saying nothing about his "Jewish background." And as he doled out jobs to his aides, Kissinger ensured that he didn't accidentally hire too many Jews. He explained that while he knew that it required ten Jews for a *minyan* (prayer service), he could not "have them all on the seventh floor" (the State Department's executive suite). Kissinger also once removed a counselor, good friend, and fellow German Jew, Helmut Sonnenfeldt, from a list of passengers for the president's plane on a trip to Germany, explaining, "I don't think too many Jews should be around."[5]

Given Nixon's prejudices, Kissinger likely felt he had something to prove. For instance, during the lengthy 1974 negotiations over Israel's withdrawal from the Sinai, Kissinger uncharacteristically reminded Nixon of his Jewishness before admitting that he found Israel's refusal to embrace America's priorities in the talks to be "terribly painful." Playing to Nixon's natural prejudices, he added, "I am Jewish. How can I want this?" together with the age-old antisemitic insinuation, "I have never seen such cold-blooded playing with the American national interest."[6]

Despite his prejudices, Nixon admired the Israelis for what he perceived to be their toughness and lack of sentimentality. So, too, did Kissinger, at least when they agreed with him. Both men, however, hated having to deal with Israel's Jewish supporters in the United States. Nixon's lifelong resentment toward East Coast elites and the media—which he, not unreasonably, identified with Jews—together with his instinctive antisemitism and anti-liberalism, sometimes drove him to distraction. In his memoirs, he warned that "the danger for Israel of relying on the prominent liberal and dove senators of both parties to come through in the event a crisis arose" was that they would "cut and run...when the chips are down." This was what he saw Jews doing vis-à-vis Vietnam, and it was therefore what Israel should expect in the future "when any conflict in the Mideast stares them straight in the face." According to Nixon, Israel's "real friends (to their great surprise) are people like Goldwater, Buckley, RN et al., who are considered to be hawks on Vietnam but who, in the broader aspects, are basically not cut-and-run people whether it is in Vietnam, the Mideast, Korea, or any place else in the world."[7]

The Israelis shared Nixon's analysis and acted accordingly, along with what we may now identify as their typical audacity. During the 1972 election, Yitzhak Rabin, then Israel's ambassador to the United States, instructed American Jews that Nixon had "done more than any other chief executive to sustain the existence of the state of Israel." He advised them to "reward men who support it, in deeds rather than in words." Nixon's Committee to Re-Elect the President mailed out literature containing this quote to over one hundred Jewish newspapers and to Jewish community leaders throughout the country. Rabin's comments constituted an obviously inappropriate intervention in American internal politics, and its violation of diplomatic protocol would likely have caused considerable public outrage had its origin been anywhere but the Israeli embassy. A few Jews did complain. Eugene Borowitz, an influential Reform rabbi, described the "heavy, unrelenting pressure the Israelis have put on American Jewry to vote for Richard Nixon" as "thoroughly demeaning to American Jews." The Reform rabbinical association passed a resolution noting its "distress" over "the reported intervention of Israel's ambassador to the United States into the coming presidential election." The Israelis naturally paid them no mind. When the issue was raised with then prime minister Golda Meir, her response echoed Stalin's famous quip about the number of troops belonging to the pope: "Have you any liberals who can supply us with Phantom [jet fighter planes]?"[8]

Nixon's prophecies and the Israelis' willingness to embrace their logic mark an important moment in the enduring conflict between American Jews' liberalism and their Zionism. There was an unavoidable logic to the position that American liberals were taking during the Nixon era, and it was the logic of global retrenchment. America had intervened in Vietnam as a liberal hegemon, and it turned out that this had been a terrible idea. Americans were baffled that other nations did not wish to be converted to their way of life at the point of a gun. Internally, moreover, the nation was tearing itself apart. The problems raised by its global empire and ensuing demands of blood and treasure were no longer sustainable. It was time, most Jewish liberals would have agreed in the early 1970s, for America to "come home," as Senator George McGovern put it in the 1972 speech in which he accepted the Democratic presidential nomination. This was the position of much of the rabbinate, none more so than America's most famous rabbi of the time, Abraham Joshua Heschel, who spoke out against the Vietnam War with the passion of a latter-day Jeremiah. But rabbis were no longer the voices that mattered in American Jewish politics. The baton had long ago passed to the executives of the representative organizations and the funders who made their jobs possible. And these people did not, as a rule, listen to latter-day prophets. They listened to wealthy and powerful men like their patrons and themselves.

Conservatives consistently made the case that, because of Israel's reliance on American power and global involvement, it was long past time for Jews to give up on liberalism altogether. Barely a month went by when this argument did not appear in some article in Norman Podhoretz's *Commentary* and in the columns of neoconservative columnists and critics. But the argument did not really find much resonance among American Jews, who would remain liberals and Democrats well into the next century. Instead, they were willing to carve out an exception for Israel as "the only democracy in the Middle East," and one that "shared America's values," even if that meant turning a blind eye to the fundamental contradiction between their dovish liberal politics and their heartfelt support for Israel as it carried out an increasingly brutal occupation in the West Bank and Gaza. George McGovern, himself the son of a Methodist pastor, nicely illustrated this phenomenon when, speaking to New Yorkers at a political rally, he attacked the Vietnam War as the "most painful and regrettable military, political, and moral blunder" in the nation's history, while stating that Israel, in contrast, "has legitimate goals, and the whole nation is united." He added his hope that the Israelis "not give up a foot of ground" until given assurances of secure borders. Leftists derided this position, then as now, as "Progressive Except for Palestine," but it also remained the unofficial ideology of most American Jews and their professional organizations.[9]

American Jews initially viewed Nixon's 1968 election victory with great trepidation. Per usual, they had voted heavily for the Democratic nominee, Vice President Hubert Humphrey, who had long championed the Zionist cause. With the nation experiencing race riots, political assassinations, and endless antiwar protests, Nixon's reputation for vindictiveness made them more nervous still. His campaign's "law and order" focus echoed those of politicians who had used such slogans to scapegoat Jews in the past. Writing in *Commentary*, Nathan Glazer viewed the landscape of Jewish involvement in the various antiestablishment movements and suggested the "possibility—almost a probability—of the rise of a stab-in-the-back myth, in which it will not only be students and professors and intellectuals who are attacked, and not only Jews in their role as members of this general community, but conceivably Jews as *Jews*." Ominously, he added, "The parallel between Weimar and America is often raised. There are many, many differences. And yet this parallel cannot be dismissed."[10]

Jews had every reason to suspect that the Nixon administration would return to the Eisenhower administration's Middle East policies, as Nixon had served as Ike's vice president. Arabists still reigned inside the State Department. And when Nixon's first secretary of state, William Rogers, announced a US peace plan that demanded significant concessions from Israel, in 1969, it inspired Jewish organizations into a massive campaign of opposition. In Philadelphia alone, the local Jewish federation planned through its community relations arm for one hundred thousand written communications to Nixon, Rogers, and key senators and congressmen. They need not have bothered, however. Behind the scenes, both Nixon and Kissinger made certain that what Kissinger termed "Bill Rogers' Middle East Insanity" went nowhere. Before the secretary of state could even discuss his ideas with Israel's leaders, Nixon sent Leonard Garment, now his de facto ambassador to American Jews, to head off Golda Meir when she came to the United States in early 1970 for a fund-raising trip. His instructions were to "slam the hell out of Rogers and his plan." There would be no successful "Rogers plan" for the Middle East so long as Henry Kissinger was around.[11]

Kissinger's machinations planted the seeds for catastrophic results. Egyptian leader Anwar Sadat, speaking through his adviser Hafiz Ismail, began to reach out to the Americans to perhaps find a way to end the state of low-level war that remained between Egypt and Israel, and even to discuss a final peace agreement in exchange for the return of Egyptian territory captured during the 1967 war. Clearly intrigued, the Israelis began discussions over what concessions they might be willing to offer for a full peace with Egypt. But Kissinger instructed the Israelis not merely to ignore Egypt's feelers, but also not to mention their interest to Rogers, who was still secretary of state at that point. "We are pushing nothing, we are wasting time," he confided to the Israelis, who eventually decided they had no choice but to go along with Kissinger's admonition, especially as he saw fit to sweeten it by arranging a secret promise to supply Israel with over a hundred US Phantom fighter jets. Sadat eventually decided that another war to avenge the humiliation of 1967 was his only choice were he ever to secure the land lost in 1967.[12]

Israel had become so popular in Congress by this time that the Nixon administration found itself in a virtual arms race to see who could claim the role of the Jewish state's most generous benefactor. Kissinger's concessions to the Israelis were no doubt extraordinary, but they were not enough. According to the 1970 Defense Procurement Act, Israel was invited by Congress to obtain "ground weapons, such as missiles, tanks, howitzers, armored personnel carriers, ordnance, etc. as well as aircraft," purely on credit. In the eyes of some of Israel's most dedicated supporters, even this was not enough. Senator Henry "Scoop" Jackson (D-WA) insisted that offering Israel better and more sophisticated weaponry all but unconditionally would encourage its leaders "to take risks at the negotiating table" for peace. Jackson's argument became yet another constant theme that the Jewish state's supporters would stick to through thick and thin for the coming half century, albeit with little in the way of evidence to support it.[13]

Resistance to this beneficence soon appeared in the form of the dovish J. William Fulbright (D-AR), who chaired the Senate Committee on Foreign Relations. Fulbright had long been deeply concerned with the activities of pro-Israel lobbyists and their connections to its government. He had even hired an investigator to see what laws were being violated and forced changes to the 1938 Foreign Agents Registration Act, embarrassing Israel and forcing a restructuring of its lobbying operations in the United States. His insistence that the law be followed likely cost him the fulfillment of his longtime ambition to be secretary of state in any future Democratic administration. But whereas Congress was dominated by doves when it came to Indochina, when attention turned to Israel the members of this species proved few and far between. Fulbright could secure only seven votes for his bill tying arms sales to a willingness on the part of Israel to negotiate a peace agreement (together with US willingness to guarantee Israel's pre-1967 borders militarily if need be). In a letter to a friend, he complained that he could not "find any substantial support in the Senate for a balanced attitude toward the two contending forces in the Middle East." He blamed this lack of support, in part, on an alliance between Zionists and "our own military establishment." Here again the hawks were lining up behind Israel and the doves were divided and defensive—another pattern that would define Congress in the coming decades.[14]

Nixon and Kissinger's appreciation of Israel's potential strategic value to their foreign policy plans rose enormously during Jordan's "Black September" of 1970. At the time, the Middle East was undergoing a degree of violent chaos that made America's exploding cities appear bucolic in comparison. The Palestine Liberation Organization (PLO) had been formed at an Arab summit in 1964 as an umbrella group made up of various factions representing different constituencies of the Palestinian people and their supporters (and funders) in the Arab world. It had little influence before 1967, however, when the failure of the Arab states to take any meaningful steps to try to address the sorry condition of Palestinian refugees led to a widespread feeling that any "liberation" from Israel's oppression would need to be undertaken by the Palestinians themselves. Most of the refugees remained either under occupation in the West Bank and Gaza or in refugee camps across the Arab world. Beginning in 1968, a group of militant, explicitly violent revolutionary factions joined the more mainstream "Fatah" in its ruling body, the Palestinian National Council (PNC). The following year, the PNC chose Fatah's Yasser Arafat as the PLO's "chairman."

It was not until October 1974 that the Arab League proved willing to recognize the PLO as the "sole, legitimate representative of the Palestinian people." In the meantime, feeling themselves forgotten by a world that failed to prioritize, or even take much notice of, the refugees' increasingly desperate plight, while simultaneously seeing themselves as a colonialized nation rather than merely displaced "refugees," many Palestinians came to support terrorism as a tactic to reclaim the world's attention. But owing to their lack of organizational discipline, or even communication, various PLO factions acted with virtually no coordination. As every tiny groupuscule sought to create ever more fantastic spectacles of violence and mass murder, the early 1970s saw what often felt like an endlessly gruesome carnival of Palestinian plane hijackings, bombings, and both individual and mass murders. Sometimes the victims were Israeli diplomats in Europe, sometimes non-Israeli Jews traveling to Israel, and sometimes schoolchildren inside Israel. Inevitably, each Palestinian attack on Jews led to a purposely "asymmetric" Israeli response, usually involving bombing missions that resulted in large numbers of civilian deaths—or "collateral damage," in the parlance of the time. As PLO terrorist cells were often armed and trained by the Soviet, Chinese, or Cuban military and intelligence agencies, funded by Arab nations in the region, and cheered on by revolutionary organizations in the West, the Middle East became another Cold War battlefield and Israel/Palestine yet another proxy war.

By 1970, the PLO had created its own somewhat anarchical mini-state inside Jordan. Its leaders overplayed their hand, however, when one of its radical factions—the Popular Front for the Liberation of Palestine (PFLP)—blew up three hijacked planes in an abandoned desert airfield, thereby humiliating King Hussein one too many times. Following a failed attempt on his life, Hussein decided to take his country back regardless of the level of brutality this might involve. The so-called Black September of 1970 involved massive attacks by Jordan's military, killing not only PLO fighters but also many thousands of Palestinian refugees living in PLO-controlled refugee camps located within Jordan's borders. The attacks appeared to backfire when Syria, backed by the Soviets, threatened to invade Jordan to rescue the PLO. Nixon and Kissinger understood the Syrians to be Soviet surrogates and were panicked by this potential expansion of the USSR's influence in the Middle East, but given the situation in both Vietnam and at home, yet another deployment abroad of US troops would have been politically impossible. So they hit upon the idea of asking the Israelis to save Hussein and fight the Syrians. After receiving assurances that if the Soviets intervened, Israel would not be asked to fight them alone, Prime Minister Golda Meir, speaking through Ambassador Rabin, agreed. The threat worked. The Syrians decided they preferred abandoning the PLO to the prospect of yet another war with Israel.[15]

Even without a war, Israel's willingness to make its military available to the United States cemented its unique role in the hearts and minds of not only the Nixon administration, but the entire US national security establishment. Kissinger informed Rabin that the president wanted Prime Minister Meir to know that he would "never forget the role played by Israel." He promised what he now called America's "Middle Eastern ally" that the United States would take Israel's willingness to use its military to serve US interests "into account in any future development." Israel benefited further in the opinions of both policymakers and the public thanks to the actions of its adversaries. PLO terrorist attacks and hijackings succeeded in reminding people of the Palestinian grievances against Israel, but not in a good way. Few Americans could summon much sympathy for masked men wearing kaffiyehs and brandishing AK-47s as they threatened, humiliated, and sometimes murdered people who looked and sounded very much like Americans, and sometimes were.[16]

By far the costliest of these terrorist operations, when judged purely from a public relations perspective, was the 1972 attack on the Olympic Village in Munich, Germany, and the eventual murder of eleven Israeli athletes during a botched rescue raid by the German police. Given the fact that so many members of the global media had gathered there to cover the Olympics, millions of Americans watched the action live on television. It thereby affixed the image of Arab-as-terrorist in their minds. This was an image that was constantly reinforced, both in the news media and in American popular culture, as Arab terrorists became the "go to" villain in many movie and television plots. (Thanks to Nixon's détente policies, Russians did not work in this role nearly as well as they once had.) Because so many Palestinian factions deployed often impenetrable Marxist jargon in support of the anti-Western "revolution" they claimed to be building, these characters were able to do double duty as both terrorists and commies in the imagination of Hollywood scriptwriters and producers, much to the delight of those among Israel's supporters who felt themselves committed to making similar arguments about the Palestinians in real life.[17]

Having failed to interest Kissinger, Nixon, or the Israelis in a peace agreement that might reclaim the territories lost in 1967, Egypt, together with Syria, launched a joint surprise attack on Israel on Yom Kippur—the holiest day on the Jewish calendar—October 6, 1973. Israel was almost entirely unprepared for the attacks and struggled to defend itself as Soviet-supplied SAM missiles shot down its bombers and fighter jets and the Arab armies marched across the Sinai and the Golan Heights. The Israelis' miscalculation can certainly be attributed to their own arrogance. Sadat had been preparing and issuing public warnings for months following his frustration with Israel and the United States and their lack of response to his peace feelers. But both US and Israeli intelligence misread his signals as mere bluster. King Hussein had even made a secret trip to Jerusalem to warn Golda Meir about a likely Syrian (and possibly Egyptian) attack.[18] But the Israelis could not imagine that Arab nations would dare to risk the consequences of another all-out war after having been so soundly defeated just six years earlier. Israel's hubris was reinforced by Kissinger's remarkable duplicity—even by Kissinger's standards—in not merely helping to engender Egypt's attack but also discouraging the

Israelis from adequately defending themselves. According to Defense Minister Moshe Dayan's testimony before Israel's 1974 Commission of Inquiry, just before the war began Kissinger offered the Israeli government strong but off-the-record warnings not to make a preemptive strike against Egypt or Syria, and not to mobilize the reserve army before the war actually started, if it wanted any help from the United States in the event of hostilities. These warnings were given after Kissinger insisted that all other Americans leave the room and no notes be taken. Dayan then canceled the air force's preemptive operation and objected to Meir's plan to mobilize the reserve. But in his frequent candid discussions with the Egyptian diplomat Hafiz Ismail, Kissinger is not known to have given any similar warning to the Egyptians. Indeed, according to Sadat's memoirs, Kissinger actually encouraged the attack, via secret messages purveyed to him through Ismail, in order to improve Egypt's negotiating position in the war's aftermath.[19]

In the days immediately following the attacks, the war looked as if it might be lost. "The Third Temple is crumbling," Dayan cried to his generals, and he even initiated discussions with Prime Minister Meir for a "demonstration" nuclear blast if the advance could not be thwarted. Three days into the war, Kissinger told Ismail that he hoped he understood that the United States was doing merely the minimum to aid Israel that was possible under the circumstances. After eight days of fighting, however, Nixon insisted, over both Kissinger's and the Pentagon's objections, on implementing a massive emergency airlift of extremely sophisticated weaponry. He did this despite his prediction to Kissinger that after Israel won the war, it would be "even more impossible to deal with than before."[20]

Israel was soon able to turn around the war so completely that its forces encircled the entire Egyptian Third Army. Together, the United States and the Soviet Union negotiated a cease-fire agreement via the UN Security Council, which the Israelis proceeded to ignore. As the Israelis continued to conquer Syrian territory and threaten the destruction of Egypt's army, Soviet premier Leonid Brezhnev sent an urgent message to Nixon, via the Soviet ambassador to the United States, Anatoly Dobrynin, and Kissinger "invit[ing]" the United States to join Moscow "to compel observance of the ceasefire without delay." The alternative, Brezhnev clearly implied, was unilateral Soviet military intervention, as Israel could not "be permitted to get away with the violation." Kissinger responded by assuring him that the United States had placed its nuclear missile force on "high alert" and raised its readiness from DEFCON 4 to DEFCON 3 (nuclear war is DEFCON 1). Kissinger, now secretary of state, gave the order himself, without even bothering to wake Nixon. He then let the Israelis know that it was time for them to finally agree to a ceasefire, though he also made it clear that he would certainly find it understandable if it took them a day or two to implement it. Viewing the conflict through the lens of a proxy Cold War battle, he later told American Jewish leaders that what he now "wanted was the most massive Arab defeat possible so that it would be clear to the Arabs that they would get nowhere with dependence on the Soviets."[21]

Nixon had unarguably come through for Israel in its time of great need, and he expected to be rewarded for it. He instructed Kissinger to get in touch with the people he usually labeled as "those dirty rotten Jews from New York," who he imagined to control the news, to make sure he received the praise he felt he deserved. "The major concern is Israel. Who saved Israel?... You have to tell them that," Nixon told him. A few minutes later he added, "Get the whole bunch in a room and say you are American first, and members of the American Jewish Community, and interested in Israel. Who is going to save Israel and who will save it in the future?"[22]

In fact, both Nixon and Kissinger were eager to lean on Israel; this was another of the rewards they felt they had earned during the war. Nixon had been planning just this for a while but had gotten sidetracked by Watergate. In February 1973, in response to another of Kissinger's arguments in favor of postponing any attempt at a comprehensive peace agreement, Nixon responded, "The time has come to quit pandering to Israel's intransigent position." After the war, Kissinger was feeling much the same way. He feared that the results of the war would push Arab regimes deeper into the Soviet orbit. During the endless, back-and-forth disengagement negotiations—at one point between January and May

1974 Kissinger and his team shuttled between Damascus and Jerusalem on twenty-five straight days—Kissinger repeatedly demanded Israeli
concessions, but, as with previous secretaries of state, he almost always
ended up empty handed and retreated in fury. To take just one of countless blowups, when in March 1975 Kissinger felt that the Israeli foreign
minister, Yigal Allon, was stalling him on the final wording of the deals
over which he had long labored, Kissinger told the president he was "outraged at the Israelis," but that his hands were tied because of the "power"
American Jews enjoyed, owing to their ability to finance political campaigns. "It is not easy to explain to the American people why we must
oppose 115 million Arabs who possess all the world's oil, permanently, on
behalf of a nation of 3 million," but there it was.[23]

The reaction among American Jews to the "Yom Kippur War" was in
many respects a repeat of 1967: panic, existential dread, and intimations
of a "second Holocaust." But this time, they were prepared. Since 1967,
American Jewish leaders had committed themselves to the creation of an
informal but still tightly knit network of literally countless communal
organizations in support of Israel's advocacy. The result was what Rabbi
Daniel Silver, Abba Hillel Silver's son, and head of the Jewish Community Relations Council, proudly termed "a continuing and systematic year-in and year-out public information campaign concerned with
maintaining for Israel the sympathy and understanding of the American
people." This network focused not only on elected officials, but also local
community leaders. It disseminated information about the Arab-Israeli
conflict via its own literature, newsreel footage, and reports of pro-Israel
rallies, speeches, and holiday celebrations that its member organizations
sponsored. As Silver observed, "up to 1967 there was a breathing space
between crises—1948, 1956, 1967. Now we live in a period of unrelenting crisis." And so the pro-Israel world prepared for permanent war.[24]

Kissinger came in for extremely harsh criticism from members of this
network, more than a few of which termed him to be a traitor to the
Jewish people. Rabbi Silver imagined in a sermon that "Israel's destruction might give [Kissinger] pause for a night or become a paragraph in
a book." Hans Morgenthau, a respected international relations scholar
whom Kissinger personally revered, went so far as to compare the pressure

he was applying to Israel to the way the West had treated Czechoslovakia in 1938 when it was threatened by Hitler.[25]

To disarm such critics, Kissinger undertook a series of off-the-record meetings with Jewish writers and intellectuals, and another with leaders of Jewish organizations. His goal was to convince them to tone down their criticism of the disengagement negotiations and, if possible, to get some help leaning on the Israelis to lighten up a bit on their demands. The intellectuals spanned the political spectrum, from the democratic socialists Irving Howe and Michael Walzer to neoconservatives such as Seymour Martin Lipset and Norman Podhoretz. There was no room for disagreement between the two poles, however, because the only issue discussed was Israel's security and how to best ensure it in the future. Kissinger posed as Israel's true savior and warned of a noticeable turn against all-out support for Israel in Congress—a phenomenon that would turn out to be 100 percent imaginary. He pointed out that, given the "critical opposition" to Israel within the international community, the perfidy of the "European vultures," and the likely power of the "extremely effective" oil embargo, Israel was "in great danger," adding, "We shouldn't kid ourselves." (The oil embargo had been instituted by the Organization of the Petroleum Exporting Countries to punish the United States, along with the Netherlands, Portugal, Rhodesia, and South Africa, for their support for Israel in the war.) He clearly had their attention. Henry Rosovsky— Dean of Harvard's Faculty of Arts and Science—asked the question that had appeared to be at the forefront of American Jewish minds since 1967: "In ten years will [Israel] still exist?" Kissinger assured him that it would, but what he needed from the assembled was "some wisdom in the Jewish community, and among friends of Israel." Sure, they could "stand up publicly for the security of Israel, and its right to legitimacy, yes. But privately you should make clear to the Israelis that you understand the situation." By "the situation," Kissinger meant that only Henry Kissinger could save Israel, and would the Israelis please get with his program already. The meeting broke up, according to the notes taken by an aide to Kissinger, "with warm expressions of gratitude."[26]

To the leaders of Jewish organizations, Kissinger went further. He complained that he could not serve Israel's interests—and prevent another Arab attack—"if the Jewish community starts climbing walls every time I am seen smiling with Sadat." He was rewarded with a pledge from Max Fisher, a Republican funder, that Jews got the message: "The Jewish community is becoming conscious of the need for a strong defense posture," Fisher said. A leading figure in national Jewish philanthropy, Fisher thereby joined a long line of false prophets of a future Jewish community conservatism that would never arrive. In neither meeting were any issues raised beyond those expressing concern for Israel's best interests, and these were always discussed exclusively in military and Cold War diplomatic terms. When one participant did try to raise the question, asking, "Is peace possible with the Palestinians?" Kissinger replied, "The Palestinians have to get a little hungrier."[27]

Kissinger also saw value in the postwar Arab oil embargo and the domestic chaos it was causing as a means of intimidating American Jews into quieting down about Israel. When he met with a group of Jewish businessmen, they were concerned that "the Arab oil embargo, coupled with anti-Israel propaganda[,] might 'pose a threat to the Jewish community in the United States.'" No matter how secure Jews became as full citizens in the United States—indeed, their success story was the story of the country's own success—their concern about an organized antisemitic campaign never fully disappeared. As a first-generation German Jew, Kissinger knew this concern as well as anyone. So he used it as a weapon to try to deflect any potential criticism of his policies.[28]

Following the upheavals of Watergate, Nixon's August 1974 resignation, and America's ignominious retreat from Vietnam, Kissinger's tenure in government, now under President Gerald Ford, ended with yet another exercise in frustration at the hands of Israel and its American Jewish supporters. With Israel continuing to resist his plans for disengagement in the Sinai and the Golan Heights, in March 1975 Kissinger convinced the new president to order a "reassessment" of US foreign policy in the region, which included a deliberate slowdown and deferral of arms deliveries pending its outcome. He announced that "every department is to be instructed to end the special relationships [with Israel]." Acting as much on the basis of paranoia and pique as on principle or policy, he imagined that American Jews were "conducting a systematic campaign" to undermine his authority and complained to Ford, "I think the Israelis are after me." Alas, Ford and Kissinger's reassessment would be a short one. With lightning speed, Israel's Washington lobbyists circulated a letter signed by seventy-six senators demanding that the president be responsive to Israel's "urgent military and economic needs," and that he "make clear, as we do, that the United States, acting in its own national interests, stands firmly with Israel in the search for peace in future negotiations." Next came Congress's cancellation of a planned sale of defensive antiaircraft weapons to Jordan. Should the pro-Israel message somehow be unclear, Bertram Gold, executive director of the American Jewish Committee, warned that "if 1975 turns out to be the year of intense pressure on Israel, there will be a very serious reaction among American Jews. We will go directly to Congress, and 1976 is not that far away."[29]

Kissinger was predictably furious. He told one aide that what was needed was "psychological warfare against Israel . . . which has treated us as no other country could," and threatened, privately, that "if the Jewish Community comes after us, we will have to go public with the whole record." Resistance, he promised, would be futile, as he instructed his State Department colleagues that "we are to see it through and even if they win it will do so much damage to the Jewish community here that it may never recover."[30]

None of this happened, of course. At the end of his extensive period of "shuttle diplomacy," Kissinger did successfully secure a "Disengagement Treaty" between Israel and Egypt and another between Israel and Syria in the spring of 1974, as well as the "the Sinai Interim Agreement" in September 1975, separating the forces of all sides and committing Egypt and Israel to forgoing use of the threat of military force against one another. Thanks in part to the careful attention he paid to cultivating his image in his memoirs and interviews, and his constant stroking of journalists, biographers, and interested pundits and historians, he later succeeded in creating a myth of himself as the supreme diplomat. The Middle East policy maven Martin Indyk, a friend of Kissinger's, titled his widely reviewed 2022 book on him *Master of the Game: Henry Kissinger and the Art of Middle East Diplomacy*. It was a nearly seven-hundred-page paean to the man's "formidable intellect." (Indyk thanked Kissinger in the acknowledgments for his "generosity and friendship," which allowed Indyk to provide an account that reflected his "deep respect for him" and his "appreciation of his statesmanship.") His book, like so many accounts, reflects the many instances in which Kissinger attempted to rewrite his record in this—as in so many conflicts in which he was involved. Documents released in the decades since the incidents in question took place have demonstrated the costs to the credibility of anyone, whether pundit or historian, who has embraced Kissinger's unsupportable self-serving version of these events and the conclusions they implied.[31]

While Kissinger's role in the Middle East may not be as stained with the blood of innocents as in Vietnam, Cambodia, Chile, or East Pakistan, to name just four nations where his policies led directly to mass murder, they are hardly worthy of the myth he worked so hard to create. After discouraging the Israelis from pursuing the possibility of a peace agreement with Egypt without a war, he then purposely disadvantaged Israel in the war that he helped ensure would happen. When it was over—and contrary to his own stated goals—Kissinger apparently felt it necessary to cave in to the Israelis in almost every respect. To secure Israel's withdrawal from the Sinai, Kissinger agreed to virtually every Israeli demand with promises of weaponry, oil, radar, shared intelligence, and help with resupply in the event of war. Most significantly, Kissinger promised that the United States would not recognize or negotiate with the PLO so long as the organization did not first recognize Israel's right to exist. He also promised that the United States would "make every effort to coordinate with Israel...with a view toward refraining from putting forward proposals that Israel would find unsatisfactory." This came pretty close to saying that the United States had farmed out its foreign policy in the Middle East to Israel and its supporters. The Israelis had defeated him only slightly less convincingly than the allegedly equally "obnoxious" Vietnamese had. And as for the prospect of actual peace between Israel and Egypt, it would take the tireless (and often thankless) efforts of a former one-term Georgia governor with no diplomatic experience whatsoever to bring that about, long after Kissinger had retired to make his fortune in private life. In the meantime, however, with Nixon gone, Kissinger was not done with the Israelis and their champions in the American political debate, and they were certainly not done with him.[32]

# CHAPTER 9

# "ZIONISM IS (NOT) RACISM"

RICHARD NIXON AND HENRY KISSINGER DID NOT CONCERN THEM-selves much with the United Nations, viewing it mostly as a debating society in which the United States and its allies were outnumbered. It annoyed them, to be certain—all those inferior peoples daring to ignore America's wishes and even pursue their own interests. When, in October 1971, a group of African nations voted to admit Communist China into the UN Security Council, the president complained to Secretary of State William Rogers about "these cannibals jumping up and down and all that.... This bunch of people who don't even wear shoes yet, to be kicking the United States in the teeth."[1]

The United Nations was important to Israel, having been instrumental in the Jewish state's creation and a barometer of its acceptance in the wider world. By 1973, however, the organization had little in common with the one that had played the pivotal role in Israel's creation a quarter century earlier. Some fifty-four countries had voted to accept Israel into the United Nations after it declared independence—but after five years, just seven of them had presented their diplomatic credentials in Jerusalem. Israel initially managed to avoid many of the earliest Cold War conflicts that divided the body, successfully forging especially warm relations with emerging African nations. Golda Meir would later recall that she was "prouder of Israel's International Cooperation Program and of the technical aid we gave to the people of Africa than I am of any other single project we have undertaken." (Tanzania's president, Julius Nyerere, called her "the mother of Africa.")[2]

But these nations, like many of those involved with the Non-Aligned Movement (a forum of 120 countries that, ostensibly, chose neutrality in the US-USSR competition), also gradually embraced the common view among Muslim, Arab, and Marxist-oriented nations that Zionism was essentially a "settler-colonial" enterprise and Jews had no place in the Middle East. It was no coincidence that during this era Israel changed the focus of its attention to South Africa, helping to build and support its racist apartheid system and aiding in its attempt to develop nuclear weapons technology—which led in 1979 to the covert testing of a nuclear device in the South Atlantic. Israel also simultaneously befriended the worst human rights abusers on the planet by providing arms and military knowhow to wherever it was welcome, including more than a few African and Latin American dictators that human rights organizations have accused of committing genocide against their own people.[3]

Israel benefited enormously from its representation, both in its Washington embassy and in its UN mission, by a silver-tongued, Oxford-educated diplomat, Abba Eban. Regardless of whether a vote went Israel's way, Eban's extraordinary eloquence in General Assembly debates reassured American Jews that Israel was getting the better of whatever argument might be taking place. President Lyndon Johnson judged his worth to be that of countless divisions in the field. An album of Eban's 1967 address to the General Assembly "sold out in New York like a Beatle's LP," according to one (wild) estimation. Exaggeration notwithstanding, this was a common view among those inclined to agree with Eban, and even among some who did not.[4]

The Palestinians, in contrast, were forced to accept the representation of other Arab nations. These were usually happy to keep up attacks on

Israel in order to unite their own populations and make cause with leftist and Soviet-supported nations around the world. But they showed little interest in persuading the persuadable. Arab and Muslim anger was often focused on Israel in the General Assembly, with the fate of the Palestinian refugees usually occupying center stage. But within the Security Council, where actual decisions got made, Israel could usually depend on the United States to thwart any measure it deemed to be of genuine significance.

In the aftermath of the Six-Day War, Israel did find itself forced to attend to UN business. This business had to do with Security Council Resolution 242, which addressed the territories Israel had conquered in the war. The resolution, sponsored by Great Britain, called for a full Israeli withdrawal, but did so in language so opaque that Israel could argue it was not called upon to do anything at all. This was thanks in significant measure to the tireless work of the US ambassador to the United Nations, the former US Supreme Court justice (and prominent American Jew) Arthur Goldberg. The resolution's key sticking point was the lack of a definite article preceding the word "territories" in the phrase "withdrawal of Israeli armed forces from territories occupied in recent conflict," at least in its English-language version (it was there in the French version, which the Israelis ignored). Arab nations, backed by the Soviets, insisted it meant every square inch. To Israel and the United States, it meant just "some" of territories now under occupation.

Israel always insisted it was ready to make a deal whenever its neighbors were willing to accept its existence and negotiate permanent borders. Arab leaders, at least in public, consistently called for a complete Israeli withdrawal from all conquered territories together with the resettlement of every last refugee who wished to return (as well as their progeny). These positions were perfectly incompatible, and it strains credulity to think either side intended them to be taken entirely seriously. In addition to the fact that allowing Arab refugees to return to their homes and villages never enjoyed even remotely significant political support in Israel, Ben-Gurion's government had ensured that it would become literally impossible. According to a US State Department study written shortly after the 1948 war, "Israeli authorities have followed a systematic program of destroying Arab houses in such cities as Haifa and in village communities in order to rebuild modern habitation for the influx of Jewish immigrants from DP camps and Europe." There were therefore "literally no houses for the refugees to return to."[5]

In public, meanwhile, the Palestinians continued to stick to their demand that Israel just disappear. The world-famous linguistics professor and left-wing foreign policy critic Noam Chomsky tells of attending meetings with senior PLO officials during the early 1970s at the invitation of Palestinian American activist and Columbia University literary scholar Edward Said. As Chomsky recalled, Said had invited him as part of his effort to increase ties between PLO officials and "people who were sympathetic to the Palestinians but critical of their policies." Chomsky found these meetings "pointless." "We would go up to their suite at the Plaza, one of the fanciest hotels in New York," he later said in an interview, "and basically just sit there listening to their speeches about how they were leading the world revolutionary movement, and so on and so forth." Chomsky discerned in the PLO "a fundamental misunderstanding of how a democratic society works.... But the Palestinian leadership simply failed to comprehend this. If they had been honest and said, 'Look, we are fundamentally nationalists, we would like to run our own affairs, elect our own mayors, get the occupation off our backs,' it would have been easy to organize, and they could have had enormous public support. But if you come to the United States holding your Kalashnikov and saying we are organizing a worldwide revolutionary movement, well, that's not the way to get public support here."[6]

These tendencies were very much on display on November 13, 1974, when PLO leader Yasser Arafat traveled to New York to address the UN General Assembly. He was accompanied by Ali Hassan Salemeh, a figure whom Israeli intelligence credited with planning the kidnapping of the Israeli athletes at the 1972 Munich Olympics. Dressed in military fatigues and with an empty pistol holster hanging from his waist—the United Nations did not allow guns, but it had no position on holsters—Arafat made the strongest case for the Palestinian cause, along with the most devastating attack on Israel, ever heard by most Americans. But he did so behind a wall of pseudo-Marxist revolutionary jargon so thick that it obscured whatever justice lay beneath it. He described Zionism as "a scheme born [for] the conquest of Palestine by European immigrants, just as settlers colonized, and indeed raided, most of Africa." He added that the Zionists were dedicated to "building colonies, everywhere cruelly exploiting, oppressing, plundering the peoples of those three continents," thereby "gladdening the hearts of imperialists and racists everywhere." These words would not have been out of place in a US Communist Party pamphlet published in the 1940s.[7]

Arafat spoke for nearly three hours and made a number of points about the conflict that would have shocked most Americans, especially American Jews, had they been able to listen to this almost perfectly inappropriate messenger without the prejudices he so intensely inspired. Arafat noted that even though the 1947 UN partition resolution had unfairly granted the Jews—whom he called "the colonialist settlers"—54 percent of what had been Palestine, they had ended up with "81 percent of the total area of Palestine." This was a significant exaggeration of a perfectly reasonable argument. Arafat also put the number of Arabs uprooted by the Israelis in the 1948 war at an even million. This was yet another exaggeration of an important point. Most historians put the number somewhere in the area of 750,000, but it is impossible to know just how many were expelled and how many chose to leave but expected to return later, after the invading Arab armies put an end to the Zionists' dream of their own country. Arafat added that the invaders had "occupied 524 Arab towns and villages, of which they destroyed 385, completely obliterating them in the process." And "having done so," he said, "they built their own settlements and colonies on the ruins of our farms and our groves." Here again, the man in the military fatigues and kaffiyeh had a point, and one that was almost never heard in American debates on the question.[8]

Arafat went on to insist that the causes of the conflict did "not stem from any conflict between two religions or two nationalisms. Neither is it a border conflict between neighboring states. It is the cause of a people deprived of its homeland, dispersed and uprooted, and living mostly in exile and in refugee camps." Again, from the Palestinian point of view, this was an entirely fair point. They had been pretty much minding their own business in 1896 when the First Zionist Congress in Basel chose Palestine as the future homeland of the Jewish people. By the time Arafat spoke in 1974, however, this hardly mattered. Israel, as the saying goes, was "real." Yes, the Palestinians were, as Edward Said put it, "victims of the victims." A series of historical injustices against the Jews culminating in one of the worst crimes in human history had inspired yet another injustice to be suffered by the Palestinians. But recognition of the latter injustice was not going to make it go away. And the fact that at the time of Arafat's address, the PLO's Palestinian National Covenant called for the "elimination of Zionism in Palestine" (Article 15) and the destruction of the "Zionist and imperialistic presence" therein (Article 22) meant that his entire approach was an obvious nonstarter.[9]

Arafat also attacked Israel's reputation with liberals and progressives by calling attention to its regressive policies abroad, in particular its close relationship with South Africa. He had a point here, too, and one that would grow stronger and more salient over time. He built on this argument by attacking what he termed Israel's "long record of hostility even towards the Jews themselves, for there is within the Zionist entity a built-in racism against Oriental Jews." But here again, in addition to being perhaps the least effective carrier of this message in the world, the PLO leader also went overboard with an otherwise meritorious argument. Oriental, or "Mizrachi," Jews did (and still do) experience considerable discrimination at the hands of Israel's Ashkenazi (European) elite. But Arafat also added that while the PLO "vociferously condemn[ed] the massacres of Jews under Nazis rule," he nevertheless insisted that "the Zionist leadership appeared more interested at that time in exploiting them as best it could in order to realize its goal of immigration into Palestine." This point was not entirely divorced from historical reality, but neither was it completely sound. And it is something that Americans were decidedly not going to concede to a man they considered a terrorist criminal. Arafat could only serve to further alienate whatever potentially sympathetic audience in the United States he may have had.

Arafat also went after the Israelis with some justice and yet more hyperbole about their treatment of their Arab minority. What he called "the small number of Palestinian Arabs who were not uprooted by the Zionists in 1948" were "at present refugees in their own homeland," he said. "Israeli law treats them as second-class citizens—and even as third-class citizens since Oriental Jews are second-class citizens—and they have been subject to all forms of racial discrimination and terrorism after confiscation of their land and property." Palestinian Israelis were, and remain, a significant minority in Israel, constituting over 20 percent of the population. And while they have many formal rights—more, democratically speaking, than in most Arab countries—they remain deeply discriminated against compared to Jewish Israelis. Until 1966, Israel's Arab towns and villages were placed under Israeli military rule, with their inhabitants subject to all manner of harsh restrictions without recourse to courts or democratic processes. Since then, they have enjoyed rights of free speech, freedom of travel, freedom of assembly, and the right to vote. But a state that defines itself as "Jewish" creates all manner of ways in which non-Jewish individuals are treated as second-class citizens—from the moment they set foot on streets named after the people they consider to be their oppressors to the inferior roads, schools, parks, and police forces they must endure. Neither occupied nor offered full equality, Arab citizens of Israel have been forced to live in a kind of existential purgatory of competing claims and loyalties, almost always an afterthought to whatever crisis was presently in the news.[10]

Finally, Arafat reached for what he must have imagined to be his ace in the hole: "Let us remember that the Jews of Europe and the United States have been known to lead the struggles for secularism and the separation of Church and State. They have also been known to fight against discrimination on religious grounds. How then can they continue to support the most fanatic, discriminatory and closed of nations in its policy?" But here, again, if he had been sincerely seeking to reach Israel's American supporters with this point, he was sadly mistaken. Even if the equation between Israel's treatment of the Palestinians and various nations' treatment of the Jews and other ethnic and religious minorities were a perfect one—and of course it was not—that hardly implied that American Jews would henceforth reconsider their support for Israel. First, people who have experienced oppression, to say nothing of mass murder, often feel that they do not have the luxury of caring too much about the treatment of others. If the Jews felt they had been "pushed off a cliff and landed on the Palestinians," as a common metaphor went at the time, well, that was just too bad.

Only the most fanatical of Israel's supporters disputed the fact that the Palestinians had suffered a catastrophic injustice in 1948. But most American Jews and other supporters of Israel agreed with the arguments of its leaders that it was the Arab nations and the Palestinians themselves who were to blame: first for refusing to accept partition; next for declaring war on Israel; and third for refusing to take responsibility for the refugees who, the Israelis insisted, had voluntarily fled in response to propaganda radio broadcasts urging them to do so. Arafat demonstrated that he was genuinely playing to a crowd of the already convinced, rather than seeking to win new converts to his cause. He closed with a clear threat, albeit one wrapped inside brilliant rhetorical flourish: "Today I have come bearing an olive branch and a freedom fighter's gun. Do not let the olive branch fall from my hand."

Arafat did not make much progress with US media. In an article that reads as typical of the time, the *New York Times* account of the speech quoted the Israeli diplomat Yosef Tekoah (whose delegation boycotted the speech) calling the PLO "murderers" and declaring that "Arafat, today, prefers the Nazi method." Tekoah insisted that "the murderers of athletes in the Olympic Games in Munich, the butchers of children in Maalot, the assassins of diplomats in Khartoum do not belong in the international community." In a subsequent *Times* "news analysis" of the speech, Tekoah would be the only person, besides Arafat, quoted by name. But the article also explained, quoting only anonymous sources, that despite Arafat's speech sounding like a "shrill prelude to a fifth Middle East war," sophisticated observers who looked past his "angry rhetoric" understood that "Arafat had to talk the way he did because the P.L.O. has its uncompromising charter and ideology, and he has to put up a show for the Arab public." In the liberal *Nation*, an editorial criticized both sides before adding, "We cannot control others, but on the American side, everybody should lower his voice and work for the coexistence which, in the Middle East, is the only alternative to holocaust."

If Yasser Arafat had set out to prove Abba Eban's famous quip that the Palestinians "never missed an opportunity to miss an opportunity," he could hardly have done a better job.[11]

Arafat's UN address would turn out to be a curtain raiser to a frontal assault on Israel's legitimacy, culminating, eighteen months later, in the November 1975 General Assembly adoption of Resolution 3379 declaring that "Zionism is a form of racism and racial discrimination."

The formal campaign for the resolution had begun the previous summer in Mexico City, at the United Nations' World Conference of the International Women's Year. That gathering decreed that women would share in "the struggle against neocolonialism, foreign occupation, Zionism, racism, racial discrimination and apartheid." American Jewish feminists who had traveled to the conference were shocked by the anti-Israel animus they encountered there. Betty Friedan, who led the US delegation, found in her delegation's resistance a determination "to combat the use of feminism itself as an anti-Semitic political tool." She came home resolved to fight for Zionism as well as feminism, further shedding her past Marxism-infused universalist beliefs. She would also later help found the celebrity-heavy "Ad Hoc Committee of Women for Human Rights" as an effort to raise consciousness about the label of "racism" being "applied solely to the national self-determination of the Jewish people."[12]

Following Mexico City, the General Assembly's "Third Committee," which was concerned with social, humanitarian, and cultural affairs, agreed by a substantial majority that Zionism was indeed a form of racism. It called upon the General Assembly to do likewise. The resolution, which enjoyed no formal enforcement power, was widely understood to be a stepping-stone for the Arab states, together with their supporters in the Soviet bloc, to try to expel Israel from world bodies such as UNESCO, the International Labor Organization, and eventually the United Nations itself. The pitch for the resolution signaled a new direction for the Palestinian struggle, making it no longer merely about the return of the lands, but instead about the ideology that had led to the Palestinians' displacement. Chomsky and Said, then quite likely the two best-known supporters of the Palestinian cause in America, and perhaps the entire world, criticized this turn. Chomsky noted the resolution's "profound hypocrisy, given the nature of the states that backed it (including the Arab states)," to say nothing of its misplaced criticism of "Zionism as such rather than the policies of the State of Israel." Said would later write, in his influential essay "Zionism from the Standpoint of Its Victims," originally published in 1979, that whatever Israel's sins, it did not help the Palestinian cause to see it "sloppily be tarnished with the sweeping rhetorical denunciation associated with racism." As with Arafat's UN address, the Palestinians' overreach undermined the genuine claims to the rights they had so long been denied.[13]

Daniel Patrick Moynihan, the late four-term US senator from New York, would owe his initial election victory to this historical moment. Moynihan had been an assistant secretary of labor, a Democratic operative, a US ambassador to India, and a Harvard faculty member. President Ford's decision to appoint him to the job of US ambassador to the United Nations in June 1975 was widely understood to be a symbol of growing conservative contempt for the world body. Moynihan, indeed, was many things: a scholar; an intellectual; a polymath; a polemicist; an Irish street-fighter, both literally and metaphorically; and an extremely high-functioning alcoholic. But one thing this intellectually ambidextrous political operator definitely was not was a diplomat—and never less so than when he chose to take up Israel's cause in the United Nations.[14]

Those who knew Moynihan were shocked to hear of his appointment. Kissinger must have known that he would have trouble containing—much less controlling—the man the *New York Times* would term "the brawler at the UN," and it remains a bit of a mystery why he agreed to the appointment. Already extremely controversial for his work in the Johnson administration, where he wrote about the breakdown of the "Negro family," and in the Nixon administration, for his promotion of a period of a "benign neglect" of America's racial problems, he was now appointed by Ford and Kissinger on the basis of a series of articles he published in *Commentary* attacking "Third World kleptocrats" and their first world "apologists." In the most important of these, titled "The United States in Opposition," and telexed from New Delhi, he suggested that other nations should feed their own people rather than complain that "Americans eat too much," and that American diplomats cease apologizing for their nation's "imperfections." Following the humiliating US evacuation from Saigon, together with the sight of a criminal president being ushered from the White House and then pardoned for his crime, this was a message that resonated with many. The *New York Times Magazine* reported that Moynihan believed he had received "a clear mandate to raise some hell," and he chose the "Zionism Is Racism" resolution to raise it with. Now fully ensconced in the bosom of the fanatically pro-Israel neoconservatives at *Commentary*, and tutored on the Zionist cause by Norman Podhoretz, Moynihan made Zionism's cause America's cause. "We are conducting a foreign policy," Kissinger was heard to complain. "This is not a synagogue." But it was too late. He had created an Irish Frankenstein.[15]

Much at Podhoretz's urging, Moynihan treated his time at the UN very much like that of a man with a 1976 New York Senate race on his mind. The "Zionism Is Racism" issue was tailor-made for any potential candidate for that office, but none more so than Moynihan. Kissinger thought the United States should "pay no attention" to the resolution, and Moynihan's insistence on using what he considered to be costly demagoguery to advance his own name at the expense of US diplomatic priorities drove him to distraction. He demanded that Moynihan clear all remarks with him in advance, which did not even come close to happening. "I will not put up with any more of Moynihan. I will not do it," he told President Ford. "He is going wild about the Israeli issues."[16]

The Israelis were deeply concerned about the resolution. Israel's UN representative, the Irish-born former chief of Israeli military intelligence and future president Chaim Herzog, wanted American Jewish organizations "in every locale to begin advocating and protesting." But the Israelis were, yet again, disappointed by what they judged to be the timidity of their American cousins. "Where were the Jewish people?" Herzog asked a reporter. "Why," he demanded, "in this city, in the midst of the largest Jewish concentration in the world, with a small Israeli delegation fighting desperately against the heaviest possible odds to defend Jewry from a major anti-Semitic attack against Jews wherever they may be," did American Jews not rise to the occasion? Why, instead, did they allow "the lead on this issue [to be] taken to its eternal credit by the United States delegation?" This was both unfair and untrue. At least fourteen major newspapers had condemned the resolution in editorials, as did fully 415 members of Congress, African American groups, Christian groups, and the president of the United States. But somehow, Pat Moynihan got all the credit. Rising to oppose the resolution, Moynihan spoke in broad rhetorical strokes with long, pregnant pauses. "The United States rises to declare before the General Assembly of the United Nations, and before the world, that it does not acknowledge"—he paused—"it will not abide by"—he paused again—"it will never acquiesce in this infamous act." "The lie is that Zionism is a form of racism. The overwhelmingly clear truth is that it is not."[17]

Coverage of the speech and the vote (72–35, with 32 abstentions) in favor of the resolution turned Moynihan into a national celebrity. "A Fighting Irishman at the UN Talks Tough—and Many Americans Feel, Talks Sense, Too," ran a *People* magazine headline above a rapturous story naming Moynihan one of the year's "25 Most Intriguing People." On *CBS Evening News*, Eric Sevareid commented that "the country is simply tired of feeling self-disgust. That explains the almost joyous response to Moynihan's passion and candor at the UN."[18]

Moynihan lasted only eight months in the UN job. Kissinger clearly signaled to friendly journalists that if Moynihan did not jump, he would be pushed. Moynihan managed to make his "resignation" a cause célèbre among conservatives, including, especially, Ronald Reagan. (Reagan, who was getting ready to challenge Ford from the Republican far right at the time, complained that it was "too bad that the Administration could not keep such a good man.") *New York Times* pundit Russell Baker asked, "What President, what Secretary of State, dares fire an Irishman who has raised his shillelagh in the cause sacred to the heart of the Jewish vote?" Moynihan claimed to be leaving the post to return to Harvard and reclaim his professorship there, insisting that he "would consider it dishonorable to leave this post and run for any office." Curiously, however, he had already switched his voting residence from Cambridge to his upstate New York farmhouse. He could not help but notice the tens of thousands of letters he was receiving from Americans urging him on. A February 1976 poll showed that support for Moynihan's actions in the United Nations stood at 78 percent among Jewish respondents, 60 percent of whom favored his entry into the New York primary race for the Democratic US Senate nomination.[19]

New York's more conservative Democrats were buyers in the market for a candidate. The 1976 Senate race was sure to become an intra–Democratic Party culture war. Paul O'Dwyer, the machine pol from times of yore and the favorite of party regulars, and Ramsey Clark, formerly Johnson's attorney general, and now on his way to the furthest reaches of anti-American leftism, were pegged early as also-rans. The real battle was between Moynihan, now the intellectual-turned-neocon culture warrior, and Congresswoman Bella Abzug, the famously outspoken feminist and left-wing Jewish liberal. Israel all but dominated campaign debate, and coincidentally, it was also where Abzug was most vulnerable. In Congress, she had once voted against selling Phantom fighter jets to Israel. She would forever deny this. Lecturing a previous Jewish congressional opponent, she had said, "This is one Jew you're not going to out-Jew." Ironically, she was now being "out-Jewed" by an Irishman. Outside her campaign headquarters, members of Meir Kahane's extremist Jewish Defense League chanted, "Israel, Yes. Bella, No," and, "A vote for Bella is a vote for Communism." Moynihan, meanwhile, had the humorous habit, when speaking to Jewish groups numbering in the hundreds, of going "off the record" so he could share secrets with them about his championing of Israel's cause in contrast with Abzug's spotty support.[20]

Moynihan's campaign certainly enjoyed the luck of the Irish. Over the July Fourth holiday weekend, for instance, he happened to be in Jerusalem—a precinct of New York for election purposes—where he was being honored by Hebrew University. By coincidence, his visit coincided with "Operation Thunderbolt," a heroic and successful Israeli raid on Uganda's Entebbe International Airport, where Palestinian and German terrorists were holding 106 hostages (almost exclusively Israeli) after hijacking an Air France flight. Upon his return to New York, Moynihan held a press conference celebrating the raid. He reminded listeners that he had gotten into trouble at the United Nations for calling Idi Amin a "racist murderer" after the Ugandan dictator had called for the "extinction" of Israel.

Moynihan was thus able to appeal to American Jews' feelings of vulnerability and their pride and relief at Israel's military prowess in kicking the asses of the terrorists and humiliating the evil dictator. He thus reaffirmed his position as a Jewish ally against the whole world, as represented by the United Nations and its embrace of the terrorist Arafat and the antisemitic "Zionism Is Racism" resolution. Whatever New Yorkers felt about any local issues that may have separated Abzug and Moynihan, these emotions carried the day. Abzug was hardly anti-Israel. Following a post-1967 tour of its captured territories, she had lionized the Jewish state for its democratic bona fides and condemned the "implacable hatred for Israel" among Arab nations. She defended it again following the 1973 war. But even if Abzug were as pro-Israel as she claimed now to be—and of course she was not—the New Leftists supporting her candidacy were not. During the campaign, she found herself forced to resign from the Women's International League of Peace and Freedom. It was her only reasonable option, given the upcoming election, after the group sent out a letter, with her name listed on the letterhead, condemning Israel's request for $2.5 billion in military aid.[21]

In *The Nation*, meanwhile, in an article by Paul Good, Moynihan found himself accused of possessing "an imperial ego to foreign relations, making him as insensitive in this realm as he was domestically." This made him "particularly unfitted to deal with people of color," Good wrote. In *Harper's*, the famed Vietnam War correspondent Frances Fitzgerald attacked Moynihan's "paranoia about communism, cultural chauvinism, manifest-destiny mythology and the go-it-alone, tough-it-out syndrome," terming him to be "possibly the most hated man in the underdeveloped world." These complaints did not move many Jews, however. Whatever they may have felt about "people of color" or Moynihan's past controversies regarding "the Negro family," most Jewish voters had decided to put the concerns of the "tribe" ahead of all others.[22]

The proverbial icing on the cake was Moynihan's endorsement by the *New York Times*. The paper's editorial board voted 11–2 to endorse

Abzug, but its publisher, Arthur Ochs Sulzberger Sr.—whose family owned the paper—overruled them and demanded an endorsement of Moynihan, leading the editorial board's chief, John B. Oakes, to resign in protest. The *Times'* embrace of the "more Zionist than thou" team was an ironic one, given the paper's history of vociferous American-Council-on-Judaism-style anti-Zionism, a position it retained longer than almost any other significant mainstream media institution. Now, its endorsement likely provided Moynihan with his razor-thin ten-thousand-vote margin of victory. Moynihan carried the Jewish vote by a large margin, while losing heavily with Blacks and other people of color.[23]

Having won the Democratic nomination, Moynihan had an easy time in the general election in a three-way race with a Conservative Party incumbent. Virtually overnight, Moynihan had ridden to not merely national but global prominence as the neoconservative scourge of America's—and Israel's—enemies. And to many American Jews, these had now become one and the same. Though Moynihan's politics would remain remarkably mercurial over his twenty-four years in the Senate, his election presaged an entirely new political constellation within America's Israel debate. Never again could a president consider a decision about Israel without facing a neoconservative campaign to ensure the Jewish state complete freedom of action, not only with regard to the Palestinians and its neighbors, but also with its superpower sponsor, the United States of America.

# CHAPTER 10

# A SEPARATE PEACE

JIMMY CARTER'S TIRELESS EFFORTS TO BRING ISRAEL AND EGYPT TOgether in a peace agreement during the 1979 negotiations at Camp David are arguably the most consequential contribution any US president has made toward Israel's security since its founding. The treaty earned the Israelis literally 100 percent of what they had so long sought: a separate peace treaty that ended not only the state of war with their most threatening neighbor, but also the freedom to carry out their other strategic and military objectives without concern of igniting regional war. (It also effectively ended the boycott of Israeli and Jewish products, people, and culture across the Arab world.) However "cold" it may have been in terms of relations between the two signatories, the agreement remained in place despite many Israeli actions that might have dislodged it: Israel's occupation of an Arab capital (Beirut); its air attacks on numerous Arab countries; its demolition of nuclear reactors in both Iraq and Syria; subsequent mini wars in Gaza against the ruling party there, the Islamic fundamentalist Hamas, and in Lebanon against Iran's guerrilla allies, Hezbollah; the occasional bombing of military targets in Syria; and the violent crushing of two Palestinian rebellions on the West Bank (the First and Second Intifadas), together with an apparently endless occupation there. But what Carter never understood was that he wanted this peace for Israel far more than American Jewish leaders did, and even more than many Israelis. He proved willing to take political risks for it that no president before or after him has been willing even to imagine. He paid for his success with a consistent campaign of vilification by these same Jewish leaders, and most of them never forgave him for the tenacity with which he pursued his vision of Middle East peace.

A former one-term governor of Georgia and surprise victor of both the Democratic presidential primary and the presidential election of 1976, Carter defeated President Ford on a strong pro-Israel platform. Before running for president, the born-again Baptist had not had much reason to give the Arab/Israeli conflict special attention, save for whatever came up in the Sunday Bible study class he taught (literally) religiously. Carter admitted that as a peanut farmer and southern governor, he knew no Arabs and had little background in Middle East diplomacy. His primary influence in thinking about Israel remained "the Bible."[1]

Carter's top aide on Jewish matters, Stuart Eizenstat, instructed the candidate that "unswerving support for Israel must be the basis for our Middle East policy," outlining "a punchy, strong pro-Israel position." The concentration of Jews in and around the nation's major population centers, as well as their prominence in the media, academia, finance, and the legal and medical professions, amplified their voices and political influence. Carter had not been the first or even the second or third Jewish choice for the presidency in 1976. But he overcame this uneasiness by insisting that the basis of his commitment to Israel's survival was "a moral imperative." This issue took precedence for him along with his promises to heal the nation in the wake of Watergate and Vietnam. Carter's choice of Senator Walter Mondale of Minnesota as his running mate was also appealing to Jews. A significant number of them had defected to the Republicans in the Nixon-McGovern race four years earlier, but Mondale was the protégé of liberal stalwart and Zionist champion Hubert

Humphrey. On Election Day, Jewish voters returned to their previous pattern, giving the Democratic nominee a 75–25 margin over incumbent Ford.[2]

In the Oval Office, Carter's political team viewed Israel in much the same way that his campaign had. Chief of Staff Hamilton Jordan explained, in a June 1977 memo, that regarding US Middle East policy, "there does not exist in this country a political counterforce that opposes the specific goals of the Jewish lobby." He added, however, albeit with considerable understatement, that while the members of the administration were "aware of [the lobby's] strength and influence," they did not "understand the basis for that strength" or how it functioned politically: "It is something that was not a part of our Georgia and Southern political experience."[3]

Carter entered office with a blueprint of how he might proceed if he decided to pursue a Middle East peace. William Quandt, whom Carter would soon hire as his top Middle East expert on the National Security Council, had already convened an influential group of professors, policy entrepreneurs, and politicians sponsored by the Brookings Institution, a centrist think tank, to examine the problem and try to come up with a workable solution to both the Palestinian problem and the Arab/Israeli conflict. Titled "Toward Peace in the Middle East," it called for staged but complete Israeli withdrawal from the occupied territories and the creation of an independent Palestinian state. But as with almost all such blue-ribbon-panel plans, it paid little attention to the question of how to get from here to there. This was a problem, given Israel's position at the time. When General Moshe Dayan, soon to be appointed Israel's foreign minister, met with Zbigniew Brzezinski, Carter's national security adviser, barely ten days into the new administration, on January 31, 1977, Dayan informed him that while the Arab nations might be ready for peace treaties, Israel was "not willing to pay the price."[4]

Carter told Brzezinski that he "would be willing to lose the Presidency for the sake of genuine peace in the Middle East," and Brzezinski believed him (though one cannot help but notice that "peace" is an odd reason to lead a president to think he might lose his job). Often speaking from his heart rather than from his advisers' talking points, Carter repeatedly brought the wrath of the professional Jewish world down on his head, beginning with a March 1977 town hall in Massachusetts, when he responded to a question on the topic by asserting, "There has to be a homeland provided for the Palestinian refugees who have suffered for many, many years." Carter was only reiterating, in slightly different language, the same position he had stated during the campaign, and he qualified his remarks by saying that Israel needed "secure borders" and the Arabs needed to recognize these so that the two sides could eventually make peace. But the words "Palestinian homeland," used for the first time by an American president, set off alarms among American Jewish leaders. To say the word "homeland" was to evoke, in the words of historian Arlene Lazarowitz, the creation of "a radical, PLO-dominated state that would be the first stage for the eventual realization of the PLO goal of destroying Israel."[5]

It did not matter that Carter thought this hypothetical entity would be linked to Jordan, rather than fully independent. Nor did it matter that he promised that the nation's "number one commitment in the Middle East" was "to protect the right of Israel to exist, to exist permanently, and to exist in peace." Much to his later regret, Carter also reiterated Henry Kissinger's assurance that the United States would not recognize the PLO "by direct conversations or negotiations" until the PLO recognized Israel's right to exist.[6]

Even recognizing the Palestinians as a people with a right to national self-determination was enough to set off the equivalent of a four-alarm fire bell among American Jewish leaders. They had reacted nearly as theatrically when, in 1975, an assistant secretary of state named Harold Saunders, speaking to an almost empty House committee hearing, had expressed the belief that "final resolution of the problems arising from the partition of Palestine, the establishment of the State of Israel, and Arab opposition to those events will not be possible until agreement is reached defining a just and permanent status for the Arab peoples who consider themselves Palestinians." The Ford administration was on its way out when Saunders made his statement, but Carter's had just begun. Rabbi Arthur Hertzberg, a prominent scholar and president of the American

Jewish Congress, would soon emerge as the most dovish of Jewish leaders and a fierce critic of the Israeli government and its neoconservative champions in the United States. But even he objected "most vehemently" to the administration's use of the term "Palestinian homeland," as he insisted that it "cannot lead to peace" and would "definitely jeopardize US interests."[7]

Carter's plans would be made immeasurably more complicated in May 1977, by the surprise defeat of Israel's long-ruling Labor Party by its right-wing rival, Likud. Likud's leader, Menachem Begin, was nothing like the tough-minded but pragmatic warrior/scholar sons and daughters of the desert that Americans associated with Israel. Rather, as the historian Jerold S. Auerbach described him, Begin "resembled a missing Old-World uncle who had suddenly reemerged from the shadows of Diaspora history." Decades in opposition and political obscurity had not much moderated the former Irgun leader. Begin and his Likud party hailed from what the Israeli political scientist Shlomo Avineri (who served as head of Israel's foreign ministry in 1975–1977, appointed by Rabin) has called Israel's "territorial school," which was dedicated to maximizing "Israeli control over as much territory as possible of the historical Land of Israel," and doing so by force, if necessary, and without regard to ancillary costs.[8]

Likud's ideological roots lay in the 1925 demand by Ze'ev Jabotinsky, the founder of Revisionist Zionism, that "the [British] Mandate be revised to recognise Jewish rights on both sides of the Jordan." Literally nothing was more important to Begin than maintaining unencumbered Israeli sovereignty over what he, without exception, called "Judea and Samaria" (referring to the West Bank territories' biblical names). He had rejected the original partition of Palestine as "illegal" and "never [to] be recognized." He would later explain, in a heartfelt note to President Reagan, that the "Jewish kingdom" was "where our kings knelt to God, where our prophets brought forth a vision of eternal peace," and where they "developed a rich civilization which we took with us in our heart and mind on our long global trek for over eighteen centuries." True, the West Bank had been briefly conquered by Jordan in 1948, but in 1967 Israel had "liberated with God's help that portion of our homeland." Begin promised that he would never allow a Palestinian state or even Jordanian control over the land. "For Zion's sake, I will not hold my peace, and for Jerusalem's sake, I will not rest," he said, quoting the biblical prophet Isaiah.[9]

Israel's lobbyists on Capitol Hill did their best to try to domesticate Begin for American audiences, pushing back against what one termed "a spate of false and unfounded statements in the media regarding the prospective new government and its leadership." Their talking points sought to dispute the "myths" that "Begin's Irgun committed a massacre at the Arab village of Deir Yassin," and that the "Irgun bombed the King David Hotel and killed innocent people." In Israel, such allegations would not have been popular, but neither would they have been much contested. Among American Jews, however, to deviate from the *Exodus*-defined discourse, in which Israel achieved the historical equivalent of immaculate conception, was to brand oneself as untrustworthy at best, an enemy at worst.[10]

Begin further complicated Carter's task with his proclivity to speak forthrightly about his plans. From Ben-Gurion onward, Israeli leaders had tended to concede to Americans' rhetorical requests while ignoring them when making their actual policy choices. Not so, Begin. He told the truth, and it was not a truth that many Americans—Jewish or not—wished to hear. He told William Quandt, for example, that he simply would "never agree to withdrawal" from the West Bank. Deploying considerable understatement, the adviser later admitted that the Carter administration "never quite figured out how to get around Begin or work through him or work over his head or behind his back. I cannot stress to you how difficult that turned out to be." Under Begin, the pace of settlement building exploded. In Begin's view and that of his followers, there was no West Bank "occupation"; there was only its "liberation." As he told one television reporter, "You don't annex your own country."[11]

Hamilton Jordan's memo to Carter had also predicted that "one of the potential benefits of the recent Israeli elections is that it has caused many leaders in the American Jewish community to ponder the course the Israeli people have taken and question the wisdom of that policy." Brzezinski had also advised Carter that "precisely because Begin is so extreme," Carter might "be able to mobilize...a significant portion of the American Jewish community" to support his plans for peace negotiations and a settlement. And this Jewish support would ease the president's path to getting "the needed congressional support." Failure has met every presidential attempt to enlist American Jews to oppose the Israeli government on almost any matter, but perhaps never quite so spectacularly as in Carter's case. Before Begin's first meeting with Carter, in May 1977, the White House received 1,552 letters addressing Carter's Middle East policies, and 95 percent were opposed; of the 359 telephone calls on the same issue, the figure was 100 percent. Among Jewish leaders, it was considered verboten to publicly disagree with Israel's leaders on any issue, no matter how trivial. Whatever criticism might be appropriate, Rabbi Alexander Schindler, chair of the Conference of Presidents of Major American Jewish Organizations, told the New York Times, should be voiced only in private, "because, to a large extent, the strength of Israel depends on the strength of the American Jewish community, on its perceived strength and its unity in support of Israel."[12]

Relations between Schindler et al. and the Carter White House deteriorated further in the ensuing weeks and months. Not long after Begin's meeting with Carter, Schindler promised, "We'll fight Carter....Jews will not vote for him in 1980. You can't scare the American Jews." When, on October 1, 1977, the governments of the United States and the USSR issued a joint communiqué regarding Middle East peace negotiations to be resumed in Geneva, and calling for a "comprehensive settlement" to finally resolve "all specific questions," this reaction was repeated. The joint statement used the same sorts of phrases that had set off Jewish leaders in the past, including, especially, its call for the "withdrawal of Israeli Armed Forces from territories occupied in the 1967 conflict," and "the resolution of the Palestinian question, including insuring the legitimate rights of the Palestinian people."[13]

To the pro-Israel editors of Near East Report, the phrase "legitimate rights of the Palestinian people" was nothing less than "a euphemism for the creation of a Palestinian state and the dismemberment of Israel." The American Israel Public Affairs Committee circulated a letter signed by 32 senators and 150 representatives accusing the administration of "devaluing" the "principles and commitments which have guided U.S. Mideast policy during the last six administrations." The letter concluded that the US-USSR communiqué was "only the latest in a series of one-sided pressures exerted recently against Israel by the Administration," one that "spell[ed] real danger for the national interests which the U.S. and Israel have long shared." It did not help with this crowd that Edward Said praised the communiqué in the *New York Times* and saluted its rare mention of Palestinian rights.[14]

Carter's White House press secretary, Jody Powell, would later describe the political reaction as "bonkers." Democratic fund-raising events were canceled. Representatives from the administration to Jewish groups were shunned. Hyman Bookbinder, the outspokenly liberal Washington representative of the American Jewish Committee, lectured the Carter people, "Obviously, you do not apparently really understand what those words mean.... 'Palestinian rights' means the destruction of Israel." A Harris poll taken at the time found 60 percent of Jews agreeing with the statement that "the president and his people have abandoned Israel."[15]

The outcry generated by the October statement had the potential to jeopardize several other important Carter administration goals, including Senate ratification of the recently signed Panama Canal treaties, the SALT II negotiations with the Soviets, and Carter's efforts to pass a comprehensive national energy policy. Evangelicals were particularly hostile, believing that Carter had literally made a deal with the devil. It further inflamed matters that Carter also took this opportunity to fight a bruising battle over his announced plan to sell advanced fighter jets to Egypt and Saudi Arabia in a deal paired with the sale of far more sophisticated weaponry, in far greater numbers (and with far more generous terms), to Israel. Egged on by Brzezinski, the president felt he needed to prevail in his first confrontation with the pro-Israel lobby, in order to convince Arab nations that he was serious about pursuing a comprehensive peace. He may have been right. Republican Party ears were largely cocked in the direction of the oil and weapons industry lobbyists who contributed so generously to their campaigns at the time. Democrats, meanwhile, were hardly eager to humiliate their party's president so early in his term.

But the bad blood lingered. Pro-Israel lobbyists went so far as to send novelizations of the eight-hour 1978 television melodrama *Holocaust* to every member of Congress as a supposed warning of what happens when Jews are left defenseless against their enemies—ignoring not only common sense, but also the fact that the very arms package they were fighting included massive amounts of sophisticated weaponry for the Jewish state. No matter. A presidential meeting with Jewish leaders broke up in mutual acrimony, with the Jewish leaders implying that the Polish-born Brzezinski's beliefs were colored by antisemitism. Ignoring all protocol, Rabbi Schindler, chair of the Presidents Conference, leaked the off-the-record contents of the meeting to the news media, thereby simultaneously demonstrating his contempt for the president and burning his bridges to the administration.[16]

Egyptian leader Anwar Sadat's surprise November 1977 announcement that he wished to fly to Jerusalem to plead the cause of peace directly to the Israeli Knesset presented the deeply religious Carter with an irresistible opportunity. It upended the US-Soviet peace initiative, but at the same time appeared to present a once-in-a lifetime opportunity to break the historical logjam between the two perennially warring parties. The problem was that, even as Sadat made his courageous overture and was warmly welcomed in Israel, Begin remained recalcitrant. He was unwilling to stop the construction of new settlements or the expansion of existing ones; unwilling to withdraw Israeli settlers from the Sinai, nor, should they stay, to permit UN or Egyptian protection for them; unwilling to acknowledge that UN Resolution 242 applied to the West Bank or the Gaza Strip; and unwilling to grant Palestinians a genuine voice in the determination of their future. Carter was stunned and began referring to Begin's position as "the six noes." Carter then came up with the audacious idea of convening a summit with the two leaders at the Camp David presidential retreat and just demanding that they hammer out a deal. It would become the first personally negotiated presidential peace agreement since Theodore Roosevelt successfully settled the 1904–1905 Russo-Japanese War.[17]

At what turned out to be a thirteen-day summit at Camp David, beginning on September 5, 1978, Carter found Sadat "always willing to accommodate" him, and so, for this reason, but also because of the personal dynamics between the two men, he told his aides he felt "very comfortable with him." With Begin it was just the opposite. Begin was "completely unreasonable," a "psycho" who demanded "a song and dance... over every word." Eventually, following thirteen days of dramatic blowups, packed bags, summoned helicopters, and drafted statements of failure at the ready, and fully twenty-three drafts of proposed agreements, Carter somehow found a formula acceptable to both sides. Israeli defense minister Ezer Weizman would later admit that he had "never seen a man more tenacious" than Carter had been in pursuit of the Camp David Accords. At the September 17 signing ceremony, Begin, who was far from famous for his sense of humor, paid tribute to Carter with the quip that to get to yes, the president had "worked harder than our forefathers did in Egypt building the pyramids." Congressman Stephen Solarz (D-NY), a strong pro-Israel voice, called the accord possibly "the most remarkable and significant diplomatic achievement in the history of the republic." Sadat, meanwhile, did wonders for the image of Arabs in the US media and with its public. After Jimmy Carter, Sadat, *Time*'s 1977 "Man of the Year," had become the living person Americans most admired, five places above Menachem Begin (causing yet another headache for American Jewish leaders).[18]

The most difficult of the negotiations' many sticking points were Israel's West Bank settlements. Carter was certain he had secured Begin's promise to cease settlement construction immediately while final negotiations about their ultimate fate could take place. He wrote this in his diary and announced it at a post-summit joint session of Congress with Begin and Sadat sitting in the audience. But Begin felt he had meant his pledge to last only three months. What Begin understood Carter to understand is ultimately unknowable. Carter would later, quite bitterly, accuse Begin of having lied on this crucial point. But the evidence is not dispositive either way. Significantly, Begin never signed the agreement that Carter and Secretary of State Cyrus Vance drew up for him that would have codified Carter's understanding. William Quandt would term this a "loose end" that had been left "vague" and "unresolved," but it would turn out to be a crucial one that risked unraveling the entire deal: Begin went home and immediately began plans to fortify and expand the settlements and soon committed to building eighteen to twenty more.[19]

Whatever Carter thought he heard from Begin, the latter never veered from his bedrock belief. Peace in exchange for the Sinai was fine, but literally nothing was ever going to dislodge Israel from "Judea and Samaria" so long as it was up to Begin. As future US ambassador to Israel Richard Jones would presciently observe in early 1982, when Israel had settled a tiny fraction of the hundreds of thousands of settlers who live on the West Bank today, "The goal has [always] been to create a matrix of Israeli control of the West Bank so deeply rooted that no subsequent Israeli government would be able to relinquish substantial chunks of that territory, even in exchange for peace." The deal Israel sought—and got—at Camp David from Egypt, thanks to Jimmy Carter, was essentially "1967 for 1948."[20]

Carter did enjoy a brief respite from criticism in the mainstream media, which celebrated the historic achievement and paid particular tribute to Carter's patience and persistence. But American Jewish leaders mostly sat on their hands. They did not object to the agreements themselves, because being more hawkish than the famously hawkish Israeli leader was like being holier than the pope. And they were certainly pleased that Carter and Sadat had ultimately proved willing to sell out the Palestinians, who, yet again, took another opportunity to miss an opportunity. (Vance sent Edward Said, a member of the Palestinian National Council, to Beirut with an offer to Yasser Arafat of US recognition of the PLO as the "sole legitimate representative" of the Palestinian people if the PLO chairman would agree to recognize Israel and join the talks, but Arafat refused even to see him.)[21]

Following the signing ceremony, Carter continued his dogged efforts to try to bridge the gaps between the two sides. During the repeated trips that he and Vance made to the Middle East, the problem continued to be Begin's unwillingness to implement what Carter had understood to be his promises at Camp David. In all of these arguments, the Israeli leader had American Jewish leaders in his corner. When, after one December 1978 trip, Vance told reporters that Israeli intransigence was blocking an agreement, the American Jewish Committee's Washington representative, Hyman Bookbinder, expressed his "outrage" over the "unfair accusations" and attacked what he called the administration's "anti-Israeli campaign." William Safire titled one of his *New York Times* columns "Carter Blames the Jews." Carter later complained that "in public showdowns on a controversial issue," the American Jewish leaders "would always side with the Israeli leaders and condemn us for being 'evenhanded' in our concern for both Palestinian rights and Israeli security."[22]

Public criticism of Israel's behavior was hardly unheard of before the Carter administration, but it had been confined largely to the far right, oil industry interests, ex–State Department officials, and the anti-Zionist American Council for Judaism. The 1967 war put Israel on the wrong side of the anti-imperialist and pro-third-world New Left, in which young American Jews were decidedly overrepresented. But these were not the kinds of voices that would be of any help to Carter's peace efforts. Unfortunately, the one group that might have helped did not survive long enough to do so. "Breira" (Choice), a group of prominent liberal rabbis and intellectuals, came together in 1972 and 1973 with a platform that read, in part, "We love Israel. We cherish the cultural treasures and the many moral examples it has given us. And we similarly affirm the richness of the Jewish experience in North America and are eager to explore and extend its possibilities." Its bona fides established, the group called on Israel "to make territorial concessions" and "recognize the legitimacy of the national aspirations of the Palestinians" so as to reach a peace agreement that reflected "the idealism and thought of many early Zionists with whom we identify."[23]

Breira's founding chairman, Rabbi Arnold Wolf, would in later decades become a close friend and confidant of a budding young Chicago politician with the odd name of Barack Hussein Obama, who happened to live across the street from his synagogue in Hyde Park. (As president-elect, Obama would eulogize Wolf in December 2008 as "a titan of moral strength and champion of social justice.") Writing in the small-circulation independent Jewish journal *Sh'ma* in March 1973, Wolf expressed the kind of disappointment with Israel that was considered near treason among his fellow Jewish leaders. "Israel colonizes the 'administered' territories without regard to international law or the rights of the indigenous Palestinian[s]," he charged, and, "increasingly, in the Jewish state, hard work is done by Arab hirelings." He lamented the cultural rehabilitation of Jabotinsky, the celebration of "generals and strategists" as opposed to "scholars" and "farmers," and closed with a near-sacrilegious admonition: "Israel may be the Jewish state; it is not now and perhaps can never be Zion."[24]

According to Max Ticktin, a scholar and rabbi employed by Hillel, the national Jewish organization serving college students, Breira hoped to create a new "grassroots based democratic structure for American Jewry" that included "youth, women and the poor." Another Breira founder, Arthur Waskow, later a prominent progressive rabbi, wondered whether progressive Jews had "a responsibility to oppose the giving of money or support" to traditional Jewish organizations, given the fact that "we feel [they] are blindly marching toward the destruction of Israel."[25]

Breira initially received quite favorable publicity in the US media, whose members were apparently intrigued by the bona fides of its founders and the newness of their message. The *Washington Post* ran a friendly profile noting that Breira's proposal for Israel "to turn its occupied territories on the West Bank into a separate Arab state and pull back to its 1967 boundaries" was frequently discussed in Israel, but not in the United States, "where criticism of what Israel does has come to be equated with an attack on Israel's existence." A *New York Times* editorial found that Breira was "overcoming...the misapprehension of many Jewish Americans that criticism of Israeli policies would be seen as a rejection of Israel." But most "major" Jewish organizations saw Breira for what it was: a challenge to their hegemony in the Jewish world and an avenue for American Jews to undercut their policy of unanimous and unquestioned support for Israel. With impressive hypocrisy, the AJC's Bookbinder professed to detect a "shrillness, a self-righteousness, a certitude" in Breira's pronouncements. The Jewish women's service organization Hadassah called the group "cheerleaders for defeatism" in one of its newsletters. (This was a particularly ironic viewpoint given the role its founder, Henrietta Szold, had played in helping to organize the binationalist Ihud movement in pre-state Palestine.) Forty-seven rabbis put their names to a letter accusing Breira of taking a position "practically identical with the Arab point of view."[26]

People who should have been its natural allies shunned and slandered the group. Arthur Lelyveld, head of the Reform rabbinate, as well as civil rights champion (and father to a future *New York Times* executive editor), accused Breira of providing "aid and comfort…to those who would cut aid to Israel and leave it defenseless before murderers and terrorists." The American Jewish Congress president, Rabbi Arthur Hertzberg, refused to speak at a meeting where a Breira representative had also been invited. Israel's ambassador to the United States, Simcha Dinitz, restated the rules in response to Breira in case anyone had forgotten: all differences of opinion between Israel and American Jews should be aired only privately; only Israelis should decide [its] policies; and no one should suggest that Israel talk to "terrorists." "These rules," as the Jewish journalist J. J. Goldberg has observed, "were quickly taken up by the Jewish leadership as sacred writ from Jerusalem," and any American Jewish leader who refused to abide by them, or even sought in any way to try to elide them, soon found himself referred to as a "former American Jewish leader."[27]

The group's fate was likely sealed in late 1976, when some of Breira's most prominent figures, including Ticktin and Waskow, attended a supposedly secret meeting with a PLO-affiliated—albeit unofficially—Arab Israeli author, Sabri Jiryis. Virtually every major Jewish organization joined in vigorous denunciation of this event. The Conference of Presidents declared that it "vigorously opposes and deplores any meetings—official or unofficial—with the P.L.O.," claiming that "the only purpose and possible result of such meetings is P.L.O. propaganda aimed at providing this terrorist federation with an image of moderation." Rael Jean Isaac, a leading member of Americans for a Safe Israel, a small, shrill, pro-settler group founded in 1971, wrote an astonishingly scurrilous thirty-page pamphlet called "Breira: Counsel for Judaism." *Commentary* published a similarly McCarthy-style attack in which Breira was accused of being "a vivid demonstration of the inroads made into the American Jewish consciousness by the campaign to delegitimize Israel."[28]

Both Isaac's and *Commentary*'s attacks rested heavily on the alleged associations of Breira's founders. Waskow, for instance, had been one of the earliest fellows at the Institute for Policy Studies, a leftist think tank, where others employed there boasted radical associations, sometimes with groups unfriendly to Israel. Carl Gershman, then a young leader of the strongly anti-Communist Young People's Socialist League (later a prominent neoconservative), declared that Waskow lived in a political world "in which the criterion of hostility to Israel [is used] to determine whether someone is anti-imperialist and 'revolutionary.'" In early 1970 Waskow had written in *Sh'ma* of the need for American Jews to challenge Israel to "deal justly and face-to-face with the Palestinian people." That same year, Jews for Urban Justice, a Washington New Left organization with which Waskow was affiliated, called on Israel to negotiate with the PLO for the creation of an independent Palestinian state in exchange for its recognition of the Jewish state. A year later, he cochaired the Ad Hoc Liberation of Palestine and Israel Committee. The group, which featured Rabbis Wolf and Arthur Green together with Noam Chomsky, the yippie leader Abbie Hoffman, and the left-wing baby doctor Benjamin Spock, among many others, published an advertisement in the *New York Review of Books* in which they urged "the American Jewish community and the American anti-war and radical movements [to] take up issues not by a mindless endorsement of one party orthodoxy or another in the Middle East but with serious study and a sensitive commitment to the liberation of both the Israeli and Palestinian people from militarism and exploitation." Members quit. Donations dried up, and the organization simply fell apart by the winter of 1977–1978. The power to speak for, and represent, American Judaism had long ago passed from rabbis and intellectuals to the professional organizations whose leaders would brook no public criticism, period. As Rabbi Ticktin, whose job at Hillel was also threatened by the brouhaha, would observe in retrospect, "We were naive about the power of the American Jewish establishment and that came out painfully when they began to attack us and limit our activity."[29]

Breira's demise was doubly unfortunate for Jimmy Carter. The group may have grown more popular had it been able to last a bit longer. And its legitimacy in the eyes of fellow Jews would undoubtedly have been boosted by the later emergence of the Israeli peace movement Shalom Achshav (Peace Now) in the wake of Sadat's visit. Shalom Achshav was led by soldiers who had fought in previous wars and promised to fight in future ones, should they turn out to be necessary; it eventually drew crowds of hundreds of thousands of Israelis for its peace rallies, and it, too, looked to American Jews for support. But Breira was no longer around to give it any. A group called American Friends of Peace Now was eventually formed, but not in time to help Carter.

The president faced yet another crisis with Jewish leaders, one that was not of his own making, when, on August 14, 1979, *Time* magazine published the news that the US ambassador to the United Nations, Andrew Young, had met privately with the PLO's UN observer, Zehdi Labib Terzi, at a July 26 dinner at the apartment of Kuwait's UN ambassador. The meeting was a violation of the promise the Israelis had extracted from Kissinger four years earlier never to speak to PLO officials until their organization recognized Israel. Owing to miscommunication within an understaffed State Department over a weekend and clumsy responses by the White House press office, followed by extremely bad faith on virtually all sides of the dispute, the meeting led to Young's forced resignation. The results were an intensification of the deterioration of the political relationship between Blacks and Jews, a weakening of what remained of the Democratic coalition that Franklin Roosevelt had forged during the New Deal, and yet another setback to the cause of Middle East peace.

Andrew Young had been a leader in the civil rights movement, an adviser to Martin Luther King Jr., a symbol of Carter's commitment to human rights abroad, and the highest-profile Black person in his administration. He was not at all shy about giving voice to his political beliefs, which were well to the left of the center of gravity in the Carter administration. Young once opined that the British had "practically invented racism." He denounced the United States' embargo of Castro's Cuba and its refusal to recognize Communist Vietnam. When Young suggested that the United States had "hundreds of people that I would categorize as political prisoners in our prisons," House Republicans instigated an unsuccessful effort to impeach him. According to Brzezinski, who opposed all of these ideas, "Carter [only] wanted him because of color."[30]

The exact circumstances that led Carter to demand Young's resignation remain murky even today. The events leading up to the explosion were in many respects a sequence of tempests in a series of teapots. Carter himself called the ban on talking to the PLO "absolutely ridiculous," and termed Kissinger's promise to the Israelis "preposterous." Moreover, it had been ignored whenever that was deemed to be necessary. Fully a year before the Terzi incident, Young had dined with a high-ranking PLO emissary and let his superiors know. Other US officials had already engaged in direct, albeit secret, talks with the PLO via intelligence channels, and the (Jewish) US ambassador to Austria, Milton Wolf, had already met with Isam Sartawi, a senior member of the PLO, three times that spring (Sartawi was later assassinated).[31]

It remains unclear who exactly leaked the news that, contrary to previous media reports, Young's meeting with Terzi had been no accident. Carter biographer Kai Bird speculated that Brzezinski, relying on an FBI surveillance transcript, may have engineered the leak in order to get rid of a potential rival for the president's ear. The purpose of the meeting with Terzi, as Young explained to Israel's UN ambassador, Yehuda Zvi Blum, was to try to prevent the submission of a draft of a Kuwaiti resolution calling for the recognition of an independent Palestinian state. Young needed the PLO to agree to the withdrawal of the resolution, or the Arab UN ambassadors would go ahead with it. Young was about to rotate into the presidency of the UN Security Council and felt himself to be acting in that capacity, rather than as US representative. In any case, the news leak of the prearranged meeting proved a disaster for Carter, whose administration prided itself on straight-shooting with the American people.[32]

Despite the fact that Young had succeeded in heading off the PLO initiative on Israel's behalf, its embassy nevertheless issued a formal protest. Bertram Gold, executive vice president of the American Jewish

Committee, insisted that "if Young did talk to the PLO on his own, he should be fired." The *New York Daily News*, then America's highest-circulation newspaper, ran a bold-type headline, "Jews Demand Firing Young." The *Washington Post* reported that Rabbi Joseph Sternstein, president of the American Zionist Federation, had wired President Carter that "only the dismissal of Ambassador Young can restore confidence in your administration." At this point, Vance felt that he had been made to look like a fool, and Carter needed to demonstrate that US policy, however "ridiculous" (and hypocritical), remained unchanged. Vance, feeling deliberately misled, told Carter that if Young did not leave, he would, giving the president no choice. "I love Andy like a brother, and I want to guide him. But he has embarrassed us too many times in the past," Carter told his aide Stuart Eizenstat. Carter would later call accepting Young's resignation "one of the most heart-wrenching decisions I had to make as president."[33]

The complicated details of the Young affair notwithstanding, by 1979 some kind of reckoning between Blacks and Jews was already a long time coming. The relationship had soured in the aftermath of the 1967 Arab-Israeli War. Black radicalism grew in influence following the 1968 murder of Martin Luther King Jr., who was staunchly pro-Israel ("Peace for Israel means security, and we must stand with all our might to protect its right to exist, its territorial integrity," King had said. "I see Israel as one of the great outposts of democracy in the world.") As Black leaders grew less and less comfortable deferring to white elites, they turned on those whites who were closest to them, both physically, in cities such as New York, and politically and socially. King had rhapsodized about the "centuries-long common struggle of the Negros and Jews, not only to rid ourselves of bondage but to make oppression of any people by others an impossibility." Now that Jews had reached the highest echelons of American society, however, many Blacks saw them to be purposely pulling the ladder out of reach of their former friends and allies.[34]

In addition to the Young contretemps, other issues had arisen to upset the former alliance. American Jewish organizations had adopted hostile positions toward any number of Black political initiatives—most importantly, affirmative action, most notably in the infamous case *Regents of the University of California v. Bakke* in 1978. In the Bakke case, Jewish organizations lined up against Black ones to convince the US Supreme Court to outlaw quotas as a means of reaching affirmative-action goals. Under Podhoretz's editorship, the AJC's *Commentary* relentlessly attacked Black leaders, occasionally edging into racist tropes and stereotypes, as the social and political agendas of the Black Power movement grew ever more ambitious. Anti-Zionist and antisemitic publications began emanating from groups such as the Student Nonviolent Coordinating Committee after the 1967 Six-Day War. A bitter New York City teachers' strike in 1968 pitted mostly Jewish teachers against mostly Black parents and school boards, featuring much ugliness in both directions before the teachers won their victory in court, leaving the Blacks angry and embittered.

This conservative drift in Jewish organizational life was accompanied by alarm about the perceived growth of Black hostility toward Jews in general. Speaking to a plenary meeting of allied Jewish organizations, the national director of the Anti-Defamation League, Benjamin Epstein, had recently presented the thesis of his 1974 book, *The New Anti-Semitism* (coauthored with the longtime ADL attorney Arnold Forster). In it, the authors attacked what Epstein defined as the new "Radical Left," led by Black and student activists, and its "all-too-frequent blindness to the centrality for Jews of Israel's survival as an independent and sovereign Jewish state." In such rhetoric, one could see the turn away from social justice and toward the defense of Israel—a historical shift from Jewish universalism to particularism. That particularism had come to define much of the professional Jewish community while simultaneously encouraging Israeli intransigence and alienating American Jews both from their historical commitment to liberalism and from their former allies among society's downtrodden.[35]

While some, mostly older, Black leaders were genuinely distressed by these developments, most appeared ready to air what they considered to be a whole package of grievances that had been building over time. An editorial in *The Afro-American* insisted that Young had been forced out of the administration due to "Jewish pressure," while reporting "rumors" that the Israelis had "bugged" Young's meeting. It advised Jews to stop "acting like spoiled children in their responses to all these events." At a meeting of two hundred Black leaders sponsored by the National Association for the Advancement of Colored People (NAACP), called in the wake of Young's resignation, speaker after speaker rose to praise Young and denounce both Israel and American Jewish leaders for their role in what one resolution called the State Department's "callous, ruthless behavior" toward Young in particular. But they denounced the conduct of US foreign policy in general as well. Little, if any, dissent on these points was evident. The respected psychologist and educator Kenneth B. Clark received a standing ovation while reading a resolution attacking Jewish organizations and intellectuals as "apologists for the racial status quo," along with Israel for what was called its "trade and military alliance" with the racist South African regime. This relationship, the Black leaders agreed, was yet "another manifestation of pro-Israelism taking precedence over American Jews' moral values and domestic political alliances."[36]

Not surprisingly, Jewish leaders chose not to turn their collective other cheek. The AJC's Bookbinder was hardly alone in accusing Black leaders of "out-and-out anti-Semitism." Others pointed to survey data demonstrating that while Jews were more sympathetic to Blacks than any other white ethnic group, Blacks were more likely than any other ethnicity to embrace negative stereotypes about Jews. Many Jews believed that Carter had cast them as scapegoats for Young's forced departure. Rabbi Schindler called the president's unwillingness to rebuke Black leaders "a pure and simple exploitation of anti-Semitism for political purposes." This was yet another false accusation against the beleaguered president. Carter had clearly said that no "American Jewish leaders or anyone else" had lobbied him to fire Young, a statement considerably more generous than a strict commitment to truthfulness would have allowed.[37]

Carl Gershman's seven-thousand-plus-word missive on the Young affair appeared in the now aggressively neoconservative *Commentary* in November 1979. Sounding like a prosecuting attorney, he accused Young of trying to turn the United States against Israel. Young, he wrote, had called Israel "an expansionist power" that engaged in "terroristic" raids on Lebanon and had "become the oppressor" of the Palestinians, and was now claiming that the Israelis "do not want peace with the PLO." Gershman also held Young responsible for boosting both the Palestinian cause and anti-Jewish feeling in the Black community. But Gershman's brief against Andrew Young was filled with McCarthyite insinuations that, together, painted a false picture both of Young and of the politics he practiced. In truth, Andrew Young, like Martin Luther King Jr., had long been a friend to Israel. In Congress, he had joined the Black Americans in Support of Israel Committee, and he had cosponsored a resolution calling for the United States to reconsider its membership in the United Nations if the organization tried to kick Israel out. He had spoken critically of the PLO's terrorist tactics and its failure to accept Resolution 242, and had said it was "vital to our own interest to guarantee Israel's survival as an outpost of democracy in the Middle East." It was also "imperative," he had added, "that the United States continue to do all that is necessary to maintain Israel's security as a nation."[38]

By this time, however, holding such views made Young something of an outlier among Black leaders, who for the most part had come to see the Palestinians' struggle as consistent with their own. This transformation was evident in the statements and travels of any number of Black leaders who made high-profile pilgrimages to Palestinian refugee camps and posed for pictures with Arafat in the aftermath of the Young affair. It can perhaps be seen most clearly in the personality of the Reverend Jesse Jackson, the former aide to King, who was present at his mentor's assassination (and literally waved his "bloody shirt" in its aftermath).

Jackson had been working to achieve a status akin to being King's successor, the symbolic "president" of Black America. And, at least insofar as the US media were concerned, his efforts were largely succeeding. In this context, Jackson soon became an almost physical lightning rod for the increasing intensity of Black-Jewish mutual recrimination. In the aftermath of the Young affair, he called Zionism a "poisonous weed" that was choking Judaism, and complained of Carter's "capitulation" to "our former allies." He added that while Jews had once been willing to "share decency" with Blacks during the civil rights movement, they had become opponents "once we began to push for our share of universal slots in institutions." Already critical of what he called Jews' "persecution complex," which he said "makes them overreact to their own suffering," he began calling for the recognition of "the just demands of the dispossessed Palestinian people." In September 1979, Jackson traveled to the Middle East, first to Israel—where Prime Minister Begin refused to meet him—and then to the Qalandiya refugee camp and to the West Bank, where Palestinian residents carried Jackson on their shoulders and chanted "Jackson! Arafat!" Next, he went on to Beirut, where he was photographed in an awkward embrace with the PLO chairman himself.[39]

Jackson's embrace of the Hitler-admiring, Jew-hating Louis Farrakhan, leader of the Nation of Islam, further enraged Jewish leaders. Jackson would later catch all kinds of hell for confiding, in what he thought was just off-the-record "black talk" with a Black reporter, that New York was "Hymietown," and that "all Hymie cares about is Israel." It would take the civil rights leader literally decades to shake the antisemitic reputation he created for himself. Jewish groups and neoconservative pundits demanded an endless series of mea culpas from him as he grew in stature during his two presidential runs—campaigns in which he was almost always greeted by Jewish protesters, catcallers, and critical op-ed articles. Even as *Commentary*'s editorship passed from Norman Podhoretz to his son John, decades later, the magazine ran regular attacks on America's Black leadership and its alleged tolerance, if not embrace, of antisemitism. These appeared with clocklike consistency (with titles such as "Black Anti-Semitism on the Rise," "The Rise of Black Anti-Semitism and How It Grows," "African Americans vs. American Jews," "Facing Up to Black Anti-Semitism," and "The Rise of Black Anti-Semitism"). Each one drove another nail into the liberal political coalition that had sustained the Democratic Party for the previous half-century.[40]

In March 1980, after Young had been replaced by his deputy, the veteran Black State Department official and establishment think-tank denizen Donald McHenry, another snafu at the United Nations further intensified anti-Carter sentiment among Jewish leaders. The United States voted to approve a Security Council resolution condemning Israeli settlements that failed to distinguish between those on the West Bank, which was under continuing Israeli military rule, and those in East Jerusalem, which Israel had effectively annexed. Carter insisted that the United States had intended to abstain, owing to the Jerusalem issue, and the vote had been "a genuine mistake—a breakdown in communications." This was true, but the excuse did little to assuage the anger the vote provoked among Jewish leaders. Senator Edward Kennedy of Massachusetts had been trailing Carter in the New York presidential primary in the weeks leading up to the UN vote, but he ended up winning it by a significant margin, rejuvenating his campaign and further weakening Carter for the general election. New York's loud-mouthed Jewish mayor Ed Koch, whom Carter had invited to lunch at the White House after the vote, went on a kind of personal public (verbal) jihad against the president for allegedly harboring anti-Israel officials in his administration—a category in which he included not only Young and McHenry, but also, rather crazily, Brzezinski, Vance, and Assistant Secretary of State Harold Saunders. He attacked the president personally, called McHenry a "bastard," and, in Carter's view, acted "like a fanatic." But Koch's campaign had its intended effect. Carter's pollster Patrick Caddell blamed "the UN vote in the Jewish community," adding, "We're getting wiped out. It's almost as if the voters know that Carter's got the nomination sewed up but want to send him a message." If so, it was a message with implications that carried over into November 1980, when Jimmy Carter became the first (and still only) Democratic presidential candidate since the 1920s to fail to win a majority of the Jewish vote.[41]

In a postmortem assessment titled "Joining the Jackals," published (of course) in *Commentary*, Moynihan, now a senator, attacked Carter for even suggesting that Young's successor, McHenry, should abstain—rather than exercise the United States' veto—on "this particularly vicious anti-Israel resolution." Moynihan did not mention that the resolution, condemning Israel's West Bank settlements, was consistent both with announced US policy and with international law—to say nothing of the commitments Carter understood Begin to have made at Camp David. The issues had become defined almost by pure emotion; facts, context, commitments, and even laws had no place in the discussion.[42]

All this set the stage for Ronald Reagan, whose presidency was characterized by an insistence that America was always right and therefore its allies were (almost) always righteous. American Jews were generally opposed to Reagan, but they found themselves in a profound conundrum when it came to Israel for this very reason. And yet, as a new constellation of pro-Israel forces came together during the Reagan years, what most American Jews felt or thought about Israel came to matter less and less. There were new political stars rising in the United States, and almost all of them presaged a powerful new Israel both in Middle East and in the corridors of power in Washington, DC.

## CHAPTER 11

# ALLIANCE FOR ARMAGEDDON

By the time of Ronald Reagan's 1980 landslide victory, the forces influencing US policy in the Middle East were already beginning to change. The views inside the Reagan administration itself were divided between the pro-Arab impulses of the national security establishment and the president's own political interests and personal sympathies. The same had been the case in previous administrations. But acting to shape Reagan's views was a new group of pro-Israel actors whose power and influence were poised to increase exponentially. These included a coterie of neoconservative writers, editors, and political operatives who were mostly, but not exclusively, Jewish; a newly politicized Christian conservative movement that shared many neoconservative goals; and an expanded and emboldened American Israel Public Affairs Committee (AIPAC) backed by the energetic, almost unanimous support of the Jewish community and its institutions, which worked hard to ensure that deference to Israel's interests dominated any and all even remotely relevant debates.

The tree of neoconservatism spawned two main branches. The first, located in Manhattan, focused on culture and was centered on *Commentary* magazine, still published by the American Jewish Committee and edited by Norman Podhoretz. The second, in Washington, was devoted to amassing political power, influence, and patronage, often under the tutelage of the *Commentary* crowd. The New York branch largely consisted of formerly left-wing Jewish intellectuals who felt themselves to have been "mugged by reality." Whereas, in Washington, Democratic anti-Communist political operatives simply flipped to become Republican anti-Communist political operations.

Broadly speaking, the New Yorkers were responsible for the battle of ideas, and the Washingtonians for implementing policy. After Pat Moynihan's 1976 Senate victory, Podhoretz apparently entertained fantasies of extending his tiny kingdom all the way to the Oval Office, with Moynihan leading the charge. One night at the senator's farm in Oneonta, New York, according to a witness, Podhoretz and his wife, Midge Decter (a fellow *Commentary* contributor), grabbed Liz Moynihan's arms and screamed, "You're standing in the way of this man becoming president! It's you, it's you, it's you." Her husband would soon disappoint both of them by refusing to run for president and by drifting back to a more traditional liberal stance during the Reagan years. When he first arrived in the Senate in 1977, however, he played the middleman, taking *Commentary*'s ideas to the Senate floor. He traded staffers and legislative priorities with another neocon heartthrob, Senator Henry "Scoop" Jackson (D-WA), and hired the children and other members of the New Yorkers' friends and family circle. (Podhoretz and Decter's son-in-law, Elliott Abrams, worked for both men.)

Initially, neoconservative ideology focused on domestic issues. These interests grew out of its adherents' concern with the takeover of the Democratic Party by the kinds of people who had nominated George McGovern in 1972. The "Zionism Is Racism" battle had been an exception to this rule: they had taken an interest in an international relations issue because of Moynihan's appointment as ambassador to the United Nations, his involvement in that issue in particular, and his ideological romance with Podhoretz and *Commentary*. When neoconservatives then began to turn to foreign policy more generally, their twin goals were to prevent the Carter administration from demanding concessions from Israel and to do whatever they could to reheat the Cold War. Twelve years of détente policies under Nixon and Kissinger, followed by four years of peacemaking attempts under Jimmy Carter, were not to their liking. To achieve their goals, they sought to seed Washington with a group of young apparatchiks who would move in and out of government in the coming decades. The political party of the followers shifted over time: first they were disaffected Democrats, and later they were right-wing Republicans. In decided contrast to the foreign policy mandarins of previous decades, they had names, as historian Susanne Klingenstein has noted, such as "Abrams, Adelman, Kampelman, Kristol, Perle, Pipes, Rostow, and Wattenberg." Scoop Jackson was not Jewish, but given his staff, his politics, and the political world in which he traveled, he might as well have been. (The Jewish Institute for National Security of America [JINSA] named an annual award after him in 1982.) The longtime Saudi diplomat Jamil Baroody, in a moment of perhaps inadvertent accuracy, once described Jackson as "more Zionist than the Zionists, more Jewish than the Jews." In purely political terms, Zionism had now become more important to Jewishness than Judaism was.[1]

Neoconservatives were united largely by what they opposed. That lengthy list included New Leftists, peace activists, civil rights leaders, student demonstrators (and their faculty sympathizers), Arabs, feminists, environmentalists, gays and lesbians, détente-oriented diplomats, and, perhaps most prominently, Jewish supporters of any or all of the above. Neocons tended to collect all such miscreants under the labels of "the movement" when discussing its scruffier elements, and "McGovernism" when referring to the Democratic Party. The ideas the neocons found so offensive had been pumped into the bloodstream of American culture, they argued, by members of what they called a "new class," a term borrowed from the Yugoslav communist scholar Milovan Djilas. This class

consisted of liberal bureaucrats, academics, journalists, and others under
the sway of what the neocons understood to be an "adversary culture"
in the making, which, having lost the nerve to fight for the old verities,
was now in the throes of what they called a "culture of appeasement."
Not coincidentally, the professions and social groups that made up this
culture were heavily populated, and in some cases dominated, by young
Jews. The neoconservatives felt they were a bulwark against all these
groups and their destruction of what they considered American values.
The neoconservatives professed to respect their elders and expected the
same from the younger generation, especially writers and political activists. Young Jewish leftists, meanwhile, were vehemently critical of the
country, of the institutions the neoconservatives held so dear, and also of
Israel. In almost perfect contrast to how leftists had viewed Israel at its
founding, most New Leftist literature on the subject of the Arab/Israeli
conflict treated Israel as a racist outpost of imperialism. According to
Mark Rudd, the Jewish leader of the protesters who took over Columbia
University's administration offices in 1968, shutting down the university and leading eventually to a violent confrontation with the police,
the issue of Israel and Palestine was what "distinguished the true anti-
imperialists from the liberals." These developments were so worrisome
to the older Jewish intellectuals who had helped to found neoconservatism that they organized a 1970 conference on the subject, which led to
a book-length collection of essays, *The New Left and the Jews*, published
the following year. A great many of the analyses it offered to explain what
its authors took to be the irrational behavior of the young thinkers and
activists veered into the realm of the personal and psychological, rather
than bothering with the political content of the protesters' concerns.[2]

When "the movement" offered up disrespect and contempt, neocons
did the same. The novelist Saul Bellow depicted the kind of disrespect
that stirred up the ire of neoconservatives in a key scene of his 1970 novel
*Mr. Sammler's Planet*. During a lecture by a fictional Columbia University professor, a heckler yells out, "Why do you listen to this effete old
shit? What has he got to tell you? His balls are dry. He's dead. He can't
come." But Bellow had actually been the recipient of a similar outburst
at one of his own lectures. Such incidents help explain the fury so many

neoconservatives directed at their putative adversaries long after their victories had already been assured.[3]

Neoconservatism was, in many respects, built on resentments. But it was inspired by one great love—Israel—a love that coincided perfectly with its obsessive hatred of the Soviet Union, and, by extension, of the Arab regimes and terrorist organizations the Soviets supported. Eugene Victor Rostow, whose very name—like that of his brother, the hawkish Kennedy/Johnson war strategist Walt Whitman Rostow—can be seen to embody the arc of neoconservative history, argued, as chair of the neocon-dominated Committee on the Present Danger, that, given what he judged to be a deepening "Arab dependence on the Soviet Union," Israel had become an "indispensable ally" in America's global struggle.[4]

Just as they seeded the staffs of senators and congressmen, the neocons' reach expanded across the culture via both new magazines, such as *The Public Interest*, and old ones, including *The New Republic*, purchased by Martin Peretz in 1974. With the backing of wealthy conservative individuals and right-wing philanthropic foundations, they also started new think tanks and burrowed into old ones. JINSA, founded in 1976 by future Reagan officials Max Kampelman and Richard Schifter, sought to turn Vietnam doves into Israel hawks, or, as Kampelman put it, "to persuade Jewish members of Congress and the Jewish community to support a strong American defense." It did not take long for names like these to appear regularly in the nation's op-ed columns and television chat shows. The denizens of the capital got their opinion advice from these outlets the way women had traditionally taken their fashion cues from *Vogue* or *Harper's Bazaar*.[5]

In this manner, they pursued what the early twentieth-century Italian Marxist philosopher Antonio Gramsci described as "cultural hegemony," especially within the world of little magazines and Washington punditry and the ranks of political mavens. During a freezing February weekend in 1983, neocons gathered at Manhattan's Plaza Hotel off of Central Park to declare victory and curse their enemies. "We are surrounded by lynch mobs just barely restrained," Podhoretz crowed, but "our work has not been in vain. We are a political community now. The resonance of what we do is greater than ever." Furthermore, he said, "there are more of us around than there were ten years ago....We are the dominant faction within the world of ideas—the most influential—the most powerful." Now, he insisted, "the liberal culture has to appease us," because "people like us made Reagan's victory."[6]

Many traditional conservatives detested the fact that traditional venues of conservative policy entrepreneurship had been colonized by a group of mostly urban Jewish former liberals and ex-Marxists. Barry Goldwater's constituency, the same folks who powered Ronald Reagan's ascendancy— mostly Republican gentiles in the South and West—did not like what they perceived as a Jewish takeover of what had been their party and movement. These resentments were partly ideological, partly cultural, and no doubt considerably turf driven. Many "paleocons," as they came to be called, meaning authentic—the original conservatives as opposed to the "neo" ones—had never quite shed their antisemitic suspicions, and the neocons, as they saw it, played exactly to type. The prominent paleocon intellectual Russell Kirk complained of writers and thinkers who "mistook Tel Aviv for the capital of the United States." Echoing the analyses of both Gramsci and the German communist student activist Rudi Dutschke—albeit from an opposite political perspective and adding more than a smidgen of antisemitism—Kirk complained of what he called a "horde of dissenters...of Jewish stock" that had "skillfully insinuated themselves into the councils of the Nixon and Reagan Administrations!"[7]

Paleocons were understandably upset to see their preeminence among conservatives challenged, but the neocons were hardly the only group to surf the Reaganite wave. A new right-wing Christian movement had arisen in opposition to the Carter presidency. They abandoned their fellow born-again Christian, Jimmy Carter, for the decidedly casual churchgoer (and America's first divorced president) Ronald Reagan. Gerald Ford had earned only 33 percent of the evangelical vote in 1976; eight years later, Reagan's share rose to 85 percent. And while their feelings about Jews might charitably be termed "conflicted," their devotion to Israel was unshakable.[8]

Christians had prayed for the return of the Jews to their biblical homeland as far back as the Reformation. But their support for the modern

Zionist movement began with the Reverend William H. Hechler, an Anglican clergyman who, already dedicated to the cause of a Jewish return to the Holy Land, grew close to Zionist founder Theodor Herzl even before the first Zionist Congress in 1897. Hechler was a disciple of John Nelson Darby, another Anglican clergyman, who, during the first half of the nineteenth century, outlined his version of how end-times prophecies about Christ's return and thousand-year reign, as predicted by the Book of Revelation, would be fulfilled. Darby's beliefs, termed "premillennial dispensationalism," constituted just one among many evangelical streams at the time. But the popularity of this interpretation of prophecy grew rapidly following the founding of Israel, and even more so in the wake of the 1967 war. Among its most successful popularizers were authors Hal Lindsey and Tim LaHaye.[9]

The *New York Times* judged Lindsey's 1970 book, *The Late Great Planet Earth* (coauthored by Carole C. Carlson), to be the best-selling book of the decade. It spawned a prime-time television program with an estimated audience of seventeen million, along with a 1975 movie that was somehow narrated by Orson Welles. Lindsey claimed that the creation of Israel was a "paramount prophetic sign" of the coming "rapture," when Christians would be swept up into heaven preceding a seven-year "tribulation" to take place on earth before Christ's return and the millennial reign. Indeed, the creation of the state of Israel would prove to be the "fuse of Armageddon," the final war at the end of the world. A dictator was "waiting in the wings somewhere in Europe," Lindsey said, who would "make Adolf Hitler and Joseph Stalin look like choirboys."[10]

Like Lindsey, the ex-minister Tim LaHaye saw in Israel's founding "the most significant of the end-time signs, even the 'super sign.'" Israel's conquest of Jerusalem sent an even stronger signal. Together with his wife, Beverly, LaHaye founded a series of important political organizations, including Concerned Christians of America, along with the influential think tank Center for National Policy. He eventually authored or coauthored eighty-five fiction and nonfiction books, most of which were devoted to helping Christians prepare for the end of days. The most successful of these were those in the Left Behind series, which eventually included sixteen books, four films, and video games, reaching sixty-five million people though the books alone. In a 1984 nonfiction work, La-Haye promoted a scenario in which Israel would ultimately become a lifeline for the United States. "As long as there is a strong Israeli air force with the capability of nuclear retaliation," LaHaye promised, "Russia will not attack the United States. . . . Before they can suppress the world with their totalitarian ideology, they must first knock out the United States. And to do that, they must first remove Israel. . . . Thus Israel's safety and military strength are our own nation's best interest for survival."[11]

LaHaye is also credited with convincing the Reverend Jerry Falwell to found the Moral Majority, the first in what would become a series of extremely influential political movements of the era based in the Christian right. Though he adopted a pose of theological discretion before secular audiences, Falwell, a Southern Baptist, also shared the premillennialist assumptions about the coming Armageddon and looked forward to its arrival. In 1980, he published *Armageddon and the Coming War with Russia*, arguing that the Bible had prophesied imminent nuclear war and concluding that this was to be welcomed because, in the end, Christ would return in glory. A mushroom cloud appeared on the front cover, and its final page reads: "WHAT A DAY THAT WILL BE!" Falwell told an interviewer in 1981, "We believe that Russia, because of her need of oil—and she's running out now—is going to move in on the Middle East, and particularly Israel because of their hatred of the Jew, and that it is at that time when all hell will break out. And it is at that time when I believe there will be some nuclear holocaust on this earth." Falwell said he considered Israel's founding on May 14, 1948, to be the most important date in history since the birth of Jesus. And while he denied this before secular and Jewish audiences, he was also on board with the premillennialist program that demanded Jews shape up before it was too late. "The Jews are returning to their land of unbelief," he warned. "They are spiritually blind and desperately in need of their Messiah and Savior." However odd such views may have sounded to journalists or Jews (or just about anyone else who was not part of the evangelical strain of Christianity), they were very much in the mainstream of the new Christian right.[12]

Falwell owed his fame and influence in significant measure to a 1960 Federal Communications Commission rule change that allowed broadcast stations to sell unprofitable airtime to churches and count it against the religious programming quotas they had to fulfill in order to retain their licenses. Mainline Protestant and Catholic churches did not feel comfortable hawking their theological wares on TV, and so the rule change meant that "televangelism" became almost the exclusive purview of right-wing evangelicals. By 1979, the year he founded the Moral Majority, Falwell's *Old Time Gospel Hour* appeared on 373 stations—more than Johnny Carson's *The Tonight Show*—and his Lynchburg, Virginia, church grew to 17,000 members with a staff of over 1,000.[13]

Before 1967, mainline Protestant churches had largely supported the Zionists against the Palestinians. Once the Israeli occupation of the West Bank and Gaza began, they came to define the conflict differently. Their misgivings about Israel became less important than they had been, however, with time, as these churches were rapidly losing both members and influence. Meanwhile, the evangelical churches grew in membership and influence. Observers who had not been paying attention to the premillennialist turn in evangelical theology were no doubt surprised to see the defense of Israel among the Moral Majority's foundational precepts. The *New York Times* did not introduce its readers to the concept of "Christians who call themselves Zionists" until 1980. By that time, however, Falwell had already traveled twice to Israel as a guest of the Begin government. There, he had warned West Bank settlers and their supporters that America was "wavering at this time in her position on the side of Israel." But he made his own support clear, saying, "I believe that if we fail to protect Israel, we will cease to be important to God." And he made sure that the Moral Majority took this responsibility extremely seriously. Item number six on its ten-point platform read, "We support the state of Israel and the Jewish people everywhere." At the group's inaugural press conference, he promised to work with anyone who shared its beliefs regarding "national defense, abortion and Israel."[14]

The Begin government evinced no qualms about embracing Israel's new friends, regardless of their theological beliefs. Indeed, right-wing religious Israelis and Christian evangelicals found much to agree on. They shared commitments to biblical exegesis, social conservatism, and militarism, and they loathed both socialism and Islam. It was no stretch for

Falwell in 1979 to be chosen the first gentile ever to receive the Likud party's "Jabotinsky Award," named after its founder (and the founder of Revisionist Zionism). Much as they had done for fans of the movie *Exodus*, though on a far larger scale, the Israelis also developed a robust tourist business for their new allies, one dedicated to Christian holy places. As early as 1980, the director of the Pilgrim Promoting Division of the Israeli Ministry of Trade and Tourism estimated that 100,000 out of 250,000 American visitors to Israel were Christian tourists. Many of these contributed generously to the construction and protection of Israel's West Bank settlements.[15]

The evangelicals, however, would prove to be a far harder sell to American Jews. Largely still liberal, many American Jews were still enthusiastic boosters of almost everything the Moral Majority had been formed to oppose: the separation of church and state, racial integration, reproductive freedom, and a dovish foreign policy, save when it involved Israel. Sociologically speaking, the two sides lived not merely in different neighborhoods in different parts of the country, but also in the functional equivalent of different universes. Leaving aside Jews' unhappy role in premillennialist eschatology—Falwell had predicted rather matter-of-factly that, when the Antichrist arrives, "of course, he'll be Jewish"—there were also quite a few problematic ideas expressed about present-day Jewish Americans in some evangelical circles. Falwell, for instance, defending his politics to a conservative Christian group, once said he understood why some of them didn't like Jews—because they "can make more money accidentally than you can on purpose."[16]

But like Begin and his Likud party, the neocons were all in with Falwell and company. Writing in *Commentary*, Irving Kristol, universally credited as neoconservatism's "godfather," wondered, "Why should Jews care about the theology of a fundamentalist preacher when they do not for a moment believe that he speaks with any authority" on theological matters? After all, he concluded, "it is their theology, but it is our Israel." Kristol insisted that Jews subjugate their liberalism to their Zionism: "This is the way the Israeli government has struck its own balance vis-à-vis the Moral Majority, and it is hard to see why American Jews should come up with a different bottom line." After all, Jews had won the fight against exclusion from the nation's country clubs, he mused in another article. Did they "now feel it necessary to take on the specter of discrimination in that Great Country Club in the Sky"?[17]

All of this was part and parcel of the neoconservative campaign by Kristol and company to convince American Jews to join them on their journey rightward. In this regard, the neocons, many of whom were former Trotskyists, saw themselves as a kind of conservative version of Marxism's notional vanguard within the Jewish community. This campaign would fail spectacularly. Jews, together with Blacks, would remain the Democrats' most loyal ethnic group, but Kristol and other neocons succeeded in convincing many Christians (and more than a few journalists) that they spoke for American Jews. This may have been the idea to begin with. It was Arthur Hertzberg's view that "what they are really selling is not neoconservatism to the Jewish community, but themselves as leaders of the Jews to the goyish community." This had the effect of further skewing the Israel-Palestine debate in a rightward direction. The neocons' success in the media and politics led to greater and greater avenues of influence in the Republican Party, where, together with the evangelical Christians and the generous contributions of a few extremely wealthy Jewish funders, they successfully converted the party to a militant version of Zionism that refused to entertain almost any compromise on Israel's retention of "Judea," "Samaria," and, most of all, an "undivided Jerusalem."[18]

The Christian Zionists' devotion to "Greater Israel" earned them a pass from the neocons for their occasional outbreaks of antisemitism. When the Reverend Pat Robertson, an evangelical entrepreneur and founder and president of the enormously popular Christian Broadcasting Network, appeared to blame a worldwide Jewish conspiracy for the downfall of Western civilization, among other things, Norman Podhoretz insisted that Robertson's pro-Israel politics "trump[ed] the anti-Semitic pedigree of his ideas." Podhoretz insisted that "Israel was, after all, the most important issue of Jewish concern," and here Robertson was "on the side of the angels." (Robertson had predicted that "war with the Soviet Union is inevitable, if I read Bible prophecy properly," and "the chances are that the U.S. will come in as a defender of Israel," and so, therefore, "it looks like everything is shaping up.") The Anti-Defamation League, initially sympathetic to the deal on offer from the Christian Zionists, under its director Nathan Perlmutter, had reversed itself under his successor, Abraham Foxman, beginning in 1987. Inspired by a 1989 declaration signed by a dozen evangelical leaders calling for a redoubled commitment to the conversion of the Jews, Foxman's ADL issued a hard-hitting report on how they were fostering racism, sexism, the persecution of homosexuals, and a general lack of respect for American pluralism. This condemnation, in turn, inspired Midge Decter to attack the ADL in her husband's magazine and to organize fully seventy-five fellow neocons to sign a full-page *New York Times* advertisement doing the same.[19]

These misgivings notwithstanding, the leaders of mainstream Jewish institutions and the premillennialist evangelicals managed to find common ground not only in support of Israel's expansion to the West Bank, but also in support of Soviet Jewish emigration. This shotgun marriage was made not in heaven, but in Washington, and it was overseen by a newly rejuvenated AIPAC, now positioned to become America's most powerful foreign policy lobby. It was not as if the pro-Israel group had been unconcerned about the plight of Soviet Jews living under especially oppressive conditions, even by Soviet standards. While the movement was undoubtedly motivated by humanitarian concerns and inspired many thousands of idealistic volunteers, it simultaneously contained crucial realpolitik value for Israel and its conservative supporters. Winning their right to emigration would mean that Soviet Jews would likely end up in Israel, something that American Jewish organizations strongly encouraged, despite the fact that many of the émigrés would have preferred the United States. A massive influx of ex-Soviet Jews could defuse the "demographic time bomb" Israel allegedly faced (meaning that the longer it held on to the occupied territories, the sooner Arab birthrates would turn Jews into a minority in lands it controlled). This is exactly what came to pass when, under Mikhail Gorbachev, the Soviet Union finally opened its doors during the final days of the 1980s. As more than a million Soviet Jewish emigrants resettled in Israel, their deep hatred of socialism and socialists moved the nation's political center of gravity further into right-wing, anti-democratic territory. For the Christian

Zionists, this all came together in one big, beautiful, pro-religion, anti-Soviet, pro-Likud, pro-Armageddon package. As one AIPAC researcher said of the Christian Zionists at the time, "Sure, these guys give me the heebie-jeebies. But until I see Jesus coming over the hill, I'm in favor of all the friends Israel can get."[20]

In its early years, AIPAC had given the impression of amateurism and ineffectiveness, though this was really a mask for the low-key manner in which it got the job done. The organization came about largely as a reaction to the October 1953 Israeli attack on the West Bank village of Qibya, then under Jordanian rule. Isaiah L. "Si" Kenen was working as a lobbyist in Congress for the American Zionist Committee for Public Affairs after having done the same job for Israel's foreign ministry. He wrote an associate that reports of the massacre had "discredited the premises of our propaganda and given the color of truth to Arab propaganda," and suggested they put together a formal operation to make Israel's case whenever circumstances made it necessary to do so.[21]

A second, no less important, impetus came in the form of complaints from then secretary of state John Foster Dulles and his assistant secretary for Near East affairs, Henry Byroade. Speaking to the Israeli ambassador to the United States, Abba Eban, they begged for mercy from the unruly amalgamation of organizations—whether Zionist, non-Zionist, or, in the case of the American Council for Judaism, anti-Zionist—professing to give voice to concerns about US policies toward Israel and always asking for meetings. (Dulles was especially annoyed at all the "various inaccuracies and distortions" he was hearing from the "Jewish fraternity" following the Eisenhower administration's short-lived decision to withhold Mutual Security funds from Israel and to support the strong censure of Israel in the UN Security Council in the wake of Qibya.) Jewish leaders had been reluctant to unite, in part for reasons of personal prerogatives; each one no doubt enjoyed being king of his own personal hill, and each of them likely nursed significant disagreements with the others ("Two Jews, three opinions...").[22]

The historian Lila Corwin Berman noted a third concern: "The more that Jews appeared as a singular political entity, the more likely they could be perceived as clannish, unassimilable and, thus, incapable of fulfilling the duties of national citizenship." But the Jews really had no choice. Administration officials insisted they could not continue to meet with sixteen separate organizations. The result was the decision to form two overarching organizations: the stand-alone American Zionist Committee for Public Affairs, which would later be renamed the American Israel Public Affairs Committee (AIPAC), and the Conference of Presidents of Major American Jewish Organizations. The former's job was to lobby Congress and help shape public opinion, and the latter's was to meet with the president, the secretary of state, and other high officials.[23]

Working with a shoestring staff in a small, cluttered office on Capitol Hill, the extremely personable and rather unassuming Kenen would corral senators and representatives to write and support legislation to supply Israel with cheap loans, generous trade terms, and bargain-basement prices for advanced weaponry. Asked to describe his job, Kenen said he needed only one sentence: "We appeal to local leadership to write or telegraph or telephone their Congressmen to urge them to call upon the President to overrule the Department of State." This was done quite informally, however, as Kenen's most important rule in this phase of AIPAC's operations was to "get behind legislation; don't step out in front of it (that is, keep a low profile)." It was a tribute to Kenen's effectiveness that a top US National Security Council official, Robert Komer, would boast, in August 1965, that the Americans had turned out to be "Israel's chief supporters, bankers, direct and indirect arms purveyors, and ultimate guarantors" to a degree that "far exceeded that which can be justified under [US Agency for International Development] economic criteria." Even the aid to the Arab nation of Jordan, in which the United States had "little other interest," was given largely to ensure Israel's safety. Komer insisted that his assessment of the sweet deal Israel received—which was written for the purposes of quieting the complaints of a small group of Jewish congressmen—be kept confidential, as "the more quiet these matters can be kept the more we can do."[24]

Kenen's successor, the hard-charging Morris J. Amitay, who took over in 1974, expanded the organization but embraced his predecessor's preference for minimal publicity designed to achieve maximum effect. He informed potential allies that lobbying for Israel in the aftermath of the 1973 war was now "a whole new ballgame," as "Israel required billions." He "wanted to make AIPAC an effective modern lobby," and aid for Israel the responsibility not of American Jewish donors, but of the US government. Amitay focused on the fact that many congressional staff members "happen[ed] to be Jewish." They were "willing," he discovered, "to look at certain issues in terms of their Jewishness," and were also "in a position to make the decision in these areas for those senators." AIPAC had faced some unwelcome scrutiny during the Kennedy administration when J. William Fulbright (D-AR), chairman of the Senate Foreign Relations Committee, launched an investigation into its funding. His researcher, the future investigative journalist Walter Pincus, found a great deal of hidden foreign funding that had been funneled into AIPAC, a clear violation of the US Foreign Agents Registration Act, and a potential propaganda point for American antisemites and enemies of Israel the world over. Fulbright wanted to expose AIPAC's activities and demand that its staff register as foreign lobbyists. Israel's friends, however, reached President Kennedy and Vice President Johnson, who wanted none of this. Johnson prevailed upon his good friend and former southern Senate colleague to carry out his investigation entirely in closed session, and to keep his findings out of the Congressional Record. Eventually, Fulbright decided it was best simply to accept AIPAC's explanation that everything it did was completely kosher, both morally and legally.[25]

AIPAC had clearly been doing something right. Fulbright, after all, credited Israel's "organized Jewish supporters" with being "the most powerful and efficient foreign policy lobby in American politics," and of "duping Americans into a policy." Both the Israelis and US administrations would come to much prefer dealing almost exclusively with AIPAC than with other Jewish groups—much less all of them—because it was a single-issue group and did not bother anyone about the kinds of social justice concerns that continued to animate many other Jewish organizations. A decade later, in mid-March 1973, President Nixon complained that he could not make any progress on Middle East peace because "Israel's lobby is so strong that the Congress is not reasonable." We have seen, in previous chapters, the lobby's role in stymying the policy initiatives of

Presidents Ford and Carter. But it was still a minor-league organization compared to the powerhouse it would soon become.[26]

AIPAC's efforts took a giant step beyond merely a legislative agenda when, in 1973, Kenen formed what he called the "Washington Truth Squad" to seek to defend Israel with "editorial writers, columnists or broadcasters" who might otherwise be critical. It would also encourage "public figures to counteract... pro-Arab or anti-Israel spokesmen." Over time, this would become a multimillion-dollar operation that dozens of organizations and literally thousands of individuals were invited to join. One *Forward* writer would observe, decades later, that "rooting out perceived anti-Israel bias in the media had become for many American Jews the most direct and emotional outlet for connecting with the conflict 6,000 miles away." It was yet another manifestation of American Jews' intense embrace of what Benedict Anderson termed "long-distance nationalism."[27]

Over time, this commitment worked political wonders. "If there is anything in the paper that smacks of criticism of Israel, my editor's phone starts ringing off the hook in the morning," said David Lamb, who covered Egypt for the *Los Angeles Times*. The same was true for almost everyone who covered the Middle East for any major media institution. As a result, "the editors shepherd through much more carefully stories about Israel than the Arab world because they know they will come under a lot of pressure," Lamb said. No doubt countless stories were skewed, or never written at all, to avoid the bother that would be certain to arise were Israel to be portrayed unfavorably by reporters, editors, and producers. They simply did not want to deal with the hassle, much less the personal abuse. "Of course, a lot of self-censorship goes on," Menachem Shalev, a former spokesman for the Israeli consulate in New York, once bragged to a reporter. "Journalists, editors, and politicians, for that matter, are going to think twice about criticizing Israel if they know they are going to get thousands of angry calls in a matter of hours. The Jewish lobby is good at orchestrating pressure." AIPAC's power to determine the acceptable parameters of debate about Israel, whether in Congress or in the media, certainly rankled. This is what former *New York Times* executive editor Max Frankel, a Jewish pro-Israel partisan, meant when he revealed, long after his retirement, that "even fervent friends of Israel, like George Mc-Govern and Ed Muskie, used to complain to me during their campaigns for president that they had to 'clear' their statements on the Middle East with Jewish censors."[28]

AIPAC was powerful, but it was not unbeatable if it went up against a determined president. It could not block the Carter administration's sale of sixty F-15s to Saudi Arabia in 1978, for example. Most portentously, it met defeat again in the first test it faced during Reagan's presidency. But it would never lose so quietly again.

The fight centered on the United States' plan to sell Saudi Arabia an airborne early warning and control system (AWACS) plane as part of a larger arms deal that originated with the Carter administration. It came out of US and Saudi fears of the spread of radical Shia Islam across the Arab world, as it was thought that it could one day threaten the Saudis' Sunni Islamic regime. By the time the Reagan team finally announced the $8.5 billion deal in April 1981, it had morphed into the single largest arms sale in history, terrifying the Israelis in the process. (Kept secret at the time was a US-Saudi plan to spend as much as $150 billion building military bases, airfields, and other military infrastructure to accommo-date this and future arms sales, which particularly appealed to Defense Secretary Caspar Weinberger, the former top executive at the defense contractor Bechtel.) Even before the announcement was made, AIPAC had secured signatures from 54 senators for a letter to the president stat-ing their "strong belief that this sale is not in the best interests of the United States and [that they] therefore recommend that you refrain from sending this proposal to the Congress." Another letter, this one signed by 224 members of the House, said much the same thing. The votes in both houses of Congress looked to be a rout in the making. But the Reagan White House retaliated by rallying the still pro-Arab security bureau-cracy, oil and weapons industry lobbyists, and the US Chamber of Com-merce. Working on behalf of all of these, Prince Bandar bin Sultan, the son of Saudi Arabia's defense minister and a nephew of its king, directed a well-funded and well-organized lobby for the sale. He hired a lobbyist who understood that, "unlike AIPAC, the Saudis and the Arab countries do not have the means to reach out into the country.... The Arab channel in this country is paper thin." The PR team therefore put the question in terms that twisted a knife into the guts of the American Jewish establishment: Were the senators "with Begin over Reagan"? Reagan embraced this narrative by complaining, "It is not the business of other nations to make American foreign policy." One Republican senator reportedly received a call from ex-president Gerald Ford—while he was at a dinner for Jewish leaders, no less—who demanded, "Are we going to let the fucking Jews run American foreign policy?" All of these interests, plus a new Republican president and a Republican majority in the Senate that did not wish to humiliate their leader, were enough to deny AIPAC its victory.[29]

The lesson AIPAC learned was that it needed to expand geographically, bureaucratically, culturally, and any other way it could think of for its next battle. Its new director, Thomas Dine, had been an aide to the Senate's liberal lion, Ted Kennedy. Dine had little connection to Jewish institutions and none at all to Israel (his gentile wife, Joan, joked to friends that he could not have located Israel on a map). But he knew how to organize a lobby. Dine is universally credited with recognizing the value of turning AIPAC into a grassroots operation with its own local chapters that could pressure lawmakers to follow their line on Israel or, if necessary, locate candidates to oppose them and help them to secure funding. It was not uncommon for the funders AIPAC located to demand the right to script a politician's positions on Israel-related matters in return for financial support. Over a period of decades, these contributions would run into the hundreds of millions of dollars.[30]

To put what he called "Jewish muscle" to work, Dine initially identified twenty-five states where grassroots campaigns could target significant populations of both Jews and evangelical Christians. AIPAC's annual budget increased from $1.2 million to $15 million during the 1980s, on its way to $50 million by the end of the century. Its membership expanded to more than 100,000 over the same period, with nine regional offices, ten satellite offices, and a staff of over 100. At roughly the same time, US public spending on military aid to Israel increased by a factor of more than 1000 percent.[31]

With these funds and an engaged membership behind it, AIPAC soon became an important player—often the most important player—not only in Israel policy debates but also in any other policy debate that was seen by AIPAC to potentially affect Israel's interests in some fashion. Speaking of his own Democratic caucus after he announced his retirement, Representative David Price (D-NC) admitted that when "AIPAC said 'jump,' we'd say 'How high?'" After one vote in which AIPAC demanded that Democratic congressmen vote in favor of aid to the murderous military junta in El Salvador, which Israel was providing with military aid, and which was also one of the few nations to support it in the United Nations, a congressman told the *Washington Post*'s Robert Kaiser, "I displayed my usual cowardice." His vote was consistent with the understanding of the unwritten law of Israel-related issues in Congress as explained to the journalist Peter Beinart decades later by a Democratic aide: "If you're labeled as anti-Israel then other members of Congress will be skeptical of everything you do even if it's only marginally related."[32]

Just how much influence AIPAC enjoyed over US policies in the Middle East, and the limits of permissible criticism of Israel or support for Palestinians, would, over time, become the most disputatious points of the entire American debate over Israel. Beginning with Dine's reign and continuing through the present, AIPAC and its (unofficially) affiliated organizations amassed so many tools of political power and influence that it was hard for anyone—even its professional opponents—to keep up with it. Unlike a typical lobby, AIPAC went beyond merely influencing congressional votes. It not only wrote legislation, but also recruited congressional candidates, and it ensured, via cut-outs, that their races were well funded against candidates who did not vote its way. It created think tanks, sent politicians (and their wives) on VIP tours of Israel, policed the public discourse, and smeared pro-Palestinian voices as antisemites, self-hating Jews, and worse. It trained college students and funded their internships across the government. It guided the hiring practices of not only senators and congressmen, but also of the Defense Department, the State Department, the Commerce Department, and other agencies, vetoing certain hires, promoting others, and often determining how much foreign aid other countries, including Israel's adversaries, might receive.

A significant portion of AIPAC's success in steering policy arose from its ability to provide congressional staff with research, talking points, and detailed drafts of the legislation it wanted passed. But as with almost everything else in American politics, the true source of its power was money. AIPAC did not endorse candidates, nor did it give away money, at least until December 2021, when it finally changed its policy and announced the creation of its own political action committee. Before that, its members raised money via advisements to friendly donors. Those candidates it approved of appeared on lists for Jewish donors nationwide, and those it did not, did not. In April 2016, Stephanie Schriock, president of EMILY's List, a political action committee that raises money to help elect women to public office, gave a short disquisition to a panel on Israel and the US election, based on her previous experience as finance director for congressional candidates:

> Before you went to the Jewish community [to raise money], you had a conversation with the lead AIPAC person in your state and they made it clear that you needed a paper on Israel. And so you called all your friends who already had a paper on Israel—that was designed by AIPAC—and we made that your paper. This was before there was a campaign manager, a policy director or a field director because you have got to raise money before you do all of that. I have written more Israel papers than you can imagine. I am from Montana. I barely knew where Israel was until I looked at a map, and the poor campaign manager would come in, or the policy director, and I'd be like, "Here is your paper on Israel. This is our policy." That means that these candidates who were farmers, schoolteachers, or businesswomen, ended up having an Israel position without having any significant conversations with anybody.

When Senator Lindsey Graham (R-SC) ran for president in 2016, he said to a group of supporters, presumably at least partially in jest, "If I put together a finance team that will make me financially competitive enough to stay in this thing.... I may have the first all-Jewish cabinet in America because of the pro-Israel funding." This was no joke, however. When Michelle Nunn, daughter of the hawkish former Democratic senator Sam Nunn of Georgia, sought to win her father's Senate seat in

2014, her campaign director put together an initial strategy memo later leaked to the media. "Michelle's position on Israel will largely determine the level of support here," it read. "There is tremendous financial opportunity, but the level of support will be contingent on her position. This applies not only to PACs, but individual donors as well."[33]

AIPAC has always pretended that its only tool was simple political persuasion, that it was just a lonely little lobby like any other—dentists or accountants, perhaps—fighting the combined interests of "Big Oil," State Department Arabists, arms manufacturers, antisemites, and so on. Every once in a while, however, it found reason to boast, lest its message of reward and punishment prove too subtle for the right people to receive it. When the chair of the Senate Foreign Relations Committee, the liberal-for-a-Republican Charles Percy, voted to approve an arms sales deal to Saudi Arabia in 1984, and suggested aloud that Israel initiate peace talks with the PLO, AIPAC responded by recruiting Congressman Paul Simon (D-IL) to run against him the next time he was up for election, promising millions in funds from Jewish contributors. Following Simon's victory, Dine proudly crowed, "All the Jews in America, from coast to coast, gathered to oust Percy....And American politicians... got the message." He had said much the same thing about the pro-Palestinian congressman Paul Findley after his defeat in the 1982 midterm election: "This is a case where the Jewish lobby made the difference. We beat the odds and defeated Findley." Another, less public boast was made at the beginning of the Clinton administration, when an AIPAC official interrupted a conversation he was having with a reporter and pushed his napkin across the table: "You see this napkin?" he asked. "In twenty-four hours, we could have the signatures of seventy senators on this napkin."[34]

The rise of AIPAC, and with it the Conference of Presidents, certainly rankled among those who might have expected to become leaders of the American Jewish community in less money-and-politics-driven times. Rabbi Arthur Hertzberg was one such dissident. Having been shoved aside from his perch as president of the venerably liberal, and increasingly irrelevant, American Jewish Congress, and retreating to his position as a congregational rabbi and writer and university professor, the Polish-born scholar/rabbi/agitator spoke disgustedly of the machine that AIPAC was building. "The AIPAC people are barely Jewish," he complained to a journalist in the mid-1980s. "They certainly don't know anything about Judaism, or Zionism for that matter. What kind of Jewish education do they have?" Hertzberg thought AIPAC was "creating more anti-Semites than it's scaring away," as it was deliberately confusing "being Jewish" with "supporting Israel" and "being an anti-anti-Semite." He predicted that "it [would] all come crashing down" on AIPAC. But in this matter, he could hardly have been more wrong.[35]

AIPAC's party line grew stronger at the expense of the Talmudic-trained rabbis, theologians, and scholars, as well as most of what constituted Judaism itself. Adultery, marriage outside the faith, eating spareribs on Yom Kippur—all these could all be forgiven—but never the public questioning of the policies of Israel's government or the righteousness of its people. This was the lesson that the rabbis who founded Breira had learned, and it would be repeated until everyone got the message. AIPAC provided its members with the proper line on whatever issue faced Israel, and the wealthy and influential among them could use this to instruct the rabbis whose synagogues they funded regarding just who they could invite to speak in their shuls and what they, themselves, might safely say in their sermons. The "new Jews" of AIPAC, as Dine termed them, not only defeated the "Arab lobby" in the US government, but vanquished the rabbis as well.

"I've believed in many things in my life, but no conviction I've ever held has been stronger than my belief that the United States must ensure the survival of Israel," wrote Ronald Reagan's ghostwriter, Robert Lindsey, in the fortieth president's purported autobiography. This may have been an overstatement, but it was not a falsehood. With 39 percent of the Jewish vote, Ronald Reagan did better with American Jews than any other Republican candidate in modern times. But this was only one of the many reasons he assumed office with strong sympathy for Israel. Reagan was also known to muse, on occasion, as to whether there might not be something to that whole Armageddon thing happening sometime soon. (He told AIPAC's Tom Dine, "You know I turn back to your ancient prophets in the Old Testament and the signs foretelling Armageddon, and I find myself wondering if we're the generation that's going to see that come about," before adding, "I don't know if you've noted any of those prophets lately but believe me, they certainly describe the times we're going through.")[36]

Reagan was not close to any Jews, however, and for the first time since Truman's presidency, his cabinet featured a total of zero sons and daughters of Moses. His biggest concern was the Cold War, and he saw Israel as integral to fighting it. "Only by full appreciation of the critical role the State of Israel plays in our strategic calculus," he announced during the 1980 campaign, "can we build the foundation for thwarting Moscow's designs on territories and resources vital to our security and our national well-being." One of his campaign workers even referred to the film version of *Exodus* when describing Israel's history. But his sympathies were not widely shared within the national security bureaucracy, where the traditional Arabist worldview continued to hold sway. This was particularly true at the Pentagon. Defense Secretary Caspar Weinberger had personally approved the Bechtel Corporation's policy of participation in the Arab boycott of Israel in his former role of general counsel. He was soon joined in the administration by his former Bechtel colleague George Shultz, who replaced the volatile, pro-Israel Alexander Haig as secretary of state. Yet even if there had been greater sympathy for Israel in the State and Defense Departments, the fact that Menachem Begin was Israel's prime minister would have made the task of anyone seeking to make its case a decidedly challenging one.[37]

Begin did not even pretend to care what the gentile world thought of what Israel did. Back in 1967, a day after the Six-Day War ended, he had told the party he founded and chaired that "one third of the Jewish nation was exterminated by the Germans." And "with a few exceptions," he noted, "the rest of the world's' [sic] nations did nothing to stop the systematic genocide." Begin had a particular nation in mind when he said this. "Six million Jews were exterminated during this generation, and the US did not save even one," he inaccurately informed then prime minister Golda Meir, when she agreed to entertain a US peace initiative in 1970.

In early 1981, he decided that Israel needed to destroy a nuclear reactor that was under construction in Iraq about ten miles southeast of Baghdad. He made this decision despite the fact that Iraq was a party to the nuclear non-proliferation treaty (as Israel was not) and would have been somewhere between ten and thirty years away from producing sufficient material for a bomb, even if it had already begun such production at the time. Iraqi leader Saddam Hussein's empty boasting notwithstanding, no such production was yet underway. (Begin, it should be noted, was likely a secret sufferer from bipolar disorder, according to a physician who treated him as prime minister, a diagnosis that was not revealed until decades later.)[38]

Begin sent US-supplied F-15 and F-16 aircraft to bomb the Iraqi reactor on June 7. This was an unambiguous act of war as well as an illegal violation of several nations' airspace. It furthermore contradicted the terms of the US sale of the aircraft, which stipulated that they be used "for defense only." Israel found itself condemned by the UN Security Council and General Assembly with no US veto. The *New York Times* described "Israel's sneak attack" as "an act of inexcusable and short-sighted aggression," while the *Los Angeles Times* called it "state-sponsored terrorism."[39]

When the Reagan administration demonstrated its displeasure by suspending the delivery of a group of F-16s, Begin went ballistic. He called the American ambassador to Israel and demanded, "Are we a vassal state? A banana republic? Are we youths of fourteen who, if they don't behave properly, are slapped across the fingers?" After reminding him about the history of US atrocities in World War II and Vietnam, he instructed the diplomat to tell his president that nobody would "frighten the great and free [Jewish] community in the United States." America's Jews, he promised, would stand by "the land of their forefathers. They have the right and duty to support [Israel]." Begin then went on, as he would do many times in the future, to equate Israel's Arab adversaries to Nazi Germany. Speaking aloud to the ambassador from a letter that he also sent directly to Reagan, he explained, "I feel as a Prime Minister empowered to instruct a valiant army facing 'Berlin' where, amongst innocent civilians, Hitler and his henchmen hide in a bunker deep beneath the surface." He and his "generation," he informed "dear Ron," had "swor[n] on the altar of God that whoever proclaims his intent to destroy the Jewish state or the Jewish people, or both, seals his fate, so that what happened from Berlin...will never happen again." Begin next phoned Jerry Falwell and, according to the reverend, asked him to "communicate to the American people, to the Christian public," that "we're not warmongers. We're trying to save our little children from annihilation." Falwell promised to do so, as "God deals with nations in relation to how they deal with Israel," and, like Begin, went on to invoke Hitler and warn of "a second holocaust on the Jewish people."[40]

The situation had few, if any, historical precedents. The leader of a tiny country, economically and militarily dependent on the United States for its survival and having committed what was unarguably an act of war using American-supplied weapons, was publicly deploying near apocalyptic rhetoric to instruct its president that he would be brooking no objections, lest it lead to another Holocaust. It was no easy task to defend Israel under these circumstances, but many took up the challenge. In the *New York Times*, for instance, former Nixon speechwriter William Safire attacked Reagan for a "policy of publicly humiliating our traditional ally," insisting that it had "made us no new friends in the Arab world and removed the trust needed to encourage Israel to take risks for peace." This argument—that the United States needed to back Israel to the hilt in all of its actions in order to give it the self-confidence "to take risks for peace"—would become another mainstay of the debate, though, once again, it was hard to see just when and where these risks, much less the peace, would materialize.[41]

Centrists such as Safire's colleague James Reston, a gentile with close connections to the State Department, were alarmed but had no idea what to do about this seemingly irrational, nuclear-armed Israeli fanatic. Reston, who reported more than opined, explained that "officials here feel that Mr. Begin is a certified disaster for Israel and the rest of the world." Yet ultimately, Congress once again lined up behind Israel. Although the Pentagon was especially unsympathetic to Israel under Weinberger, many in the building were not unhappy to see the Iraqi program get clipped. Reagan, aware of the strong evangelical support Begin enjoyed, decided he could live with it as well. He said of the country that had just carried out a daring bombing mission that it was hard for him "to envision Israel as being a threat to its neighbors." Months later, Begin came to the United States, where he and Reagan agreed to formalize a mutual defense agreement aimed, in Reagan's eyes, at the real enemy: the Soviet Union.[42]

Not long after these incidents, the venerated rabbi and philosopher David Hartman authored an influential article titled "Auschwitz or Sinai." Hartman had moved to Jerusalem in 1971 from Montreal (and inspired much of his congregation to move with him). There he had founded the Shalom Hartman Institute, named for his father—a religious think tank devoted to issues of individual and collective morality. "It is both politically and morally dangerous for our nation to perceive itself essentially as the suffering remnant of the Holocaust," he warned. Doing so led Jews to proclaim that "no one can judge the Jewish people," a phenomenon he termed "morally arrogant" and "self-righteous." The attitude was antithetical, he said, to "an increased sensitivity about all human suffering," and in making such statements, "a basic Judaic principle is violated." But Begin and his champions in the United States were not interested in such questions. To them, the Holocaust, and the world's indifference, had given the Jewish people special license to do exactly what Hartman had warned against: to refuse "to take the moral criticism of the world seriously because the uniqueness of our suffering places us above the moral judgment of an immoral world."[43]

A similar sort of dance took place a few months later when, with little warning and no diplomatic preparation whatsoever, Begin announced that Israel would unilaterally extend its "laws, jurisdiction and administration" to Syria's Golan Heights, which had been captured in the 1967 war. The Reagan administration objected, as did countless newspaper editorial boards. Liberal Jews evinced concern, while both neoconservatives and evangelicals cheered. They were cheering an Israel that, thanks in part to their efforts, could do whatever it wished, whenever it wished. Prime Minister Begin proudly told the Knesset that he had purposely chosen not to consult the US president because "no one will dictate our lives to us, not even the United States." Right again.[44]

# CHAPTER 12

# WAR: WHAT IS IT GOOD FOR?

MENACHEM BEGIN'S GO-IT-ALONE ATTITUDE MAY HAVE DISCOMFITED American Jew and gentile alike, but the discomfort did not actually translate into any meaningful obstacles for his policies. The Reagan administration's reactions to both the attack on Iraq's nuclear reactor and the Golan annexation were temporary and toothless. But this period of successfully papering over problems between Israel and the United States—and with its Jews—was about to come to an end. On June 6, 1982—a year after the attack on the nuclear reactor, and twenty-five years after it had begun the Six-Day War—Israel launched a brutal preemptive strike against the PLO in Lebanon, inspiring the people who had previously found a way to defend every action of its government to engage in public dissent.

The Israelis had long wanted to secure the border with Lebanon, where they had been fighting an on-again, off-again war with the PLO, and, by extension, the Syrians. They chose the attempted assassination of Shlomo Argov, Israel's ambassador to Britain, in London, as their catalyst.

The assassination attempt was actually the work of a small renegade PLO group under the direction of an enemy of PLO chairman Arafat, Abu Nidal, who had been supplied not by Syrian but by Iraqi intelligence. But Begin cared even less about distinctions among PLO enemies than he did about the doctrinal differences among his conservative Christian friends: "They're all PLO," he told his briefers, and ordered the invasion. Begin viewed all perceived enemies of the Jews in a continuous, almost linear fashion—not unlike the manner in which the biblical Israelites had viewed the nation of "Amelek," their eternal enemy across historical epochs. To Begin, the PLO was composed of "Arab Nazis." Israel needed to "avoid another Treblinka," he said, and kill "Little Hitler" (Arafat) in "his bunker." In response to birthday greetings from Ronald Reagan, he informed the president that the Israeli military would soon be closing in on "Hitler and his henchmen."[1]

Arafat had stated that in the months leading up to the war none of the attacks against Israelis had originated from PLO camps. Even so, US secretary of state Alexander Haig had let the Israelis know that should they experience an "internationally recognized provocation," they had a green light to start their war, just so long as they did it quickly and cleanly, "like a lobotomy." By attempting an assassination, Abu Nidal had obliged, providing a pretext for the invasion. Israel initially portrayed its objectives for "Operation Peace for Galilee" to be extremely limited, as Haig demanded. Begin promised Reagan that Israel sought only to clean out a security zone twenty-five miles deep on the Lebanese side of the border, with the aim of putting PLO rockets out of range. This was consistent with the assurances that Israeli defense minister Ariel Sharon had given the Begin cabinet before its members approved the operation. But in reality, Sharon had already given his commanders orders to march all the way to Beirut and destroy the entire PLO army. The attack also included the saturation bombing of Beirut itself, and with it, the destruction of much of the city that had long been considered the "Paris of the Middle East." According to Haim Rubovitch, former head of the Directorate of Israel's intelligence service Shin Bet, who served in Lebanon during the war, it was "the wild west." He recalled that "total chaos set in. We made arrests in crazy numbers.... We arrested countless people for no reason." Haig was shocked by the operation's massive scale, a far cry from the one he apparently imagined when he had given his winking approval. He warned the Israelis that "the continued bombing of Beirut would destroy what remains of the goodwill of your friends in the United States." He may have meant it, or he may not have, but it didn't matter, because the Israelis did what they wanted, and soon enough Haig was replaced by George P. Shultz.[2]

At least initially, the invasion looked to be a success. Following a US-brokered cease-fire, Arafat and his army were forced to evacuate Lebanon; Arafat left for his new headquarters in Tunisia on August 30 before a cheering crowd of thousands. (Other PLO fighters were sent to Cyprus en route to Tunisia and other friendly nations, including Jordan, Syria, Iraq, Sudan, and North and South Yemen.) Speaking to the fifth annual convention of Jerry Falwell's Moral Majority in Jerusalem, the Israeli ambassador to the United States, Moshe Arens, described the war as "a great victory, not only for Israel but also for the free world." Negative publicity notwithstanding, for a time this looked to be true. Falwell organized a trip for more than fifty clergy from the United States to travel to Israel, and then to be escorted to the battlefields in Lebanon by the Israel Defense Forces. When they returned, he explained to his followers that the Israelis "were, in fact, with surgical precision caring for the welfare of the private citizen," and insisted that "every Christian in America" should "spend extra time and effort at rebuilding Israel's image in this country."[3]

On September 14, 1982, however, the situation changed considerably when a Syrian national assassinated Lebanon's Christian president, Bachir Gemayel. A local warlord and leader of the fascist-style Phalange Party founded by his father, Gemayel had allied himself and the Lebanese Forces, a militia group staffed largely by Maronite Christians, with Israel in order to win Lebanon's ongoing battle for control of the country against the PLO and its Syrian supporters. That's when all hell broke loose. Israeli troops surrounded two heavily populated Palestinian refugee camps near Beirut (Sabra and Shatila) between September 15 and 18 and invited the deceased Gemayel's army into the camps. There, to no one's surprise, given the circumstances, they proceeded to massacre as many as two thousand Palestinians, nearly all of them unarmed civilians. The

Israeli army not only prevented refugees from escaping, but also lofted flares—as requested by the Phalangists—to light up the sky and thereby assist the murderers in their gruesome task. (One must note that our knowledge of the details of these conversations is incomplete due to the fact that, decades later, the Mossad continued to insist before Israeli courts that it could not locate the documents necessary to explain its role.)[4]

Following an international outcry and massive protests inside Israel, an official Israeli Commission of Inquiry found Sharon guilty of enabling the massacre and forced his resignation as defense minister. (According to what was then an unpublished, secret addendum to the commission's report, Gemayel was quite explicit in describing his murderous plans— "It is possible we will need several Deir Yassins," he had told the Israelis, referring to the massacres carried out against Palestinians by Begin's Irgun terrorists during the 1948 war.) Begin, who had been widowed shortly before the war began, sank into a deep depression from which he never recovered. He resigned in September 1983 with the words, "I cannot go on any longer." But he had set the terms of debate over the massacre, and, by extension, the war itself, when, ignoring Israel's undeniable role in enabling the Phalangist massacre of the Palestinians, he insisted that "Goyim are killing goyim" and "the whole world is trying to hang Jews for the crime."[5]

Meanwhile, quick action by AIPAC and its allies in Congress kept Israel from suffering adverse consequences in Washington. Both Reagan and Shultz sought to ensure that Congress would do nothing "to endorse and reward Israel's policies," but what Congress delivered instead was a $250 million increase in Israel's supplemental assistance. "This brought home to me vividly Israel's leverage in our Congress," Shultz later wrote. "I saw that I must work carefully with the Israelis if I was to have any handle on congressional action that might affect them."[6]

Congress's action notwithstanding, Operation Peace for Galilee inspired an entirely new sort of Israel/Palestine debate in the United States. As had happened with Vietnam, seeing the war's brutality on television shocked American sensibilities, especially as it had occurred in what had been one of the world's most cosmopolitan cities (and one in which countless Western reporters lived and worked). Reporting from a hotel rooftop as the buildings around him went up in flames, NBC's John Chancellor must have shocked many viewers when he spoke of a "savage Israel...an imperialist state that we never knew existed before," that was now "solving its problems in someone else's country" (though he later admitted that his choice of words might have been misguided at the time).[7]

Nevertheless, for the first time, criticism of Israel's tactics and aims by Jews themselves pierced through the walls erected by Jewish officialdom. The arguments began, just as they had since 1967, with dueling signed statements by notable intellectuals on both sides. The critics' letter, however, this time featured not only traditional leftist critics of Israel, but also respected voices in the Jewish community. Philip Klutznick and Nahum Goldmann, both past presidents of the World Jewish Congress, joined former French premier Pierre Mendès France in a call for Israel to retreat from Beirut and begin negotiations with the PLO. (Goldmann also specifically criticized using the Holocaust "as an excuse for the bombing of Lebanon," which he termed "a kind of Hillul Hashem [sacrilege], a banalization of the sacred tragedy of the Shoah [Holocaust], which must not be misused to justify politically doubtful and morally indefensible policies.") Sixty-seven American Jewish scholars, writers, and rabbis signed an advertisement expressing "grave misgivings" over the fighting in Lebanon and advocating "national self-determination" for Palestinians. They asked, "Is it not time for us as supporters of Israel to speak out critically about those Israeli policies we know to be mistaken, self-defeating, and contrary to the original Zionist vision?" The signatories were among the most famous and admired names in Jewish cultural life, including the authors Saul Bellow, E. L. Doctorow, Alfred Kazin, and Irving Howe and the scholars Meyer Schapiro, Daniel Bell, Nathan Glazer, and Seymour Martin Lipset. Glazer and Lipset, frequent contributors to Podhoretz's *Commentary*, also authored a *New York Times* op-ed saying the war was "ill-advised" and calling on Israel to "recognize that Palestinian nationalism is as legitimate as Jewish nationalism"—a radical statement in the context of American Jewish life at the time. Other staunch Israel supporters agreed. Rita Hauser, a Republican Jewish activist, found Israel's role "shameful" and "shocking"—it was "simply something that Jews, Israelis, are not supposed to do." A third of the delegates of the Central Conference of American [Reform] Rabbis voted in favor of a resolution that expressed concern "for the soul of Israel and of the Jewish people." Even I. F. Stone was impressed by the reaction. He noted to a reporter that Jewish dissent over the nation's foreign policy was "much more widespread than ever before." People who used to call him and Noam Chomsky "stooges of the P.L.O.," he said, were now joining him in petitions for peace.[8]

Interestingly, one of the ways that the stalwarts in the organized Jewish community responded was to agree with Hauser, and therefore declare that what had happened could not possibly have happened. "The history of the Jewish people is too full of massacres and pogroms, and the injunctions of Jewish law are too powerful a force in Jewish consciousness to have permitted or even countenanced a Jewish role in this awful incident," insisted Julius Berman, the chairman of Conference of Presidents of Major American Jewish Organizations, in a press release. "Any suggestion that Israel took part in it or permitted it to occur must be categorically rejected." But, of course, it had happened. Israeli Jews understood this. Indeed, over 10 percent of Israel's population showed up at a massive protest demonstration hastily organized by Peace Now outside Tel Aviv's city hall, demanding an accounting from their government.[9]

The rejuvenation of Peace Now four years after its founding provided an important sense of legitimacy to dovish American Jews concerned about Israel's direction under Begin and Sharon. It brought back to the forefront the very kinds of Israelis whom Americans had learned to love. Its leaders were former generals, intelligence officers, and soldier/scholars, such as the historian Mordechai Bar-On, former staff chief to Moshe Dayan in the IDF, and Yehoshafat Harkabi, an influential former chief of military intelligence and counterterrorism adviser to two Israeli prime ministers. No less important were those Israeli writers that Americans cherished in their imaginations as the voices of the Israel they so admired, who also spoke up for Peace Now. These included the dashing, brilliant novelist and kibbutznik Amos Oz, a founder of the organization, and his comrades David Grossman, A. B. Yehoshua, Yehuda Amichai, and Amos Elon. Showing up on op-ed pages, in book tours, and in synagogue speaking engagements, these voices helped to legitimize the concerns of American Jews who felt Israel had lost its way.

A 1983 survey by the American Jewish Committee found that 48 percent of American Jews were "often troubled by the policies of the current Israeli government." Suddenly, the doors that the rabbis of Breira had found shut in their faces just a few years earlier were pushed open—at least some of them, partway and for the moment. "Our powerful communal disposition has always been to support Israel and rally around the flag," said Leonard Fein, a trusted adviser to Jewish federations and founder and editor of the respected Jewish general interest magazine, *Moment*. "The problem is that the flag now is in a suburb of Beirut, and that's a long way to go for a rally. Some people dropped off along the way—at the Litani River, [in Southern Lebanon] to be exact." "All of the exclamation points are being bent now into question marks," was the way the influential Reform rabbi Balfour Brickner, of the Stephen Wise Free Synagogue in Manhattan, put it to a *New York Times* reporter.[10]

It was not as if traditional boundaries disappeared. New Jewish Agenda (NJA)—a successor organization to Breira, but with a younger demographic, and led by veterans of the antiwar, feminist, and gay rights movements of the late 1960s—found itself no more welcome in the world of professional organizations than Breira had been. Its advertisements condemning the invasion and arguing on behalf of Palestinian rights in the language of typical anti-imperialist discourse (as well as Jewish texts) appeared above the signatures of 600 American Jews, including 39 rabbis. It eventually boasted 23 chapters and 2,500 members, but it never really achieved critical mass beyond movement types and college students. Its $118,000 1982 budget came to almost exactly one-twentieth of the amount earned at a single fund-raising dinner addressed by Menachem Begin, where NJA members chanted and held protest signs outside.[11]

Journalists naturally took notice of the changing atmosphere surrounding the Israel/Palestine debate. Tom Hundley, a foreign correspondent with the *Chicago Tribune* for nineteen years, found that "suddenly every-one realized that Israel could be criticized and the world went on." The *Washington Post*'s Al Friendly, previously noted for his letter to Israel's press coordinator about having been "happy" to have won awards for his pro-Israel reporting, because it had been a case where "the white hats licked the black ones," now wrote to condemn the "slaughters" he had witnessed. His headline read "Israel: Recollections and Regrets." He decried the Israeli government's "full capitulation to the religious ex-tremists" as well as its "shameless abandonment of Resolution 242." He wondered whether he had been "expecting more than was possible—that Israel could remain the country with a conscience, a home for honor, a treasury for the values of mind and soul," instead of what it had now become: "merely a nation like any other, its unique splendor lost."[12]

Neoconservative pundits reacted furiously to the newly critical report-ing on Israel and sought to destroy the personal and professional reputa-tions of those whom its members deemed responsible. One of the earliest of these counterattacks was penned, unsurprisingly, by Martin Peretz, owner and self-appointed editor-in-chief of *The New Republic*. Returning from an IDF-escorted trip to Lebanon, Peretz warned readers, "Much of what you have read in the newspapers about the war in Lebanon—and even more of what you have seen and heard on television—is simply not true." Peretz particularly objected to what he termed reporters' "relent-less trolling of the PLO and its partisans about civilian casualties." For the truth, he relied instead on an unnamed "Arab friend" in Jerusalem, who he said had "coyly" admitted to him that "Arabs exaggerate." This was a remarkably generous description in the Peretz lexicon, given the fact that he typically termed Arabs to be "violent, fratricidal, unreliable, primitive and crazed," "cruel, belligerent, [and] intolerant," and "murder-ous and grotesque," among other epithets. His exceptional friend not-withstanding, Arabs could not be trusted as sources: "I actually believe that Arabs are merely feigning outrage when they protest what they call American (or Israeli) 'atrocities,'" he said. Sadly, Arabs possessed a "na-tional characterological inability to compromise"; they also "behave[d] like lemmings." In Peretz's view, one could almost be grateful to the Is-raelis for killing so many of them, what with their attachment to "closed schools, rapes, molestations," and so on. Peretz's hope, he told an interviewer, was to see Israel turn the Palestinians "into just another crushed nation, like the Kurds or the Afghans," referencing peoples that had been (temporarily) crushed by the Iraqi and Soviet dictatorships, respectively. As *The New Republic* literary editor Leon Wieseltier admitted not long afterward, "Marty really put the fear of the devil into the media after Lebanon."[13]

Causing an even greater stir was Norman Podhoretz's July 1982 *Commentary* essay "J'Accuse." Borrowing his title from the famous Émile Zola essay from the days of the trial of Alfred Dreyfus, Podhoretz insisted that everyone who refused to take Israel's side was guilty "not merely of anti-Semitism but of the broader sin of faithlessness to the interests of the United States and indeed to the values of Western civilization as a whole." Like Peretz, Podhoretz insisted that the criticism Israel now faced had nothing to do with its actions, which had been, without exception, exemplary. It was instead a mere manifestation of heretofore hidden antisemitism and Jewish self-hatred on the part of those who had previously felt compelled to hide it. Before the invasion, Podhoretz said, he had detected "unambiguously venomous attacks on Israel" only in "marginal sectors of American political culture like the *Village Voice* and the *Nation* on the far Left"—whose circulations dwarfed that of *Commentary*, which he slyly sought to equate with the lunatic right-wing Liberty Lobby. Now, however, he was reading similarly critical comments from the likes of the liberal *New York Times* columnist Anthony Lewis, the much-respected Harvard University political scientist Stanley Hoffmann, and former assistant secretary of state Harold Saunders. "Their persistent hectoring of Israel" was "endangering Israel's very existence." He mocked the notion that Israel's critics could have had any motive save its destruction.[14]

Podhoretz was particularly incensed by Lewis, whose use of the word "exterminate" to describe Israel's plan for the PLO's presence in Lebanon he judged to be a purposeful equation of Israeli Jews with Nazis. In Podhoretz's view, this was typical of Jews like Lewis, who had "the effrontery to instruct Israel on how to insure its security," along with "the shamelessness to pronounce moral judgment upon the things Israel does to protect itself." Even more offensive than Lewis's "constant hectoring" on the *Times* op-ed page was its editors' willingness to publish authors who did not even pretend to like Israel. "Thus no sooner had the Israelis set foot in Lebanon than the Palestinian-American professor Edward Said was to be found on the Op-Ed page of the *New York Times*." He further complained that "books by Said like *The Question of Palestine* had been widely and sympathetically reviewed in the very media he indiscriminately denounce[d] for being anti-Arab."

Perhaps the worst offender for Podhoretz in his lengthy list of indictments was former assistant secretary of state George W. Ball. In Podhoretz's view, Ball, writing in *Foreign Affairs*, the prestigious publication of the Council on Foreign Relations, saw fit to "claim to be telling the Israelis harsh truths for their own good as a real friend should, on the evident assumption that he had a better idea than they did of how to ensure their security, and even survival." In the Johnson administration, Ball had been a famous dove, constantly warning against the folly of war in Vietnam. (He had also been Jimmy Carter's first choice to be secretary of state, but Carter was warned that anyone who wrote so critically of Israel could not hope to be confirmed in the Senate.) Fighting a two-front war, Podhoretz sought to simultaneously delegitimize all criticism of Israel and revive America's attachment to foreign military adventures—and Ball was understood to be the enemy in both cases. That Ball's critique of US support for Israel could be treated respectfully in any forum—much less *Foreign Affairs*—was doubly offensive. According to Podhoretz and the neocons he led, "Israel has dramatically refuted the 'lessons of Vietnam,'" and now, thanks to Israel, America was ready to go to war again.[15]

Alas, rather than refuting the "lessons of Vietnam," Israel's Lebanon adventure reinforced them. Israel had attempted to solve a political problem by military means and entered into a quagmire that would entrap its troops for decades. At Sabra and Shatila, it experienced its own version of America's massacre at My Lai. Israel had undermined its global reputation and seen its soldiers kill and be killed without improving its citizens' physical security in any discernible way. The Lebanon incursion split the citizenry down the middle and gave rise to a massive peace movement demanding accountability that had been previously lacking. Most significantly, it discredited Israel's political leadership, which was revealed as simultaneously dishonest and incompetent, leaving its citizens divided and dispirited about their future. And finally, it actually increased the threat the country faced. The PLO in southern Lebanon was not replaced by Israel-friendly Phalangists, but by a far more threatening adversary, Hezbollah, a powerful Shi'ite militia acting as a proxy for both the Iranians and the Syrians. Hezbollah reduced Lebanon's ability to control its own borders and threatens Israel today with advanced weaponry in a fashion that the Palestinians could never have imagined. Such judgments, however, were beside the point, which was to warn journalists and others who might cast a critical eye on Israel: Cross our line and you know what to expect.

Israel's defenders had reason to be concerned about the turn the debate was now taking in the US media, but Israel enjoyed advantages in that arena that could not be measured in column inches. Back in 1965, when the *Washington Post* reported that Israel seemed like "a little America," it would have been easy to point out the myriad and fundamental differences between the two. From the outset of the Arab/Israeli conflict through to the present, as the cultural historian Michelle Mart has demonstrated, Israelis came to be viewed by Americans, whether journalists or not, as "surrogate Americans." Jewish Israelis were "insiders" sharing in a "Judeo-Christian civilization," while Arabs were and would remain "outsiders."[16]

What's more, for much of the 1970s and 1980s, thanks to the actions of the PLO, "Arab" often implied "terrorist" in American popular culture. The 1977 blockbuster film *Black Sunday* featured a football stadium full of Americans held hostage by a joint team of Palestinian and German terrorists. The Americans survive only because of the wit and bravery of an Israeli Mossad agent, who saves the day, while the FBI stands all but paralyzed on the (literal) sidelines. This was something that Arabs, especially desperate, disenfranchised Palestinian Arabs, were never going to be able to overcome in the minds of either journalists or their audiences. The fact of the frequently close relationships between so many Hollywood executives and stars with Israeli politicians and diplomats only provided another incentive to champion the Israeli cause whenever possible in film, television, and other pop culture forms. Three separate films were made in the aftermath of Israel's spectacular rescue of its citizens from Uganda's Entebbe Airport in 1974; yet another one appeared in 2018. No wonder, in John le Carré's 1983 novel *The Little Drummer Girl*, a Palestinian bomb maker laments, just before he is killed by Israeli agents, "Why are we not making Hollywood movies about great struggle?"[17]

As a dark-skinned and (mostly) Muslim people, Palestinians remained "other" to Americans in a way Israeli Jews were not. It is no coincidence, in this regard, that the first personality to break through into the mainstream discourse on behalf of the Palestinian cause was the Columbia University professor and overall Renaissance man Edward Said. Handsome, impeccably attired in bespoke Saville Row suits, enviably eloquent, enormously respected in the academy for his trailblazing literary criticism—and a concert-level pianist to boot—this Princeton- and Harvard-educated Christian Palestinian living in exile on the Upper West Side of Manhattan presented as the very opposite of Yasser Arafat or any other PLO spokesperson. Rather, he was someone to whom American journalists—and by extension their audiences— could relate.

Said made his first appearance as a pro-Palestinian voice in the mainstream media in 1973 on the *New York Times* op-ed page. There, he argued that the Palestinians were viewed, when viewed at all, as merely "the disruptor of Israel's existence," not unlike "cigarette ash." When Said was given time to speak on a mainstream media outlet, readers and viewers were likely in for a shock, and the institution's owner would be on the receiving end of protests from outraged Jewish groups and individuals. With the possible exceptions of Said's friend and fellow world-famous intellectual dissident Noam Chomsky—or perhaps the unrepentant Stalinist press critic Alexander Cockburn, or the acid-tongued novelist Gore Vidal—no one given even occasional access to the mainstream media was remotely as critical of the coverage Israel enjoyed in the mainstream media. Over time, however, Said came to question the value of his role in the debate. He found, he said, a "deep media compliance...so that effective, and especially narrative, renderings of the Palestine-Israel contest are either attacked with near-unanimous force or ignored."[18]

The fact that for many years it often felt as if Edward Said was the only Palestinian whose phone number appeared in the Rolodexes of the entire population of US media bookers added only further to the frustration of the eloquent-but-angry leftist literary theorist. According to an assessment published in *The Guardian* two years before his death from leukemia in 2003, Said was "arguably the most influential intellectual of our time." Reviewing his memoir five years earlier, Janny Scott of the *New York Times* had called him "one of the most influential literary and cultural critics in the world." And yet, upon his passing, the *Times'* editors assigned his obituary to Richard Bernstein, a pro-Israel neoconservative, who authored an account filled with critical comments about Said's political beliefs. The piece was then buried deep inside the paper—a practice usually reserved for dead dictators. Moreover, from the time of his death to the present, Said has never been replaced. Literally no one in the Palestinian camp ever came to be treated as a sufficiently respected commentator worthy of a regular presence on political chat shows or influential op-ed pages. According to one scholar's research, published in 2020, during the previous fifty years fewer than 2 percent of the nearly 2,500 op-ed articles published in the *New York Times* that addressed Palestinians and the issues facing them were authored by Palestinians. This was twice the percentage achieved by the *Washington Post*, however. In *The New Republic* during this fifty-year period, the magazine published over 500 articles on the subject, and the number of Palestinians invited to contribute totaled zero.[19]


It can be a fraught matter to try to address media coverage of Israel in a critical manner, because it can so easily sound as if one is falling into age-old antisemitic tropes. And contemporary antisemites do continue to deploy these with increasing frequency both in the United States and abroad—something Israel's defenders are always pointing out as a means of ensuring that the discussion never takes place. But the fact is that many owners of media institutions, as well as editors, publishers, producers, reporters, and especially pundits, are Jewish, and therefore can have emotional and sometimes family attachments to Israel (your author included). And even if they aren't Jewish, many of the people they work with, and with whom they socialize, or who sign their checks, are. And since the natural position of American Jews since 1967 has been to care deeply about Israel's safety and security, the manner in which news about it is reported has become a matter of often obsessive concern. In a few cases, certain wealthy Jews have appeared to purchase media properties with the explicit goal of ensuring that Israel receives favorable coverage. This was unquestionably the case with Martin Peretz and *The New Republic* during the thirty-four years he owned it, as well as with real estate magnate Mortimer Zuckerman, who was an activist owner (and self-appointed columnist) for *US News and World Report*, *The Atlantic Monthly*, and the *New York Daily News* while at the same time serving as chairman of the Conference of Presidents of Major American Jewish Organizations. The same goes without saying about Norman Podhoretz's *Commentary*, which was funded for decades by the American Jewish Committee.

Few Arabs and zero Palestinians enjoy these cultural connections. When the respected television journalist Don Hewitt, creator of *60 Minutes* on CBS, broadcast a tough report on the October 1990 "massacre" at the Temple Mount, in which Israeli police fired at a crowd of Muslim worshippers, killing seventeen of them, Lawrence Tisch, the network's CEO and a major contributor to Jewish causes, accused Hewitt of "betraying his people." More recently, when a multinational publisher purchased the popular website Politico in a deal valued at over $1 billion, its CEO said that every employee must understand that "support for Israel" was a condition of employment. Within the media, controversy over the sale of the news organization centered exclusively around union organizing at the company; the demand that it publish only supportive journalism about Israel received barely any mention at all. If one were one to substitute the word "Palestinians" for "Israel" in this or any of the above stories, they become impossible to imagine. These are all advantages in the media, and, by extension, in politics and public opinion, that are literally beyond measurement—all the more so because the specter— and accusation—of antisemitism that accompanies the topic serves as a powerful tool of self-censorship before the issue is even raised.[20]

To the Israelis and their allies, however, these advantages were not (and would never be) enough. The discord inspired by the Lebanon invasion served as a significant shock to their system. As part of their effort to reclaim their advantages, the Israelis commissioned a survey of newspaper coverage of the conflict: according to Ambassador Moshe Arens, only fourteen of forty-eight outlets studied earned a positive rating. The Anti-Defamation League commissioned a separate study of the coverage of the Lebanon war and found a "lack of objective perspective," a term that—ironically—had no objective meaning, given who was making the judgment, but certainly sounded critical. More extreme groups, such as the far-right Americans for a Safe Israel, filed a petition with the Federal Communications Commission demanding the revocation of NBC's broadcast license owing to its allegedly harsh coverage of Israel during the war. So furious was Ariel Sharon that he filed a $50 million lawsuit against *Time* magazine for allegedly overstating his role in inviting the massacres at Sabra and Shatila. Sharon lost his suit, but he won considerable support from American Jewish leaders, who made the cause of alleged bias against Israel in the media a first-order priority for Jewish community professionals and a new battlefield for Israel, fought together with its American soldiers.[21]

To try to figure out how to press what they perceived to be their innate advantages in the media, the Israelis invited a group of American journalists and media experts to Jerusalem in the summer of 1983 to plot out a strategy to improve the treatment it received. When the fact of the meeting was revealed, many in the media found the idea comical, but they could not ignore it, given the feelings of so many of their readers, viewers, and listeners. After all, this was a time when the American-reared Israelis Moshe Arens and Benjamin Netanyahu were among the most frequently booked guests on Ted Koppel's ABC news program *Nightline*—easily the most influential news program on television—while it refused to book any PLO representatives. "We don't feel the PLO is a counterpoint to Israel," explained its top producer, Rick Kaplan, who was among the journalists who met with the Israelis. Both ABC and the *Washington Post* agreed to allow representatives of Israel and American Jewish organizations inside their newsrooms to observe their newsgathering and reporting process, in search of evidence of anti-Israel bias—a concession that would be unthinkable for almost any other lobby or self-interested organization.[22]

The post-Lebanon period also led to the creation of a small industry of censorious pro-Israel organizations with the aim of doing what Peretz, Podhoretz, and others had done during the war: discrediting anyone in the media who dissented from the pro-Israel position. These well-funded groups, including the Committee for Accuracy in Middle East Reporting in America (CAMERA) and Facts and Logic About the Middle East (FLAME), made the *New York Times* their main target. Rarely, if ever, have any of their studies found the paper's coverage to be fair or balanced. In fact, the *Times'* overall coverage—like that of the US media as a whole—was favorable to the Israeli point of view, even as the paper did begin to display an unprecedented willingness to both question the official version of events and tell the story of Israel's victims. Compared to the coverage in the *Times'* French counterpart, *Le Monde*; its British competitor, *The Guardian*; and even Israel's own excellent newspaper, *Haaretz*, the *Times'* coverage—like almost all US mainstream coverage—displayed a decidedly pro-Israel hue. Palestinians often died in the passive voice, as if no one in particular was dropping the bombs or aiming the missiles that killed them. During the 1982 incursion, the combined news coverage of the *New York Times*, the *Washington Post*, and the *Los Angeles Times* justified Israel's actions twice as often as those of its Arab adversaries.[23]

Ironically, while the *New York Times* is often the first example cited by pro-Israel media critics for alleged pro-Palestinian bias, it is also the first example cited by pro-Palestinian media critics for its alleged pro-Israel bias. This is due in part to the fact of its being by far the most influential and important foreign-news source in the United States—indeed, in the English-speaking world. Former Begin spokesman Zev Chafets explained that within the Israeli government attention was paid to the *Times* correspondent first, with whoever was US ambassador to Israel at the time following closely behind. The paper had "primacy" because "if it was in the *Times* it was automatically going to be everywhere else." The *Times'* coverage of Israel was no less a focus of attention owing to its special status as what might be called the "hometown" paper of American Jewry. ("I love the *Times* like it was my child or my parent," explains Miriam Nessler in Paul Rudnick's 2020 play *Coastal Elites*. "On the census, when they ask for religion, I don't put Jewish, I put the *New York Times*.") When former *Times* Jerusalem Bureau chief Jodi Rudoren took the job as editor of the Jewish *Forward* in 2019, she told a former colleague, Ben Smith, that she hoped to make it the "Jewish *New York Times*." His reply: "But the *New York Times* is already the Jewish *New York Times*." That Smith, the *Times'* media columnist at the time, was a former reporter at *The Forward* was perhaps merely coincidental, but neither was it surprising, given what Rudoren described as "radical overrepresentation" of Jews in the mainstream media.[24]

The perception of the *Times'* Israel/Palestine coverage was complicated, however, by the legacy of Arthur Hays Sulzberger, the paper's publisher from 1935 to 1961. If a novelist wished to create a character to represent the genuinely "self-hating" Jew, he could do worse than model it after Sulzberger. Sulzberger was an antisemite in his hiring practices and an anti-Zionist in his politics. He directed the paper's indefensibly—whether judged by moral, intellectual, or journalistic standards—scant coverage of the Shoah as it took place. (When accused by a fellow editor of being antisemitic, his reply was, "Well, maybe I am.") In 2010, the *Times* executive editor Joseph Lelyveld admitted that this history had led to a "deep-seated feeling that the *New York Times* was made up of self-hating Jews," and, by extension, that it was reflexively hostile to Israel. (Ironically, the man speaking was the son of Rabbi Arthur Lelyveld, the former president of the American Jewish Congress, who had accused Breira rabbis and scholars of wishing to leave Israel "defenseless before murderers and terrorists.")[25]

Almost certainly, the single most influential writer in describing the reality of the 1982 war for Americans was *Times* foreign correspondent Thomas Friedman, who by 2002 had become the recipient of three Pulitzer Prizes. A graduate of Brandeis with a master's degree in modern Middle East studies from Oxford, Friedman was traumatized by what he had seen in the aftermath of Sabra and Shatila. As a self-described "three-day-a-year Jew" who had always treated Israel as a "badge of pride," he now found himself shocked into another place entirely. "The Israel I met on the outskirts of Beirut," he insisted, in his massively best-selling book on the war, *From Beirut to Jerusalem*, "was not the heroic Israel I had been taught to identify with." And so he "buried...every illusion I held about the Jewish state." Friedman felt that "something had gone terribly wrong" with that country. Even so, his employer was not ready to take this voyage with him—or even to trust his eyewitness reporting. When Friedman filed a story describing what he had seen in the air and on the ground—"Israeli planes, gunboats and artillery rained indiscriminate shellfire all across West Beirut today"—and his editors excised the word "indiscriminate," Friedman protested: "You are afraid to tell our readers and those who might complain to you that the Israelis are capable of indiscriminately shelling an entire city." And they were. *Times* editors, like most journalists, and indeed most Americans, could not believe Israel would do this even as it was reported by their own Jewish Brandeis grad reporter who had personally witnessed what he was describing.[26]

In a lengthy 2011 study of the history of the *Times*' coverage of Israel produced for Harvard University's Shorenstein Center for the Press and Politics, former *Times* reporter Neil A. Lewis Jr. found a pattern that was extremely sympathetic, almost *Exodus*-like, for a period of decades. The Palestinians, in contrast, were defined largely as a diplomatic problem for the nations of the region, without the status of a people entitled to self-determination. The paper's tone began to change in the late 1970s, and the study attributed this to a series of factors, including journalistic ones, such as the lack of a close relationship with Menachem Begin's government ministers in comparison to that enjoyed by reporters with Israel's Labor Party, and "the development of non-governmental organizations (NGO's) within Israel as advocates for the Palestinians[,] which gave Western journalists a ready and credible source which could be used to criticize the Israeli government." No less powerful were what Lewis described as "the political actions of the Israeli government itself, notably the questionable invasion of Lebanon and its frequent brutal tactics employed to quell Palestinian unrest and threats of violence," along with its continually expansionist settlement policies, "often spoken about in epochal biblical terms," and, finally, the "emergence of Palestinian nationalism" and the sympathy this engendered in those who witnessed it.[27]

Even with all these changes, however, the parameters of the *Times'* coverage were almost always defined by Israel. For instance, Lewis noted, the word "Nakba"—the commonly used term among those sympathetic to the Palestinians to describe the "catastrophe" of 1948—did not appear in the paper of record until 1998. What's more, as the Friedman incident demonstrated, *Times* editors would sometimes—one has no idea how frequently—find occasion to censor their writers if they strayed too far from the pro-Israel position, even when those reporters were experts on the topic and their editors were not. In 1981, for instance, former Jerusalem correspondent David Shipler was assigned by the paper's *Book Review* to write about Jacobo Timerman, a Jewish Argentinian journalist and human rights advocate who had been jailed by that US-supported, neo-fascist regime before being allowed to emigrate to Israel. Timerman had been a hero to the US press when he had written about Argentina's crimes, but when Shipler quoted him saying that he had grown ashamed of being an Israeli, because of how the nation treated the Palestinians, the article was killed. Shipler described the silencing of Timerman on Israel—as opposed to Argentina—as "purely political in that they didn't want a person of Timerman's stature criticizing Israel."[28]

The more one knows about the inner workings of the *Times*, the more its consistent, if sometimes subtle, pro-Israel slant becomes understandable, even predictable. When A. M. "Abe" Rosenthal, executive editor of the paper from 1977 to 1988—and likely the last word in killing Shipler's piece and censoring Friedman—became a columnist for the paper's op-ed page the year of his forced retirement, his obsession with defending Israel at every turn came to verge on the ridiculous. (On November 30, 1947, when the *Times* reported Israel's victory in the UN partition vote the day before, it was twenty-five-year-old A. M. Rosenthal's byline that appeared atop its front page. The use of the initials, rather than his given name, Abraham, was done by order of the publisher, Arthur Hays

Sulzberger, who thought a name that was too Jewish would seem inappropriate for a *New York Times* reporter "in the showcase." Other "Abrahams" on the paper were similarly instructed.) Rosenthal's 2006 obituary in the Jewish *Forward*, written by an Orthodox Jewish former *Times* reporter he had hired to be its religion reporter, was headlined, "Abe Rosenthal: Editor and Advocate for Israel." The description was decidedly understated. Rosenthal's successor, Max Frankel, was his adversary at the paper in every way except one. "I was much more deeply devoted to Israel than I dared to assert," Frankel admitted afterward in his memoirs. "Fortified by my knowledge of Israel and my friendships there, I myself wrote most of our Middle East commentaries. As more Arab than Jewish readers recognized, I wrote them from a pro-Israel perspective." (In this regard, both Rosenthal and Frankel resembled the longtime gentile editorial page editor of the *Wall Street Journal*, Robert Bartley, who was comfortable admitting that "Shamir, Sharon, Bibi—whatever those guys want is pretty much fine by me.")[29]

The relationships between *Times* journalists and the Israelis charged with selling the country's image to Americans were evident in manifold ways. When Israel's New York consul general, Uri Savir, was called home in 1992, for example, he was treated to a farewell skit in his honor performed by two *Times* reporters, along with TV news anchors Dan Rather and Peter Jennings and the Hollywood stars Kathleen Turner and Ron Silver. (Rather would also address a 1992 fund raiser for the Jewish settlement inside Arab East Jerusalem, where he warned of a potential "Arab population explosion.") Sydney Gruson, vice chairman of the New York Times Company for much of this period, was a board member of the Council for a Beautiful Israel, an American/Israeli environmental group; David Shipler spoke at one of its fund raisers. Among Shipler's successors as Jerusalem correspondent, following Friedman, was Ethan Bronner, who was married to an Israeli woman; while he had the job, his son enlisted in the Israel Defense Forces. Jeffrey Goldberg, who himself served in the IDF, guarding Palestinian prisoners, before becoming an acclaimed journalist and editor-in-chief of *The Atlantic*, was offered the job of the paper's top Jerusalem correspondent, but turned it down. Once again, putting the word "Palestinian" in any of the above sentences would require the construction of an alternate universe. But for America's most influential news source, they barely raised an eyebrow.[30]

American Jews found themselves caught in a very special nightmare in late November 1985 when the news broke that US authorities had arrested an American Jew and his wife for spying on the US government for Israel. Jonathan and Anne Pollard had been desperately seeking to enter the Israeli embassy, begging for asylum, at the time of his arrest, on November 21, 1985, but its gates had remained locked. Anne attempted to flee but was arrested the next day.

The spying itself should not have shocked anyone. Israeli intelligence agencies had long been active in the United States. Indeed, they had conducted a number of extremely audacious operations, including the likely theft of enough highly enriched uranium from a small nuclear processing plant in Apollo, Pennsylvania, to make at least ten nuclear bombs. But Pollard was a home-grown American Jew. As if created in a laboratory by antisemitic scientists, he was fanatically committed to Israel—but he liked money, too. Raised as the son of a successful professor of microbiology at Notre Dame, Pollard told people that Israel had been with him "every waking moment since I can remember. The first flag I remember was the Israeli flag." Pollard and his wife enjoyed payments of hundreds of thousands of dollars in secret bank accounts, expensive jewelry, lavish meals, and long stays in five-star hotels and resorts across Europe, where they often traveled with the phony Israeli passports they had been issued.

Psychologically, Pollard was a mess. While working for Navy Field Operational Intelligence, he had his security clearance revoked in 1981 because of the avalanche of lies he was telling about his alleged back-channel relationship with South African spies. He was ordered to seek psychiatric treatment. Beginning in 1984, he began passing classified data to the Israeli Bureau of Scientific Relations, a top-secret office that answered directly to the prime minister and was originally created to guard the secrets of Israel's nuclear weapons effort and to secretly secure the materials it needed. Over time, Pollard managed to steal enough secret documents, according to federal prosecutors, "to fill a room...ten feet by six feet by six feet." Many of the documents contained technical information on National Security Agency projects designed to intercept foreign communications and to protect the identity of US agents and communications abroad. US intelligence officials told *The New Yorker's* Seymour Hersh that much of this information had made its way to the Soviets as well, either because there was a mole in Mossad or because the Israelis had traded it in exchange for emigration permits for Soviet Jews. And while the Israeli government insisted that Pollard had been run as a "rogue operation," this was a lie. But to protect its lies, Israel offered only the most pro forma cooperation with US efforts to recover, or at least understand, what information had been lost.

Pollard's lawyers made a deal with US authorities for a guilty plea in exchange for a twenty-year sentence. But Defense Secretary Caspar Weinberger upended that arrangement by sending the judge a still-secret briefing letter just before sentencing. The Pollards' own self-generated publicity did not help their cause. Anne Pollard told viewers on CBS's *60 Minutes* that she and her husband had only done "what our moral obligation was as Jews," and that she had "no regrets." In a letter to the *Jerusalem Post*, Pollard described his plea deal as a "judicial crucifixion," and then proceeded to violate the terms of his agreement by pleading his case in a pre-sentencing jailhouse interview with the same paper. Based on Weinberger's last-minute intervention, coupled with both Pollards' lack of remorse, Jonathan received a sentence of life in prison, while Anne got five years.[31]

For American Jews, Pollard was a veritable Frankenstein monster come to life, a Julius and Ethel Rosenberg–style case, but with Zionism playing the role originally cast for international communism. Not surprisingly, the official reaction of many American Jews was to reject the Pollards entirely. The American Jewish Committee's Hyman Bookbinder, for example, later said that Jews "wanted to wash our hands of him," lest support "give the wrong impression that American Jews are willing to do anything and everything that seems to be beneficial to Israel." After Pollard's sentencing, *Times* pundit William Safire warned that the Pollard case only encouraged "anti-Semites who charge that Jews everywhere are at best afflicted with dual loyalty and at worst are agents of a vast fifth column."

Israelis, yet again, were decidedly unimpressed by their American cousins' sensitivities. The liberal scholar Shlomo Avineri mocked what he judged to be the "nervousness, insecurity, and even cringing" of American Jews before their gentile neighbors. Pollard said much the same thing, albeit in language laced with bitterness and accusations of betrayal. With an impressive display of chutzpah, the Jew who had received hundreds of thousands of dollars to spy on his country for Israel attacked other Jews as nothing more than "pocket-book Zionists." To Pollard, mere "dual loyalty" was insufficient; Israel was entitled to "the unequivocal loyalty of every diaspora Jew—even if that entails placing one's life in harm's way." In a letter to a group of far-right Israeli politicians, Pollard even celebrated the Jewish terrorists—whom he called "patriots"—who had blown a leg off of one Arab mayor and the foot off of another in a series of 1980 Israeli car bombings. He said his only regret was the fact that the bombers had only done "half a job."[32]

From the standpoint of both American patriotism and simple human decency, Pollard was becoming more monstrous by the day. Even so, his support grew among Jews in Israel and in the United States. Initially, it appeared mostly among Orthodox rabbis, who routinely called him a "political prisoner." Eventually, however, even Reform and Conservative rabbis joined in, both individually and through their national bodies. (The ubiquitous lawyer and television pundit Alan Dershowitz went so far as to compare Pollard to Colonel Dreyfus.) Pollard was given Israeli citizenship in 1995 and eventually became a bargaining chip between the two countries. The Israelis sought to trade his freedom in exchange for fulfilling their legal obligations under agreements they had reached, under US auspices, with the Palestinians. The US Department of Defense and intelligence agencies continued to resist these deals, and so the saga went on until Pollard was finally paroled in 2015, having served the statutory minimum thirty years of his life sentence. In November 2020, President Donald Trump's Justice Department lifted Pollard's parole restrictions. On December 30, Pollard flew to Israel on a private jet provided by the right-wing American Jewish billionaire Sheldon Adelson, where he was met on the tarmac by Prime Minister Benjamin Netanyahu. Pollard praised the prime minister and kissed the ground in front of him, and

Netanyahu informed the American that he was "home." The two men then recited the "Shehecheyanu," a blessing of thanksgiving, together. Days later, on his final day in office, January 20, 2021, Trump pardoned Aviem Sella, the Israeli Air Force officer who had recruited Pollard. Sella had fled the United States at the time of Pollard's arrest, but had been indicted on three counts of espionage in absentia in 1987. Israel never agreed to extradite him, and he never served any time for his crimes.[33]

What is most impressive about the evolution of the Pollard case over time is the self-confidence of the Jews who came to support him. Pollard's crimes fit the antisemitic stereotype to perfection. He made himself into an even uglier caricature with his increasingly shrill jailhouse support for Jewish terrorists and his contempt for the patriotic American Jews who had kept their distance. And yet, much as they may have wished to, American Jews could not walk away from him. Israel wanted Pollard free, and so, therefore, did they; his crimes and their own concerns about the antisemitic stereotypes his behavior may have reinforced among gentile Americans would have to be set aside for another day.


On December 9, 1987, an IDF truck crashed into a line of cars, killing four passengers in the Jabalia refugee camp just outside Gaza City. The victims' funerals turned into mass demonstrations, and these developed into a spontaneous popular uprising—later known as the First Intifada. It was led not by the PLO in Tunis, or even recognized local authorities, but by stone-throwing young people who were apparently ready to risk whatever punishment came their way in order to demonstrate their resistance to continued Israeli rule. The Israeli reaction came swiftly. Prime Minister Rabin instructed his military to put down the teenage rock throwers with "might, power, beatings." So Israel's internal security service, the Shin Bet, went about grabbing the protesters off the streets and methodically breaking their bones. Within just three days, over three hundred Palestinians were being treated for these and even more severe injuries. Soon these same Palestinian teenagers were giving interviews to US journalists as they lay with arms and legs in traction—creating yet another public-relations disaster for the Jewish state.[34]

Rabin was unmoved. "What can we do now, go back to killing?" he asked his cabinet. Jewish leaders in the United States were in a panic but were reluctant to criticize or even disagree in public with Rabin, whose relationship with them spanned decades. In an off-the-record meeting with them, Henry Kissinger endorsed Rabin's strategy. He told them Israel needed to suppress the uprising "brutally and rapidly," adding, "The first step should be to throw out television, a la South Africa."[35]

The great transformation that the intifada inspired in the US debate was the humanization of the Palestinians. A key moment in this process was a weeklong broadcast on *Nightline*, in April 1988, that featured Israelis and Palestinians arguing with one another (they were physically separated by a symbolic wall). The series culminated in a town-hall-style meeting that was also rebroadcast on PBS stations, becoming a television event with few, if any, precedents. The series provided information and perspectives never previously seen or heard on American television. American viewers learned about what Palestinians had been forced to endure under Israeli rule. "Israel systematically destroyed 379 of 475 Arab villages" after 1948, one correspondent explained, and it had "dynamited another 1,300 homes in the West Bank and Gaza" since 1967. West Bank Palestinians had experienced the forced expulsion of "many teachers, doctors, lawyers, journalists, the natural leaders of the Palestinian community," as well as "highly visible brutal beatings, at times virtually random." These comments were more than offset by those sympathetic to Israel, who painted the PLO as a threat to its existence and the intifada as "a new kind of war for Israeli troops." But perhaps the most important aspect of the show was the (admittedly brief) replacement of Yasser Arafat's reviled image in the public sphere with a series of well-spoken, highly educated West Bank Palestinian diplomats, scholars, and professionals—including especially the scholars and soon-to-be Palestinian diplomats Saeb Erekat and Dr. Hanan Ashrawi—wearing Western attire and speaking directly to American audiences on behalf of their cause.[36]

Jews were hardly immune to the sympathetic picture these Palestinians painted. Even before the *Nightline* program aired, in February 1988, a *New York Times* op-ed, written by what were then likely Israel's four best-known literary figures—the poet Yehuda Amichai, the journalist

Amos Elon, and the novelists Amos Oz and A. B. Yehoshua—had urged American Jews to speak up. Titled "Israel Must End the Occupation," it condemned Rabin and company for their "refusal to face up to the root causes" of the conflict—a failure the authors termed "both immoral and futile." Albert Vorspan, a leading voice of Reform Jewry, mused aloud in the *New York Times Magazine* that following the "euphoric mood after the Six-Day War," when American Jews had "felt 10 feet tall," they were now "suffering under the shame and stress of pictures of Israeli brutality televised nightly" and would have liked "to crawl into a hole." Vorspan deemed this depressing reality to be "the price we pay for having made of Israel an icon—a surrogate faith, surrogate synagogue, surrogate God."[37]

Rabbi Arthur Hertzberg, who, when he headed the American Jewish Congress, had made life so difficult for Jimmy Carter whenever the president had dared to utter the words "Palestinian" and "homeland" in the same sentence, now became an open and bitter critic of Israeli behavior and of the sorts of Jewish leaders he himself had been until his 180-degree turnaround. "American Jews preferred to see Israel as it was depicted by Leon Uris in *Exodus*, in which Israelis were painted as totally noble and Arabs were the Middle Eastern equivalent of the murderous Indians of Hollywood Westerns," he wrote. "When support for Israel became the 'secular religion' of most American Jews, Israel had to be presented as a homeland that was superior to all other homelands." Throughout these *Exodus*-influenced decades, Hertzberg admitted, "most American Jews have not wanted to know what was really happening in Israel." Now, however, they found themselves face-to-face with the "uncomfortable fact that there is a right wing in Israel that is so insistent on its ideology that it would rather live amid violence than search for compromises." The problem with American Jewish leaders, as he judged them, however, was their addiction to personal briefings and high-profile dinners with top Israeli officials and other Jewish leaders at fund-raising events and such. "To be in open conflict with a sitting Prime Minister, even one of a divided government, is a disaster for any leader within the Jewish establishment. He will be treated coolly in Jerusalem. He will not be able to return home to tell his board of trustees of his intimate conversation with the Prime Minister in Jerusalem, or carry messages of supposed importance between Jerusalem and Washington."[38]

As was now the custom whenever Israel's behavior caused controversy at home, the argument over its harsh response to the intifada soon transformed into an argument about bias in the media coverage it received. In *Commentary*, Norman Podhoretz professed to see "the opening of a third phase in the Arab war against Israel." This time, "instead of troops and tanks and planes, the Arabs resorted to stones and Molotov cocktails; and instead of dispatching trained operatives to murder Jewish civilians, they sent young Palestinians into the streets of Gaza and the West Bank against Israeli soldiers." He judged this alleged conspiracy to be "enormously effective," as "it had the intended result of shifting the balance of sympathy among liberals decisively to the side of the Palestinians and against the Israelis," and thereby "creat[ing] a groundswell of liberal support for the establishment of a Palestinian state in those territories." Rather typically of his analytical structures, Podhoretz compared this development to the Holocaust, only this time with liberal American Jews playing the role of Hitler's henchmen. "After Hitler," he mused, "we had vowed over and over that we would never again stand by in helpless passivity and watch a community of our fellow Jews being destroyed for the crime of being Jewish. And yet this time it was worse, much worse. This time we were not merely passive. This time we helped the destruction along."[39]

Though many tried, few could match Podhoretz for anti-liberal vitriol. One could see the contest underway in *The New Republic*, however, which styled itself, in the words of its flamboyant literary editor, Leon Wieseltier, as "the cops" of the discourse on Israel. In this angry debate, nearly thirty years after its appearance, *Exodus* remained a touchstone. Neoconservative pundit Charles Krauthammer complained that "no one shunned association with Otto Preminger's Israel" (leaving aside its entirely imaginary existence). He attacked, instead, the "escapism" that had led Israel's critics "to believe that unilateral autonomy or unilateral withdrawal or a PLO state will rid Israel of the Palestinian issue. In fact, it will turn Israel into the Palestinian issue. The question will then not be who rules Nablus. It will be who rules Haifa." Owner and editor-in-chief Martin Peretz, as he had done so frequently in the past, cast the problem as a racial one: its cause was "the generic afflictions of Arab politics, the principled resistance to compromise, the intoxicating effects of language, the endless patience for vengeance."[40]

But the combination of images of Israeli troops deliberately breaking the bones of rock-throwing teenagers—or teenagers who happened to be present while others threw rocks—combined with the presentation of dignified, eloquent, homegrown spokespeople for the Palestinians—both reaching directly into the homes of Americans—had created new conditions for debate, and these attacks no longer enjoyed the resonance they had only six years earlier. In the same issue of *The New Republic* containing Peretz's and Krauthammer's fulminations, one could find Wieseltier taking American Jewish leaders to task for "throwing sand in the eyes of the American Jewish community, morally pampering it," and generally treating Israel as if it were still the country so many *Exodus*-influenced Jews had imagined it to be. The pro-Israel side had long refused to grant any legitimacy to Palestinian arguments, but denial had become politically unsustainable. The Cold War was receding, and the Israel/Palestine conflict was coming into focus in an entirely different light, one with countless prismatic effects depending on the angle chosen by any given viewer. Ironically, the debate over Israel/Palestine would only grow more vituperative as it became more difficult for its traditional powers to police it.[41]

# CHAPTER 13

# "FUCK THE JEWS"

BETWEEN FRANKLIN ROOSEVELT'S VICTORY IN 1932 AND DONALD Trump's loss in 2020, only two incumbent US presidents—one Democrat and one Republican—failed to win reelection. Not at all coincidentally, both found themselves facing the electorate on the wrong side of the American Israel Public Affairs Committee and the leaders of the American Jewish establishment. Obviously, multiple factors contributed to their losses, and it is impossible to attribute responsibility to just one. But with 45 percent of the Jewish vote in 1980, Jimmy Carter's was the worst performance by a Democrat since 1920. And George H. W. Bush's 11 percent share of the Jewish vote in 1992 proved to be easily the worst by a Republican since Barry Goldwater's blowout in 1964.[1]

The first Bush's tenacity in taking on Israel during his presidency remains rather mysterious, given the ideological flexibility that characterized his political career. The Texan by way of Greenwich Country Day School, Phillips Academy, and Yale had readjusted his positions so frequently that by the time Ronald Reagan named him as his running mate in 1980, people joked that Bush had placed "his principles" in a "blind trust." He prided himself on his ability to bond with leaders of other countries. But early on, Bush came to hate the Israeli prime minister that he had to deal with as president—Yitzhak Shamir—with an uncharacteristic passion. Robert Gates, who served as Bush's deputy assistant for national security affairs before being named CIA director (during what would become decades of service in national security positions under Democratic and Republican presidents), later noted that of all the presidents he had served, literally "every" one of them would, at some point in his presidency, "get so pissed off at the Israelis that he couldn't speak." They would all "rant and rave around the Oval Office" out of "frustration about knowing that there was so little they could do about it because of domestic politics." But when asked if he could think of a single leader Bush "actively disliked," Gates named only Shamir. This lack of sympathy opened the door for Bush's secretary of state and lifelong close confidant, James Baker, to treat Israel pretty much as the State Department had almost always wished to, but had been stymied from doing so by the president's own wishes, together with the calculations of his political advisers about where his true interests lay.[2]

Shamir had replaced Menachem Begin as both head of the Likud party and prime minister in 1983, serving in the latter role just for a year before becoming prime minister again from 1986 to 1992. A former pre-state terrorist, and later, a Mossad agent, Shamir had chosen his Hebrew name after a mythological worm, or perhaps a substance—the text is unclear on this point—described in the Talmud as having the ability to burrow through stone, iron, and diamond. Taciturn by nature, he was also uncomfortable speaking English. Shamir communicated none of Begin's old-world charm, moral seriousness, or disarming honesty. More substantively, his political views had apparently been fired in the kiln of some of the most uncompromising of the pre-state Jewish terror cells.

At an April 1989 meeting, during Shamir's second term as prime minister, Bush told the Israeli leader that his plans for accelerated settlement construction in the West Bank were "an issue of great concern to us." Shamir responded that "the settlements ought not to be such a problem." This was what every Israeli leader had told every American president since the settlement-building process had begun soon after the 1967 war. The "problem" was always Arab recalcitrance, Palestinian terrorism, and the lack of an acceptable partner for peace—whatever. But just as Jimmy Carter had misunderstood Menachem Begin at Camp David on this very issue and felt himself to have been betrayed afterward, so, too, did Bush when he learned that Shamir was merely giving him a brush-off. When Shamir went back home and announced the creation of even more settlements on the West Bank, Bush felt Shamir had played him for a "fool."[3]

The source of the problem was the influx into Israel of over a million Soviet Jews in the wake of the slow-motion collapse of the Soviet Union. With the unflinching support of AIPAC, neoconservatives, and evangelicals, Shamir sought to exploit the housing crisis as an opportunity to not only defuse the "population bomb" that threatened the state's Jewish majority but also to further entrench the occupation. Bush, according to aides, went "ballistic" when he learned that Shamir was planning to house massive numbers of Soviet immigrants in the occupied territories, including East Jerusalem. He had understood from Shamir that fewer than 1 percent of the new immigrants would be housed in all the territories combined.[4]

As the United States knit together a multinational coalition to expel Saddam Hussein's forces from Kuwait, following the Iraqi dictator's August 1990 invasion of that tiny, oil-rich nation, Bush and Baker succeeded in keeping Israel out of the Gulf War—a necessity for retaining the support of the Arab and Muslim-majority nations in the coalition. This was not easy to achieve, as Iraq had launched forty-two Scud missiles into Israel proper. While they did little material damage, the missile threat forced much of the country's population into bomb shelters with gas masks at the ready. The Israelis longed to retaliate but agreed to hold back in return for a $2 billion bump in their annual US aid package.[5]

High on the drug of a smashing military victory, Baker took the opportunity of a newly scrambled postwar political order—owing not only to the invasion, but also the chaos in what was about to become, in December 1991, the "former Soviet Union"—to try to pick up where Jimmy Carter had left off and solve the Arab/Israeli conflict. Baker was not much on scripture, and his heart surely did not bleed for the plight of the Palestinians. But he liked making deals, and he thought he saw an opening. Bush expected to coast to reelection in 1992 with or without significant Jewish support. Moreover, as lifelong Republicans who had made their fortunes in the Texas oil industry, both Baker and Bush came into office with few ties, both in terms of personal relationships and in terms of ideological concerns, to Israel and the American Jewish community. They were uniquely willing, therefore, to put the screws on Israel.

Meanwhile, the PLO had continued its nearly perfect record of terrible political judgment by noisily taking the side of Saddam Hussein during the war. The United States had already cut off all dialogue with the PLO following a series of particularly brutal terrorist attacks both in Israel and against Jews abroad. Yasser Arafat had not ordered them, but he also refused to condemn them. Iraq's quick collapse in the five-week war, ending in February 1991, left Arafat and company weakened by every measure: morally, diplomatically, and financially. Baker likely reasoned that it was a propitious time to get the Palestinians to accept conditions they had hitherto been unwilling to consider. Why he thought he could steamroll Shamir into offering them anything at all, however, is likely explained only by hubris.

Baker revived Jimmy Carter's idea of a Geneva conference for all concerned parties, including the Russians, with the hope of settling everything once and for all. The only Palestinians the Israelis would agree to talk to, however, were those without direct ties to the PLO who did not live in East Jerusalem. Following painstaking negotiations, the sides agreed to allow East Jerusalemites to be included in a Palestinian/Jordanian delegation. It took eight trips back and forth to the nations in question, coupled with considerable bouts of screaming, cajoling, and (likely) lying, but Baker finally got his conference. It began in Madrid on October 30, 1991, and would continue in the form of topically based working groups in various locations through November 1993. Bush and Baker touted the fact that they had, for the first time, succeeded in gathering all the parties involved to meet face-to-face—an implicit recognition of Israel by its neighbors. With regard to "facts on the ground," however, nothing changed. Shamir had gone along with Baker's plans for a conference, albeit after imposing demanding conditions, but he proved unwilling to consider parting with even a millimeter of the West Bank, thereby strangling any hopes for a "land for peace" deal in its metaphorical cradle. Israel was going to continue expanding Jewish settlements in the West Bank and expected US taxpayers to lay out the cash to make it happen.

Conflict between Shamir and Bush and Baker had been simmering well before the failed conference began. In June 1990, Baker all but invited it by going public with, for a diplomat, remarkably undiplomatic language before the House Committee on Foreign Affairs. After complaining of what he considered to be a series of needlessly provocative Israeli actions, he theatrically announced the phone number for the White House switchboard and added, "When you're serious about peace, call us." When he heard that Israel's deputy foreign minister had accused the United States of building its Israel policy "on a foundation of distortion and lies," he had the fellow barred from even entering the State Department building. Robert Gates, then the deputy national security adviser, had met the same Israeli official and been so "offended" by what he termed to be his "glibness," and his "arrogance and outlandish ambition," that he told his boss, National Security Adviser Brent Scowcroft, that he ought not to be allowed on White House grounds either. The gentleman's name: Benjamin Netanyahu.[6]

Yet another conflict between the United States and Israel arose in June 1991, when Israel asked the United States to guarantee $10 billion in loans to build housing for newly arriving Soviet immigrants. Bush and Baker had made clear that any loan guarantees had to be conditioned on a halt to Israeli settlement in the occupied territories—trading settlements for resettlement, wags put it. The Israelis had been assured by their allies at AIPAC that Congress could make the loans happen with or without Bush and Baker's support. But relations between Bush, Baker, and AIPAC had begun badly and got worse from there. Baker had first addressed the group's annual conference in May 1989, speaking more bluntly than any secretary of state had done before him. He called on

Israel to "lay aside, once and for all, the unrealistic vision of a greater Israel," to stop all settlement construction, to forget about the annexation of any part of the occupied territories, and to reach out to the Palestinians "as neighbors who deserve political rights." All of these positions were consistent with those of previous administrations, and Baker followed them with a similar list of necessary concessions to be asked of the Palestinians, including an end to the intifada, a change in the PLO charter calling for Israel's destruction, and a willingness to reach out to the Israelis. But the businesslike presentation and the lack of fulsome praise to which all AIPAC audiences had become accustomed set heads spinning and clearly presaged trouble ahead.[7]

AIPAC began organizing in Congress to pass legislation to give Israel its unconditional $10 billion loan guarantee. It appeared to have the votes until Bush asked for a 120-day delay. Jewish leaders organized a "fly-in" of pro-Israel activists to tell their congressmen to ignore the settlement issue and approve the loans unconditionally. On September 12, a furious Bush called a press conference in which he complained of being "up against some powerful political forces" in Congress who were fighting to undermine his administration's policies on behalf of Israel. These "forces" enjoyed what the president called "a thousand lobbyists" in Congress, while he was just "one lonely little guy" seeking to do what was right. He reminded everyone that the United States gave Israel "the equivalent of $1,000 for every Israeli citizen." At the time, Bush was enjoying a post–Gulf War approval rating of nearly 70 percent, and he was not about to lose a key foreign policy vote in Congress. His "remarks punctured [Congress's] balloon like a blowtorch," one journalist reported. The loan guarantee legislation died, and even the Israeli population eventually obliged. Ending a lengthy period of political instability, in June 1992 Israelis voted to replace Shamir with Washington's old friend, Labor Party leader Yitzhak Rabin.[8]

With Shamir gone, the deal went so smoothly one had to wonder what all the fuss was about. In order to get the loan guarantees, Rabin agreed to cancel construction of six thousand planned housing units in the West Bank but was given permission by the Bush administration to finish building the eleven thousand already begun. These could be added to as necessary to accommodate the "natural growth" of the population already living in the settlements as well as whatever Israel decided constituted a "security area"—all of which would end up covering roughly half of the entire West Bank and the entirety of East Jerusalem. In other words, in the post-Shamir agreement the Bush administration almost completely caved in to the Israelis. Its terms clearly demonstrated that the administration's problem had been less about Israel's desire to deepen and extend its occupation than about Shamir's unwillingness to provide the necessary fig leaf to hide it. And yet Israel's champions were so angry at Bush and Baker that they were blind to what had just happened. One could hardly imagine a more tasteless criticism than that leveled by Norman Podhoretz, who complained, in *Commentary*, that "if one might reasonably say that with Shamir in power Israel was being raped, one might also say that with Shamir out of the way the victim decided to lie back and enjoy it."[9]

In March 1992, the histrionic Jewish ex–New York mayor Ed Koch, who after his three terms in office had become a motor-mouthed pundit, "reported" that Baker had privately told Jack Kemp, a Republican congressman from New York, "Fuck the Jews, they don't vote for us anyway." The *New York Post* trumpeted the alleged quote in a front-page banner headline: "BAKER'S 4-LETTER INSULT." Koch almost certainly had the story wrong (as did the *New York Times'* William Safire, who relied on him). Baker's version of the conversation had him replying to the prediction that AIPAC would not appreciate the administration's position on the loan guarantees by saying, "Screw them, they don't vote for us," meaning AIPAC, not "Jews." Kemp's version was even milder, failing to include the expletive and portraying Baker as merely explaining that there was no need for the congressman to campaign within the Jewish community because, "Well, they don't vote for us."[10]

But despite the frequent disconnect between his brain and his mouth, Koch was considered a credible source by Jewish leaders and laity alike. And while he (and therefore Safire) may have been wrong in the details, they were not wrong in the bigger picture. In the eyes of most Jewish leaders, most members of the mainstream media, and most inside-the-beltway politicos, AIPAC did equal "Jews." Refusing, therefore, to give Israel the money it wanted for the expansion of settlements in the occupied territories (thereby further reducing the potential for a two-state solution) was understood to be the equivalent of saying, "Fuck 'em." And so even though he ended up extending the loan guarantees on extremely generous terms, Bush in 1992 lost more than half of the Jewish vote he had earned in 1988, and the election along with it.[11]

Ironically, Bush's tribulations coincided with a low point for AIPAC, as Israel's new (and old) prime minister, Yitzhak Rabin, was all but telling it (yet again) to get lost. When he met with AIPAC's leaders not long after defeating Shamir, he attacked them bitterly for siding with Likud in all matters. As J. J. Goldberg put it, he "dismissed as a fraud their claim that they supported whatever government Israel chose." Rabin let AIPAC know that he would be grateful if it allowed Israel to handle its relations with the US government without its help. This was just the first of a number of pins the Israelis had at the ready to puncture the self-importance of American Jews and the organizations they supported on Israel's behalf. Rabin's finance minister, Avraham Shochat, observed that Israel had no need for the "Israel Bonds" that American Jews were so fond of buying and selling, because it could find better borrowing rates on the open market. Deputy Foreign Minister Yossi Beilin informed Americans that Israel no longer needed their contributions at all; Israel was now a rich country. Speaking to members of the Presidents Conference, he twisted the knife even more deeply when he instructed them to stop stifling dissent among Jews. "We want you to disagree with us," he told them. These sentiments were apparently too shocking for the Jewish leaders to hear, much less obey. Hadassah ex-president Ruth Popkin replied, "We can't do that. Our job here is to defend you."[12]

Israel's most admired cultural figures were also sending similar signals of impending divorce, laced with the usual contempt for the whole idea of diaspora life. Amos Oz told American Jews that they were curating a museum of Jewishness, while in Israel they were living the real thing. A. B. Yehoshua called American Jews "neurotics," owing to the sad circumstances of their "divided existence." And Shlomo Avineri, who had mocked what he believed was American Jews' hypersensitivity about Jonathan Pollard's spying, went so far as to suggest that they were living no less a life of "exile" than those Jews in the Soviet Union or Iran.[13]

A similar loosening of ties was underway within the larger American Jewish community. Writing in 1996, Steven M. Cohen, then the leading analyst of American Jewish social and political trends, found that "journalists, social scientists, Jewish communal leaders, and Israeli officials, among others, have surmised that American Jews have grown less enamored of Israelis, less interested in Israel, and less active in supporting Israel by way of travel, study, political activism, and philanthropic contributions." He attributed these developments to what he termed "four major flash points." These were the 1982 Sabra and Shatila massacres, Jonathan Pollard's 1985 arrest, the late 1987 and early 1988 intifada, and "the post-election bargaining in the winter of 1988–1989, which raised what became known as the 'Who is a Jew?' question." As it stood, the definition of "Jew," for Israeli politicians, appeared to delegitimize the authority of all but the most ultra-Orthodox of American rabbis, and with it, mainstream American Jewish religious practice. The increasingly narrow legal definition of the term was implicitly insulting to all but the most traditionally Orthodox American Jews.[14]

Arnold Eisen, a scholar of Judaism and American Jewish culture who would soon become the first non-rabbi to lead the Conservative Jewish Theological Seminary, noted in an essay for the American Jewish Committee that "the 'myth' of Israel that nourished the American Jewish imagination and helped to sustain American Jewish identity for much of this century no longer function[ed] with anything like its former power." Gone were the "larger-than-life images of a people reborn, a desert reclaimed, the weak grown strong, and the ideal made actual." They had been replaced by "TV news accounts of occupation and intifada, [and] resurgent religious fundamentalism." Eisen might also have mentioned that Israel's origin story had become unsustainable for many young Jews. As the Israelis opened their archives to a new generation of historians, the myths they had created about the nation's founding—with enthusiastic American Jewish cooperation—fell by the wayside. As Eisen concluded, the result was that "many American Jews born since 1948, let alone

students born since 1967, do not really know what to do with Israel."
What they needed in order to support the foundation of their Jewishness
was "an Israel which in its existence, vitality, and might validates our still
fragile sense of Jewish life in the shadow of the death camps. We need a
country that supports our claim to higher moral standards, illustrating
for all to see Jewish teachings of social justice and compassion in action."
But that was not the Israel they had. And the commitment, both political
and psychological, of American Jewish leaders to a clearly mythical vision
of Israel—the Israel of Leon Uris's and Otto Preminger's *Exodus*—left
them ill prepared to deal with a world in which Israel would come to be
understood by many Jews, especially young American Jews, as more of
a burden than an inspiration. These conflicting forces would only grow
in the coming years, as a new Democratic administration attempted to
negotiate the changing world of American Jewish politics and an even
more complex—and confusing—constellation of forces defining the apparently never-ending Israeli/Palestinian conflict.[15]

# CHAPTER 14

# DISCOURSE MATTERS

WHEN BILL CLINTON WON THE 1992 PRESIDENTIAL ELECTION WITH A whopping 80 percent of the Jewish vote, it provided him with a kind of permission to aggressively pursue a peace agenda that asked far more of Israel than any previous president had. It appeared to work for a while. Yitzhak Rabin and Yasser Arafat met on the White House lawn on a beautiful mid-September afternoon in 1993, shook hands, and signed the Oslo I Accord, named after the city in Norway where the negotiations for the peace agreement began. Countless Jewish tears were shed on the White House lawn that day, your author's included, when, during his speech, the usually blunt, unsentimental ex-general, Rabin—he of the "might, power, beatings" order during the First Intifada—cried out to the Palestinian people, "We say to you today in a loud and a clear voice: Enough of blood and tears. Enough. We have no desire for revenge. We harbor no hatred towards you. We, like you, are people who want to build a home, to plant a tree, to love, to live side by side with you in dignity, in empathy, as human beings." Oslo II, signed two years later, would supplement Oslo I (together they are known as the "Oslo Accords"). To those assembled, Rabin spoke words that sounded as if they could have fallen out of the Old Testament. One could be forgiven for believing that it was all taking place inside a dream. In a way, it was: one that lasted roughly seven years—and cost Rabin his life—before the world woke up to a reality of Palestinian terrorism, asymmetric Israeli military retaliation, a return to power of Israel's right wing, and never-ending fusillades of accusation and recrimination from all sides during the final days of the second Clinton administration.[1]

In Israel, the philosopher and scholar of Hebrew literature Menachem Brinker was in the process of concluding that "the task of Zionism is very nearly completed. That is to say, the problem that Zionism set out to address is just about solved. Soon we will be living in a post-Zionist era, and there will no longer be a good reason for a Zionist movement to exist alongside the State of Israel." Given the central role that the movement had played in the creation of American Jews' identity, this presumed a radical reorientation that few, if any, were now prepared to accept. With the traditional agenda apparently a thing of the past, American Jewish leaders turned inward. The 1990–1991 National Jewish Population Study had shocked them with the finding that each year, more than half of the American Jews who got married were marrying gentiles—and these marriages rarely resulted in children who considered themselves to be members of the Jewish community. (The 1957 figure had been 3.5 percent.) This news caused panic among Jewish leaders and moved them to recommit themselves to prioritizing a "Jewish continuity agenda" that had been brewing for nearly four decades. (Both *Commentary* and *Look*, as early as 1963 and 1964, respectively, had claimed that Jews in America were "vanishing.")[2]

But now the frog's kettle was boiling. "American Jewish life is in danger of disappearing, just as most American Jews have achieved everything we ever wanted: acceptance, influence, affluence, equality," warned Alan Dershowitz on the first page of his 1997 book, *The Vanishing American Jew*. In 1996, Prime Minister Benjamin Netanyahu, referring to the rising American intermarriage rates, spoke of "a Silent Holocaust." By this time, Zionism had come to dominate Jewish leaders' thinking so profoundly that they had chosen to look to Israel, and especially to its military, to rescue American Jewry from the dangers of assimilation. The "Project Birthright" program—nicknamed "Project Hook-Up"—which offered young Jews a free ten-day group trip to Israel (and maybe the opportunity to find a Jewish mate)—had its origins in this moment.[3]

The theologian Mordecai Kaplan had warned in 1948 that "Eretz Israel–centered education [was] bound to have a ruinous effect on the happiness and character" of Jewish children. But secular American Jews had long ago failed to heed Kaplan's warning. Instead, they had embraced the twin poles of the defense of Israel and the sacralization of the Holocaust as the near sum-total of Jewish identity. (One senses that in 1976, when the "godfather" of neoconservatism, Irving Kristol, explained that his connection to Judaism consisted entirely of "the Holocaust and the founding of the state of Israel," he was likely speaking for countless American Jews of his and subsequent generations.) And with the transformation of Israel's popular image from the mythical nation portrayed in *Exodus* to the nation that was occupying the West Bank and Gaza, and the gradual natural fading of the memory of the Holocaust, that identity grew too weak to sustain itself. Young Jews were marrying gentiles in numbers that alarmed their parents and grandparents, to say nothing of the resulting demographic threat that their non-Jewish offspring might pose to future Jewish political power. The result was a significant shrinkage in the number of people who remained passionately and politically engaged with the Israel/Palestine issue, and the subsequent domination of the discourse by those most devoted to their respective causes: ultra-religious Jews, neoconservatives, and evangelical Christian Zionists, who virtually all sought to undermine the fragile peace process then underway.[4]

The American Israel Public Affairs Committee also joined in, albeit behind the scenes, and usually beneath the camouflage of pro-peace rhetoric. Its leaders had no doubt felt humiliated by the Rabin government's desire to shut them out of its relations with its American counterpart. Nor were they at all comfortable with what was now being asked of them by that same government—to lobby for aid to the new, post-Oslo "Palestinian National Authority" made up of people they had previously referred to as "PLO terrorists." What's more, AIPAC's key funders, and therefore its staff and board of directors, were by this time dominated by Republicans, and most of them had forged personal relationships with Likud politicians during the party's decade and a half in power. Its executive director, Neal Sher, previously head of the Nazi-hunting Office of Special Investigations in the US Justice Department, would describe soliciting support from his organization for the peace agreements as being "like pulling teeth." AIPAC board members and staffers did not throw tomatoes or scream obscenities at Israel's US ambassador, the historian Itamar Rabinovich, when he appeared in public. But right-wing American Jewish protesters sometimes did, and it often became a trial for him to appear anywhere, whether in a synagogue or a public gathering, to argue on behalf of Israeli/Palestinian peace. These events always threatened to become another (literal) food fight.[5]

Ironically, the news of the agreement worked out by Israeli and Palestinian negotiators caught the Clinton team by surprise. The Americans had not been privy to the secret Oslo talks, which had begun in 1993 with the participation of Palestinian and Israeli academics and negotiators. The Clinton administration, in fact, was invited into the process just in time to arrange the celebration in Washington and assume its funding. It was to be a cold, almost frigid peace. Waiting backstage for the White House ceremony to begin, Clinton was anxious about the possibility that Arafat might try to kiss him (as this was a typical greeting among Arab leaders). To prevent that from happening, Tony Lake, the president's national security adviser, suggested that he hold Arafat's shoulders when greeting him, and drive his thumbs into them should the PLO leader seek to move in for a kiss. This turned out not to be necessary, but it spoke to both the fraught quality and the initial euphoria the accord excited, together with its political fragility, given Arafat's continued identification with terrorism in the eyes of the US public.[6]

The first major battle of the post–Oslo I era occurred in 1995 when AIPAC decided to push through legislation designed to force the Clinton administration to move the US embassy in Israel from Tel Aviv to Jerusalem. Israel had declared Jerusalem as its capital in 1950, but only two nations—Costa Rica and El Salvador—recognized it as such. Jordan asserted in 1953 that East Jerusalem had the status of *amana*, or trusteeship, making it essentially a second capital of Jordan. When the AIPAC tried to push the 1995 legislation through, Israel's leaders privately opposed the move, realizing that preempting negotiations over Jerusalem would be taken as bad faith, possibly undermining any hopes they had to work out their myriad disagreements with the Palestinians over the future shape of Palestine. No issue—not even the Palestinian "right of return"—would be more complicated to address than how to handle the future of Jerusalem, and everyone involved understood that it needed to be saved for last. But no Israeli government could take a public position against AIPAC's move, and almost no one in Congress saw much profit in opposing it. As Rabinovich would later write, the "embarrassing" legislation came about because "elements of the Israeli and Jewish right saw a golden opportunity to strengthen, so they thought, Israel's hold on Jerusalem, to earn political dividends and cause political damage to the Clinton administration, Rabin and the Oslo process, which they vehemently opposed."[7]

The law passed with only token opposition and with veto-proof majorities in both houses. Just three weeks afterward, on November 5, 1995, a right-wing religious zealot, Yigal Amir, murdered the prime minister at a Tel Aviv peace rally—ironically, the first time Rabin had ever openly embraced the movement. Rabin's murder inspired a brief moment of retrospection and temporary respite from the Oslo-related acrimony, and, at the same time, a rise in concern about the increasing turn to violence on the part of Israel's radical right. This period soon ended, however, as violence (and counterviolence) emanating from the West Bank, Gaza, and Lebanon erupted in its wake. Usually these conflicts were between Israelis and Palestinians, but tensions rose as well between right-wing Israelis, especially settlers, who opposed the peace agreement, and its supporters, violence that led eventually to Rabin's murder. Following a failed 1996 election campaign by Rabin's Labor Party successor and longtime political rival Shimon Peres, Israel voted in yet another narrow, right-wing Likud government. It was led by Benjamin Netanyahu, a hardline opponent of the peace process who enjoyed close ties to US neoconservatives and evangelicals. Indeed, he had been assiduously working with them to undermine Rabin before the assassination.

Just as Begin and Shamir had done to Clinton's predecessors, Netanyahu drove his American counterparts crazy—only more so. After their first meeting—after listening to the young Israeli leader lecture him about the alleged realities of the region—Clinton, described as finding Netanyahu to be "nearly insufferable," turned to an aide and asked, "Who the fuck does he think he is? Who's the fucking superpower here?" He vowed that he would no longer "put up with [his] bullshit," but of course he would end up putting up with plenty more. Netanyahu often went out of his way to demonstrate his contempt for the Democratic president. Immediately before one meeting with the president, in January 1998, for instance, Netanyahu joined Jerry Falwell—a man who regularly accused Clinton of literally being a murderer and a sex criminal—as Falwell led an assembled crowd to chant, "Not One Inch!"[8]

For all his bluster and occasional overreach, Netanyahu would turn out to be a remarkably canny politician. He did not want to formally renounce the peace process. He wanted the Palestinians to kill it for him. Much as Richard Nixon had done with his pretend-support for civil rights as president in the 1970s, the Israeli leader sought to find ways to inspire anger—even rioting—by Palestinians while speaking platitudes of peace in the process. Netanyahu consistently insisted that Arafat arrest Palestinians whom Israel deemed "terrorists" to demonstrate his fealty to the peace process, and then pretended to be shocked when his demands were rejected. When the riots and resistance arrived, frequently in the form of new terrorist attacks on Israeli civilians, both in the territories and inside Israel proper, Netanyahu reneged on the promises made by his predecessor and launched retaliatory attacks on heavily populated targets. This destructive dynamic returned the debate in the United States to the familiar footing of the pre-peace era. American Jews—particularly the younger ones—may have been "distancing" themselves from Israel, and some were even beginning to organize on behalf of the Palestinians, but the middle-aged and elderly folk who ran the venerable community organizations were now back at work doing what they did best: lionizing Israel and demonizing the Palestinians.[9]

Meanwhile, a spirited debate on almost every aspect of the increasingly beleaguered peace process took place in the *New York Times* op-ed pages. Anthony Lewis led the peace camp, Thomas Friedman and James Reston occupied the middle ground, and William Safire and former executive editor A. M. "Abe" Rosenthal formed an implacable right flank. The AIPAC-inspired Jerusalem Embassy Act had set a deadline of May 31, 1999, for the Clinton administration to complete the embassy's move to Jerusalem, but it also contained an escape clause allowing the president to waive it for six-month intervals, in order "to protect the national security interests of the U.S."—something every president would do every six months until it was Donald Trump's turn (he moved the embassy on May 14, 2018, the seventieth anniversary of the day Israel had declared itself into existence). But after the bill's November 8, 1995, passage, just weeks after the White House handshake, Safire and Rosenthal were hammering Clinton endlessly for refusing to make the move right away. The former attacked Clinton three years before the deadline for embracing the notion of a "P.L.O. beachhead in Jerusalem," and for attempting "to circumvent" the law since its signature. Returning to an old theme of the pro-Israel pundits, he insisted that "by deferring to Arabs who insist that Israel's claim to Jerusalem is invalid, generations of State Department Arabists have been unevenhandedly insulting our ally." In a later column, titled "Gun to the Head," Safire announced, "This generation's battle for Jerusalem has begun. With two attacks on Israeli civilians punctuated by the public 'kiss of death' bestowed by Yasser Arafat on a terrorist leader, militant Arabs have shown that they intend to make Jerusalem their capital at the point of a gun." So, naturally, Safire added, "Prime Minister Benjamin Netanyahu, in the face of Arafat's 10 major broken security promises, has stopped letting Israel be the salami under the Palestinian knife."[10]

Safire, a former advertising executive who had served as Nixon's speechwriter before being given a column on the *Times* op-ed page, was at least a skilled writer and a canny, albeit often dishonest, practitioner of the pundit's profession. He could make a strong case so long as he was able to determine the premises of his argument. This was not the case, however, with Abe Rosenthal, who, when eased out of the job of executive editor of the paper, was given a column on its op-ed page as consolation. According to his son, the *Times* journalist Andrew Rosenthal, his tenure as the paper's executive editor had, by this time, "turned him into a crazy person," and this was nowhere more evident than in his obsession with criticism of Israel. Rosenthal, born in 1922, had been traumatized as a youth—as had so many other Jews of his generation—upon learning of America's and the world's failure to respond effectively to Hitler's Holocaust, and he viewed virtually all news from the Middle East from this psychological prism, much as Menachem Begin had professed to see Hitler in Arafat's bunker. A comically clumsy writer, Rosenthal more than once saw fit to quote parts of his previous columns in which he had also quoted himself from yet another column. In this manner, he achieved the unique journalistic achievement of literally quoting himself quoting himself. Rosenthal rarely convinced anyone who did not already agree with him, but his arguments provided a valuable window into the not uncommon neuroses that continued to drive many older American Jews when confronted with what they understood to be threats to Israel. His opinion columns also can provide insight into the paper's prejudices during his twenty-six-year reign in top *Times* editorial positions (managing editor from 1969 to 1977 and executive editor from 1977 to 1986).[11]

Like Leon Uris, Rosenthal described a world in which Israel behaved in morally flawless fashion; literally every problem in the Middle East arose from the evil inclinations of its adversaries, with an assist from their feckless and frequently dishonest supporters in the United States. In September 1996, for instance, Rosenthal authored a column in defense of a badly bungled Mossad assassination operation in Jordan aimed at a visiting Hamas leader; the attempt had infuriated King Hussein, who was Israel's ally, and inspired worldwide condemnation. The problem here, according to Rosenthal, was not Israel's violation of the sovereignty and laws of one of the only two Arab countries with whom it had made peace; rather, it was, as it always was, the Arabs and their irrational hatred of the Jewish state in their midst. Employing a defense that might have been published on any day during his twelve-year tenure as a *Times* pundit, Rosenthal wrote, "One day, terrorism may end—a still-distant day when the Arab world ends its half-century war against Israel, permanently." But until then, he argued, Israel was within its rights to do whatever it pleased wherever it pleased. The rest of the world may not approve, but it was Rosenthal's view—one that the *Times* was willing to regularly publish on the most prestigious page in all of American journalism—that "every time Israeli citizens are murdered by Palestinian terrorism, the world's leaders respond by spitting on their graves."[12]

Safire and Rosenthal were balanced by the other writers on the page, with Anthony Lewis being the most passionate defender of the Palestinians, and Thomas Friedman likely being the most influential among both readers and government officials. (Though he was still writing, James "Scotty" Reston was by this time long past his prime.) Lewis addressed the conflict in largely idealistic terms, speaking as an archetypal liberal Jew who was constantly disappointed with what he saw as Israel's political intransigence and moral insensitivity. Friedman favored the common journalistic tactic of always seeking to apportion blame to "both sides," or what might be termed "ontheonehandism." On the one hand, "there are Palestinian extremist groups that are nourished by terrorism against Jews—and it doesn't matter who's in power in Israel, how active the U.S. is, or whether peace talks are moving or stalled." But on the other, "Mr. Netanyahu's leadership has been incompetent. Yes, he has floated the idea of a Palestinian mini state in the West Bank and Gaza. But while Mr. Netanyahu has leaked those ideas to the Israeli press, he has never shared them with the Palestinians or developed any realistic strategy for working with Palestinians to achieve his ends." Friedman was a congenital optimist as well as a liberal Zionist, and his columns often illustrated the frequent contradictions these two positions increasingly entailed.[13]

Friedman saw his train leaving the station and felt hopeless to stop it, much less turn it around. And his coverage, however unwelcome by "pro-Israel" partisans, nevertheless embraced far more of their version of the narrative than it did that of the Palestinians—indeed, far more, as well, than the hard-nosed coverage in Israel's counterpart to the *Times*, *Haaretz*. True, Israel was no longer immune to strong criticism in the mainstream media, and the unsigned editorials in places like the *Times*, the *Washington Post*, and the *Los Angeles Times* now echoed many of these same concerns. But only on the rarest of occasions was a writer or thinker associated with a straightforward pro-Palestinian perspective of the kind preached by Edward Said or Noam Chomsky ever invited to their pages. There were not even any voices as critical of Israel as those being published in *Haaretz* at the time, such as those of the paper's regular columnists Tom Segev, Orit Shochat, Akiva Eldar, Uzi Benziman, Danny Rubinstein, Gideon Levy, Gideon Samet, and Amira Hass.[14]

Bill Clinton shared the deep scriptural connection to Israel that Democratic presidents Truman, Johnson, and Carter had demonstrated before him. He would later recall how, when he was the governor of Arkansas, his "old pastor and mentor" W. O. Vaught had said to him, "Bill, I think you're going to be President someday.... [T]here's one thing above all you must remember: God will never forgive you if you don't stand by Israel."[15]

As president, he had been deeply moved by what he felt was the visionary leadership of Yitzhak Rabin, and he desperately wanted to carry out the agreements that had been negotiated to ensure what he understood to be their collective political legacy. He saw the conflict in much the way Thomas Friedman described it and proved remarkably tenacious in trying to bridge the gap between the two sides. Clinton brought Netanyahu and Arafat together with King Hussein in October 1998 for a summit in Wye River, Maryland, to try to save the peace process, and they managed to hammer out a deal reviving the promises the two sides had made five years earlier. They negotiated as well a clear timetable for their respective trade-offs. Clinton even traveled to Gaza—the first president ever to do so—and was met with enthusiastic crowds. There, he watched (with Arafat and Netanyahu) as the PLO officially eliminated the twenty-six clauses in its charter calling for Israel's destruction.

All of these debates came to a head in dramatic fashion in July 2000, as Clinton tried, one last time, to convince both sides to make the painful compromises necessary to turn the Oslo Accords into a genuine "two-state solution." He chose Camp David to bring the Israelis and Palestinians together, no doubt for the symbolism it held as the location where Jimmy Carter had brought Anwar Sadat and Menachem Begin together twelve years earlier. The Israelis had replaced Netanyahu's far-right government with one led by Labor's Ehud Barak, former chief of staff of the IDF and its most highly decorated officer. Like Rabin, he appeared to enjoy sufficient legitimacy on security-related issues with the Israeli public to be able to deliver on promises of peace, however painful the compromise involved. But as Clinton's adviser Aaron David Miller would admit twenty years after the fact, "The Camp David summit—ill-conceived and ill-advised—should probably never have taken place." By that time Barak's coalition was already teetering on the brink of collapse. The Israeli leader looked to a summit as a potential path to saving his government. Clinton was initially skeptical, but tended, eventually, to go along with everything Barak wanted. Arafat, meanwhile, was dead set against it, seeing an Israeli/American trap. He expected to be ganged-up on by Clinton and Barak to make a bad deal and then be blamed by both when he refused. He agreed to attend only if Clinton promised in advance that there would be "no finger-pointing" in the event of no final deal. Clinton made the promise and then proceeded to break it. He supported Barak at virtually every turn—acting, in Miller's words, not as an honest broker but as "Israel's lawyer." When the talks failed, Clinton then proceeded to point his finger exclusively at Arafat.[16]

It is literally impossible to accurately summarize what was agreed to during this summit given the Rashomon-like conflicting accounts offered by its participants following its failure. Much of the most energetic disputation it inspired was dedicated to picking apart the media accounts intended to answer these questions. Broadly speaking, there's no question that Clinton eventually succeeded in cajoling Barak into making the Palestinians a serious offer of statehood, one that not only surpassed anything any Israeli leader had publicly suggested in the past, but also anything the Israeli public had been prepared to accept in advance of the talks. Barak broke his own campaign promise, which he had made just a year earlier, by agreeing to a division of Jerusalem. But as Miller pointed out, Barak's proposals were still "nowhere close to what Arafat needed, even if the Palestinian leader had been interested in closing a deal." Arafat could not accept permanent Israeli sovereignty over significant sections of the Arab parts of Jerusalem, including the third-holiest site in Islam, the "Haram al-Sharif" (Noble Sanctuary) where Al-Aqsa Mosque is located (and where the prophet Muhammed is said to have ascended to Heaven in the seventh century CE). Alas, to Jews the same spot is known as Har Habayit, or the "Temple Mount," where, allegedly, Solomon's Temple stood. Hence, as the location of that temple's "Western Wall," it symbolizes to many Judaism's holiest place. According to a *New York Times* report, the leaders of both Saudi Arabia and Egypt had "all but threatened Mr. Arafat with political excommunication" if he agreed to accept Israel's proposals for the city, and he had every reason to fear for his life if he resisted these warnings. The Palestinian "right of return" issue remained unsolved as well, a particularly important point given the fact that the United Nations classified fully 3.6 million Palestinians as "refugees" at the time.[17]

Notwithstanding the weaknesses of the Israeli/American offer—and there were many, as I describe below—Palestinian negotiators were handicapped by a set of structural contradictions that, as a people, they had historically been free to ignore when peace remained a distant dream. The problem lay in the radically different circumstances of the now millions of refugees and descendants of refugees, as well as the demands of other Arab nations regarding sovereignty of the Holy Land. There are Palestinians who live in Israel proper as semi-citizens. Others live under an increasingly brutal occupation on the West Bank and what is frequently termed—with only some exaggeration—an "open-air" prison in Gaza. There are also countless Palestinians who live in fetid, unsanitary refugee camps in Israel and across the Arab world. Still others live as stateless residents, often exploited workers with few rights elsewhere in the world. Some are settled into comfortable professional lives as businessmen, academics, and the like. These groups all have different interests that cannot be easily adjudicated—to say nothing of the Arab leaders who insist that any agreement must include complete Arab sovereignty over the religion's many holy sites. These leaders really don't mind if the Palestinians remain a convenient focus of anger against Israel and the West among their own undemocratic, badly served populations.

The problem of these complicated, conflicting interests was independent of the more obvious one of factionalism, which in the past had sometimes led one group within the PLO to plot bombings and assassinations aimed at another, and in more recent years had led Hamas and the Palestinian Authority to nearly go to war with one another. So long as peace remained impossible, these differences were merely rhetorical. If an actual peace agreement had been placed on the table, they would have had to be addressed—and addressed in a way that satisfied, or at least placated, all the interests involved. This was, alas, impossible then, and it is likely impossible now. It is much simpler to continue to demand justice for Palestinians and the return of their lands to the descendants of the families who lost them in 1948, 1967, and since then. Coincidentally, this alternative also frees Israel from having to face its own responsibilities in solving the conflict, allowing it instead to rely on its military prowess to "manage" the conflict and maintain what is a remarkably favorable status quo for its citizens.

The deadly Second Intifada began in September 2000 and helped to ensure that Arafat and the Palestinians would receive the lion's share of the blame when the negotiators went home empty-handed. In President Clinton's estimation, Israeli prime minister Barak "showed particular courage, vision, and an understanding of the historical importance of this moment," in contrast to Arafat, who persisted in stubborn rejectionism. The pro-Israeli US negotiator Dennis Ross blamed the failure to reach an agreement on "a mindset that has plagued the Palestinians throughout their history," a tendency to "fall back on blaming everyone else for their predicament" that "perpetuates the avoidance of responsibility." Barak insisted that it was the result of the fact that the Palestinians were "products of a culture in which to tell a lie...creates no dissonance. They don't suffer from the problem of telling lies that exists in Judeo-Christian culture. Truth is seen as an irrelevant category."[18]

Many conservatives were relieved that the talks failed. In a column filled with falsehoods, the *Times'* William Safire complained that Barak had not only broken his election pledge, by agreeing to a divided Jerusalem, but had also "offered Arafat virtually all the West Bank, including the vital Jordan Valley, requiring the uprooting of 40,000 Israeli settlers. He offered what amounts to right of return of thousands of Palestinians to Israel, backed up by a reported huge commitment by Clinton to pay Palestinians around the world to not return. 'Not enough,' smiled Arafat. He went home to the cheers of intransigent Palestinians in Gaza and the praise of Egypt's unyielding Hosni Mubarak." The Arabs, Safire announced, were "delighted at the one-way flow of concessions because they now see Jerusalem 'in play.'" Safire's scorn was to be expected, but Thomas Friedman's analysis was hardly less one-sided. Barak, he wrote, had offered Arafat the "unthinkable" and the "unprecedented." It had been "a historic compromise proposal that would have given Palestinians control of 94 to 96 percent of the West Bank and Gaza— with all the settlements removed, virtually all of Arab East Jerusalem, a return to Israel of a symbolic number of Palestinian refugees and either the right of return to the West Bank and Gaza or compensation for all the others."[19]

Unfortunately, everyone involved had been asked to ensure that no written records would be kept regarding the various proposals made and which parts had achieved tentative agreement from either side, lest they be used as political weapon against Barak in the event of the talks' failure—as, in fact, they were anyway, albeit without written evidence. And because the Palestinian perspective was absent from the mainstream debate, the many caveats contained in Barak's allegedly unthinkable and unprecedented offer went unacknowledged and therefore undiscussed. But, of course, the truth was a far more complicated manner. Yes, after refusing for a week even to engage in negotiations while at Camp David and ostentatiously snubbing Arafat at every turn, Barak did appear to tentatively agree to terms that went well beyond what Israel had offered in the past or where most observers expected him to go in the talks. And, in retrospect, there is no doubt that, given the wisdom of hindsight based on events that have since transpired, the Palestinians should certainly have swallowed their objections, secured their statehood, and begun to build from there (just as they should also have at countless intervals since the 1917 Balfour Declaration). Here was yet another Palestinian "missed opportunity." Yet examined carefully, the deal in question, which was crafted by Clinton and tentatively accepted by Barak with significant caveats—rather than "offered" by Israel—left a great deal to be desired if

Palestine was to be expected to survive as a sovereign independent state, leaving aside the complicated question of "justice."[20]

The problems with the proposed Camp David deal went far deeper than just the fact that the Israelis were to retain sovereignty over key parts of Arab East Jerusalem. While Barak proposed giving the Palestinians 91 percent of West Bank lands, he was also insistent about Israel being able to keep and expand its settlements on the remaining 9 percent that it chose to keep. (Recall that 100 percent of the West Bank would still have left the Palestinians with what amounted to just 22 percent of what had been pre-1948 Palestine.) Israel also insisted on retaining direct military control over significant parts of what was to be Palestine. According to Ahmed Qureia (known as "Abu Ala"), the Palestinians' top negotiator and the Speaker of its parliament, the plan "would have carved Israeli-controlled cantons out of the West Bank and dashed any hopes for a viable, territorially contiguous Palestinian state." It looked to the Palestinians like a plan for a South African–style "Bantustan." Israel's foreign minister, Shlomo Ben-Ami, a member of Israel's negotiating team, drafted a number of Barak's responses to Clinton's suggestions. He nevertheless concluded, "If I were a Palestinian, I would have rejected Camp David, as well." Barak made much the same point in defending his record as an unreconstructed hawk to the Israeli public. He titled one op-ed, published in Hebrew, "I Did Not Give Away a Thing." And finally, Barak had a poor record of keeping to previous agreements and had backed off of even elements of the Oslo agreements that Netanyahu had agreed to; he also backed out at the last minute from a separate Israeli/Syrian peace agreement negotiated between 1992 and 1996, once he discovered the concessions Israel would have made under it to be deeply unpopular with voters, infuriating Bill Clinton at the time.[21]

Given the hegemony of the Barak/Clinton narrative in America's Israel/Palestine debate, it should not surprise anyone that when the Palestinian perspective was finally given voice, it would shake up the consensus considerably. The corrective came almost a year later in the form of a one-two punch of extremely lengthy reconsiderations published in the *New York Times* and the *New York Review of Books*. The former was a 5,681-word retrospective by Jerusalem bureau chief Deborah Sontag, the latter a 7,834-word autopsy cowritten by Clinton's (Jewish) National Security Council Middle East expert, Robert Malley, together with Hussein Agha, a member of the Palestinian negotiating team. Both articles emphasized that both sides had made mistakes during the talks. As Sontag put it, she sought to upend the belief that "Mr. Barak offered Mr. Arafat the moon at Camp David last summer," and that "Mr. Arafat turned it down, and then 'pushed the button' and chose the path of violence." Rather, she said, "there were missteps and successes by Israelis, Palestinians and Americans alike." Malley and Agha both criticized Arafat's failure "to present a cogent and specific counterproposal," but they devoted the bulk of their essays to providing evidence to dispute the monochromatic picture of what Malley and Agha called "Ehud Barak's unprecedented offer and Yasser Arafat's uncompromising no."[22]

The reaction was swift but volcanic. William Safire denounced his own newspaper. "Do not swallow this speculative rewriting of recent events," he warned readers. "The overriding reason for the war against Israel today is that Yasser Arafat decided that war was the way to carry out the often-avowed Palestinian plan. Its first stage is to create a West Bank state from the Jordan River to the sea with Jerusalem as its capital. Then, by flooding Israel with 'returning' Palestinians, the plan in its promised final phase would drive the hated Jews from the Middle East." *The New Republic* ran a forensic analysis of the Sontag piece by Israeli writer (and former Begin government spokesman) Yossi Klein Halevi that ran roughly as long as the Sontag article itself. He accused her of "lazy reporting, errors of omission, questionable shading, and an indifference to the basic fact that the Palestinian decision to wed diplomacy with violence, not American and Israeli miscues, damned the search for peace." He then lay literally every flaw in the negotiations, as well as 100 percent of the responsibility for the violence that followed, at the feet of the Palestinians. Clinton himself was quoted complaining about Sontag's emphasis as well. "What the hell is this? Why is she turning the mistakes we made into the essence?" he was reported to have asked an aide.[23]

The Malley/Agha article was more authoritative than Sontag's, but likely less influential, as it ran in the *New York Review* rather than on the front page of the *New York Times*. This was a shame, as it was more detailed, allowed for greater subtlety, and was written by two longtime participants in the process, people who had actually witnessed the events in question. The complexity of their argument, coupled with their undeniable knowledge of both what took place and how it fit into the recent history of the region, left critics with little but ad hominem attacks to maintain their one-dimensional narrative of Israeli beneficence and Palestinian rejectionism. Accusing Malley of having written "revisionist history" without any apparent understanding of the meaning of the term, Mortimer Zuckerman, then both publisher of the *New York Daily News* and chairman of the Conference of Presidents of Major American Jewish Organizations, also joined in the attack. "Rob Malley was the most pro-Arab member of the National Security Council," he wrote in his article with a Palestinian adviser, and he was in Camp David only in a junior capacity. Moreover, he asserted, "There is one truth, period: The Palestinians caused the breakdown at Camp David and then rejected Clinton's plan in January." The ADL's Abe Foxman resorted to McCarthyite tactics: having no evidence with which to contest the authors' arguments, he accused Malley of "playing someone's agenda"; then he followed up with the all-but-perennial complaint, "I don't think this is the right time to cast doubts over Israel's intentions." Meanwhile, Morton Klein, president of the Zionist Organization of America, who tended to occupy the right-most position among the Jewish community's leadership, this time spoke for its consensus: "Whether their account is accurate or not is irrelevant. . . . I reject any discussion of what happened."[24]

In January 2001, just as Bill Clinton was preparing to turn the White House over to George W. Bush, Israeli and Palestinian negotiators made one final attempt to square the circle. Meeting in the Red Sea resort town of Taba, the Israelis sweetened the deal with more generous land swaps, greater control over Arab East Jerusalem, and an explicit Israeli recognition of the "right" (but not the practice) of return. Unfortunately, negotiations were suspended owing to the fact that Barak's government was poised to fall. By the time of these talks, polls had demonstrated that Barak only had the support of one-third of the Israeli voting population, and an even smaller fraction of the seated members of the Knesset. He had no chance of receiving the popular mandate he would have needed to move forward with a painful peace agreement. Moreover, here, again, exactly what was agreed to remains highly contentious, as none of it was ever put down on paper. All the conversations and concessions were floated in purely hypothetical terms in order to protect both sides in the event of failure. The only written record we have are notes taken by an observer from the European Union.[25]

The fact that the talks in Taba took place at all implied a significant triumph of hope over experience. Things were already falling apart. On September 28, 2000, Israel's provocative right-wing opposition leader Ariel Sharon paid a visit to the Temple Mount (or Haram al-Sharif, to Muslims) in Jerusalem's Old City, accompanied by an estimated 1,000-person security detail. The frustration of the Palestinians in the territories in the wake of Camp David's failure had reached a boiling point, as Sharon well knew. Yet another cycle of violence began as protesters threw rocks at Jewish worshippers at the Western Wall, directly below the Mount, and Israeli police responded with live ammunition, killing four and wounding as many as two hundred. Later in the day, three more Palestinians and one Israeli were killed. Next, a twelve-year-old Palestinian boy was killed in crossfire in Gaza, and this was filmed and broadcast to the world. Over the next few days, an Israel Border Police officer— a Druze, as it happened—was shot by a Palestinian gunman and left to bleed to death at Joseph's Tomb in Nablus, and two IDF reservists were brutally beaten to death by a mob in the West Bank Palestinian city of Ramallah after accidentally taking a wrong turn. The mood in Israel shifted, in the eyes of foreign ministry official Shlomo Ben-Ami, "from the belief that peace was possible into the mindset of bloody retribution, a religion-based war of murder, blood and vengeance."[26]

The Second Intifada that arose in response to Sharon's visit, and the accompanying violence on both sides to which it ultimately led, would be fought not with rocks but with automatic weapons, and it included assaults on Jews during prayer services, a suicide bombing on a school bus, and other suicide bombers blowing themselves up amid crowds of teenagers in a Tel Aviv disco as well as in a Jerusalem pizza parlor.

During the four-plus years that followed Sharon's visit to the Temple Mount, 1,038 Israelis and 3,189 Palestinians lost their lives, according to the calculations of Israel's internal security service, the Shin Bet, and the Israeli human rights organization B'Tselem (In the Image of God). Israeli forces arrested some 6,000 Palestinians and demolished 4,100 Palestinian homes during this same period. As the *Haaretz* columnist Gideon Levy would observe on the twentieth anniversary of these events, "For Israel, the second intifada morphed into the nightmare of exploding buses and suicide bombers, years of unremitting horror and dread for the country's citizens. For the Palestinians, these were years of brutal suppression, extensive bloodshed, sieges, closures, lockdowns, checkpoints, mass arrests, and also combat and sacrifices that got them nowhere." In February 2001, in the midst of this escalating violence, Israelis chose Ariel Sharon—now politically rehabilitated following the censure he had experienced for his role in helping to enable the 1982 massacres at Sabra and Shatila—as their prime minister. With Republican George W. Bush about to replace Bill Clinton in America's own deeply contested 2000 presidential election, peace between Israel and the Palestinians suddenly appeared to be a more distant goal than ever before.[27]

# CHAPTER 15

# THE CONSEQUENCES OF CHAOS

THE MIDDLE EAST OF THE SECOND INTIFADA WAS A WILD, OFTEN LAW-less place, especially in the occupied territories. Palestinians launched suicide bombings in which those who sacrificed themselves in order to murder Israelis were promised not only the rewards of Heaven but also generous payments to their surviving family members by supportive Arab regimes. The so-called al-Aqsa Martyrs' Brigades conducted over 150 attacks between 2000 and 2005. Meanwhile, Israel finished construction on an elaborate—and largely effective—system of electronic fences, patrol roads, and observation towers that it called a "separation barrier." Most of the rest of the world termed it a "wall," and the International Court of Justice ruled it illegal. The 440-mile-long route the system eventually took had the effect of unilaterally annexing approximately 10 percent of the West Bank and 38 percent of what had previously been Palestinian land in East Jerusalem. Many Jewish settlers, however, responded to the violence with violence of their own. While most of the incidents involved relatively small-scale threats and intimidation, a cadre of Jewish terrorists bent on vengeance captured random Palestinians for the purposes of torture and murder, often receiving the blessings of their religious authorities in advance. One entire Palestinian village was forced to evacuate all of its 150 citizens because, its members claimed, the "gunfire, stone-throwing, physical assaults and vandalism had become unbearable"—raising uncomfortable echoes of the pogroms visited upon Jews in nineteenth- and early twentieth-century Eastern Europe.[1]

The violence reached a climax on March 28, 2002, when suicide bombers attacked a public Passover seder at the Park Hotel in Netanya, killing twenty-nine Israelis and wounding dozens more. Prime Minister Ariel Sharon responded by canceling Israel's promise, made as part of the Oslo Accords, to keep Israeli troops out of Palestinian-controlled population centers. Starting with the northern West Bank cities of Nablus and Jenin, he ordered the IDF to stamp out the rebellion. With the unflinching support of the US president, the conservative Republican George W. Bush, what followed was a series of sustained Israeli bombing campaigns, random beatings, and, most controversially, a series of targeted assassinations.[2]

The Israeli assassination program had been around long enough to become a matter of legend. The Mossad routinely sent killers to whatever nation its targets happened to be residing in, and their audacious murders and daring escapes made them heroes at home and to American Jews and gentiles alike. Mossad maintained the public pretense that it never had any involvement in these murders and didn't even know what the questioner was talking about. ("If you want to shoot, shoot, don't talk," a retired IDF general and former defense ministry official, Amos Gilad, once explained, quoting Clint Eastwood's "Dirty Harry" character. "[T]he Mossad's reputation is to do fantastic operations, allegedly, clandestine, without publicity," he said.)[3]

Excitement grew when the unlucky target happened to be an ex-Nazi or a famous Arab terrorist. But the program was expanding to include religious figures, especially those associated with the Gaza-based Hamas organization, people who inspired terrorists but had not personally engaged in terrorist acts. It would soon also expand to scientists of many nationalities who were understood to be helping Iran with its (allegedly peaceful) nuclear program. Sometimes the targets were former inciters who had changed their ways and called for peace, but somehow no one at Mossad had gotten the news. Though the Israelis sought to go to great lengths to avoid it, family members, neighbors, and sometimes children would often turn out to be "collateral damage" in these assassinations. Even today, as the assassination program continues, its history remains shrouded in mystery: Israel's High Court of Justice ruled in April 2021 that declassification could "endanger national security," regardless of how old the cases might be.[4]

Aside from stating the usual prohibitions that most countries have against murder, the Oslo agreements forbade Israeli troops from entering Palestinian-controlled territory for any reason. The Israelis didn't care and did nothing to hide the fact that their undercover agents were operating there routinely. "There is complete justification for the implementation of the principle 'He who tries to kill you, kill him first,'" Yisrael Meir Lau, the country's Ashkenazi chief rabbi, told one journalist. Israel was fighting a "mandatory war," demanding "acts of self-defense, initiative and daring." Few human rights organizations embraced the rabbi's interpretation, however. They noted that the assassinations violated the 1907 Hague Convention, which clearly states that occupying forces are forbidden from infringing on the rights of the host nation's citizens. Israel also refused to provide any evidence that the people it was killing were, in fact, who it said they were or had done what they were alleged to have done. Amnesty International found that Israeli forces had "committed violations of international law during the course of military operations in the West Bank towns of Jenin and Nablus, including war crimes." Amnesty was not reporting in a one-sided way: an earlier report had termed Palestinian terrorist attacks against Israeli citizens to be "crimes against humanity." But Israel and its supporters rejected these reports, attacked the human rights organizations as biased, and sought to prevent them from doing their jobs.[5]

Israeli governments had long been at odds with the human rights organizations operating both inside Israel and within the occupied territories.

Israel's defenders consistently argued that it was the "only democracy in the Middle East" and that it alone among the countries in the region lived up to Western standards of human rights protections. But this was true only for Jews. Israeli Palestinians may have had more recognized rights than most of the citizens of the Arab dictatorships surrounding it—a point Israel's defenders never tired of making—but when it came to actually enforcing those rights, they often proved a mirage. Israeli Palestinians could not remotely depend on the web of legal protections, personal relationships, and military, judicial, and police sympathies that their fellow Jewish citizens simply took for granted. Israel's official investigation into the lives of its Arab inhabitants in 2003, known as the Or Commission Report, found that they could not depend on its police force to "demonstrate systematic and egalitarian enforcement of the law." This was another way of describing the persistent institutional discrimination Arabs had faced since the state's founding. Human rights groups won an important victory when, in 1999, the Israeli Supreme Court ruled that the "routine" torture of prisoners was illegal. In any case, the violence-minded settlers were more than happy to take matters into their own hands. Palestinians on the West Bank lived a life of near lawlessness between local authorities, roving gangs of self-appointed enforcers, Islamic decrees, and both Israeli troops and Jewish vigilantes.[6]

Israel's battles with the likes of Amnesty International, Human Rights Watch, and its own B'Tselem became a regular feature of US news coverage in this period, but they did not much affect US public opinion. Most Americans apparently accepted the argument that human rights violations were a necessity in a nation beset by terrorism. These feelings only intensified after September 11, 2001. Before the 9/11 attacks, one poll showed a 41–13 percent preference for the Israeli position over that of the Palestinians among Americans questioned; afterward, in the same poll, it was 55–7 percent.[7]

Even before the planes crashed into the World Trade Center and the Pentagon, neoconservatives had begun a campaign to justify another US-backed war against the Palestinians. During a three-day period in August 2001, three pundits, for example, argued in the *Washington Post* that Israel should launch yet another war. Michael Kelly, former editor-in-chief of *The New Republic*, began his piece by terming Ariel Sharon's visit to the Temple Mount a "pretext" for Palestinian violence, and mocked "the aggressively delusional" people who still failed to understand that "the Palestinians are the aggressor": "They started the conflict, and they purposely drive it forward with fresh killing on almost a daily basis." The Palestinians saw the Second Intifada "not as a sporadically violent protest movement but as a war," and Israel should respond accordingly. Kelly said Secretary of State Colin Powell's call for both sides to reduce tension was "beyond stupid": "It is immoral, hypocritical, obscene. It is indefensible." Powell and others had simply failed to recognize that "Israel is at war with an enemy that declines, in its shrewdness and its cowardice, to fight Israel's soldiers but is instead murdering its civilians, its women and children."[8]

Kelly's column was followed by that of another former *New Republic* editor, Charles Krauthammer, who had since decamped to Rupert Murdoch's *Weekly Standard*. Krauthammer described the conflict as if filing his story from inside Israel's propaganda ministry. "No country," he claimed, "can sustain what Israel is sustaining." Now that Arafat had "reject[ed] Israel's offer of a Palestinian state with its capital in a shared Jerusalem," he had unleashed a "terror campaign [with which] he intends to bring a bleeding, demoralized Israel to its knees, ready to surrender." Krauthammer, a recipient of the 2002 "Guardian of Zion" award from Israel's Bar-Ilan University, recommended war: "a lightning and massive Israeli attack on every element of Arafat's police state infrastructure" with a simultaneous attack on Arafat's rivals, Gaza's Hamas and Islamic Jihad—though he referred to them as Arafat's "allies"—as "the only way" to solve the crisis.[9]

On the third day came a column by George F. Will, the paper's most famous columnist ever since he had been hired to write an op-ed column for the paper in 1974. A secular conservative Christian, Will called for Israel to launch "a short war—a few days; over before European and American diplomats' appeasement reflexes kick in." Its purpose should be "to kill or capture those terrorists (and those who direct them) whom Arafat has permitted to remain at large," and "to destroy the Palestinian Authority's military infrastructure." Will insisted that Israel claim "all of Jerusalem," and thereby "signal the end of all talk about the indivisibility of Jerusalem." He, too, attacked US policy, blaming the State Department under the presumably dovish Secretary Powell as a "brackish and bottomless lagoon of obtuseness" when it came "to whatever Israel does in self-defense."[10]

Once again, talk of a "second Holocaust" filled the US media. One leader of a national Jewish organization announced that he was "convinced that we are facing a threat as great, if not greater, to the safety and security of the Jewish people than we faced in the '30s." Ron Rosenbaum, a respected Jewish biographer of Hitler, warned that "there's likely to be a second Holocaust. Not because the Israelis are acting without restraint, but because they are, so far, acting with restraint despite the massacres making their country uninhabitable." George Will would cite Rosenbaum's column in one of his own titled " 'Final Solution,' Phase 2." A New York Jewish paper ran the headline "THE NEW KRISTALLNACHT" above a story about a terrorist attack in Netanya; Charles Krauthammer repeated the phrase in the *Washington Post*, writing "This is Kristallnacht transposed to Israel." The Anti-Defamation League's Abe Foxman began his provocatively titled 2003 book *Never Again? The Threat of the New Anti-Semitism* by insisting that he was "convinced that we currently face as great a threat to the safety and security of the Jewish people as the one we faced in the 1930s—if not a greater one." This irrational panic occurred, it should be noted, more than five years after Israel's minister of communication, science, and the arts, Shulamit Aloni, advised her fellow Jews, at the 1996 Independence Day celebration, that "the world has changed; our place among the nations of the world is secure and stable. The struggle for physical survival is over. Only people with anachronistic mind-sets are still scaring us with fears of the past...seizing the sensations of victimization and persecution, preaching for isolation."[11]

This apparent never-ending psychosis—together with 9/11—would prove a boon for Israel's cause in the United States. A report summarizing thirteen polls taken in the aftermath of the attacks found large majorities agreeing with the view that most Palestinians sided with America's attackers. Support for the establishment of a Palestinian state fell to less than a third of those questioned. Many Americans shared the view that the attacks were at least partially inspired by America's association with, and support for, Israel. Only a tiny minority, however, told pollsters that the United States should therefore distance itself from the Jewish state. Rather, fully 93 percent believed that Israel and the United States should be working together to meet the threat of Islamic terrorism worldwide, and 84 percent believed that Israel should do whatever was necessary to find and destroy terrorists, who threatened to do serious harm to its citizens or nation. "You're either with us or you're with the terrorists," was George W. Bush's simplistic formula. Israel was "with us."[12]

This was all music to the ears of neoconservatives, who now dominated debate as never before. The Second Intifada had driven a stake through the heart of the Israeli peace movement and similarly devastated the political parties that supported it. The Israeli peace movement's decline robbed dovish American Jews of the legitimizing blessing that well-known Israeli writers, intellectuals, and (best of all) ex-generals could bestow upon them with their speaking tours of the United States and newspaper op-eds. Some brave (or reckless) writers or organizational figures may have tentatively floated the notion that it might be preferable were Israel to act with restraint, but there was virtually no one doing this in the mainstream US political debate. In the political climate of the Second Intifada, almost no one was willing to assign any responsibility to Israel for the ongoing violence between Israel and the Palestinians. What pro-Palestinian voices there were in these debates were largely in "Letters to the Editor" sections, and then published only in response to articles that spoke with the authority of the publication itself. For instance, Hussein Ibish, then employed as communications director of the American-Arab Anti-Discrimination Committee, wrote to the *Washington Post* to complain that "instead of urging Israel to comply with international law and end the occupation, [Michael] Kelly urges Israel to 'go right ahead and escalate the violence' and 'destroy, kill, capture and expel the armed Palestinian forces.'" But when Palestinians said such things about their Israeli enemies, he noted, "the United States demands their arrest, and Israel sends its death squads to execute them." His letter was one of four printed, and it appeared at the very bottom of the *Post*'s page.[13]

Democrats had emerged from 9/11 slightly less hawkish than Republicans, meaning that their leaders approved of the United States attacking only those nations and organizations that might credibly be tied to the attacks, rather than ones we just didn't happen to like. This reticence inspired yet another effort by conservatives, neo and otherwise, to try to convince American Jews to abandon the party they had stuck with since the beginning of the New Deal. (This was doubly ironic, as George W. Bush, in October 2001, became the first US president to make support for an independent Palestinian state official US policy.) William Safire picked up the cudgel that so many conservatives had been wielding since Lyndon Johnson began complaining about Jewish opposition to the Vietnam War thirty-five years earlier. The argument boiled down to the contention that if Jews really cared about Israel, they would desert the Democrats, who simply made an exception to their overall dovishness for Israel, and embrace the Republican Party, where hawkish support for military adventurism was consistent with its overall philosophy and therefore more reliable. In a column headlined "Democrats vs. Israel," published in the *New York Times* during the annual meeting of the American Israel Public Affairs Committee (AIPAC) in the spring of 2002, Safire insisted that Democrats were now in the process of "transmogrifying the Arab aggressor into the victim," though the reporting of his own newspaper belied the specifics of what he claimed as evidence. Here, yet again, Safire sought to carry on an argument that had now, for decades, been hosted by *Commentary*. It had featured American Jewish Committee staffer and sociologist Milton Himmelfarb (1967, 1981); his brother-in-law, the "godfather" of neoconservatism Irving Kristol (1973, 1984, 1999); AJC historian and Holocaust scholar Lucy Dawidowicz (1984); Harvard's Martin Peretz; professor of Yiddish Literature Ruth Wisse (1993); and many others. Kristol may have started it, but each of the others echoed his complaints about what he termed, in 1999, "the political stupidity of American Jews," albeit to little effect. Most Jews remained Democrats then and still remain so today.[14]

In the deeply contested 2000 presidential election in which the US Supreme Court eventually awarded him the presidency, George W. Bush earned just 19 percent of the Jewish vote. His opponent, Bill Clinton's vice president and a former senator, Al Gore, already enjoyed strong ties with Jewish leaders. He did not exactly hurt himself with this constituency by choosing Joe Lieberman, a politically hawkish senator, as his running mate. Lieberman was often described as the Senate's first Orthodox Jew. (Though Lieberman did attend an Orthodox Washington synagogue, he described himself only as an "observant Jew," rather than an Orthodox one.) With the Soviet Union consigned to the dustbin of history, Bush initially chose to side with the wing of the Republican Party that sought to return to its pre–World War II isolationist roots in foreign policy. "If we're an arrogant nation, they'll resent us," he said while running for president; but "if we're a humble nation, but strong, they'll welcome us." But 9/11 turned Bush around by 180 degrees. Guided by his vice president and now mentor in all matters, former defense secretary Dick Cheney, together with Defense Secretary Donald Rumsfeld, Bush expanded the definition of US national security beyond that of any previous administration. Henceforth, under Bush, the United States would "rid the world of evil-doers." A US military response against Al-Qaeda and the Taliban government in Afghanistan was widely supported across virtually the entire political spectrum. But the next question the members of the Bush administration asked themselves almost immediately was whether to attack Iraq as well.[15]

Anyone in search of a "Protocols of the Elders of Zion"–style conspiracy theory to explain the Bush administration's foreign and defense policies would have found particularly rich material in the myriad connections, coauthorships, editorships, and interlocking board memberships of the various organizations that connected the neoconservatives inside and outside the Bush administration agitating for a US attack on Iraq. Michael Lind, a foreign policy writer with ambidextrous politics, noted the apparent paradox at the time: "Most Jewish Americans are politically hostile to George W. Bush, whose alliance with the Christian right disturbs them. Yet the younger Bush has, in practice, been influenced more by the Israel lobby than by the oil lobby." This reliance was due, he suggested, to the post-9/11 loss of influence of the State Department, which continued to support Palestinian statehood and the peace process, together with the rise of "a cadre of pro-Israel hawks" allied with Undersecretary of Defense Paul Wolfowitz.[16]

The son of Polish Jewish immigrants, and fluent in six languages, Wolfowitz had been the model for the Straussian political apparatchik character in Saul Bellow's final novel, 2001's *Ravelstein*. A former Senate staffer for Henry "Scoop" Jackson who received his PhD while studying under the nuclear war theorist Albert Wohlstetter, Wolfowitz was deeply enmeshed in the world of Jewish neoconservatism. In 2002, the Jewish Institute for National Security of America (JINSA) gave Wolfowitz its Henry M. "Scoop" Jackson Distinguished Service Award for promoting a strong partnership between Israel and the United States, and the *Jerusalem Post*, describing him as "devoutly pro-Israel," named him its "Man of the Year." A frequent guest at AIPAC conferences even while in office, Wolfowitz helped the organization raise funds by speaking to invitation-only gatherings for big donors.[17]

Wolfowitz's deep connections to AIPAC, the neocons, and Israel were particularly important in the debates of how the United States was misled into its disastrous war in Iraq. After 9/11 Wolfowitz had argued for the United States to attack Iraq rather than Afghanistan. And it was Wolfowitz who found the political justification for such a war. "For bureaucratic reasons," he admitted to *Vanity Fair*, "we settled on one issue, weapons of mass destruction, because it was the one reason everyone could agree on." The fact that the case for war would turn out to be based on false information—and that it was promoted by Wolfowitz, given his reputation and associations—would, to no small degree, color the perception that the disastrous war was launched at least partially to benefit Israel rather than the United States.[18]

In addition to Wolfowitz, a former JINSA board member, Douglas Feith, who was now Bush's deputy undersecretary of defense, together with the chair of Bush's Defense Policy Board, Richard Perle, another former Scoop Jackson staffer, had coauthored a 1996 paper with David Wurmser, now a special assistant to the (extremely hawkish) undersecretary of state for arms control, John Bolton. (Israel's ambassador to the United States labeled Bolton "a secret member of Israel's own team" during his tenure as Bush's UN representative.) The paper, titled "A Clean Break: A New Strategy for Securing the Realm," was written at the behest of Benjamin Netanyahu, who was then not yet prime minister but an extremely ambitious Likud politician. The report called for "removing Saddam Hussein from power in Iraq" as "an important Israeli strategic objective in its own right," together with a war on the Palestinian Authority.[19]

Another paper, this one authored exclusively by Feith in 1997, suggested that Israel reoccupy "the areas under Palestinian Authority control." A year later, in 1998, under the rubric of a neoconservative foreign policy think tank, the Project for the New American Century, ten members of the future Bush administration—including Wolfowitz, Rumsfeld, Perle, and Feith—signed a letter arguing for a unilateral US invasion of Iraq. This missive was followed up in early 2001 by Wurmser, then ensconced at another conservative think tank, the American Enterprise Institute, who wrote up war plans for Israel and the United States "to strike fatally, not merely disarm... the regimes of Damascus, Baghdad, Tripoli, Tehran, and Gaza." These arguments were heavily promoted inside the White House by Elliott Abrams, a former Scoop Jackson staffer and Norman Podhoretz's and Midge Decter's son-in-law. Following his criminal conviction for lying to Congress about the Iran/Contra scandal during the Reagan administration, Abrams received a presidential pardon from the first president Bush, and the job of national security staffer in charge of Middle East policy from the second.[20]

As the administration was debating how to respond to the Al Qaeda attacks, and much of the rest of the country remained in a state of shock and fear, neoconservatives leapt into what they accurately viewed as a political void. Charles Krauthammer and others had taken the position—in the years immediately following the end of the Cold War—that as the world's only "unipower" (that is, its only remaining superpower), the United States could pretty much do whatever it wished with its military. At the same time, Harvard scholar Samuel Huntington's argument for a "clash of civilizations" between Islam and the West led many to the conclusion that a civilizational war was not only unavoidable but desirable. The fact that this meshed with Israel's interests implied that for those advocating these actions, it was understood as a given that the United States should attack some as yet undetermined combination of Israel's Arab adversaries. For neoconservatives and many others, the interests of the United States and Israel were now identical, and a global war against radical Islam was therefore justified wherever what Bush called these "evildoers" reared their heads. Israel could now play the role that Benjamin Netanyahu, as prime minister, later described as a "defensive shield of Western civilization in the heart of the Middle East." New York's *Jewish Week* put the case rather starkly in a headline reading, "America: The New Israel."[21]

The neoconservatives presented Americans with a lengthy list of nations they believed should be invaded or, at the very least, attacked. Nine days after the 9/11 attack, forty neoconservatives (and others) sent an open letter to George W. Bush insisting that he target not only Saddam Hussein, but also Syria and Iran, if the latter did not stop supporting Hezbollah, as well as Hezbollah itself. "Even if evidence does not link Iraq directly to the attack," it read, "any strategy aiming at the eradication of terrorism and its sponsors must include a determined effort to remove Saddam Hussein from power in Iraq." Its authors reminded Bush that "Israel has been and remains America's staunchest ally against international terrorism." Writing in the *Wall Street Journal*, Seth Lipsky, a neoconservative and the former editor of the [Jewish] *Forward*, called for US attacks "from Afghanistan to Iran to Iraq to Syria to the Palestinian Authority." *The New Republic*'s editors demanded that the Bush administration "move ruthlessly to prevent Iran from acquiring the deadliest arsenal of all." *Weekly Standard* editor William Kristol preferred an immediate "military strike against Iranian nuclear facilities." Charles Krauthammer argued in the *Washington Post* that after the United States was done with Afghanistan, Syria should be next, followed by Iran and Iraq. Norman Podhoretz, writing in *Commentary*, termed George W. Bush's mission to be to fight what he called "World War IV—the war against militant Islam." Among his favored targets: Iraq, Iran, North Korea, Syria, Lebanon, and Libya as well as Saudi Arabia, Egypt, and the Palestinian Authority.[22]

The panic, paranoia, and uncertainty that followed 9/11 led to accusations of disloyalty against anyone who failed to get with the program or who even dared to question what it might be. Andrew Sullivan was not a neoconservative, but he had been the editor of *The New Republic* and a protégé of Martin Peretz. Five days after the attack, Sullivan pontificated that "the middle part of the country—the great red zone that voted for Bush—is clearly ready for war. The decadent Left in its enclaves on the coasts is not dead—and may well mount what amounts to a fifth column." (Those "decadent" untrustworthy Gore voters, Sullivan failed to note, exceeded those voting for Bush by slightly more than half a million.)[23]

As was now the new "normal," neoconservative arguments in the wake of 9/11 hewed much closer to the views held by evangelical Christians than they did to those of American Jews. A Gallup poll found "that among the major religious groups in the United States, Jewish Americans are the most strongly opposed to the Iraq war." Ambivalence abounded. As the pundit Michael Kinsley put it in October 2002, "Among Jewish Americans, including me, there are people who hold every conceivable opinion about war with Iraq with every variation of intensity, including passionate opposition and complete indifference." Meanwhile, the age-old worries about gentiles blaming the Jews for the wars they fought also arose again. David Harris, at the helm of the American Jewish Committee, feared that a failed war in Iraq would lead Americans to turn to the "scapegoat for bigots for centuries"—its Jews. All of these competing arguments within the Jewish community led to a far more complicated picture than that usually painted in the media, where "Jewish interests" continued to be defined as "supporting Israel," as the neocons had so far successfully defined them.[24]

Jews also worried about being blamed for the 9/11 attack itself. Their concerns had nothing to do with the band of so-called 9/11 "Truthers," who counted the (fictitious) number of Jews who allegedly stayed home from work in the World Trade Center's Twin Towers that day, or who saw the hand of the Mossad in the attack itself—these deranged individuals could be safely ignored. Rather, their concerns were grounded in the commonsense belief that when Islamic terrorists attacked the United States, they were likely to have been inspired by the United States' long support for Israel. But neoconservative pundits and Jewish leaders insisted that the attack and US foreign policy were unrelated. They did so in part because they wished to argue that US support for Israel brought with it no significant costs, and also because if it were true, then the obvious fix would be to change the policy and reduce US support for Israel.

Ironically, the first prominent person to lay out the case against the neoconservative war party turned out to be the paleocon pundit and sometime Republican presidential candidate Patrick J. Buchanan. A fascinating and quite charming personality in the American punditocracy, Buchanan had danced along the far-right fringe of respectable discourse for decades. His easy amiability and perennial good humor helped to make his semi-fascistic political views palatable to television producers and radio programmers and their audiences. Buchanan had grown up in a culturally isolated Catholic community where Spain's longtime dictator Francisco Franco and Joseph McCarthy were counted as heroes. He championed the Chilean dictator Augusto Pinochet and the racist government of apartheid-era South Africa, flirted with supporting the former KKK grand wizard David Duke, and even evinced a soft spot for accused Nazi war criminals. Regarding the Middle East, he manifested a traditional far-right distaste for Israel, exacerbated by a fury born of the neoconservative displacement of himself and his fellow paleoconservatives from the center of conservative thought and power. During the first Gulf War, under the first President Bush, he had notoriously claimed, from his perch on television's *McLaughlin Group*, that "there are only two groups that are beating the drums...for war in the Middle East—the Israeli Defense Ministry and its amen corner in the United States."[25]

Buchanan's 5,200-word cover story appeared in March 2003, just as Washington's war fever was reaching its highest pitch. Buchanan leaned heavily on guilt-by–Jewish association. It was published in *The American Conservative*, which, despite its name, displayed heterodox ideological proclivities, with both left- and right-wing voices united in support of an old-fashioned isolationist foreign policy, together with a profound hostility to Israel that sometimes slipped into naked antisemitism. Alongside conspiracy-friendly Buchanan, the magazine also featured the sometimes pro-Nazi Taki Theodoracopulos (who would become its editor) and Philip Weiss, a former journalist whose bizarre, conspiracy-driven musings on Jews and Israel on his eponymous website, Mondoweiss, put a period on the end of what had once been a successful journalistic career.[26]

Noting the host of nations that various neoconservatives had nominated for attack, Buchanan asked, "*Cui Bono*? For whose benefit these endless wars in a region that holds nothing vital to America save oil, which the Arabs must sell us to survive? Who would benefit from a war of civilizations between the West and Islam?" His answer: "One nation, one leader, one party. Israel, Sharon, Likud." He then guided the reader through a potted history of what he understood to be Israel's all-but-criminal manipulation of US politics up to the present day. He charged the neoconservatives with seeking to "ensnare our country in a series of wars that are not in America's interests," and with "colluding with Israel to ignite those wars and destroy the Oslo Accords." He insisted that they were "deliberately damaging U.S. relations with every state in the Arab world that defies Israel or supports the Palestinian people's right to a homeland of their own," and "alienat[ing] friends and allies all over the Islamic and Western world through their arrogance, hubris, and bellicosity." The upshot, he continued, was that "President Bush is being lured into a trap baited for him by these neocons that could cost him his office and cause America to forfeit years of peace won for us by the sacrifices of two generations in the Cold War." (Luckily for Bush, Buchanan was unaware that the president's own mother, former First Lady Barbara Bush, had greeted him on the phone with the question, "How's the first Jewish president doing?")[27]

What Buchanan did not understand, or at least did not say, was that for many American Jewish neoconservatives, there was no distinction to be made between the defense of Israel and the defense of the United States. With countless American Jews, these identities had thoroughly merged. To be a patriotic American meant to support your government in war, and so, too, to be a patriotic Jew meant to support Israel. To be an American Jew meant supporting both and questioning neither—at least when Israel was involved. It was less a conspiracy than an identity. The idea that the interests of these two nations—these two parts of the beating heart of American Jewish identity, could diverge became, for many, literally unthinkable. The fact that one of these countries was a tiny beleaguered Middle Eastern nation and the other a global superpower nearly seven thousand miles away meant little when it came to Israel's and America's supposed "shared values" and shared enemies. Martin Peretz put this clearly during the 2006 Israeli war with Hezbollah: "Let's face it: Aside from fighting for themselves, the Israelis are also fighting for us." Norman Podhoretz, readers may recall, had accused anyone who did not approve of Israel's invasion of Lebanon twenty-four years earlier "not merely of anti-Semitism but of the broader sin of faithlessness to the interests of the United States and indeed to the values of Western civilization as a whole."[28]

Their arguments, while hardly convincing in a normative sense, tracked almost perfectly with those of leftists who viewed Israel merely as an organ of American imperialism. In any case, Buchanan's arguments could be summarily dismissed in the mainstream debate because of who it was that was making them: a far-right crank with a particular bee in his bonnet about Israel, resulting from his brand of Joe McCarthy–style right-wing Catholicism, pre–World War II isolationism, soft antisemitism, and occasional sympathy for accused Nazi war criminals. With friends like Pat Buchanan, the Palestinians hardly needed enemies. The next set of Israel's critics would not be so easy to dismiss.

## CHAPTER 16

# WARS OF WORDS

THE 9/11 ATTACKS LEFT MANY MARKS ON AMERICAN LIFE ARISING FROM the combination of fear, paranoia, anger, and confusion they inspired. A byproduct of this miasma of emotion would be a significant narrowing of what was considered to be responsible political opinion. And given the ethnic and religious makeup of the hijackers and their champions abroad, no issue would turn out to be as sensitive to this trend as the debate over the US role in the Middle East. In the halls of Congress and in much of the mainstream media, any questioning of America's essential goodness, its moral purpose in the world, and the necessity of standing up for its allies in the region was considered the equivalent of disloyalty. Perhaps our behavior in the world had not been perfect, and yes, some Middle East inhabitants might have genuine grievances against us, but to say so aloud, much less to enumerate reasons why, was, in the parlance of the time, "to let the terrorists win." And it should come as no surprise that nowhere was the post-9/11 debate policed more energetically than in the case of America's support for Israel.

Beyond the borders of congressional and cable news and op-ed-page debates, liberals and leftists had been marching steadily in a pro-Palestinian direction for decades. Evidence of this transformation could be seen in the pages of small-circulation left-wing opinion magazines such as *The Nation* and *Mother Jones* or alternative *Village Voice*–like newspapers. Aside from these, and the occasional outburst from a Hollywood celebrity (often rapidly withdrawn), the one place where the Palestinians were consistently seen to wear the white hats, and Israelis the black ones, was on the campuses of America's elite universities.

Under most circumstances, it matters little what students and professors think about politics. College protesters made themselves matter during the Vietnam era because they were willing to throw themselves into marches, demonstrations, and eventually riots that upset the balance of society beyond the confines of their campuses. (And it is far from clear, based on a reading of public opinion data, that they did not do far more harm to the antiwar cause than good.) Anti-Israel sentiment on campuses was unlikely to affect US public opinion, much less its foreign policy. But there were two reasons why the issue did rise to the level of a genuine national controversy. First was a concern among elites generally that future generations of America's leaders were being raised by their professors to overturn decades of US foreign policy consensus and that this portended dramatic changes ahead both for Israel and for America's role in the world (and, to be fair, this was exactly what their professors intended). Second was the fact that almost all upper-middle-class American Jewish high school students go on to college. Most do so, however, having been educated about Israel in a Leon Uris–type of ideological bubble. In college, they enter an alternative universe in which Israel is understood to be the oppressor and the Palestinians their victims. This caused cognitive dissonance, and the result was often panic. Their parents, meanwhile, were also often panicked to learn that the hundreds of thousands of dollars of tuition they were paying were resulting in their children coming home with arguments they believed to be not merely wrong, but personally (and painfully) offensive. This was especially true given what had become the central role that support for Israel now played in defining secular American Jews' identity.

The leftist turn against Israel had many causes. But "the most obvious one," as *Haaretz*'s veteran political columnist Chemi Shalev would write in his valedictory column, "especially for the younger generation," was "the unbearable discrepancy between the idyllic Israel they were sold and their realization of reality on the ground." Israel had become a conservative cause, whereas academia had moved steadily leftward. Indeed, on many campuses, liberals were now the conservatives and conservatives were entirely nonexistent.[1]

On campus, the humanities had undergone a considerable epistemological transformation since the parents of twenty-first-century students had closed their last textbook. As the revolutionary movements of the 1960s collapsed in violence and recrimination, many of the most sophisticated thinkers of the era, along with their idealistic followers, sought refuge inside the academy. Many of the former set out to determine what had gone wrong and to train the next generation of student activists to do a better job. While each discipline brought its own approach to contemporary politics, most humanities faculty members in America's top universities shared a similar set of Marxist-tinged assumptions. Like the ideologies of the 1960s, they implied a rapaciousness on the part of the United States and other Western nations vis-à-vis the downtrodden of the world. Professors—and their students—accused their elders of helping to justify injustices and inequalities that previous scholarship barely acknowledged to exist. They tied the pursuit of "knowledge" directly to the creation of these oppressive structures, and hence wanted to see it dismantled and rebuilt to reflect a new, anti-racist, anti-colonialist pedagogical agenda. In this universe, Israel functioned as a mini America, spreading misery, doing the bidding of an imperialist power in the service of "settler colonialism," and being rewarded with billions in aid and endless propaganda published by a compliant corporate media. Soon enough, as the scholar of Jewish campus life, Rachel Fish, pointed out from the vantage point of 2022, "the state of Israel [became] an obsession of today's university, a linchpin around which an extraordinary volume of discourse, pedagogy, and politics revolves."[2]

The anti-Israel tilt in academia manifested itself in any number of ways. A group calling itself Students for Justice in Palestine supported demonstrations and teach-ins featuring lectures, film presentations, and theatrical "Israel Apartheid" performances, together with often obnoxious disruptions of Israel-related lectures and rallies. A growing number of Jewish students joined these groups, especially the organization Jewish Voice for Peace (JVP), which claimed to be the fastest-growing Jewish organization on campus. Even at Brandeis, America's most Jewish (secular) university, students formed a JVP chapter and applied to become a constituent member of the school's Hillel organization. Although they were rejected, they still collected a thousand student signatures for a petition that demanded their admittance.[3]

The foundational text for the epistemological transformation in the humanities within the academy was Edward Said's *Orientalism: Western Conceptions of the Orient*, published in 1978. (Ironically, Said decided to write the book only after his friend Noam Chomsky declined his suggestion that the two coauthor one on media misperceptions of the Middle East.) Ranging across an astonishing number of sources in different disciplines and at least a half dozen languages, Said explained that the term "Orientalism" was intended to explain, culturally and ideologically, how "a mode of discourse with supporting institutions, vocabulary, scholarships, imagery, doctrines, even colonial bureaucracies and colonial styles" supported imperialist modes of thought and action. It was a form of what the French philosopher Michel Foucault termed "power-knowledge," by which Western nations shaped not only the beliefs of their own citizens, but also those of the nations they conquered and controlled via mechanisms originally described by the Italian communist philosopher Antonio Gramsci. In leading the West "to take up a position of irreducible opposition to a region of the world it considered alien to its own," Said deduced, Orientalism—a handmaiden to imperialism—excused, and even celebrated, all manner of brutality under the banner of "progress." Flawed as Said's analysis may have been in the eyes of many specialists in the myriad fields into which its polymathic author ventured, his critique proved a powerful tool to interrogate the ideas put forth by established academics who cultivated cozy relationships with government agencies, global corporations, and other sources of political power.[4]

Translated into thirty-six languages (including Hebrew) and published all over the world, the book's popularity on America's elite college campuses drove its conservative critics to distraction. According to one calculation,

*Orientalism* appeared on the syllabi of 868 courses in American colleges and universities, and this count included only syllabi available online in 2013. Israel's former ambassador to the United States, the American-born Michael Oren, sporting two degrees from Columbia University, reported in his 2015 memoir that he believed it had become the "single most influential book in the humanities." And while he based his assessment on a nine-year-old, statistically sketchy survey of Harvard students, he was likely not wrong. In March 2002, Martin Kramer, of the aggressively "pro-Israel" watchdog organization Campus Watch, specifically blamed what he called the "empire" Said had built for having laid the intellectual groundwork for the worldview that left Americans "unprepared for the events of 9/11." Kramer wrote an entire book on the topic and argued in multiple forums that congressional control of the field's federal research funds was necessary. Middle Eastern studies programs and research centers had to be "held accountable for how they serve the needs of the American public or the United States government." The famously Islamophobic Daniel Pipes, who headed up Middle East Forum, Campus Watch's parent organization, made a similar argument, insisting that university-based scholars were "financed by the public and are thus accountable in some way to the public." Together, the two were instrumental in promoting legislation in 2003 that would have demanded government control over the content of what was taught about US foreign policy on college campuses. It passed the House of Representatives but never made it into law.[5]

Having failed in Congress, however, the battle was joined in academia itself. One result was the rapid expansion of "Israel studies" programs, centers, and endowed chairs in universities across America. The Taub Foundation's Fred Lafter donated $3.5 million to get New York University's program off the ground, saying it was in order to fill the "void" he identified within Middle Eastern studies departments, where he believed the issues were "cast in an Arabic point of view." (The program's "advisory board" included not scholars in the field but right-wing Jewish funders, such as the [now disgraced] billionaire Michael Steinhardt and the former CEO of CBS Laurence Tisch.) Recent numbers are hard to come by, but by the 2011–2012 school year, fully 316 schools included in one study offered 625 courses that focused specifically on Israel, as well as 752 other Israel-related courses. These courses no doubt enjoyed considerable overlap with others offered in the nation's more than 250 Jewish studies departments and programs, which also saw significant growth in guest lectures and funding during the same period.[6]

One should not draw any nefarious conclusions about any of the individual scholars teaching in these programs and departments—indeed, this book is deeply indebted to their work. But in academia, perhaps only slightly less frequently than in business or politics, he who pays the piper often gets to call the tune. There are no Israel studies programs supporting explicitly anti-Zionist scholars. It would be no easy task locating one that was willing to risk even hosting a debate about Israel and Palestine with such a scholar, lest it anger an important funder. Many such programs are actually run by Israeli professors themselves, and all walk a fine line between scholarship and boosterism, with a necessary sensitivity to every potential political pitfall. When, in 2022, the University of Washington returned a gift to a Jewish funder who had been contacted by the right-wing organization "Stand With Us," after a professor's name had appeared on a petition of Jewish scholars who were critical of Israel's behavior during its May 2021 bombing of Gaza, this was, ironically, the second time a funder had demanded money back from an Israel studies program over the politics of a professor in the state of Washington. (The first had taken place in 2017, at Western Washington University.) Following an outcry among faculty at the university and from scholars in related fields, the University of Washington managed to save the program (albeit at a reduced level of funding) and find a replacement chair for the scholar in question, Professor Liora Halperin. But the threat—and the university's initial willingness to contravene its own rules regarding a donor's power over gifts already given—no doubt caused a chill among many other scholars who might have to rely on such funding the future.[7]

Save for Jewish parents and grandparents, most of the general public would have had little familiarity with how the debate over Israel and Palestine was being presented on college campuses, or much reason to care. But pundits and politicians who paid more than casual attention to the issue did have reason to care. Especially in New York and other places where Jews—and, hardly coincidentally, many of the nation's most influential media institutions—were concentrated, college curricula soon became a crucial political battleground. It grew in significance each year as word of the unsympathetic views of Israel being taught at top universities seeped into family discussions at Thanksgiving and other holidays. Not surprisingly, the most heated controversy over the teaching of the Israel/Palestine conflict on campus occurred not long after 9/11 at New York City's only Ivy League school, Columbia University. The problem began when a Palestinian American assistant professor, Joseph Massad—a former mentee of Said's—taught a class called "Palestinian and Israeli Politics and Societies." Massad apparently used a number of unflattering terms in class to describe Israel, including calling it a "racist, settler-colonial state," and the class became its own sort of mini war zone on campus. According to one student, "Professor Massad was unable to speak more than five sentences without being interrupted during his lecture," and he "listened calmly and responded kindly to every interruption." But another student claimed to have been told in class, during a discussion of Israel's invasion of Gaza, "If you're going to deny the atrocities being committed against the Palestinian people, then you can get out of my classroom."[8]

According *The Nation*'s Scott Sherman, Massad said that "unregistered individuals and auditors" appeared in his class, and Massad believed they were "there to heckle him and monitor his teaching." In any case, a few individuals secretly filmed his class. "The David Project," a Boston-based organization devoted, in its own words, to rooting out "dishonest discussion and discourse about the Mideast on college campuses," showed up to jump-start a student petition for Columbia to fire Massad and sanction some of his colleagues who appeared to share his views. The project was part of a multimillion-dollar effort begun in March 2002 by a network of national Jewish organizations to "'take back the campus' by influencing public opinion through lectures, the Internet and coalitions," according to Sherman. It had "ties" to the American Israel Public Affairs Committee (AIPAC), the Anti-Defamation League (ADL), and the American Jewish Committee (AJC), though its funding and structure always remained rather murky.[9]

The project recruited Jewish students to speak about their feelings and experiences on camera. It eventually created six versions of the video, titled *Columbia Unbecoming*, made up of student complaints about their professors, with each one being shown to different preselected audiences. Many of the students—quite a few of whom had their faces purposely distorted for the video, the way mobsters do when they testify against their bosses—expressed unhappiness with comments and statements that professors either wrote in newspapers and scholarly articles, or were heard to utter at rallies, rather than in academic settings. The film's foundational argument, that Jews were "under attack at Columbia or that the faculty is anti-Semitic," was a "crazy, crazy exaggeration," according to Robert Pollack, the Jewish former dean of the university's Columbia College, who had helped to raise millions for Columbia's Israel and Jewish programs. Indeed, Columbia was the first Ivy League school to promote a Jew, Lionel Trilling, to a tenured position in its English Department. It has since garnered the highest percentage of Jewish students in its student body of any Ivy League school, more than 30 percent higher than its nearest competitor. Its sister school, Barnard, has the second-highest single population of Jewish students at any major school in the country, missing out on a tie with Brandeis by a single percentage point. Columbia has an Institute for Israel and Jewish Studies with enormously robust programs; a well-funded, well-attended, and well-staffed Hillel chapter; and some of the most distinguished Jewish faculty members of any university in the world.[10]

Even so, the videos did the trick, creating what the ancient Talmudic sage Rabbi Yossi ben Zimra called *motzira*: a combination of gossip and slander that led to a perception of chaos to those outside. The extreme right-wing Zionist Organization of America sponsored "The Middle East and Academic Integrity on the American Campus," a day-long denunciation session on the Columbia campus. Campus Watch called for Massad to be fired in countless press releases and op-eds, including one published by the *Wall Street Journal*. The *New York Sun*, a small, neoconservative paper run by the right-wing Jewish editor and media entrepreneur Seth Lipsky, launched a lengthy barrage of attacks against Massad and his colleagues, with nearly hourly coverage of the students' complaints. The *New York Daily News* published a lurid "special report" headlined "Poison Ivy: Climate of Hate Rocks Columbia University." The article proclaimed that "dozens of academics are said to be promoting an I-hate-Israel agenda, embracing the ugliest of Arab propaganda, and teaching that Zionism is the root of all evil in the Mideast." Massad's photo appeared in an editorial under the headline "Columbia: Fire This Professor." Given that New York City has the largest Jewish community in the world outside of Israel, its politicians naturally found the cause irresistible. Congressman Anthony Weiner (D-NY), who was planning a mayoral run, demanded that Columbia dismiss Massad for his "anti-Semitic rantings." The city's sitting mayor, Michael Bloomberg, asked Columbia to investigate the students' complaints, as did the ADL's Abe Foxman, though City Council Speaker Gifford Maxim warned of a potential "whitewash." The ubiquitous Jewish attorney and television pundit Alan Dershowitz showed up on campus to denounce, perhaps not so surprisingly, Edward Said, who had died two years earlier.[11]

Columbia's president, Lee Bollinger, tried to quiet the crisis by offloading the issue to an ad hoc committee of the faculty. When it finally issued its report, the committee found that the problem was less with Columbia itself than with those seeking to make a national issue of what was being taught in its classrooms. Yes, members of the Columbia faculty, including, especially, Massad, had made critical comments about Israel that were likely inappropriate in an academic setting. But the committee found "no evidence of any statements made by the faculty that could reasonably be construed as anti-Semitic." What the investigation did turn up, however, was "a broader environment of incivility on campus, with pro-Israel students disrupting lectures on Middle Eastern studies and some faculty members feeling that they were being spied on." Made-up charges were then repeated and manipulated by "pro-Israel" propagandists and then trumpeted by opportunistic politicians and careless and often disingenuous journalists and neoconservative pundits. The New York Civil Liberties Union said the committee had "properly identifie[d] the threats to academic freedom posed by the 'involvement of outside organizations in the surveillance of professors,'" but criticized it for failing to "adequately...place the intrusion into the academy by outside organizations in a broader political context." One student gave up his Middle East major regretfully, blaming what he called "outside instigation" that "wasn't really about Columbia, or even Massad. It was about Edward Said. It was as if all those forces had been waiting until he was gone to make a case against him."[12]

The row hardly ended with the committee report, however. Rashid Khalidi, the director of Columbia's Middle East Institute in its School of International and Public Affairs, former president of the Middle East Studies Association, editor of the *Journal of Palestine Studies*, and, not least in importance, the son of Palestinian parents and the holder of the university's Edward Said Chair in Modern Arab Studies, had previously cotaught a course on Israel and Palestine with Rabbi Arthur Hertzberg. He now found himself barred by the New York chancellor of education, Joel Klein, from participating in a public school education program for teachers. The disinvite came shortly after the *Sun* trumpeted his planned participation while reporting that the American Jewish Committee had attacked Khalidi's "record of brazen, openly biased and distorted statements about Israel."[13]

Back at Barnard, meanwhile, another controversy arose when Nadia Abu El-Haj, an American anthropologist with a Palestinian father, came up for tenure. Her 2001 book, *Facts on the Ground: Archaeological Practice and Territorial Self-Fashioning in Israeli Society*, had been chosen by the Middle East Studies Association of North America as one of the winners of its 2002 Albert Hourani Book Award. Three different tenure committees approved her. That's when a group led by an American-born West Bank settler named Paula Stern, who owned a small technical writing business, started sending out Internet petitions calling on Columbia to reject El-Haj, insisting that her scholarship was substandard and corrupted by an alleged hatred of Israel. Questioned about these charges by enterprising reporters, Stern admitted that the information contained in her petition might not be "100 percent accurate." Even so, she was joined in her effort by a former Columbia student, Bari Weiss, who had participated in the *Columbia Unbecoming* project. Weiss had published an op-ed in Israel's *Haaretz* complaining that El-Haj did not deserve tenure at Barnard because her scholarship was nothing more than an anthropological manifestation of Said's *Orientalism*. Weiss apparently misunderstood Said's work as an argument that "there is no such thing as truth or fact. Instead, there is only identity." The effort failed, and El-Haj received tenure in 2007; as of this writing, she codirects Columbia's Center for Palestine Studies.[14]

Having lost this battle, Weiss—who would go on to forge a successful (and lucrative) career, first as a *New York Times* pundit, and later as an independent writer who specialized in exposing "cancel culture" on campuses and in the mainstream media—then went after Massad yet again. When Massad was granted tenure in 2015, Weiss published an article in Mosaic Magazine, funded by the right-wing Jewish Tikvah Fund, titled "How to Fight Anti-Semitism on Campus." There, she complained that Massad had been promoted "despite the sustained and strong opposition of student whistleblowers, concerned alumni, and others." This opposition had apparently continued despite the fact that Massad had somehow turned "untold numbers of naïve students into unwitting tools of anti-Semitism." Weiss went on to attack another of Massad's colleagues, Hamid Dabashi, a professor of Iranian studies and comparative literature, as a "bigot." She suggested that his presence "at a university whose biggest donors include well-known and proud supporters of Israel [was] a wonder and a scandal." The idea that the pro-Israel donors and alumni should somehow control, or even influence, the tenure process could hardly be more offensive to the fundamental tenet of academic freedom that a great university like Columbia attempts to uphold. But it was an idea that was becoming increasingly popular among pro-Israel partisans, who were growing ever more panicky about what was being taught on campus. In November 2021, with apparently unintended irony, Weiss's website announced the formation of a new—albeit uncredited and still largely imaginary—university to one day be located in Texas. Its mission statement explained, "The reality is that many universities no longer have an incentive to create an environment where intellectual dissent is protected, and fashionable opinions are scrutinized."[15]

The controversy at Columbia would turn out to be a mere curtain-raiser to a far larger collision between the vision of Israel now common in academia—as well as in most of the rest of the world beyond America's borders—and its portrayal in mainstream US political discourse. It began in March 2006, when two highly regarded "Realist" international relations scholars gave voice to some of the harshest criticism of Israel—and the role it played in US foreign policy—heard in mainstream debate certainly since Patrick Buchanan's 2003 *American Conservative* article (and perhaps going back to Yasser Arafat's UN speech twenty-eight years earlier).

In their interrogation of the role of what they called "the Israel Lobby," Stephen Walt and John J. Mearsheimer authored first a 34,000-plus-word Harvard working paper along with a 13,000-plus-word article in the *London Review of Books*, and later a 484-page book on the subject. They argued that thanks in significant measure to the efforts of "the Lobby," the United States had become an "enabler" of Israeli expansion in the occupied territories. The United States was therefore "complicit in the crimes perpetrated against the Palestinians" and had earned the enmity of Arabs and Muslims the world over. Most controversially, they insisted that the Lobby's pressure was the critical element in the US decision to undertake its catastrophic invasion of Iraq.[16]

What made this effort so significant was the comprehensiveness of the authors' indictment, together with the prestige they enjoyed and the prominence of their publications. Walt and Mearsheimer were not leftists, Arabs, Muslims, or members of a pro-Palestinian organization. They were not friends, much less students, of Edward Said or Noam Chomsky. Their work was usually published not in *The Nation* or *The Village Voice*, but in *Foreign Affairs*, the prestigious publication of the Council on Foreign Relations, and the peer-reviewed journal *Security Studies*. Walt was the Robert and Renée Belfer Professor of International Affairs at Harvard University and formerly the academic dean at its John F. Kennedy School of Government. He had previously taught at Princeton and the University of Chicago, along with visiting stints at the Brookings Institution and Carnegie Endowment for International Peace. Mearsheimer was a US Air Force veteran and the R. Wendell Harrison Distinguished Service Professor at the University of Chicago, the former chair of its Department of Political Science, and a member of the American Academy of Arts and Sciences. It would have been hard, at the time of publication, to find two more respected international relations scholars anywhere in the English-speaking world.

It is true that despite these credentials, their argument was sometimes sloppy. First, much of what they attributed to the influence of "the Israel Lobby" could easily have been at least partially credited to other forces, especially in their arguments about the US invasion of Iraq. Walt and Mearsheimer credited both AIPAC and neoconservatives with more influence over Bush's decision to go to war than they likely deserved. True, they were able to quote AIPAC's executive director, Howard Kohr, bragging of "quietly lobbying Congress to approve the use of force in Iraq," and called this "one of AIPAC's successes over the past year." But AIPAC leaders brag about all sorts of things; it does not make them true. Was "the Lobby" really the "critical element" identified by the authors in the decision to go to war? The authors promised "abundant evidence" on this point, but nowhere among their 1,399 footnotes did they make good on that claim.[17]

President Bush, after all, had repeatedly expressed outrage about "the guy who tried to kill my dad." He said repeatedly that he wanted to rid the world of "evil," and, given his combination of arrogance and religious fervor, coupled with his near total ignorance of geography, history, and culture, he apparently believed this to be possible. The more cynical pro-war voices—including those of his top three advisers, Vice President Dick Cheney, Secretary of Defense Donald Rumsfeld, and Secretary of State Condoleezza Rice, along with CIA Director George Tenet—had demonstrated no particular devotion to Israel. None were Jews or neoconservatives. Each was clearly motivated by a belief that Saddam Hussein represented a genuine national security threat to the United States, or at least to key national interests. These included not only access to oil, but also strategic dominance of the entire region. One can agree that, just below this level, Wolfowitz, Feith, Wurmser, Abrams, and others were putting Israel's security near the pinnacle of their concerns. But to imply that they bamboozled their bosses into supporting their views with lies about weapons of mass destruction and phony connections between Iraq and al-Qaeda is both naïve and, at least arguably, overly conspiratorially minded.[18]

Second, the authors offered up "the Lobby" as virtually the only deter-minant of US Middle East policy—a proposition that is all but impos-sible to defend. Noam Chomsky was particularly critical on this point. He insisted that US support for Israel provided "a huge service" for the United States, the Saudis, and energy corporations by "smashing secu-lar Arab nationalism," which he said "threatened to divert resources to domestic needs." He thought it silly to argue that the US government was somehow in the grip of "an all-powerful force that it cannot escape." Ironically, Chomsky's criticism was mirrored by the conservative mag-azine *The Economist*, whose editors insisted that the Walt/Mearsheimer argument "feels like an attempt to absolve America of responsibility for a decision it took by and for itself."[19]

To be fair, the authors had set themselves to what was likely an im-possible task. No less a scholar/practitioner than William Quandt has observed that "pro-Israel groups are often most influential when they do nothing at all to influence policy," as they have what he calls "the law of anticipated reaction" on their side: "Alternative courses of action are frequently rejected because of the expectation of negative reaction from pro-Israeli groups and their supporters in Congress." The fact is that "real tests of strength are rare," thanks to the effectiveness of anticipated re-action, which works just as well "in shaping policy as the mobilization of support in a confrontation would." Ben Rhodes, a Jewish national secu-rity adviser to President Obama, said much the same thing when he ad-mitted that, when it comes to making Middle East policy, "the last thing we need is any static on Israel. . . . [I]t's just not worth the headache." This dynamic is more effective in preventing action than in initiating it, but it has the added attractiveness of operating invisibly. Former US ambassa-dor to Israel Samuel Lewis admitted as much when, speaking of what he mislabeled as the "Jewish lobby," he observed that they "can and do set limits on the freedom of action that the White House feels like it has." But do these factors explain the invasion? Not at all. Bush's march of folly was based on any number of misguided motivations, and only a few of these were related in any way to Israel.[20]

Third, while Walt and Mearsheimer did make it clear that they were not blaming "the Jews"—"Any notion that Jewish Americans are disloyal citizens is wrong... [T]hose who lobby on Israel's behalf are acting in ways that are consistent with longstanding political traditions"—they failed to clarify the fact that whereas the decision makers in key Jewish organizations, such as AIPAC and the Conference of Presidents, were Likud-supporting hardliners, most American Jews were not. The organized Jewish world was decidedly non-democratic: it represented its conservative funders' views with far greater fealty than it did the views of those in whose name its leaders professed to speak. Opinion survey after opinion survey consistently demonstrated support for a far more dovish foreign policy, both for the United States and for Israel, among American Jews than these organizations demanded from Congress and the president. This, together with some mention of the Jewish organizations that sought to speak for these views at the time—such as the New Israel Fund, Americans for Peace Now, Partners for a Progressive Israel, Ameinu, Brit Tzedek v'Shalom, Jews for Racial and Economic Justice, T'ruah (The Rabbinic Call for Human Rights), and the Tikkun Community, among others—might have taken the edge off of the charge of Jewish conspiracy-mongering, even if none enjoyed even a fraction of the power or funding that would have been needed to challenge AIPAC's overall influence.[21]

Where the authors' argument was most successful was in its portrayal of the lengths to which Israel's supporters would go to ensure that the public discussion of the conflict mirrored the narrow parameters that AIPAC and its allies defined as acceptable. "The Lobby," they wrote, "strives to ensure that public discourse portrays Israel in a positive light, by repeating myths about its founding and by promoting its point of view in policy debates. The goal is to prevent critical comments from getting a fair hearing in the political arena. Controlling the debate is essential to guaranteeing U.S. support because a candid discussion of U.S.-Israeli relations might lead Americans to favor a different policy." Ironically, the treatment of Walt and Mearsheimer's work may be the best illustration of this process we have. In no other area of debate would a scholarly argument get a fraction of the attention the authors received, or the personal opprobrium they endured. As the Paris-based columnist William Pfaff wrote in the *International Herald Tribune*, "The venom in the attacks made on [Walt and Mearsheimer] risks the opposite of its intended effect by tending to validate the claim that intense pressures are exercised on publishers, editors, writers, and on American universities to block criticism, intimidate critics, and prevent serious discussion of the American-Israeli relationship." Writing for an audience of his fellow scholars, the diplomatic historian Andrew Preston made much the same point. The most "remarkable" aspect of the entire affair, he noted, was "just how, well, unremarkable it is...[to say] that politically active pro-Israel Americans have dominated debate within the United States to such an extent that they have made it all but impossible for America to be even-handed in the Middle East. For anyone who has followed U.S. politics and foreign policy of the last forty years, even if only in passing, this is not exactly breaking news." And yet, as Preston noted, "rarely has a major book, especially one written by esteemed scholars and published by a reputable press, been received so harshly by so many reviewers.... Using personal, mostly ad hominem attacks and scattershot but totally spurious charges of anti-Semitism, some of the most shrill, hysterical reviewers... have been guilty of nothing less than character assassination." This was, if anything, an understatement.[22]

Within days of the appearance of the Harvard working paper and the article in the *London Review of Books*, Walt and Mearsheimer found themselves described as "crackpots" (Martin Peretz); "smelly" (Christopher Hitchens); "conspiratorial" (the ADL); and "liars" and "bigots," as well as authors of a book that "could have been written by Pat Buchanan, by David Duke, Noam Chomsky, and some of the less intelligent members of Hamas" (Alan Dershowitz); "as scholarly as [John Birch Society founder] Robert Welch and [disgraced red-baiting Wisconsin senator Joseph] McCarthy—and just as nutty" (Max Boot); the authors who "put The Protocols of the Elders of Zion to shame" (Josef Joffe); the authors of a study that "resembles nothing so much as Wilhelm Marr's 1879 pamphlet 'The Victory of Judaism over Germandom'" (Ruth Wisse); and the authors of "a meretricious, dishonest piece of crap" (Congressman Jerold Nadler [D-NY]). Writing in *The New Republic*, Jeffery Goldberg called their book "the most sustained attack, the most mainstream attack, against the political enfranchisement of American Jews since the era of Father Coughlin," likening it to the views of Louis Farrakhan, David

Duke, Pat Buchanan, Mel Gibson, and Charles Lindbergh. His review followed Benny Morris's assessment, also published in *TNR*, calling the work "a travesty... riddled with shoddiness and defiled by mendacity." Congressman Eliot Engel (D-NY) found himself musing that, "given what happened in the Holocaust, it's shameful that people would write reports like this."[23]

According to reporting by *The Forward*, Harvard "received 'several calls' from 'pro-Israel donors' expressing concern about the Walt-Mearsheimer paper." It reported that one contributor the university heard from was Robert Belfer, whose $7.5 million gift to the Kennedy School had endowed Walt's chair. In an apparent panic over the firestorm of criticism and possible financial fallout, the Kennedy School disassociated itself from the working paper and agreed to add Alan Dershowitz's non-scholarly rebuttal to its website. Dershowitz judged the working paper to be "so dependent on biased, extremist and anti-American sources, as to raise the question of motive." In case anyone had any doubt what that motive might be, Dershowitz spelled it out: the paper had raised "the ugly specter of 'dual loyalty,' a canard that has haunted Diaspora Jews from time immemorial."[24]

These attacks were unsupportable. Unlike the case of Patrick Buchanan, there was not a hint of antisemitism in Walt and Mearsheimer's writing, or even what might fairly be called "anti-Zionism." The authors did not take issue with the fact of Israel's existence, nor did they call for its destruction. They did not compare Israelis to Nazis or seek to dehumanize them in any way. They did not "[target] ... the state of Israel, conceived as a Jewish collectivity," or "[deny] the Jewish people their right to self-determination, e.g., by claiming that the existence of a State of Israel is a racist endeavor" (as the European Union's International Holocaust Remembrance Alliance defines the term "antisemitism," in a definition so expansive that numerous Jewish groups and Jewish studies scholars have rejected it as unfair to honest critics of Israel). They did not even "[apply] double standards by requiring of it a behaviour not expected or demanded of any other democratic nation," another requirement of the definition. Yes, many of the people they criticized were Jews, but how could it have been otherwise? Israel is the Jewish state, and Jews, especially neoconservative Jews, formed the backbone of political support for the policies they sought to critique. This is the conundrum that faces all critics of either Israel or its network of (mostly) Jewish supporters in the United States.[25]

By the time of the Walt/Mearsheimer controversy, the array of organizations and individuals who undertook to enforce the pro-Israel parameters of debate had grown considerably. AIPAC was undoubtedly the most important and the most effective of these, but, as we have seen, there was also Campus Watch, The David Project, the Committee for Accuracy in Middle East Reporting in America (CAMERA), The Israel Project, Honest Reporting, Stand with Us, NGO Watch, the Israel on Campus Coalition, and, later, the anonymously funded and operated Canary Mission. All were working pretty much the same ideological police beat, albeit in different intellectual neighborhoods. Together with pro-Israel pundits associated with magazines like *The New Republic*, *Commentary*, and *The Weekly Standard*, the preferred style of argument for any critic of Israel was personal vituperation rather than reasoned argument.

In leveling these attacks, the writers were, whether they were aware of it or not, taking up the cause put forth by Ruth Wisse, Harvard's Martin L. Peretz Professor of Yiddish Literature, during a 2007 program at the Center for Jewish History in New York for young, aspiring Jewish journalists. Wisse had instructed them to think of themselves not as honest and independent-minded public intellectuals—in the mold of, say, Nathan Glazer or Michael Walzer, with whom she happened to be sharing the stage. Rather, she said, they were "soldiers" in Israel's cause, armed with pens rather than Uzis. This was, of course, not only awful advice for any aspiring journalist or intellectual, but also just about the most un-Jewish attitude a person could hold. After all, the Talmudic tradition is devoted to endless ethical and intellectual disputation. ("The ways and nature of these people, the Jews, are like fire, as, were it not for the fact that the Torah was given to the Jewish people, whose study and observance restrains them, no nation or tongue could withstand them," God is quoted as saying in Beitzah 25b:7.) But it would also stand as evidence that there is nothing unusual about older Jews instructing younger Jews to put the good of Israel above all other concerns, including their professional credos. Another term for this sort of advice might be "dual loyalty."[26]

The term is poison in public discussions of Israel and raising it almost always leads to charges of antisemitism. But it is also an undeniably genuine phenomenon. For instance, at an American Jewish Committee symposium held at the Library of Congress in 2006, the brilliant Jewish novelist Cynthia Ozick announced, "I have a dual loyalty—total loyalty to the country where I live and the same feeling toward Israel." She was attacked for this by the Israeli novelist A. B. Yehoshua—not for being disloyal to the United States, but for being insufficiently committed to Israel.[27]

In early 2020, *The Forward* published an editorial by a Jewish New York City schoolteacher. Based on her experiences in six different schools where she had been employed, she said she judged the schools' respective connections to Israel to be "the most essential attribute" of their identity. At these institutions, she noted, "Hatikvah," the Israeli national anthem, was more commonly heard than the Pledge of Allegiance or the "Star-Spangled Banner," and Israeli national holidays were taught with greater reverence than either religious or American ones. "Veteran's Day was never discussed, but Yom HaZikaron, Israel's Memorial Day, had special projects and assemblies," the teacher noted. She also quoted her fellow faculty members saying to student assemblies, "You don't belong in America"; "Israel is your country"; and "The IDF are your soldiers." Joshua Shanes, an Orthodox Jewish scholar who serves as director of the Arnold Center for Jewish Studies at the College of Charleston, sends his children to a Jewish day school in Illinois where Israel is referred to as "our homeland." He observed the presence of the Israeli flag at many synagogues as well as the fact that while "most synagogues that recite a blessing for America and/or its military forces also recite one for Israel and its military forces," some "ONLY do so for Israel."[28]

The public assault on the character of the scholars Walt and Mearsheimer may have been extreme in its size and scope, but it was hardly unique.

In and around 2006, the year they published their initial critique, similar controversies arose across the US mainstream media. These involved Richard Cohen, a Jewish *Washington Post* columnist with decades of experience; Tony Judt, a much-admired Jewish European historian and contributing editor to *The New Republic*; Jimmy Carter, the former (obviously) non-Jewish president of the United States; and Steven Spielberg, the Jewish film director who is among the only creative people in the business who can get his blockbuster movies funded at the snap of his fingers. All four controversies resulted in apologies of sorts—or at least extensive explanations—by those being accused, designed to keep the wolves at bay. And, as with Walt and Mearsheimer, each example acted as a kind of cautionary tale for anyone considering stepping outside the permissible boundaries.

Cohen had penned a column wondering if perhaps the creation of Israel had a been "a mistake" that "produced a century of warfare and terrorism." CAMERA attacked his "historical ignorance and appeasement mentality," and the American Jewish Committee published a study titled "The New Anti-Semitism," featuring a lengthy argument about Cohen's alleged self-hatred. Cohen was grouped together with others whom the author Alvin Rosenfeld deemed to be "proud to be ashamed to be Jews." Cohen responded by writing an entire book about Israel that functioned as a 273-page abject apology. Cohen's new view: "What a marvelous people these Jews were!" What's more, Cohen now found the ridiculous version of Israel's history presented in the film *Exodus* to be accurate, "more or less."[29]

Tony Judt, a British-born historian who had lived in Israel as a young man and served as a volunteer in the IDF auxiliary, did not cave nearly so easily. In 2003, he published an essay in the *New York Review of Books* titled "Israel: The Alternative." In it he argued that Israel had "imported a characteristically late-nineteenth-century separatist project into a world that has moved on, a world of individual rights, open frontiers, and international law. The very idea of a 'Jewish state'—a state in which Jews and the Jewish religion have exclusive privileges from which non-Jewish citizens are forever excluded—is rooted in another time and place. Israel, in short, is an anachronism." Judt was summarily fired as a contributing editor at *TNR*, where he had been among its most frequent essayists, and pilloried elsewhere. Three years later, he was scheduled to give a talk on "The Israel Lobby and U.S. Foreign Policy" to a nonprofit organization that regularly rented space from the Polish consulate in New York. But after receiving calls from top officials at both the ADL and the American Jewish Committee, Krzysztof Kasprzyk, the Polish consul general, canceled the talk, just an hour before it was to begin.[30]

As Kasprzyk explained to reporters, the callers "were…exercising a delicate pressure." The AJC's executive director, David Harris, told journalists that he had made his call "as a friend of Poland" to let Kasprzyk know "that Tony Judt was not a universally popular figure in the Jewish community"—as if this were somehow a proper criterion for who should be allowed to speak to the organizations that rented space in the consulate for private meetings. When Judt published a collection of his work in 2008, he omitted the offending essay. In 2011, at a Paris conference sponsored by the *New York Review of Books* in Judt's honor, a year after he had passed away from amyotrophic lateral sclerosis (Lou Gehrig's disease), the *Review*'s longtime editor and founder, the much-revered Robert Silvers, insisted that Judt's article had merely posed his suggestion as a "thought experiment," which was not true. The intention, once again, appeared to be to make Judt's article disappear.[31]

Jimmy Carter may have become a much admired ex-president, but he was still not strong enough to resist the pressure that came after he published a book in November 2006 provocatively titled *Palestine: Peace, Not Apartheid*. The ADL's Abraham Foxman responded by calling Carter a "bigot" and denouncing him in paid newspaper advertisements across America. Alan Dershowitz called the book an "anti-Israel screed," and Martin Peretz termed it a "tendentious, dishonest and stupid book," adding in various blog posts that the former president of the United States was "a Jew-hater," a "jackass," and "a downright liar." Less biased sources were hardly any more sympathetic. The liberal pundit Michael Kinsley, in Slate, the web magazine he founded, called Carter's book "moronic," and the comparisons he drew between Israel and South Africa "foolish" and "unfair." The former executive editor of the *New York Times*, William Keller, also attacked the book in the ultra-liberal *New York Review of Books*. Almost all the attention paid to its contents focused on the book's title. Following the attacks, Carter chose to issue an "Al Het," which is a prayer Jews usually say on Yom Kippur to atone for their sins and ask God for forgiveness. He added, "We must not permit criticisms for improvement to stigmatize Israel."[32]

The most interesting of these cases involved the Hollywood icon Steven Spielberg. The director chose to make a movie about the patient, long-term Mossad campaign, launched by Israeli prime minister Golda Meir, to murder every one of the Palestinian terrorists who participated in the massacre of Israel's athletes at the 1972 Olympics. Spielberg hired Tony Kushner, the outspoken left-wing playwright and critic of Israel, to write the script. The film, *Munich*, examined the moral ambivalence experienced by the Mossad agents who were asked to carry out the vengeance murders, without ever implying anything but evil intentions on the part of the Palestinian kidnappers.

*Munich* inspired political attacks by Leon Wieseltier in *TNR* and David Brooks in the *New York Times* even before its December 2005 release. Both writers accused the director of treating the terrorists and the Mossad agents as moral equivalents. Brooks's criticism, in particular, was filled with false and misleading accusations wrapped in an almost comical injection of whataboutism. He thought the film unfair, he wrote, because, "in 1972, Israel was just entering the era of spectacular terror attacks and didn't know how to respond. But over the years Israelis have learned that targeted assassinations, which are the main subject of this movie, are one of the less effective ways to fight terror." This was nonsense. Mossad did not get to the Munich murderer Atef Bseiso until 1992. Moreover, Brooks had to know that the robust Mossad assassination program continued then, as it does today. The vast majority of *Rise and Kill First*, the Israeli journalist Ronen Bergman's massive history of the Mossad's assassination program, published in 2018, is devoted to killings (and failed killings) that took place after the ones portrayed in the movie. Brooks also complained that "in Spielberg's Middle East, there is no Hamas or Islamic Jihad. There are no passionate anti-Semites, no Holocaust deniers like the current president of Iran, no zealots who want to exterminate Israelis." This is both irrelevant and wrong. Indeed, to emphasize the reality of the terrorist attacks that inspired the murders, the director employed actual news footage from the coverage of the massacre, and neither Iran nor Hamas nor Islamic Jihad had anything to do with the story. Hamas was not founded until February 1988. Islamic Jihad was founded earlier, in 1983, but was active almost exclusively in Lebanon. Neither could have had anything to do with the 1972 Olympic massacre. Once the film appeared, *Commentary*'s reviewer, Gabriel Schoenfeld, termed it "a blatant attack on Israel in virtually every way, shape, and form." Perhaps the most spectacular attack on the film, however, came from *Washington Post* columnist Charles Krauthammer, who compared Spielberg, the primary patron behind the creation of the Shoah Foundation, director of the Holocaust epic *Schindler's List*, and the youngest person ever to be accorded Hebrew University's Scopus Award, to Iranian president Mahmoud Ahmadinejad, who had questioned the actuality of the Holocaust: "It takes a Hollywood ignoramus to give flesh to the argument of a radical anti-Semitic Iranian," Krauthammer wrote.[33]

Spielberg, the creative genius responsible for billions of dollars in movie receipts in the past, had the resources to hire high-powered PR firms to defend the film and his reputation. He also secured the services of Dennis Ross, the pro-Israel presidential adviser; former State Department spokesman Mike McCurry; and Eyal Arad, the chief PR consultant for Israeli prime minister Ariel Sharon. Ignoring the specifics of the attacks, Spielberg trotted out his Zionist bona fides, telling an interviewer, "I made this picture as a committed Jew, a pro-Israeli Jew and yet a human Jew. I made this movie out of love for both of my countries, USA and Israel," the two countries for which, Spielberg added, he would "be prepared to die." Kushner, perhaps America's greatest playwright since Arthur Miller, also had sufficient resources to shield himself from his harshest critics. He published an imaginary conversation with his *mishpocheh* (family) in which he called himself "an American and a proudly Diasporan Jew." He argued therein that his "criticism of Israel has always been accompanied by declarations of unconditional support of Israel's right to exist," and added, "I have written and spoken of my love for Israel." (Kushner would experience another attempt to silence his criticism of Israel when, in 2011, John Jay College at the City University of New

York decided first to give him an honorary degree, then saw that decision reversed by "pro-Israel" partisans on the university's board of trustees, only to have that decision reversed in an emergency board meeting following an outcry over the original reversal.)[34]

Each person targeted in the attacks described in this chapter, including the two tenured professors Walt and Mearsheimer, had at least some of the resources they needed to withstand the abuse they encountered and emerge afterward with damage only to their reputations, and perhaps their future job prospects. But as much as these campaigns to silence critics of Israel were directed at specific individuals, they were no less intended to intimidate others, especially those who were far less able to survive, either professionally or politically, the predictable onslaught of criticism against anyone who dared transgress the boundaries of what the pro-Israel voices defined to be acceptable. Ironically, this was true despite the fact that these boundaries were almost constantly in motion.

# CHAPTER 17

# "BASICALLY, A LIBERAL JEW"

During a friendly interview at New York's venerable Temple Emanu-El in January 2018, America's first Black president joked to the audience that he was "basically, a liberal Jew." This was actually awfully close to the truth. All that was necessary was to substitute the word "Zionist" for "Jew," as so many American Jews implicitly do. Obama shared the liberal Zionist belief that Israel had to be pushed and prodded into saving itself from an illiberal, anti-democratic, quasi-apartheid future. But like so many liberal Zionists, Obama was better at inspirational speeches than political combat. In his post-presidential memoir, he recalled a moment when his deputy national security adviser, Ben Rhodes, arrived in his office "looking particularly harried" after spending an hour with a "highly agitated liberal Democratic congressman" who had expressed nervousness about the president's opposition to Israel's settlements. "I thought he opposes settlements?" Obama asked. "He does," Rhodes replied, but "he also opposes us doing anything to actually stop settlements." Little did the president know that this ironic quip would end up defining his own administration as well.[1]

In many respects, Barack Obama's career can be viewed as the realization of what the independent scholar Marcus Raskin once called "the We Shall Overcome Moment" in American politics. This was especially true for America's still quite liberal Jewish community. In 1992, barely more than thirty years old, Obama, a recent graduate of Columbia University and Harvard Law School, married Michelle Robinson, and the couple moved into a condominium in Chicago's leafy and unusually integrated Hyde Park neighborhood. The building happened to be located across the street from the KAM Isaiah Israel synagogue, then led by Rabbi Arnold Jacob Wolf. Back in 1973, Wolf had been one of the founders of Breira, the liberal Jewish group that had called for recognition of "the national aspirations of the Palestinians." During Breira's brief life, which lasted only until 1977, the American Jewish establishment had vociferously denounced Wolf and his fellow organizers for making their criticisms of Israel in public. By the time the Obamas became Wolf's neighbor, however, many American Jews had moved closer to the beliefs Breira had enunciated way back then. Obama and Wolf became friends, and Obama found himself in sympathy with much of what Wolf had been preaching all those years.

When he was a young lawyer and budding politician, Obama's most significant mentors and generous political donors were also liberal Jews, as was his most important political adviser, David Axelrod. In his memoir, Obama noted that some of his "most stalwart friends and supporters" came from Chicago's Jewish community. He admired how Jewish voters remained progressives while other white ethnic groups did not. He said he felt himself bound to Jews by "a common story of exile and suffering," and that this made him "fiercely protective" of their rights. But Obama's friendship with the pro-Palestinian scholar Rashid Khalidi, then teaching at the University of Chicago, together with the now decades-long links between the Palestinians and Black leaders, which initially flowered during the Carter administration's Andrew Young controversy, had also helped to sensitize him to the Palestinian narrative of the "Nakba" and "the conditions under which Palestinians in the occupied territories were forced to live." And from a purely pragmatic viewpoint, Obama had come to the conclusion that, in the wider world, America's association with Israel's mistreatment of the Palestinians and West Bank occupation "continued to inflame the Arab community and feed anti-American sentiment across the Muslim world." The bottom line was that "the absence of peace between Israel and the Palestinians made America less safe."[2]

Here, Obama was stating something taken to be obvious in many, if not most, places in the world. It was especially well understood at the time within the US military. General James Mattis, who later became Donald Trump's first secretary of defense, told a 2013 meeting of the Aspen Security Forum, "I paid a military security price every day as a commander of CENTCOM because the Americans were seen as biased in support of Israel." General David Petraeus, Mattis's predecessor at CENTCOM, who went on to become Barack Obama's director of central intelligence, had made strikingly similar comments three years earlier when, testifying before the Senate Armed Services Committee, he admitted that "Arab anger over the Palestinian question limits the strength and depth of U.S. partnerships with governments and peoples in the region."[3]

Candidate Obama had proven remarkably candid about his disagreements with Israel while at the same time demonstrating an unusually intimate relationship with Israeli culture. In an interview with the influential Jewish journalist Jeffrey Goldberg, Obama spoke with impressive sophistication and (for him) considerable emotion about his attachment to the Jewish people and their culture as well as Israel and its culture, but also of the dangers he believed Israel faced if it continued on a path of endless occupation. He mentioned his fondness for the novels of Philip Roth, and of the work of Israeli writer David Grossman, especially the latter's searing 1988 book on Israel's treatment of the Palestinians, *The Yellow Wind*. (Being a skilled politician, in addition to a bona fide intellectual, Obama said he also enjoyed "more popular writers like Leon Uris.") He waxed eloquent about his "enormous emotional attachment and sympathy for Israel, mindful of its history, mindful of the hardship and pain and suffering that the Jewish people have undergone, but also mindful of the incredible opportunity that is presented when people finally return to a land and are able to try to excavate their best traditions and their best selves": "And obviously," he went on, flipping what had become the now traditional identification of the Black freedom struggle with that of the Palestinians, "it's something that has great resonance with the African American experience." Sounding more like Martin Luther King Jr. than his successors in the civil rights movement, Obama called "the idea of a secure Jewish state...a fundamentally just idea," and said his commitment to Israel's security was "non-negotiable." At the same time, he publicly advised a Jewish group in Cleveland not to buy into the view that "unless you adopt an unwavering pro-Likud approach to Israel, you're anti-Israel." Anticipating pushback, he noted—again, truthfully, but also bravely—"One of the things that struck me when I went to Israel was how much more open the debate was around these issues in Israel than they are sometimes here in the United States."[4]

Not surprisingly, Obama's mild criticisms inspired multiple attacks of heartburn in official Jewish circles, whose members had grown accustomed to candidates who spoke exclusively in the language of "shared values," the "only democracy in the Middle East," and "unbreakable partnerships" as they pocketed generous donations. In his post-presidential *A Promised Land*, Obama identified what he called a "whisper campaign" in this period that sought to portray him as "insufficiently supportive— or even hostile toward—Israel." And "as far as many AIPAC board members were concerned," he wrote of the American Israel Public Affairs Committee, "I remained suspect, a man of divided loyalties." It was hardly AIPAC alone. As *The Forward* said in an editorial, during the 2008 Democratic primary season, "the attacks on Obama have metastasized into a wide-ranging assault on his associations." Debra Feuer, counsel for the American Jewish Committee, sent a confidential memo to her counterparts at other organizations criticizing Obama's views on the Middle East, Iran, and Syria and attacking him for having once appeared at a fund raiser headlined by Edward Said. Morton Klein, head of the far-right Zionist Organization of America, complained that "Barack

Obama doesn't understand the continuing Arab war against Israel"; he called the notion of an Obama presidency "frightening." Klein was joined by Malcolm Hoenlein, then executive vice president of the Conference of Presidents of Major American Jewish Organizations, who told *Haaretz* that Obama's talk of "change" could prove "an opening for all kinds of mischief" and expressed what he termed "a legitimate concern over the zeitgeist around the campaign." (He later denied using these specific words and said he had been discussing the candidates generally, but others who were present confirmed *Haaretz*'s report.) A number of press releases highlighted Obama's middle name, Hussein, as well as his deceased father's background (Barack Hussein Obama Sr., a Kenyan, was originally Muslim and later atheist; father and son had long been estranged). Sidney Blumenthal, a close confidant of Hillary Clinton, circulated a picture to journalists and politicos of Obama dressed up for his half-brother's wedding in Indonesia in what appeared to be traditional Muslim garb, no doubt to imply the possibility that the future president was really a Muslim. Blumenthal also implored journalists to go to Kenya to investigate Obama's family background.[5]

Obama's alleged "foreignness" became a familiar trope in the mainstream media. For instance, during a Democratic presidential debate, Tim Russert, host of NBC's *Meet the Press*, demanded over and over that Obama reject the kind words spoken about him by the antisemitic leader of the Nation of Islam, Louis Farrakhan, so that Jews might feel a bit more comfortable with him. Obama repeatedly did this, but it hardly ended matters—even in Russert's own questioning that day, much less among Jewish leaders. It is impossible to say how much of the conservative hostility toward Obama was driven by racist fears and prejudice. But given the ease with which Donald Trump took over the Republican Party eight years later, at the end of Obama's two terms in office— earning himself nearly a quarter of the Jewish vote in the process—one may fairly conclude that the correct answer would not be "none." Obama himself endorsed Ben Rhodes's view that, together with his "expressions of concern for ordinary Palestinians" and his "friendships with certain critics of Israeli policy, including an activist and Middle East scholar named Rashid Khalidi," his real problem among the haters was the fact of his being "a Black man with a Muslim name who lived in the same neighborhood as Louis Farrakhan."[6]

Obama was elected president in 2008 with an estimated 79 percent of the Jewish vote at a moment when neoconservatives were still licking their wounds. Boosting the disastrous and dishonestly promoted Iraq War had discredited neoconservatives with the larger public, and their eagerness to question the patriotism of those who—like Obama—had had the good sense to counsel caution had all but eliminated their remaining influence in the Democratic Party. Meanwhile, the evangelical "pro-Israel" movement had grown enormously and embraced ever more extremist views of the Israeli/Palestinian conflict. Its new public face was the Pentecostal pastor John Hagee, head pastor of an eighteen-thousand-member San Antonio church, host of a popular television program, and a massively best-selling author. Hagee had overtaken many of his competitors in both popularity and influence. A "Spirit-centered Zionist," Hagee's preaching focused foremost on Genesis 12:3, in which God said to Abraham, "I will make you into a great nation. . . . I will bless those who bless you, and whoever curses you I will curse; and all peoples on earth will be blessed through you." What this meant, he said, was that Israel was "the gateway to God's blessing."[7]

Like his predecessors in the pro-Israel evangelical political space, Hagee looked forward to a final rapture and the confrontation between Jesus and Satan that it would ultimately usher in. The best way to get things going, he mused, was for either Israel or the United States—preferably both together—to launch an attack on Iran, which he hoped would lead Russia to invade Israel. Then, as outlined in the Book of Ezekiel, the world would experience an "inferno [that would] explode across the Middle East, plunging the world toward Armageddon." And woe unto those who failed to get with God's program. "Could it be that America," Hagee asked, "who refuses to defend Israel from the Russian invasion, will experience nuclear warfare on our east and west coasts?" Here again, it's a yes, due to Genesis 12:3. In the meantime, Hagee explained, the head of the European Union, who was really, in fact, Satan at that future time (incarnated as the Antichrist), would rule "a one-world government, a one-world currency and a one-world religion" for three and a half years, accompanied by a "false prophet," whom the Bible also foretold. All of this was imminent, he said, something he considered so obvious as to require no explanation ("One need only be a casual observer of current events to see that all three of these things are coming into reality"). At this point the Antichrist would declare himself to be God and demand to be worshipped from within a rebuilt Temple in Jerusalem. Another three and a half years would pass, to make up the complete seven-year "tribulation" period, and then the Antichrist would find himself confronted by China at Armageddon. At the end of that great final battle, Jesus would finally make his long-awaited return on a white horse and send these two evildoers—the Antichrist and the false prophet—into a "lake of fire burning with brimstone" (Revelation 20:10). He would also dispense with the rest of the world's nonbelievers, including, unfortunately, all the world's remaining Jews, except for the ones who had become Christians after the rapture.[8]

Hagee also had some interesting things to say about the Shoah. It seems that the Jews of the Holocaust had perished because "God sent a hunter," meaning, of course, Adolf Hitler. In explaining why God would allow this to happen, Hagee had a ready-made answer: God's "top priority for the Jewish people" was "to get them to come back to the land of Israel." Had it not been for "the disobedience and rebellion of the Jews," in refusing to accept Jesus Christ as their lord and savior, maybe God (and Hitler) would have allowed them to catch a break. But because the Jews had continued to manifest their stubbornness "to this very day," they should not expect things to go well when all the accounts were finally settled, theologically speaking. Should anyone—say, a Jew who lost a loved one during the Shoah—find these remarks at all problematic, Hagee had a reply at the ready: "I didn't write it, Jeremiah wrote it. It was the truth, and it is the truth."[9]

In 2009, Hagee founded what immediately became the largest pro-Israel membership organization in the world, Christians United for Israel (CUFI), which claimed two million members at its founding, later rising to seven million. He later added a lobbying arm to it called the "CUFI Action Fund," run by the former head of the right-wing Christian Family Research Council, Gary Bauer. It began with a multimillion-dollar budget and dozens of paid lobbyists, who set their minds to working against President Obama and on behalf of Prime Minister Netanyahu. Hagee warned, "If I were a candidate, especially in the Republican Party, I'd be aware of how many voters will cast their vote principally on Israel."[10]

Polls of Jewish voters during Obama's presidency remained strongly negative on Hagee, with polls finding those who opposed cooperating with the man and his organization outnumbering those in favor by five (or even ten) to one. But the people who put themselves forth in the media as Jewish spokespeople did not see a problem. Elliott Abrams and *The Weekly Standard*'s Jennifer Rubin were happy to sign off on the same bargain that their ideological forefathers—and in Abrams' case, his in-laws—had made in the past with Jerry Falwell and Pat Robertson: forget the antisemitism and the rooting for the rapture, they advised. Business was business and Israel came first. "American Jews ought to notice that there are actually more evangelicals in this country than Jews by about 20 or 30 to 1," Abrams insisted. "With the Jewish population shrinking as a percentage of the American people, Christians are an increasingly critical base of support for Israel—and groups like CUFI are begging us to accept their help. We should accept it with gratitude and enthusiasm."[11]

Invited to address AIPAC's annual conference in 2007, Hagee had chosen to keep his theological ruminations to himself. Instead, speaking as "an emissary of 50 million Christians," he said, "Please know that what I say to you now is a sentiment shared by millions of Christians across America and around the world. Today, in the world of freedom, the proudest boast is 'Ani Yisraeli—I am an Israeli.'" Of the countless ironies embedded in this moment was the fact that Hagee was talking to a group with the word "American" as the first one in its name, and yet here he was praising an entirely different country as the world's "proudest," and receiving massive applause for having done so. Rabbi Eric Yoffie, then president of the Union for Reform Judaism, attacked AIPAC's leaders for inviting Hagee, arguing that they were whitewashing his offensive beliefs in exchange for the massive funds that evangelicals raised for pro-Israel organizations, and further alienating young Jews from their cause. But nobody in AIPAC really cared what a bunch of Reform rabbis—or even the vast majority of American Jews—thought. AIPAC had become a "pro-Israel" lobby—not, as antisemites and people using incautious or outdated terminology thought, a "Jewish" one. The conservative Christian takeover of the Republican Party, together with AIPAC's rapid right-wing drift, meant that to the degree that any genuine debate on Israel and the Palestinians was to be had, it would have to happen exclusively among Democrats.[12]

The political space on the leftward side of the debate expanded during Obama's presidency as well. This manifested itself in two ways simultaneously. The first was the launching of J Street, which called itself a "pro-peace, pro-Israel lobby." J Street was unique in that it played on the same field as the other respectable Jewish establishment organizations while at the same time openly criticizing the Israeli government. This meant redefining the term "pro-Israel" and taking on AIPAC in the process. That AIPAC was now behaving as a weapon that Bibi Netanyahu aimed at Obama gave J Street a perfect opportunity to define itself as an organization of unapologetic liberal Zionists who promised to have the back of their popular president. In ending the policy of *omertà* regarding public criticism of Israel, J Street gave voice to political positions far more consistent with the ambivalence American Jews felt toward Israel than AIPAC did with its unswerving fealty to Netanyahu's aggressively illiberal government. And Obama did what he could for the organization, inspiring the unconcealed consternation of the leaders of traditional Jewish organizations by including J Street's president, Jeremy Ben-Ami, in his presidential briefings.

Just how comfortable were American Jews seeing their misgivings about Israel expressed in public, however, remained a complicated question, one whose emotional resonance ran far deeper than could be measured by any opinion poll. Leonard Fein, the thoughtful liberal Zionist founder of *Moment* magazine, offered a glimpse of these sorts of conflicting crosswinds when he averred, during the Walt/Mearsheimer debate, "We don't trust the Palestinians, we worry about Iran, we haven't a clue about how you get from here to peace, we don't take America's support for granted and even if we did, we are not exactly proud to have to depend on that support." And therefore, he admitted, despite whatever disagreements many liberal Jews had with the hardline positions that leading Jewish organizations adopted, "we are not entirely upset that 'out there,' in the public square, those who speak authoritatively on Israel's behalf—meaning, principally, AIPAC and the Conference of Presidents—are considerably more rigid, more hawkish, if you will, than we are."[13]

Early in his presidency, Obama learned the price of crossing AIPAC. Consistent with the policies he campaigned on, he sought to restart peace negotiations by asking Israel to freeze West Bank settlement expansion, as this show of good faith might help bring the Palestinians back to the negotiating table. As he explained in his memoir, "given the asymmetry in power," he "thought it was reasonable to ask the stronger party to take a bigger first step in the direction of peace."[14]

"Reasonable," alas, was likely the last quality that might impress anyone involved in America's Israel/Palestine debate. AIPAC responded with a letter signed by 329 House members asking Obama to make his requests to Israel "privately"—that is, without any pressure to actually address them. As if reading from a time-honored script, Alan Dershowitz, in a *Wall Street Journal* op-ed titled "Has Obama Turned on Israel?" quoted the Conference of Presidents' Malcolm Hoenlein, warning that "President Obama's strongest supporters among Jewish leaders are deeply troubled by his recent Middle East initiatives, and some are questioning what he really believes." (Dershowitz also made reference to Obama's "friendships with rabidly anti-Israel characters like Rev. Jeremiah Wright and historian Rashid Khalidi"—a quote that also appeared virtually word for word in another *Journal* op-ed by Norman Podhoretz.) The Republicans, meanwhile, committed to opposing literally everything Obama proposed, but especially whatever he proposed that the Israelis also opposed. According to Obama, "the White House phones started ringing off the hook, as members of my national security team fielded calls from reporters, leaders of American Jewish organizations, prominent supporters, and members of Congress, all wondering why we were picking on Israel.... [T]his sort of pressure continued for much of 2009."[15]

Obama was hardly naïve. Sounding like a sophisticated student of the more reasonable aspects of the arguments that Walt and Mearsheimer had made, he said he fully understood that taking on Israel and its allies "exacted a domestic political cost that simply didn't exist when I dealt with the United Kingdom, Germany, France, Japan, Canada, or any of our other closest allies." That was why "members of both parties worried about crossing the American Israel Public Affairs Committee," and "even stalwart progressives were loath to look less pro-Israel than Republicans." Almost all American politicians had to face up to the fact that "those who criticized Israeli policy too loudly risked being tagged as 'anti-Israel' (and possibly anti-Semitic) and confronted with a well-funded opponent in the next election."[16]

But Obama stuck with his plan, at least at first. With the greatest reluctance, Israel eventually agreed to freeze new settlement building for ten months, albeit with exceptions for all of East Jerusalem, all public buildings "essential for normal life," and all buildings whose foundations had already been laid—and only for ten months. Key was the exemption for construction already underway, which, according to figures provided by Peace Now, would be fully 1,712 buildings that had been begun in the year of the proposed freeze alone. And within eight days of the freeze's alleged commencement, Israel announced a planned expansion of the Gilo neighborhood in annexed East Jerusalem, before issuing tenders for new construction in three more such neighborhoods. Despite these gaps—and following intense lobbying by both the Obama administration and European governments—the Palestinians eventually agreed to rejoin the peace talks, which began again in late 2010, just three weeks before the putative "freeze" was to end. Vice President Joe Biden flew to Jerusalem to help get the talks off the ground. But just as the wheels on Air Force Two hit the ground, Israel's interior minister announced a near doubling of the number of proposed dwellings for the ultra-Orthodox East Jerusalem neighborhood of Ramat Shlomo. Biden was furious: "I condemn the decision by the government of Israel to advance planning for new housing units," read a Biden statement that his office issued after he chose to show up ninety minutes late for dinner with Netanyahu. Obama's secretary of state, Hillary Clinton, also unloaded on Netanyahu, in a forty-eight-minute phone call in which she ticked off numerous demands. Netanyahu ignored all of them and, soon enough, political reality set back in. Just in case the House members' letter had failed to impress, AIPAC secured seventy-six senators' signatures on an April 2010 letter asking the president to "reaffirm the unbreakable bonds that tie the United States and Israel together and diligently work to defuse current tensions" with Israel.[17]

As Obama saw it, AIPAC had adopted Israel's position "even when Israel took actions that were contrary to U.S. policy." While J Street made progress building itself into an institution with the power to survive in an unfriendly atmosphere, it was hardly a counterweight to the power amassed by its rivals. Ben Rhodes would later lament that vis-à-vis Israel and Palestine, "there was constant pressure from the right, and I never felt any from the left.... You had J Street and you had public-opinion polls, but...I don't think there was a significant set of people representing a left point of view in Congress." In the mainstream media, the balance of power was, if anything, even more one-sided. Rhodes found it "striking" the degree to which "the drivers of opinion on foreign policy come almost entirely from the right. If you look at who's on television and the opinion pages, it's dominated by the right." Moreover, "if you look at the right, it's all the same people revolving through the foreign-policy establishment over decades, and it's not the power of their ideas, it's the power of financing and coordination. Every one of these little groups like the Emergency Committee for Israel had a bigger budget than anyone pushing back against them."[18]

Rhodes was certainly right. While Arab American groups did seek to organize themselves on AIPAC's model, they met with precious little success. As a result, there was really no such thing as a pro-Palestinian or Palestinian American group sufficiently influential to make itself felt on the presidential or even congressional level. The net result, as a Congressional Quarterly report put it two years into Obama's first term, was that

"President Obama, who came into office with grand hopes of revitalizing the peace process, quickly found himself isolated and eventually boxed in by the ferocity of lawmakers' support for Israel." That Obama's position consistently proved to be the most popular one among not only all Americans, but also among American Jews, carried no politically measurable weight in this debate.[19]

It should shock no one that playing handmaiden to Likud proved profitable for Republicans. They began raising "pro-Israel" money at a far faster clip than ever before and even overtook Democrats on this score during the 2014 midterm elections. Part of the credit belonged to Hagee and his fellow evangelicals, who gave generously to fund settlements and West Bank land grabs as well as to support candidates who advocated these policies. But the real hero of this effort would turn out to be the right-wing Jewish billionaire and Las Vegas–based gambling magnate Sheldon Adelson.

"It is impossible to overstate the significance that Sheldon Adelson along with his wife Miriam had on shaping US policy with regard to Israel," observed Republican Jewish Coalition executive director Matt Brooks in a tribute to the couple. This was no exaggeration. Adelson liked to call himself "the richest Jew in the world." He wasn't, but he was certainly the richest Jewish Republican funder devoted to an extremist position in the Arab-Israeli conflict. Adelson told *Jewish Week* that "the two-state solution is a stepping-stone for the destruction of Israel and the Jewish people." And if "Israel won't be a democratic state," Adelson said in a 2014 address, "[s]o what?" To *The New Yorker* he said he hoped the United States would bomb Iranian cities with nuclear weapons because "I really don't care what happens to Iran. I am for Israel." Adelson even abandoned AIPAC in 2007 over the organization's (admittedly reluctant) willingness to support then Israeli prime minister Ehud Olmert's request for direct US funding to the Palestinian Authority, during a brief moment when peace between the parties appeared at least remotely possible (but remained threatened by the rejectionism of Hamas, then growing rapidly in influence among Palestinians).[20]

Adelson frequently found himself under criminal investigation for his alleged ties to organized crime, official bribery, money laundering, and the use of prostitution for his business interests. (An average of forty to sixty prostitutes walked the floors of Adelson's Venetian Macao Resort Hotel in Macau on weekends, outnumbering security personnel, according to company documents, which also reported that the women were "frequently under 18 years" old and were trafficked from China's inner provinces by "vice syndicates.") He paid $47 million in fines in 2013 to avoid criminal charges. His money stayed clean enough, however, to be deposited in Republican coffers.[21]

The billionaire's special status in Israel first made news in 1991, when Adelson and his Israeli/American bride-to-be received permission to hold their wedding reception inside Israel's Knesset. According to the body's Speaker, this extremely unorthodox use of Israel's parliament had been arranged, without the knowledge of its members, as "a private evening honoring donors to Israel" by its then deputy foreign minister, Benjamin Netanyahu. Adelson continued to fund Netanyahu's career and the luxurious lifestyle he and his wife enjoyed. But it was not until July 2007, when Adelson launched a shamelessly pro-Netanyahu free daily newspaper, *Israel Hayom* (Israel Today)—and later named his wife, Miriam Adelson, as its publisher—that the extent of their alliance was fully revealed. The only political interventions he insisted upon involved Netanyahu: the prime minister was to be the hero in all the stories in which his name appeared.[22]

*Israel Hayom* proved to be something new and perhaps unique in the history of journalism: a free daily newspaper that people actually wanted to read. The Adelsons spent freely enough on talent that many of Israel's best journalists could not resist their entreaties. The "Bibi-ton," as Israelis called it—combining Netanyahu's nickname with the Hebrew word for newspaper, *iton*—was also sometimes referred to as "Bibi's Pravda" by Jews from the former Soviet Union. By 2010, *Israel Hayom* was the highest-circulation newspaper in Israel, dwarfing the left-leaning *Haaretz*, one of the world's great newspapers, by more than six to one in circulation numbers. It put other formerly profitable newspapers out of business entirely. Adelson soon bought up a number of other media properties in Israel, which then took the same pro-Netanyahu editorial stance. In doing so, he skirted Israel's otherwise tough political funding restrictions and made the equivalent of uncontrolled, unaudited contributions to Netanyahu's various political campaigns. Over time, the value of the resulting PR Netanyahu received would be worth many hundreds of millions of dollars. No other politician in the country enjoyed anything like it.[23]

In the United States, Adelson's method was to fund politicians, pressure groups, and media properties and devote all these resources simultaneously to shifting US policy in Israel in a direction consistent with Netanyahu's interests and demands. Money was no object when it came to this objective. Adelson bought Nevada's largest paper, the *Las Vegas Review-Journal*, using a cut-out holding company to hide his identity. To accomplish this, he paid $140 million for the paper, which happened to be $38 million more than what the entire chain that it was part of had sold for just nine months earlier. Adelson's family foundation also secretly funded JNS.org, a right-wing Jewish news service that passed its propaganda on to the American Jewish news organizations that subscribed to it. JNS.org was just one of countless organizations Adelson and his wife funded to further their far-right agenda for Israel in both Israel itself and in the United States.[24]

Nowhere was the power of the Adelsons' purse more evident than inside the Republican Party. During the 2012 presidential campaign, Adelson's millions literally dictated the positions taken by GOP presidential candidates. The disgraced former Republican House Speaker Newt Gingrich told NBC's Ted Koppel that Adelson supported him because "he knows I'm very pro-Israel. That's the central value of his life." Well, now Gingrich was pro-Israel. But back in 2005, he had authored an article calling on the US government to defend "the Palestinian people's right to have a decent amount of land," and condemned "the desire of some Israelis to use security as an excuse to grab more Palestinian land." If necessary, he had argued, the United States should even be willing to "employ financial or other leverage to compel the Israeli government to behave reasonably on the issue of settlements." And, going even further, Gingrich had called it "vital to our credibility in the entire Middle East that we insist on an end to Israeli expansionism," and also "vital to our humanitarian duty to the Palestinian people that we protect the weaker party from the stronger power." The Newt Gingrich who had been gifted with a $20 million contribution from Sheldon and Miriam Adelson for his presidential campaign turned out to have very different views in 2012. Gingrich had decided that the Palestinians were merely an "invented" people who "had a chance to go many places" but apparently preferred military occupation and refugee-camp living. When Gingrich flamed out in the contest for the Republican presidential nomination, Adelson provided another $30 million to the Republican nominee, Mitt Romney, eventually bringing his overall giving to the party in that cycle to $92.7 million. At the time, this was by far the largest amount any one donor had ever given to candidates in a single campaign. But Adelson himself set new records in 2016 and again in 2020. He also cohosted an event for Romney inside Jerusalem's famous King David Hotel, where Benjamin Netanyahu, the candidate's former colleague from the Boston-based investment firm Bain Capital, now prime minister of Israel, showed up to support the Republican nominee.[25]

Two years later, in March 2014, as the 2016 Republican presidential primary was still in what pundits call its "beauty contest" phase, Adelson summoned all the contestants to his Venetian hotel in Las Vegas under the aegis of the Republican Jewish Coalition to have them parade their ideological wares. Those who came all sought to leave with the crown of his multimillion-dollar contributions. They were joined by Ron Dermer, Netanyahu's close confidant, who had emigrated to Israel from the United States after working for the right-wing Republican pollster Frank Luntz and was now Israel's ambassador to the United States. During New Jersey governor Chris Christie's turn before the party's putative godfather, he committed the apparently unforgivable faux pas of using the term "occupation" to refer to the occupation. Christie soon rushed back and, according to press reports, "apologized in a private meeting," though this failed to secure him the prize of Adelson's beneficence.[26]

Adelson, however, was not the only Republican Jewish billionaire who committed tens of millions of dollars to Republicans to push the Likud line during the Obama era (and after). The New York hedge-fund magnate Paul Singer not only gave millions of his own, but created a network of similarly minded right-wing Jewish multimillionaires to do so as well. Barack Obama was likely being overly kind in his memoir when he wrote that "most congressional Republicans had abandoned any pretense of caring about what happened to the Palestinians." If any one of them did actually care, he or she understood the need to keep this information to themselves. The financial power of Adelson, Singer, and others, combined with the intense commitment of the party's evangelical base to Israel's permanent control over the Golan Heights, the West Bank, and every inch of Jerusalem, defined an extremely narrow path for any Republican politician who hoped for a successful political future. (Adelson and prominent evangelicals often joined forces. Since the beginning of 2012, Adelson has donated at least $4.6 million to Hagee's Christians United for Israel [CUFI], for example, and since 2015 he has given over $22 million to another organization, called the Maccabee Task Force, headed by CUFI's former executive director. The task force was dedicated to defending Israel on college campuses.)[27]

Over time, the radicalism of these extremely well-funded anti-Obama forces grew to a fevered pitch. "I've never seen as much enmity toward a president by American Jews as I do toward Obama," said the Adelson-funded Zionist Organization of America's Morton Klein. "I've never heard people say, as they say to me, 'I hate him,'" as if that somehow negated Obama's sky-high approval ratings among Jews. Klein repeatedly tried to convince AIPAC to bar Obama from its annual meetings, because "every chance he gets he blames Israel." Media mogul and Presidents' Conference chairman Mortimer Zuckerman complained that "from the start of his presidency, Mr. Obama has undermined Israel's confidence in U.S. support." Taking a page from Adelson, he was particularly angry about Obama's use of the term "settlements" to describe Israel's settlements. Daniel Pipes of the Middle East Forum rather crazily insisted that Obama was "enforcing Islamic law, a precedent that could lead to other forms of compulsory Shariah compliance." The uber-Islamophobic Jewish blogger Pamela Geller, who is funded by mainstream Jewish philanthropies and was a frequent speaker on cable TV and at conservative political gatherings, even more nuttily accused Obama of "advancing jihad against the oath of office that he took," and "agitating Muslims against Jews." With apparent seriousness, she asked, "Will he declare war on Israel?"[28]

While such talk was not only profoundly divorced from reality—to say nothing of its distance from the views of the vast majority of Jewish voters—it only occasionally resulted in any sort of rebuke from polite society, even among liberal Jews. The novelist Cynthia Ozick remained a beloved figure in literary Manhattan even as she described America's first Black president, in 2010, as "a clever, sly, shrewd, ideologically radical Third-World minded enemy of Israel" who was committed to "sell[ing] Israel down the river." Incredibly, she also compared President Obama to Hitler, musing that "the German Jews at least had enough perspective not to vote for der Fuhrer... but American Jews, content in our fleshpots, are likely to be fully self-destructive." When an apparently disturbed owner of an Atlanta Jewish newspaper suggested that perhaps it would be a good idea if the Israelis had Obama assassinated (and was then forced to resign and sell the paper), it became clear that the price of such talk was higher than the Obama-hating Jews had calculated. And yet it hardly abated at all.[29]


When, shortly after his January 2009 inauguration, President Obama announced he would fly to Cairo in April to give a high-profile speech addressing the Muslim world, without so much as a stop in Israel in either direction, Israelis began to complain. Speaking with friendly journalists and others, they said Obama lacked the typical American "special feeling" for Israel they had come to expect from American politicians. Deputy national security adviser Ben Rhodes noted that, to address this alleged problem, American Jewish groups working on behalf of Israel frequently sought to script the president, hoping to help him show that he felt Israel's concern in his *kishkas*—a Yiddish word meaning, in this context, "gut," that Rhodes said he heard more than any other from Jewish leaders.[30]

Obama finally traveled to Israel in March 2013, and he wowed the place. He spoke to an audience of mostly young Israeli Jews and Arabs at Hebrew University in Jerusalem in a manner so "deft, nuanced, broadly empathetic," in the judgment of *New Yorker* editor David Remnick, that he successfully "soothed anxieties about American commitment" while simultaneously mollifying Israelis' concerns about his *kishkas*. "Make no mistake," the president assured his audience. "Those who adhere to the ideology of rejecting Israel's right to exist might as well reject the earth beneath them and the sky above, because Israel is not going anywhere. Today, I want to tell you—particularly the young people—that so long as there is a United States of America, *Ah-tem lo lah-vad* [You are not alone]." At the same time, however, Obama sought to prick Israeli consciences over the increasing inhumanity of what was now looking to be a permanent occupation. "It is not fair," he insisted, "that a Palestinian child cannot grow up in a state of her own. Living their entire lives with the presence of a foreign army that controls the movements not just of those young people but their parents, their grandparents, every single day. It's not just when settler violence against Palestinians goes unpunished. It's not right to prevent Palestinians from farming their lands; or restricting a student's ability to move around the West Bank; or displace Palestinian families from their homes." Then, demonstrating some of the audacity of hope that had guided him on his amazing journey in the first place, he declared, "Neither occupation nor expulsion is the answer. Just as Israelis built a state in their homeland, Palestinians have a right to be a free people in their own land."[31]

Most reviews of Obama's talk echoed Remnick's enthusiasm, occupying a space somewhere between reverential and rhapsodic. *The New Republic*'s usually quite skeptical Israeli analyst, Yossi Klein Halevi, termed it "the most passionate Zionist speech ever given by an American president," and credited it with "end[ing] the debate here about whether or not he is a friend of Israel." On the opposite end (or perhaps just outside) of the relevant spectrum of opinion, Hussein Ibish, then a resident scholar at the Arab Gulf States Institute in Washington, called the speech "without question the strongest ever made by a senior American politician on the Israeli-Palestinian conflict." He judged it "plainly designed to speak directly to the Israeli and Palestinian peoples over the heads of their political leaderships. It was an exercise in public diplomacy par excellence, intended to change the tone and atmosphere, and public perceptions of

Obama himself, presumably as an adjunct to actual diplomatic efforts to lay the groundwork for eventually resuming negotiations." But there was the rub. As Jeffrey Goldberg noted at the time, had Obama given the same speech to AIPAC at one of its annual conventions, "he definitely would have been booed."[32]

Before leaving for Israel, Obama sat down with Goldberg in order to set the stage for his trip and boiled his concerns down to a set of questions, the same ones, as it happened, that formed the most pressing concern of the rapidly dwindling tribe of liberal Zionists: "I think, there comes a point where you can't manage this anymore, and then you start having to make very difficult choices. Do you resign yourself to what amounts to a permanent occupation of the West Bank? Is that the character of Israel as a state for a long period of time? Do you perpetuate, over the course of a decade or two decades, more and more restrictive policies in terms of Palestinian movement? Do you place restrictions on Arab-Israelis in ways that run counter to Israel's traditions?" he asked, before adding that "nobody has provided me with a clear picture of how this works in the absence of a peace deal." Invoking Hillel the Elder, the famous Jewish philosopher from the first century BCE, Obama asked, "If not now, when? And if not you, Mr. Prime Minister, then who?" Alas, the question did not much interest Bibi Netanyahu. And as Netanyahu went, so went AIPAC et al. Barack Obama was brilliant at reaching hearts and changing minds. What he could not do was alter the increasingly brutal "facts on the ground."[33]

In Washington, AIPAC and its allies continued their assault on Obama's policies, undermining the political appointment of anyone whose positions on Israel did not jibe with their own. AIPAC tended to work quietly among staffers on Capitol Hill, and with journalists, off the record. The most frequently quoted individual on matters of Jewish concern in the mainstream media was almost certainly Abe Foxman, the Anti-Defamation League's national director. A veritable perpetual motion machine when it came to returning journalists' emails and phone calls, Foxman displayed a kind of genius when offering up Solomonic soundbites on deadline.

His primary concern was to draw lines in the sand over which forms of criticism of Israel might be considered permissible and which revealed the dark heart of an antisemite lurking beneath a person's comment. But in doing so, Foxman was not speaking merely for himself. By the end of his three-decade reign in 2015, he headed up a powerhouse organization boasting a $60 million budget and a full-time staff of over three hundred, with countless consultants, part-timers, National Commission members, and others who brought the number well into the thousands. And while these individuals were spread out across twenty-seven separate offices, they were answerable only to Foxman. (With one of Sheldon Adelson's private jets at Foxman's disposal, the threat of a visit from headquarters was never far away for potential deviationists.) When asked, for a sympathetic *New York Times* profile, who in the organization besides himself a reporter might interview, Foxman was unable to come up with a single name. While he no doubt enjoyed the limelight, behind the scenes he turned the ADL into "first and foremost a fund-raising organization," according to a staffer there. He owed his super-hero status to what another Jewish professional termed the "guilt and gelt generation" of American Jews. "You worshiped at the altar of Israel by contributing. Jewish observance [became] raising money, not going to the synagogue," said David Clayman, a high-ranking American Jewish Congress official, of Foxman's success. The ADL cannot be said to have ignored other forms of alleged discrimination under Foxman's reign, but it prioritized only one. As one of Foxman's top lieutenants once informed an ADL regional representative, who was apparently too distant from home base to have gotten the memo, "Your little Christian-Jewish dialogue is very nice but remember, whatever you do with your inter-group relations, the end game is always Israel."[34]

During the 1990s, the ADL had operated a spying operation devoted to the activities of left-wing organizations, including the American Civil Liberties Union, Arab American groups, dovish Jewish groups, and even a congressman, Ronald V. Dellums (D-CA), sharing what it found with the Israeli government. As a result of these illegal activities, the FBI raided its San Francisco and Los Angeles offices in 1993. But even when acting lawfully, Foxman's ADL often behaved as if it were in the "defamation" business, rather than its opposite. For instance, when in 2009 the enormously respected PBS journalist Bill Moyers broadcast a less than laudatory commentary about Israel's Gaza invasion, Foxman accused the liberal icon of "moral equivalency, racism, historical revisionism, and indifference to terrorism." When Human Rights Watch issued a critical report of Israeli actions in the same war, Foxman told reporters, "Human Rights Watch's approach to these problems is immorality at the highest level." Under Foxman, the ADL's moral calculations grew so complex that he somehow concluded that it was the job of the organization to lend its help to prevent Congress from passing resolutions condemning the conduct of genocide—specifically, that committed by Turks against the Armenians during World War I. Foxman did not dispute the (undisputable) fact that the genocide took place. Rather, he argued that it would be inconvenient for Turkish (and Israeli) Jews if Congress took note of it.[35]

The liberal journalist Peter Beinart raised a series of complicated questions about the role of American Jewish organizations in an article in the *New York Review of Books* published in 2010, as well as in a book published two years later. The former boy-wonder editor of Martin Peretz's *New Republic* was part of the way along in what would become a lengthy journey leftward into dovish Jewish politics. His credibility as a critic was augmented not only by his former hawkishness, but also by his observant Jewish lifestyle, Orthodox synagogue membership, the Jewish day-schooling of his children, and his generally respectful attitude toward his Jewish elders. In other words, he was no Stephen Walt or John Mearsheimer, much less a Pat Buchanan, and therefore a much tougher target for the slings and arrows that such open criticism could be certain to inspire.

In his article, Beinart warned that "for several decades, the Jewish establishment has asked American Jews to check their liberalism at Zionism's door, and now, to their horror, they are finding that many young Jews have checked their Zionism instead.... Because their liberalism is real, they can see that the liberalism of the American Jewish establishment is fake." He predicted that if American Jewish leaders did not "change course, they will wake up one day to find a younger,

Orthodox-dominated, Zionist leadership whose naked hostility to Arabs and Palestinians scares even them, and a mass of secular American Jews who range from apathetic to appalled."[36]

Beinart's thesis was "examined...in the uppermost precincts of organized U.S. Jewry and became fodder for lunchtime chats," according to "insiders" quoted by the Jewish Telegraphic Agency. "Everyone's read it and everyone is talking about it," said Mark Pelavin, the associate director of the Reform movement's Religious Action Center. This may have been true behind closed doors, but before the public, the reaction was pretty much déjà vu. Beinart's bona fides did not protect him from being called "strident" by *The New Republic*'s Jonathan Chait, and "pseudo-courageous" by its literary editor, Leon Wieseltier. Peretz's former assistant there, James Kirchick, complained that Beinart was "joining the anti–'Jewish establishment' bandwagon." *The Atlantic*'s Jeffrey Goldberg (who later hired him) termed Beinart's argument "utopian" and not "too interested in the forces that seek the elimination of Israel." *Commentary*'s Noah Pollak insisted that Beinart was eager to join "the Israel bashers" before going on to equate Beinart's criticism with those of Noam Chomsky, the post-Zionist historian Avi Shlaim, and, of course, Walt and Mearsheimer. AIPAC's Steven Rosen responded, with unintended irony, that Beinart could not possibly be correct, moreover, because "AIPAC's income from donations is now five times what it was in 2000, and sixty times what it was when I joined the organization in 1982."[37]

Beinart's warnings were vindicated in 2013, when the Pew Foundation published the most in-depth look at American Jews' beliefs and values in many decades. While the vast majority defined themselves as pro-Israel, just 43 percent of those questioned agreed that "caring about Israel" was an "essential" part of being Jewish. In fact, Israel was only one percentage point more popular as a definitional category than "having a good sense of humor." What's more, Israel's centrality declined precipitously among younger Jews—"caring about Israel" fell to just 30 percent among those under thirty.[38]

It was hard not to notice, moreover, that when questioned about the Israeli/Palestinian conflict, the views of most American Jews were far closer to those of the liberal Zionists at J Street than to those of the

hardline hawks represented by AIPAC and the Presidents' Conference—
which continued to bar J Street from membership—to say nothing of
those even further to their right. While these organizations almost always parroted the Likud line, American Jews remained stubbornly dovish: only 17 percent supported Israel's settlement policy, and just 38
percent thought Israel's government was sincerely seeking peace. And,
once again, consistent with Beinart's arguments, a mere 23 percent of
Jews between the ages of eighteen and twenty-nine believed the Israeli
government was sincerely pursuing peace. Quizzed about how out of
touch (and undemocratic) they were, the leaders of these organizations
basically responded that it was the fault of the people whose views they
failed to represent. Asked about this, Foxman was unmoved. What mattered, after all, were the funders. "Listen," he explained in one interview,
"there's a lot of organized Jewish life, and these are the people that pay
the bills."[39]

The power of money to dictate the parameters of allowable speech
was the reason why so many synagogues barred J Street president Jeremy
Ben-Ami from speaking, and instead sponsored trips to the annual AI-
PAC convention. It took only one donor threatening to withhold a major
donation to ensure that a specific voice went unheard—something that
was almost always done in secret. A 2013 report by the Jewish Council
for Public Affairs, based on an online survey of over five hundred mostly
Reform and Conservative rabbis, found that nearly half held "views on
Israel that they won't share publicly, many for fear of endangering their
reputation or their careers." The survey found that 43 percent of rabbis
who identified as dovish reported feeling "very fearful" of expressing their
true views on Israel, compared to just 29 percent of moderates and 25
percent of hawks. A full 74 percent of the dovish rabbis reported feeling
"very" or "somewhat" fearful of expressing their views. Rabbi Jill Jacobs,
executive director of T'ruah, a liberal rabbinic human rights organization
with 1,800 member rabbis, admitted that "rabbis are just really scared
because they get slammed by their right-wing congregants, who are often
the ones with the purse strings. They are not necessarily the numerical
majority, but they are the loudest."[40]

The undeniable truth was that by the middle of Barack Obama's second presidential term, American Jews could rarely discuss Israel among themselves without participants erupting in anger and acrimony. The gulf between American Jews' dogged commitment to liberalism and their emotional attachment to Zionism had grown too vast to bridge. Some chose one, and some chose the other, but almost all felt that their opponents were not merely wrong but engaging in fundamental betrayal.

The Jerusalem-based Jewish People Policy Institute, which was created by the Jewish Agency in 2002 to bridge gaps of understanding between Israeli and diaspora Jews, in its 2015 report, said there was "a sense of crisis" within American Jewish communities, whose members found it "increasingly difficult... to discuss Israel because of the bitter political disputes these discussions spark." Israel's treatment of the Palestinians and apparent lack of interest in genuine peace was the most frequently voiced complaint, but it was hardly the only one. The report's authors also addressed "a long litany of complaints about Israel's refusal to respect American Jewish identity as legitimate in areas that relate to them directly," such as conversion, the treatment of non-Orthodox streams of Judaism, chief rabbinate policy, the never-ending "Who is a Jew?" question, and, in particular, Netanyahu's failure to keep his word on a long-negotiated compromise that would have allowed women to pray at the Western Wall in Jerusalem with rights (almost) equal to those of men. In addition, their dogged liberalism "led to alienation from Israel on numerous civil rights issues, especially those related to Israel's treatment of its minorities, whether among Arab Jews, immigrant Jews, or foreign, non-Jewish workers."[41]

More and more, it was becoming clear that despite the efforts of American Jewish officialdom to paper over differences to create the pretense of a united front on behalf of Israel, this had become a losing battle. The rise of Israeli illiberalism was everywhere evident, with increasing ultra-Orthodox influence over politics, creeping West Bank annexation, and consistent attempts, on the part of Netanyahu, to bend Israel's once proudly independent judiciary to his will. The American/Israeli pollster Dahlia Scheindlin credited Israel's 18th Knesset (2009–2013) with having "introduced anti-liberal and anti-democratic legislation and normalized offensive, ultranationalist, anti-Arab rhetoric in social discourse." As a result, the sorts of Israeli civil society organizations US liberals funded as a reflection of their own values saw themselves targeted for censorship and defunding and often received violent, threatening messages that were amplified by the Adelsons' Netanyahu-friendly media landscape. The demands being made on American Jews by an increasingly illiberal Israel that consistently demonstrated its disdain for diaspora life became ever more obvious and unbridgeable.[42]

Michael Oren, an American-born and Ivy League–educated Jewish historian, had emigrated to Israel, served in the IDF, and launched a political career that eventually landed him as ambassador to the United States during Obama's first term. In the spring of 2015, he published a memoir and a series of provocative op-ed articles that helped to demonstrate the gulf that had arisen between the views of Israeli and American Jews. Like so many of his fellow Israeli Jews, he believed the worst about Obama. He postulated that what he termed the president's "abandonment" by his mother's "two Muslim husbands" had left behind a psychological need for "acceptance by their co-religionists," which would explain his allegedly anti-Israel foreign policy.[43]

Even Abe Foxman found Oren to be "veer[ing] into the realm of conspiracy theories" regarding Obama. But the balance of Oren's armchair psychiatry can be properly understood as an attack on American Jews, given how much the community admired him. Lest there be any confusion on this point, however, Oren was good enough to make his attack explicit: he "could not help questioning whether American Jews really felt as secure as they claimed. Perhaps persistent fears of anti-Semitism impelled them to distance themselves from Israel and its controversial policies. Maybe that is why so many of them supported Obama." Oren singled out the "malicious" op-ed page of the *New York Times*, "once revered as an interface of ideas, now sadly reduced to a sounding board for only one, which often excluded Israel's legitimacy." He complained that the "unflattering dispatches" at the *Times* were "written by Jews working for a paper long under Jewish ownership." (In fact, Arthur Ochs Sulzberger Jr., who had been at the helm of the paper since 1997, was raised Episcopalian, and one can only wonder about Oren's nostalgia for a newspaper whose Jewish owners were famous for their anti-Zionism.) Sadly, Oren noted, "the presence of so many Jews in print and on the screen rarely translates into support for Israel.... The pinch I felt reading articles censorious of Israel sharpened into a stab whenever the names on the bylines were Jewish. Almost all of the world's countries are nation-states, so what, I wondered, drove these writers to nitpick at theirs?"[44]

Oren's attack embodied two time-honored antisemitic canards. The first was that American Jews remained politically paralyzed by the fear of antisemitism. This is a profoundly ridiculous contention given the size and scope of the American Jewish organizations devoting themselves to supporting Israel and the amount of money they were able to raise. The second was that the true country of America's Jews was not the one in which they lived and to which they pledged their allegiance, but Israel, where they did not live, vote, or pay taxes, and in whose military they did not serve. To triple the irony implicit in his attack, he went on to equate American Jewish distaste for Netanyahu to historical antisemitic attitudes, as if this were the only conceivable motivation for criticism of a politician whose values consistently offended their own, and who treated their concerns as a matter of indifference when not openly demonstrating his contempt. Oren insisted that "the antagonism sparked by Netanyahu" among American Jews somehow resembled that traditionally triggered by the Jews in gentiles. "We were always the ultimate Other—communists in the view of the capitalists and capitalists in communist eyes, national-ists for the cosmopolitans and, for jingoists, the International Jew." And he did not stop there. At one point he claimed that some "saw assailing Israel as a career enhancer—the equivalent of Jewish man bites Jewish dog—that saved several struggling pundits from obscurity." Others he compared to "upper class American Jews of German ancestry," noting their historic scorn for Jewish immigrants from Eastern Europe—"the Yiddish speaking rabble who allegedly made all Jews look bad." Still oth-ers, he wrote, "largely assimilated, resented Israel for further complicat-ing their already conflicted identity."[45]

Oren is no doubt sincere in his complaints. But the irony of a former American Jewish academic achieving political success (together with
book sales in the United States) by deploying age-old antisemitic slanders
against the American Jewish journalists and scholars who had been his
friends and colleagues in his past life is a little too thick to escape notice.
Such have long been a staple of Israelis' political and cultural rhetoric.
Throughout their history, Israelis have proven unwilling to demonstrate
respect for the ways and mores of American Jewish religious practices,
refusing legitimacy to their denominations, refusing to recognize conversions practiced by their rabbis, and denying women equal access to religious sites, while simultaneously demanding 100 percent fealty to what
Israel defined as its security interests, no questions asked.

This contempt became ever more naked under Netanyahu as Christian Zionists and wealthy right-wing donors provided whatever resources
he felt he needed without having to listen to the constant complaints of
American Jewish liberals. Gary Rosenblatt, the longtime editor and publisher of the *Jewish Week* of New York, tells of attending briefings with
journalists that Netanyahu held during his visits to the United States. In
one case, he attended two held on the same day. At the first, Netanyahu
met with "major media figures"; at the other, with "the same number of
editors of Jewish newspapers from around the country." At the former,
Netanyahu was "warm, friendly and upbeat from the outset." At the latter he was "ornery... challenging and dismissive." Rosenblatt said he witnessed many similar scenes over the years and believed they represented
"the prime minister's attitude not just toward the Jewish press but toward
American Jewry in general," adding that "Netanyahu has said in private
that as long as he has the support in America of evangelical Christians,
who vastly outnumber Jews, and the Orthodox Jewish community, he
is in good shape." And yet, for most of this period, American Jewish
organizations had not only reinforced the Israeli view, but also enforced
a policy of *omertà* regarding all criticism. By the end of Barack Obama's
presidency, many Jews had opted out entirely from the essentially vicar-
ious experience of defining their Jewishness in terms of the interests of
a country where Jews did not appear to be physically threatened, whose

values increasingly conflicted with their own, and whose leaders apparently held them and their religious identities in contempt.[46]

Their power and influence in Congress notwithstanding, Netanyahu and AIPAC could not, ultimately, control every aspect of US foreign policy. Presidents, as Ronald Reagan and George H. W. Bush had shown, could take on Israel and win if they were willing to take the fight public. The Israelis were forced to relearn this lesson in 2015, when a reelected Obama, together with the leaders of China, Russia, the United Kingdom, France, and Germany (approved and partially financed by the European Union), signed an interim nuclear deal with Iran. The agreement included lifting some important international sanctions in exchange for Iran pausing its nuclear program for the coming ten years and came with impressively invasive verification measures. Its signatories hoped and expected that it would be the first step toward not only blunting the threat of a "Muslim bomb," but eventually reintegrating Iran into the international community. That was not how Netanyahu saw it, however. The Israelis had been lobbying for a joint US/Israeli attack on Iran's nuclear facilities and were at times poised to undertake one on their own, but had been dissuaded by the president's advisers. Netanyahu was furious when US officials informed him of secret negotiations with Iran (and he was immediately suspected by US officials of having leaked it to the media). The two leaders already had a tortured relationship—Netanyahu treated Obama with even greater condescension than he had previous presidents. During one meeting, as Netanyahu delivered a lengthy political lecture to the president, the latter, struggling to maintain his cool, patiently said, "Bibi, you have to understand something. I'm the African American son of a single mother, and I live here, in this house. I live in the White House. I managed to get elected president of the United States. You think I don't understand what you're talking about, but I do." He did not need any political lectures from Israel's prime minister.[47]

But Netanyahu, apparently unimpressed, kept at it over the next weeks and months. He could not believe that Obama had acted against both his advice and the political pressure he had brought to bear on the president over the Iran nuclear deal. Furious, the Israeli prime minister went beyond what any leader of any putative US ally had done before and tried to publicly undermine a sitting US president's policy. Israel's ambassador to the United States, the former right-wing US political consultant Ron Dermer, cut a deal with the Republican Speaker of the House, John Boehner, to have Netanyahu invited by Republicans—who controlled both houses of the legislature at the time—to address a joint session of Congress in order to attack the deal. Neither the Israelis nor the Republican leaders even mentioned the plan to the president, who learned about it, along with the rest of the world, in a press release.

Although most polls showed majority Jewish support for Obama's position, Citizens for a Nuclear Free Iran, an AIPAC offshoot, reportedly raised between $20 million and $40 million for a campaign to oppose it. As Peter Beinart later noted, one AIPAC official called it "one of the most significant mobilization efforts in our organization's history." The head of the Orthodox Union Advocacy Center concurred, terming the campaign "the biggest mobilization in the community that we have ever seen." The relentless propaganda campaign had its effects, even with liberal American Jews, who remained vulnerable to stoked fears of a "second Holocaust"—this time in the form of a potential Iranian nuclear attack on Israel. When Obama granted an interview to the editor of the Jewish newspaper *The Forward*, its editor, Jane Eisner, accused him of employing "incendiary language" against opponents of the deal, citing his use of the phrase "warmongers" to describe them. But, as Obama told her, he never used the phrase. The fact that the editor of a small, liberal Jewish paper, whose editors had to be thrilled to be granted a presidential interview, could level a false accusation against the president himself on behalf of Netanyahu's defenders demonstrates just how deep the reach of the prime minister's anti-Obama campaign went. As Obama felt compelled to explain, he had "at no point...ever suggested that those who are critical of the deal are 'warmongers.'" Instead, he had argued, "if we reject the deal, the logical conclusion is that if we want to prevent Iran from getting a nuclear weapon, military strikes will be the last option remaining."[48]

The lengths to which "pro-Israel" AIPAC allies would go to police the Israel debate was again made clear by a series of incidents around this time involving Washington's premier Democratic think tank, the Center for American Progress (CAP). The center's founder and first president, John Podesta, previously Bill Clinton's chief of staff, had headed up Barack Obama's presidential transition team. He had successfully sought to avoid arguments about Israel during his seven-year reign, which began in 2003. But after Podesta turned over the reins to CAP's cofounder, longtime Hillary Clinton staffer Neera Tanden, at the end of 2010, the issue crept to center stage. The problem lay with the center's newsy weblog, *Think Progress*, whose contributors, in late 2011 and 2012, published a series of posts and tweets critical of Israel, of AIPAC, and of what these mostly young writers judged to be efforts to draw the United States into war with Iran. It's fair to say that more than a few of these posts and tweets might have been more thoughtfully articulated had they been accorded closer editorial scrutiny before they were posted. But anything critical of Israel published by the center would have done the trick.

Thanks to a public campaign led by Josh Block, a former spokesperson for AIPAC, these posts and tweets inspired a multipronged attack against CAP. Ben Smith, then reporting for Politico, noted that CAP's stance had "shaken up the Washington foreign policy conversation and broadened the space for discussing a heretical and often critical stance on Israel heretofore confined to the political margins." Jason Isaacson, of the American Jewish Committee, told reporters of his concern about the "very troubling things that have been written on a pretty regular basis by certain people associated with the organization." Abe Foxman also worried about statements made under CAP's aegis that he felt were "anti-Semitic and borderline anti-Semitic." Rabbi Abraham Cooper, associate director of the Simon Wiesenthal Center, joined in with a complaint to President Obama's Jewish community liaison, Jarrod Bernstein, who called the situation at CAP "troubling" and not reflective of "this administration," though, of course, the Obama administration played no role in dictating content in blog posts at *Think Progress*.

As the controversy rose in prominence, an apparently panicked Tanden emailed Podesta and other top CAP officials to say she had received a furious phone call from Ann Lewis, who was another close adviser to Hillary Clinton, as well as a frequent speaker at AIPAC events and those of its sister organization, the American Israel Education Fund. Lewis was speaking, as Tanden understood her, both on behalf of AIPAC and, as both women no doubt understood, out of concern for Hillary Clinton's future presidential campaign. Lewis read Tanden the riot act about *Think Progress*'s treatment of Israel, accusing it of, among other sins, failing to balance its criticism of Israel with compliments for its virtues. Tanden responded by instituting a policy under which any mention of Israel on the website would be subject to its own, organization-wide, prepublication editorial review. The Iranian-born contributing writer Ali Gharib was told to expect to "never" again be allowed to write about AIPAC or any other American Jewish organization. Tanden also apparently directed the retroactive removal of all references to Israel and American Jewish groups from a previously published CAP report on Islamophobia in the US media. Gharib and another *Think Progress* writer, Eli Clifton, soon left the organization under murky circumstances. Matt Duss, who oversaw much of CAP's Middle East policy work, was told to rein in his staff and his own writings. He left CAP in 2014 to become president of the Foundation for Middle East Peace before rising to prominence as chief foreign policy adviser to Senator Bernie Sanders (D-VT).*

CAP soon reaped the rewards of these actions. Again, according to internal emails later published in the media, its officers celebrated the fact that AIPAC's deputy director of policy and government affairs, Jeff Colman, had been "very positive" in his response to the steps taken and was pleased to see that the organization "now was moving in the right direction." An AIPAC event was coming up, and CAP's chief of staff, Ken Gude, enthused, in one email, "I bet we get a lot of invitations to

---

* I was a Senior Fellow at CAP from its founding in 2003 through the end of 2016. Although I was not involved with *Think Progress*, I authored a weekly media-focused column titled "Think Again" for much of this time. One such column was referenced in the coverage of this controversy, and when it was over, Tanden asked me to please avoid the subjects of Israel and AIPAC in future columns. I agreed to do so, as foreign policy generally was not a topic I had been hired by CAP to address in my work. I should also note here that it was in his capacity as president of the foundation noted above that Duss oversaw the grant I received that I mention in my acknowledgments to this book.

attend." He added, "And it's very likely that I'm going to Israel on one of their upcoming trips." Leaders of other groups, including officers of the American Jewish Committee and the National Jewish Democratic Council, joined in the praise.[49]

But this response did not satisfy Tanden, who decided, in November 2015, that in order to further cement CAP's "pro-Israel" credentials, she would host none other than Benjamin Netanyahu for a friendly, public chat in the think tank's offices. According to a report in the Huffington Post, the decision came after intense lobbying by the Israeli embassy augmented by "pressure" from AIPAC. The announcement of the invitation, however, led to an uproar among CAP's liberal staffers. After all, not only had Israel become a clearly conservative cause, and Netanyahu the leader of what were increasingly illiberal forces in Israel, but he was also waging a not-so-secret war against America's Democratic president at the moment of the invitation. Why in the world, wondered much of Washington, was Washington's premier Democratic Party–aligned think tank appearing to side with his tormentor? Reports of angry internal meetings were leaked to the press by CAP staffers. Matt Duss said, of his former employer, "the idea that CAP would agree to give him bipartisan cover is really disappointing," since "this is someone who is an enemy of the progressive agenda, who has targeted Israeli human rights organizations throughout his term, and was re-elected on the back of blatant anti-Arab race-baiting." The public discussion came off, however, largely without incident. Tanden asked the prime minister a series of mostly friendly questions, as did the invited members of the audience. In another leaked email, from Tanden to Podesta, Tanden expressed her relief that, while the Netanyahu invitation had been a difficult decision to make, and the internal rebellion unpleasant to handle, angry AIPAC complaints would now be a thing of the past. By the time Hillary Clinton made Podesta CEO of her 2016 presidential campaign, with Tanden a top unofficial adviser (and Ann Lewis head of "Jewish Women for Hillary"), the matter was pretty much forgotten. AIPAC and company had forced yet another showdown between Zionism and liberalism, and the latter again lost.[50]

These events came on the heels of the Iran debate's most dramatic moment: Netanyahu's speech to both houses of Congress denouncing the deal. The Israeli leader became only the second person ever to enjoy the honor of speaking to Congress three times, the other being Winston Churchill. But while his harsh words played well with Israelis at home and with Republicans in the United States, for Democrats this was a bridge too far. Netanyahu's previous embrace of Jerry Falwell and John Hagee, his open support for Mitt Romney, and his airtight alliance with the Adelsons did not help him get the votes he needed to defeat the president on the Iran agreement and may have cost him. Signing one's name to an AIPAC-drafted letter was one thing; humiliating the president in the midst of a hard-fought battle, in which the opposing party had lined up 100 percent on the other side, was quite another. What's more, the Netanyahu speech plus AIPAC's massive campaign against the deal had failed to sway a majority of American Jews, who, according to a survey conducted by the *Jewish Journal* in July 2015, found that 49 percent of American Jews supported the nuclear deal with Iran while just 31 percent were opposed. More than fifty Democrats refused to attend the speech. Netanyahu got himself twenty-nine standing ovations as he bet the house on his persuasive powers. As far as Iran went, however, he went home with empty pockets.[51]

The Obama era ended much as it had begun, with impotent, futile gestures toward Israeli-Palestinian peace by the administration and hysterical and dishonest attacks on the president and his advisers by the Israelis and their champions. The proximate cause—much as it had been for another scorned champion of peace for Israel, Jimmy Carter—was a UN vote. Having seen his diplomatic efforts go down in flames, in December 2016 US secretary of state John Kerry laid out a potential peace plan that had no hopes whatever of being adopted—as Donald Trump had already been elected president. Kerry then instructed the United States' UN ambassador to abstain rather than vote no on a Security Council Resolution declaring Israeli settlements in the Palestinian territories to have "no legal validity," and thus to constitute "a flagrant violation under international law." The resolution therefore passed unanimously.[52]

Obama had not allowed any such anti-Israel resolution to go forward during the previous seven years and had been alone among American presidents in having so protected Israel. Literally every other American president since the occupation began had either supported these condemnations or abstained on the vote. Between 1967 and 1988, fully fifty-seven resolutions condemning Israeli actions had made it through the Security Council, with twenty-one of them coming during Reagan's presidency. The two Bush presidencies along with Bill Clinton's yielded eighteen more. Yet Obama's single abstention, coming after seven years of shielding Israel, was somehow taken as evidence of his administration's perfidy. Netanyahu attacked it as "old-world bias against Israel," and immediately announced the construction of thousands of new homes in East Jerusalem (the Obama presidency had already seen the addition of over 100,000 Israeli settlers on the West Bank and in East Jerusalem). Israel Katz, a senior government minister from Netanyahu's ruling Likud party, speaking of a president who had negotiated with Congress to ensure the passage of literally the largest military aid package from one country to another in the annals of human history, said Obama had "reached a new low when he turned his back on America's ally Israel."[53]

These views were consistently echoed in the United States, especially on the nation's most influential editorial pages. Seventy-eight senators signed a letter condemning the vote, and one, Lindsey Graham (R-SC), told CNN he planned to ask Congress to rescind all funding for the United Nations unless it reversed the entire world's virtually unanimous position on the illegality of Israel's settlements. But with what was becoming typical irony, the Obama position was actually much more popular than Lindsey Graham's with a plurality of Americans: indeed, according to an extensive poll by the Pew Research Center, fully 60 percent of Democrats supported far stronger action in opposition to Israel's occupation, including imposing economic sanctions or more serious action. And for the first time ever, more self-described liberal Democrats, a category that included a near majority of America's Jews, said they sympathized with the Palestinians more than they did with Israel. These sympathies had no policy implications to speak of in the present, but they were evidence of a possible transformation of the debate in years to come.[54]

# CHAPTER 18

# COMING UNGLUED

IF THE 2016 PRESIDENTIAL ELECTION HAD BEEN A GAME SHOW IN WHICH contestants competed to find newer and more extravagant means to praise Israel's virtues and attack its adversaries, it might have been called *Can You Top This?* As the liberal Jewish journalist Peter Beinart aptly observed early in the nomination process, the seventeen Republican presidential candidates represented three sometimes "overlapping" positions on the Israel/Palestine question: those who believed the Israeli military occupation should continue "indefinitely"; those favoring "expelling Palestinians from Israel"; and those "deny[ing] that Palestinians exist[ed] at all."[1]

Though it included only two serious candidates, the Democratic side proved more diverse. Hillary Clinton hewed close to the AIPAC-defined parameters of the debate, paying rhetorical tribute to the idea of a Palestinian state just so long as Israel was free to dictate all the conditions under which it might one day come into existence. As a candidate for the US Senate in New York in 2000, she had been the target of robocalls from Republican opponents expressing shock over the fact that, as First Lady, she had accepted the greeting of a kiss on both cheeks from Yasser

Arafat's wife, Suha Arafat, at a diplomatic reception. She was damned if she was going to leave herself open to any more such attacks. As Obama's first secretary of state, Clinton had had many strong disagreements with Netanyahu, and these sometimes grew heated. But as a presidential candidate, she might as well have been on Israel's public relations payroll. According to candidate Clinton, Ariel Sharon's 2000 visit to the Temple Mount, which set off the Second Intifada, had not been provocative at all; it was long past time to move the US embassy to Jerusalem—and maybe the US Justice Department had been a little too hard on poor Jonathan Pollard. Clinton did not, like some Republicans, deny the existence of the Palestinians; she simply ignored them. In one speech on the Middle East given at the Brookings Institution's Saban Center—named after and paid for by Clinton's own close adviser and major funder, the Israeli-born billionaire Haim Saban—she said the word "Israel" or "Israeli" forty times, but "Palestine" or "Palestinians" not even once. When her adviser for Jewish affairs, Ann Lewis, was asked about the overall thrust of Clinton's Middle East policy, she replied, reversing the usual relationship between the leader of a superpower and one of its client states, "The role of the president of the United States is to support the decisions that are made by the people of Israel."[2]

Clinton's only meaningful competition for the 2016 Democratic presidential nomination was the independent socialist senator Bernie Sanders of Vermont, and in his coalition, one could glimpse the dawning of a new era for Democrats and Israel. Sanders, who as a Jewish boy in Brooklyn had attended Hebrew school, and who was Bar Mitzvahed in 1954—spoke more openly and critically about Israel than any previous Democratic presidential candidate, saying on the campaign trail the kinds of things that previously had been voiced exclusively in private. He was particularly critical of Israel's December 2008 invasion of Gaza. Israel had "every right in the world to destroy terrorism," but that did not justify "some 10,000 civilians who were wounded and some 1,500 who were killed," Sanders thundered at an April 2016 Democratic Party debate held in Brooklyn (where Clinton's national campaign office happened to be located). Clinton surrogate Eliot Engel, a US congressman from New York and soon to be chairman of the House Committee on

Foreign Affairs, called Sanders's comments "disgraceful and reprehensible," as they gave "radical left-wing elements in the party more license to attack Israel." But they earned the loud applause of the attending audience. The progressive Brooklyn rabbi Andy Bachman correctly noted that Sanders "spoke to this growing rift in the Democratic Party—it was proof of a major crisis in the Jewish community that no major Jewish organization has resolved or figured out to handle." (Ironically, in 2020 Engel would lose his seat in a Democratic primary to a Black candidate, Jamal Bowman, who spoke in Sanders-style rhetoric about the importance of "establishing a true Palestinian state where they can have safety and security and self-determination as well.") And the trends among self-described liberal Democrats—a heavily Jewish category—continued to move in Sanders's direction. By 2017, support for Israel and the Palestinians was now basically equal among Democrats in general, but among self-described "liberal Democrats," the Palestinians were now ahead. All Democrats under thirty would also come to view Palestinians more favorably than Israelis, as evidenced by a Pew survey released in May 2022. What's more, fully 42 percent of Jews surveyed that year by the Pew Research Center thought Trump was "favoring the Israelis too much," nearly double the proportion of Christians who said they felt this way.[3]

While the Democratic contest revealed the transformation underway in the party's Israeli/Palestine discourse, the Republican side reached ever greater heights of absurdity, culminating in Donald Trump's nomination and election. Trump had no particular knowledge of, or views on, Israel, save for an adherence to a number of the antisemitic stereotypes he had picked up from his notoriously racist father and during his own career as a real estate shyster (this was only partially mitigated by the conversion of his favorite child, Ivanka, to Orthodox Judaism, preceding her marriage to Jared Kushner, a Modern Orthodox Jew, in 2009). Trump was more than happy to share some of these tropes during the campaign, even when speaking to Jewish audiences. "You're not going to support me because I don't want your money," he announced to Sheldon Adelson's Republican Jewish Coalition. Speaking to another right-wing Adelson-funded organization, the Israeli American Council, he opined, apparently thinking he was offering compliments: "You're brutal killers, not nice people at all."

But Trump went on to predict, inaccurately, that Jews were "going to be my biggest supporters," because, he said, Democrats were proposing to raise taxes on the super wealthy. Apparently he was unaware that by this time the vast majority of Jews had been voting for the party that supported the poor and working class for more than eighty years.[4]

The unmistakable tolerance and often unsubtle promotion of antisemitism by Trump and his allies in the Republican Party had a far darker side than this casual ribbing, however. They almost constantly stoked hatred toward the liberal Jewish billionaire philanthropist George Soros, for example, whom conservatives treated as an all-purpose bogeyman, often with exaggerated features in the traditional antisemitic fantasy of the Jew as puppet master. During the final days of the 2016 campaign, Trump ran a commercial attacking Soros, Goldman Sachs CEO Lloyd Blankfein, and Federal Reserve chair Janet Yellen—all of them Jews—claiming they were seeking to control the world. During the 2018 midterm elections, House majority leader Kevin McCarthy warned on Twitter that Soros and his fellow Jewish billionaires Michael Bloomberg and Tom Steyer were trying "to BUY this election!" Fox Business Network host Lou Dobbs invited a guest to make the ridiculous argument that the (largely imaginary) migrant caravan supposedly about to "invade" the United States at its Mexican border was part of a plan hatched by the "Soros-occupied State Department." This notion was picked up by his Fox colleague Maria Bartiromo, who asked, "Who do you think is behind these caravans? A lot of speculation that it was George Soros." This led Congressman Louie Gohmert, a Texas Republican, to say, again on Fox News, that "the Democrats—perhaps Soros, others—may be funding this, thinking it's going to help them." These themes continued to figure prominently in Republican campaigns through all the national elections that followed 2016. The 2022 midterm elections, for instance, featured Republican candidates refusing to renounce supporters with neo-Nazi ties, employing antisemitic dog whistles, and attempting to blame George Soros for everything from crime to abortion to promoting a "globalist agenda, a new world order."[5]

That right-wing antisemites were also enamored with Israel was hardly the contradiction it first appeared. First, many were evangelicals, who, as we have seen, had eschatological reasons for their affection for the Jewish state. Second, right-wingers admired Israel's harsh treatment of its Muslim minority, those living under its occupation and those with whom it occasionally went to war. Trump himself credited Israel with its allegedly "unbelievable job" of internal racial profiling, adding that America demonstrated weakness in this area because "we're trying to be so politically correct in our country and this is only going to get worse." Third, right-wing nationalists have long combined their antisemitic beliefs with support for Zionism. The neo-Nazi Richard Spencer, recognized as a leader of US "alt-right" forces, explained, "You could say that I am a white Zionist in the sense that I care about my people, I want us to have a secure homeland for us and ourselves. Just like you want a secure homeland in Israel."[6]

American Jews may have been offended by Trump—they voted approximately three to one against him in both 2016 and 2020—but Israelis polled the reverse. (The Americans felt that "Israelis insulted our former president, whom we loved; now you love our current president, whom we hate," as two op-ed writers put it.) In Israel, Benjamin Netanyahu's government did not mind the exploitation of antisemitic resentments in other countries—which, in the eyes of many Israelis, only strengthened their case that Jews belonged in Israel—and anyway, it was more than balanced out in fellow illiberal democracies by pro-Israel (really anti-Muslim) policies. When Prime Minister Viktor Orban of Hungary made Soros public enemy number one in his 2018 reelection campaign, using Nazi-style graphics to demonize the eighty-seven-year-old Holocaust survivor, the Netanyahu government actually joined in the slander.[7]

Members of Netanyahu's coalition were more than happy to run interference for Trump so long as he delivered for them on the things they really cared about. This became clear following the horrific October 27, 2018, mass murder at the Tree of Life synagogue in the Squirrel Hill section of Pittsburgh, when Trump announced that he would be visiting. Protesters marched through the neighborhood with signs containing messages such as "President Hate is not welcome in our state," and the Tree of Life rabbi pleaded with Trump to please stay away. Trump didn't care. He showed up anyway, and Israeli ambassador Ron Dermer flew in to meet him. Naftali Bennett, then the leader of Israel's pro-settler Jewish Home Party and former minister of diaspora affairs (and later Netanyahu's successor), took to Twitter to defend the president as well. He also felt it necessary to try to equate the far-right antisemitic murderer in Pittsburgh with Israel's enemies in the Arab world, saying that "the hand that fires missiles is the same hand that shoots worshippers."[8]

That a massive increase of antisemitic violence had accompanied Trump's political rise was undeniable. An Anti-Defamation League report that happened to be released a day before the Tree of Life shooting found that before Trump's 2016 election, antisemitic harassment of Jews was relatively rare. Afterward, however, it became a daily occurrence. The ADL estimated that about 3 million Twitter users posted or reposted at least 4.2 million antisemitic tweets in English in just Trump's first year—a 57 percent increase in what it defined as antisemitic incidents. Of the tweets judged to be antisemitic, fully 80 percent came from the political right, and nearly 40 percent of these featured the pro-Trump hashtags #MAGA and #KAG. Here again, the Israelis ran interference for the president. When Trump and Netanyahu held a joint press conference in February 2017, an Israeli journalist mentioned the "rise in anti-Semitic incidents" since Trump's election and asked whether his administration was "playing with xenophobia and maybe racist tones." Trump gave a nonsensical response about his electoral college victory before pivoting to the fact that his daughter and son-in-law were Jews. Netanyahu immediately stepped in to swear that "there is no greater supporter of the Jewish people and the Jewish state than President Donald Trump." Trump had not even been in office thirty days at the time. But just a few weeks earlier, in his remarks on International Holocaust Remembrance Day, he had somehow failed to mention the fact that any of the victims were Jews. (This is a favored tactic of "soft" Holocaust denialism.) Here, yet again, he found Netanyahu squarely in his corner. When asked about Trump's conspicuous omission, the man who fancied himself the representative of all the world's Jews could only repeat, "This man is a great friend of the Jewish people and the State of Israel." American Jews' concerns about him were therefore "misplaced." Trump complemented these arguments in August 2019 by insisting that American Jews owed their allegiance not to the United States but to Israel. He called Netanyahu "your prime minister" and insisted that for a Jew to vote for a Democrat "shows either a total lack of knowledge or great disloyalty [to Israel]."[9]

Trump supporters tended to answer accusations of antisemitism with the typical "whataboutism" that characterizes so much of the debate on Jews and Israel-related topics. Rather than addressing the very real concerns about the president, his movement, and his party, they responded by accusing Democrats of coddling antisemites in their own ranks. The party had begun to welcome Muslims into its coalition and saw two of them elected to Congress: Michigan's Rashida Tlaib, a daughter of Palestinian immigrants (with family still living in the West Bank), and Ilhan Omar of Minnesota, a former Somali refugee. Both spoke about Israel in a fashion rarely, if ever, previously heard in Congress, creating an entirely new set of controversies.

By focusing her criticism on Israel's American supporters, and doing so, on occasion, using language loaded with antisemitic tropes that she likely did not understand herself, Omar sometimes gave her allies heartburn and her enemies a sword. For instance, in 2019, it was discovered that back in 2012, she had tweeted that "Israel has hypnotized the world, may Allah awaken the people and help them see the evil doings of Israel." For some Jews, this language was especially offensive because the word "hypnotized" evoked medieval charges of occult powers. Another time, also in 2019, Omar told an audience, "I want to talk about the political influence in this country that says it is okay to push for allegiance to a foreign country." AIPAC and the ADL typed the "dual loyalty" keys on their computers and pushed send. "The charge of dual loyalty not only raises the ominous specter of classic antisemitism, but it is also deeply insulting to the millions upon millions of patriotic Americans, Jewish and non-Jewish, who stand by our democratic ally, Israel," AIPAC tweeted. "[Omar's] comments were anti-Semitic. Accusing Jews of having allegiance to a foreign government has long been a vile anti-Semitic slur used to harass, marginalize and persecute the Jewish people for centuries," wrote the ADL's executive director, Jonathan Greenblatt. While being pilloried not only by Republicans and neoconservative pundits, but even many Democrats, Omar did what Republicans never did in such circumstances: she apologized. "I heard from Jewish orgs. that my use of the word 'Hypnotize' and the ugly sentiment it holds was offensive," she tweeted. She also made it clear she was "disavowing the anti-Semitic trope I unknowingly used, which is unfortunate and offensive." But this became a kind of pattern. Omar also said that support for Israel in Congress was "all about the Benjamins baby," hip-hop slang for hundred-dollar bills, suggesting that Israel's support was bought and paid for by AIPAC and its allies. Again, this was extremely clumsily articulated and definitely deserved an apology. But the reference to the Puff Daddy rap song lyric—and the 2002 buddy comedy starring Ice Cube—aside, in substance, what Omar was saying was not terribly different from what many Jews had long said themselves, usually in private, to one another. Back in 1980, Rita Hauser, a pro-Israel Republican lawyer, had warned in a *Commentary* magazine symposium that President Carter's proposed campaign finance laws "eliminated the strongest weapon the Jewish community exercised in influencing the selection of nominees in both political parties." (And subsequently, none other than Donald Trump would endorse Omar's argument when, in November 2021, the ex-president expressed his regret over the passing of the days when Israel "literally owned Congress.")[10]

Her apology notwithstanding, Omar continued to insist that the questions she sought to raise, however clumsily, demanded attention. "Because Rashida [Tlaib] and I are Muslim . . . a lot of our Jewish colleagues, a lot of our constituents, a lot of our allies, go to thinking that everything we say about Israel to be anti-Semitic because we are Muslim," she observed. In addition to this being racist and unfair, she added, it meant that "nobody ever gets to have the broader debate of what is happening with Palestine. So for me, I want to talk about the political influence in this country that says it is okay for people to push for allegiance to a foreign country. And I want to ask, why is it okay for me to talk about the influence of the NRA, of fossil fuel industries, or Big Pharma, and not talk about a powerful lobby?"[11]

That the congresswoman had a point in both respects could not have been less relevant to the arguments she inspired. AIPAC launched a campaign against the two Muslim women that, much to the delight of Republicans, attempted to paint all Democrats in their ideological colors. During the 2020 presidential campaign, it produced an advertisement that featured two little girls wrapped in Israeli and American flags against a desert background. But this image was mixed in with frightening photos of the two Muslim representatives, while a voiceover accused "the radicals in the Democratic Party" of "pushing their anti-Semitic and anti-Israel policies down the throats of the American people." Following an outcry, including announcements from Democratic presidential candidates Elizabeth Warren and Bernie Sanders that they would be skipping AIPAC's annual conference that year, the group backed off a bit. AIPAC said it was offering an "unequivocal apology to the overwhelming majority of Democrats in Congress who were rightfully offended by the inaccurate assertion that the poorly worded, inflammatory advertisement implies." No apology, however, was forthcoming to Tlaib or Omar, and AIPAC continued its campaign against the two without pause in the coming years. It also began including Representatives Alexandria Ocasio-Cortez (D-NY) and Cori Bush (D-MO) in its attacks. All four were women of color as well as critics of Israel. And all of them started receiving death threats. Omar's communications director, Jeremy Slevin, tweeted that "the language AIPAC uses in paid ads to smear and vilify [Omar] is virtually identical to the language used in death threats she gets." But AIPAC was unmoved. Not only did the advertisements continue, but AIPAC sent out fund-raising emails specifically tied to its attacks on Omar, asking people to contribute funds so that it might continue its campaign.[12]

Republicans were largely spared such treatment. In 2019, for instance, the retired army colonel Douglas Macgregor offered the observation, during an interview, that Trump's national security adviser at the time, John Bolton, had "become very, very rich and is in the position he's in because of his unconditional support for the Israeli lobby." He also said, of Trump's secretary of state, Mike Pompeo, that he "has his hands out for money from the Israeli lobby." In a previous appearance, seven years earlier, with Russian state television, he had credited AIPAC "and it's [sic] subordinate elements or affiliated elements that represent enormous quantities of money" with amassing "enormous influence" and "power in Congress." The White House had announced—rather incredibly—Macgregor's appointment as US ambassador to Germany, but when his comments were made public, he was given the consolation prize of a job as a senior adviser to the acting secretary of defense. After leaving the administration, he was heard to complain that "Jews are just gonna destroy white power completely, and destroy America as a white country." Nevertheless, he found himself frequently invited on Tucker Carlson's Fox News program, where both men praised the actions of Russia's Vladimir Putin. Despite all this, at least until he left the Trump administration, Macgregor's vitriolic antisemitism rated nary a whisper among Jewish groups or in the mainstream media.[13]

Almost comical attempts to argue that antisemitism was present in both Republicans and Democrats in equal measure—the Beltway addiction to "bothsidesism"—followed. In January 2021, for example, American Jewish Committee CEO David Harris attempted to equate Omar's criticisms of US policy toward Israel and the Palestinians with the lunatic ravings of the right-wing QAnon-spouting congresswoman Marjorie Taylor Greene (R-GA). Rather than drawing attention to AIPAC's heavy-handed tactics in Congress, Greene was concerned about Jewish-owned space lasers controlled by Jewish bankers—she specifically mentioned the Rothschilds—starting California wildfires. She was also upset with the survivors of the horrific 2018 Parkland school massacre in Florida, because, she said, they were lying in order to collect their payments from George Soros. Greene also shared videos in which Holocaust deniers explained how "Zionist supremacists have schemed to promote immigration and miscegenation." That her lunatic beliefs appealed to so many Republicans is consistent with a fact that became obvious during the Trump presidency, that David Harris should have known, and that is backed up by a consistent set of survey data: that conservatives are more likely to hold antisemitic attitudes than liberals, with young conservatives, in particular, being the most likely to believe false stereotypes about Jews.[14]

No doubt the biggest concern among Israel's supporters in the United States during the Trump administration was the rapid growth of the movement to "Boycott, Divest and Sanction" (BDS) Israel among college students and liberal and left-wing activists. Judged by its stated goals, the BDS movement was an abject failure. None of the groups that voted to support it had the power to influence divestment or US policy. Not a single major American university, corporation, or even labor union actually chose to boycott Israel. The effect on the Israeli economy of those scattered institutions that did endorse the idea was literally invisible. The BDS movement never did succeed in reaching enough Americans for even a remotely significant number of them to form an opinion on it. According to a Pew Research Center survey released in May 2022, just 5 percent of Americans questioned said they supported the movement (with 2 percent doing so "strongly"). Fully 84 percent said they had never heard of it. But what BDS "did not fail at," as Samuel and Carol Edelman wrote in an essay collected in *The Case Against Academic Boycotts of Israel*, was inspiring "weeks, months, and even years of constant attacks against Israel, portraying it as a pariah nation, an occupier, a human rights violator, a racist nation, and a denier of Palestinian rights" on America's college campuses. And its success—in this narrow but crucial venue for American Jews—could be judged in the profoundly disproportional backlash it created.[15]

The academic version of the BDS campaign was founded in 2005 by Omar Barghouti, then (ironically) a graduate student at Tel Aviv University. It called on all universities and related institutions to refuse to participate in any activities—whether conferences, classes, or journals—that enjoyed any institutional affiliation with the Israeli government until such time as the goals of the movement were met. But the actual goals of the BDS movement were never clearly defined, and hence always remained a matter of dispute. If one took Barghouti as a guide, his goal was most definitely not a "two-state solution," but the replacement of Israel with a Palestine in which some, but not all, Jews would be allowed to remain. At various times, he called for, "at minimum, ending Israel's 1967 occupation and colonization, ending Israel's system of racial discrimination, and respecting the right of Palestinian refugees to return to their lands from which they were ethnically cleansed during the 1948 Nakba." He went so far as to say, "I am completely and categorically against bi-nationalism because it assumes that there are two nations with equal moral claims to the land." In 2013 he proclaimed that "no Palestinian— rational Palestinian, not a sell-out Palestinian—will ever accept a Jewish state in Palestine."[16]

The movement's greatest weakness was its inability to craft a credible theory of meaningful success. The official BDS website calls not only for the unrestricted right of return for all Palestinian refugees, but also an end to the "occupation and colonization of all Arab lands," again mean- ing the end of the state of Israel as founded in 1948. Understood liter- ally, it demanded that the Israeli people turn over their country to their sworn enemies. Just how they might be convinced to do so, however, was a question for which BDS adherents had no coherent response. Was the very same US government that had backed Israel to the hilt in virtually every conflict it had ever had with the Palestinians now going to reverse its entire foreign policy and force Israel to dismantle itself? When pressed on such issues, BDS proponents invariably changed the subject to the successful example of the global boycott of South Africa. Pressed further, however, on the many fundamental differences between contemporary Israel and late twentieth-century South Africa, and the myriad reasons why success in one could hardly guarantee success in the other, all practi- cal discussion tended to be replaced by rhetorical tropes such as the need to be on "the right side of history."[17]

The inability of the movement's leaders to think strategically mirrored a fundamental tension at the heart of the Palestinians' historical strug- gle. Its leaders sometimes act, in the words of US State Department and National Security Council official Robert Malley, as if they see them- selves as avatars of "a national liberation movement, whose leaders are militants, whose objective is independence and whose main currency is resistance." At other times, however, they view themselves as head- ing a "political party, whose leaders are statesmen, whose objective is institution-building, and whose main currency is negotiations." BDS served the former goal even as it simultaneously undermined the latter. It had no means to improve the material conditions of the lives of the Pal- estinians who were forced to live in refugee camps, under occupation, in exile, or even under discriminatory conditions inside Israel. Its practical energies were exclusively devoted to inspiring a popular movement to consistently condemn Israel. It had no plan beyond that.[18]

The movement's focus on college students and academics created another set of complications. By demanding a boycott of Israeli scholars, BDS adherents sought to undermine the fundamental purpose of a university: the unimpeded pursuit of knowledge and enlightenment. Although they argued that they did not seek to suppress individual Israeli voices, only those who represented its government, practically speaking this was a distinction without a difference. When academics travel abroad to attend conferences and seminars, they do so with university funds. Given the fact that virtually all Israeli universities are publicly funded, Israeli academics became automatic targets for silencing. In pursuing this line of protest, the movement ended up trying to silence the very Israelis who were likely to be among the country's most vocal supporters of Palestinian dignity and independence. And yet, despite these contradictions, the movement grew like kudzu among progressive student groups and faculty organizations on the nation's most elite college campuses—as illustrated by its endorsement by Harvard's student newspaper, *The Crimson*, in April 2022, in an editorial by the paper's editorial board. This naturally led to considerable panic among Jewish parents, college administrators, and the sorts of people who worried about the views of America's future leaders.[19]

The BDS movement's greatest success was likely achieved among university faculty associations and student governments. The American Studies Association's 2013 BDS endorsement was followed by ones from the Association for Asian American Studies, the African Literature Association, the Critical Ethnic Studies Association, the Native American and Indigenous Studies Association, the Middle East Studies Association, and many others. Dozens of student governments also endorsed the campaign at a rapid pace (and are likely continuing to do so as you are reading this book). "Israel Apartheid Week" became an annual event on many campuses.

Ironically, the ambiguity of the movement's aims, as well as its cloudy-to-the-point-of-nonexistent theory of change, would turn out to be one of its great strengths, especially on campus. In this respect, together with some of its tactics, the movement recalled the heyday of the Communist Party of the United States (CPUSA). During the 1930s and 1940s, countless CPUSA members believed they were fighting for racial equality, peaceful relations between nations, and an end to the threat of nuclear annihilation. Its leaders, however, were interested merely in discrediting the United States in Europe and the third world as they built up the reputation of Stalin and his murderous minions. Now, countless young people on campus understood themselves to be marching and chanting for the dignity of the Palestinians and a peaceful end to the brutality inherent in Israel's occupation, unaware that the movement's leaders sought the end of Israel entirely (and, in many cases, such as Barghouti's, the expulsion of most of its Jewish inhabitants). The movement's idealistic varnish no doubt attracted garden-variety student leftists similar to those of earlier generations that had protested earlier US policies, such as those relating to Southeast Asia, Central America, or South Africa. Unfortunately, BDS adherents also borrowed tactics from the communists on occasion, winning votes and taking over academic organizations in the proverbial dead of night, by scheduling campus-wide debates and student government resolutions on or near Jewish holidays, thereby making it impossible for many Jews to participate.

Rather than communism, or even Marxism of any variety, the movement relied on the theory of "intersectionality," which, by the early 2000s, had grown extremely popular among campus and other leftists. Originally developed by the legal scholar Kimberlé Williams Crenshaw—and consistent with, if not a direct successor to, Edward Said's "Orientalism"— intersectionality provided a "lens through which you can see where power comes and collides, where it interlocks and intersects." What this theory meant in practice was a responsibility on the part of progressives to support not only the causes that inspired them personally, but also those of peoples deemed to be "oppressed" by the dominant group or ideology— a category in which Palestinians were all but universally understood to qualify. It was an ideal theory for a college seminar room in which students could draw connections to different forms of perceived oppression and sound out connections between them that appeared both morally and intellectually compelling. As a strategic foundation for political action, however, it was a disaster. Because each cause was really about every other cause, it paralyzed adherents from devoting the time and effort to understand, and therefore attempt to address, the dynamics that drove each one. Moreover, it often prevented speakers from sticking to any one subject. The problem of Zionist "settler colonialism" intertwined with US racial oppression and stolen land from Native Americans, US-Western capitalism despoiling the earth as it simultaneously propped up white supremacy across the globe. When "everything" matters, then nothing is likely to get done. Attention, after all, is a limited resource in the best of times. In the immediate matter of the summer of 2020, however, when the Black Lives Matter movement exploded across the country, Trump supporters used the support voiced by movement spokespeople for the BDS movement to attempt to discredit it among the larger Jewish community.[20]

Back in 2016, fifty Black organizations meeting under the BLM umbrella had accused Israel of pursuing "genocide" against Palestinians. "Being committed to a fight for global freedom, we saw no choice, really, to not include a critique of the way the U.S. enables the state-sanctioned killing on [sic] an occupation of black and brown people globally across the diaspora," explained Janae Bonsu, one of the drafters of the BLM platform. "Our freedom fight knows no borders, so that has to include unequivocal support for the Palestinian struggle for freedom and peace." Many found it significant that members of the St. Louis Metropolitan Police Department, which had violently suppressed a protest in Ferguson, Missouri, following the 2014 police shooting (twelve times) of Michael Brown, an unarmed Black teenager, had been trained in "crowd control" in Israel (as part of an ADL-sponsored program that would be put on pause in 2002 owing to its "high risk, low reward"). So when Alexandria Ocasio-Cortez compared the police violence directed toward Black protesters in Ferguson, Missouri, to Israel firing at demonstrators on its border with Gaza, she was tapping into a rich history that had tied together supporters of Black Lives Matter and Palestinian solidarity groups—one that included large numbers of young Jews who had become increasingly disaffected with and alienated from Israel.[21]

BDS supporters found themselves denounced and shunned (and then denounced again) by all the remotely mainstream Jewish organizations, with the partial exception of J Street, which was itself denied membership in the President's Conference, and T'ruah. The typical response among Jewish leaders and their funders was to create a new group, or an off-shoot of their old ones, specifically dedicated to fighting BDS on campus. "Funders," explained Kenneth Stern, speaking of his experience working at the American Jewish Committee, "who were parents and grandparents of college students, were deeply concerned about anti-Israel activity on campus," and they wanted the organizations they supported to do something to counteract it. But because these organizations remained committed to the mythical *Exodus* narrative of a nearly flawless Israel, they could not really enter the discussion in a way in which their arguments were likely to be convincing. One reason for this handicap was, yet again, a question of money. A number of anti-BDS organizations, including Aish Hatorah, an Orthodox group that sponsors trips to Israel for college students, and gives them lessons in *hasbara* (Israeli propaganda) to help them argue the case for Israel back home, as *The Forward* revealed in 2019, were secretly receiving funding from the Israeli government, which had allotted millions to the cause and fought court battles to keep this information secret. Curiously, one of the largest gifts, $1.3 million, was bestowed on John Hagee's Christians United for Israel. Even more remarkably, Sheldon Adelson had chosen to pony up over $22 million to the "Maccabee Task Force," with CUFI's former chief, David Brog, at its helm. The Israelis added insult to injury by publishing dossiers on pro-BDS activists and stopping rabbis, professors, and even Peter Beinart at Ben-Gurion Airport for questioning. On occasion Israeli authorities even expelled such visitors—thereby further diminishing the nation's reputation for respecting free expression and democratic debate.[22]

A few Jewish groups, including the anonymously authored Canary Mission, began sending out blacklists of professors and even students believed to support BDS. The explicit goal was to intimidate them into silence, for fear of being denied jobs and scholarships. In June 2017, following the annual "Celebrate Israel" parade in Manhattan, then minister of strategic affairs Gilad Erdan announced the launch of a new digital campaign, replete with a phone app that students could use to report on unfavorable comments made by their professors or fellow students about Israel. The app, developed by the Interdisciplinary Centre in Herzliya, together with the Israeli-American Council and the Maccabee Task Force—all three of which were funded by Sheldon Adelson—included a prewritten note complaining to deans and other university personnel. Meanwhile, Canary Mission accused BDS enthusiasts on campus of "defending terror-financiers," "spreading anti-Semitism," and "supporting violent protesters." It began publishing BDS supporters' names and photos with the explicit goal of destroying their professional future. In 2021, Natalie Abulhawa, a young athletic trainer who had been targeted by the Canary Mission, was fired by the Agnes Irwin School, an All-Girls College Preparatory School near Philadelphia, after members of the school's community raised concerns over pro-Palestine social media posts. A year later she remained unemployed. "It is your duty," its website proudly announced, "to ensure that today's radicals are not tomorrow's employees."[23]

Jewish and Israel studies professors did not need to be told not to invite pro-BDS speakers to their campuses, even for the purpose of debate with Israel supporters. And if they had any thoughts otherwise, there were more than enough private funders—or university personnel who dealt with private funders—to set them straight. At publicly funded universities, local officials often found BDS events an irresistible target. At Brooklyn College, New York State assemblyman Dov Hikind—who represented a district heavily populated by ultra-Orthodox Jewish constituents—demanded the resignation of the school's president because of her willingness to allow a joint lecture by BDS founder Omar Barghouti and the pro-BDS literary scholar Judith Butler. Inspired by a lengthy document compiled by the far-right Zionist Organization of America, and filled with falsehoods, exaggerations, and McCarthyite insinuations, New York state legislators sought to radically cut back funding for Brooklyn's parent institution, the City University of New York (CUNY). The tactic appeared on the verge of success until a way to have the cut deleted from the final legislation was found in a last-minute budget agreement with Governor Andrew Cuomo. This was only one of many assaults on CUNY related to the issue, however. The university has

proven willing to protect free speech while simultaneously seeking to dis-
courage students and faculty from raising the question repeatedly. A similarly farcical set of events could be found at the University of California,
orchestrated—ultimately unsuccessfully—by another right-wing Jewish
organization, the "AMCHA Initiative." ("AMCHA," the group's website
explains, "is the Hebrew word meaning 'your people' and also connotes
'grassroots,' 'the masses,' and 'ordinary people.'")[24]

The fight naturally extended to Congress. While Ilhan Omar and
Rashida Tlaib were the only Democratic representatives to endorse the
BDS movement during the Trump administration, most Democrats felt
a need to tread around it cautiously. BDS supporters were often the same
politically dedicated activists who volunteered for election campaigns
and registered people to vote in primaries—the very people candidates
needed to win elections. BDS opponents even succeeded in destroying—
at least temporarily at this writing—the Constitutional protection that
boycotts have long enjoyed as "free speech," going back to the nation's
founding, when a three-judge panel of the Federal court's 8th Circuit
ruled that the state of Arkansas had the right to demand that anyone
who worked for, or did business with the state of Arkansas, must sign
a pledge to refuse to adhere to the boycott or forfeit twenty percent of
their compensation. The decision was celebrated by the American Jewish
Committee, which had celebrated numerous boycotts in the past.[25]

The debate spilled into social media, of course, as well as other media.
Facebook admitted to suppressing posts from people supporting BDS
or criticizing Israel's human rights record. In the mainstream media, no
prominent political columnist publicly supported BDS. When, in 2018,
the African American CNN commentator Mark Lamont used the BDS
slogan in a speech at a United Nations event and called for a "free Palestine from the river to the sea," the ADL condemned him for allegedly
"promot[ing] divisiveness and hate." He was immediately fired by CNN.
In 2021, a young Associated Press reporter found herself fired as well, owing, apparently, to blogposts she had made as a member of Jewish Voice
for Peace and Students for Justice in Palestine while a student at Stanford University—though the issues she covered for AP had nothing to
do with the Middle East. The Israelis were so concerned about budding

support for Palestinians on campus that, on occasion, their diplomats were known to contact college administrators to try to prevent pro-BDS professors—and even graduate students—from being allowed to teach courses on the conflict.[26]

In both 2017 and 2019, congressional representatives, working with AIPAC, introduced a bill condemning BDS. It eventually passed in the House by a vote of 398–17, with a companion bill passing 77–23 in the Senate, though the two were never conferenced and enacted into law. Omar responded with a bill affirming the "right to participate in boycotts in pursuit of civil and human rights at home and abroad." It attracted only six cosponsors, but these included the revered civil rights leader John Lewis (D-GA). It also enjoyed the endorsements of both J Street and the American Civil Liberties Union, among other liberal groups. Republicans, predictably, used the legislation as yet another cudgel with which to beat Democrats over the head for alleged softness on antisemitism. Marco Rubio (R-FL) lambasted House Speaker Nancy Pelosi for "allow[ing] the radical, anti-Semitic minority in the Democratic Party to dictate the House floor agenda."[27]

Donald Trump naturally jumped into the BDS fray as well. In December 2019, the president signed an executive order empowering the US Department of Education to add discrimination on the basis of "religion" to the categories of offenses that allowed the government to withhold funds from a college or educational program under Title VI of the 1964 Civil Rights Act. Education Secretary Betsy DeVos, a right-wing extremist, had appointed Kenneth Marcus, a dedicated right-wing anti-BDS activist, to be her civil rights chief. Within days of the order's announcement, two extremely sensitive former Columbia University students, with impressively long memories, filed legal action under the new rules. The first, Jonathan Karten, complained of, among other things, a report about an alleged speech by the Palestinian American professor Joseph Massad given at Oxford University seventeen years earlier. The second, by Jaimie Kreitman, addressed the "hostility and toxicity" Kreitman said she had experienced while a grad student sometime during the 1980s. Apparently, "a professor thought that [her] thesis was completely subjective and that it wasn't worthy of a graduate's level."[28]

The Trump administration's Title VI change was not designed to prevent any actual discrimination. Jewish students already had all the protections they needed under the act's coverage of discrimination on the basis of a "group's actual or perceived ancestry or ethnic characteristics," or "actual or perceived citizenship or residency in a country whose residents share a dominant religion or a distinct religious identity." The principal drafter of the order's definition of discrimination, Kenneth Stern, denounced its deployment and predicted that "students and faculty members will be scared into silence." While there definitely were incidents that raised genuine concern about antisemitic harassment on some campuses, the alleged remedy—as well as the rhetoric that accompanied it—was entirely inconsistent with the scope of the problem. In 2017, four scholars at Brandeis University conducted an in-depth study of the issue at four high-profile campuses and found that "Jewish students are rarely exposed to antisemitism on campus," and that "Jewish students do not think their campus is hostile to Jews." Further, they wrote, "the majority of students disagree that there is a hostile environment toward Israel on campus," and "support for BDS is rare." They concluded that "Israel and Jews are not a top concern for students." Scholars associated with the Jewish studies program at Stanford University found a similar picture of campus life among six California campuses. Students interviewed "reported low levels of antisemitism or discomfort," and by and large agreed that they "felt comfortable as Jews" on campus. "When they did encounter discomfort, they traced it either to the carelessness of student speech or to tensions within campus debates about the Israel-Palestine conflict." But "they held both supporters and critics of Israel responsible for creating this environment."[29]

Back in the halls of power in Washington and Jerusalem, it was difficult to determine where Donald Trump's Middle East policies ended and Benjamin Netanyahu's wish list began. Past US presidents had at least tried to negotiate with, and sometimes even threaten, Israeli leaders before (eventually) giving in. Regarding the Palestinians, they had often sought to restrain Israel from doing anything that would make peace unachievable under any circumstance, even if they proved reluctant to pressure Israel to take any immediate steps toward a peaceful resolution of the conflict. Not so Donald Trump.

Trump's extraordinary largesse to the Israelis was due in part to the similarities in how he and Benjamin Netanyahu viewed the world. While the Israeli leader did not indulge all of Trump's most bizarre beliefs and personality quirks, the two men shared a remarkable number of both personal and political prejudices. Both politicians were profoundly corrupt, even compared to their respective colleagues and predecessors, and each sought desperately to cling to power while faced with the possibility of being imprisoned in the event of political defeat for the various crimes they appeared to have committed (in Netanyahu's case, while in office, and in Trump's both in and out of office). Both leaders also displayed degrees of racism, nativism, and ethnocentrism that were considered extreme even by the standards of the racist, nativist, and ethnocentric parties they led. Politically, both were aspiring authoritarians who were eager to forge alliances with fellow illiberal politicians consolidating power based on ethnonationalist appeals in places such as Russia, Turkey, Poland, the Czech Republic, Slovakia, Hungary, the Philippines, Brazil, Egypt, Oman, Azerbaijan, the Gulf states, Saudi Arabia, and elsewhere. Neither evinced any patience, much less respect, for democratic niceties such as freedom of speech, freedom of the press, or the separation of powers. The fact that so many of the regimes they courted engaged in the exploitation of antisemitism at home for political gain was, at least for Netanyahu, more than offset by their more intense focus on the Islamic threat they believed they faced from their own citizens, the refugees flooding their borders, and the fiery rhetoric emanating from Iran and elsewhere that led those regimes to wish to work with Israel. Common enemies bred friendships of convenience. Netanyahu repeatedly excused Trump's antisemitism and that of his political allies. So did Trump's Jewish Republican supporters, who were willing to make the same tradeoff that had appealed to the neoconservatives of a previous generation, when they had chosen to embrace antisemitic but pro-Zionist evangelical preachers beginning in the 1970s. As long as Trump was willing to indulge Netanyahu, they were willing to indulge Trump.[30]

On a personal, psychological level, both leaders were also paranoid, pathologically dishonest, and eager to blame others when the natural consequences of their actions eventually manifested themselves. Each tacitly

encouraged violence against political adversaries. It is an intriguing coincidence that both Netanyahu and Trump lived much of their respective lives
beneath the shadow of a powerful father figure whose prejudices they each
apparently inherited. Netanyahu's father, Benzion Netanyahu, had treated
all of Jewish history as a march from one Holocaust to another; Trump's
real-estate mogul father had attended a Ku Klux Klan rally and consistently
discriminated against Black home buyers and renters. Both Trump and Netanyahu were also, not surprisingly, essentially friendless, insisting on un-
stinting loyalty from cronies and colleagues but showing none in return.[31]

This convergence was exclusively a matter of political convenience
rather than any shared affection between the two men, and Trump
became furious with Netanyahu when the Israeli failed to endorse his
efforts to steal the 2020 election. Trump dismissed Netanyahu in a December 2021 interview with the words, "I haven't spoken to him since.
Fuck him." But it was not Netanyahu whom Trump was seeking to
please with his embrace of the Israel leader's wish list. Rather, it was his
base, which, when it came to Israel, was made up almost exclusively of
evangelical Christians and Sheldon Adelson.[32]

Adelson donated an estimated $426 million to Donald Trump and
the Republican Party between 2016 and 2020 to buy support for Israel's right-wing government, and this was one sale on which Trump can
honestly say he delivered. Upon becoming president, he appointed David Friedman and Jason Greenblatt to carry out US Israel policy under
the watchful eye of his Jewish son-in-law, Jared Kushner. All three had
worked with (or for) Trump in the real estate business before taking on
these responsibilities, and none of them had any experience in diplomacy
or specialized knowledge of the Middle East. Their only qualifications for
their jobs in the administration were their relationships to Trump and
their support for Jewish extremist organizations.

For instance, Friedman, a bankruptcy lawyer, had previously suggested that unless Arab citizens of Israel decided "to support the state,"
Israel should reconsider its policy of "bestowing upon them the benefits of citizenship." He considered liberal Jews to be "smug advocates of
Israel's destruction," and compared J Street to "Kapos during the Nazi
regime"—that is, the Jews who aided in their own genocide. Trump also

appointed former congressman Mike Pompeo (R-KS), an evangelical Christian Zionist who believed Christianity to be engaged in a "holy war" with Islam, as his CIA director, and then as secretary of state. It was no coincidence that when Pompeo campaigned for Trump while on official duty during the 2020 election—a violation of the federal Hatch Act's limits on partisan political activity, according to the State Department's Office of Special Counsel—he did so by giving a partisan speech at the Republican National Convention from Jerusalem.[33]

Kushner, meanwhile, by far the most important and influential among the group, had grown up in a family that was intimately tied up with funding the settler movement. It was not merely that Israel was seeking to deepen its relationship with the Gulf states, and particularly with Saudi Arabia, during Trump's presidency that led to Kushner's interest in the region. He was also indebted to Middle East financial institutions for stepping in with hundreds of millions of dollars to save his family's real estate business while he served in the White House. Moreover, he was apparently planning to raise additional capital in the region in his post–White House career for an investment fund he began shortly after his father-in-law lost the 2020 election. The size and scope of Kushner's payoff was revealed, however, in April 2022, when the *New York Times* broke the news that the Saudi sovereign wealth fund had agreed to funnel at least $2 billion to Kushner's new firm, Affinity Partners. In return, the Saudis received not only nearly 40 percent off of the firm's regular management fees, but an additional "stake of at least 28 percent" of Kushner's firm. Kushner got the money despite the fact that a panel charged with screening its investments, especially investments of this magnitude, "cited concerns." According to the *Times*, "those objections included 'the inexperience of the Affinity Fund management'; the possibility that the kingdom would be responsible for 'the bulk of the investment and risk'; due diligence on the fledgling firm's operations that found them 'unsatisfactory in all aspects'; a proposed asset management fee that 'seems excessive'; and 'public relations risks.'" These warnings were cast aside, however, by the Saudi crown prince, Mohammed bin Salman (MBS), who ultimately exercises control over the fund. Hardly coincidentally, President Trump was heard to brag to a reporter about the lengths to which he went to prevent Congress from holding MBS accountable for the brutal murder and dismemberment of US-based journalist Jamal Khashoggi, when he said, as Bob Woodward reported in his book *Rage*, "I saved his ass. I was able to get Congress to leave him alone. I was able to get them to stop." As the *Times* also noted, "Mr. Kushner played a leading role inside the Trump administration defending Crown Prince Mohammed after U.S. intelligence agencies concluded that he had approved the 2018 killing and dismemberment of Jamal Khashoggi, . . . who had criticized the kingdom's rulers." To complete the circle, in May 2022, the *Wall Street Journal* revealed Kushner's plans to invest "millions of dollars of Saudi Arabia's money in Israeli startups." (The Israeli government and its supporters in the US lobbying community had been energetically lobbying both Congress and the Trump administration, and later its successor, to ignore the killing and proceed to deepen its ties with the Saudis; software tracking the victim's phone was later discovered to be that of the Israeli spy company Pegasus.)[34]

These were just a few of the blessings Trump bestowed on Israel during his one term as president. Others included:

- The transfer of the US embassy from Tel Aviv to Jerusalem.
- Recognition of Israeli sovereignty, just before Netanyahu faced an election vote, over the Golan Heights, making the United States the only nation to do so (despite a unanimous 1982 Security Council resolution, which included the United States, that termed Israel's annexation of the territory to be "null and void and without international legal effect"), and the encouragement of what would turn out to be, according to Peace Now, a 63 percent increase in settlement construction during Trump's presidency. (It was Republican President George W. Bush who declared, on June 4, 2009, that "the United States does not accept the legitimacy of continued Israeli settlements. This construction violates previous agreements and undermines efforts to achieve peace.")
- The end of the official use of the term "occupied territories" and an end to the US practice of labeling its products as such, rather than as coming from "Israel" itself.

- The February 2020 presentation of Jared Kushner's comically biased "peace plan," which invited Israel to annex some 20 percent of the West Bank and maintain full control over security, borders, and air space, thereby ensuring a permanent occupation of the West Bank and the enshrinement of what numerous human rights organizations have termed "apartheid."
- A cutoff of all aid to, and official US government communications with, the Palestinian Authority.
- The closing of the US consulate in East Jerusalem that had served Palestinians since 1844 (in breach of the 1995 Oslo II agreement) and the forced shuttering of the PLO's offices in Washington.
- Massive arms sales to Israel and continued and intensified support for repressive Gulf Arab monarchies in the UAE and Bahrain, as well as an endorsement of Morocco's territorial claims over the occupied Western Sahara in contravention of long-standing US policy, UN Security Council resolutions and a decades-long independence campaign by the Polisario Front.
- Unilateral US withdrawal from the Joint Comprehensive Plan of Action (JCPOA) with Iran (commonly known as the Iran nuclear deal).
- Strong support for anti-BDS legislation, especially that related to shutting down campus speech critical of Israel.
- The willingness—though his administration did not succeed before time ran out—to define human rights organizations that criticized Israel as "antisemitic."
- A Presidential Medal of Freedom (the United States' highest honor) for Miriam Adelson.[35]

Many Israel partisans had long argued that if only the United States fully allied itself with Israel's aims and showed the Palestinians and the Arab nations that they could not rely on US pressure to force Israeli concessions, Palestinians would finally realize that it was time to make the best peace deal possible and give up their unrealistic dreams of replacing the Jewish state and returning to their (now nonexistent) ancestral homes. Trump's policies did make significant progress in winning Israel the recognition of a group of Arab nations that shared an enemy (Iran) and could mostly be bought off with promises of generous US military aid and weapons sales—and, in the case of Morocco, an endorsement of its territorial claims. The agreements were promoted as the "Abraham Accords," and American Jews could not help but celebrate this important advance in Israel's acceptance in the region. But an Israeli/Palestinian peace deal was never further away from realization than following Trump's unilateral concessions.

According to a number of military and intelligence specialists in Israel and the United States, including Gadi Eisenkot, former head of the Israel Defense Forces; Danny Citrinowicz, who headed the Iran Branch of IDF's Military Intelligence Research and Analysis Division; former Mossad chief Yossi Cohen; and former defense minister Moshe Ya'alon, the US withdrawal from the JCPOA was a mistake—as Ya'alon put it, "the main mistake of the last decade." Iran was released from all restrictions and international inspections—rules with which it had appeared to be complying. Absent the robust inspection regime that had been in place under the agreement, Iran—which continued to adhere to the accord long after the United States itself had violated its terms—was finally left to improve its nuclear program with more efficient cascades of centrifuges and uranium stockpiles at higher capacities. It also achieved far greater levels of both decentralization and clandestine activity, which enabled Iranians to make their nuclear facilities increasingly invulnerable to attack. In June 2022, the Israeli news site Ynet reported that several Israeli generals, including the chief of Military Intelligence, had also argued in favor of a return to the pact. The macho posturing of Trump and Netanyahu in torching the accord succeeded only in creating a far more ominous threat to Israel from Iran than would have been the case had the United States stuck with the Obama administration's negotiated agreement. The Obama deal had kept Iran's nuclear capabilities in check. This is among the reasons, no doubt, why the American Jewish Committee CEO, David Harris, argued for a US attack on Iran in late December 2021, just as Netanyahu had consistently done throughout Trump's presidency, according to the (officially vetted) memoir of ex–US defense secretary Mark Esper. Meanwhile, a number of other Jewish leaders, echoing a statement crafted by former general and CIA director David Petraeus, former secretary of defense Leon Panetta, and others, called for "high-profile military exercises by the U.S. Central Command, potentially in concert with allies and partners, that simulate what would be involved in such a significant operation, including releasing air-to-ground attacks on hardened targets," should Iran continue on its post-agreement path.[36]

Virtually none of the "pro-Israel" hardliners who originally advocated these policies proved willing to admit their error, and it's unlikely that Trump even concerned himself with what his unprecedented indulgence of Israel might or might not achieve. What he did likely understand, however, was the fact that this policy of consistent concession would appeal to many of the increasingly conservative and politically active 10 percent of American Jews who, like Friedman, Greenblatt, and Kushner, identified as Orthodox and were now voting Republican. But while their numbers were increasing, they were not yet sufficiently numerous to carry much weight politically. Indeed, the vast majority of American Jews would grow even more supportive of the deal, reaching a figure of 68 percent in support restoring it according to a poll of 800 registered Jewish voters undertaken in the spring of 2022. This support came as both AIPAC and the Israeli government were gearing up to amass yet another campaign, this time to try to prevent the US from reversing the Trump administration's withdrawal from the accord, albeit under necessarily considerably less favorable terms. Far more likely is that Trump and company had two specific political targets in mind. One was quite obviously Sheldon Adelson and the hundreds of millions of dollars he committed to the cause. But the second, no less significant target was the evangelical Christian population that made up the most loyal component of Trump's base, and whose 2020 voting pattern matched the polling preferences of Israelis in supporting the president. (Numerous conservative Christian groups—not only Hagee's CUFI, but also countless others, including relatively unknown ones such as the United States–Israel Education Association, based in Alabama—had long been in the business of ferrying US representatives to the West Bank and helping to lobby for support for the settlements there.)[37]

Saying the quiet part out loud once again, Trump complained at an August 2020 campaign rally that while he had moved the US embassy in

Israel to Jerusalem "for the evangelicals," he found it "amazing that—the evangelicals are more excited by that than Jewish people. It's incredible." More than a year after he left office, he was still evincing shock, telling an interviewer that he found it "incredible" how little Jewish support he received. His explanation was that "Jewish people in this country, many of them, do not like Israel." Had he been even slightly self-aware, Trump might have considered the fact that one of the people he had invited to the Jerusalem embassy ceremony was Pastor Robert Jeffress, who taught his followers that because Jews had allegedly "led people away from God," they would, like Muslims, unfortunately, end up "in a pit of Hell."[38]

During a spirited 2020 Democratic primary campaign, the second- and third-place challengers, Bernie Sanders and Elizabeth Warren, attacked AIPAC and embraced policies conditioning US aid to Israel on a demand for better behavior. But in the end, former vice president Joe Biden brought the party back to its previous ambivalently pro-Israel position. Its election platform eschewed the word "occupation." It denounced the goals of the BDS movement but reluctantly agreed that it qualified as constitutionally protected speech. It opposed the expansion of Israeli settlements but praised Jerusalem as the "undivided" capital of Israel. Biden won the historically typical three-quarters-plus of American Jewish votes.

Meanwhile, a group called the Democratic Majority for Israel raised millions of dollars, first to attack Sanders—ironically, the only Jew in the race, and certainly the only presidential candidate who ever worked on an Israeli kibbutz—during the presidential primaries, and then to try to intervene at the local level to defeat pro-Palestinian candidates, whom it accused of seeking to "sow hatred of Israel." These efforts failed in almost every case. Omar and Tlaib were returned to Congress. Despite his seniority as chair of the House Foreign Affairs Committee, Representative Eliot Engel of New York—who had voted with Netanyahu rather than with Obama on the Iran deal—lost in a landslide to Jamal Bowman, who eagerly joined the admittedly tiny "squad" of representatives led by Alexandria Ocasio-Cortez that insisted on challenging the party's seventy-year policy of deference to Israel.[39]

Bibi Netanyahu greeted Biden's presidency with a brazen assassination of Iran's top nuclear scientist. This was followed by the announcement (later reversed by his successor) of yet another massive expansion of housing units in the West Bank and East Jerusalem in locations chosen, as if by design, to make it all but impossible to implement any sort of two-state solution that might be acceptable to Palestinians at any time in the future. (Fully 600 of the 2,600 proposed units would have been in Palestinian territory even under Jared Kushner's biased proposals.) The IDF expanded the scope of its military exercises into Palestinian areas it had deliberately avoided for the previous seven years, ignoring earlier promises to allow their inhabitants to live their lives in relative peace.[40]

The Biden administration's response was that there would be no conditioning of aid to Israel; no thought of moving the embassy from Jerusalem; no reconsideration of the arms sales or other concessions made by Trump to support Arab recognition of Israel; and no overt pressure on Israel to take any steps to move toward peace with the Palestinians. Meanwhile, Linda Thomas-Greenfield, Biden's choice to be US ambassador to the United Nations, made the administration's promised priorities clear at her confirmation hearing before the Senate Foreign Relations Committee when she affirmed that the United States would be "standing against the unfair targeting of Israel, the relentless resolutions that are proposed against Israel unfairly." "It goes without saying," she said, "that Israel has no closer friend than the United States and I will reflect that in my actions at the United Nations."[41]

The Democratic Party, according to poll after poll, was now evenly divided on whether to root for Israel or the Palestinians in their never-ending conflict. Its younger members leaned heavily in the direction of the Palestinians, while seventy-eight-year-old Joe Biden kept his feet planted firmly in the party's pro-Israel past. But below the presidential level, among Democrats, liberals, young Jews, and even young evangelicals, the foundations that had always undergirded America's support for Israel had grown decidedly shaky—a problem for Biden and company that would only grow in size and scope as his presidency progressed.

# CONCLUSION

# NOT "OVER"

As Joe Biden assumed office in January 2021, having earned an estimated 77 percent of the Jewish vote, the Israeli/Palestinian conflict barely rated as an item on the White House agenda. Writing in an online Jewish publication, Tablet, in January, former Israeli ambassador to the United States Michael Oren announced that "the Arab-Israeli conflict is dead." The following month, the Palestinian diplomats and scholars Hussein Agha and Ahmad Samih Khalidi came to the same conclusion in the pages of in the Council on Foreign Relations' journal, *Foreign Affairs*: "The official Arab-Israeli conflict has ended."[1]

The Palestinians had indeed lost their place on the Middle East's center stage. In the Arab world, hostility toward Israel was displaced by a de facto coalition between Israel, the United States, and most of the Arab states against Iran and its scattered allies, anchored by the Abraham Accords between Israel, the Gulf nations, Sudan, and Morocco (with the implicit support of Saudi Arabia). Meanwhile, during the domestic turbulence of the four consecutive deadlocked elections the Israelis found themselves forced to conduct between 2019 and 2021, the issue of peace with the Palestinians rarely even arose as a topic of serious discussion. When the nation's new leader, Naftali Bennett, flew to New York to address the UN General Assembly and Jewish Federations of North America in September 2021, he made no mention at all of the peace process or the occupation in either forum. Just before he arrived, Bennett's office let it be known to reporters that "there is no diplomatic process with the Palestinians, nor will there be one."[2]

Bennett's reticence was especially remarkable given that barely ninety days earlier, the Israelis and the Palestinians had been at war. The conflict had grown out of a series of raids by Israeli police on the Al-Aqsa Mosque, Islam's third-holiest shrine, which sits atop Jerusalem's Temple Mount, Judaism's holiest shrine, inside the gates of the Old City, during the holy Muslim month of Ramadan. Two miles north, in the East Jerusalem neighborhood of Sheikh Jarrah, Israelis had been using a complicated set of legal maneuvers to evict the Palestinians and replace them with Jewish families, giving fresh inspiration to what were now years' worth of angry demonstrations and counterdemonstrations, each one threatening to explode into violence. A week after the first police raid, a Jewish mob marched through the city chanting "Death to Arabs" and attacking random Palestinians in its path. More evictions and police raids followed. On the final night of Ramadan, police used tear gas, stun grenades, and rubber-tipped bullets aimed at Al-Aqsa worshippers. Palestinian protests spread across the West Bank and into Israel proper, where random mobs on both sides began attacking civilians in mixed cities. The IDF killed eleven protesters on the West Bank, and the country appeared to be on the verge of civil war.[3]

When the Palestinian Authority canceled what would have been its first democratic election in fifteen years and began rounding up and jailing—and occasionally killing—its opponents, Hamas leaders sensed an opportunity to unite disaffected Palestinians under their banner by claiming that Hamas was the defender of Islam's holy sites and leader of their resistance. Hamas began firing rockets into Israel proper, attacks that Human Rights Watch would later label "war crimes." The Israelis responded, as always, asymmetrically. Their eleven-day bombing campaign, "Operation Guardian of the Walls," resulted in more than 256 deaths in Gaza (including 66 children) and injured nearly 2,000, according to Hamas. The Israelis counted 4,360 rockets and mortars launched at Israeli population centers. Owing to the effectiveness of the US-Israeli Iron Dome antimissile system and the inaccuracy of the Palestinian rockets, the death toll was limited to twelve civilians on the Israeli side, of whom two were children. The conflict was clearly not "over."[4]

While the punditocracy remained largely pro-Israel, however, what no doubt shocked many of Israel's supporters was the willingness of so many in the mainstream media to report from an unapologetic Palestinian perspective. The *Washington Post* ran a more than five-thousand-word investigation of Palestinian life under occupation, which it portrayed as a hellish landscape made up of constant humiliation, frequent settler violence, and occasional (and almost always unpunished) IDF killings. The *New York Times* published a heartbreaking front-page photo montage of dead Palestinian children, killed in Gaza by Israel's bombing, beneath the headline "They Were Only Children." Just four days earlier, another heavily produced and promoted story appeared on page one titled "Life Under Occupation: The Misery at the Heart of the Conflict." These stories were followed by a twenty-two-minute documentary on the *Times* website about the brutal police-state tactics employed by Israeli soldiers enforcing the occupation in the Palestinian city of Hebron, on behalf of the 850 Israeli settlers who lived there. It was directed by a filmmaker who had formerly served in the IDF and described exclusively in the words of the Israeli soldiers who enforced it.[5]

The photos alone came as a shock to the *New York Times* audience. The ADL's Abe Foxman emerged from retirement to announce the cancellation of his *Times* subscription over the stories, tweeting that he had read the paper for sixty-five years, but "today's blood libel of Israel and the Jewish people on the front page is enough." Rabbi Abraham Cooper of the Simon Wiesenthal Center called the pictures "libelous against the Jewish state," and further complained that they were published "amidst a tsunami of antisemitic attacks by pro-Hamas forces across the United States." The *Times*, he insisted, had gone from "being the paper of record for the United States of America—the world's greatest democracy—to becoming the newspaper of record for Hamas."[6]

The war that some Palestinians had come to call their "Unity Intifada" coincided with the final days of Bibi Netanyahu's term as prime minister. Biden's team was thrilled when Netanyahu's political opponents managed to cobble together a hydra-headed, left/right, religious/secular, Jewish/Arab coalition to finally end Netanyahu's twelve-year reign in June 2021. (Months earlier, Biden had waited an unmistakably symbolic full month before returning the Israeli prime minister's call of congratulations to him after his own election.) Adding to Bennett's precarious position, his sixty-one-member coalition included thirteen lawmakers from the right and far right, including Bennett himself. Given that fragility, the threat of Netanyahu's return lingered like what one Israeli columnist termed "a bear in the basement." Biden and company did their utmost to avoid poking the bear by making difficult public demands on Bennett's government that might give a single legislator the urge to switch sides and bring Netanyahu back into power.

As the onetime head of the Judea-Samaria-Gaza Settlers Council, founder of a far-right political party, and Israel's first Orthodox Jewish leader, Bennett was every bit as committed to settlement expansion as any of his predecessors. His stated position: "We won't annex territories and won't create a Palestinian state." But, once in office, he sought to further entrench the occupation whenever possible, and with it, practices that, on the West Bank at least, clearly fit the International Criminal Court's legal definition of "apartheid." Palestinians living under military occupation in the same geographical location as Israeli settlers did not enjoy a fraction of the latter's rights. In fact, they enjoyed barely any rights at all. What's more, they found themselves vulnerable to a growing epidemic of vigilante violence from Jewish settlers in this period. Settler attacks were carried out with virtual impunity, often with the implicit support of the Israeli military, rising to more than 400 in just the first five months of 2022, a rate that nearly doubled that of the previous year. In those instances where authorities did intervene, just 4 percent of the settlers accused of what Major General Yehuda Fuchs, the commander of Israeli troops in the West Bank, called "settler terrorism" ever found themselves facing actual charges. The 88 Palestinians killed by the Israeli military and police (in addition to three killed by Israeli civilians) during Bennett's year in office, was also a massive jump of more than 60 percent above the last year of Netanyahu's rule.[7]

Biden's team tried to minimize the significance of Bennett's relentless efforts to expand and entrench the occupation, at least in public. It did blacklist a state-sanctioned private high-tech spyware company, NSO, whose wares had been deployed against US diplomats, dissidents, and human rights workers worldwide, and privately managed to prevent Israel from building new settlements in Israeli-annexed East Jerusalem that would have made any future sharing of the city impossible, but only temporarily. But, breaking a campaign promise, it did not re-open the US consulate in East Jerusalem that, before it was closed by Trump, had served Palestinians there since 1854, as the Israelis continued to object. In May 2022, moreover, as Biden was preparing for a visit to Jerusalem, as was very nearly custom by now, the Israeli Defense Ministry announced its approval of plans for building 4,000 new housing units in Jewish settlements in the West Bank in addition to the 1,300 units it had announced the previous October. The reaction, once again, was muted at best. The Biden administration "strongly opposed" the decision but took no other action, as the Israelis insisted to the Biden team that the survival of its teetering ruling coalition, having already lost its one-vote majority, demanded such actions, as the "bear" continued to roam the basement, eager to pounce, until those efforts finally failed in June 2022, and the Bennett government announced that Israelis would go to the polls for the fifth time in barely more than three years.[8]

When Bennett's government finally collapsed, he resigned and was replaced as prime minister on an interim basis by the former journalist, Yair Lapid, who had founded and led the centrist party, Yesh Atid ["There is a Future"]. Not long afterward, Israel caused a worldwide uproar in the human rights community by simultaneously raiding seven Palestinian human rights and civil society organizations it deemed "terrorist," owing to their alleged connections to the Popular Front for the Liberation of Palestine (PFLP). Its forces confiscated property, sealed off office doors, and posted official notices declaring the groups illegal. But the Israelis were unable to substantiate their charges to anyone who asked for proof, including the US CIA. Back in mid-July, before the raids but after Israel had announced the "terrorist" designations of the groups in question, twenty-two Democratic representatives sent a letter to Secretary of State Blinken complaining that "a reported lack of evidence to support this decision raises concerns that it may be a deeply repressive measure, designed to criminalize and silence prominent and essential Palestinian human rights organizations." Following the raids, Israel found its actions condemned by over 150 global organizations organized by Human Rights Watch, nine members of the European Union, and eight liberal American Jewish groups operating under the umbrella "Progressive Israel Network." New Israel Fund CEO Daniel Sokatch opined in the *Forward* that "Israel is not acting like the 'only democracy in the Middle East' as it declares itself to be. American Jews should urge our leaders to tell Israel: Cease and desist from persecuting human rights defenders—their work is critical to your democracy." Despite Israel's inability to substantiate its charges, the Biden government was willing only to "voice [their] concern," and then only via their ambassador, rather than Secretary of State Blinken, much less the president himself. Bibi Netanyahu was already running hard in the coming election with the support of Israel's most extremist right-wing parties; doing nothing to improve his chances was clearly the administration's primary—and perhaps—only priority.[9]

Among American Jews, public political criticism of Israel had traveled well beyond its previously heavily policed borders, but American Jewish leaders continue to deny this. As late as February 2022, William Daroff, the CEO of the Conference of Presidents, would straight-facedly tell a reporter, "I believe the broad consensus of American Jewry is pretty much in one place." He termed the Jewish state to be both "a central force of who we are as a Jewish community" and "part and parcel and a key foundation of 21st century American Judaism." Yet, as Israel's former consul general in Boston, who is now executive director of J Street, Nadav Tamir, far more accurately explained, Israel had long taken the support of diaspora Jewry for granted, "expecting it to serve as a vital resource to generate pro-Israel support, a cash machine for unconditional funding." At the same time, "the attitude of the Israeli religious establishment toward the non-Orthodox denominations of Judaism has left a large majority of the Jewish people"—that is, 90 percent of American Jews—"out in the cold." These tensions were exacerbated by Israel's drift toward illiberalism, both at home and in its relationships abroad. All of this, he concluded, "led to a situation where the Jewish nation has become more of a divisive element for Jews than a unifying force."[10]

Among the many incidents that demonstrated the truth of Tamir's diagnosis was the profound disjunction that arose over Russia's February 2022 invasion of Ukraine. The US Jewish community was almost wholly united in support of the victims, both proud of and awed by the bravery and eloquence of its unlikely leader, the Jewish former comedian Volodymyr Zelensky. The Israelis, meanwhile, took a much more circumspect attitude toward the conflict, seeking to retain its good relations with the Russian dictatorial strongman Vladimir Putin at the expense of the country his military was in the process of destroying with near-genocidal aggression. This was so even though Putin supplemented his attacks with a barrage of shockingly antisemitic propaganda, going so far as to equate Zelensky (who lost much of his family in the Shoah) and company to Hitler and the Nazis.[11]

Following an alarming increase in reported global antisemitic incidents in the wake of the May 2021 war, some of them violent, Jewish leaders, led by the Anti-Defamation League and the American Jewish Committee, organized what they expected to be a mass rally in Washington "in Solidarity with the Jewish People." It drew a mere two thousand attendees. Many "pro-peace" Jewish organizations, including J Street, Americans for Peace Now, and T'ruah, boycotted the gathering, because its organizers had refused to distinguish between antisemitism and harsh criticism of Israel. The demand on the part of the organizers that anti-Semitism and anti-Zionism be understood to be indistinguishable was no longer accepted by much of the Jewish community, and hence was undermining any hopes for a unified response to what all agreed was an alarming rise in antisemitic attacks, both physical and rhetorical.[12]

AIPAC poured metaphorical oil on this fire when, after finally deciding in December 2021 to create a super PAC that would donate directly to congressional candidates, it announced, in April 2022, that it was endorsing over one hundred Republicans who had enlisted in Donald Trump's campaign to destroy American democracy. Boasting million-dollar contributions from right-wing Republicans, including Home Depot co-founder Bernie Marcus and hedge fund manager Paul Singer, AIPAC sought to defeat progressive candidates in Democratic primaries with advertisements that never even mentioned Israel.

It invested an eye-popping $6 million in just one Democratic primary to ensure the defeat of yet another woman of color who had been critical of Israel, former Maryland Congresswoman Donna Edwards. Weeks later, continuing to act as a kind of death star for progressive Democrats facing members of the party's centrist wing, it invested another $4.2 million in defeating the liberal Zionist Congressman Andy Levin. A member of a Michigan Jewish dynasty, Levin had not only authored the "Two-State Solution

Act" in the House, designed to ensure that Israel did not close off the possibility of one day making peace with the Palestinians, but also provided a
neighboring representative, Palestinian-American Muslim Rashida Tlaib,
with strong statements of friendship and support. This was a particular concern for his opponents because, as one former AIPAC President David Victor
emailed Levin supporters, "Andy sincerely claims to be a lifelong Zionist,
proud Jew and defender of Israel.... So when Andy Levin insists he's pro-
Israel, less engaged Democratic colleagues may take him at his word." Unlike
most of AIPAC's more than $26 million investment in the 2022 Democratic
primary process—$10.5 million of which was devoted strictly to attack ad-
vertisements—this race did feature Israel as a key issue. J-Street came across
with $700,000 for Levin; Bernie Sanders rallied with him and Tlaib; and
members of the left-wing Jewish group IfNotNow showed up in the district
to knock on doors wearing "Jews for Andy" t-shirts. AIPAC could therefore
declare a victory over those Democrats who were moving with the majority
of the party toward a more sympathetic view of the Palestinians and more
critical one of Israel, albeit one funded with right-wing Republican money.[13]

In yet another hard-fought primary in Brooklyn and Manhattan that
followed, AIPAC took credit for helping to defeat yet another woman of
color—an Asian American woman named Yuh-Line Niou—in a tight race
with the more centrist Dan Goldman, who was also opposed by two other
progressive candidates of color. (Niou, who had been endorsed by the Democratic Socialists of America, said she strongly supported the free speech
rights of BDS activists, without explicitly supporting the movement itself.)
What was distinctive about this intervention was the fact that AIPAC hid
its participation under the name of a previously unknown cut-out, apparently understanding that among this heavily Jewish population, its support
might be perceived negatively by voters. With an impressive (and revealing)
display of chutzpah, the organization proceeded to attack its rival J Street for
accepting a one million dollar donation from George Soros—an attack that
J Street noted was consistent with the "fear mongering and hate-mongering"
about the Hungarian-born Holocaust survivor that the head of the ADL had
termed in other contexts to be a "gateway to anti-Semitism."[14]

Even more controversially, AIPAC's Republican insurrectionists included
Representative Jim Jordan of Ohio, who refused to cooperate with the

committee investigating the January 6, 2021, attack on the Capitol; Representative Pete Sessions of Texas, who had secretly met with "Stop the Steal" leaders just days before Trump's attempted coup; and Representative Scott Perry of Pennsylvania, an unashamed fan of white supremacist and antisemitic "replacement theory" conspiracies, and who was known to compare Democratic leaders to the Nazis. AIPAC's list originally excluded Wyoming representative Elizabeth Cheney, the vociferously "pro-Israel" Republican who had been deemed persona non grata by her party for refusing to embrace its anti-democratic crusade. This decision was later reversed, however, apparently in response to the outcry its exposure inspired.[15]

When asked by a *Washington Post* reporter whether there was anything at all "a candidate who supports Israel could support that would rule them out for AIPAC's support," Howard Kohr, the organization's president could not, offhand, come up with a single example. But given that only 4 percent of American Jews, in 2022, put Israel at the top of their list of concerns—and they are divided on the issue—and that the vast majority voted for Joe Biden, and opposed the efforts of Trump and his Republican followers to steal the election and delegitimize the new administration, what AIPAC (with unintended irony) called its "United Democracy Project" clearly undermined its bona fides as a supporter of American democracy. Former AIPAC executive director Tom Dine announced that if the organization he helped build was going to embrace "antidemocratic people who believe the last election was a fraud and they support the January 6 insurrection," he would "not give them a dime." Even Abe Foxman expressed the rarest of criticism of the organization with which he had allied the ADL for the nearly three decades he spent at its helm. "Sad mistake!," Foxman complained in a tweet. "Israel's security depends on America being a strong democracy." Together with its continued attacks on President Biden's attempt to restore US participation in President Obama's Iran accord, AIPAC's heavy-handed intervention in the 2022 primaries and general election proved one fact conclusively: Whatever claim AIPAC may have enjoyed as the perceived political representative of the broad Jewish community in the United States had, by this time, clearly become a thing of the past.[16]

Israel was clearly growing increasingly unpopular among young people in general, among liberals, and among Jews, especially young Jews. Donald

Trump, with his typical political sophistication and subtlety, professed to discover, as ex-president, that "the Jewish people in the United States either don't like Israel or don't care about Israel." He was, for once, only partially wrong. In a survey undertaken by the liberal-leaning Jewish Electorate Institute, 34 percent of American Jews agreed with the statement "Israel's treatment of Palestinians is similar to racism in the U.S.," and fully 22 percent agreed that Israel was committing "genocide." According to the Pew Research Center's extensive investigation of Jewish American attitudes undertaken in 2020, the vast majority continued to support the creation of a Palestinian state alongside Israel. But should that potential solution disappear—as had already very nearly happened—they were roughly evenly divided between ending Israel's Jewish identity and allowing Israel to formally annex the West Bank. In every one of these categories, young Jews were consistently more critical of Israel than their parents or grandparents were or ever had been.[17]

Evidence of the intensity of the disaffection can be seen in a May 23, 2021, letter to President Biden signed by more than five hundred "proud alumni" of his presidential campaign. Based both on the names of the signatories and on the composition of Democratic presidential campaign staffs generally, one can safely infer that a large percentage of the signers were Jewish. The letter demanded all manner of changes to US policy in the name of the "pursuit of justice, peace, and self-determination for Palestinians." They wanted to "ensure U.S. aid no longer funds the imprisonment and torture of Palestinian children, theft and demolition of Palestinian homes and property, and annexation of Palestinian land," and called on Biden to insist that the Israeli government put an end to the "violent attacks by Israeli mobs that operate with the protection of Israeli police." They also wanted an end to Israel's "blockade of Gaza, which has made it an uninhabitable open-air prison," together with an investigation of "whether Israel's most recent assault on Gaza violates the Leahy Law, prohibiting U.S. military aid from funding foreign military units implicated in the commission of gross violations of human rights." As a Jewish campaign alumnus explained at the time, "There's no question that there are many Jewish staffers on the Hill that are told one version of history growing up but now have a much more evenhanded analysis of the conflict.... We would sing 'Hatikva' but not really interrogate how Israel came to be, and there was no real mention of Palestinian people at all." The harsh criticism of Israel was now coming, as the saying goes, "from inside the house."[18]

Critics noticed a spate of novels and short stories by American Jewish writers in which Israelis were portrayed in far less admirable terms than in the past. While Philip Roth had been relatively lonely in painting complicated portraits of often larger-than-life Israeli characters in a series of novels beginning with 1969's *Portnoy's Complaint*, major American Jewish writers of the early 21st century including Jonathan Safran Foer (*Here I Am*), Michael Chabon (*The Yiddish Policemen's Union*), Nicole Krauss (*Forest Dark*), Nathan Englander (*What We Talk About When We Talk About Anne Frank*), and Joshua Cohen (*The Netanyahus*, winner of the 2022 Pulitzer Price for Fiction) all had much harsher messages to communicate. This alleged trend led one Tel Aviv-based professor to yearn for the days when Leon Uris's "heroic and sentimental" 1958 novel, *Exodus* (adapted two years later into a successful film starring Paul Newman), celebrated the transformation of the Jewish people from subjugation in Europe to emancipation in the Middle East.[19]

Even more disturbing to American Jewish leaders was the May 19, 2021, letter signed by ninety-three rabbinical and cantorial students representing all denominations save Orthodoxy. It began with the words, "Blood is flowing in the streets of the Holy Land," and went on to complain that so many Jewish institutions—the very ones with which many of its signatories hoped to soon begin their careers as Jewish leaders and teachers—had been "silent when abuse of power and racist violence erupts in Israel and Palestine." It then detailed various crimes Israel was committing against the Palestinians, using the term "apartheid" to describe the "two separate legal systems for the same region." Once a "flying buttress" that "held up the American Jewish community from the outside," as the veteran Jewish affairs journalist Marc Tracy wrote, in a lengthy *New York Times Magazine* article that focused on the students' complaints, Israel was now tearing American Jews apart. The rabbinical and cantorial students' harsh language proved a particularly ominous harbinger to older Jewish leaders, given the fact that they represented the future not just of the academy, but of American Judaism itself. As one of the signatories quoted by Tracy explained, "there's an assumption among American Jews that the more people learn about Zionism, the more Zionist they will become." But, he added, "I think that's wrong."[20]

What's more, an all but unbridgeable gulf had opened between the political beliefs of Israeli and American Jews. The fact that Israeli voters were significantly more politically conservative in almost every respect than American Jews was consistent with differences in the two groups' socioeconomic and educational status. But for decades now, the former were moving further and further rightward as the latter remained steadfast in their commitment to political liberalism. According to data compiled in 2022 by the Israel Democracy Institute, fully 62 percent of Israeli Jews now considered themselves to be "right-wing," with just 24 percent in the center and a mere 11 percent as left-identifying. Meanwhile, according to the Pew Research Center survey, in 2020, American Jews remained "among the most consistently liberal and Democratic groups in the US population. Seven in ten Jewish adults identify with or lean toward the Democratic Party, and half describe their political views as liberal." This conflict came, increasingly, to encroach on views of issues facing Israel. A 2016 Pew poll found nearly 80 percent agreement among Israeli Jews that they ought to be entitled to privileges over Israeli non-Jews. Nearly 50 percent agreed that "Arabs should be expelled or transferred" from Israel. The latter figure would turn out to be a higher percentage than those favoring a two-state solution, according to a later Pew poll—views that, again, were almost perfectly contradicted by those of the majority of American Jews, with young Jews on either side of the divide further exacerbating the two trends.[21]

Writing in late 2021, Gil Troy, a McGill University historian and Zionist activist, proposed the term "Identity Zionism" to define Jews who "cherish Israel" and resist the "shrill elite of rabidly anti-Zionist professors, rabbis and activists." The latter constituted what Troy, writing earlier that year with the Soviet refusenik turned right-wing Israeli politician Natan Sharansky, defined as "Un-Jews," who complain of "the conflation of Israel with the Jewish people." Troy specifically mentioned the signatories of the rabbinical and cantorial students' letter as being in the latter category. These definitions suffer from an obvious inability to account for the likes of the huge ultra-Orthodox, intensely anti-Zionist Satmar sect of Hasidim—whose anti-Zionism is rooted in Masechet Ketubot (111a) in the Talmud, which they believe instructs Jews not to restore Jewish sovereignty until Messianic times—to say nothing of the history of the Jewish people's proud addiction to limitless disputation. (Once again: "Two Jews, three opinions…") Even so, by demanding fealty to Israel as a necessary condition of Jewish identity, Troy and Sharansky did articulate the usually unspoken ideological commitment that runs throughout the modern history of secular American Jewish life—redefining, but ultimately restating, what Rabbi Michael Meyer, writing in 1994, described as "the minimal litmus test of [American] Jewish identification."[22]

They were, however, fighting a rear-guard and likely losing battle. Ever since the Jewish state's founding in the aftermath of the Holocaust, and especially since the 1967 war, support for Israel has been the central project of secular American Jewry and the central definitional identity for most American Jews. For many years, this commitment rejuvenated their communities and provided a healthy, unifying theme at a time when theology ceased to matter much and the liberal politics that had replaced it grew ever more divisive. True, Israel's actions frequently overrode American Jews' traditional commitment to their liberalism. But the combination of the young Jewish state's perceived vulnerability, together with the constantly reinforced reification of the Shoah, sustained the unity of a community whose "dovishness stopped at the delicatessen door"—as one wag put it—well into the twenty-first century. Not incidentally, it also helped to ensure not merely Israel's survival, but its eventual blossoming into an economically dynamic and militarily powerful regional superpower.

At the same time, American Jewish identity, especially in the aftermath of the Six-Day War, became, for the non-Orthodox, vicariously defined with Israel. And that definition had precious little in common with the everyday lives of American Jews. Back in 1971, for instance, a Wheeling, West Virginia, rabbi named Martin Siegel wrote of an experience that was no doubt repeated in temples and synagogues all across post-1967 America. A heavily decorated Israeli colonel came to his synagogue and bragged before a rapturous audience of worshippers about "how many Arabs *we* had killed, how many tanks *we* had captured." The congregants, Siegel observed, "literally bounced with delight in their seats." It was, he lamented, as if they actually believed that "*I, the shoe salesman, killed an Arab; I, the heart specialist, captured a tank.*" What remains of Jewish culture and belief beyond Zionism and reverence for those lost in the Shoah has become, at least for the non-Orthodox, increasingly difficult for most Jews to identify with, much less define—which accounts, at least in part, for the commonly stated belief among so many Israeli intellectuals that secular American Judaism is a doomed—and rather ridiculous—phenomenon.[23]

Jews who lived through the traumatic events of the mid-twentieth century, along with their children and grandchildren, felt the Shoah, the founding of Israel, and the perceived threat of its destruction in the days preceding the Six-Day War to be something that happened to them personally. One can understand their willingness to defend Israel as a kind of miracle of redemption that arose from the ashes of European Jewish civilization. (The Greek origins of the English word "holocaust" itself lay in the "burnt offerings" of ritual animal sacrifice.) They were therefore willing to support, without much questioning, just about anything Israeli leaders said was necessary to assure its security and survival. During the 1982 Israeli invasion of Lebanon, Elie Wiesel, the eloquent de facto face of Shoah survival, made the point with admirable clarity: "The nations that kept silent during the Holocaust ought to keep silent now as well. The world that then condemned itself by its silence has lost all right to judge Israel now."[24]

By the second decade of the twenty-first century, the Shoah and Israel's founding had become, for most young American Jews, both ancient and distant matters. Israel's unquestioning defense made little sense to those whose only experience of Israel was of an increasingly illiberal nation that allied itself with the American right wing, that helps to arm and train the military and intelligence agencies of repressive regimes across the world, and that occupies another people's land, denies these people even the most basic political rights, and occasionally launches bombing raids against a population forced to live without access to dependable electricity, clean water, and, oftentimes, food and shelter. Rather than the refuge from antisemitism that their parents and grandparents understood a Jewish state to be, young Jews experience Israel as a motivation for attacks on Jews by pro-Palestinian mobs and anti-Israel activists. And finally, many Israelis, including, especially, Israeli political and religious authorities, continue to show virtually no respect for American Jewish religious practice.

In 1945, Jean-Paul Sartre's book-length essay *Anti-Semite and Jew* offered the thesis that "the sole tie that binds [one Jew to another] is the hostility and disdain of the societies which surround him." To the degree that there was ever any truth to this vastly overstated claim, it lost its relevance with the founding of the state of Israel, which gave Jews, both in Israel and the diaspora, a clear purpose: the defense of the state combined with the sanctification of those murdered in the Shoah. Today, however, young American Jews have been voting with their feet—running, not walking, away from the Israel-and-the-Holocaust-grounded Judaism of their parents and grandparents. The 2020 Pew study found that compared to their elders sixty-five years old and up, barely half as many Jews between the ages of eighteen and twenty-nine identified with Reform or Conservative Judaism. And Jews who defined themselves as belonging to no denomination or religion have proven unlikely to pass along their Jewish identity to their children, much less their commitment to defending Israel. While older American Jews still told pollsters that they "supported Israel," fewer than half of Jewish adults under the age of thirty described themselves as even "somewhat" emotionally attached to the Jewish state, and many of those who retained that attachment were strongly opposed to its actions. But of those American Jews who did feel an emotional attachment to Israel, fully 87 percent agreed that one could be both "pro-Israel" and critical of Israeli government policies. A generation earlier, fewer than half of all Jews had held that view. Moreover, 58 percent of American Jews supported restricting military aid to Israel to prevent its use in the occupied territories. Still, this same view, if spoken publicly, would likely result in de facto excommunication from most of the major Jewish organizations that allege to speak on behalf of American Jews.[25]

American Jews have never been much for synagogue attendance. Barely 20 percent of Jews attend regularly, a figure that would be far lower if we excluded the Orthodox from the calculation. Resources devoted to defending every action undertaken by Israel's government might instead have been devoted to Jewish education, community service, and the Jewish tradition of social justice known as *tikkun olam*, all of which have gone begging in recent decades. Clearly a reimagining of what it means to be a diasporic Jew is necessary if the community is to retain even a significant fraction of those drifting away from the faith, much less find a way to grow again. But American Jewish institutions' relentless focus on—and demands for—fealty to Israel, tied to the Holocaust and antisemitism, are the only cards that mainstream Jewish leaders know how to play, and thus make any such renaissance difficult to imagine. As if harkening back to Sartre, Malcolm Hoenlein, the Conference of Presidents' executive vice president, explained, in February 2022, that while many people liken the contemporary threat of antisemitism to "1933, 1938"—that is, Hitler's Holocaust—"it's not 1938 because of the State of Israel. I think that is the big difference." But Hoenlein saw a silver lining in the fact that "antisemitism is going to awaken a lot of young people to a sense of community because they feel vulnerable, they feel alone." The idea that young American Jews might be attracted by a commitment to *tikkun olam*—while at the center of growth for groups like "Bending the Arc"—held little appeal to Hoenlein and his fellow Conference of Presidents members. In 2022, for instance, the Jewish Federations of North America removed advocacy for gun control, voting rights, and LGBTQ protections from its "Public Priorities" statement. Its top priority: "Jewish communal security and support for Israel." Not long afterward, the Anti-Defamation League CEO, Jonathan Greenblatt, made it clear, point blank, that according to his organization's definition, "to those who still cling to the idea that antizionism is not antisemitism—let me clarify this for you as clearly as I can—antizionism *is* antisemitism," adding, for emphasis, "I will repeat: *antizionism is antisemitism.*" And while he allowed that, although some groups on the left "might not have armed themselves or engaged in an insurrection designed to topple our government," they were no less a matter of concern than the violent insurrectionists, owing to the slogans they chanted, the tweets they posted, and the pro-Palestinian speakers they invited to speak on their campuses. This was true, he added, even for Jewish organizations that "attempt[ed] to use their Judaism as a shield."[26]

It is a particularly sad commentary on the state of American Jewish leaders' estimation of their own inner resources that, when panic set in during the early 1990s over the future "continuity" of American Judaism, owing to the threats posed by intermarriage and "distancing," instead of seeking to find answers internally among their educational, religious, and community organizations, they turned immediately to Israel—and especially to its military—to try to give young Jews a reason to remain in the fold. It is also no accident that by far the largest community investment in this effort has been the nonprofit "Birthright" program, which has now given over seven hundred thousand young American Jews a free trip to Israel, under the watchful guidance of its military, since 1994. This program has reportedly been supported by some $50 billion in donations. But the fact that much of this funding has made its way into the Israeli economy, rather than being put to use by the many desperately underfunded and understaffed institutions serving young Jews in the United States, was understood from the start to be a feature, rather than a bug, of the system its organizers put in place. That its single largest donor has been the funder of both US and Israeli right-wing illiberalism and extremism, Sheldon Adelson, may or may not have played a role in defining the ideological indoctrination its participants receive. But whatever its cause, the belief that Israel can be credibly presented to young people via what a former spokesman for the program described as "the Leon Uris version of Israel's history"—which is so obviously belied by the reality they see there on the ground—makes it hardly likely that young American Jews will buy what their elders are selling.[27]

One of the great changes in the larger US debate over Israel in recent times that has helped to fundamentally transform its content has been the Internet-enabled explosion of available information about the region from virtually every ideological perspective. For the first time in the more than eighty-year battle for control of the narrative of the Israeli/Palestinian conflict, one can now find just as many journalists covering the Palestinians' plight as are singing Israel's praises. In the former's corner is, among others, the brilliant, merciless reporting of Nathan Thrall—former director of the International Crisis Group's Arab-Israeli Project—which has appeared in the *New York Review of Books*, *New York Times* magazine, *The Guardian*, and elsewhere alongside additional pro-Palestinian essays and reportage. The newly revived *Jewish Currents*, founded as a Communist Party vehicle during the early Cold War, now provides an independent Jewish anti-Zionist perspective. Its prominence and newfound legitimacy has been buoyed by the presence of former liberal Zionist stalwart Peter Beinart, whose conversion to binationalism sent shockwaves through the communities of many of his former allies. In late 2021, *The Nation* hired Mohammed El-Kurd, a Palestinian activist from Sheikh Jarrah, giving him the new title of "Palestine reporter," to add to its staff of almost exclusively pro-Palestinian reporters and columnists. The post–Martin Peretz *New Republic* also switched sides and began publishing articles with titles such as "Israel's Never-Ending War Against Palestinian Health." The liberal *American Prospect* takes a similarly critical perspective toward Israel. Anchored by the emotional attachments and frequently unmatched eloquence of one of its founders, the liberal philosopher Michael Walzer, the democratic socialist journal *Dissent* remained a place of enormous sympathy for Israel among its longtime contributors, while its younger editors and writers skewed heavily in the direction of pro-Palestinianism.

Ideological commitment to the Palestinian struggle can now be found among any number of left-wing Internet sites and progressive publications, their on-the-ground reporting combined with exhortatory, often provocative rhetoric. (It should be noted that the writers taking the pro-Palestinian side in the debate on sites like Mondoweiss and The Electronic Intifada are hardly less eager to demonize their opponents than those on the "pro-Israel" side, though none can be said to enjoy even remotely commensurate influence. As *New York Times* executive editor Dean Baquet testified in 2014, "Just as many critics who say we are biased against Israel, I get just as many emails saying the opposite. I promise you—and just as virulent.")[28]

At the same time, the field has also grown ever more crowded on the Jewish right wing. *Commentary*, cut loose by the American Jewish Committee in December 2006, carries on its tradition of relentless attacks on Israel's critics, with a particular focus on the alleged apostasies of pro-Palestinian Blacks and liberal Jews. It is now under the direction of John Podhoretz, Norman Podhoretz's son—or "John P. Normanson," as he was referred to when in the employ of Sun Myung Moon's *Washington Times*, where his colleagues often read his column aloud to one another in a ritual they termed "Podenfreude." (His roughly $500,000 2019 remuneration package for a magazine with a mere twenty-four thousand paid subscriptions may be the the highest pay-per-reader compensation ratio in the history of American journalism.) The daily website Tablet takes a similarly aggressive "Pro-Israel" stance. Like *The New Republic* during the more than thirty years that Martin Peretz owned and edited it (though often embracing some of the wildest Trump-inspired conspiracy theories—it once even published a piece attacking the character of Holocaust survivors), Tablet peppers its assaults on those outside the pro-Israel fold with a smattering of well-regarded critics and independent intellectuals. Its publisher, Nextbook Inc., is generously funded by a member of the board of directors of the extremely Trump-friendly Tikvah Fund, which is chaired by Norman Podhoretz's son-in-law, the one-time Iran/Contra scandal criminal pardoned by President George H. W. Bush, Elliott Abrams. Tikvah also supplied funds for the intellectually oriented *Jewish Review of Books*, modeled after the *New York Review of Books*, but with the opposite stance on the Israel/Palestinian conflict. Its magazine, *Mosaic*, which claims to be "advancing Jewish thought," is even more hardline.[29]

These publications were joined on the pro-Israel right wing by the daily newsletter *Jewish Insider*, as well as a newly reincarnated *New York Sun* under the same editorship that had found what students were learning at Columbia University in the early 2000s so alarming. The *Sun*'s funder also paid for the far-right Internet journal Algemeiner, which published a steady stream of right-wing pro-Israel propaganda. *SAPIR*, yet another new entry in this intellectual category, is a journal edited by the Jewish right-wing *New York Times* columnist Bret Stephens, a relentless Israel partisan. It is funded by an Israel-based foundation, the Maimonides Fund, that does not disclose the identity of its donors (though educated guesses are easily made by those willing to search through the necessary disclosure forms). The issue of a funder's identity is important for any institution, but in this case, it is especially so, as the Israeli government has in the past committed many millions of dollars in secret to organizations and institutions supportive of Israeli interests, especially in the United States. In doing so, the Israelis are employing a model the CIA used in the 1950s, when it sought to counter Soviet propaganda efforts. The CIA's hush-money payments to the publishers of intellectual journals were intended to enable those outlets to reach people who were suspicious of more forthright efforts at public diplomacy. As *The Forward* reported, moreover, many US pro-Israel organizations have shown considerable reluctance to report the contributions they have received, even though the US Foreign Agents Registration Act, originally passed in the 1930s to battle pro-Nazi propaganda efforts, requires that they do so. For the *Times* to bless such an arrangement, given its editors' oft-stated concerns with even "the appearance of a conflict of interest," was unusual to say the least.[30]

Between these poles are the general-interest sources intended for a Jewish audience, such as the venerable *Forward*, whose English-language version was reinvented in 1990 and which still manages to publish the Yiddish newspaper it began in 1897. It is joined by the news agency JTA (Jewish Telegraphic Agency, begun in The Hague in 1917); both were mostly pro-Israel but open to harsh criticism, along with the monthly magazine *Moment* (originally founded by the liberal Zionist Leonard Fein in 1975). These sources augment the English-language version of *Haaretz* (founded in 1918, making it Israel's longest-running publication), which was open to far harsher criticism, and, as noted earlier, was unmatched anywhere in its relentless reporting and commentary on both Israeli and Palestinian politics. In addition to these were the *Times of Israel* (founded in 2012); Israel's most trafficked news site, Ynet; and a 2021 entry, *Sources*, a thoughtful journal founded by the Hartman Foundation. What's more, interested parties could easily find themselves inundated with information from literally dozens of organizations dedicated to spreading news that suited their aims, collated especially for an individual's interests and delivered via email alerts, Facebook, Twitter, and other forms of social media, augmented for scholars and other interested parties by a burgeoning collection of academic journals open to virtually all political and intellectual perspectives.*

In other words, for the first time since the debate over Zionism in the United States began, virtually anyone could access a steady stream of reasonably accurate, detailed information about the Israeli/Palestinian conflict from multiple ideological and intellectual perspectives. And yet political reality remained largely unchanged. As J Street president Jeremy Ben-Ami observed during the May 2021 Gaza war, it may be that "the Democratic Party is clearly now willing and able to speak out in a much more balanced manner about issues related to Israel." But while the rhetoric was different, the politics were not. For all the criticism Israel received in the wake of the war, opponents could not convince even a tenth of their colleagues in either the House or the

---

* I should note that among the publications mentioned, I have been, during the course of my career, a columnist for *The Nation* (for twenty-five years), *The Guardian*, *The Forward*, *Moment*, and *The American Prospect*. I have also been a frequent contributor to *Haaretz* and an occasional contributor to *The New Republic* during the decades of Martin Peretz's ownership.

Senate to place any meaningful restrictions on the US military aid it received. President Biden, while on a celebratory visit to Israel in July 2022, attributed the entire phenomenon of Democratic dissent over America's Israel policies as the politically insignificant "mistake" of just "a few" of the party's members.[31]

Palestinian supporters succeeded in colonizing university Middle East studies departments, student and faculty organizations, and far-left political organizations and media institutions, but even so, the BDS movement in which they had invested so heavily had virtually no concrete achievements to show for its efforts in terms of genuine boycotts of Israel, whether inside or outside of academia. The movement's goal of creating sufficient pressure, either on Israel or on a future US government, to demand that Israeli Jews turn their country over to what has apparently already become an Arab majority "between the river and the sea" is not something any sane supporter of Israel ever need worry about. As Israel continues to refuse the Palestinians even a modicum of democracy and human dignity, it will almost certainly continue to grow less and less popular among Democrats, young people, and Jews. But will this change US policy? Nothing in the recent or even distant past—or in the continued stranglehold that money, power, organizational structure, and clearly defined paths to personal career advancement continue to hold over the shape of US foreign policy—leads one to such a conclusion.[32]

Despite all the deserved criticism that Israeli treatment of the Palestinians has inspired in recent decades, Israel retains the powerful argument that it has no credible "partner" for peace. The Palestinian Authority that rules on the West Bank has sacrificed whatever credibility it once enjoyed among Palestinians owing to decades of corruption, ineffectiveness, and authoritarianism, along with its perceived co-optation by Israeli security services. (It has not faced voters since 2006.) Hamas leaders sometimes make statements indicating that they may one day be open to a discussion of a two-state solution with Israel, but at the same time, as recently as March 2002, it was still celebrating terrorist attacks inside Israel itself. But given the organization's commitment to a politically charged, fundamentalist brand of Islam, the repression of its opponents, and support for terrorism, almost no one concerned with the survival of the Jewish state would dream of demanding that it accommodate itself to Hamas's demands—much less dissolve itself, as so many Palestinian supporters claim it must, in order to offer the many millions of

Palestinian refugees scattered around the world a literal "right of return." And while it is also true that Israel bears considerable responsibility for creating the factors that led to this sorry situation, that is hardly an effective—or even responsible—argument for demanding that such risks be undertaken in the foreseeable future. One could, no doubt, find people on both the Palestinian and Israeli sides who, under the proper conditions, could imagine making sufficient concessions to end the conflict and enable realization of the ever-distant "two-state solution," but such a vision appears each day to be less a realistic goal than an excuse for inaction. According to a March 2022 survey undertaken for the American Jewish Committee, a majority of Israeli millennials agreed that "there is no viable solution to the Israeli-Palestinian conflict," while fewer than a fifth of American Jews questioned said the same.[33]

Many people involved in the US political debate on Israel look away from these realities, but, when combined, they give every impression of making any sort of peace impossible for the foreseeable future. As Haim Rabinovich, a twenty-five-year veteran of Israel's security service, the Shin Bet, who rose to its number three position, put it in a February 2022 interview, "The majority of Israelis don't want to rule another people. But they are indifferent to this issue. The vast majority of Israelis don't really experience the control of the Palestinians on an everyday basis." He called the occupation "not moral, not Jewish, not principled," before adding, "Do you think the Palestinians will get used to it? That will never happen."[34]

Following a failed attempt during the 2021 Gaza war to pause US weapons deliveries to Israel, led by Bernie Sanders in the Senate and members of the Alexandria Ocasio-Cortez "squad" in the House, debate in Congress moved on to a proposal to add $1 billion to the $38 billion in aid that was already assured to Israel—thanks to Barack Obama—to replace the Iron Dome missiles Israel had fired to head off the missiles fired by Hamas during the conflict. The opposition managed only 9 nay votes in the House versus 420 in favor. During the debate over the extra money, Rashida Tlaib attacked Israeli "apartheid," inspiring a furious reaction from Representative Ted Deutch (D-FL). Deutch announced, "I cannot allow one of my colleagues to stand on the floor on the House of Representatives and label the Jewish democratic state of Israel an apartheid state.... [T]hat's anti-semitism." These comments turned out to be a kind of try-out for Deutch's next job, that of CEO of the American Jewish Committee, which was announced in February 2022.[35]

But far more than the funding issue at hand, Tlaib had identified the next major battlefield in the debate. Shortly before she spoke, Human Rights Watch had issued a 213-page report (boasting 866 footnotes) following much shorter (unfootnoted) reports by the Jerusalem-based human rights group B'Tselem and a lengthy legal brief by the Israeli lawyer Michael Sfard, published by the Tel Aviv–based group Yesh Din, that found Israel guilty of maintaining "apartheid" in the occupied territories by treating the two ethnic populations there with sharply unequal legal standards. Furthermore, a 2021 survey of qualified Middle East scholars found 65 percent agreement with the statement that Israel now practiced "a one state reality akin to apartheid." Perhaps most surprising, according to a survey undertaken around the same time by the Democratic-leaning Jewish Electorate Institute, so did 25 percent of American Jews, including 38 percent of those under the age of forty.[36]

The apartheid argument exploded on the final day of January 2022, just before the venerable London-based human rights organization Amnesty International released a report titled "Crime of Apartheid: The Government of Israel's Systematic Oppression Against Palestinians." Four years in the making, the 280-page report (boasting fully 1,559 footnotes) made the case that Israel's "apartheid" was not restricted to the West Bank but included—and had always included—its treatment of Palestinian citizens of Israel as well. In the organization's judgment, "Jewish Israelis form a group that is unified by a privileged legal status embedded in Israeli law, which extends to them through state services and protections regardless of where they reside in the territories under Israel's effective control." Amnesty, moreover, accused Israel of having pursued, since its founding, "a policy of establishing and maintaining a Jewish demographic hegemony and maximizing its control over land to benefit Jewish Israelis while restricting the rights of Palestinians and preventing Palestinian refugees from returning to their homes." That policy was extended to the West Bank and Gaza Strip after 1967, Amnesty asserted. Unlike the previous reports, Amnesty International's was understood by all concerned to be a call to arms. Its purposely incendiary rhetoric was almost certainly designed to inspire others to join the worldwide movement to pressure Israel into ending the special privileges that Jews enjoyed—by virtue of the fact that, as Benjamin Netanyahu put it in March 2019, it was "the national state, not of all its citizens, but only of the Jewish people"—up to, and including, dissolving itself, as the BDS movement also suggested.[37]

The Amnesty report carried significant weight in the debate, owing to the organization's reputation for accuracy. Many democratic governments, including that of the United States, had relied on the findings laid out in its reports since its 1961 founding. (And it did so even with this report, in its annual "2021 Country Reports on Human Rights Practices," released in April 2022.) But because Amnesty officials had circulated the report in advance of its release, and because of its obvious political intent, attacks on the content heralded its arrival. It almost immediately became a kind of propaganda ping-pong ball, hit back and forth between Israel's die-hard supporters, its attackers, and those caught in the middle. The Israeli government initially tried to convince the organization not to publish it, maintaining that it was "false, biased," and, of course, "antisemitic." When those efforts failed, its Ministry of Foreign Affairs called Amnesty "just another radical organization which echoes propaganda, without seriously checking the facts." The ministry added that the report relied on "lies shared by terrorist organizations." The Israelis insisted that the allegations endangered Jews the world over—a charge repeated almost word for word by the Anti-Defamation League, which claimed that the report would "likely... lead to intensified antisemitism around the world." The Conference of Presidents, AIPAC, the ADL, the American Jewish Committee, the Jewish Federations of North America, and B'nai B'rith International issued a rare joint statement calling the report an "unbalanced, inaccurate, and incomplete review" that "inexplicably focuse[d] on one aim: to demonize and delegitimize the Jewish and democratic State of Israel."[38]

Speaking to an Israeli reporter, Malcolm Hoenlein took credit on behalf of the fifty-three-member Conference of Presidents for "mobilization of all the organizations right away" to contact members of Congress and write "statements that they were encouraged to make" against the report. William Daroff, the group's CEO, added, "We were engaged in an effort to communicate with key members of Congress, with key members of the Biden administration, with key members of other governments and other NGOs." Among American officials, the US ambassador to Israel, Tom Nides, rejected its findings, as did almost all the senators and members of Congress from both political parties who mentioned it. Nine centrist House Democrats, including former Democratic National Committee chairwoman Debbie Wasserman Schultz, issued a statement terming the report to be "baseless," "biased," and "steeped in antisemitism." It was "part of Amnesty's broad, decades-long campaign," she said, "to criminalize and delegitimize the world's only Jewish state." Not long after the report's release, Israel announced that it would not be cooperating with the United Nations' own investigation into the incidents and practices the Amnesty report had described. Like clockwork, a letter appeared that was signed by sixty-eight senators—thirty-seven Republicans and thirty-one Democrats—asking Secretary of State Antony Blinken to "lead a multinational effort...to end the [United Nations Human Rights Council's] permanent Commission of Inquiry [COI] on the Israeli-Palestinian conflict," terming it to be "the latest endeavor by UNHRC to discredit the only Jewish state" in a manner that would be "likely to further fuel antisemitism worldwide."[39]

As we've seen, the "anti-Zionism equals antisemitism" equation was by now an old warhorse, as it had long been deployed to shut down criticism—to say nothing of branding virtually all Palestinians as antisemites—without the inconvenience of having to deal with the substance of any given charge. The fact of Amnesty's 280 pages and 1,559 footnotes can hardly be said to have affected any side's calculations. Fourteen Israeli human rights organizations—both Jewish and Arab—while not endorsing the details of the report itself, condemned the attacks on Amnesty, also in a rare joint signed statement, writing, "Many of the most pre-eminent scholars of Jewish life, history and persecution have warned that the struggle against antisemitism in the world is being weakened by the unbearable, inaccurate and instrumentalized use to which the antisemitism accusation is lodged for political ends, in order to avoid debate about Israel's oppressive policies towards the Palestinians."[40]

Inside Israel, the word "apartheid" had long ago lost its power. It had been used in Israel's internal debate at least as early as 2002, sometimes as a warning, other times as a description of current reality. One can find such statements by journalists and politicians of every ideological stripe—including former prime ministers, attorneys general, top military and intelligence officials, opposition leaders, and even the man who, as I write this, holds the office of Israel's presidency, Isaac Herzog. As recently as December 2021, David Grossman, likely Israel's most famous living writer, mused, "Maybe it should no longer be called an 'occupation,' but there are much harsher names, like 'apartheid,' for example." After the report's publication, in May 2022, Israel's High Court of Justice approved the eviction of over a thousand Palestinians from a cluster of villages in the desert frontier area in the South Hebron Hills called "Masafer Yatta" to make way for Israeli military exercises. *Haaretz*'s editors insisted, "In view of the selective expulsion based on nationality, it will no longer be possible to refute the argument that an apartheid regime has replaced the military occupation in the territories. Occupation is temporary by definition; apartheid is liable to persist forever. The High Court approved it." (The Israelis did not make their defenders' task any easier when, shortly thereafter, the IDF apparently killed the beloved Palestinian/American journalist Shireen Abu Akleh, during protests immediately following the decision, and then refused to cooperate with all international efforts to investigate the incident, including a request from fifty-seven US Democratic senators and representatives. In a particularly shocking scene broadcast across the world by social and other media, Israeli police were then filmed firing stun grenades at the men who carried her casket and beating them with batons before thousands of mourners who had gathered to pay tribute to her.)[41]

In Amnesty's report, as in many others, the accusation of the "crime of apartheid" was tied directly to the definition offered in the 1988 Rome Statute that created the International Criminal Court. The statute defined apartheid in terms of "inhumane acts" undertaken "in the context of an institutionalized regime of systematic oppression and domination by one racial group over any other racial group or groups and committed with the intention of maintaining that regime." As precious few people actually read the Amnesty report—or the Rome Statute, or any of the other "apartheid" reports—almost no one understood the word's legal meaning in the context in which it was being used. Therefore, pretty much every argument about

Israeli "apartheid" turned on the degree to which Israel's treatment of its Arab population, whether in the occupied territories or in Israel proper, could be fairly equated with Afrikaners' treatment of South African Blacks—with which most people associated the term. In *The Nation*, BDS movement founder Omar Barghouti, writing with the Jewish Voice for Peace executive director Stefanie Fox, asked, in one headline, "Is This Israel's South Africa Moment?" Shortly after the report's release, one could find fully six attacks in the *Wall Street Journal* published in the previous ten days. Most made reference to South Africa and insisted—with the Israeli government and mainstream American Jewish organizations—that even to raise the notion of such a comparison was to evince, or at least exploit, antisemitism.[42]

American "liberal Zionist" organizations—that is, those who represent the views of roughly half of American Jews—found themselves, per usual, caught in the middle. Understanding the word's power in the US debate and its association with South Africa, groups such as J Street, Ameinu, T'ruah, Americans for Peace Now, Partners for Progressive Israel, and New York Jewish Agenda took a nuanced position distancing themselves from the word "apartheid," especially as applied to pre-1967 Israel, while trying to shift the debate to the details that Amnesty had uncovered, in the hopes of convincing American—and even perhaps Israeli—Jews to take the criticisms seriously.[43]

Interestingly, the only major player in the media to refuse to engage with the Amnesty report at all was the Israel debate's most important and influential forum, the *New York Times*. Its reaction was complete silence, as if no such report had appeared. Even after the report had inspired vociferous responses from the Israeli government, from the US government, and from "pro-Israel" groups, "pro-peace" groups, "pro-Palestinian" groups, and other human rights organizations, along with members of Congress, senators, and countless local elected officials across America, anyone who relied on the *Times* as their most trusted news source when it came to Israel—a population, it may be assumed, heavily populated by American Jews—would never have heard of the report at all. A *Times* spokesman responded to a query about this with the explanation that the paper had "covered the debate over Israel's treatment of Palestinians, both the accusations by rights groups that Israel practices apartheid as well as with on-the-ground reporting of the underlying conditions that give rise to these arguments. While it is not our practice to cover every report published by NGOs, these issues have been and will continue to be an essential part of our Mideast coverage." (At the time, the *Times* had already run four of the five stories it would eventually publish on the issues raised by comments made by the comedian Whoopi Goldberg about the Holocaust on the television chitchat program *The View*.) America's "paper of record" did, eventually, reverse itself and decide to cover the report after all, fully fifty-five days after its release had been reported, and then only in a decidedly pro forma piece, buried deep inside the day's news, and with no discussion of the enormous controversy its publication had caused. It was as if the news were simply too painful to be dealt with by America's most important and influential news organization on all matters, but most especially when it came to Israel and American Jews.[44]

The much-admired essayist and novelist Joan Didion once observed that while the "question of the US relationship with Israel" was discussed with "considerable intellectual subtlety in Jerusalem and Tel Aviv," this was not so in the United States. "In New York and Washington and in those academic venues where the attitudes and apprehensions of New York and Washington have taken hold," she said, the topic turned evenings "toxic." The issue of Israel had become "unraisable, potentially lethal, the conversational equivalent of an unclaimed bag on a bus. We take cover. We wait for the entire subject to be defused, safely insulated behind baffles of invective and counter-invective. Many opinions are expressed. Few are allowed to develop. Even fewer change."[45]

Didion was inspired at the time by a statement by Harvard University president and former secretary of the treasury Lawrence Summers, whom she quoted as saying that "criticisms of the current government of Israel could be construed as 'anti-Semitic in their effect if not their intent.'" She was speaking to an audience at the New York Public Library in late 2002, but her statement would have been just as relevant had she made it fifty years earlier or twenty years later. In this book, I have tried to tell the story of why that is, and why it matters, not just for Israel and for American Jews, but for the sake of civil discourse upon which all hopes for democracy must finally rest.[46]

# ACKNOWLEDGMENTS

First of all, thanks to everyone at Basic Books who worked, or will work, on my book. Writing a book is both a lonely and a collective process, and many of its most important and committed contributors necessarily remain unsung. They are nevertheless deeply appreciated.

Believe it or not, I began researching this book over forty years ago. In the spring of 1980, I spent a semester at Tel Aviv University, where I was lucky enough to study the Israeli/Palestinian issue with faculty members Itamar Rabinovich, Shimon Shamir, and Arnon Gutfeld, among others. Upon returning to my home college, Cornell, I wrote my honors thesis in history, on the relationship between the Vietnam War, the Six-Day War, and the origins of Jewish neoconservatism, under the invaluable guidance of my lifelong academic mentor, Walter LaFeber, finishing in 1982. I must have had an inkling of my future, as I saved all the index cards upon which I took notes from the interviews and readings I did for that essay, which was also read by Benedict Anderson and Isaac Kramnick. A few of my notes actually ended up in these pages.

While earning my master's degree in international relations at Yale from 1984 to 1986, I did independent study courses on Israel's wars with Donald Kagan and took classes on military history with Paul Kennedy and on the role of intellectuals in public debate with visiting professor Edward Said. I then picked up my formal research in 1991 as a history (and Jewish studies) PhD student at Stanford University. I spent a year researching a doctoral dissertation on the impact of the founding of the state of Israel on American liberalism. I even signed a book contract for it before deciding to switch topics and writing what eventually became my fourth book, *When Presidents Lie*. Although I did not end up writing about Israel for my dissertation, however, I did write a series of papers on the topic for my professors during my years at Stanford, and again, saved all those notes and files. They made it into this book too.

At Stanford I worked most closely with my dissertation adviser, Barton J. Bernstein, and on Jewish history and sociology with Steven Zipperstein and Arnie Eisen, respectively. What originally inspired my interest in Jewish history and culture, however, was an adult education class on rabbinical literature that I took in the late 1980s under the auspices of the Fabrangen Havurah in Washington, DC, taught by the rabbi and professor Max Ticktin. Max died at the age of ninety-four in 2016, but I remain deeply appreciative of his role in inducting me into a rich intellectual tradition that has been important to my life ever since. I would also like to thank other scholars, teachers, and rabbis who aided me on this intellectual journey. First and foremost among these is my now close friend Rabbi David Gelfand of Temple Israel of New York, with whom I studied Torah on a weekly basis for over a decade. Also crucial to my Jewish education were the scholars associated with the Hadar Institute, especially the theologian and teacher Rabbi Shai Held.

I've written more columns and articles on the subject covered in this book than I can count for more publications than I can remember, and I have taken many reporting trips to Israel and the West Bank. These have included a trip with the Foundation for Middle East Peace, then under the guidance of Matt Duss. (The foundation was also the source of a $20,000 research grant accorded me in 2016.) I went on a second research trip to the same places that year under the auspices of the Schusterman Center for Israel Studies at Brandeis University, following an intense period of study of Israel at Brandeis itself, then under the leadership of the rabbi and professor David Ellenson. (The Nation Institute, which no longer exists, also contributed $5,000 in 2016 to this same worthy cause.) Neither organization, however, enjoyed any input into this book.

I set out to write this book itself sometime in 2015. While writing many drafts between then and now, I benefited enormously from the expert editorial advice and editing from my good friends J. J. Goldberg,

Kai Bird, Brian Morton, and (well, she's more than a friend) Laura Hercher. After the galleys were published and sent out, I received some important help from two people whose work I respected and whom I asked for blurbs but know only professionally. Well beyond the call of duty, Hussein Ibish volunteered a nearly 7,000-word memo filled with useful corrections and a lengthy arguments that immensely improved my final version. David Myers also offered a bunch of helpful suggestions. These now put me more deeply in each scholar's debt. The value of the combined knowledge, expertise, and patience of these people with my work (and my, um, personality) can hardly be overestimated, and the book's analysis is far richer and more nuanced, to say nothing of more concise, than it would have been without their generous help. To be perfectly honest, however, I cannot imagine that these people, or anyone else, will agree with everything in this book, and so should not be held responsible.

In addition to Laura's love and [shocker!] patience, I also remain in the debt of my many friends who listened to me talk about the book over the years who will just have to know who they are, given how long these acknowledgments already are. One person who deserves special mention, however, is my daughter and hero, Eve Rose Alterman, who, as I said in my dedication, has taught me far more than I (or anyone) would have wished to learn about strength, and fortitude, and grace. I hope the book is worthy of her. I also hope she reads it one day.

Finally, my gratitude to my long-suffering parents, Ruth and Carl Alterman, who will be (just about) eighty-eight and ninety-two, respectively, at the time of the book's publication. Alas, for the twelfth time in the past thirty years, I must regretfully admit that whatever mistakes somehow remain in this book are entirely their fault.

—ERA, 8/31/22

# NOTES

### Introduction: Working on a Dream

1. Amnon Cavari, "Six Decades of Public Affection: Trends in American Attitudes Toward Israel," in *Israel and the United States: Six Decades of US Israeli Relations*, ed. Robert O. Freedman (Boulder: Westview Press, 2012), 100–123.

2. Calev Ben-Dor, "Amazon Prime's Human Factor: American Negotiators and the Failure of the Oslo Peace Process," *Fathom*, September 2021, https://fathomjournal.org/amazon-primes-human-factor-american-negotiators-and-the-failure-of-the-oslo-peace-process.

3. David Nirenberg, *Anti-Judaism: The Western Tradition* (New York: W. W. Norton, 2013), 1; Vyacheslav Karpov and Manfred Svensson, *Secularization, Desecularization, and Toleration: Cross-Disciplinary Challenges to a Modern Myth* (London: Palgrave Macmillan, 2020), 199.

4. Uri Abulof, *The Mortality and Morality of Nations* (New York: Cambridge University Press, 2015), 130; David Remnick, "The Outsider," *New Yorker*, May 17, 1998, https://archives.newyorker.com/newyorker/1998-05-25/flipbook/080.

5. Amos Oz, "A Look at Israel Turning 50," *Washington Post*, April 26, 1998, www.washingtonpost.com/archive/opinions/1998/04/26/a-look-atisrael-turning-50/474ce999-c897-4fa1-ac82-303b38f19b7e.

6. Leon Hadar, "American Jewish Fantasies of Israel: Coping with Cognitive Dissonance," *Washington Report on Middle East Affairs* 10, no. 3 (August/September 1991), 27.

7. Anshel Pfeffer, "'The Netanyahus' Is About So Much More than Netanyahu," *Haaretz*, November 11, 2021, www.haaretz.com/israel-news/.premium.HIGHLIGHT-an-unexpected-expose-of-what-netanyahu-really-thinks-about-u-s-jews-1.10376990; Benjamin Taylor, "Philip Roth's Last Laugh," *Paris Review*, July 2, 2020, www.theparisreview.org/blog/2020/07/02/philip-roths-last-laugh.

8. Ofira Seliktar, *Divided We Stand: American Jews, Israel, and the Peace Process* (Westport, CT: Praeger, 2002), 75.

9. Shaul Magid, "Rethinking American Jewish Zionist Identity: A Case for Post-Zionism in the Diaspora (Based on the Writings of R. Menachem Froman)," in *Beyond Jewish Identity: Rethinking Concepts and Imagining Alternatives*, ed. Jon A. Levisohn and Ari Y. Kelman (Boston: Academic Studies Press, 2019), 113–143.

10. Kenneth Stern, *The Conflict over the Conflict* (Toronto: New Jewish Press, 2020), 3–4, 11–12.

11. Hasia R. Diner, "Zion and America: The Formative Visions of Abba Hillel Silver," in *Abba Hillel Silver and American Zionism*, ed. Mark A. Raider, Jonathan D. Sarna, and Ronald W. Zweig (New York: Routledge, 1997), 48; Edward S. Schapiro, *We Are Many: Reflections on American Jewish History and Identity* (Syracuse, NY: Syracuse University Press, 2005), 172.

12. "The Father of Israel Is Dead," *Windsor Star*, December 3, 1973, https://news.google.com/newspapers?id=vlc_AAAAIBAJ&sjid=41IMAAAAIBAJ&pg=1709,731564&dq.

13. Aluf Benn, "And Then Biden Will Ask: 'Bennett, Where Did the Palestinians Disappear To?,'" *Haaretz*, August 25, 2021, www.haaretz.com/israel-news/.premium.HIGHLIGHT-and-then-biden-will-ask-bennett-where-did-the-palestinians-disappear-1.10150062.

14. Benedict Anderson, *Imagined Communities: Reflections on the Origin and Spread of Nationalism* (New York: Verso, 1983); Alain Dieckoff, "The Jewish Diaspora and Israel: Belonging at Distance?" *Nations and Nationalism* 23, no. 2 (April 2017): 271–278.

15. Response to a question at a conference of American Jewish and Israeli leaders, Sodom, Israel, December 1985; Nathan J. Robinson, "How the Media Cracks Down on Critics of Israel," *Current Affairs*, February 21, 2021, www.currentaffairs.org/2021/02/how-the-media-cracks-down-on-critics-of-israel.

16. Walter Laqueur, *A History of Zionism: From the French Revolution to the Establishment of the State of Israel* (New York: MJF Books, 1972), 61; Alan Wolfe, *At Home in Exile: Why Diaspora Is Good for the Jews* (Boston: Beacon Press, 2014), 17; A. B. Yehoshua, "The Meaning of Homeland," in *The A. B Yehoshua Controversy: An Israel-Diaspora Dialogue on Jewishness, Israeliness, and Identity*, ed. and trans. from Hebrew by Noam Marans and Roselyn Bell (New York: Dorothy and Julius Koppelman Institute on American Jewish–Israeli Relations and American Jewish Committee, 2006), 5–13.

17. David Ellenson, "Reform Zionism Today: A Consideration of First Principles (2014)," in *The Zionist Ideas: Visions for the Jewish Homeland*, ed. Gil Troy (Philadelphia: Jewish Publication Society, 2018), 438; Abigail Pogrebin, "The View from Here: What Happens When We're Told Our Judaism Isn't Judaism," in *Twenty-Five Essays About the Current State of Israeli-American Jewish Relations* (Washington, DC: American Jewish Committee, 2018), www.ajc.org/sites/default/files/pdf/2018-06/Twenty-Five%20Essays%20about%20the%20Current%20State%20of%20Israeli-American%20Jewish%20Relations.pdf.

18. Alfred Kazin, *New York Jew* (New York: Knopf, 1978), 278; Richard M. Cook, *Alfred Kazin's Journals* (New Haven, CT: Yale University Press, 2011), 421; Saul Bellow, "A Jewish Writer in America—II," *New York Review of Books*, November 10, 2011, www.nybooks.com/articles/2011/11/10/jewish-writer-america-ii.

19. Norman Podhoretz, "My Negro Problem—and Ours," *Commentary*, February 1963, 93–101; Norman Podhoretz, "The State of World Jewry," *Commentary*, December, 1983, 39; Martin Peretz, "Ha'aretz: 'Restraint Is Not Possible,'" *New Republic*, February 12, 2008, https://newrepublic.com/article/40004/haaretz-quotrestraint-not-possiblequot.

20. Michael Calderone, "David Gregory Clarifies Netanyahu 'Leader of the Jewish People' Comment," Huffington Post, September 16, 2012, www.huffpost.com /entry/david-gregory-netanyahu_n_1888329; Bennett Cohen and Jerry Greenfield, "We're Ben and Jerry. Men of Ice Cream, Men of Principle," *New York Times*, July 28, 2021, www.nytimes.com/2021/07/28/opinion/ben-and-jerry-israel.html; Anshel Pfeffer, "American Jews Aren't Soldiers in Israel's Political Wars," *Haaretz*, July 29, 2021, www.haaretz.com/israel-news/.premium.HIGHLIGHT-american-jews -aren-t-soldiers-in-israel-s-political-wars-1.10053659.

21. Jonathan Greenblatt, *It Could Happen Here: Why America Is Tipping from Hate to the Unthinkable—and How We Can Stop It* (New York: HarperCollins, 2022), 224; Eric Alterman, "Altercation: Israel Fumes at Ice Cream Company," *American Prospect*, July 23, 2021, https://prospect.org/world/altercation-israel-fumes-at-ice -cream-company; Lydia Saad, "Americans Still Favor Israel While Warming to Palestinians," Gallup, March 19, 2021, https://news.gallup.com/poll/340331 /americans-favor-israel-warming-palestinians.aspx; "Jewish Americans in 2020," Pew Research Center, May 11, 2021, www.pewresearch.org/religion/2021/05/11 /jewish-americans-in-2020; Judah Ari Gross, "US Jewish Leaders Warn of Growing Antisemitism, Say They Helped Fight Amnesty Report," *Times of Israel*, February 16, 2022, www.timesofisrael.com/us-jewish-leaders-warn-of-growing-antisemitism -say-they-helped-fight-amnesty-report.

22. J. J. Goldberg, *Jewish Power: Inside the American Jewish Establishment* (New York: Addison Wesley, 1996), 218–219; "A Portrait of Jewish Americans," Pew Research Center on Religion and Public Life, October 13, 2013, www.pewforum .org/2013/10/01/jewish-american-beliefs-attitudes-culture-survey; "Jewish Americans in 2020"; Dov S. Zakheim, "American Jewry and Israel: Tension and Prospects," in *Twenty-Five Essays*; Ben Sales, "Mega-Donors Are Taking over Jewish Philanthropy, New Study Says," Jewish Telegraphic Agency, March 26, 2018, www .jta.org/2018/03/26/united-states/mega-donors-taking-jewish-philanthropy-new -study-says.

23. "Jewish Americans in 2020"; Eric Alterman, "The Last Few Years Have Spelled a Resounding End to the 'Jewish Vote,'" *The Nation*, November 30, 2020, www.thenation.com/article/politics/american-jewish-vote. Ben Samuels, "Israel Only Western Country to Prefer Trump Over Biden, Pew Finds," *Haaretz*, June 22, 2022, https://www.haaretz.com/israel-news/2022-06-22/ty-article/.highlight /survey-most-of-the-world-prefers-biden-to-trump-but-not-israel/00000181-8ba3 -d2c2-a3a5-cbbf21fe0000.

24. Aaron David Miller, "Lost in the Woods: A Camp David Retrospective," Carnegie Endowment for International Peace, July 13, 2020, https://carnegieen dowment.org/2020/07/13/lost-in-woods-camp-david-retrospective-pub-82287.

## Chapter 1. Zionism for Thee, but Not for Me

1. *Washington Post*, May 15, 1948, A1; Amnon Cavari and Elan Nyer, "From Bipartisanship to Dysergia: Trends in Congressional Actions Toward Israel," *Israel Studies* 19, no. 3 (2014): 1–28; Michael T. Benson, *Harry S. Truman and the Founding of Israel* (Westport, CT: Praeger, 1997), 190; E. Ray Canterbery, *Harry S Truman: The Economics Of A Populist President* (Singapore: World Scientific, 2014) 17.

2. William Davidson Talmud, Sanhedrin 98a, Sefaria, www.sefaria.org/Sanhe drin.97b.14.

3. Walter Laqueur, *A History of Zionism: From the French Revolution to the Establishment of the State of Israel* (New York: MJF Books, 1972), 75–83, 211–213; Leora Halperin, *The Oldest Guard: Forging the Zionist Settler Past* (Stanford, CA: Stanford University Press, 2021).

4. Melvin L. Urofsky, *American Zionism from Herzl to the Holocaust* (Garden City, NY: Anchor/Doubleday, 1975), 23.

5. Samuel Goldman, "The Real Reason Americans Support Israel (Hint: It's Not AIPAC)," Tablet, February 15, 2019, www.tabletmag.com/jewish-news-and-poli tics/280492/the-real-reason-americans-support-israel.

6. Melvin Urofsky, *Louis D. Brandeis: A Life* (New York: Pantheon, 2009), 413.

7. Presidential Address, 8th Annual Convention of the CCAR, July 6, 1897, *Yearbook of the Central Conference of American Rabbis* 7 (1897–1898): x–xii.

8. Ira M. Sheskin and Arnold Dashefsky, "Jewish Population in the United States, 2012," in *American Jewish Year Book 2012*, ed. Arnold Dashefsky and Ira M. Sheskin (Cham, Switzerland: Springer, 2013), 143–211.

9. Quoted in Urofsky, *Brandeis*, 400.

10. Urofsky, *Brandeis*, 16, 399; Susanne Klingenstein, *Jews in the American Academy, 1900–1940* (Syracuse, NY: Syracuse University Press, 1998), 40.

11. Louis D. Brandeis, "The Jewish Problem: How to Solve It," speech, April 25, 1915, archived at Louis D. Brandeis School of Law Library, https://louisville.edu /law/library/special-collections/the-louis-d.-brandeis-collection/the-jewish-prob lem-how-to-solve-it-by-louis-d.-brandeis.

12. The letter, dated April 24, 1916, is quoted in "Anti-Semitic Letter from Ex-president Taft Up for Auction," History News Network, www.historynewsnet work.org/article/162644.

13. Urofsky, *Brandeis*, 419.

14. Shai Afsi, "The Bride Is Beautiful, but She Is Married to Another Man: Historical Fabrication and an Anti-Zionist Myth," *Shofar* 30, no. 3 (Spring 2012): 35–61; Israel Zangwill, *The Commercial Future of Palestine* (London: Greenberg, 1901), 10, 15; Benny Morris, *One State, Two States* (New Haven, CT: Yale University Press, 2009), 35–36.

15. Kai Bird, *Crossing Mandelbaum Gate: Coming of Age Between the Arabs and Israelis, 1956–1978* (New York: Scribner, 2010), 369.

16. "Balfour Declaration—Original Text, English (1917)," Israeli-Palestinian Conflict: An Interactive Database, Economic Cooperation Foundation, https://ecf.org.il /media_items/297; David Tal, *The Making of an Alliance: The Origins and Development of the US-Israel Relationship* (New York: Cambridge University Press, 2022), 29.

17. Samuel Report, 1921, United Nations Information System on the Question of Palestine, https://unispal.un.org/UNISPAL.NSF/0/349B02280A930813052565 E90048ED1C; "British White Paper of June 1922 on Palestine—English," Israeli-Palestinian Conflict: An Interactive Database, Economic Cooperation Foundation, https://ecf.org.il/media_items/439.

18. "Peel Commission Full Report (1937)," Israeli-Palestinian Conflict: An Interactive Database, Economic Cooperation Foundation, https://ecf.org.il/media _items/290; "British White Paper of 1939," Avalon Project, Yale Law School, Lillian Goldman Law Library, https://avalon.law.yale.edu/20th_century/brwh1939.asp;

John B. Judis, *Genesis: Truman, American Jews, and the Origins of the Arab/Israeli Conflict* (New York: Farrar, Straus and Giroux, 2014), 250.

## Chapter 2. The Horror

1. Melvin Urofsky, *We Are One: American Jewry and Israel* (Garden City, NY: Doubleday, 1978), 104.

2. Marc Lee Raphael, *Abba Hillel Silver: A Profile in American Judaism* (New York: Holmes and Meier, 1989), xiv.

3. David Wyman, *The Abandonment of the Jews: America and the Holocaust, 1941–1945* (New York: New Press, 1984), 20; Melissa Dinsman, *Modernism at the Microphone: Radio, Propaganda, and Literary Aesthetics During World War II* (New York: Bloomsbury, 2015).

4. Peter Grose, *Israel in the Mind of America* (New York: Knopf, 1983), 122–123.

5. Grose, *Israel in the Mind of America*, 126, 132.

6. Richard Breitman and Alan J. Lichtman, *FDR and the Jews* (Cambridge, MA: Belknap Press of Harvard University Press, 2013), 319, 209.

7. Ben Hecht, "A Champion in Chains," *Esquire*, October 1942, https://classic .esquire.com/article/1942/10/1/a-champion-in-chains.

8. Urofsky, *We Are One*, 103–104; Peter Novick, *The Holocaust in American Life* (New York: Mariner Books, 2000), 40–44.

9. Aaron Berman, *Nazism, the Jews and American Zionism* (Detroit: Wayne State University Press, 1990), 119–120.

10. Berman, *Nazism*, 183; Michael N. Barnett, *The Star and the Stripes: A History of the Foreign Policies of American Jews* (Princeton, NJ: Princeton University Press, 2016), 144–145.

11. Bruce Hoffman, *Anonymous Soldiers: The Struggle for Israel, 1917–1947* (New York: Knopf, 2015), 413.

12. Bruce J. Evensen, *Truman, Palestine, and the Press: Shaping Conventional Wisdom at the Beginning of the Cold War* (Westport, CT: Greenwood Press, 1992), 64; Milton Himmelfarb, "AJC Position on the Jewish State," December 31, 1947, memo to members of staff, Committee on Palestine, American Jewish Committee, AJC files, Wiener Library, New York.

13. Hoffman, *Anonymous Soldiers*, 13.

14. J. Samuel Dinin, "Zionist and Pro-Palestinian Activities," *American Jewish Year Book 5705: September 18, 1944 to September 7, 1945*, vol. 46, ed. Harry Schneiderman (Philadelphia: Jewish Publication Society of America, 1944), 169–186; Jack Ross, *Rabbi Outcast: Elmer Berger and American Jewish Anti-Zionism* (Washington, DC: Potomac Books, 2011), 59.

15. Grose, *Israel in the Mind of America*, 226; Susan E. Tift and Alex S. Jones, *The Trust: The Private and Powerful Family Behind* The New York Times (New York: Little, Brown, 1996), 215–219.

16. Samuel Halperin, *The Political World of American Zionism* (Detroit: Wayne State University Press, 1961), 151.

17. Monty Noam Penkower, "American Jewry and the Holocaust: From Biltmore to the American Jewish Conference," *Jewish Social Studies* 47, no. 2 (1985): 95–114.

18. Solomon Schechter, *Seminary Addresses and Other Papers* (New York: Burning Bush Press, 1959), 93, 101.

19. Israel Knox, "American Judaism: ZOA Blueprint: Are We to Be Israel's Colony Culturally?," *Commentary*, August 1948, www.commentarymagazine.com/articles/american-judaism-zoa-blueprintare-we-to-be-israels-colony-culturally.

## Chapter 3. In the Arena

1. Dennis Ross, *Doomed to Succeed: The U.S.-Israel Relationship from Truman to Obama* (New York: Farrar, Straus and Giroux, 2015), loc. 221–226, Kindle.

2. Monty Noam Penkower, "The Venting of Presidential Spleen: Harry S. Truman's Jewish Problem," *Jewish Quarterly Review* 94, no. 4 (2004): 615–624.

3. John B. Judis, *Genesis: Truman, American Jews, and the Origins of the Arab/Israeli Conflict* (New York: Farrar, Straus and Giroux, 2014), 79, 121, 249–250; Anglo-American Committee of Inquiry, *Report to the United States Government and His Majesty's Government in the United Kingdom*, Lausanne, Switzerland, April 20, 1946, at Avalon Project, Yale Law School, Lillian Goldman Law Library, https://avalon.law.yale.edu/20th_century/angch01.asp.

4. Penkower, "Venting"; Sidney Hertzberg, "This Month in History," *Commentary*, January 1946, 39; Foreign Relations of the United States, 1948, The Near East, South Asia, and Africa, vol. 5, part 2 [Focus on Israel], ed. Herbert A. Fine and Paul Claussen (Washington, DC: Government Printing Office, 1976), 593, https://history.state.gov/historicaldocuments/frus1948v05p2.

5. Tom Segev, *A State at Any Cost* (New York: Farrar, Straus and Giroux, 1999), 395; email to the author, May 8, 2021.

6. Evan Wilson, *A Calculated Risk: The U.S. Decision to Recognize Israel* (Covington, KY: Clerisy Press, 2008), 12, 28; Foreign Relations of the United States, Diplomatic Papers, 1945, The Near East and Africa, vol. 8, ed. Herbert A. Fine, Ralph R. Goodwin, John P. Glennon, Rogers P. Churchill, and Laurence Evans (Washington, DC: Government Printing Office, 1969), 751ff, https://history.state.gov/historicaldocuments/frus1945v08.

7. Thomas W. Lippman, "The View from 1947: The CIA and the Partition of Palestine," *Middle East Journal* 61, no. 1 (Winter 2007): 17–28.

8. Aaron Berman, *Nazism, the Jews and American Zionism* (Detroit: Wayne State University Press, 1990), 148, 14; "Christianity and the Holocaust," United States Holocaust Memorial Museum, www.ushmm.org/collections/bibliography/christianity-and-the-holocaust; "Population of Germany from 1800 to 2020," Statista, www.statista.com/statistics/1066918/population-germany-historical.

9. Carl Hermann Voss and David A. Rausch, "American Christians and Israel, 1948–1988," *American Jewish Archives Journal* 40, no. 1 (1988): 41–81.

10. "Testimony of Reinhold Niebuhr," *Jewish Frontier* 13, no. 2 (February 1946): 38–39.

11. David Ben-Gurion, Testimony Before the Anglo-American Committee of Inquiry, *Jewish Frontier* 13, no. 4 (April 1946): 51; Shabbatai Tebbeth, *Ben-Gurion: The Burning Ground, 1886–1948* (New York: Houghton Mifflin, 1987), 188–189; Stephen Wise, *The Personal Letters of Stephen Wise*, ed. Justine Wise Polier and James Waterman Wise (Boston: Beacon Press, 1956), 269.

12. Reinhold Niebuhr, "Jews After the War," part 2, *The Nation* 5, no. 155 (February 28, 1942): 253–255.

13. Giora Goodman, " 'Palestine's Best': The Jewish Agency's Press Relations, 1946–1947," *Israel Studies* 16, no. 3 (2011): 16; Lilly Schultz Papers, courtesy of Debra Shultz.

14. Henry Wallace, "The Conquerors of the Negev," *New Republic*, November 10, 1946, 4.

15. I. F. Stone, "Palestine Pilgrimage" (December 8, 1945), reprinted in I. F. Stone, *The Best of I. F. Stone*, ed. Karl Weber (New York: PublicAffairs, 2006), 213–218.

16. Stone, "Palestine Pilgrimage"; I. F. Stone, "Jewry in a Blind Alley," *The Nation*, November 24, 1945; I. F. Stone, "Born Under Fire," *New Republic*, May 31, 1948; I. F. Stone, *Underground to Palestine and Reflections Thirty Years Later* (London: Hutchinson, 1979 [1946]), 215–217; Susie Linfield, *The Lions' Den: Zionism and the Left from Hannah Arendt to Noam Chomsky* (New Haven, CT: Yale University Press, 2019), 239, 241.

17. Elliot E. Cohen, "An Act of Affirmation," *Commentary* 1, no. 1 (November 1945): 1–2.

18. Author's interview with Alfred Kazin, New York City, December 1993; Eric Alterman, with Kevin Mattson, *The Cause: The Fight for American Liberalism from Franklin Roosevelt to Barack Obama* (New York: Viking Press, 2012), 253.

19. Hannah Arendt, "The Jewish State: Fifty Years After," *Commentary* 1, no. 7 (May 1946): 9; Hannah Arendt, "To Save the Jewish Homeland: There Is Still Time," *Commentary* 5, no. 5 (May 1948): 400–405.

20. *Boston Globe*, February 10, 1948, 15.

21. James Reston, "Bipartisan Policy on Holy Land Seen," *New York Times*, January 27, 1948, 8, https://timesmachine.nytimes.com/timesmachine /1948/01/27/85181689.html?pageNumber=8. See also Jeffrey Gurock, ed. *American Jewish History*, vol. 8, *American Zionism: Mission and Politics* (London: Routledge, 1998), 11.

22. Kermit Roosevelt, "The Partition of Palestine: A Lesson in Pressure Politics," *Middle East Journal* 2, no. 1 (January 1948): 4–16; Daniel Rickenbacker, "The Arab League's Propaganda Campaign in the US Against the Establishment of a Jewish State (1944–1947)," *Israel Studies* 25, no. 1 (January 2020): 1–25.

23. David Tal, *The Making of an Alliance: The Origins and Development of the US-Israel Relationship* (New York: Cambridge University Press, 2022), 40; Congressional Record, February 24, 1947, www.govinfo.gov/content/pkg/GPO-CRECB -1947-pt1/pdf/GPO-CRECB-1947-pt1-36.pdf; David Schoenbaum, *The United States and the State of Israel* (New York: Oxford University Press, 1993), 29.

24. Palestinius, "Palestine's Mood After UNSCOP: The Yishuv Ponders Partition," *Commentary*, October 1947, www.commentary.org/articles/palestinius/pales tines-mood-after-unscopthe-yishuv-ponders-partition.

25. Ofer Aderet, "Why the Mysterious Swede Who Drew Up Israel's Map Favored the Jews," *Haaretz*, November 25, 2017, www.haaretz.com/israel-news /.premium-why-the-mysterious-swede-who-drew-up-israel-s-map-favored-the -jews-1.5626801.

26. H. Lowenberg, Palestinian Correspondent, "United Nations Progress Report," June 29, 1947, in AJC Archives, www.ajcarchives.org/ajcarchive/Digital Archive.aspx.

27. Monty Noam Penkower, "Juda Leib Magnes: The Last Year," *American Jewish Archives Journal* 71, no. 11 (2019): 67–113; Wilson, *Calculated Risk*, 245.

28. Harry S. Truman, *Memoirs*, vol. 2, *Years of Trial and Hope* (Garden City, NY: Doubleday, 1956), 140.

29. Michael Cohen, *Truman and Israel* (Berkeley: University of California Press, 1990), 127; Earl G. Harrison, Harrison Report, July 1945, available at Dwight D. Eisenhower Presidential Library, www.eisenhowerlibrary.gov/sites/default/files/re search/online-documents/holocaust/report-harrison.pdf.

30. Ritchie Ovendale, "The Palestine Policy of the British Labour Government, 1945–1946," *International Affairs* 55, no. 3 (1979): 409–431.

31. Michael J. Cohen, "Truman and Palestine, 1945–1948: Revisionism, Politics and Diplomacy," *Modern Judaism* 2, no. 1 (February 1982): 1–22; Judis, *Genesis*, 242.

32. Cohen, *Truman and Israel*, 83.

33. Judis, *Genesis*, 276; Tal, *Making of an Alliance*, 45.

34. Simon A. Waldman, *Anglo-American Diplomacy and the Palestinian Refugee Problem, 1948–51* (New York: Palgrave Macmillan, 2015), 36; Jeffrey Herf, "The U.S. State Department's Opposition to Zionist Aspirations During the Early Cold War: George F. Kennan and George C. Marshall in 1947–1948," *Journal of Cold War Studies* 23, no. 4 (Fall 2021): 153–180.

35. Bruce J. Evensen, *Truman, Palestine, and the Press: Shaping Conventional Wisdom at the Beginning of the Cold War* (Westport, CT: Greenwood Press, 1992), 113, 135; "Red 'Fifth Column' for Palestine Feared as Ships Near Holy Land," *New York Times*, January 1, 1948, 1.

36. "Memorandum by the President's Special Counsel (Clifford) to President Truman," March 8, 1948, Foreign Relations of the United States, 1948, The Near East, South Asia, and Africa, vol. 5, part 2, Clifford Papers, 605, https://history .state.gov/historicaldocuments/frus1948v05p2/d79.

37. "Memorandum by the President's Special Counsel (Clifford) to President Truman."

38. David Holly, *Exodus 1947* (Annapolis, MD: Naval Institute Press, 1995); Evensen, *Truman, Palestine, and the Press*, 130.

39. "Draft Memorandum by the Director of the Office of United Nations Affairs (Rusk) to the Under Secretary of State (Lovett)," drafted by David McClintock, May 4, 1948 (not sent), Foreign Relations of the United States, 1948, The Near East, South Asia, and Africa, vol. 5, part 2, 501.BB Palestine/5–448, https://his tory.state.gov/historicaldocuments/frus1948v05p2/d210; Frank E. Manuel, *The Realities of American-Palestine Relations* (Washington, DC: Public Affairs Press, 1949), 133; Evensen, *Truman, Palestine, and the Press*, 52.

40. Melvin Urofsky, *We Are One: American Jewry and Israel* (Garden City, NY: Doubleday, 1978), 169.

41. "Statement Made by the United States Representative at the United Nations [Warren] (Austin) Before the Security Council on February [24] 1948," Foreign Relations of the United States, 1948, The Near East, South Asia, and Africa, vol. 5, part 2, https://history.state.gov/historicaldocuments/frus1948v05p2/d57; Zev Ganin, "The Limits of American Jewish Political Power: America's Retreat from Partition, November 1947–March 1948," *Jewish Social Studies* 39, nos. 1/2 (Winter–Spring 1977): 1–36.

42. Department of State Bulletin, March 7, 1948, 296; Penkower, "Juda Leib Magnes."

43. "The Switch on Palestine," *New York Times*, March 21, 1948, 111; Bruce J. Evenson, "A Story of 'Ineptness': The Truman Administration's Struggle to Shape Conventional Wisdom on Palestine at the Beginning of the Cold War," *Diplomatic History* 15, no. 3 (July 1991): 339–359.

44. George M. Elsey, Michael T. Benson, Abba Eban, and Raymond H. Geselbracht, *Harry S. Truman and the Recognition of Israel* (Independence, MO: Harry S. Truman Library, 1998), 18.

45. Clark Clifford, with Richard Holbrooke, *Counsel to the President: A Memoir* (New York: Random House, 1991), 1.

46. Clifford, *Counsel*, 1.

47. Michael Ottolenghi, "Harry Truman's Recognition of Israel," *Historical Journal* 47, no. 4 (2004): 963–988.

48. Clifford, *Counsel*, 10–12.

49. Judis, *Genesis*, 315–318.

## Chapter 4. Jew vs. Jew

1. Quoted in Michelle Mart, *Eye on Israel: How Americans Came to View Israel as an Ally* (Albany: State University of New York Press, 2006), 56, 23; "Israel at the Poles," *Washington Post*, August 1, 1951, 26; "Israel's Tenth," *New York Times*, April 24, 1958; Congressional Record, cited in Bat-Ami Zucker, "The Genesis of the Special Relationship Between the United States and Israel, 1948–1973," *American Jewish Archives Journal* 44, no. 2 (1992), https://sites.americanjewisharchives .org/publications/journal/PDF/1992_44_02_00_zucker.pdf.

2. Michelle Mart, "Eleanor Roosevelt, Liberalism, and Israel," *Shofar* 24, no. 3 (Spring 2006): 58–89; Peter Grose, *Israel in the Mind of America* (New York: Knopf, 1983), 314.

3. See "Babylonian Talmud, Tractate Kethuboth," Folio 110a, in Kethuboth, trans. Samuel Daiches and Israel W. Slotki, ed. I. Epstein, https://halakhah.com /kethuboth/kethuboth_110.html.

4. Theodore Sasson, "Mass Mobilization to Direct Engagement: American Jews' Changing Relationship to Israel," *Israel Studies* 15, no. 2 (2010): 176; Jonathan Sarna, "A Projection of America as It Ought to Be: Zion in the Mind's Eye of American Jews," in *Envisioning Israel: The Changing Images and Ideals of North American Jews*, ed. Allon Gal (Jerusalem: Magnes Press; Detroit: Wayne State University Press, 1996), 41–42.

5. Lawrence Grossman, "Transformation Through Crisis: The American Jewish Committee and the Six-Day War," *American Jewish History* 86, no. 1 (1998): 27–54. Glazer is quoted in Charles Silberman, *A Certain People: American Jews and Their Lives Today* (New York: Summit Books, 1985), 204.

6. Matthew Berkman, "Antisemitism, Anti-Zionism, and the American Racial Order: Revisiting the American Council for Judaism in the Twenty-First Century," *American Jewish History* 105, no. 1/2 (January/April 2021): 139; Marianne Sanua, *Let Us Prove Strong: The American Jewish Committee, 1945–2006* (Waltham, MA: Brandeis University Press, 2007), 24.

7. Mordecai Kaplan, "Needed: A New Zionism," *The Reconstructionist* 20, no. 9 (1954): 11.

8. Zvi Ganin, *An Uneasy Relationship: American Jewish Leadership and Israel, 1948–1957* (Syracuse, NY: Syracuse University Press, 2005).

9. A. D. Gordon, "Some Observations" (1911), in *The Zionist Idea: A Historical Analysis and Reader*, ed. Arthur Hertzberg (Philadelphia: Jewish Publication Society, 1997), 277.

10. Matthew Berkman, "Coercive Consensus: Jewish Federations, Ethnic Representation, and the Roots of American Pro-Israel Politics" (PhD diss., University of Pennsylvania, 2018), 208–211; Ganin, *Uneasy Relationship*, 36.

11. For the full text of the agreement, see "David Ben-Gurion: American Jews and the Diaspora—The Ben-Gurion Blaustein Agreement," August 23, 1950, Zionism: Zionism and Israel Information Center, https://zionism-israel.com/hdoc/Ben-Gurion-Blaustein_Zionism_Diaspora.htm.

12. Milton Himmelfarb, "Observations on the Impact of Israel on American Jewish Ideologies," *Jewish Social Studies* 21, no. 1, Papers and Proceedings of the Joint Conference on the Impact of Israel on the American Jewish Community (January 1959): 83–84; Natan Aridan, *Advocating for Israel: Diplomats and Lobbyists from Truman to Nixon* (New York: Lexington Books, 2019), 205; Zeev Sternhell, *The Founding Myths of Israel: Nationalism, Socialism, and the Making of the Jewish State*, trans. David Maisel (Princeton, NJ: Princeton University Press, 1998), 47.

13. Jack Wertheimer, "American Jews and Israel: A 60-Year Retrospective," in *American Jewish Year Book 2008*, vol. 108, ed. David Singer and Lawrence Grossman (New York: American Jewish Committee, 2008), 12.

14. Ganin, *Uneasy Relationship*, 102. See also *Israel Studies* 25, no. 3 (Fall 2020): 1–80, with several articles on the topic, and Arthur Hertzberg, "American Zionism at an Impasse," *Commentary* 8 (October 1949): 341–345.

15. Ganin, *Uneasy Relationship*, 157.

## Chapter 5. Standing Up and Standing Down

1. Walter L. Hixson, *Israel's Armor: The Israel Lobby and the First Generation of the Palestine Conflict* (New York: Cambridge University Press, 2019), 77.

2. Fouad Ajami, *The Dream Palace of the Arabs: A Generation's Odyssey* (New York: Pantheon, 1998), xvi.

3. Khaled Elgindy, *Blind Spot: America and the Palestinians from Balfour to Trump* (Washington, DC: Brookings Institution Press, 2019), 51, 57.

4. Yfaat Weiss, *A Confiscated Memory: Wadi Salib and Haifa's Lost Heritage* (New York: Columbia University Press, 2011), 37.

5. Adam Shatz, "We Are Conquerors," *London Review of Books* 41, no. 20 (October 29, 2019): 37–42; Michael R. Fischbach, *Records of Dispossession: Palestinian Refugee Property and the Arab Israeli Conflict* (New York: Columbia University Press, 2003), 58–68; "How Israel Legalized Theft," *Haaretz*, March 18, 2022, www.haaretz.com/opinion/editorial/.premium-how-israel-legalized-theft-1.10682279; Peter Beinart, "Teshuvah: A Jewish Case for Palestinian Refugee Return," *Jewish Currents*, May 11, 2021, https://jewishcurrents.org/teshuvah-a-jewish-case-for-palestinian-refugee-return.

6. Avi Shlaim, "The Debate About 1948," *International Journal of Middle East Studies* 27, no. 3 (1995): 287–304.

7. The 750,000 figure corresponds to a 1950 estimate from the United Nations Relief and Work Agency for Palestine Refugees in the Near East (UNRWA). See "Palestine Refugees," UNRWA, www.unrwa.org/palestine-refugees, accessed May

28, 2022; Benny Morris, "On Ethnic Cleansing," *New Left Review* 26 (March/April 2004), https://newleftreview.org/issues/II26/articles/benny-morris-on-ethnic-cleansing; "Migration of Eretz Yisrael Arabs Between December 1, 1947, and June 1948," June 30, 1948, from Hashomer Hatzair (Yad Yaari) Archive, file 95-35.27(3), trans. Akevot Institute for Israeli-Palestinian Conflict Research, archived at *Haaretz*, www.haaretz.co.il/st/inter/Heng/1948.pdf; Tom Segev, "'A State at Any Cost: The Life of David Ben-Gurion,' with Tom Segev," speech to Center for Israel Studies, American University, October 15, 2019, Center for Israel Studies, American University, posted by AUCollege, November 14, 2019, YouTube, www.youtube.com/watch?v=G_nVaFVRm4M.

8. Shlaim, "The Debate About 1948"; Avi Shlaim, "Husni Zaim and the Plan to Resettle Palestinian Refugees in Syria," *Journal of Palestine Studies* 15, no. 4 (Summer 1986): 26–31; Avi Shlaim, "The Two-State Solution—Illusion and Reality," *Palestine-Israel Journal* 26, no. 3–4 (2021), www.pij.org/articles/2144/the-twostate-solution—illusion-and-reality; Mordechai Bar-On, *Gates of Gaza: Israel's Road to Suez and Back, 1955–57* (New York: Palgrave Macmillan, 1995), 89.

9. Irene Gendzier, "US Policy in Israel/Palestine, 1948: The Forgotten History," *Middle East Policy* 18, no. 11 (Spring 2011): 42–53; Hixson, *Israel's Armor*, 68; Natan Aridan, *Advocating for Israel: Diplomats and Lobbyists from Truman to Nixon* (New York: Lexington Books, 2019), 63.

10. Andrew Lapin, "Explosive New Israeli Documentary 'Tantura' Is Prompting Calls to Excavate a Possible Palestinian Mass Grave," Jewish Telegraphic Agency, January 25, 2022, www.jta.org/2022/01/25/culture/tantura-an-explosive-new-israeli-documentary-is-prompting-calls-to-excavate-a-possible-palestinian-mass-grave.

11. Gershom Gorenberg, "The War to Begin All Wars," *New York Review of Books* 56, no. 9 (May 28, 2009), www.nybooks.com/articles/2009/05/28/the-war-to-begin-all-wars; Shlaim, "The Debate About 1948"; Walid Khalidi, "Why Did the Palestinians Leave, Revisited," *Journal of Palestine Studies* 34, no. 2 (Winter 2005): 42–54; Benny Morris, *1948: A History of the First Arab-Israeli War* (New Haven, CT: Yale University Press, 2008); Benny Morris, *The Birth of the Palestinian Refugee Problem, 1947–1949* (Cambridge: Cambridge University Press, 1988); Benny Morris, "The New Historiography: Israel Confronts Its Past," in *Making Israel*, ed. Benny Morris (Ann Arbor: University of Michigan Press, 2007), 11–29; Ofer Aderet, "State Archive Error Shows Israeli Censorship Guided by Concerns over National Image," *Haaretz*, January 5, 2022, www.haaretz.com/israel-news/.premium.MAGAZINE-state-archive-error-shows-israeli-censorship-guided-by-concerns-over-national-image-1.10517841; Ofer Aderet, "'Unpleasant' War Crimes: The Secret Docs Israel Insists on Censoring," *Haaretz*, October 18, 2021, www.haaretz.com/israel-news/.premium.HIGHLIGHT.MAGAZINE-war-crimes-and-unpleasantness-israel-s-censorship-list-1.10301458.

12. "Israel and the Arab Refugees," *Hearings Before the Committee on Foreign Affairs, House of Representatives*, 82nd Cong., 1st sess., June 1951 (Washington, DC: US Government Printing Office, 1951), 1498.

13. Hixson, *Israel's Armor*, 68, 77.

14. Matthew Berkman, "Coercive Consensus: Jewish Federations, Ethnic Representation, and the Roots of American Pro-Israel Politics" (PhD diss., University of Pennsylvania, 2018), 242.

15. David Tal, *The Making of an Alliance: The Origins and Development of the US-Israel Relationship* (New York: Cambridge University Press, 2022), 75–76; Isaac Alteras, "Eisenhower, American Jewry, and Israel," *American Jewish Archives Journal* 4, no. 4 (1986): 72–89; Herbert F. Weisberg, "Reconsidering Jewish Presidential Voting Statistics," *Contemporary Jewry* 32, no. 3 (2012): 215–236; J. J. Goldberg, *Jewish Power: Inside the American Jewish Establishment* (Reading, MA: Addison-Wesley, 1996), 155.

16. Aridan, *Advocating*, 67, 124; David Shoenbaum, *The United States and the State of Israel* (New York: Oxford University Press, 1993), 95.

17. Uri Bialer, *Israeli Foreign Policy: A People Shall Not Dwell Alone* (Blooming-ton: University of Indiana Press, 2020), 61.

18. Benny Morris, "The Israeli Press and the Qibya Operation, 1953," *Journal of Palestine Studies* 25, no. 4 (1996): 40–52.

19. David A. Nichols, *Eisenhower 1956: The President's Year of Crisis—Suez and the Brink of War* (New York: Simon and Schuster, 2011), 220.

20. Ray Takeyh and Steven Simon, *The Pragmatic Superpower: Winning the Cold War in the Middle East* (New York: W. W. Norton, 2016), 119.

21. Alteras, "Eisenhower, American Jewry and Israel"; Naomi W. Cohen, *Not Free to Desist: The American Jewish Committee, 1906–1966* (Philadelphia: Jewish Publication Society of America, 1972), 323–324; Lawrence Grossman, "Transfor-mation Through Crisis: The American Jewish Committee and the Six-Day War," *American Jewish History* 86, no. 1 (1998): 27–54.

22. Philip A. Walker Jr., "Lyndon B. Johnson's Senate Foreign Policy Activism: The Suez Canal Crisis, a Reappraisal," *Presidential Studies Quarterly* 26, no. 4 (Fall 1996): 996–1008.

23. Donald Neff, *Fallen Pillars: U.S. Policy Towards Palestine and Israel Since 1945* (Washington, DC: Institute for Palestine Studies, 1995), 99; Alteras, "Eisen-hower, American Jewry and Israel"; Geoffrey Phillip Levin, "Another Nation: Israel, American Jews, and Palestinian Rights, 1948–1977" (PhD diss., New York Univer-sity, 2019), 13–14.

24. "President Eisenhower Radio Address on the Situation in the Middle East," February 20, 1957, Jewish Virtual Library, www.jewishvirtuallibrary.org/jsource /History/ikewarn1.html; Aridan, *Advocating*, 139; David Ben-Gurion, *Israel: A Per-sonal History* (New York: Funk and Wagnalls, 1971), 509; Dwight D. Eisenhower, *The White House Years*, vol. 2, *Waging Peace, 1956–1961* (New York: Doubleday, 1965), 74.

25. George W. Ball, "The Coming Crisis in Israeli-American Relations," *Foreign Affairs*, Winter 1979/80, www.foreignaffairs.com/articles/israel/1979-12-01/com ing-crisis-israeli-american-relations; "Memorandum of a Telephone Conversation Between the Israeli Ambassador (Eban) and the Secretary of State, Washington, March 3, 1957, 10:25 p.m.," Foreign Relations of the United States, 1955–1957, Arab-Israeli Dispute, 1957, vol. 17, https://history.state.gov/historicaldocuments /frus1955-57v17/d187; Lila Corwin Berman, *The American Jewish Philanthropic Complex* (Princeton, NJ: Princeton University Press, 2020), 93–96; Alteras, "Eisen-hower, American Jewry and Israel."

## Chapter 6. A New "Bible"

1. Bradley Burston, "The 'Exodus' Effect: The Monumentally Fictional Israel That Remade American Jewry," *Haaretz*, November 9, 2012, www.haaretz.com /the-exodus-effect-of-leon-uris-on-u-s-jewry-1.5197397; M. M. Silver, *Our Exodus: Leon Uris and the Americanization of Israel's Founding Story* (Detroit: Wayne State University Press, 2010), 89.

2. Silver, *Our Exodus*, 84–86; "Uris, Leon," *Encyclopedia Judaica*, vol. 16 (Jerusalem: Encyclopedia Judaica, 1971), 10.

3. Frances G. Couvares, *Movie Censorship and American Culture* (Amherst: University of Massachusetts Press, 1996), 152; Nora Sayre, *Running Time: Films of the Cold War* (New York: Dial, 1982), 18.

4. Tony Shaw and Giora Goodman, *Hollywood and Israel: A History* (New York: Columbia University Press, 2022), loc. 645, Kindle.

5. Edward S. Shapiro, *A Time for Healing: American Jewry Since World War II* (Baltimore: Johns Hopkins University Press, 1995), 20; Gary Fishgall, *Gregory Peck: A Biography* (New York: Scribner's, 2002), 124.

6. Michelle Mart, *Eye on Israel: How Americans Came to View Israel as an Ally* (Albany: State University of New York Press, 2006), 25–28. *The Juggler* is occasionally shown on TCM. For a synopsis and other film details, see TCM, www.tcm.com /tcmdb/title/27793/the-juggler#overview. I saw it on January 14, 2020, and viewed *Sword in the Desert* on TCM on January 26, 2021. For information on *Sword*, see TCM, www.tcm.com/tcmdb/title/92168/sword-in-the-desert#overview.

7. Silver, *Our Exodus*, 92; Shaw and Goodman, *Hollywood and Israel*, loc. 2498, 2530.

8. Burston, "'Exodus' Effect"; Stephen J. Whitfield, "Value Added: Jews in Postwar American Culture," in *American Jewish History*, vol. 4, *American Jewish Life, 1920–1990*, ed. Jeffrey Gurock (New York: Routledge, 1997), 77; Norman Mirsky, "Nathan Glazer's American Judaism After 30 Years: A Reform Opinion," *American Jewish History* 77 (December 1987): 237; Amy Kaplan, *Our American Israel* (Cambridge, MA: Harvard University Press, 2019), loc. 1739, Kindle; Dov Waxman, *Trouble in the Tribe: The American Jewish Conflict over Israel* (Princeton, NJ: Princeton University Press, 2016), 29.

9. Shaul Mitelpunkt, *Israel in the American Mind: The Cultural Politics of US-Israeli Relations, 1958–1988* (New York: Cambridge University Press, 2018), loc. 35–39, Kindle; Shaw and Goodman, *Hollywood and Israel*, loc. 1752.

10. Silver, *Our Exodus*, 170–171; Natan Aridan, *Advocating for Israel: Diplomats and Lobbyists from Truman to Nixon* (New York: Lexington Books, 2019), 184; Kaplan, *Our American Israel*, loc. 1739; Patricia Erens, *The Jew in American Cinema* (Bloomington: University of Indiana Press, 1985), 217, 219; Rachel Weissbrod, "*Exodus* as a Zionist Melodrama," *Israel Studies* 4, no. 1 (1999): 129–152; Mitelpunkt, *Israel in the American Mind*, loc. 76.

11. Jeremy Salt, "Facts and Fiction in the Middle Eastern Novels of Leon Uris," *Journal of Palestinian Studies* 14, no. 3 (Spring 1985): 54–63; Ruth Gruber, *Exodus 1947: The Ship That Launched a Nation* (New York: Union Square Press, 1999); David Holly, *Exodus, 1947* (Annapolis, MD: Naval Institute Press, 1995).

12. Idith Zertal, *From Catastrophe to Power: The Holocaust Survivors and the Emergence of Israel* (Berkeley: University of California Press, 1998), 32–43.

13. Henry Gonshak, "Tough Jews, Schlemiels, and 'Shickses': Leon Uris' Exodus," *Response* 69 (1999): 100–117; Shaw and Goodman, *Hollywood and Israel*, loc. 1624.

14. Amy Weiss, "1948's Forgotten Soldiers? The Shifting Reception of American Volunteers in Israel's War of Independence," *Israel Studies* 25, no. 1 (January 2020): 149–172; Silver, *Our Exodus*, 66–72.

15. Weissbrod, "*Exodus* as a Zionist Melodrama."

16. Dan Wakefield, "Israel's Need for Fiction," *The Nation*, April 11, 1959, 318–319; Claudia Roth Pierpont, *Roth Unbound: A Writer and His Works* (New York: Farrar, Straus and Giroux, 2013), 13–14; Silver, *Our Exodus*, 117–120.

17. Silver, *Our Exodus*, 202–204; Shaw and Goodman, *Hollywood and Israel*, loc. 1721; "Israeli Leader to Talk on Novel and Film 'Exodus,'" *Los Angeles Times*, January 2, 1961, B30.

18. Kaplan, *Our American Israel*, loc. 1417, 1524, 1547; Silver, *Our Exodus*, 44.

19. Shaw and Goodman, *Hollywood and Israel*, loc. 1880, 1900; Lawrence Davidson, *America's Palestine: Popular and Official Perceptions from Balfour to Israeli Statehood* (Gainesville: University of Florida Press, 2001), 215.

20. Silver, *Our Exodus*, 170–171.

21. "Exodus," *Monthly Film Bulletin* 28, no. 329 (June 1961): 75; Silver, *Our Exodus*, 209; "We Must Not Be Lulled by Peace Talk—Dayan," *Jerusalem Post*, May 2, 1956, 1.

22. Benny Morris, "Beyond the Gates of Gaza," *Jerusalem Post*, June 30, 1989, A11.

23. Oscar Handlin, "Ethics and Eichmann," *Commentary*, August 1960, www.commentary.org/articles/oscar-handlin/ethics-eichmann; Eric Alterman, "Happy Birthday, 'National Review'! Too Bad You Haven't Grown Any Wiser with Age," *The Nation*, December 3, 2015, www.thenation.com/article/archive/happy-birthday-national-review-too-bad-you-havent-grown-any-wiser-with-age.

24. Lucy S. Dawidowicz, "United States, Israel and the Middle East," *American Jewish Year Book 1961*, vol. 62, ed. Morris Fine and Milton Himmelfarb (Philadelphia: Jewish Publication Society of America, 1961), 193.

25. Martin Kramer, "The Truth of the Capture of Adolf Eichmann," Mosaic, June 1, 2020, https://mosaicmagazine.com/essay/history-ideas/2020/06/the-truth-of-the-capture-of-adolf-eichmann.

26. Burston, "'Exodus' Effect"; Aviva Halmish, "Exodus, the Movie—Half a Century Later," *Jewish Film and New Media* 5, no. 2 (Fall 2017): 123–142; Judy Maltz, "The Last Relic of the Exodus, and Its Incredible Journey to Israel," *Haaretz*, January 6, 2022, www.haaretz.com/israel-news/2022-01-06/ty-article-magazine/.highlight/the-last-relic-of-the-exodus-and-its-incredible-journey-to-israel/0000017f-edb6-ddba-a37f-effe050d0000.

27. Shaul Magid, "Feelings and the Israel/Palestine Conflict," Tablet, June 3, 2021, www.tabletmag.com/sections/community/articles/feelings-and-israel-palestine-conflict; Kenneth Bob, Facebook, November 23, 2020.

28. Burston, "'Exodus' Effect"; John F. Kerry, *Every Day Is Extra* (New York: Simon and Schuster, 2018), 444.

## Chapter 7. Six Days That Shook the World

1. Walter L. Hixson, *Israel's Armor: The Israel Lobby and the First Generation of the Palestine Conflict* (New York: Cambridge University Press, 2019), 128; Dan Kurzman, *Ben-Gurion: Prophet of Fire* (New York: Simon and Schuster, 1983), https://religiondocbox.com/Judaism/65549105-Ben-gurion-prophet-of-fire.html.

2. Amos Elon, "A Very Special Relationship," *New York Review of Books*, January 15, 2004, www.nybooks.com/articles/2004/01/15/a-very-special-relationship.

3. Avner Cohen, *The Worst Kept Secret: Israel and the Bomb* (New York: Columbia University Press, 2010), 70; Khaled Elgindy, *Blind Spot: America and the Palestinians from Balfour to Trump* (Washington, DC: Brookings Institution Press, 2019), 69.

4. Moshe Shemesh, "The IDF Raid on Samu': The Turning-Point in Jordan's Relations with Israel and the Palestinians," *Israel Studies* 7, no. 1 (2002): 139–166; Clea Lutz Bunch, "Strike at Samu: Jordan, Israel, the United States, and the Origins of the Six-Day War," *Diplomatic History* 32, no. 1 (2008): 55–76; Tom Segev, *1967: Israel, the War, and the Year That Transformed the Middle East* (New York: Metropolitan Books, 2005), 149.

5. Y. Harkabi, *Arab Attitudes to Israel* (Jerusalem: Keter Publishing House, 1972), 277.

6. Rashid Khalidi, *The Hundred Years War on Palestine: A History of Settler Colonialism and Resistance, 1917–2017* (New York: Metropolitan Books, 2019), 103.

7. Gilbert Achcar, *The Arabs and the Holocaust: The Arab-Israeli War of Narratives* (New York: Henry Holt, 2009), 215.

8. Richard B. Parker, ed., *The Six-Day War: A Retrospective* (Gainesville: University of Florida Press, 1996), 204; "Memorandum from the Joint Chiefs of Staff to Secretary of Defense McNamara," August 25, 1967, Foreign Relations of the United States, 1964–1968, vol. 19, Arab-Israeli Crisis and War, 1967, ed. Harriet Dashiell Schwartz (Washington, DC: Government Printing Office, 2004), https://history.state.gov/historicaldocuments/frus1964-68v19/d427; Michael R. Fischbach, *The Movement and the Middle East* (Stanford, CA: Stanford University Press, 2019), loc. 59–60. See also William Quandt, *Peace Process: American Diplomacy and the Arab-Israeli Conflict Since 1967* (Washington, DC: Brookings Institution, 1993), 510–512.

9. Michael Oren, *Six Days of War* (New York: Oxford University Press, 2002), 59–60; Bunch, "Strike at Samu."

10. Shlomo Ben-Ami, *Scars of War: Wounds of Peace: The Israeli-Arab Tragedy* (New York: Oxford University Press, 2006), 100; Abba Eban, *Personal Witness: Israel Through My Eyes* (New York: G. P. Putnam's Sons, 1992), 382–383; Roland Popp, "Stumbling Decidedly into the Six-Day War," *Middle East Journal* 60, no. 2 (Spring 2006): 281–309; David Remnick, "The Seventh Day: Why the Six-Day War Is Still Being Fought," *New Yorker*, May 28, 2007, www.newyorker.com/magazine/2007/05/28/the-seventh-day.

11. Anthony Weiss, "Long Suppressed, 'Censored Voices' Speaks Out About Six-Day War," Jewish Telegraphic Agency, February 1, 2015, www.jta.org/2015/02/01/culture/long-suppressed-censored-voices-speaks-out-about-six-day-war.

12. Shaul Mitelpunkt, *Israel in the American Mind: The Cultural Politics of US-Israeli Relations, 1958–1988* (New York: Cambridge University Press, 2018), loc.

132, Kindle; Bill Mauldin, "Not a Litterbug Among Them, Those Israeli Troops," *New Republic*, June 24, 1967, 6; "Israel's Swift Victory," *Life*, Special Edition, June 23, 1967; *Lightning out of Israel: The Six-Day War in the Middle East* (New York: Associated Press, 1967); Amy Kaplan, *Our American Israel* (Cambridge, MA: Harvard University Press, 2019), loc. 1941, Kindle.

13. Edward S. Shapiro, *A Time for Healing: American Jewry Since World War II* (Baltimore: Johns Hopkins University Press, 1992), 207–208; A. J. Heschel, *Israel: An Echo of Eternity* (New York: Farrar, Straus and Giroux, 1969), 195–199; Arthur Hertzberg, "Israel and American Jewry," *Commentary*, August 1967, www.commentary.org/articles/arthur-hertzberg/israel-and-american-jewry.

14. Howard M. Sachar, *A History of the Jews in America* (New York: Knopf, 1992), 736; Menahem Kaufman, "The Case of the United Jewish Appeal," in *Envisioning Israel: The Changing Ideals and Images of North American Jews*, ed. Allon Gal (Jerusalem: Magnes Press; Detroit: Wayne State University Press, 1996), 232; Shapiro, *Time for Healing*, 210–211; Tony Shaw and Giora Goodman, *Hollywood and Israel: A History* (New York: Columbia University Press, 2022), loc. 2400, Kindle.

15. Henry Roth, "Kaddish," *Midstream*, January 1977, 54–55.

16. Joshua Muravchik, *Making David into Goliath* (New York: Encounter Books, 2014), 12; Gabriel Piterberg, "Zion's Rebel Daughter," *New Left Review* 48 (November/December 2007), https://newleftreview.org/issues/II48/articles/gabriel-piterberg-zion-s-rebel-daughter; Susie Linfield, *The Lion's Den: Zionism and the Left from Hannah Arendt to Noam Chomsky* (New Haven, CT: Yale University Press, 2019), 78.

17. Milton Himmelfarb, "In Light of Israel's Victory," *Commentary*, October 1967, 59; Benjamin Balint, *Running Commentary: The Contentious Magazine That Transformed the Jewish Left into the Neoconservative Right* (New York: PublicAffairs, 2010), 110; Irving Howe, *A Margin of Hope: An Intellectual's Autobiography* (San Diego: Harcourt, Brace, Jovanovich, 1982), 251, 286; Maurice Isserman, "Steady Work: Sixty Years of Dissent," *Dissent*, January 23, 2015, www.dissentmagazine.org/online_articles/steady-work-sixty-years-of-dissent.

18. Shaul Magid, "Re-Thinking American Jewish Zionist Identity: A Case for Post-Zionism in the Diaspora (Based on the Writings of R. Menachem Froman)," in *Beyond Jewish Identity: Rethinking Concepts and Imagining Alternatives*, ed. Jon A. Levisohn and Ari Y. Kelman (Boston: Academic Studies Press, 2019), 113–143; Arthur Hertzberg, "Some Reflections on Zionism Today," *Congress Monthly* 44, no. 3 (March/April 1977): 3–7.

19. Lawrence Grossman, "Transformation Through Crisis: The American Jewish Committee and the Six-Day War," *American Jewish History* 86, no. 1 (1998): 27–54; Matthew Berkman, "Coercive Consensus: Jewish Federations, Ethnic Representation, and the Roots of American Pro-Israel Politics" (PhD diss., University of Pennsylvania, 2018), 281.

20. Bat-Ami Zucker, "The Genesis of the Special Relationship Between the United States and Israel, 1948–1973," *American Jewish Archives Journal* 44, no. 2 (1992).

21. Grossman, "Transformation Through Crisis"; Emet Ve-Emunah, *Statement of Principles of Conservative Judaism*, 2nd ed. (New York: United Synagogue Book Service, 1988), 37, 38; "Reform Judaism: A Centenary Perspective," Central

Conference of American Rabbis, 1976, www.ccarnet.org/rabbinic-voice/platforms /article-reform-judaism-centenary-perspective; Jack Wertheimer, "American Jews and Israel: A 60-Year Retrospective," *American Jewish Year Book 2008*, vol. 108, ed. David Singer and Lawrence Grossman (New York: American Jewish Committee, 2008): 3–79; David Ellenson, "Envisioning Israel in the Liturgies of North American Liberal Judaism," and Chaim I. Waxman, "The Changing Religious Relationship: American Jewish Baby Boomers and Israel," in Gal, *Envisioning Israel*.

22. Peter Novick, *The Holocaust in American Life* (New York: Houghton Mifflin, 1990), 148–149; Marc Ellis, *Beyond Innocence and Redemption: Confronting the Holocaust and Israeli Power* (San Francisco: Harper and Row, 1990); Emil L. Fackenheim, *To Mend the World: Foundations of Post-Holocaust Jewish Thought* (Bloomington: Indiana University Press, 1994), 14.

23. Arnold Jacob Wolf, "Overemphasizing the Holocaust," in *Unfinished Rabbi: Selected Writings of Arnold Jacob Wolf*, ed. Jonathan Wolf (Chicago: Ivan R. Dee, 1998); Novick, *Holocaust in American Life*, 10.

24. Ruth R. Wisse, "Israel and the Intellectuals: A Failure of Nerve?," *Commentary*, May 1988, www.commentarymagazine.com/articles/israel-the-intellectuals -a-failure-of-nerve; Melanie Kaye/Kantrowitz, "Stayed on Freedom: Jews in the Civil Rights Movement and After," in *Cornerstones of Peace: Jewish Identity, Politics and Democratic Theory* (New Brunswick, NJ: Rutgers University Press, 1996), 104–122.

25. Arnold M. Eisen, "Israel at 50: An American Jewish Perspective," *American Jewish Year Book 1998*, vol. 98, ed. David Singer and Ruth R. Seldin (New York: American Jewish Committee, 1998), 47–71; A. Diana Forster, Ira M. Sheskin, and Kenneth D. Wald, "The Political Consequences of Trauma: Holocaust Exposure and Emotional Attachment to Israel Among American Jews," *Contemporary Jewry* 40 (May 2020): 209–236; Nina Glick Schiller, "Long-Distance Nationalism," in *Encyclopedia of Diasporas: Immigrant and Refugee Cultures Around the World*, vol. 1, *Overviews and Topics*, ed. Melvin Ember, Carol R. Ember, and Ian Skoggard (New York: Kluwer Academic / Plenum Publishers, 2005), 570; "Jewish Americans in 2020," Pew Research Center, May 11, 2021, 20, www.pewresearch.org/religion/2021/05/11/jewish-americans-in-2020.

26. Lucy Dawidowicz, "American Public Opinion," in *American Jewish Year Book 1968*, vol. 69, ed. Morris Fine and Milton Himmelfarb (New York: American Jewish Committee; Philadelphia: Jewish Publication Society of America, 1968), 205; Michael E. Staub, *Torn at the Roots: The Crisis of Jewish Liberalism in Postwar America* (New York: Columbia University Press, 2012), 128; Marshall Sklare, "Lakeville and Israel: The Six-Day War and Its Aftermath," *Midstream* 18, no. 8 (1968): 10–11; David Tal, *The Making of an Alliance: The Origins and Development of the US-Israel Relationship* (New York: Cambridge University Press, 2022), 143, 167.

27. Thomas Friedman, *From Beirut to Jerusalem* (New York: Farrar, Straus and Giroux, 1989), 454–455; Saul Friedlander, *Where Memory Leads: My Life* (New York: Other Press, 2016), 148.

28. Neve Gordon, *Israel's Occupation* (Berkeley: University of California Press, 2008), 1; Nathan Thrall, "A Day in the Life of Abed Salama," *New York Review of Books*, March 19, 2021, www.nybooks.com/daily/2021/03/19/a-day-in-the -life-of-abed-salama; Jorgen Jensehaugen, "Terra Morata: The West Bank in

Menachem Begin's Worldview," *Contemporary Levant* 5, no. 1 (2020): 54–63; "Crime of Apartheid: The Government of Israel's System of Oppression Against Palestinians," Amnesty International, February 1, 2022, www.amnestyusa.org /endapartheid, 16

29. Raja Shehadeh, "State of Exception," *The Nation*, July 1, 2019, www.then ation.com/article/noura-erakat-justice-for-some-book-review; Gershom Gorenberg, *The Accidental Empire: Israel and the Birth of the Settlements, 1967–1977* (New York: Times Books, 2007), 100.

30. Aviezer Ravitsky, *Messianism, Zionism and Jewish Religious Radicalism* (Chicago: University of Chicago Press, 1996), esp. 110–116, 118–129, 144; Yehuda Gershoni, "The Torah of Israel and the State," *Tradition: A Journal of Orthodox Jewish Thought* 12, no. 34 (Winter/Spring 1972): 25–34.

31. Eliyahu Avihayil, *Le-or ha-shahar* (Jerusalem, 1982), 107, 118–119, as cited in Ravitsky, *Messianism, Zionism*, 128; Richard L. Hoch, "Sovereignty, Sanctity, and Salvation: The Theology of Rabbi Tzvi Yehuda ha-Kohen Kook and the Actions of Gush Emunim," *Shofar* 13, no. 1 (1994): 90–118.

32. Walter L. Hixson, *Israel's Armor: The Israel Lobby and the First Generation of the Palestine Conflict* (New York: Cambridge University Press, 2019), 169; Adam Raz, "Israel Claimed Its 1967 Land Conquests Weren't Planned. Declassified Documents Reveal Otherwise," *Haaretz*, June 3, 2021, www.haaretz.com/israel-news /.premium.HIGHLIGHT-israel-said-67-land-conquests-weren-t-planned-declassi fied-documents-say-otherwise-1.9873297; Associated Press, "West Bank Settlement Population Surged During the Trump Era, Report Says," *Times of Israel*, January 27, 2021, www.timesofisrael.com/west-bank-settler-population-surged-during -trump-era-report-says; Ofer Aderet, "Archives Reveal What Israeli Left-Wing Leaders Truly Thought on Early Settlement Efforts," *Haaretz*, January 5, 2022, www.haaretz.com/israel-news/.premium.HIGHLIGHT-archives-reveal-left-wing -leaders-rabin-and-peres-true-policy-on-early-settlements-1.10514049; Michael Sfard, "Yes, It's Israeli Apartheid. Even Without Annexation," *Haaretz*, September 7, 2020, www.haaretz.com/israel-news/.premium-yes-it-s-israeli-apartheid-even -without-annexation-1.8984029.

33. Shaiel Ben-Ephraim, "Distraction and Deception: Israeli Settlements, Vietnam, and the Johnson Administration," *Diplomatic History* 42, no. 3 (June 2018): 456–483; Hixson, *Israel's Armor*, 149; Lyndon B. Johnson, *The Vantage Point: Perspectives of the Presidency, 1963–1969* (New York: Holt, Reinhart and Winston, 1972), 297.

34. Tevi Troy, "How the GOP Went Zionist," *Commentary*, December 2015, www.commentarymagazine.com/articles/gop-went-zionist; "Why the South Must Prevail," *National Review*, August 25, 1957, reproduced at Adam Gómez, Wordpress, https://adamgomez.files.wordpress.com/2012/03/whythesouthmustpre vail-1957.pdf; "U.S. Presidential Elections: Jewish Voting Record," Jewish Virtual Library, www.jewishvirtuallibrary.org/jsource/US-Israel/jewvote.html.

35. Barney Ross, "Show of Shows Nets $80,000 for War Fund," *New York Times*, March 14, 1944, 15.

36. Pamela Pennock, *The Rise of the Arab American Left: Activists, Allies, and Their Fight Against Imperialism and Racism, 1960s–1980s* (Chapel Hill: University of North Carolina Press, 2017), 254; Geoffrey Levin, "American Jewish Insecurities and the End of Pro-Arab American Politics in Mainstream America, 1952–1973,"

*Arab Studies Journal* 25, no. 1 (Spring 2017): 30–58; Michael Kramer, "Blacks and Jews," *New York Magazine*, February 4, 1985, https://nymag.com/news/features/49091.

37. *The Militant*, February 1969, quoted in Arnold Foster and Benjamin R. Epstein, *The New Anti-Semitism* (New York: McGraw-Hill, 1974), 137, 51.

38. Leo Huberman, "Israel Is Not the Main Enemy," *Monthly Review* 19, no. 5 (October 1967): 8–9.

39. James Ridgeway, "Freak-Out in Chicago," *New Republic*, September 16, 1967, 9–12; "Letter from the Palmer House," *New Yorker*, September 23, 1967, 56–88.

40. I. F. Stone, "Holy War," *New York Review of Books*, August 3, 1967, www.nybooks.com/articles/1967/08/03/holy-war. See also Robert Alter, "Israel and the Intellectuals," *Commentary*, October 1967, 46–52.

41. Martin Peretz, "The American Left and Israel," *Commentary*, November 1967, www.commentarymagazine.com/articles/the-american-left-israel; Alter, "Israel and the Intellectuals."

42. "Benny Morris: I Haven't Found Evidence of Arab Radio Broadcast Asking Palestinians to Flee in 1948," Oslo, September 27, 2014, posted by Med Israel for fred, October 6, 2014, YouTube, www.youtube.com/watch?v=eNwTk2lpBtU; Walid Khalidi, "Why Did the Palestinians Leave, Revisited," *Journal of Palestine Studies* 34, no. 2 (Winter 2005): 42–54.

43. I. F. Stone, "Gangsters or Patriots?," *The Nation*, January 12, 1946; Michael Walzer and Martin Peretz, "Israel Is Not Vietnam," *Ramparts*, July 1967, www.unz.com/print/Ramparts-1967jul-00011.

44. Henry P. Van Dusen, "'Silence' of Church Leaders on Mideast," letter to the editor, *New York Times*, July 7, 1967, 32, https://timesmachine.nytimes.com/timesmachine/1967/07/07/90367283.html?pageNumber=28; Joshua Michael Zeitz, "'If I Am Not for Myself...': The American Jewish Establishment in the Aftermath of the Six-Day War," *American Jewish History* 88, no. 2 (June 2000): 253–286; Samuel Goldman, *God's Country: Christian Zionism in America* (Philadelphia: University of Pennsylvania Press, 2018), 14; Naomi W. Cohen, *American Jews and the Zionist Idea* (Hoboken, NJ: KTAV Publishing, 1975), 137.

45. Hixson, *Israel's Armor*, 188–195, 209; Natan Aridan, *Advocating for Israel: Diplomats and Lobbyists from Truman to Nixon* (New York: Lexington Books, 2019), 237; Edward Tivnan, *The Lobby: Jewish Political Power and American Foreign Policy* (New York: Simon and Schuster, 1987), 67.

46. Michael Wyschogrod, "The Jewish Interest in Vietnam," *Tradition: A Journal of Orthodox Jewish Thought* 8, no. 4 (1966): 5–18.

47. Glen Frankel, *Beyond the Promised Land: Jews and Arabs on a Hard Road to a New Israel* (New York: Simon and Schuster, 1994), 222; Tivnan, *The Lobby*, 119; Edward Giock, *The Triangular Connection: America, Israel, and American Jews* (Boston: George Allen and Unwin, 1982), 97.

48. Amos Oz, "Four Cups for the Seder Against the Occupation," letter to the editor, *Davar*, August 22, 1967, online at Proquest, www.proquest.com/openview/f13e182a4f836f335d6ba87ae61dd994/1?pq-origsite=gscholar&cbl=26627; Yeshayahu Leibowitz, *Judaism, Human Values, and the Jewish State* (Cambridge, MA: Harvard University Press, 1992), 226.

49. Alain Finkielkraut, *The Imaginary Jew* (Lincoln: University of Nebraska Press, 1994), 132; Benedict Anderson, *Imagined Communities: Reflections on the Origin and Spread of Nationalism* (New York: Verso, 1983).

## Chapter 8. A Jew (and an Antisemite) for All Seasons

1. Robert Dallek, *Nixon and Kissinger: Partners in Power* (New York: HarperCollins, 2006), 93, 206, 250, 434; Debbie Lord, "Billy Graham–Richard Nixon Tapes: The One Time Graham's Image Was Tarnished," *Atlanta Journal-Constitution*, February 21, 2018, www.ajc.com/news/national/billy-graham-richard-nixon-tapes-the-one-time-graham-image-was-tarnished/DCj06gfORZJLYa30cLawWL; Stephen J. Whitfield, "Nixon and the Jews," *Patterns of Prejudice* 44, no. 5 (2010): 432–453.

2. Walter Isaacson, *Kissinger, A Biography* (New York: Simon and Schuster, 1992), 893; Gil Rabak, "A Jew for All Seasons: Henry Kissinger, Jewish Expectations, and the Yom Kippur War," *Israel Studies Forum* 25, no. 2 (2010): 1–25.

3. Eric Alterman, *Lying in State: Why Presidents Lie and Why Trump Is Worse* (New York: Basic Books, 2020), 121; Isaacson, *Kissinger*, 560; Seymour Hersh, *The Price of Power: Kissinger in the Nixon White House* (New York: Simon and Schuster, 1983), 84.

4. Alterman, *Lying in State*, 121.

5. Rabak, "A Jew for All Seasons"; Jeremi Suri, *Henry Kissinger and the American Century* (Cambridge, MA: Harvard University Press, 2007), 250–252; Hersh, *Price of Power*, 322–323.

6. Foreign Relations of the United States, 1969–1976, vol. 23, Arab-Israeli Dispute, 1969–1972, ed. Steven Galpern (Washington, DC: Government Printing Office, 2015), 338.

7. Richard Nixon, *RN: The Memoirs of Richard Nixon* (New York: Grosset and Dunlop, 1978), 66.

8. Dallek, *Nixon and Kissinger*, 410–411; Lewis Coser and Irving Howe, eds., *The New Conservatives: A Critique from the Left* (New York: Quadrangle, 1974), 78; Eugene Borowitz, "The Heavy, Unrelenting Pressure the Israelis Have Put on U.S. Jewry to Vote for Nixon Is Thoroughly Demeaning," *New York Times*, October 9, 1972, 31; Melvin Urofsky, *We Are One: American Jewry and Israel* (Garden City, NY: Doubleday, 1978), 389; Kenneth Kolander, "Phantom Peace: Henry 'Scoop' Jackson, J. William Fulbright, and Military Sales to Israel," *Diplomatic History* 41, no. 3 (June 2017): 567–593.

9. "McGovern Backs Goals of Israel," *New York Times*, June 23, 1967.

10. Nathan Glazer, "Revolutionism and the Jews: 3—The Role of the Intellectual," *Commentary*, February 1971, www.commentarymagazine.com/articles/revolutionism-the-jews3-the-role-of-the-intellectual.

11. Joseph Kraft, "Those Arabists in the State Department," *New York Times Magazine*, November 7, 1971, 38; Hersh, *Price of Power*, 135, 290; Salim Yaqub, *Containing Arab Nationalism: The Eisenhower Doctrine and the Middle East* (Chapel Hill: University of North Carolina Press, 2004).

12. Boaz Vanetik and Zaki Shalom, "The White House Middle East Policy in 1973 as a Catalyst for the Outbreak of the Yom Kippur War," *Israel Studies* 16, no. 1 (Spring 2011): 53–78.

13. Kolander, "Phantom Peace."

14. Kolander, "Phantom Peace."

15. Ziv Rubinovitz, "Blue and White 'Black September': Israel's Role in the Jordan Crisis of 1970," *International History Review* 32, no. 4 (2010): 687–706.

16. Bruce Riedel, "Fifty Years After Black September in Jordan," *Studies in Intelligence* 64, no. 2 (June 2020), Central Intelligence Agency, www.cia.gov/static /a0e9e907ebef070b8d13a714867f1e5b/Black-September-Jordan.pdf.

17. Melani McAlister, *Epic Encounters: Culture, Media, and U.S. Interests in the Middle East Since 1945* (Berkeley: University of California Press, 2005), 180.

18. Bruce Riedel, "Enigma: The Anatomy of Israel's Intelligence Failure Almost 45 Years Ago," Brookings Institution, September 15, 2017, www.brookings.edu /research/enigma-the-anatomy-of-israels-intelligence-failure-almost-45-years-ago.

19. Rami Rom, Amir Gilat, and Rose Mary Sheldon, "The Yom Kippur War, Dr. Kissinger, and the Smoking Gun," *International Journal of Intelligence and Counter-Intelligence* 31, no. 2 (2018): 357–373; Salim Yaqub, "The Nixon Administration's Policy Towards the Arab Israeli Conflict from 1969 to 1973," in *The Cold War in the Middle East, 1967–73*, ed. Nigel J. Ashton (New York: Routledge, 2008), 35–58.

20. Avner Cohen, "When Israel Stepped Back from the Brink," *New York Times*, October 13, 2013, www.nytimes.com/2013/10/04/opinion/when-israel-stepped -back-from-the-brink.html; Ribak, "A Jew for All Seasons."

21. Arnon Gutfeld and Boaz Vanetik, "'A Situation That Had to Be Manipulated': The American Airlift to Israel During the Yom Kippur War," *Middle Eastern Studies* 52, no. 3 (2016): 419–447; William Quandt, *Peace Process: American Diplomacy and the Arab–Israeli Conflict Since 1967*, 3rd ed. (Berkeley: University of California Press, 2005), 123–124; Galen Jackson and Mark Trachtenberg. "A Self-Inflicted Wound? Henry Kissinger and the Ending of the October 1973 Arab-Israeli War," *Diplomacy and Statecraft* 32, no. 3 (2021): 554–578; "189. Memorandum of Conversation," Subject: Meeting with Jewish Leaders (Philip Klutznik Group), New York, June 15, 1975, 12:15–2:35 p.m., Foreign Relations of the United States, 1969–1976, vol. 26, Arab-Israeli Dispute, 1974–1976, https://history.state .gov/historicaldocuments/frus1969-76v26/d189.

22. Hersh, *Price of Power*, 135; Ribak, "A Jew for All Seasons."

23. Salim Yaqub, *Imperfect Strangers: Americans, Arabs, and U.S.–Middle East Relations in the 1970s* (Ithaca, NY: Cornell University Press, 2016), 113; Gil Troy, *Moynihan's Moment: America's Fight Against Zionism as Racism* (New York: Oxford University Press, 2013), 36.

24. Matthew Berkman, "Coercive Consensus: Jewish Federations, Ethnic Representation, and the Roots of American Pro-Israel Politics" (PhD diss., University of Pennsylvania, 2018), 287.

25. Troy, *Moynihan's Moment*, 36; Ribak, "A Jew for All Seasons."

26. Zaki Shalom, "Kissinger and the American Jewish Leadership After the 1973 War," *Israel Studies* 7, no. 1 (2002): 195–217.

27. "189. Memorandum of Conversation."

28. Rabak, "A Jew for All Seasons," 18.

29. Arlene Lazarowitz, "American Jewish Leaders and President Gerald R. Ford: Disagreements over the Middle East Reassessment Plan," *American Jewish History* 98, no. 3 (2014): 175–200; George W. Ball, "The Coming Crisis in Israeli-American Relations," *Foreign Affairs* (Winter 1979/1980), www.foreignaffairs.com/articles

/israel/1979-12-01/coming-crisis-israeli-american-relations; David Tal, *The Making of an Alliance: The Origins and Development of the US-Israel Relationship* (New York: Cambridge University Press, 2022), 199–200.

30. Natan Aridan, *Advocating for Israel: Diplomats and Lobbyists from Truman to Nixon* (New York: Lexington Books, 2019), 284.

31. Ball, "Coming Crisis"; Martin Indyk, *Master of the Game: Henry Kissinger and the Art of Middle East Diplomacy* (New York: Knopf, 2021); Isaac Chotiner, "The Lessons of Henry Kissinger's Diplomacy," *New Yorker*, November 29, 2021, www .newyorker.com/news/q-and-a/the-lessons-of-henry-kissingers-diplomacy; Jackson and Trachtenberg, "A Self-Inflicted Wound?"

32. "Memorandum of Agreement Between the Governments of Israel and the United States," September 1, 1975, Foreign Relations of the United States, 1969–1976, vol. 26, Arab-Israeli Dispute, 1974–1976, https://history.state.gov/historical documents/frus1969-76v26/d227 diplomacy.

### Chapter 9. "Zionism Is (Not) Racism"

1. Associated Press, "Haldeman Diary Shows Nixon Was Wary of Blacks and Jews," *New York Times*, May 18, 1994, A19; Tim Naftali, "Ronald Reagan's Long-Hidden Racist Conversation with Richard Nixon," *Atlantic*, July 30, 2019, www .theatlantic.com/ideas/archive/2019/07/ronald-reagans-racist-conversation-richard -nixon/595102.

2. Michael Brenner, *In Search of Israel: The History of an Idea* (Princeton, NJ: Princeton University Press, 2018), 154.

3. Sasha Polakow-Suransky, *The Unspoken Alliance: Israel's Secret Relationship with Apartheid South Africa* (New York: Pantheon, 2010).

4. Asaf Siniver, *Abba Eban: A Biography* (New York: Overlook, 2016), 252–253.

5. "Policy Paper Prepared in the Department of State," March 15, 1949, 501.MA Palestine/3-1749, Annex 2 in "Memorandum by the Coordinator on Palestine Refugee Matters (McGhee) to the Under Secretary of State (Webb)," March 15, 1949, 501.BB Palestine/3-1549, Foreign Relations of the United States, 1949, The Near East, South Asia, and Africa, vol. 6, https://history.state.gov/historicaldocuments /frus1949v06/d533.

6. Mouin Rabbani, "Reflections on a Lifetime of Engagement with Zionism, the Palestine Question, and American Empire: An Interview with Noam Chomsky," *Journal of Palestine Studies* 41, no. 3 (Spring 2012): 92–120.

7. These and all subsequent quotes from the speech are drawn from "Yasser Arafat's 1974 UN General Assembly speech," Wikisource, https://en.wikisource.org /wiki/Yasser_Arafat's_1974_UN_General_Assembly_speech.

8. The dispute over the figures in question is covered in Hussein Ibish, "A 'Catastrophe' That Defines Palestinian Identity," *Atlantic*, May 14, 2018, www.the atlantic.com/international/archive/2018/05/the-meaning-of-nakba-israel-palestine -1948-gaza/560294.

9. Edward Said, "Zionism from the Standpoint of Its Victims," *Social Text* 1 (Winter 1979): 7–58; "The Palestinian National Charter: Resolutions of the Palestine National Council, July 1–17, 1968," Avalon Project, Yale Law School, Lillian Goldman Law Library, https://avalon.law.yale.edu/20th_century/plocov.asp.

10. See, for instance, Sammy Smooha, *Arabs and Jews in Israel*, 2 vols. (New York: Routledge, 1992).

11. Paul Hofmann, "Dramatic Session," *New York Times*, November 14, 1974, A1; Paul Hofmann, "Arafat's Message," *New York Times*, November 15, 1974; "The Olive Branch and the Gun," *The Nation*, November 20, 1974.

12. Gil Troy, "When Feminists Were Zionists," Tablet, March 8, 2013, www .tabletmag.com/jewish-arts-and-culture/books/126348/when-feminists-were-zionists.

13. Noam Chomsky, *The Fateful Triangle: The United States, Israel and the Palestinians* (Boston: South End Press, 1983), 184; Said, "Zionism from the Standpoint of Its Victims."

14. Eric Alterman, "Moynihan Rules," *New York Magazine*, May 2, 1994, 43–50.

15. Tom Buckley, "Brawler at the UN," *New York Times Magazine*, December 7, 1975, www.nytimes.com/1975/12/07/archives/brawler-at-the-un-pat-moynihan -the-kid-from-hells-kitchen-has-a.html.

16. Gil Troy, *Moynihan's Moment: America's Fight Against Zionism as Racism* (New York: Oxford University Press, 2013), 133, 154.

17. Troy, *Moynihan's Moment*, 125, 154–155; Buckley, "Brawler at the UN."

18. *People*, December 29, 1975–January 5, 1974, 27; Eric Sevareid, "Commentary," *CBS Evening News with Walter Cronkite*, January 13, 1976.

19. Russell Baker, "Dangerous Case of English," *New York Times*, January 31, 1976, 20; Patrick Andelic, "Daniel Patrick Moynihan, the 1976 New York Senate Race and the Struggle to Define American Liberalism," *Historical Journal* 57, no. 4 (2014): 1111–1133.

20. Jonthan Soffer, *Ed Koch and the Rebuilding of New York City* (New York: Columbia University Press, 2010), 99.

21. Leandra Ruth Zarnow, *Battling Bella: The Protest Politics of Bella Abzug* (Cambridge, MA: Harvard University Press, 2018), 244–245.

22. Paul Good, "The Mask of Liberalism," *Nation* 221, no. 21 (December 20, 1975): 654; Frances Fitzgerald, "The Warrior Intellectuals," *Harper's*, May 1976, 58.

23. Godfrey Hodgson, *The Gentleman from New York: Daniel Patrick Moynihan: A Biography* (Boston: Houghton Mifflin, 2000), 271; Andelic, "Daniel Patrick Moynihan."

## Chapter 10. A Separate Peace

1. Jimmy Carter, *The Blood of Abraham: Insights into the Middle East* (Fayetteville: University of Arkansas Press, 2007), 29.

2. Arlene Lazarowitz, "Ethnic Influence and American Foreign Policy: American Jewish Leaders and President Jimmy Carter," *Shofar* 29, no. 1 (Fall 2010): 112–136; John Ehrman, *The Rise of Neoconservatism* (New Haven, CT: Yale University Press, 1995), 123.

3. "Memorandum from the President's Assistant (Jordan) to President Carter," June 1977, Foreign Relations of the United States, Arab-Israeli Dispute, vol. 8, January–July 1977, ed. Adam M. Howard (Washington, DC: Government Printing Office, 2013), 283.

4. Carter, *Blood of Abraham*, 21; "Toward Peace in the Middle East," in *Journal of Palestine Studies* 6, no. 2 (Winter 1977): 195–205; Seth Anziska, *Preventing*

*Palestine: A Political History from Camp David to Oslo* (Princeton, NJ: Princeton University Press, 2018), 22–23.

5. Lazarowitz, "Ethnic Influence."

6. Zbigniew Brzezinski, *Power and Principle: Memoirs of the National Security Adviser, 1977–1981* (New York: Farrar, Straus, and Giroux, 1983), 97; "Clinton, Massachusetts, Remarks and a Question-and-Answer Session at the Clinton Town Meeting," March 16, 1977, American Presidency Project, University of California, Santa Barbara, www.presidency.ucsb.edu/documents/clinton-massachusetts-re marks-and-question-and-answer-session-the-clinton-town-meeting.

7. Saunders to House Foreign Affairs Subcommittee on the Middle East, November 12, 1975, Mideast Web, www.mideastweb.org/saunders.htm; Jerold S. Auerbach, "Are We One? Menachem Begin and the Long Shadow of 1977," in *Envisioning Israel: The Changing Images and Ideals of North American Jews*, ed. Allon Gal (Jerusalem: Magnes Press; Detroit: Wayne State University Press, 1996), 335–351.

8. Auerbach, "Are We One?"; Shlomo Avineri, "Ideology and Israel's Foreign Policy," *Jerusalem Quarterly* 37 (1986): 3–13.

9. Avi Shlaim, "The Iron Wall Revisited," *Journal of Palestine Studies* 41, no. 2 (2012): 276; Mark Tessler, "The Political Right in Israel: Its Origins, Growth, and Prospects," *Journal of Palestine Studies* 15, no. 2 (1986): 12–55; Anziska, *Preventing Palestine*, 213; Isaiah 62:1.

10. Daniel Strieff, "The President and the Peacemaker: Jimmy Carter and the Domestic Politics of Arab-Israeli Diplomacy, 1977–1980" (PhD diss., London School of Economics, 2013), 62.

11. Jeremy Pressman, "Explaining the Carter Administration's Israeli-Palestinian Solution," *Diplomatic History* 37, no. 5 (2013): 1117–1147; Joshua Muravchik, *Making David into Goliath* (New York: Encounter Books, 2014), 128.

12. Brzezinski, *Power and Principle*, 95–96; Strieff, "The President and the Peacemaker," 80–81; Arthur Samuelson, "The Dilemma of American Jewry," *The Nation*, April 1, 1978, 368.

13. Phillip Ben, "We'll Fight Against Carter," *Maariv*, June 13, 1977, 1; "Joint US-Soviet Statement of the Middle East," October 1, 1977, Center for Israel Education, https://israeled.org/resources/documents/joint-u-s-soviet-statement-middle -east.

14. "Carter's Blunder," *Near East Report*, October 5, 977; AIPAC, quoted in Darren J. McDonald, "Blessed Are the Policy Makers: Jimmy Carter's Faith-Based Approach to the Arab–Israeli Conflict," *Diplomatic History* 39, no. 1 (2015): 470; Edward W. Said, "Palestinians," 1977, in *The Politics of Dispossession: The Struggle for Palestinian Self-Determination, 1969–1994* (London: Vintage, 1994), 30–32.

15. "Interview with Jody Powell," December 17–18, 1981, transcript, Miller Center, University of Virginia, http://web1.millercenter.org/poh/transcripts/ohp_1981 _1217_powell.pdf; Arlene Lazarowitz, "Ethnic Influence"; Anziska, *Preventing Palestine*, 90; Ehrman, *Neoconservatism*, 125.

16. Strieff, "The President and the Peacemaker," 159–164.

17. Lawrence Wright, *Thirteen Days in September: Carter, Begin, and Sadat at Camp David* (New York: Knopf, 2014), 42.

18. Wright, *Thirteen Days*, 264–265; Kai Bird, *The Outlier: The Unfinished Presidency of Jimmy Carter* (New York: Crown, 2021), 283–284; "Carter the Tenacious,"

*Washington Star*, November 1, 1978; Robert G. Kaiser, "After the Summit, a Wave of Bipartisan Euphoria for Carter," *Washington Post*, September 19, 1978, A1; "Anwar Sadat, Man of the Year," *Time*, January 2, 1978; George Gallup, *The Gallup Poll: Public Opinion 1978* (Lanham, MD: Rowan and Littlefield, 1979), 1.

19. William B. Quandt, "Personal Notes on the Camp David Summit, 5–17 September 1978," Peace Research Institute, Oslo. See, especially, September 15, 1978, available at Prio, www.prio.org/utility/DownloadFile.ashx?id=1816&type=publica tionfile.

20. Anziska, *Preventing Palestine*, 182–183.

21. Khaled Elgin, *Blind Spot: America and the Palestinians from Balfour to Trump* (Washington, DC: Brookings Institution Press, 2019), 102. Said also described his trip privately to the author during a 1992 luncheon on the Stanford University campus.

22. Jonathan Alter, *His Very Best: Jimmy Carter, a Life* (New York: Simon and Schuster, 2020), 388; William Safire, "Carter Blames the Jews," *New York Times*, December 18, 1978; Strieff, "The President and the Peacemaker," 211; Lazarowitz, "Ethnic Influence."

23. Michael E. Staub, *Torn at the Roots: The Crisis of Jewish Liberalism in Postwar America* (New York: Columbia University Press, 2012), 281.

24. Arnold Jacob Wolf, "Will Israel Become Zion?," in *The Zionist Ideas: Visions for the Jewish Homeland*, ed. Gil Troy (Philadelphia: Jewish Publication Society, 2018), 316–317.

25. Jack Wertheimer, "Breaking the Taboo: Critics of Israel and the American Jewish Establishment," in Gal, *Envisioning Israel*, 399–408.

26. Marjorie Hyer, "US Jews Beginning to Go Public in Criticism of Israel," *Washington Post*, May 3, 1976, A2; "Israel's Dilemma," *New York Times*, May 11, 1976, 32.

27. J. J. Goldberg, *Jewish Power: Inside the American Jewish Establishment* (Reading, MA: Addison-Wesley, 1996), 207.

28. Bernard Gwertzman, "American Jewish Leaders Are Split over Issue of Meeting with P.L.O.," *New York Times*, December 30, 1976, 45; Rael Jean Isaac, *Breira: Counsel for Judaism* (New York: Americans for a Safe Israel, 1977).

29. Carl Gershman, "Between War and Peace: The Issues in the Middle East Conflict," *Crossroads* 2, no. 6 (June 1971); Michael R. Fischbach, *The Movement and the Middle East* (Stanford, CA: Stanford University Press, 2019), 70–75; Joseph Shattan, "Why Breira?," *Commentary*, April 1977, 60–65; Max Ticktin Oral History, American Jewish Peace Archive, http://ajpeacearchive.org/peace-pioneers1 /max-ticktin.

30. Bird, *Outlier*, 464.

31. Bird, *Outlier*, 463–465; Michael R. Fischbach, *Black Power and Palestine: Transnational Countries of Color* (Stanford, CA: Stanford University Press, 2009), 188.

32. Bird, *Outlier*, 469.

33. Bird, *Outlier*, 472, 490.

34. Michael Stevens, "A Lesson from Martin Luther King," *Jerusalem Post*, May 1, 2013, www.jpost.com/opinion/op-ed-contributors/a-lesson-from-martin-luther -king-311732; Jonathan Rieder, *The Word of the Lord Is upon Me: The Righteous*

*Performance of Martin Luther King, Jr.* (Cambridge, MA: Harvard University Press, 2010).

35. Matthew Berkman, "Coercive Consensus: Jewish Federations, Ethnic Representation, and the Roots of American Pro-Israel Politics" (PhD diss., University of Pennsylvania, 2018); Arnold Forster and Benjamin R. Epstein, *The New Anti-Semitism* (New York: McGraw Hill, 2018 [1974]).

36. Fischbach, *Black Power*, 189–192.

37. John Herbers, "Aftermath of the Andrew Young Affair: Blacks, Jews and Carter All Could Suffer Greatly," *New York Times*, September 6, 1979, A18; Edward Cowan, "President Asserts Jewish Leaders Did Not Pressure Him to Dismiss Young," *New York Times*, September 24, 1979, A15.

38. Carl Gershman, "The Andrew Young Affair," *Commentary*, November 1979, www.commentarymagazine.com/articles/carl-gershman-2/the-andrew-young-affair; Fischbach, *Black Power*, 184.

39. Fischbach, *Black Power*, 193–210.

40. Rick Atkinson, "Jackson Denounces 'Hounding' from Jewish Community," *Washington Post*, February 22, 1984.

41. "Remarks of President Jimmy Carter to Community and Civic Leaders," New York, March 11, 1980, Jimmy Carter Presidential Library and Museum, www .jimmycarterlibrary.gov/digital_library/sso/148878/153/SSO_148878_153_09.pdf; Edgar M. Bronfman, "On Israel, Cut Out the Abuse," *New York Times*, March 22, 1980, 21; Hamilton Jordan, *Crisis: The Last Year of the Carter Presidency* (New York: G. P. Putnam's Sons, 1982), 234.

42. Daniel Patrick Moynihan, "Joining the Jackals," *Commentary*, February 1981, www.commentarymagazine.com/articles/joining-the-jackalsrdquo.

## Chapter 11. Alliance for Armageddon

1. Sidney Blumenthal, *The Rise of the Counter Establishment: The Conservative Ascent to Political Power* (New York: Union Square Press, 2008), 124; Susanne Klingenstein, " 'It's Splendid When the Town Whore Gets Religion and Joins the Church': The Rise of the Jewish Neoconservatives as Observed by the Paleoconservatives in the 1980s," *Shofar* 21, no. 3 (2003): 83–98; Jacob Heilbrunn, *They Knew They Were Right: The Rise of the Neocons* (New York: Doubleday, 2008), 115.

2. Peter Steinfels, *The Neoconservatives: The Men Who Are Changing America's Politics* (New York: Simon and Schuster, 1979), 47–48; Justin Vaisse, *Neoconservatism: The Biography of a Movement* (Cambridge, MA: Belknap Press of Harvard University Press, 2010), 73–84; Benjamin Balint, *Running Commentary: The Contentious Magazine That Transformed the Jewish Left into the Neoconservative Right* (New York: PublicAffairs, 2010); Yuri Slezkine, *The Jewish Century* (Princeton, NJ: Princeton University Press, 2004), 349; Michael R. Fischbach, "The New Left and the Arab-Israeli Conflict in the United States," *Journal of Palestine Studies* 49, no. 3 (Spring 2020), www.palestine-studies.org/en/node/1650341; Mordecai S. Chertoff, ed., *The New Left and the Jews* (New York: Pitman, 1971).

3. Eric Alterman, with Kevin Mattson, *The Cause: The Fight for American Liberalism from Franklin Roosevelt to Barack Obama* (New York: Viking Press, 2012), 258.

4. John Ehrman, *The Rise of Neoconservatism* (New Haven, CT: Yale University Press, 1995), 125.

5. Dan Raviv and Yossi Melman, *Friends in Deed: Inside the US-Israel Alliance* (New York: Hyperion, 1994), 228.

6. Raviv and Melman, *Friends in Deed*, 228; Antonio Gramsci, "The Intellectuals," in *Selections from the Prison Notebooks of Antonio Gramsci*, ed. and trans. Quintin Hoare and Geoffrey Nowell Smith (New York: International Publishers, 1971); Alfred Kazin, "Saving My Soul at the Plaza," *New York Review of Books*, March 31, 1983, www.nybooks.com/articles/1983/03/31/saving-my-soul-at-the-plaza.

7. Russell Kirk, "The Neoconservatives: An Endangered Species," Heritage Foundation, December 15, 1988, www.heritage.org/political-process/report/the-neocon servatives-endangered-species.

8. Corwin Smidt, "Evangelicals and the 1984 Election: Continuity or Change?," *American Politics Quarterly* 15, no. 4 (October 1987): 419–444.

9. Samuel Goldman, *God's Country: Christian Zionism in America* (Philadelphia: University of Pennsylvania Press, 2018), 7.

10. Ray Walters, "Paperback Talk," *New York Times*, April 6, 1980, T7; Hal Lindsey, with Carole C. Carlson, *The Late Great Planet Earth* (Grand Rapids, MI: Zondervan, 1970), 43–44, 17; Colin Shindler, "Likud and the Christian Dispensationalists: A Symbiotic Relationship," *Israel Studies* 5, no. 1 (Spring 2000): 153–182.

11. Tim LaHaye, *The Coming Peace in the Middle East* (Grand Rapids, MI: Zondervan, 1984), 167.

12. Daniel K. Williams, *God's Own Party: The Making of the Christian Right* (New York: Oxford University Press, 2010), 194, 171; Jerry Falwell, *Armageddon and the Coming War with Russia* (n.p.: Jerry Falwell, 1980); Stephen Spector, *Evangelicals and Israel: The Story of American Christian Zionism* (New York: Oxford University Press, 2009), 27; John Herbers, "Armageddon View Prompts a Debate," *New York Times*, October 24, 1984 (quoting Falwell interview with Robert Scheer, *Los Angeles Times*, March 4, 1981), www.nytimes.com/1984/10/24/us/armageddon -view-prompts-a-debate.html.

13. Daniel K. Williams, "Jerry Falwell's Sunbelt Politics: The Regional Origins of the Moral Majority," *Journal of Policy History* 22 (April 2010): 133.

14. Ronald R. Stockton, "Christian Zionism: Prophecy and Public Opinion," *Middle East Journal* 41, no. 2 (Spring 1987): 234–253; David K. Shipler, "1,000 Christian 'Zionists' in Jerusalem," *New York Times*, September 25, 1980, in Goldman, *God's Country*, 167; Melani McAlister, *Epic Encounters: Culture, Media, and U.S. Interests in the Middle East Since 1945* (Berkeley: University of California Press, 2005), 103–105.

15. William Claiborne, "Israelis Look on U.S. Evangelical Christians as Potent Allies in Battle with Arab States," *Washington Post*, March 23, 1981, www .washingtonpost.com/archive/politics/1981/03/23/israelis-look-on-us-evangelical -christians-as-potent-allies-in-battle-with-arab-states/5259c395-4bb7-43dc-a289 -e6a0a0b1511c.

16. *Roanoke Times and World News*, September 14, 1979, B-1; "Falwell Antichrist Remark Sparks Anti-Semitism Charges," *J.*, January 22, 1999, www.jweekly .com/1999/01/22/falwell-antichrist-remark-sparks-anti-semitism-charges.

17. Irving Kristol, "The Political Dilemmas of American Jews," *Commentary*, July 1984, www.commentary.org/articles/irving-kristol/the-political-dilemma

-of-american-jews, and "Why Religion Is Good for the Jews," *Commentary*, August 1994, www.commentary.org/articles/irving-kristol/why-religion-is-good-for-the-jews, both reprinted in Irving Kristol, *The Neoconservative Persuasion: Selected Essays, 1942–2009* (New York: Basic Books, 2011), 259–271, 286–291.

18. Author's interview with Arthur Hertzberg at his home in Connecticut, Summer 1992.

19. Norman Podhoretz, "In the Matter of Pat Robertson," *Commentary*, August 1995, www.commentary.org/articles/norman-podhoretz/in-the-matter-of-pat-robertson; Claiborne, "Israelis Look"; Midge Decter, "The ADL vs. the 'Religious Right,'" *Commentary*, September 1994, www.commentary.org/articles/midge-decter-3/the-adl-vs-the-religious-right.

20. Robert O. Smith, *More Desired Than Our Owne Salvation: The Roots of Christian Zionism* (New York: Oxford University Press, 2013), 169; Stephen J. Whitfield, "Necrology," *Jewish Quarterly Review* 94, no. 4 (Autumn 2004): 666–671.

21. Walter L. Hixson, *Israel's Armor: The Israel Lobby and the First Generation of the Palestine Conflict* (New York: Cambridge University Press, 2019), 90–94.

22. Hixson, *Israel's Armor*, 94–95.

23. Hixson, *Israel's Armor*, 94–95; Lila Corwin Berman, *The American Jewish Philanthropic Complex* (Princeton, NJ: Princeton University Press, 2020), 97.

24. Lloyd Grove, "The Men with Muscle," *Washington Post*, June 14, 1991, www.washingtonpost.com/archive/lifestyle/1991/06/14/the-men-with-mus cle/2b49e828-af4f-44e6-b2bd-4ec1af61332b; Abba Eban, *Personal Witness: Israel Through My Eyes* (New York: G. P. Putnam's Sons, 1992), 219–221; Natan Aridan, "Israel Lobby," *Israel Studies* 24, no. 2 (2019): 128–143; Shaul Mitelpunkt, *Israel in the American Mind: The Cultural Politics of US-Israeli Relations, 1958–1988* (New York: Cambridge University Press, 2008), loc. 107–108, Kindle.

25. Mitchell Baird, "Israel Lobby Power," *Midstream*, January 1987, 8; Edward Tivnan, *The Lobby: Jewish Political Power and American Foreign Policy* (New York: Simon and Schuster, 1987), 83; Randall Bennett Woods, *Fulbright: A Biography* (New York: Cambridge University Press, 1995), 111, 258, 309–310; James William Fulbright, *The Crippled Giant: American Foreign Policy and Its Domestic Consequences* (New York: Random House, 1972), 109, 135. Years later, AIPAC targeted Fulbright for defeat in his reelection campaign. Hixson, *Israel's Armor*, 138–141.

26. Boaz Vanetik and Zaki Shalom, "The White House Middle East Policy in 1973 as a Catalyst for the Outbreak of the Yom Kippur War," *Israel Studies* 16, no. 1 (Spring 2011): 53–78; Dov Waxman, "The Pro-Israel Lobby in the United States," in *Israel and the United States: Six Decades of US Israeli Relations*, ed. Robert Freedman (Boulder: Westview Press, 2012), 88; Daniel Streiff, "The President and the Peacemaker: Jimmy Carter and the Domestic Politics of Arab-Israeli Diplomacy, 1977–1980" (PhD diss., London School of Economics, 2013), 89.

27. Matthew Berkman, "Coercive Consensus: Jewish Federations, Ethnic Representation, and the Roots of American Pro-Israel Politics" (PhD diss., University of Pennsylvania, 2018), 152; Michael Massing, "The Israel Lobby," *The Nation*, May 23, 2002, www.thenation.com/article/archive/israel-lobby.

28. Robert I. Friedman, "Selling Israel to America," *Mother Jones*, February–March 1987, 20–27; Max Frankel, *The Times of My Life with* The Times (New York: Delta, 1999), 404.

29. Charles Mohr, "Saudi AWACs Deal Rises to $8 Billion," *New York Times*, August 22, 1981, A1; Arnon Gutfeld, "The 1981 AWACS Deal: AIPAC and Israel Challenge Reagan," *Mideast and Policy Studies* 157, Began-Sadat Center for Security Studies, Bar-Ilan University, Ramat Gan, Israel, November 2018, https://besacenter.org/wp-content/uploads/2018/11/157-MONOGRAPH-The-1981-AWACS-Deal-Gutfeld-WEB.pdf; David Schoenbaum, *The United States and the State of Israel* (New York: Oxford University Press, 1993), 279; "Ronald Reagan: The President's News Conference," October 1, 1981, American Presidency Project, University of California, Santa Barbara, www.presidency.ucsb.edu/ws/index.php?pid=44327; Steven R. Weisman, "Reagan Says U.S. Would Bar a Takeover in Saudi Arabia That Imperiled Flow of Oil," *New York Times*, October 2, 1981, www.nytimes.com/1981/10/02/world/reagan-says-us-would-bar-a-takeover-in-saudi-arabia-that-imperiled-flow-of-oil.html; Tivnan, *The Lobby*, 145, 157.

30. Tivnan, *The Lobby*, 137.

31. J. J. Goldberg, *Jewish Power: Inside the American Jewish Establishment* (Reading, MA: Addison-Wesley, 1996), 218–219, 224, 201–203.

32. Ben Samuels, "Retiring Democratic Lawmaker: When AIPAC Told Us to Jump, the Party Used to Ask 'How High?'" *Haaretz*, October 27, 2021, www.haaretz.com/us-news/.premium-retiring-democratic-lawmaker-when-aipac-told-us-to-jump-we-used-to-say-how-high-1.10330326; Robert G. Kaiser, "Relationship," *Washington Post*, May 27, 1984, www.washingtonpost.com/archive/opinions/1984/05/27/relationship/0bfb78e1-c97f-40a8-a0b1-024018ac9146; Peter Beinart, "How a Defender of Palestinian Rights Lost His Way," *Jewish Currents*, May 2, 2022, https://jewishcurrents.org/how-a-defender-of-palestinian-rights-lost-his-way.

33. "Opening Night, Pundits, Pollsters and Politicos," J Street 2016 National Gala, April 17, 2016, posted by J Street, n.d., YouTube, www.youtube.com/watch?v=DnJrYrBhR9s; Jewish Telegraphic Agency, "Dear Lindsey Graham: Some Jokes Only Jews Can Make," *Jerusalem Post*, April 22, 2015, www.jpost.com/diaspora/dear-lindsey-graham-some-jokes-only-jews-can-make-398971; James Homan, "The Nunn Memos: 10 Key Passages," Politico, June 29, 2014, www.politico.com/story/2014/07/michelle-nunn-memos-10-key-passages-109463.

34. Goldberg, *Jewish Power*, 269–270, 273; Don Oberdorfer, "Sen. Percy Says He Has No Regrets About Votes on Middle East Issues," *Washington Post*, December 7, 1984, www.washingtonpost.com/archive/politics/1984/12/07/sen-percy-says-he-has-no-regrets-about-votes-on-middle-east-issues/e978e475-85d9-49d7-8476-543695fdedd7; Jeffrey Goldberg, "Real Insiders: A Pro-Israel Lobby and an FBI Sting," *New Yorker*, July 4, 2005; Nicholas Laham, *Selling AWACS to Saudi Arabia: The Reagan Administration and the Balancing of America's Competing Interests in the Middle East* (Westport, CT: Praeger, 2002), 67.

35. Tivnan, *The Lobby*, 165–166.

36. Raviv and Melman, *Friends in Deed*, 306. Ronald Reagan, *An American Life* (New York: Simon and Schuster, 1990), 410.

37. Reagan, *An American Life*, 410; Seth Anziska, *Preventing Palestine: A Political History from Camp David to Oslo* (Princeton, NJ: Princeton University Press, 2018), 162; Joe Conason, "'Most Antagonistic' Toward Israel? That Would Be Ronald Reagan's Defense Secretary," Real Clear Politics, January 10, 2013, www.realclearpolitics.com/articles/2013/01/10/most

_antagonistic_toward_israel_that_would_be_ronald_reagans_defense_secretary _116635.html.

38. Arye Naor, "Lessons of the Holocaust Versus Territories for Peace, 1967–2001," *Israel Studies* 8, no. 1 (2003): 130–152; Donald G. Boudreau, "The Bombing of the Osirik Reactor," *International Journal on World Peace* 10, no. 2 (1993): 21–37; Dan Reiter, "Preventive Attacks Against Nuclear Programs and the 'Success' at Osiraq," *Nonproliferation Review* 12, no. 2 (July 2005): 355–371; Målfrid Braut-Hegghammer, "Revisiting Osirak: Preventive Attacks and Nuclear Proliferation Risks," *International Security* 36, no. 1 (Summer 2011): 101–132; Hal Brands and David Palkki, "Saddam, Israel and the Bomb: Nuclear Alarmism Justified?," *International Security* 36, no. 1 (Summer 2011): 133–166. "How Long Would It Take for Iraq to Obtain a Nuclear Explosive After Its Research Reactor Began Operation?," CRS Report for Congress, House Committee on Foreign Affairs, Hearings: Israeli Attack on Iraq, 97th Cong., 1st sess., June 25, 1981; Judy Kovel-Itzkovich, "Begin Center Furious over Revelations of Former PM's Mental State," *Jerusalem Post*, May 23, 2018, www.jpost.com/health-science/begin-center-furious-over-reve lations-of-former-pms-mental-state-558182.

39. Raviv and Melman, *Friends in Deed*, 197; "Israel's Illusion," *New York Times*, June 9, 1981, A14; Jonathan Steele, "Carte Blanche for a War on the World," Dawn, June 8, 2002, www.dawn.com/news/41201.

40. "Transcript of Prime Minister Begin's Statement to the US Envoy to Israel," *New York Times*, December 21, 1981, www.nytimes.com/1981/12/21/world/transcript -of-prime-minister-begin-s-statement-to-the-us-envoy-to-israel.html; Daniel G. Hummel, *Covenant Brothers: Evangelicals, Jews and US-Israeli Relations* (Philadelphia: University of Pennsylvania Press, 2019), 170.

41. William Safire, "Reagan 'Suspends' Israel," *New York Times*, December 24, 1981, A23.

42. James Reston, "Washington: The Old and New Jerusalem," *New York Times*, December 23, 1981, A19, www.nytimes.com/1981/12/23/opinion/washington-the -old-and-new-jerusalem.html; Raviv and Melman, *Friends in Deed*, 199–200.

43. David Hartman, "Auschwitz or Sinai?," in *The New Jewish Canon*, ed. Yehuda Kurtzer and Claire E. Sufrin (Boston: Academic Studies Press, 2020), originally published in *Jerusalem Post*, December 12, 1982, and reprinted at Shalom Hartman Institute, www.hartman.org.il/auschwitz-or-sinai.

44. William Claiborne, "Israel, in Sudden Move, Annexes Golan Heights," *Washington Post*, December 15, 1981, A1.

## Chapter 12. War: What Is It Good For?

1. Kai Bird, *The Good Spy: The Life and Death of Robert Ames* (New York: Random House, 2014), 288; Gerald Cromer, *A War of Words: Political Violence and Public Debate in Israel* (London: Frank Cass, 2004), 116; David Schoenbaum, *The United States and the State of Israel* (New York: Oxford University Press, 1993), 282; UPI, "Begin Compares Arafat to Hitler," August 5, 1982, www.upi.com/Ar chives/1982/08/05/Begin-compares-Arafat-to-Hitler/2671397368000.

2. George W. Ball, "Error and Betrayal in Lebanon" (Washington, DC: Foundation for Middle East Peace, 1984), 35; Yossi Melman and Dan Raviv, *Friends in Deed: Inside the U.S.-Israel Alliance* (New York: Hyperion, 1994); Patrick Tyler, *A*

*World of Trouble: The White House and the Middle East from the Cold War to the War on Terror* (New York: Farrar, Straus and Giroux, 2009), 279; Seth Anziska, *Preventing Palestine: A Political History from Camp David to Oslo* (Princeton, NJ: Princeton University Press, 2018), 208; Amos Harel, "'We Arrested Countless Palestinians for No Reason,' Says Ex–Top Shin Bet Officer," *Haaretz*, February 17, 2022, www .haaretz.com/israel-news/.premium.HIGHLIGHT.MAGAZINE-we-arrested -countless-palestinians-for-no-reason-says-ex-top-shin-bet-officer-1.10618087.

3. Colin Schindler, "Likud and the Christian Dispensationalists: A Symbiotic Relationship," *Israel Studies* 5, no. 1 (2000): 153–182; Daniel G. Hummel, *Covenant Brothers: Evangelicals, Jews and US-Israeli Relations* (Philadelphia: University of Pennsylvania Press, 2019), 172–173.

4. Thomas Friedman, "Four Days," *New York Times*, September 26, 1982, A19; Shaul Mitelpunkt, *Israel in the American Mind: The Cultural Politics of US-Israeli Relations, 1958–1988* (New York: Cambridge University Press, 2018), loc. 298, Kindle; Ofer Aderet, "Mossad Says Can't Find Files on 1982 Lebanon Massacre," *Haaretz*, April 5, 2022, www.haaretz.com/israel-news/.premium-israel-s-mossad -can-t-find-docs-on-1982-lebanon-massacre-lawyer-tells-court-1.10721596.

5. Rashid I. Khalidi, "The Sabra and Shatila Massacre: New Evidence," Institute for Palestine Studies, https://oldwebsite.palestine-studies.org/content/sabra-and -shatila-massacre-new-evidence, accessed April 28, 2022; Michael Kramer, "The Jerusalem Scenario," *New York Magazine*, October 11, 1982, 25.

6. George P. Shultz, *Turmoil and Triumph: My Years as Secretary of State* (New York: Scribner, 1993), 112.

7. Robert I. Friedman, "Selling Israel to America," *Mother Jones*, February– March 1987, 20–27; Paul Jabert, "'News Speak' About the Lebanon War," *Journal of Palestine Studies* 14, no. 1 (1984): 16–35.

8. Mark Chmiel, "The Witness of Elie Wiesel," *Tikkun*, December 1, 2002, https://read.dukeupress.edu/tikkun/article-abstract/17/6/61/83012/Elie-Wiesel -and-the-Question-of-Palestine; Paul L. Montgomery, "Discord Among U.S. Jews over Israel Seems to Grow," *New York Times*, July 15, 1982, A16; Steven T. Rosenthal, *Irreconcilable Differences? The Waning of the American Jewish Love Affair with Israel* (Waltham, MA: Brandeis University Press, 2001), 167.

9. Anziska, *Preventing Palestine*, 221.

10. Arthur Hertzberg, "Begin and the Jews," *New York Review of Books*, February 18, 1982, www.nybooks.com/articles/1982/02/18/begin-and-the-jews; Montgomery, "Discord Among U.S. Jews"; Jewish Telegraphic Agency, "Survey Shows U.S. Jews Overwhelmingly Committed to Israel's Security but Deeply Divided over the Policies of the Current Israeli Government," *Daily News Bulletin* 61, no. 175 (September 15, 1983): 2, http://pdfs.jta.org/1983/1983-09-15_175.pdf.

11. David R. Verbeeten, *The Politics of Nonassimilation: The American Jewish Left in the Twentieth Century* (DeKalb: Northern Illinois University Press, 2017), 132.

12. Neil A. Lewis, "Israel in *The New York Times* over the Decades: A Changed Narrative and Its Impact on Jewish Readers," Joan Shorenstein Center on the Press, Politics and Public Policy, Harvard University, Spring 2012, https://shorensteincen ter.org/wpcontent/uploads/2012/03/d69_lewis.pdf; Alfred Friendly, "Israel: Recollections and Regrets," *Washington Post*, June 29, 1982.

13. *Haaretz*, December 9, 1982; Eric Alterman, *Sound and Fury: The Washington Punditocracy and the Collapse of American Politics* (New York: HarperCollins, 1992), 195–196.

14. Norman Podhoretz, "J'Accuse," *Commentary*, July 1982, www.commentary magazine.com/articles/podhoretz/jaccuse.

15. George W. Ball, "The Middle East: How to Save Israel in Spite of Herself," *Foreign Affairs*, April 1977. See also, for instance, George W. Ball, "The Coming Crisis in Israeli-American Relations," *Foreign Affairs*, Winter 1979/1980, www.for eignaffairs.com/articles/israel/1979-12-01/coming-crisis-israeli-american-relations.

16. Robert H. Estabrook, "Affluence, Gaiety, Seen in Israel," *Washington Post*, February 23, 1965.

17. Michelle Mart, *Eye on Israel: How America Came to View Israel as an Ally* (Albany: State University of New York Press, 2006), x, 66–67, 93; Dana H. Allin and Steven N. Simon, *Our Separate Ways: The Struggle for the Future of the US-Israel Alliance* (New York: PublicAffairs, 2016), 210; Tony Shaw and Giora Goodman, *Hollywood and Israel: A History* (New York: Columbia University Press, 2022), loc. 2863, 3743, Kindle.

18. Edward Said, "Arab and Jew: 'Each Is the Other,'" *New York Times*, October 14, 1973; Edward Said, "Permission to Narrate," *London Review of Books* 6, no. 3 (February 16, 1984), www.lrb.co.uk/the-paper/v06/n03/edward-said/permission -to-narrate.

19. Maya Jaggi, "Between the Lines," *Guardian Weekly*, December 13, 2001, www.theguardian.com/GWeekly/Story/0,3939,617489,00.html; Janny Scott, "Palestinian Confronts Time: For Columbia Literary Critic, Cancer Is a Spur to Memory," *New York Times*, September 19, 1998, B7; Richard Bernstein, "Edward Said, Leading Advocate of Palestinians, Dies at 67," *New York Times*, September 25, 2003, www.nytimes.com/2003/09/25/obituaries/edward-said-leading-advo cate-of-palestinians-dies-at-67.html; Maha Nassar, "US Media Talks a Lot About Palestinians—Just Without Palestinians," 972, October 2, 2020, www.972mag .com/us-media-palestinians.

20. Friedman, "Selling Israel to America"; "New Politico Owner Says Will Enforce pro-Israel Policy," *Haaretz*, October 17, 2021, www.haaretz.com/israel-news /new-politico-owner-says-will-enforce-pro-israel-policy-1.10301503.

21. Friedman, "Selling Israel to America"; Tony Schwartz, "ADL Criticizes TV over Coverage of Lebanon," *New York Times*, October 21, 1982, C30; Thomas Friedman, "Time Magazine and Sharon Settle the Libel Suit He Filed in Israel," *New York Times*, January 23, 1986, B8.

22. Friedman, "Selling Israel to America."

23. Raymond Stock, "Prestige Press at War: The New York Times and Le Monde in Lebanon, August 1–September 26, 1982," *Middle East Journal* 39, no. 1 (Summer 1985): 317–340.

24. Lewis, "Israel in *The New York Times*"; "Now Playing: Coastal Elites," *New Yorker*, September 28, 2020, www.newyorker.com/goings-on-about-town/theatre /coastal-elites-09-28-20; Jodi Rudoren, Zoom YIVO Institute for Jewish Research symposium on the Jewish press, September 13, 2021.

25. Gay Talese, *The Kingdom and the Power* (New York: Random House, 1969), 216.

26. Thomas Friedman, *From Beirut to Jerusalem* (New York: Farrar, Straus and Giroux, 1989), 164, 166; Friedman, quoted in Jerold S. Auerbach, "Are We One? Menachem Begin and the Long Shadow of 1977," in *Envisioning Israel: The Changing Images and Ideals of North American Jews*, ed. Allon Gal (Jerusalem: Magnes Press; Detroit: Wayne State University Press, 1996), and in Rashid Khalidi, *The Hundred Years' War on Palestine: A History of Settler Colonialism and Resistance, 1917–2017* (New York: Metropolitan Books, 2020), 149.

27. Lewis, "Israel in *The New York Times*."

28. Lewis, "Israel in *The New York Times*."

29. Samuel Friedman, "In the Diaspora: Abe Rosenthal, American Jew," *Jerusalem Post*, May 15, 2016, www.jpost.com/opinion/columnists/in-the-diaspora-abe-rosenthal-american-jew; Laurel Leff, "A Tragic 'Fight in the Family': *The New York Times*, Reform Judaism and the Holocaust," *American Jewish History* 88, no. 1 (March 2000): 3–51; Ari L. Goldman, "Abe Rosenthal: New York Times Editor and Advocate for Israel," *The Forward*, May 19, 2006, https://forward.com/news/985/abe-rosenthal-new-york-times-editor-and-advocate; Max Frankel, *The Times of My Life and My Life with* The Times (New York: Random House, 1999), 401; Bret Stephens, "Eye on the Media by Bret Stephens: Bartley's Journal," *Jerusalem Post*, November 21, 2002.

30. Seth Ackerman, "Israel and the Media: An Acquired Taste," in *Wrestling with Zion: Progressive Jewish-American Responses to the Israeli-Palestinian Conflict*, ed. Tony Kushner and Alisa Solomon (New York: Grove Press, 2003), 63.

31. The details about Pollard's activities are drawn from David K. Shipler, "Close US-Israel Relationship Makes Keeping Secrets Hard," *New York Times*, December 25, 1985, A1; Shimon Shiffer, "From Disposable Asset to National Hero: The Full Pollard Spy Saga," Ynet News, September 14, 2015, www.ynetnews.com/articles/0,7340,L-4700225,00.html; Seymour Hersh, "The Traitor," *New Yorker*, January 18, 1999, 26–33; Robert I. Friedman, "The Secret Agent," *New York Review of Books* 36, no. 16 (October 26, 1989), www.nybooks.com/articles/1989/10/26/the-secret-agent; Fred Kaplan, "Just Punishment," Slate, July 29, 2015, www.slate.com/articles/news_and_politics/war_stories/2015/07/jonathan_pollard_was_one_of_the_worst_traitors_of_the_20th_century_he_deserved.html; Jonathan S. Tobin, "The Pollard Spy Case, 25 Years Later," *Commentary*, March 1, 2011.

32. Gil Troy, "National Insecurity: The Case for Jonathan Pollard," Tablet, November 16, 2010, www.tabletmag.com/jewish-news-and-politics/50505/national-insecurity; Tobin, "The Pollard Spy Case"; James D. Besser, "The Jonathan Pollard Case: A Reflection of Our Fears," Jewish Telegraphic Agency, June 28, 2002, www.jta.org/2002/06/28/ny/the-jonathan-pollard-case-a-reflection-of-our-fears.

33. Julian E. Barnes, "Jonathan Pollard, Convicted Spy, Completes Parole and May Move to Israel," *New York Times*, November 20, 2020, www.nytimes.com/2020/11/20/us/politics/jonathan-pollard-parole-ends.html; Boaz Bismuth, "Home at Last: Jonathan Pollard Arrives in Israel," *Israel Today*, December 30, 2020, www.israelhayom.com/2020/12/30/home-at-last-jonathan-pollard-arrives-in-israel.

34. Rosenthal, *Irreconcilable Differences*, 98.

35. Tyler, *A World of Trouble*, 344; Barbara Vobeja, "Kissinger Said to Urge 'Brutal Force,'" *Washington Post*, March 6, 1988, www.washingtonpost.com/archive

/politics/1988/03/06/kissinger-said-to-urge-brutal-force/710e5742-8f09-4ee8 -a491-82acf58b03ef.

36. *Nightline*, "This Week in the Holy Land," ABC News, April 25–29, 1988, shows 1806–1810.

37. Albert Vorspan, "Soul Searching," *New York Times Magazine*, May 8, 1988, 6, 40.

38. Arthur Hertzberg, "The Illusion of Jewish Unity," *New York Review of Books*, June 16, 1988, www.nybooks.com/articles/1988/06/16/the-illusion -of-jewish-unity; Jonathan Marcus, "The US Jewish Community and Israel During the 1980s," *International Affairs* 66, no. 3 (July 1990): 545–558; Murray Polner, "Present Tense, 1973–1990: Seeing the World Through Jewish (Prophetic) Eyes," *Serials Review* 18, no. 4 (1992): 11–20.

39. Norman Podhoretz, "Israel: A Lamentation from the Future," *Commentary*, March 1989, www.commentary.org/articles/norman-podhoretz/israel-a-lamenta tion-from-the-future.

40. Charles Krauthammer, "No Exit," and Martin Peretz, "Occupational Hazards," *New Republic*, March 14, 1988, 29–31, 14–20.

41. Leon Wieseltier, "Summoned by Stones," *New Republic*, March 14, 1988, 20–28.

## Chapter 13. "Fuck the Jews"

1. Glenn Frankel, "A Beautiful Friendship?," *Washington Post*, July 16, 2006, www.washingtonpost.com/wp-dyn/content/article/2006/07/12/AR2006 071201627_3.html.

2. Robert M. Gates, interview by Timothy J. Naftali et al., July 23–24, 2000, 88, George H. W. Bush Oral History Project, Miller Center, University of Virginia, https://millercenter.org/the-presidency/presidential-oral-histories/robert-m-gates -deputy-director-central.

3. Maureen Dowd and Thomas L. Friedman, "The Fabulous Bush and Baker Boys," *New York Times Magazine*, May 6, 1990, 34–67.

4. Glenn Frankel, "As Peres Prepares to Govern, US-Israel Relations Hit Low," *Washington Post*, April 29, 1990, www.washingtonpost.com/archive/poli tics/1990/04/29/as-peres-loses-bid-to-govern-us-israeli-relations-hit-a-low/e247dbe7 -4140-44e2-8d5c-82a405d6af9a.

5. Kathleen Christison, "Splitting the Difference: The Palestinian-Israeli Policy of James Baker," *Journal of Palestine Studies* 24, no. 1 (1994): 39–50.

6. John M. Goshko, "U.S. Faults Israel on Territories," *Washington Post*, May 23, 1989, www.washingtonpost.com/archive/politics/1989/05/23/us-faults-isra el-on-territories/4f7931d9-c89d-4c9a-9279-50d0e2e5031b; Dana H. Allin and Steven N. Simon, *Our Separate Ways: The Struggle for the Future of the US-Israel Alliance* (New York: PublicAffairs, 2016), 52; "Robert Gates: The Man Who Would Ban Netanyahu from the White House," *Haaretz*, January 14, 2014, www.haaretz .com/.premium-he-d-ban-bibi-from-white-house-1.5310858.

7. Thomas L. Friedman, "Baker, in a Middle East Blueprint, Asks Israel to Reach Out to Arabs," *New York Times*, May 23, 1989, www.nytimes.com/1989/05/23 /world/baker-in-a-middle-east-blueprint-asks-israel-to-reach-out-to-arabs.html.

8. George H. W. Bush, "The President's News Conference," September 12, 1991, American Presidency Project, University of California, Santa Barbara, www.presi dency.ucsb.edu/ws/?pid=19969.

9. Christison, "Splitting the Difference"; Norman Podhoretz, "Israel and the United States: A Complex History," *Commentary*, May 1998, www.commentary magazine.com/articles/israel-and-the-united-states-a-complex-history.

10. James Baker and Susan Glasser, *The Man Who Ran Washington: The Life and Times of James A. Baker III* (New York: Doubleday, 2020), loc. 9858–9895, Kindle; Mark S. Mellman, Aaron Strauss, and Kenneth D. Wald, "Jewish American Voting Behavior, 1972–2008: Just the Facts," July 2012, Solomon Project, Berman Jewish DataBank, www.jewishdatabank.org/content/upload/bjdb/599/N-Jewish_Ameri can_Voting_Solomon_Project_2012_Main_Report.pdf.

11. Mellman et al., "Jewish American Voting Behavior, 1972–2008."

12. J. J. Goldberg, *Jewish Power: Inside the American Jewish Establishment* (Reading, MA: Addison-Wesley, 1996), 31; Steven Bayme, *Israel and American Jewry: Oslo and Beyond*, Jerusalem Center for Public Affairs, January 15, 2008, archived at Policy Commons, https://policycommons.net/artifacts/1171965/israel-and-american -jewry/1725094; Michael E. Staub, *Torn at the Roots: The Crisis of Jewish Liberalism in Postwar America* (New York: Columbia University Press, 2012), 347.

13. Arnold Eisen, "A New Role for Israel in American Jewish Identity," Institute on American Jewish-Israeli Relations, American Jewish Committee, 1992.

14. Steven M. Cohen, "Did American Jews Really Grow More Distant from Israel, 1983–1993?—A Reconsideration," in *Envisioning Israel: The Changing Images and Ideals of North American Jews*, ed. Allon Gal (Jerusalem: Magnes Press; Detroit: Wayne State University Press, 1996), 352–373.

15. Eisen, "A New Role for Israel."

### Chapter 14. Discourse Matters

1. I was among those invited to the ceremony that day and refer here to the feelings I experienced, as well as those of a number of people to whom I spoke. "Remarks by PM Yitzhak Rabin at Signing of DOP-13-Sep-93," September 13, 1993, Israel Ministry of Foreign Affairs, www.mfa.gov.il/mfa/foreignpolicy/peace /mfadocuments/pages/remarks%20by%20pm%20yitzhak%20rabin%20at%20sign ing%20of%20dop%20-%2013.aspx.

2. Menachem Brinker, "The End of Zionism? Thoughts on the Wages of Success," in *Zionism: The Sequel*, ed. Carol Diament (New York: Hadassah, 1998), 293–299; Deborah Dash Moore, *American Jewish Identity Politics* (Ann Arbor: University of Michigan Press, 2009), 17.

3. Alan Dershowitz, *The Vanishing American Jews* (New York: Little, Brown, 1997), 1; Lila Corwin Berman, "With Huge Gifts to Birthright Israel, Wealthy Donors Influence American Jewish Identity," Inside Philanthropy, September 30, 2020, www.insidephilanthropy.com/home/tag/Birthright+Israel.

4. Mordecai Kaplan, "The Future of the American Jew (1948)," in *The Zionist Idea: A Historical Analysis and Reader*, ed. Arthur Hertzberg (Philadelphia: Jewish Publication Society, 1997), 539–541; Alexander Bloom, *Prodigal Sons: The New York Intellectuals and Their World* (New York: Oxford University Press, 1986), 143.

5. Dan Flesher, *Transforming America's Israel Lobby: The Limits of Its Power and the Potential for Change* (Washington, DC: Potomac Books, 2009), 46–47.

6. George Stephanopoulos, who was present, related these events to me a few hours after they took place on September 23, 1993, in my apartment in Washington, DC.

7. Itamar Rabinovich, "The Jerusalem Hijack," *Haaretz*, August 7, 2003, www.haaretz.com/life/books/1.5357637.

8. Anshel Pfeffer, *Bibi: The Turbulent Life and Times of Benjamin Netanyahu* (New York: Basic Books, 2018), 240.

9. Anthony Lewis, "By the Sword," *New York Times*, August 25, 1997.

10. William Safire, "Move the Embassy," *New York Times*, July 1, 1996, A13; William Safire, "Gun to the Head," *New York Times*, September 10, 1997, A23.

11. Charles Kaiser, "My Father the Communist: The *New York Times*' Andrew Rosenthal on Iraq, Times Select, and His Father's Secret Past," Radar, November 2, 2007, via Internet Archive, https://web.archive.org/web/20081022094112/http://www.radaronline.com/features/2007/11/andrew_rosenthal_abe_rosenthal_new_york_times_1.php; Eric Alterman, *Sound and Fury: The Making of the Punditocracy* (New York: HarperCollins, 1992), 135–145.

12. A. M. Rosenthal, "The Amman Story," *New York Times*, October 14, 1997, A27; A. M. Rosenthal, "Spitting on the Graves," *New York Times*, August 1, 1997, A31.

13. Thomas Friedman, "The Terrorist Question," *New York Times*, August 4, 1997, A17.

14. Jerome Slater, "Muting the Alarm: The *New York Times* vs. *Haaretz*, 2000–2006," *International Security* 32, no. 2 (Fall 2007): 84–120.

15. William J. Clinton, *My Life* (New York: Knopf, 2004), 464.

16. Aaron David Miller, "Lost in the Woods: A Camp David Retrospective," Carnegie Endowment for International Peace, July 13, 2020, https://carnegieendowment.org/2020/07/13/lost-in-woods-camp-david-retrospective-pub-82287; Rob Malley and Hussein Agha, "Camp David: The Tragedy of Errors," *New York Review of Books*, August 9, 2001, www.nybooks.com/articles/2001/08/09/camp-david-the-tragedy-of-errors.

17. Aaron David Miller, *The Much Too Promised Land: America's Elusive Search for Arab-Israeli Peace* (New York: Bantam Books, 2008), 305–307; Lee Hockstader, "'Unique Opportunity' Lost at Camp David," *Washington Post*, July 30, 2000, A1; William B. Quandt, "Clinton and the Arab-Israeli Conflict," *Journal of Palestine Studies* 30, no. 2 (Winter 2001): 26–40.

18. "President William J. Clinton Statement on the Middle East Peace Talks at Camp David," July 25, 2000, Avalon Project, Yale Law School, Lillian Goldman Law Library, https://avalon.law.yale.edu/21st_century/mid027.asp; Dennis Ross, "Camp David: An Exchange," *New York Review of Books*, September 20, 2001, www.nybooks.com/articles/2001/09/20/camp-david-an-exchange; Benny Morris, "Camp David and After: An Exchange (An Interview with Ehud Barak)," *New York Review of Books*, June 13, 2002, www.nybooks.com/articles/2002/06/13/camp-david-and-after-an-exchange-1-an-interview-wi.

19. William Safire, "Why Is Arafat Smiling?," *New York Times*, July 27, 2000, A25; Thomas Friedman, "Arafat's War," *New York Times*, October 13, 2000, 33.

20. Shlomo Ben-Ami, *Prophets Without Honor: The 2000 Camp David Summit and the End of the Two-State Solution* (New York: Oxford University Press, 2022), 108.

21. Lee Hockstader, "A Different Take on Camp David Collapse," *Washington Post*, July 24, 2001, www.washingtonpost.com/archive/politics/2001/07/24/a-differ ent-take-on-camp-david-collapse/bb315457-af34-4428-aa89-d3c72f8a5731; Deborah Sontag, "And Yet So Far: A Special Report. Quest for Mideast Peace: How and Why It Failed," *New York Times*, July 26, 2001, A1; Ehud Barak, "I Did Not Give Away a Thing," *Yediot Aharonot*, August 29, 2003; "Fmr. Israeli Foreign Minister: 'If I Were a Palestinian, I Would Have Rejected Camp David,'" Democracy Now, February 14, 2006, www.democracynow.org/2006/2/14/fmr_israeli_foreign_min ister_if_i; Raphael Cohen-Almagor, "History of Track Two Peace Negotiations: Interview with Hussein Agha," *Israel Studies* 26, no. 1 (2021): 47–72; Tanya Reinhart, "How Barak Failed the Peace With Syria," trans. Irit Katriel, *Yediot Aharonot*, July 2000, https://staticweb.hum.uu.nl/uilots/Tanya.Reinhart/personal/Political%20 Work/HowBarakFailedWithSyria.html.

22. Sontag, "And Yet So Far"; Malley and Agha, "Camp David: The Tragedy of Errors."

23. William Safire, "Not Arafat's Fault?," *New York Times*, July 20, 2001, A17; Yossi Klein Halevi, "State of Despair: A Tour of Israel Under Siege," *New Republic*, August 6, 2001; Morris, "Camp David and After."

24. Marc Perelman, "Clinton Aide Attacked for Offering 'Revisionist' Take on Camp David," *Haaretz*, April 8, 2001, www.haaretz.com/1.5371768; Eric Alterman, "West Bank Dreamin'," *The Nation*, August 23, 2001, www.thenation.com /article/archive/west-bank-dreamin.

25. "Israel and Palestine: After the War Is Over," *Economist*, April 11, 2002, www.economist.com/special-report/2002/04/11/after-the-war-is-over; Sontag, "And Yet So Far"; Halevi, "State of Despair."

26. Yotam Berger, "7 Years After Lynching of Soldiers, Israel to Give Convicted Palestinian Policeman New Trial," *Haaretz*, February 12, 2017, www.haaretz .com/israel-news/.premium-israel-to-give-ramallah-lynching-perpetrator-new -trial-1.5433259; Shlomo Ben-Ami, *Prophets Without Honor* (New York: Oxford University Press, 2022), 139.

27. Gideon Levy, "The Second Intifada, 20 Years On: Thousands Died in a Struggle That Failed," *Haaretz*, September 26, 2020, www.haaretz.com/is rael-news/.premium.MAGAZINE-the-second-intifada-20-years-on-thousands -died-in-a-struggle-that-failed-1.9185099.

## Chapter 15. The Consequences of Chaos

1. Joel Greenberg, "Jewish Settlers' Zeal Forces Palestinians to Flee Their Town," *New York Times*, October 21, 2002, A1.

2. Jack Kelley, "Israel Hunts Terrorists amid Controversy," *USA Today*, August 21, 2001, A1. (Note: Kelley was forced to resign from *USA Today* in 2004 when it was found that he had invented some stories and plagiarized others. I have not relied on him for any details that did not also appear elsewhere.)

3. Jiyar Gol, "Israel's Mossad Suspected of High-Level Iran Penetration," BBC News, February 6, 2022, www.bbc.com/news/world-middle-east-60250816.

4. Steven R. David, "Israel's Policy of Targeted Killing," *Ethics and International Affairs* 17, no. 1 (2003): 111; Ronen Bergman, *Rise and Kill First: The Secret History of Israel's Targeted Assassinations* (New York: Random House, 2018), esp. 493–515; "Israel, a Country Fleeing Its Past," *Haaretz* (editorial), April 12, 2021, www .haaretz.com/opinion/editorial/israel-a-country-fleeing-its-past-1.9702565.

5. Joel Greenberg, "Amnesty Accuses Israeli Forces of War Crimes," *New York Times*, November 4, 2002, www.nytimes.com/2002/11/04/international/middleeast /04RIGH.html.

6. "Israeli Arabs: The Official Summation of the Or Commission Report," September 2, 2003, Jewish Virtual Library, www.jewishvirtuallibrary.org/the-official -summation-of-the-or-commission-report-september-2003.

7. Dana H. Allin and Steven N. Simon, *Our Separate Ways: The Struggle for the Future of the US-Israel Alliance* (New York: PublicAffairs, 2016), 55.

8. Michael Kelly, "Mideast Myths Exploded," *Washington Post*, August 15, 2001, www.washingtonpost.com/archive/opinions/2001/08/15/mideast-myths-exploded /f82c5c23-3c67-47dc-94e1-5fee03eb4396.

9. Charles Krauthammer, "Mideast Violence: The Only Way Out," *Washington Post*, August 16, 2001, A25, www.washingtonpost.com/archive/opinions /2001/08/16/mideast-violence-the-only-way-out/8b952c56-216d-420d-897b-3b1ff de504bb.

10. George F. Will, "A War and Then a Wall," *Washington Post*, August 17, 2001, A23, www.washingtonpost.com/archive/opinions/2001/08/17/a-war-and -then-a-wall/7a49a076-b01d-408d-914f-0ff90922f182.

11. Leon Wieseltier, "Hitler Is Dead: Against Ethnic Panic," *New Republic*, May 27, 2002; Abraham Foxman, *Never Again? The Threat of the New Antisemitism* (New York: Harper One, 2003), 4; Amy Wilentz, "How the War Came Home," *New York*, May 6, 2002, https://nymag.com/nymetro/news/politics/international/fea tures/5972; Gulie Ne'eman Arad, "The Shoah and Israel's Political Trope," in *Divergent Jewish Cultures: Israel and America*, ed. Deborah Dash Moore and S. Ilan Troen (New Haven, CT: Yale University Press, 2001), 208.

12. Sid Groeneman and Gary A. Tobin, "American Public Opinion Toward Israel and U.S. Policy in the Middle East: Post September 11, 2001," n.d., Institute for Jewish and Community Research, online at Policy Commons, https://policycommons .net/artifacts/1171671/american-public-opinion-toward-israel-us-policy-in-the-mid dle-east/1724800; Patrick E. Tyler, "Shock of Sept. 11 Is Making Americans More Supportive of Israel, Polls Suggest," *New York Times*, May 13, 2002, A8; Bob Kemper, "Bush Support Fades as Nation Moves On," *Chicago Tribune*, September 10, 2002, www.chicagotribune.com/news/ct-xpm-2002-09-10-0209100261-story.html.

13. Hussein Ibish, in "Middle East Rage," *Washington Post*, August 17, 2001, www.washingtonpost.com/archive/opinions/2001/08/17/middle-east-rage/c695f ccc-83a9-4c30-8699-20eadd539e24.

14. William Safire, "Democrats vs. Israel," *New York Times*, April 22, 2002, www.nytimes.com/2002/04/22/opinion/democrats-vs-israel.html; Todd Purdum, "State Dept. Report Investigating Arafat's Links to Terror Is at Odds with Israeli Claims," *New York Times*, May 3, 2002, A10; Irving Kristol, "On the Political Stupidity of the Jews," *Azure* (Autumn 1999), reprinted at *Tikvah*, https://tikvahfund .org/uncategorized/on-the-political-stupidity-of-the-jews; Eric Alterman, "Jews Are

Still Liberal," Center for American Progress, April 19, 2020, www.americanprog ress.org/issues/general/news/2012/04/19/11420/think-again-jews-are-still-liberal.

15. Laurie Goodstein, "Democrats: The Observances. Lieberman Balances Private Faith with Life in the Public Eye," *New York Times*, August 18, 2000, www .nytimes.com/2000/08/18/us/democrats-observances-lieberman-balances-private -faith-with-life-public-eye.html; Gerald M. Popper, "The 2000 Presidential Election: Why Gore Lost," *Political Science Quarterly* 116 (2001): 201–223; Peter Waldman and Hugh Pope, " 'Crusade' Reference Reinforces Fears War on Terrorism Is Against Muslims," *Wall Street Journal*, September 21, 2001, www.wsj.com/articles /SB1001020294332922160.

16. Michael Lind, "Distorting U.S. Foreign Policy: The Israel Lobby and American Power," *Washington Report on Middle East Affairs*, May 2002, www.wrmea .org/002-may/distorting-us-foreign-policy-the-israel-lobby-and-american-power .html.

17. Frank Rich, "The Booing of Wolfowitz," *New York Times*, March 11, 2002, A17.

18. Sam Tanenhaus, "Bush's Brain Trust," *Vanity Fair*, July 2003.

19. Eric Alterman, *Lying in State: Why Presidents Lie and Why Trump Is Worse* (New York: Basic Books, 2020), 210–216; Institute for Advanced Strategic and Political Studies, Study Group on a New Israeli Strategy Toward 2000, "A Clean Break: A New Strategy for Securing the Realm," PalestineRemembered.com, December 27, 2004, www.palestineremembered.com/Acre/Articles/Story1351.html.

20. Douglas Feith, "A Strategy for Israel," *Commentary*, September 1997, www .commentarymagazine.com/articles/douglas-feith/a-strategy-for-israel. For David Wurmser's work at AEI in 2001, see www.aei.org/profile/david-wurmser.

21. Samuel Huntington, *The Clash of Civilizations and the Remaking of the World Order* (New York: Simon and Schuster, 1996); Herb Keinon, "Netanyahu in Berlin Calls French Plan 'Surprising' as Merkel Puts Brakes on Diplomatic Efforts," *Jerusalem Post*, February 17, 2016, www.jpost.com/israel-news/politics-and-diplomacy /netanyahu-in-berlin-calls-french-plan-surprising-as-merkel-puts-brakes-on-diplo matic-effort-445076; Gary Rosenblatt, "After 9/11, I Wrote a Jewish Week Headline Comparing the US to Israel. Here's Why I Regret It," Jewish Telegraphic Agency, September 10, 2021, www.jta.org/2021/09/10/opinion/after-9-11-i-wrote-a-jewish -week-headline-comparing-the-us-to-israel-heres-why-i-regret-it.

22. Eric Alterman, "Neocon Dreams, American Nightmares," *The Nation*, August 10, 2006, www.thenation.com/article/archive/neocon-dreams-american-night mares; John Mearsheimer and Stephen Walt, "The Israel Lobby," *London Review of Books* 28, no. 6 (March 23, 2006), www.lrb.co.uk/the-paper/v28/n06/john-mear sheimer/the-israel-lobby.

23. Timothy Noah, "Al Gore, Andrew Sullivan, and 'Fifth Column,' " Slate, December 2, 2002, https://slate.com/news-and-politics/2002/12/gore-sullivan-and -fifth-column.html.

24. Michael Kinsley, "What Bush Isn't Saying About Iraq," Slate, October 24, 2002, https://slate.com/news-and-politics/2002/10/what-bush-isn-t-saying-about -iraq.html; Laurie Goodstein, "Divide Among Jews Leads to Silence on Iraq War," *New York Times*, March 15, 2003, A7.

25. Eric Alterman, "Semites and Anti-Semites: The Pat and Abe Show," *The Nation*, November 5, 1991, 520.

26. Jewish Telegraphic Agency, "Respected British Magazine Publishes Defense of Nazi German Troops," *Times of Israel*, May 18, 2018, www.timesofisrael.com /respected-british-magazine-publishes-defense-of-nazi-german-troops; David Bernstein, "Mondoweiss Is a Hate Site," *Washington Post*, May 4, 2015, www.washing tonpost.com/news/volokh-conspiracy/wp/2015/05/04/mondoweiss-is-a-hate-site.

27. These and subsequent quotes are drawn from Patrick J. Buchanan, "Whose War? A Neoconservative Clique Seeks to Ensnare Our Country in a Series of Wars That Are Not in America's Interest," *American Conservative*, March 24, 2003, 2–7, www.theamericanconservative.com/articles/whose-war; Peter Baker, *Days of Fire: Bush and Cheney in the White House* (New York: Doubleday, 2014), 204.

28. Martin Peretz, "The New War: Just Cause," *New Republic*, July 27, 2006, www.tnr.com/doc.mhtml?i=20060807&s=peretz080706; Norman Podhoretz, "J'Accuse," *Commentary*, July 1982, www.commentarymagazine.com/articles/pod horetz/jaccuse.

## Chapter 16. Wars of Words

1. Chemi Shalev, "Farewell to Haaretz and All Its Readers—but Especially American Jews," *Haaretz*, December 31, 2020, www.haaretz.com /israel-news/2020-12-31/ty-article/farewell-to-haaretz-and-all-its-readers-but-espe cially-american-jews/0000017f-f1dc-da6f-a77f-f9de828b0000; Ben Samuels, "With New Congress, Israel Loses Two of Its Best Friends in Washington," *Haaretz*, January 3, 2021, www.haaretz.com/us-news/.premium.HIGHLIGHT-with-new-con gress-israel-loses-two-of-its-best-friends-in-washington-1.9419833.

2. Zachary Lockman, *Contending Visions of the Middle East: The History and Politics of Orientalism* (New York: Cambridge University Press, 2004), 155; Rachel Fish, "Can the Academy Be Saved from Anti-Zionism?," *SAPIR* 5 (Spring 2022), https:// sapirjournal.org/zionism/2022/05/can-the-academy-be-saved-from-anti-zionism.

3. Alan Wolf, "Free Speech, Israel, and Jewish Illiberalism," *Chronicle of Higher Education*, November 17, 2006, B6; Gal Beckerman, "JVP: Harsh Critic of Israel, Seeks a Seat at the Communal Table," *The Forward*, April 13, 2011, https://forward .com/news/137016/jvp-harsh-critic-of-israel-seeks-a-seat-at-the-com.

4. Edward W. Said, *Orientalism* (New York: Vintage, 1979), 328.

5. Joshua Muravchik, "Enough Said: The False Scholarship of Edward Said," *World Affairs* 175, no. 6 (2013): 9–21; Thomas L. Lippman, "Islam and Its Discontents," *Washington Post*, December 11, 1983, www.washingtonpost.com /archive/entertainment/books/1983/12/11/islam-and-its-discontents/296f339c -479a-46dc-9cf8-0a020f5f1cc1; Dov S. Zakheim, "Mr. Oren's Planet: A Bogus Account from Israel's Man in Washington," *National Interest*, August 21, 2015, https://nationalinterest.org/feature/mr-oren%E2%80%99s-planet-bogus-account-is rael%E2%80%99s-man-washington-13648; Martin Kramer, "Middle East Studies Fails in America," Middle East Forum, March 14, 2002, www.meforum.org/167 /middle-east-studies-fails-in-america; Martin Kramer, *Ivory Towers on Sand: The Failure of Middle East Studies in America* (Washington, DC: Washington Institute for Near East Policy, 2001), www.academia.edu/171206/Ivory_Towers_on_Sand _The_Failure_of_Middle_East_Studies_in_America.

6. Nacha Cattan, "NYU Center: New Addition to Growing Academic Field," *The Forward*, May 2, 2003, www.meforum.org/campus-watch/8410

/nyu-center-new-addition-to-growing-academic-field; Arnold Dashefsky, Ira M. Sheskin, and Pamela J. Weathers, "Academic Resources," in *American Jewish Year Book 2018*, ed. Arnold Dashefsky and Ira M. Sheskin (Cham, Switzerland: Springer, 2019), 775–851.

7. Francie Diep, "'It's Outrageous': 2 Donor Conflicts Reveal Tensions for Jewish-Studies Scholars," *Chronicle of Higher Education*, February 28, 2022, www .chronicle.com/article/its-outrageous-2-donor-conflicts-reveal-fraught-tensions-for -jewish-studies-scholars.

8. Jennifer Senior, "Columbia's Own Middle East War," *New York Magazine*, January 19, 2005, https://nymag.com/nymetro/urban/education/features/10868.

9. Scott Sherman, "The Mideast Comes to Columbia," *The Nation*, March 16, 2005, www.thenation.com/article/archive/mideast-comes-columbia. To see one of the six iterations of *Columbia Unbecoming*, see "Columbia Unbecoming 2004," Vimeo, https://vimeo.com/89896944.

10. See "Colleges with the Best Jewish Life," *College Transitions*, July 15, 2020, www.collegetransitions.com/blog/colleges-with-the-best-jewish-life. Data from the College Transitions website.

11. Senior, "Columbia's Own Middle East War"; Sherman, "Mideast Comes to Columbia"; Douglas Feiden, "Hatred 101: Columbia's Learning Curve on Israel," *New York Daily News*, November 21, 2004, www.monabaker.org/2015/10/02/ha tred-101-columbias-learning-curve-on-israel.

12. "Intimidation Charges at Columbia (4 Letters)," *New York Times*, January 23, 2005, www.nytimes.com/2005/01/23/opinion/intimidation-charges-at-co lumbia-4-letters.html; Karen W. Arenson, "Columbia Panel Clears Professors of Anti-Semitism," *New York Times*, March 31, 2005, www.nytimes.com/2005/03/31 /nyregion/columbia-panel-clears-professors-of-antisemitism.html (the language of the report's summary belongs to the *Times*, not the report itself); Jane Kramer, "The Petition: Israel, Palestine, and a Tenure Battle at Barnard," *New Yorker*, April 7, 2008, www.newyorker.com/magazine/2008/04/14/the-petition; New York Civil Liberties Union to Lee C. Bollinger, Re: Report of the Ad Hoc Committee, letter, April 6, 2005, NYCLU, www.nyclu.org/en/letter-nyclu-calls-columbia-committee -report-inadequate.

13. Nathaniel Popper, "N.Y. School Board Bans a Controversial Arab Professor," *The Forward*, February 25, 2005, www.forward.com/articles/2741; Joyce Purnick, "Some Limits on Speech in Classrooms," *New York Times*, February 28, 2005, www.nytimes.com/2005/02/28/nyregion/some-limits-on-speech-in-classrooms .html.

14. Kramer, "The Petition"; Eric Alterman, "Motzira-Making on the Right," *The Nation*, April 17, 2008, www.thenation.com/article/archive/motzira-making-right.

15. Bari Weiss, "How to Fight Anti-Semitism on Campus," Mosaic, May 20, 2015, https://mosaicmagazine.com/response/israel-zionism/2015/05/how-to-fight -anti-semitism-on-campus; Paul Kanelos, "We Can't Wait for Universities to Fix Themselves. So We're Starting a New One," November 8, 2021, Bari Weiss Substack, https://bariweiss.substack.com/p/we-cant-wait-for-universities-to.

16. This formulation can be found in Michael Massing, "The Storm over the Israel Lobby," *New York Review of Books*, May 11, 2006, www.nybooks.com/arti cles/2006/06/08/the-storm-over-the-israel-lobby.

17. Leonard Fein, "Letter to Stephen Walt Concerning 'The Israel Lobby,'" September 2007, Berman Jewish Policy Archive, www.bjpa.org/search-results/publica tion/15930.

18. John J. Mearsheimer and Stephen M. Walt, *The Israel Lobby and U.S. Foreign Policy* (New York: Farrar, Straus and Giroux, 2007), 242; Melvin P. Leffler, "The Decider: Why Bush Chose War in Iraq," *Foreign Affairs*, November/December 2020, www.foreignaffairs.com/reviews/review-essay/2020-10-13/decider; Michael J. Mazarr, *Leap of Faith: Hubris, Negligence, and America's Greatest Foreign Policy Tragedy* (New York: PublicAffairs, 2019); Eric Alterman, *Lying in State: Why Presidents Lie and Why Trump Is Worse* (New York: Basic Books, 2020).

19. Noam Chomsky, "The Israel Lobby?," ZNet, March 28, 2016, https://chomsky.info/20060328. *The Economist* is quoted in Itamar Rabinovich, "Testing the Israel Lobby Thesis," Brookings Institution, March 1, 2008, www.brookings .edu/articles/testing-the-israel-lobby-thesis.

20. Dan Flesher, *Transforming America's Israel Lobby: The Limits of Its Power and the Potential for Change* (Washington, DC: Potomac Books, 2009), 95–96; "Occupied Thoughts: Former Deputy National Security Advisor Ben Rhodes with Peter Beinart," February 11, 2021, posted by Foundation for Middle East Peace, YouTube, www.youtube.com/watch?v=g3_P1UWVAi0&ab_channel=Foundationfor MiddleEastPeace.

21. Mearsheimer and Walt, *The Israel Lobby*, 147.

22. John Mearsheimer and Stephen Walt, "The Israel Lobby," *London Review of Books* 28, no. 6 (March 23, 2006), www.lrb.co.uk/the-paper/v28/n06/john-mear sheimer/the-israel-lobby; William Pfaff, "The Mearsheimer-Walt Paper on America's Israel Lobby," *International Herald Tribune*, April 4, 2006; Christopher L. Ball, Andrew Preston, David Schoenbaum, and Tony Smith, "The Israel Lobby and U.S. Foreign Policy: Roundtable Review," H-Diplo Roundtables 8, no. 18 (2007), www .h-net.org/~diplo/roundtables/PDF/IsraelLobby-Roundtable.pdf.

23. The quotes can be found in Massing, "The Storm"; Juan Cole, "Breaking the Silence," Salon, April 19, 2006; Eric Alterman, "AIPAC's Complaint," *The Nation*, April 13, 2006, www.thenation.com/article/archive/aipacs-complaint; Jeffrey Goldberg, "The Usual Suspect," *New Republic*, October 8, 2007; Benny Morris, "And Now for Some Facts," *New Republic*, April 28, 2006; John J. Mearsheimer, Stephen M. Walt, Aaron Friedberg, Dennis Ross, Shlomo Ben-Ami, and Zbigniew Brzezinski, "The War over Israel's Influence," *Foreign Policy*, July–August 2006, 56–66: Dov Waxman, "Review: Beyond Realpolitik: The Israel Lobby and US Support for Israel," *Israel Studies Forum* 22, no. 1 (Winter 2007): 97–114.

24. Gal Beckerman, "Scholars Debate 'Israel Lobby' Article," *The Forward*, October 6, 2006, https://forward.com/news/4845/scholars-debate-e2-80-98israel -lobby-e2-80-99-article; Alan Dershowitz, "Debunking the Newest—and Oldest— Jewish Conspiracy: A Reply to the Mearsheimer-Walt 'Working Paper,'" Harvard Law School Working Paper, 2006, www.comw.org/warreport/fulltext/0604der showitz.pdf.

25. "Definition of Anti-Semitism," European Commission, https://ec.europa.eu /info/policies/justice-and-fundamental-rights/combatting-discrimination/racism -and-xenophobia/combating-antisemitism/definition-antisemitism_en.

26. I was present at the discussion described above, which was cosponsored by *New Voices* and *Azure* magazines and took place at the Center for Jewish History in Manhattan in 2007.

27. Roselyn Bell, "At Century's End, at a Century's Beginning," American Jewish Committee Symposium, May 2006.

28. Anonymous, "I've Taught at Six Different Jewish Day Schools. They Are Preaching Dual Loyalty to Israel," *The Forward*, February 21, 2020, https://forward.com/opinion/439563/ive-taught-at-six-jewish-day-schools-theyre-preaching-dual-loyalty-to; Joshua Shanes, Facebook, Drachim—A New Path Forward for Israel/Palestine, February 8, 2021, and May 6, 2022, www.facebook.com/groups/221480179475787 (quoted with permission).

29. Richard Cohen, "Hunker Down with History," *Washington Post*, July 18, 2006; Alvin H. Rosenfeld, "Progressive Jewish Thought and the New Antisemitism," American Jewish Committee, December 2006, at Internet Archive, https://web.archive.org/web/20100312025251/http://www.ajc.org/atf/cf/%7B42D75369-D582-4380-8395-D25925B85EAF%7D/PROGRESSIVE_JEWISH_THOUGHT.PDF; Eric Rozenman, "Israel Is a Mistake—Is Mistaken," Committee for Accuracy in Middle East Reporting and Analysis, July 19, 2006, www.camera.org/article/israel-is-a-mistake-is-mistaken; Richard Cohen, *Israel: Is It Good for the Jews?* (New York: Simon and Schuster, 2014), 2, 4–5.

30. Tony Judt, "Israel: The Alternative," *New York Review of Books*, October 23, 2003, www.nybooks.com/articles/2003/10/23/israel-the-alternative.

31. Michael Powell, "Polish Consulate Says Jewish Groups Called to Oppose Historian," *Washington Post*, October 9, 2006, A10. (I was in attendance at the Paris conference in question.)

32. Michael Kinsley, "It's Not Apartheid," Slate, December 11, 2006, https://slate.com/news-and-politics/2006/12/jimmy-carter-s-moronic-new-book-about-israel.html; Joseph Lelyveld, "Jimmy Carter and Apartheid," *New York Review of Books*, March 29, 2007, www.nybooks.com/articles/2007/03/29/jimmy-carter-and-apartheid; Associated Press, "Carter Apologizes to Jews," *New York Times*, December 23, 2009, A13.

33. Leon Wieseltier, "Hits," *New Republic*, December 19, 2005, www.tnr.com/article/washington-diarist-2; David Brooks, "What 'Munich' Left Out," *New York Times*, December 11, 2005, D14; Gabriel Schoenfeld, "Spielberg's 'Munich,'" *Commentary*, February 2006, www.commentary.org/articles/gabriel-schoenfeld/spielbergs-munich; Tony Kushner, "Defending 'Munich' to My Mishpocheh," *Los Angeles Times*, January 22, 2006, www.latimes.com/archives/la-xpm-2006-jan-22-op-kushner22-story.html. See also Rachel Abramowitz, "'Munich'?," *Los Angeles Times*, January 23, 2006, www.latimes.com/archives/la-xpm-2006-jan-23-et-munich23-story.html; Shai Ginsberg, "An American Reflection: Steven Spielberg, the Jewish Holocaust and the Israeli-Palestinian Conflict," *Miguk'ang* 34, no. 1 (2011): 45–76.

34. Michelle Goldberg, "The War on 'Munich,'" Salon, December 20, 2005, www.salon.com/2005/12/20/munich_3; Kushner, "Defending 'Munich'"; Abramowitz, "'Munich'?"; Winne Hu, "In Reversal, City University Trustees Approve Honorary Degree for Tony Kushner," *New York Times*, May 9, 2011, www

.nytimes.com/2011/05/10/nyregion/in-reversal-cuny-votes-to-honor-tony-kushner
.html; Tony Shaw and Giora Goodman, *Hollywood and Israel: A History* (New York: Columbia University Press, 2022), loc. 4218, Kindle.

## Chapter 17. "Basically, a Liberal Jew"

1. "Obama Used to Joke with Staff That He's 'Basically a Liberal Jew,'" *Jerusalem Post*, January 26, 2018, www.jpost.com/american-politics/obama-used-to-joke -with-staff-that-hes-basically-a-liberal-jew-539929; Barack Obama, *A Promised Land* (New York: Crown, 2020), 652.

2. Peter Beinart, "On Gaza, Israel Is Losing the Obama Coalition," *Haaretz*, July 31, 2014, www.haaretz.com/opinion/.premium-israel-is-losing-the-obama-coa lition-1.5257687; Obama, *Promised Land*, 657.

3. Emily Hauser, "CENTCOM Commander: Unresolved Israeli-Palestinian Conflict Meant 'I Paid a Military Security Price Every Day,'" Daily Beast, July 26, 2013, www.thedailybeast.com/centcom-commander-unresolved-israeli-palestinian -conflict-meant-i-paid-a-military-security-price-every-day; William B. Quandt, "Israeli Palestinian Peace Prospects in Context," in *Pathways to Peace: America and the Arab-Israeli Conflict*, ed. Daniel Kurtzer (London: Palgrave Macmillan, 2012), 4.

4. Jeffrey Goldberg, "Obama on Zionism and Hamas," *Atlantic*, May 12, 2008, www.theatlantic.com/international/archive/2008/05/obama-on-zionism-and -hamas/8318; Eric Alterman, "(Some) Jews Against Obama," *The Nation*, March 6, 2008, www.thenation.com/article/archive/some-jews-against-obama.

5. Obama, *Promised Land*, 629; Alterman, "(Some) Jews"; Anshel Pfeffer, "U.S. Jewish Leader Worried by Thrust of White House Campaigns," *Haaretz*, February 12, 2008, www.haaretz.com/1.4990144; Larry Cohler-Esses, "Hoenlein Backing Off Apparent Swipe at Obama," *New York Jewish Week*, February 13, 2008, www .jta.org/2008/02/13/ny/hoenlein-backing-off-apparent-swipe-at-obama; Josh Gerstein, "Dad's Muslim-to-Atheist Conversion Omitted by Obama in Cairo," Politico, June 4, 2009, www.politico.com/blogs/under-the-radar/2009/06/dads-mus lim-to-atheist-conversion-omitted-by-obama-in-cairo-018888.

6. Obama, *Promised Land*, 629; Alterman, "(Some) Jews."

7. Daniel G. Hummel, *Covenant Brothers: Evangelicals, Jews, and U.S.-Israeli Relations* (Philadelphia: University of Pennsylvania Press, 2019), 186–187.

8. Sarah Posner, "Pastor Strangelove," *American Prospect*, May 21, 2006, https:// prospect.org/features/pastor-strangelove; John Hagee, *Jerusalem Countdown*, revised and updated (Chicago: Frontline, 2007).

9. Rachel Tabachnick, "Saving Jews from John Hagee," ZEEK / *The Forward*, February 15, 2010, https://zeek.forward.com/articles/116367.

10. Nathan Guttman, "Are Christian Zionists the 800 Pound Gorilla in the Pro-Israel Room?," *The Forward*, July 16, 2015, http://forward.com/news/312078/are -christian-zionists-the-800-pound-gorilla-in-the-pro-israel-room.

11. Jennifer Rubin, "Onward, Christian Zionists: The Fastest Growing Israel Support Group in America," *Weekly Standard*, August 2, 2010, reprinted at *Washington Examiner*, www.washingtonexaminer.com/weekly-standard/onward-chris tian-zionists.

12. Stephen Spector, *Evangelicals and Israel: The Story of American Christian Zionism* (New York: Oxford University Press, 2009), 172.

13. Leonard Fine, "The American Zionist Left," undated, Berman Jewish Policy Archive, www.bjpa.org/content/upload/bjpa/leon/Leonard%20Fein%20American%20Zionist%20Left.pdf.

14. Obama, *Promised Land*, 632.

15. Jonathan Broder, "Israel: The Ties That Bind," *CQ Weekly*, October 15, 2011, http://public.cq.com/docs/weeklyreport/weeklyreport-000003963858.html; Alan Dershowitz, "Has Obama Turned on Israel?," *Wall Street Journal*, July 12, 2009, www.wsj.com/articles/SB124649366875483207; Norman Podhoretz, "Why Are Jews Liberals?," *Wall Street Journal*, September 10, 2009, www.wsj.com/articles/SB10001424052970203440104574402591116901498.

16. Obama, *Promised Land*, 633.

17. Agence France-Presse, "US Senators Press Clinton on Mideast Peace," YNet, April 14, 2010, www.ynetnews.com/articles/0,7340,L-3875693,00.html.

18. "Occupied Thoughts: Former Deputy National Security Advisor Ben Rhodes with Peter Beinart," February 8, 2021, in *Occupied Territory*, podcast, Foundation for Middle East Peace, https://fmep.org/resource/occupied-thoughts-former-deputy-national-security-advisor-ben-rhodes-with-peter-beinart.

19. Obama, *Promised Land*, 629; David Klion, " 'There's a Lot of New Ground for Democrats to Fight Over': A Q&A with Ben Rhodes," *The Nation*, November 9, 2018, www.thenation.com/article/archive/ben-rhodes-interview-obama-democrats-foreign-policy; Jonathan Broder, "Israel: The Ties That Bind," *CQ Weekly*, October 11, 2011, http://public.cq.com/docs/weeklyreport/weeklyreport-000003963858.html.

20. Jacob Magid, "Backed by Deep Pockets, Adelson Made His Mark with an Unwavering Focus on Israel," *Times of Israel*, January 13, 2021, www.timesofisrael.com/backed-by-deep-pockets-adelson-made-mark-with-unwavering-focus-on-israel; Connie Bruck, "The Brass Ring," *New Yorker*, June 30, 2008, www.newyorker.com/magazine/2008/06/30/the-brass-ring; Robert Slater, with Wesley G. Pippert, "The Adelson Effect," *Moment*, May/June 2014, https://momentmag.com/author/robert-slater-with-wesley-g-pippert.

21. Matt Isaacs, "Sheldon Adelson Bets It All," *Mother Jones*, March/April 2016, www.motherjones.com/politics/2016/02/sheldon-adelson-macau-casinos-lawsuit; Chris McGreal, "Sheldon Adelson: The Casino Mogul Driving Trump's Middle East Policy," *The Guardian*, June 8, 2018, www.theguardian.com/us-news/2018/jun/08/sheldon-adelson-trump-middle-east-policy; Robert D. McFadden, "Sheldon Adelson, Billionaire Donor to G.O.P. and Israel, Is Dead at 87," *New York Times*, January 12, 2021, A1.

22. Amir Tibon and Talk Shalev, "Scenes from a Marriage," Huffington Post Highline, n.d., https://highline.huffingtonpost.com/articles/en/bibi-obama.

23. Tibon and Shalev, "Scenes"; "The Bibi-ton Bomb," *The Economist*, February 14, 2015, www.economist.com/middle-east-and-africa/2015/02/12/the-bibi-ton-bomb; Adam Taylor, "Pink Champagne, Cuban Cigars and Sheldon Adelson: How Benjamin Netanyahu Got Accused of Corruption," *Washington Post*, February 28, 2019, www.washingtonpost.com/world/2019/02/28/pink-champagne-cuban-cigars-sheldon-adelson-how-benjamin-netanyahu-got-accused-corruption.

24. Ravi Somaiya, Ian Lovett, and Barry Meier, "Sheldon Adelson's Purchase of Las Vegas Paper Seen as a Power Play," *New York Times*, January 2, 2016, A1; Josh

Nathan-Kazis, "Sheldon Adelson's Jewish Media Secrets Revealed," *The Forward*, December 22, 2015, https://forward.com/news/327694/move-over-rupert-sheldon -adelsons-secret-media-reach-revealed.

25. Eli Clifton, "Sheldon Adelson's Legacy of Underwriting American Militarism," Responsible Statecraft, January 12, 2021, https://responsiblestatecraft .org/2021/01/12/sheldon-adelsons-legacy-of-underwriting-american-militarism; Eric Alterman, "Sheldon Adelson and the End of American Anti-Semitism," *The Nation*, February 8, 2012, www.thenation.com/article/archive/sheldon-adelson -and-end-american-anti-semitism; Jason Zengerle, "Sheldon Adelson Is Ready to Buy the Presidency," *New York*, September 9, 2015, https://nymag.com/intelli gencer/2015/09/sheldon-adelson-is-ready-to-buy-the-presidency.html; McFadden, "Sheldon Adelson, Billionaire Donor."

26. Thomas L. Friedman, "Sheldon Adelson: Iran's Best Friend," *New York Times*, April 5, 2014, www.nytimes.com/2014/04/06/opinion/sunday/friedman -sheldon-irans-best-friend.html.

27. Alex Kane, "Sheldon Adelson's Far Right Alliance Will Serve Israel Long After His Death," 972, January 13, 2021, www.972mag.com/sheldon-adelson-evan gelicals-israel; Clifton, "Sheldon Adelson's Legacy."

28. Mortimer Zuckerman, "Obama's Jerusalem Stonewall," *Wall Street Journal*, April 28, 2010, www.wsj.com/articles/SB10001424052748703465204575208711846560650; Laura Meckler, "Jewish Donors Warn Obama on Israel," *Wall Street Journal*, May 19, 2011, www.wsj.com/articles/SB10001424052748703509104576331661918527 1545; Daniel Pipes, "Pipes: 'Rushdie Rules' Reach Florida," *Washington Times*, September 20, 2010, www.washingtontimes.com/news/2010/sep/20/rush die-rulesreach-florida.

29. Merrill Joan Gerber, "True Believer: My Friendship with Cynthia Ozick," *Salmagundi*, Summer 2018, https://salmagundi.skidmore.edu/articles/111-true -believer-my-friendship-with-cynthia-ozick; Uriel Heilman, "Obama Assassination Column Raises Question: Why Do Some Jews See Obama as So Sinister?," Jewish Telegraphic Agency, updated January 3, 2013, www.jta.org/2012/01/24 /politics/obama-assassination-column-raises-question-why-do-some-jews-see -obama-as-so-sinister.

30. "Occupied Thoughts: Former Deputy National Security Advisor Ben Rhodes with Peter Beinart."

31. "Remarks of President Barack Obama to the People of Israel," March 21, 2013, Obama White House, https://obamawhitehouse.archives.gov/the-press-of fice/2013/03/21/remarks-president-barack-obama-people-israel; David Remnick, "Obama in Israel: A President at Large," *New Yorker*, March 21, 2013, www.new yorker.com/news/daily-comment/obama-in-israel-a-president-at-large.

32. Yossi Klein Halevi, "Obama's Big Israel Breakthrough," *New Republic*, March 21, 2013, https://newrepublic.com/article/112730/obama-israel-speech-big-break through; Hussein Ibish, "Outsourcing Peace," *Foreign Policy*, March 21, 2013, https://foreignpolicy.com/2013/03/21/crowdsourcing-peace.

33. Jeffrey Goldberg, "Obama to Israel—Time Is Running Out," Bloomberg, March 2, 2014, www.bloomberg.com/opinion/articles/2014-03-02/obama-to-is rael-time-is-running-out.

34. James Traub, "Does Abe Foxman Have an Anti-Anti-Semite Problem?," *New York Times Magazine*, January 14, 2007, www.nytimes.com/2007/01/14/magazine /14foxman.t.html; Peter Beinart, *The Crisis of Zionism* (New York: Times Books, 2012), 44; Dan Flesher, *Transforming America's Israel Lobby: The Limits of Its Power and the Potential for Change* (Washington, DC: Potomac Books, 2009), 126.

35. Robert I. Friedman, "The Enemy Within: How the Anti-Defamation League Turned the Notion of Human Rights on Its Head, Spying on Progressives and Funneling Information to Law Enforcement," *Village Voice*, May 11, 1993, 27–32; Eric Alterman, "The Defamation League," *The Nation*, January 28, 2009, www.the nation.com/article/archive/defamation-league; Aryeh Neier, "The Attack on Human Rights Watch," *New York Review of Books*, November 2006, www.nybooks .com/articles/2006/11/02/the-attack-on-human-rights-watch.

36. Peter Beinart, "The Failure of the American Jewish Establishment," *New York Review of Books*, June 10, 2010, www.nybooks.com/articles/archives/2010/jun/10 /failure-american-jewish-establishment.

37. Ron Kampeas, "Pro-Israel, with Questions: Beinart Pins His Thesis to the Synagogue Door," *Jewish Telegraphic Agency*, May 25, 2010, www.jta.org /2010/05/25/politics/pro-israel-with-questions-beinart-pins-his-thesis-to-the-syna gogue-door; Ami Eden, "Responding to Beinart," *Jewish Telegraphic Agency*, May 24, 2010, www.jta.org/2010/05/24/culture/responding-to-beinart; Eric Alterman, "Israel Agonistes," *The Nation*, June 2, 2010, www.thenation.com/article/archive /israel-agonistes.

38. "A Portrait of Jewish Americans," Pew Research Center on Religion and Public Life, October 13, 2013, www.pewforum.org/2013/10/01/jewish-american-beliefs -attitudes-culture-survey. Note: These numbers were similar to those published in the 2020 follow-up to the 2013 survey.

39. Connie Bruck, "Friends of Israel," *New Yorker*, August 25, 2014, www .newyorker.com/magazine/2014/09/01/friends-israel; Beinart, *Crisis of Zionism*, 44; Josh Nathan-Kazis, "Jews Express Wide Criticism of Israel in Pew Survey but Leaders Dismiss Findings," *The Forward*, October 2, 2013, https://forward.com/news /israel/184900/jews-express-wide-criticism-of-israel-in-pew-surve; David Samuels, "Q&A with Abe Foxman, Head of the Anti-Defamation League," Tablet, December 20, 2013, https://orangecounty.adl.org/news/abe-foxman-on-why-2013-was -bad-for-the-jews.

40. Sarah Posner, "Too Hot for Shul: Rabbis Seek Healthy Israel Dialogue After Gaza," Religion Dispatches, September 22, 2014, https://religiondispatches.org /too-hot-for-shul-rabbis-seek-healthy-israel-dialogue-after-gaza; Laurie Goodstein, "Talk in Synagogue of Israel and Gaza Goes from Debate to Wrath to Rage," *New York Times*, September 22, 2014, www.nytimes.com/2014/09/23/us/rabbis-find -talk-of-israel-and-gaza-a-sure-way-to-draw-congregants-wrath.html.

41. Shmuel Rosner and Michael Herzog, "Jewish Values and Israel's Use of Force in Armed Conflict: Perspectives from World Jewry," Jewish People Policy Institute, 2015, www.jppi.org.il/uploads/Jewish_Values_and_Israels_Use_of_Force_in _Armed_Conflict-JPPI.pdf.

42. Dahlia Scheindlin, "The Israeli Zionist Left: Sources of Failure and Renewal," Friedrich Ebert Stiftung, October 2020, www.fes.org/il/shop/the-israeli

-zionist-left-sources-of-failure-and-renewal; Elisheva Goldberg, "The Making of an Echo Chamber," *Jewish Currents*, March 11, 2020, https://jewishcurrents.org/the -making-of-an-echo-chamber.

43. Michael Oren, "How Obama Opened His Heart to the 'Muslim World,'" *Foreign Policy*, June 19, 2015, https://foreignpolicy.com/2015/06/19/barack-obama -muslim-world-outreach-consequences-israel-ambassador-michael-oren.

44. Michael B. Oren, *Ally: My Journey Across the American-Israeli Divide* (New York: Random House, 2015), 268, 247, 266–267; Jonathan Broder, "Sound and Fury: Michael Oren's Anti-Obama Memoir," *Newsweek*, June 27, 2015, www.news week.com/2015/07/10/michael-oren-anti-obama-memoir-347759.html.

45. Oren, *Ally*, 216–217, 267; "How Obama Abandoned Israel," *Wall Street Journal*, June 16, 2015, www.wsj.com/articles/how-obama-abandoned-israel -1434409772; Elliott Abrams, "The Ally That Wasn't," *Commentary*, September 2015, www.commentarymagazine.com/articles/elliott-abrams/ally-wasnt; Chemi Shalev, "Michael Oren: American Jewish Journalists Lead Media's Anti-Israeli Assault," *Haaretz*, June 15, 2015, www.haaretz.com/oren-u-s-jewish-journalists-lead -medias-anti-israeli-assault-1.5372323.

46. Gary Rosenblatt, "Why Benjamin Netanyahu Treated the Jewish Media with Contempt," *New York Jewish Week*, June 10, 2021, https://jewishweek.timesofisrael .com/why-benjamin-netanyahu-treated-jewish-media-with-contempt.

47. Aaron David Miller, "The Curious Case of Benjamin Netanyahu," *Foreign Policy*, May 30, 2012, https://foreignpolicy.com/2012/05/30/the-curious -case-of-benjamin-netanyahu; Seth Freedman, "Why the Benjamin Netanyahu Tape Is No Real Shocker," *The Guardian*, July 26, 2010, www.theguardian.com /commentisfree/2010/jul/26/binyamin-netanyahu-tape-israeli-palestinian-politics; Jeffrey Goldberg, "The Obama Doctrine," *Atlantic*, April 2016, www.theatlantic .com/magazine/archive/2016/04/the-obama-doctrine/471525.

48. Peter Beinart, "AIPAC Refuses to Learn from Its Mistakes on Iran," *Jewish Currents*, January 30, 2022, https://jewishcurrents.org/aipac-refuses-to-learn -from-its-mistakes-on-iran; Jane Eisner, "The Full Transcript of Forward Editor-in-Chief's Interview with Obama," *The Forward*, August 31, 2015, http:// forward.com/news/320091/read-the-transcript-of-forward-editor-in-chiefs-inter view-with-barack-obama/#ixzz3kW7MYyoz.

49. Glenn Greenwald, "Leaked Emails from Pro-Clinton Group Reveal Censorship of Staff on Israel, AIPAC Pandering, Warped Militarism," The Intercept, November 5, 2015, https://theintercept.com/2015/11/05/leaked-emails-from-pro-clinton-group -reveal-censorship-of-staff-on-israel-aipac-pandering-warped-militarism.

50. This account relies on the author's own experience as well as the following: Ben Smith, "Israel Rift Roils Democratic Ranks," Politico, December 7, 2011, www .politico.com/story/2011/12/israel-rift-roils-democratic-ranks-069929; Ben Smith, "What's 'Anti-Semitic'?," Politico, December 9, 2011, www.politico.com/blogs /bensmith/1211/Whats_antiSemitic.html; Peter Wallsten, "Center for American Progress, Group Tied to Obama, Under Fire from Israel Advocates," *Washington Post*, January 19, 2012, www.washingtonpost.com/politics/center-for-america -progress-group-tied-to-obama-accused-of-anti-semitic-language/2012/01/17/gIQA crHXAQ_story.html; Nathan Guttman, "AIPAC Tries to Brand Israel as Liberal Cause," *The Forward*, March 10, 2013, http://forward.com/articles/172475

/aipac-tries-to-brand-israel-as-liberal-cause; Greenwald, "Leaked Emails"; Jessica Schulberg and Ryan Grim, "Netanyahu Successfully Lobbies to Address Progressive Think Tank During DC Visit," Huffington Post, October 30, 2015, www.huffpost.com/entry/netanyahu-center-for-american-progress_n_56301482 e4b0631799100532; Nahal Toosi, "Bibi Turns on the Charm for Liberals," Politico, November 10, 2015, www.politico.com/story/2015/11/benjamin-netanyahu-center -for-american-progress-21569.

51. "New poll: U.S. Jews support Iran deal, despite misgivings," *Jewish Journal*, July 23, 2015, jewishjournal.com/news/united-states/176121/.

52. Barak Ravid, "Analysis: Kerry's Speech Was Superbly Zionist, Pro-Israel, and Three Years Too Late," *Haaretz*, December 29, 2016, www.haaretz.com/israel -news/.premium-kerry-s-speech-superbly-azionist-pro-israel-3-years-too-late-1.5479462.

53. Lara Friedman, "Israel's Unsung Protector: Obama," *New York Times*, April 10, 2016, www.nytimes.com/2016/04/12/opinion/international/israels-unsung-pro tector-obama.html; Avi Shlaim, "Believe It or Not, Barack Obama Had Israel's Best Interest at Heart," *The Guardian*, January 17, 2017, www.theguardian.com/com mentisfree/2017/jan/17/barack-obama-netanyahu-trump-israe; Carol Morello and Ruth Eglash, "Netanyahu Blasts U.N., Obama over West Bank Settlements Resolution," *Washington Post*, December 23, 2016, www.washingtonpost.com/world /netanyahu-calls-un-resolution-on-settlements-shameful/2016/12/23/2d45fbac -c94c-11e6-bf4b-2c064d32a4bf_story.html.

54. Peter Baker, "A Defiant Israel Vows to Expand Its Settlements," *New York Times*, December 26, 2016, A1; "Public Uncertain, Divided over America's Place in the World," Pew Research Center, May 5, 2016, www.pewresearch.org/poli tics/2016/05/05/public-uncertain-divided-over-americas-place-in-the-world.

## Chapter 18. Coming Unglued

1. Peter Beinart, "Given the U.S. Presidential Candidates' Views on Palestinians, I Miss Obama Already," *Haaretz*, November 9, 2015, www.haaretz.com/world -news/given-u-s-candidates-views-on-palestinians-i-miss-obama-already-1.5418759.

2. Beinart, "Given the U.S."; Peter Beinart, "Israel's New Lawyer: Hillary Clinton," *Haaretz*, August 11, 2014, www.haaretz.com/opinion/.premium-israels-new -lawyer-hillary-clinton-1.5258957. Note: I received one of the robocalls so described.

3. Giovanni Russonello, "Criticize Israel? For Democratic Voters, It's Now Fair Game," *New York Times*, November 1, 2019, www.nytimes.com/2019/11/01 /us/politics/democrats-israel-polls.html; Jason Horowitz, "Criticizing Israel, Bernie Sanders Highlights Split Among Jewish Democrats," *New York Times*, April 15, 2016, A1; "Jamaal Bowman Wants to Be the Bridge Between His Jewish and Black Constituents," interview with Yehuda Kurtzer, Jewish Telegraphic Agency, December 22, 2020, www.jta.org/2020/12/22/opinion/jamaal-bowman-wants-to-be-the -bridge-between-his-jewish-and-black-constituents; "Republicans and Democrats Grow Even Further Apart in Views of Israel, Palestinians," Pew Research Center, January 23, 2018, www.pewresearch.org/politics/2018/01/23/republicans-and -democrats-grow-even-further-apart-in-views-of-israel-palestinians; Becky A. Alper, "Modest Warming in U.S. Views on Israel and Palestinians," Pew Research Center, May 26, 2022, https://www.pewresearch.org/religion/2022/05/26/modest-warm ing-in-u-s-views-on-israel-and-palestinians.

4. Jonathan Mahler, "Donald Trump Courts Wary Jewish Voters," *New York Times*, March 20, 2016, www.nytimes.com/2016/03/21/us/politics/donald-trump -jews.html; Eric Alterman, "Trump's Executive Order on Anti-Semitism Isn't About Protecting Jews," *The Nation*, December 19, 2019, www.thenation.com/article/ar chive/executive-order-anti-semitism.

5. Kevin McCarthy (@kevinmccarthy), Twitter, October 24, 2018 (later de-leted), screenshot at Devan Cole, "House Majority Leader Deletes Tweet Saying So-ros, Bloomberg, Steyer Are Trying to 'Buy' Election," CNN, October 28, 2018, www .cnn.com/2018/10/28/politics/tom-steyer-mccarthy-tweet/index.html; Aaron Blake, "How the Trumps and Conservative Media Helped Mainstream a Conspiracy Theory Now Tied to Tragedy," *Washington Post*, October 29, 2018, www.washingtonpost.com /politics/2018/10/29/how-trumps-conservative-media-helped-mainstream-conspiracy -theory-now-tied-tragedy; Eric Alterman, "Chronicle of Deaths Foretold," *The Na-tion*, November 8, 2018, www.thenation.com/article/archive/trump-rhetoric-violence; Ben Samuels, "Holocaust Comparisons, Soros Conspiracies Dominate U.S. Republican Messaging," *Haaretz, August* 14, 2022, www.haaretz.com/us-news/2022 -08-14/ty-article/.highlight/holocaust-comparisons-soros-conspiracies-dominate -u-s-republican-messaging/00000182-9bca-d9bc-affb-fbde193f0000.

6. Tessa Stuart, "Why Trump Calls for Racial Profiling After Attacks," *Roll-ing Stone*, September 19, 2016, www.rollingstone.com/politics/politics-features /why-trump-calls-for-racial-profiling-after-attacks-103371; "Richard Spencer Tells Israelis They 'Should Respect' Him: 'I'm a White Zionist," *Haaretz*, August 16, 2017, www.haaretz.com/israel-news/richard-spencer-to-israelis-i-m-a-white-zionist -respect-me-1.5443480.

7. Natan Sharansky and Gil Troy, "Can American Jews and Israeli Jews Stay Together as One People?," Mosaic, July 19, 2018, https://mosaicmagazine.com/essay /israel-zionism/2018/07/can-american-and-israeli-jews-stay-together-as-one-people. See also Eric Alterman, "Benjamin Netanyahu, Friend of the Far Right," *Le Monde Diplomatique*, September 2019, https://mondediplo.com/2019/09/13netanyahu.

8. Libby Lenkinski, "How Trump and Netanyahu Made American Antisemitism Come Alive," Evolve, December 31, 2020, https://evolve.reconstructingjudaism .org/howtrumpandnetanyahumadeamericanantisemitismcomealive.

9. "U.S. Image Suffers as Publics Around World Question Trump's Leadership," Pew Research Center, June 26, 2017, www.pewresearch.org /global/2017/06/26/u-s-image-suffers-as-publics-around-world-question-trumps -leadership; Jay Reeves, "Days After Synagogue Massacre, Online Hate Is Thriv-ing," Associated Press, November 1, 2018, https://apnews.com/article/a0099d8f 60054deab9ed433b453bc8bd; Mark Landler, "Support for the President in Pitts-burgh, but It's Coming from Israel," *New York Times*, November 1, 2018, A20; Alterman, "Chronicle of Deaths"; Gershom Gorenberg, "Netanyahu Doesn't Think Trump Has a Jewish Problem. And That's a Problem," *Washington Post*, Febru-ary 17, 2017, www.washingtonpost.com/news/global-opinions/wp/2017/02/17/net anyahu-doesnt-think-trump-has-a-jewish-problem-and-thats-a-problem; Philip Rucker, "Trump, Frustrated by Unpopularity with Jews, Thrusts Israel into His Culture War," *Washington Post*, August 22, 2019, www.washingtonpost.com/pol itics/trump-frustrated-by-unpopularity-with-jews-thrusts-israel-into-his-culture -war/2019/08/21/81557d10-c428-11e9-b72f-b31dfaa77212_story.html.

10. Ilhan Omar (@IlhanMN), Twitter, January 21, 2019, https://twitter.com/IlhanMN/status/1087580654194384896; "What Did Ilhan Omar Say?," transcript, Institute for Policy Studies, March 6, 2019, https://ips-dc.org/what-did-ilhan-omar-say-heres-the-full-transcript-of-her-response-to-a-question-about-anti-semitism; AIPAC (@AIPAC), Twitter, March 1, 2019, https://twitter.com/aipac/status/1101596692548333575; Jonathan Greenblatt, "Omar's Comments Are Wrong. Plain and Simple," *USA Today*, March 6, 2019, www.usatoday.com/story/opinion/2019/03/06/ilhan-omars-comments-were-anti-semitic-rhetoric-says-adl-talker/3078821002; Cody Nelson, "Minnesota Congresswoman Ignites Debate on Israel and Anti-Semitism," NPR, March 7, 2019, www.npr.org/2019/03/07/700901834/minnesota-congresswoman-ignites-debate-on-israel-and-anti-semitism; "Liberalism and the Jews," *Commentary*, October 1980, www.commentary.org/articles/robert-alter-2/liberalism-the-jews-a-symposium; Ben Samuels, "Trump: 'Israel Literally Owned Congress' Until a Decade Ago," *Haaretz*, November 1, 2021, www.haaretz.com/us-news/trump-israel-literally-owned-congress-until-a-decade-ago-1.10344379.

11. Zack Beauchamp, "The Ilhan Omar Anti-Semitism Controversy, Explained," Vox, March 6, 2019, www.vox.com/policy-and-politics/2019/3/6/18251639/ilhan-omar-israel-anti-semitism-jews; Nelson, "Minnesota Congresswoman Ignites Debate"; Karen Zraick, "Ilhan Omar's Latest Remarks on Israel Draw Criticism," *New York Times*, March 1, 2019, www.nytimes.com/2019/03/01/us/politics/ilhan-omar-israel.html.

12. Ron Kampeas, "AIPAC Apologizes for Ads That Called Some Democrats 'Radicals' Pushing 'Anti-Semitic' Policies," Jewish Telegraphic Agency, February 8, 2020, www.jta.org/2020/02/08/united-states/aipac-apologizes-for-ad-that-said-radical-democrats-were-maybe-a-greater-threat-than-isis; Jeremy Slevin (@jeremyslevin), Twitter, August 11, 2021, https://twitter.com/jeremyslevin/status/1425479000487571466; Ben Samuels, " 'Putting Her Life at Risk': Ilhan Omar Staff Slams AIPAC over Aggressive Campaign Ads," *Haaretz*, August 12, 2021, www.haaretz.com/us-news/.premium-putting-her-life-at-risk-ilhan-omar-slams-aipac-over-aggressive-campaign-ads-1.1011151. I received one such email on February 13, 2019. See image at Mairav Zonszein, Facebook, February 12, 2019, www.facebook.com/photo?fbid=10157153874468793&set=a.10151093148953793.

13. Amir Tibon, "Senior Trump Admin. Official Says Politicians Get 'Very Rich' by Supporting Israel," *Haaretz*, February 16, 2020, www.haaretz.com/us-news/.premium-senior-trump-admin-official-says-politicians-get-very-rich-by-supporting-israel-1.9308451; David Samuels, "American Racist," Tablet, June 11, 2020, www.tabletmag.com/sections/news/articles/kevin-macdonald-american-anti-semitism.

14. Lior Zalzman, "A 'Jewish Space Laser' Sounds Funny. But Marjorie Taylor Greene's Anti-Semitism Is No Laughing Matter," Jewish Telegraphic Agency, February 3, 2021, www.jta.org/2021/02/03/opinion/a-jewish-space-laser-sounds-funny-but-marjorie-taylor-greenes-anti-semitism-is-no-laughing-matter; David Harris (@DavidHarrisAJC), Twitter, January 31, 2021, https://twitter.com/DavidHarrisAJC/status/1355868748104806404; Ben Sales, "Conservatives Are More Likely Than Liberals to Hold Anti-Semitic Views, Survey Finds," Jewish Telegraphic Agency, April 22, 2021, www.jta.org/2021/04/22/united-states/conservatives-are-more-likely-than-liberals-to-hold-anti-semitic-views-survey-finds.

15. Adam Kirsch, "The Great Jewish American Liberal Academic Anti-Anti-Zionist Freak-Out," Tablet, December 2, 2014, www.tabletmag.com/sections/arts-letters/articles/academic-boycotts; Samuel Edelman and Carol Edelman, "When Failure Succeeds: Disinvestment as Delegitimation," in *The Case Against Academic Boycotts of Israel*, ed. Cary Nelson and Gabriel Noah Brahm (Chicago: Members for Scholars Rights, 2015), 235–243; Alper, "Modest Warming."

16. Ali Mustafa, " 'Boycotts Work': An Interview with Omar Barghouti," Electronic Intifadah, May 31, 2009, http://electronicintifada.net/content/boycotts-work-interview-omar-barghouti/8263; "Omar Barghouti—Strategies for Change," video, Dag Hammarskjöld Society, Vimeo, https://vimeo.com/75201955.

17. The BDS movement's website is at https://bdsmovement.net.

18. Robert Malley, "An Anti-Imperialist Father and His American Diplomat Son," *Jewish Currents*, February 4, 2021, https://jewishcurrents.org/an-anti-imperialist-father-and-his-american-diplomat-son.

19. "In Support of Boycott, Divest, Sanction and a Free Palestine," *Harvard Crimson*, April 29, 2022, www.thecrimson.com/article/2022/4/29/editorial-bds.

20. Kimberlé Williams Crenshaw, "Mapping the Margins: Intersectionality, Identity Politics, and Violence Against Women of Color," *Stanford Law Review* 43, no. 6 (July 1991): 1241–1299.

21. Emma Green, "Why Do Black Activists Care About Palestine?," *Atlantic*, August 18, 2016, www.theatlantic.com/politics/archive/2016/08/why-did-black-american-activists-start-caring-about-palestine/496088. See also ADL memo, June 9, 2020, https://s3.us-east-1.amazonaws.com/jewish-currents/JC-ADL_DX_memo_2020-06-pages.pdf.

22. Kenneth Stern, *The Conflict over the Conflict: The Israel/Palestine Campus Debate* (Toronto: New Jewish Press, 2020), 11–12; Aiden Pink, "US Groups Failed to Disclose Grants from Israeli Government," *The Forward*, August 31, 2020, https://forward.com/news/israel/453286/us-pro-israel-groups-failed-to-disclose-grants-from-israeli-government; "Brief of T'ruah and J Street as Amici Curiae in Support of Plaintiff-Appellant and Reversal," Arkansas Times LP v. Mark Waldrop et al., Appellate Case 19-1378, April 15, 2019, online at Georgetown Law, www.law.georgetown.edu/icap/wp-content/uploads/sites/32/2019/04/19-1378-filed-brief.pdf. For the Maccabee Task Force, see www.maccabeetaskforce.org/about.

23. Noa Kattler Kupertz, "I Was Publicly Blacklisted by a Shadowy Website for My Views on Israel," *The Forward*, January 30, 2018, https://forward.com/scribe/393278/i-was-publicly-blacklisted-by-a-shadowy-website-for-my-views-on-israel; Josh Nathan-Kazis, "REVEALED: Canary Mission Blacklist Is Secretly Bankrolled by Major Jewish Federation," *The Forward*, October 3, 2018, https://forward.com/news/411355/revealed-canary-mission-blacklist-is-secretly-bankrolled-by-major-jewish; Ishmael N. Daro, "How an App Funded by Sheldon Adelson Is Covertly Influencing the Online Conversation About Israel," Buzzfeed, September 20, 2018, www.buzzfeednews.com/article/ishmaeldaro/act-il-social-media-astroturfing-israel-palestine; Massarah Mikati, "She was fired for being publicly pro-Palestine. One year later, no one is hiring her," *The Philadelphia Inquirer*, August 23, 2022, www.inquirer.com/news/agnes-irwin-fires-pro-palestine-employee-20220823.html.

24. Eric Alterman, "The BDS Campaign's Unpopular Front," *Democracy* 47 (Winter 2018), https://democracyjournal.org/magazine/47/the-bds-campaigns-unpopular-front; "About Amcha Initiative," https://amchainitiative.org/about.

25. Andrew Demillo, "Appeals court upholds Arkansas' Israel boycott pledge law, *The Washington Post*, June 22, 2022, https://www.washingtonpost.com/politics /appeals-court-upholds-arkansas-israel-boycott-pledge-law/2022/06/22/54efa492 -f24e-11ec-ac16-8fbf7194cd78_story.html.

26. "Israel/Palestine: Facebook Censors Discussion of Rights Issues," Human Rights Watch, October 8, 2021, www.hrw.org/news/2021/10/08/israel/palestine -facebook-censors-discussion-rights-issues; Associated Press, "Mark Lamont Fired from CNN After His Speech on Israel Draws Outrage," November 30, 2018, NBC News, www.nbcnews.com/news/us-news/marc-lamont-hill-fired-cnn-after-his -speech-israel-draws-n942151; "I Will Not Yield My Values: Fired AP Journalist Emily Wilder Speaks Out After Right-Wing Smears," Democracy Now, May 25, 2021, www.democracynow.org/2021/5/25/journalist_emily_wilder_ap_firing; Murtaza Hussein, "Israeli Diplomat Pressured UNC to Remove Teacher Who Criticized Israel," The Intercept, September 28, 2021, https://theintercept.com/2021/09/28 /israel-palestine-unc-academic-freedom.

27. Eric Alterman, "Does Anyone Take B.D.S. Seriously?," *New York Times*, July 30, 2019, A27.

28. Stewart Ain, "This Student Is Taking on Columbia in First Test of Trump's Title VI Order," *New York Jewish Week*, January 14, 2020, https://jewishweek.times ofisrael.com/columbia-complaint-tests-limits-of-anti-zionist-speech; Danielle Siri, "N.Y.'s Columbia University Rattled by Jewish Students' Complaints, Filed in Wake of Trump's Anti-Semitism Order," *Haaretz*, December 24, 2019, www.haaretz.com /us-news/.premium-trump-s-anti-semitism-executive-order-prompts-jewish-students -to-speak-up-in-u-s-ca-1.8317033; Hanna Dreyfus, "Columbia University Students Pass College's First Ever BDS Referendum," *New York Jewish Week*, September 29, 2020, https://jewishweek.timesofisrael.com/columbia-university-students-pass-its -first-ever-bds-referendum.

29. Elizabeth Redden, "Pro-Israel Groups Question Federal Funds for Middle East Centers," Inside Higher Ed, September 18, 2014, www.insidehighered.com /quicktakes/2014/09/18/pro-israel-groups-question-federal-funds-middle-east-cen ters; Stephen Zunes, "Trump's Dangerous Appointment to Key Civil Rights Position: Kenneth Marcus," *The Progressive*, November 3, 2017, https://progressive.org /dispatches/trumps-dangerous-appointment-to-civil-rights-Kenneth-Marcus; Peter Baker and Maggie Haberman, "Trump Targets Anti-Semitism and Israeli Boycotts on College Campuses," *New York Times*, December 10, 2019, A20; Alterman, "Trump's Executive Order on Anti-Semitism"; Graham Wright, Michelle Shain, Shahar Hecht, and Leonard Saxe, "The Limits of Hostility: Students Report on Antisemitism and Anti-Israel Sentiment at Four US Universities," Cohen Center for Modern Jewish Studies, Brandeis University, 2017, www.brandeis.edu/cmjs/noteworthy/ssri /limits-hostility-campuses.html; Ari Y. Kelman, Abiya Ahmed, Ilana Horwitz, Jeremiah Lockwood, Marva Shalev Marom, and Maja Zuckerman, "Safe and on the Sidelines: Jewish Students and the Israel-Palestine Conflict on Campus," Research Group of the Concentration in Education and Jewish Studies, Stanford University, 2017, at Berman Jewish Policy Archive, www.bjpa.org/bjpa/search-results?search=safe+on+the+sidelines.

30. Alterman, "Benjamin Netanyahu, Friend of the Far Right."

31. Mary Trump, *Too Much and Never Enough: How My Family Created the World's Most Dangerous Man* (New York: Simon and Schuster, 2020); Anshel

Pfeffer, *Bibi: The Turbulent Life and Times of Benjamin Netanyahu* (New York: Basic Books, 2018), 15–28.

32. Barak Ravid, "Trump Blasts Netanyahu for Disloyalty: 'F**k Him,'" Axios, December 21, 2021, www.axios.com/trump-netanyahu-disloyalty-fuck-him -276ac6cc-3f70-4fba-b315-c82a59603e67.html.

33. Brendan Cole, "Sheldon Adelson Gave Trump and Republicans over $424 Million Since 2016," *Newsweek*, January 12, 2021, www.newsweek.com/sheldon-adelson -donald-trump-republicans-donations-1560883; Lazar Berman, "No Longer US Ambassador, David Friedman Is Sticking to His Sledgehammers," *Times of Israel*, February 8, 2021, www.timesofisrael.com/no-longer-us-ambassador-david -friedman-is-sticking-to-his-sledgehammers; Kate Kelly, David Kirkpatrick, and Alan Rappeport, "Seeking Backers for New Fund, Jared Kushner Turns to Middle East," *New York Times*, November 26, 2021, A1; Edward Wong, "The Rapture and the Real World: Mike Pompeo Blends Beliefs and Policy," *New York Times*, March 30, 2019, www.nytimes.com/2019/03/30/us/politics/pompeo-christian-policy.html; Josh Alvarez, "Trump's Ambassador to Israel Is Truly Terrifying," *Washington Monthly*, March 23, 2017, https://washingtonmonthly.com/2017/03/23/trumps-ambassador-to-israel-is-truly -terrifying; Associated Press, "Probe Finds Trump Officials Repeatedly Violated Hatch Act," *U.S. News and World Report*, November 10, 2021, www.usnews.com/news/politics /articles/2021-11-10/probe-finds-trump-officials-repeatedly-violated-hatch-act.

34. David D. Kirkpatrick and Kate Kelly, "Trump Threw Saudi Arabia a Lifeline After Khashoggi's Death. Two Years Later, He Has Gotten Little in Return," *Washington Post*, October 2, 2020, www.washingtonpost.com/national-security /trump-threw-saudi-arabia-a-lifeline-after-khashoggis-death-two-years-later-he-has -gotten-little-in-return/2020/10/02/699af7f6-04d5-11eb-8879-7663b816bfa5_ story.html; Dion Nissenbaum and Rory Jones, "Jared Kushner's New Plans to Invest Saudi Money in Israel," *Wall Street Journal*, May 7, 2022, www.wsj.com/articles /jared-kushners-new-fund-plans-to-invest-saudi-money-in-israel-11651927236?mod =djemalertNEWS; David D. Kirkpatrick and Kate Kelly, "Before Giving Billions to Jared Kushner, Saudi Investment Fund Had Big Doubts," *New York Times*, April 10, 2022, www.nytimes.com/2022/04/10/us/jared-kushner-saudi-investment-fund .html; Bob Woodward, *Rage* (New York: Simon and Schuster, 2021), 227; Ronen Bergman and Mark Mazetti, "Israeli Companies Aided Saudi Spying Despite Khashoggi Killing," *New York Times*, July 17, 2021, A1, www.nytimes.com/2021/07 /17/world/middleeast/israel-saudi-khashoggi-hacking-nso.html.

35. Amnon Cavari, "Trump and Israel: Exploiting a Partisan Divide for Political Gains," *Israeli Studies* 27, no. 1 (Spring 2022): 156–181.

36. Amir Tibon, "Three Years Late, Israelis Finally Hear the Truth About Trump," *Haaretz*, November 27, 2021, www.haaretz.com/us-news/2021-11-27 /ty-article/.highlight/netanyahu-mossad-years-late-israel-hear-truth-trump-iran /0000017f-da72-d42c-afff-dff265140000; Emanuel Fabian, "Military Intelligence, Backs Iran Deal, Breaking with IDF, Mossad," *Times of Israel*, June 22, 2022, https://www.timesofisrael.com/military-intelligence-backs-revived-iran-deal -breaking-with-idf-chief-mossad/; Peter Beinart, "AIPAC Refuses to Learn from Its Mistakes," *Jewish Currents*, January 32, 2022, https://jewishcurrents.org/aipac -refuses-to-learn-from-its-mistakes-on-iran; Ben Samuels, "Netanyahu Urged Trump to Strike Iran, Ex-defense Chief Suggests in Censored Book," *Haaretz*, May

10, 2022, www.haaretz.com/us-news/.premium-netanyahu-urged-trump-to-strike
-iran-ex-defense-chief-suggests-in-censored-book-1.10789522.

37. Lazar Berman, "From Iron Dome to Supply Chains, US Christian Group Quietly
Shaping US-Israel Ties," *Times of Israel*, January 7, 2002, www.timesofisrael.com/from
-iron-dome-to-supply-chains-us-christian-group-quietly-shaping-us-israel-ties; Jewish
Electorate Institute National Survey, March 28-April 3, 2022, www.jewishelectorate
institute.org/wp-content/uploads/2022/04/Jewish-Electorate-Institute-National-Jewish
-Survey-Topline-Results-040322.pdf.

38. Ron Kampeas, "Donald Trump: I Could Run for Prime Minister of Israel,"
*The Forward*, November 1, 2021, https://forward.com/fast-forward/477523/donald
-trump-i-could-run-for-prime-minister-of-israel; Matthew Haag, "Robert Jeffress,
Pastor Who Said Jews Are Going to Hell, Led Prayer at Jerusalem Embassy," *New
York Times*, May 14, 2018, www.nytimes.com/2018/05/14/world/middleeast/rob
ert-jeffress-embassy-jerusalem-us.html.

39. Sam Brodey and Hanna Trudo, "Biden and Sanders Teams Stand Off over
Israeli 'Occupation,'" Daily Beast, July 21, 2020, www.thedailybeast.com/biden
-and-sanders-teams-stand-off-over-israeli-occupation; Eric Alterman, "In New
York, Zionism and Liberalism Faced Off—and Liberalism Won," *The Nation*, July
1, 2020, www.thenation.com/article/politics/eliot-engel-israel.

40. Jackson Diehl, "Netanyahu's Reaction to Biden's Victory Is Appalling," *Washington Post*, December 6, 2020, www.washingtonpost.com/opinions/global-opinions
/netanyahus-reaction-to-bidens-victory-is-appalling/2020/12/06/c920146e-357b
-11eb-b59c-adb7153d10c2_story.html; Amira Hass, "Why Is the Israeli Military Ex-
ercising in These Palestinian Villages for the First Time in 7 Years?," *Haaretz*, February 3, 2021, www.haaretz.com/israel-news/.premium.MAGAZINE-why-is-the-idf
-exercising-in-these-palestinian-villages-for-first-time-since-2013-1.9509405.

41. Mark Rod, "Biden's U.N. Ambassador Nominee Pledges to Support Israel
at the U.N," *Jewish Insider*, January 27, 2021, https://jewishinsider.com/2021/01
/linda-thomas-greenfield-confirmation.

## Conclusion: Not "Over"

1. Danielle Ziri, "Over Three-Quarters of U.S. Jews Voted for Biden in Election,
Poll Finds," *Haaretz*, November 4, 2021, www.haaretz.com/us-news/.premium
-over-three-quarters-of-u-s-jews-voted-for-biden-in-election-poll-finds-1.9288692;
Lydia Saad, "Americans Still Favor Israel While Warming to Palestinians," Gallup,
March 19, 2021, https://news.gallup.com/poll/340331/americans-favor-israel-warm
ing-palestinians.aspx; Michael Oren, "The Death of the Arab-Israeli Conflict,"
Tablet, January 12, 2021, www.tabletmag.com/sections/israel-middle-east
/articles/death-of-arab-israeli-conflict; Hussein Agha and Ahmad Samih Khalidi, "A
Palestinian Reckoning: Time for a New Beginning," *Foreign Affairs*, March/April 2021,
www.foreignaffairs.com/articles/middle-east/2021-02-16/palestinian-reckoning.

2. Jonathan Lis, "'No Diplomatic Process with the Palestinians,' Source Close to
Bennett Says After Gantz Meets Abbas," *Haaretz*, August 30, 2021, www.haaretz
.com/israel-news/.premium-gantz-meets-with-abbas-in-ramallah-to-discuss-secu
rity-economy-1.10163773.

3. Patrick Kinglsey, "After Years of Quiet, Israeli-Palestinian Conflict Exploded.
Why Now?," *New York Times*, May 16, 2021, A1.

4. "Palestinian Rockets in May Killed Civilians in Israel, Gaza," Human Rights Watch, August 12, 2021, www.hrw.org/news/2021/08/12/palestinian-rockets-may -killed-civilians-israel-gaza.

5. Steve Hendrix, Shira Rubin, and Sufian Taha, "Highway of Hope and Heartbreak," *Washington Post*, November 22, 2021, www.washingtonpost.com/world /interactive/2021/israel-palestinians-two-state-solution; Mona El-Naggar, Adam Rasgon, and Mona Boshnaq, "They Were Only Children," *New York Times*, May 26, 2021, A1, www.nytimes.com/interactive/2021/05/26/world/middleeast/gaza-israel -children.html; David M. Halbfinger and Adam Rasgon, "Life Under Occupation: The Misery at the Heart of the Conflict," *New York Times*, May 22, 2021, A1, www .nytimes.com/2021/05/22/world/middleeast/israel-gaza-conflict.html.

6. Abraham Foxman (@FoxmanAbraham), Twitter, May 28, 2021, https://twit ter.com/FoxmanAbraham/status/1398316595722735628; Aaron Bandler, "Former ADL Head Says He's Canceling NYT Subscription over Front Page 'Blood Libel,'" *Jewish Journal*, May 28, 2021, https://jewishjournal.com/news/337152/former-adl -head-says-hes-canceling-nyt-subscription-over-front-page-blood-libel.

7. Hagar Shazif, "Charges Are Pressed Only in 4% of Settler Violence Cases," *Haaretz*, February 7, 2022, www.haaretz.com/israel-news/.premium.MAGAZINE -charges-are-pressed-in-just-4-of-settler-violence-cases-1.10595783; Patrick Kingsley, "As Violence Rises in the West Bank, Settler Attacks Raise Alarm," *New York Times*, February 12, 2022, A4; Oren Ziv, "'Same agenda, just more subtle': Bennett-Lapid government's first year in numbers," 972.org, June 19, 2022, https://www .972mag.com/bennett-lapid-first-year-numbers/.

8. Laura Kelly, "State: US 'Strongly Opposes' Israeli Settlement Expansion," *The Hill*, October 26, 2021, https://thehill.com/policy/international/578564-state-us-strongly -opposes-israeli-settlement-expansion; Ronan Farrow, "How Democracies Spy on Their Citizens," *New Yorker*, April 18, 2022, www.newyorker.com/magazine/2022/04/25 /how-democracies-spy-on-their-citizens; Barak Ravid, "Israel to Approve 4,000 Housing Units for Jewish Settlers in Occupied West Bank," Axios, May 6, 2022, www .axios.com/2022/05/06/israel-settlements-approval-west-bank-biden-visit.

9. Isaac Scher, "CIA unable to corroborate Israel's 'terror' label for Palestinian rights groups," *The Guardian*, August 22, 2022, www.theguardian.com/world/2022/aug/22 /cia-report-israel-palestinian-rights-groups; "Joint Statement: Over 150 Organizations Demand International Community Stand Against Raids and Closures of 7 Palestinian Organizations," Human Rights Watch, August 22, 2022, www.hrw.org/news /2022/08/22/joint-statement-over-150-organizations-demand-international-commu nity-stand-against; "Pro-Israel Organizations Urge Secretary Blinken to Address Israel's Persecution of Palestinian Civil Society Organizations," Progressive Israel Network, August 24, 2022, www.progressiveisraelnetwork.org/us-jewish-organizations-letter -urging-secretary-blinken-to-address-israels-persecution-of-palestinian-civil-society/ Daniel Sokatch, Israel is criminalizing Palestinian human rights defenders. American Jews must push the US to intervene," *The Forward*, August 25, 2022, forward.com /opinion/515623/israel-criminalizing-palestinian-human-rights-defenders-american -jews-us-intervene/; Ron Kampeas, "Biden administration: Israel has yet to justify shuttering of Palestinian human rights groups," Jewish Telegraphic Agency, April 18, 2022, www.jta.org/2022/08/18/united-states/biden-administration-israel-has-yet-to -justify-shuttering-of-palestinian-human-rights-groups.

10. Judah Ari Gross, "US Jewish Leaders Warn of Growing Antisemitism, Say They Helped Fight Amnesty Report," *Times of Israel*, February 16, 2022, www.timesofisrael.com/us-jewish-leaders-warn-of-growing-antisemitism-say-they-helped-fight-amnesty-report; Nadav Tamir, "Israel's Relations with Diaspora Jewry: Can the Rift Be Healed? A Practical Start," *Jerusalem Strategic Tribune*, November 2021, https://jstribune.com/nadav-tamir-israel-relations-with-diaspora-jewry.

11. Yonat Shimron, "US Jews Furiously Raise Money, Send Delegations to Help Ukraine," Religion News Service, March 12, 2022, https://religionnews.com/2022/03/12/us-jews-furiously-raise-money-send-delegations-to-help-ukraine; Bernard Avishai, "Israel and the Triangular Crisis of Ukraine, Iran, and Palestine," *New Yorker*, April 1, 2022, www.newyorker.com/news/daily-comment/israel-and-the-triangular-crisis-of-ukraine-iran-and-palestine; Jason Stanley, "The Antisemitism Animating Putin's Claim to 'Denazify' Ukraine," *The Guardian*, February 27, 2022, www.theguardian.com/world/2022/feb/25/vladimir-putin-ukraine-attack-antisemitism-denazify.

12. Judah Ari Gross, "US Jewish Leaders Warn"; Ron Kampeas, "Israel Link Keeps Leftist Jewish Groups from Planned DC Antisemitism Rally," *Times of Israel*, July 9, 2021, www.timesofisrael.com/israel-link-keeps-leftist-jewish-groups-from-planned-dc-antisemitism-rally.

13. Ben Samuels, "Democrat With Unprecedented AIPAC Backing Slated to Win Maryland Primary," *Haaretz*, July 20, 2022, www.haaretz.com/us-news/2022-07-20/ty-article/.highlight/aipac-backed-democrat-slated-to-win-maryland-primary-buoyed-by-pro-israel-group/00000182-1b5a-df36-adaa-7bdf95ad0000; Chris McGreal, "Pro-Israel group pours millions into primary to defeat Jewish candidate," *The Guardian*, July 29, 2022, www.theguardian.com/us-news/2022/jul/29/pro-israel-lobby-aipac-andy-levin-democratic-races.

14. Ben Samuels, "Pro-Israel Candidates Win Key Primaries in New York, Florida," *Haaretz*, August 24, 2022, www.haaretz.com/us-news/2022-08-24/ty-article/.highlight/pro-israel-candidates-win-key-primaries-in-new-york-florida/00000182-cd91-db88-a7c7-cfb587f70000; AIPAC (@AIPAC), "George Soros has a long history...," Twitter, August 24, 2022, twitter.com/AIPAC/status/1562496370241851396?s=20&t=i-LhTt__0MgTWugSy4tmig; J Street (@jstreetdotorg), "The ADL called attacks, fear-mongering and hate-mongering about George Soros 'a gateway to antisemitism,'" Twitter, August 24, 2022, twitter.com/jstreetdotorg/status/1562538310400360449?s=20&t=i-LhTt__0MgTWugSy4tmig; Matthew Kassel, "Yuh-Line Niou adds Israel policy to website, mulls possible third-party run," *Jewish Insider*, August 30, 2022, jewishinsider.com/2022/08/yuh-line-niou-israel-bds-mondaire-jones-working-families-party/.

15. Alan Salomont and Nancy Buck, "AIPAC Is on the Wrong Side of Democracy," *Boston Globe*, April 18, 2022, www.bostonglobe.com/2022/04/14/opinion/aipac-is-wrong-side-democracy/?event=event12; Ben Samuels, "After Haaretz Report, AIPAC Changes Course and Endorses Rep. Liz Cheney," *Haaretz*, April 30, 2022, www.haaretz.com/us-news/.premium.HIGHLIGHT-after-haaretz-report-aipac-changes-course-and-endorses-rep-liz-cheney-1.10771644.

16. Dave Weigel, "The Trailer: Your hour-by-hour guide on what to watch in four states tonight," *The Washington Post*, August 9, 2022, www.washingtonpost.com/politics/2022/08/09/trailer-your-hour-by-hour-guide-what-watch-four-states

-tonight/; "2022 National Survey of Jewish Voters," Jewish Electorate Institute, April 13, 2022, www.jewishelectorateinstitute.org/2022-national-survey-of-jewish-voters; Rabbi Laura Geller and Rabbi John L. Rosove, "Letter to the Editor: On AIPAC and its pro-Israel mission," *Jewish Journal*, August 23, 2022, jewishjournal.com/letters_to_the_editor/350970/on-aipac-and-its-pro-israel-mission/.

17. John Wagner, "Trump Says Jewish Americans 'Don't Like Israel or Don't Care About Israel," *Washington Post*, December 17, 2021, www.washingtonpost.com/politics/trump-jews-israel/2021/12/17/12f68c2c-5f50-11ec-ae5b-5002292337c7_story.html; "2022 National Jewish Survey"; "Jewish Americans in 2020," Pew Research Center, May 11, 2021, www.pewresearch.org/religion/2021/05/11/jewish-americans-in-2020; "100+ Jewish Leaders and Elected Officials Defend JFREJ Against ADL Attacks," Jews for Racial & Economic Justice, August 8, 2022, www.jfrej.org/news/2022/08/75-jewish-leaders-elected-officials-voice-defend-jfrej-from-adl.

18. Ben Samuels, "These Young Jewish Staffers Are Bringing Their Disillusionment with Israel to Capitol Hill," *Haaretz*, May 26, 2021, www.haaretz.com/israel-news/.premium-these-young-jewish-staffers-bring-their-disillusionment-with-israel-to-capitol-hill-1.9847059; "Dear President Biden," Medium, posted by Matan Arad-Neeman, May 23, 2021, https://matan-aradneeman.medium.com/dear-president-biden-b19600918a67.

19. Noam Gil, "Why Are American-Jewish Authors Obsessed With the 'Ugly Israeli'?" *Haaretz*, August 18, 2022, www.haaretz.com/us-news/2022-08-18/ty-article-magazine/.highlight/why-so-many-american-jewish-authors-mock-israelis-in-their-novels/00000182-b0de-d5c6-a59f-b8df64e80000.

20. Marc Tracy, "Inside the Unraveling of American Zionism," *New York Times Magazine*, November 2, 2021, www.nytimes.com/2021/11/02/magazine/israel-american-jews.html; Chelsea Mandell, Emily Holtzman, Frankie Sandmel, Hannah Bender, Jenna Shaw, and Josh Nelson, "'Gates of Tears': Rabbinical and Cantorial Students Stand for Solidarity with Palestinians," *The Forward*, May 13, 2021, https://forward.com/scribe/469583/gates-of-tears-rabbinical-and-cantorial-students-stand-for-solidarity-with.

21. Carry Keller-Lynn, "Jewish Israeli voters have moved significantly rightward in recent years, data shows," *Times of Israel*, August 29, 2022, www.timesofisrael.com/israeli-jewish-voters-moved-significantly-rightward-in-recent-years-data-shows/; "8. U.S. Jews' Political Views," Pew Research Center, May 11, 2020, www.pewresearch.org/religion/2021/05/11/u-s-jews-political-views/; "Israel's Religiously Divided Society," Pew Research Center, March 8, 2016, https://www.pewforum.org/2016/03/08/israels-religiously-divided-society/.

22. Gil Troy, "We Need to Focus on the Jews That Love Israel, Not Those Who Are Anti," *Jerusalem Post*, November 9, 2021, www.jpost.com/opinion/we-need-to-focus-on-the-jews-that-love-israel-not-those-who-are-anti-opinion-684524; Natan Sharansky and Gil Troy, "The Un-Jews," Tablet, June 16, 2021, www.tabletmag.com/sections/news/articles/the-un-jews-natan-sharansky; Michael A. Meyer, foreword to Yosef Gorny, *The State of Israel in Jewish Public Thought* (New York: New York University Press, 1994), x; William Davidson Talmud, Ketubot 111a, Sefaria, www.sefaria.org/Ketubot.111a.6?ven=William_Davidson_Edition_-_English&vhe=William_Davidson_Edition_-_Vocalized_Aramaic&lang=bi.

23. Martin Siegel, "Diary of a Suburban Rabbi," ed. Mel Ziegler, *New York*, January 18, 1971, 27.

24. Mark Chmiel, "The Witness of Elie Wiesel," *Tikkun*, December 1, 2002, https://read.dukeupress.edu/tikkun/article-abstract/17/6/61/83012/Elie-Wiesel -and-the-Question-of-Palestine?redirectedFrom=PDF.

25. Jean-Paul Sartre, *Anti-Semite and Jew* (New York: Schocken, 1948), 9; "Jewish Americans in 2020"; Tracy, "Inside the Unraveling."

26. Gross, "US Jewish Leaders Warn"; Ron Kampeas, "Jewish Federations Umbrella Group Removes Gun Control and LGBTQ Advocacy from Policy Priority List," JTA, Jewish Telegraphic Agency, February 27, 2022, www.jta.org/2022/02/17 /politics/jewish-federations-umbrella-group-removes-gun-control-and-lgbtq-advocacy -from-policy-priority-list; "Remarks by Jonathan Greenblatt to the ADL Virtual National Leadership Summit," Anti-Defamation League, May 1, 2022, www.adl.org /news/remarks-by-jonathan-greenblatt-to-the-adl-virtual-national-leadership-summit.

27. "Birthright Celebrates $70 Million in Donations from the Adelsons This Year," *Times of Israel*, June 18, 2018, www.timesofisrael.com/birthright-cele brates-70-million-in-donations-from-the-adelsons-this-year; author's phone interview with Birthright director of communications Deborah Camiel, 2010; Hadas Binyamin, "Philanthropy and the 'Jewish Continuity Crisis,'" Public Books, April 6, 2021, www.publicbooks.org/philanthropy-and-the-jewish-continuity-crisis.

28. Natalie Shure, "Israel's Never-Ending War Against Palestinian Health," *New Republic*, May 24, 2021, https://newrepublic.com/article/162495/israel-war -palestinian-health-care-gaza; Erika Allen, "Dean Baquet on Israel Coverage, Innovation and the Web," *New York Times*, September 10, 2014, www.nytimes .com/2014/09/10/insider/events/dean-baquet-on-israel-coverage-innovation-and -the-web.html.

29. Hannah Rosen, "Oedipus and Podhoretz," *New York*, January 5, 1998, https://nymag.com/nymetro/news/media/features/1968; For Podhoretz's remuneration package, see "Commentary Inc.," Nonprofit Explorer, ProPublica, https://proj ects.propublica.org/nonprofits/organizations/133610041. Tablet's notorious attack on Holocaust survivors, since disappeared from the Internet, is discussed in Jeffrey Goldberg, "Tablet Magazine's Ghastly Attack on Holocaust Survivors," *Atlantic*, July 19, 2012, www.theatlantic.com/national/archive/2012/07/tablet-magazines -ghastly-attack-on-holocaust-survivors/259974.

30. Rafaella Goichman, "This Anti-BDS Initiative Failed. So Israel Throws Another $30 Million at It," *Haaretz*, January 30, 2022, www.haaretz.com/israel-news /.premium.MAGAZINE-this-anti-bds-initiative-failed-so-israel-throws-another -100-million-nis-at-it-1.10565661; Aiden Pink, "US Pro-Israel Groups Failed to Disclose Grants from Israeli Government," *The Forward*, August 30, 2020, https:// forward.com/news/israel/453286/us-pro-israel-groups-failed-to-disclose-grants -from-israeli-government. For more on *SAPIR*'s funding, see Eric Alterman, "Altercation: The Dark Money Funding a Times Columnist's Magazine," *American Prospect*, March 18, 2022, https://prospect.org/politics/altercation-dark-money -funding-times-columnists-magazine, and "Altercation: CBS News Hires a Prevaricating Trumpoid," *American Prospect*, April 1, 2022, https://prospect.org/politics /altercation-cbs-news-hires-prevaricating-trumpoid.

31. Sean Sullivan and Anne Gearan, "Biden Is Increasingly at Odds with Other Democrats over Israel," *Washington Post*, May 19, 2021, www.washingtonpost.com /politics/biden-democrats-israel-palestinians/2021/05/18/0d78da76-b7ed-11eb -a5fe-bb49dc89a248_story.html Jacob Kornbluh, "'There are a few of them': Biden on Democrats critical of Israel," *The Forward*, July 13, 2022, forward.com/fast -forward/510325/there-are-a-few-of-them-biden-on-democrats-critical-of-israel/.

32. Eric Alterman, *Who Speaks for America? Why Democracy Matters in Foreign Policy* (Ithaca, NY: Cornell University Press, 1998); "Jews now a 47% minority in Israel and the territories, demographer says," *Times of Israel*, August 31, 2022, www.times ofisrael.com/jews-now-a-minority-in-israel-and-the-territories-demographer-says/

33. Gershom Gorenberg, "Israel Just Showed Its Strategy on Settlement Boycotts: Gaslighting," *Washington Post*, December 15, 2021, www.washingtonpost.com /opinions/2021/12/14/israel-horizon-europe-deal-settlement-boycotts-gaslighting; "AJC's Surveys of American and Israeli Jewish Millennials: A Comparison," American Jewish Committee, www.ajc.org/Jewish-Millennial-Survey-2022.

34. Amos Harel, "'We Arrested Countless Palestinians for No Reason,' Says Ex-Top Shin Bet Officer," *Haaretz*, February 17, 2022, www.haaretz.com/israel -news/.premium.HIGHLIGHT.MAGAZINE-we-arrested-countless-palestinians -for-no-reason-says-ex-top-shin-bet-officer-1.10618087.

35. Donna Cassata, "Democratic Tensions over Israel Erupt Again as House Backs Funds for Iron Dome System," *Washington Post*, September 23, 2021, www .washingtonpost.com/powerpost/israel-iron-dome-democrats-house/2021/09/23/5f 2fa47e-1cb2-11ec-8380-5fbadbc43ef8_story.html; "American Jewish Committee Announces Appointment of Congressman Ted Deutch as Next Chief Executive Officer," American Jewish Committee, Global Voice, February 28, 2022, www.ajc .org/news/american-jewish-committee-announces-appointment-of-congressman -ted-deutch-as-next-chief.

36. "A Threshold Crossed: Israeli Authorities and the Crimes of Apartheid and Persecution," Human Rights Watch, April 27, 2021, www.hrw.org /report/2021/04/27/threshold-crossed/israeli-authorities-and-crimes-apartheid-and -persecution; "A Regime of Jewish Supremacy from the Jordan River to the Mediterranean Sea: This Is Apartheid," B'Tselem, January 12, 2021, www.btselem .org/publications/fulltext/202101_this_is_apartheid; Michael Sfard, "Executive Summary: The Occupation of the West Bank and the Crime of Apartheid. Legal Opinion," Yesh Din, June 2020, https://s3-eu-west-1.amazonaws.com/files.yesh -din.org/Apartheid+2020/Apartheid++Summary+ENG.pdf; Marc Lynch and Shibley Telhami, "Academic Experts Believe That Middle East Politics Are Actually Getting Worse," *Washington Post*, September 17, 2021, www.washingtonpost.com /politics/2021/09/17/academic-experts-believe-that-middle-east-politics-are-actu ally-getting-worse; "July 2021 National Survey of Jewish Voters," Jewish Electorate Institute, July 13, 2021, www.jewishelectorateinstitute.org/july-2021-national-sur vey-of-jewish-voters.

37. "Crime of Apartheid: The Government of Israel's System of Oppression Against Palestinians," Amnesty International, February 1, 2022, www.amnesty usa.org/endapartheid, 14; Bill Chappell, "Netanyahu Says Israel Is 'Nation-State of the Jewish People and Them Alone,'" NPR, March 11, 2019, www.npr

.org/2019/03/11/702264118/netanyahu-says-israel-is-nation-state-of-the-jewish
-people-and-them-alone.

38. "2021 Country Reports on Human Rights Practices," US Department of State, Bureau of Democracy, Human Rights, and Labor, April 12, 2022, www.state.gov/reports/2021-country-reports-on-human-rights-practices; Eric Alterman, "The Times Goes AWOL on Amnesty and 'Apartheid,'" *American Prospect*, February 11, 2022, https://prospect.org/politics/altercation-times-goes-awol-on-amnesty-and-apartheid.

39. Gross, "US Jewish Leaders Warn"; Reuters and Ben Samuels, "U.S. State Department Rejects Amnesty's Apartheid Claim Against Israel," *Haaretz*, February 1, 2022, www.haaretz.com/us-news/u-s-state-department-rejects-amnesty-s-apartheid-claims-against-israel-1.10583830; Barak Ravid, "Israel Says It Won't Cooperate with UN Human Rights Probe," Axios, February 18, 2022, www.axios.com/israel-un-human-rights-investigation-gaza-violence-d254cc25-55d7-4151-bcb6-b8d98091c386.html; Letter to Antony Blinken, United States Senate, March 28, 2022, www.portman.senate.gov/sites/default/files/2022-03/2022-03-28%20Letter%20to%20Sec%20Blinken%20on%20UNHRC%20Commission%20of%20Inquiry%20on%20Israel.pdf.

40. "14 Israel Rights Groups Jump to Amnesty's Defence Following Apartheid Report," Middle East Monitor, February 4, 2022, www.middleeastmonitor.com/20220204-14-israel-rights-groups-jump-to-amnestys-defence-following-apartheid-report.

41. Caroline Morganti, "Israeli Leaders Talk About Israel and Apartheid. So Why Can't We?," *Haaretz*, May 18, 2008, www.haaretz.com/opinion/.premium-israelis-talk-about-apartheid-why-can-t-we-1.5414290; Alterman, "Times Goes AWOL"; "Israel's High Court of Justice, the Occupation's Rubber Stamp," *Haaretz*, May 8, 2022, www.haaretz.com/opinion/editorial/israel-s-high-court-of-justice-the-occupation-s-rubber-stamp-1.10784957; Emir Nader (@EmirNader), Twitter, May 13, 2022, https://twitter.com/EmirNader/status/1525071210589077504; Ellen Francis, "Al Jazeera to Refer Killing of American Journalist to War Crimes Court," *Washington Post*, May 27, 2022, www.washingtonpost.com/world/2022/05/27/aljazeera-journalist-killing-israel-shireen-abu-akleh-icc; Agence France-Presse, "US Lawmakers Seek FBI Probe into Palestinian Journalist's Death," France 24, May 20, 2022, www.france24.com/en/live-news/20220520-us-lawmakers-seek-fbi-probe-into-palestinian-journalist-s-death.

42. Omar Barghouti and Stefanie Fox, "Is This Israel's South Africa Moment?," *The Nation*, February 7, 2022, www.thenation.com/article/world/israel-apartheid-amnesty-report; tally of *Wall Street Journal* articles per Google search using search terms "Israel" and "apartheid" with "Wall Street Journal" undertaken on February 12, 2022.

43. Mari Cohen and Alex Kane, "Why Liberal Zionist Groups Won't Say 'Apartheid,'" *Jewish Currents*, February 10, 2022, https://jewishcurrents.org/why-liberal-zionist-groups-wont-say-apartheid.

44. Patrick Kingsley, "U.N. Investigator Accuses Israel of Apartheid, Citing Permanence of Occupation," *New York Times*, March 23, 2022, www.nytimes.com/2022/03/23/world/middleeast/israel-apatheid-un.html; Alterman, "Times

Goes AWOL"; Eric Alterman, "Altercation: Right Answers Celebrated; Speaking Truths Not So Much," *American Prospect*, February 18, 2022, https://prospect.org /politics/altercation-right-answers-celebrated-speaking-truths-not-so-much.

45. Joan Didion, "Fixed Opinions, or The Hinge of History," *New York Review of Books*, January 16, 2003, www.nybooks.com/articles/2003/01/16/fixed-opinions -or-the-hinge-of-history.

46. Didion, "Fixed Opinions."

# INDEX

Credit: Maresa Patterson

**Eric Alterman** is Distinguished Professor of English, Brooklyn College, City University of New York. From 1995 to 2020, he was *The Nation*'s "Liberal Media" columnist, and he is now a contributing writer to the magazine as well as to *The American Prospect*, where he writes the weekly "Altercation" newsletter. In the past, he has been a Senior Fellow of the Center for American Progress, the World Policy Institute, and The Nation Institute; a columnist for *Rolling Stone*, *Mother Jones*, *The Guardian*, The Daily Beast, *The Forward*, *Moment*, and the *Sunday Express* (London); and a contributor to *The New Yorker*, *The Atlantic*, and *Le Monde Diplomatique*, among other publications. He has also been named a Media Fellow at the Hoover Institution at Stanford University, a Schusterman Foundation Fellow at Brandeis University, a Fellow of the Society of American Historians, and a member of the Usage Panel of the *American Heritage Dictionary of the English Language*.

Alterman is the author of the national best-seller *What Liberal Media? The Truth About Bias and the News* as well ten other books, and he has received the George Orwell Prize, the Stephen Crane Literary Award, and the Mirror Award for media criticism (twice). He holds a PhD in US history from Stanford (minoring in Jewish Studies), an MA in international relations from Yale, and a BA from Cornell. He tweets at @eric_alterman and has an open Facebook page at facebook.com/alterman.eric. He lives in Manhattan and can be reached at ealterman@brooklyn.cuny.edu.